FOUNDATIONS OF MARKETING

Third Edition

William M. Pride
Texas A & M University

O. C. Ferrell
University of New Mexico

Houghton Mifflin Company   BOSTON   NEW YORK

To Jim and Yvonne Pride
To Linda Ferrell

Vice President, Executive Publisher: George Hoffman
Executive Editor: Lisé Johnson
Marketing Manager: Nicole Mollica
Sponsoring Editor: Mike Schenk
Development Editor: Suzanna Smith
Editorial Associate: James Hamilton
Editorial Assistant: Katilyn Crowley
Project Editor: Shelley Dickerson
Art/Design Manager: Jill Haber
Cover Design Director: Tony Saizon
Senior Photo Editor: Jennifer Meyer Dare
Senior Composition Buyer: Chuck Dutton
Senior New Title Project Manager: Pat O'Neill

Cover image, and cover image used in preface: © Patrick Bennett/Getty Images

Printed in the U.S.A.

Library of Congress Control Number: 2007940549

Instructor's Exam Copy—
ISBN 13: 978-0-547-00467-9
ISBN 10: 0-547-00467-2

For orders, use student text ISBNs—
ISBN 13: 978-0-618-97337-8
ISBN 10: 0-618-97337-0

1 2 3 4 5 6 7 8 9 — CRK — 12 11 10 09 08

Resources for Instructors

Foundations of Marketing includes a comprehensive package of teaching materials.

 **Online Teaching Center**

Online Teaching Center instructor's web site   Redesigned to enhance ease-of-use. Content includes sample syllabi, downloadable text files from the *Instructor's Resource Manual*, PowerPoint® slides, *CRS (Classroom Response System) "Clicker"* content, *Integrated Lecture Outlines* (lecture outlines with suggested placement of PowerPoints, video clips, overheads, and more), and more.

Test Bank   Provides more than 3,200 test items including true/false, multiple choice, and essay questions, with correct answers, difficulty ratings, main text page references, and applications.

HMTesting CD (powered by Diploma™)   Computerized version of the Test Bank. Allows instructors to select, edit, and add questions, or generate randomly selected questions to produce a test master for easy duplication.
Includes Online Testing and Gradebook functions.

Instructor's Resource Manual   Written by the text's authors. Includes a complete set of teaching tools, exercises, hints, and solutions.

Marketing Deals with Products, Price, Distribution, and Promotion

- The Marketing Mix
  - Four marketing activities—product, pricing, distribution, and promotion—that a firm can control to meet the needs of customers within its target market

Product / Pricing / Distribution / Promotion → Target Market

Basic and Premium PowerPoint slide presentations   Basic slides offer helpful PowerPoint lecture outlines. The Premium PowerPoint slides include additional material such as advertisements, surveys and graphs, videos, and important terms.

Course Management Systems with **Eduspace** powered by **Blackboard** and **Blackboard/WebCT**   Allow instructors to create and customize online course materials to use in distance learning, distributed learning, or as a supplement to traditional classes. Each system includes most instructor resources and more.

EDUSpace®
Houghton Mifflin's Online Learning Tool
BUSINESS

CRS (Classroom Response System) "Clicker" Content   Question-and-answer slides are ideal for any classroom.

Marketing videos   Videos for use with the end-of-chapter video cases.

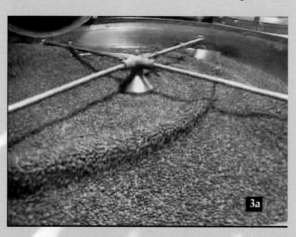

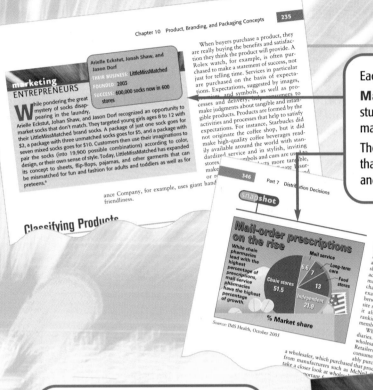

Each chapter includes two **boxed features**.

Marketing Entrepreneurs features introduce students to exciting and innovative new players in the marketing industry.

The **Snapshot** features present graphs and summaries that offer quick insights with marketing-related statistics and figures.

The **Careers in Marketing** appendix introduces students to issues they will face when they are ready to enter the work force, such as marketing careers, job searches, résumé writing, and interviewing skills.

There's also...

The **...And Now** features tie together the chapter concepts introduced in the opening vignette.

A **Chapter Review** summarizes the major topics discussed.

A list of **key concepts** reinforces marketing vocab.

End-of-Chapter review content:

■ Issues for Discussion and Review

■ Marketing Applications

■ Online Exercises

■ GlobalEdge Exercise

■ Video Case

A comprehensive **Glossary** defines more than 600 important marketing terms.

 **HM NewsNow** A story from the Associated Press applicable to the textbook subject area periodically updated with a PowerPoint presentation that includes a summary of the story, related video content, and review questions.

Online color transparencies These PDF versions of the Premium PowerPoints, and can be used with an overhead projector.

Author Website *www.prideferrell.net* provides teaching tips, exercises, classroom activities, additional cases, podcasts, as well as other resources.

Resources for Students

 All of the major student resources are tied to, and are available through, the **Multimedia eBook,** an interactive PDF version of the textbook.

Pride/Ferrell Marketing Study Center with **HMBusinessSpace** at www.college.hmco.com/ pic/prideferrellfom3e contains the following:

- ■ **Audio Chapter Summaries** and **Audio Chapter Quizzes** are available in mp3 format.
- ■ **ACE and ACE+ online self-tests**
- ■ **HM NewsNow.** PowerPoint presentations of headlines from the Associated Press that relate to the marketing industry. Includes an AP NewsFeed.
- ■ **The Interactive Marketing Plan.** An exciting, hands-on digital way to learn how marketing plans are developed and executed.
- ■ **Flashcards.**

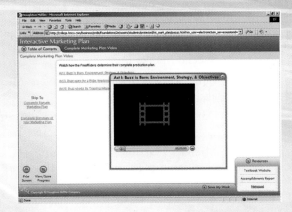

- ■ **Online Glossary & Chapter Summary.**
- ■ **Career Center.** Downloadable "Personal Career Plan Worksheets" and links to various marketing careers websites will help students explore their options and plan their job search.

Comments and Suggestions

We invite your comments, questions, and criticisms, and your suggestions will be sincerely appreciated. Please e-mail us at w-pride@tamu.edu or OCFerrell@ mgt.unm.edu, or call 979-845-5857 (Pride) or 505-277-3468 (Ferrell). You can also send a feedback message through the website at **www.prideferrell.com**.

Thanks

The authors would like to thank the hundreds of reviewers who have provided invaluable feedback over the years as we have written and revised our introductory marketing titles, and also the over 500 faculty across the country who responded to marketing research specifically designed to help create *Foundations of Marketing*.

A special faculty advisory board assisted in making decisions during the development of this text and its instructional package. For being "on-call" and available to answer questions and make valuable suggestions, the authors are grateful to those who participated: William Motz, *Lansing Community College*; Carol Rowey, *Community College of Rhode Island*; Morris A. Shapero, *University of South Florida*; Melodie Philhours, *Arkansas State University*; Patricia Bernson, *County College of Morris*; Eva Hyatt, *Appalachian State University*; Thomas Kanick, *Broome Community College*; Gayle Marco, *Robert Morris University*; Stanley Garfunkel, *Queensborough Community College*; Stephen Goodwin, *Illinois State University*; William Carner, *University of Texas-Austin*; Mohan Agrawal, *California Polytechnic State University*; Jean-Luc Grosso, *University of South Carolina-Sumter*; Gloria Bemben, *Finger Lakes Community College*; Betty Jean Hebel, *Madonna University*; Barry McCarthy, *Irvine Valley College*; Donna Leonowich, *Middlesex Community College*; and Melissa Moore, *Mississippi State University*.

Gwyneth V. Walters assisted in research, editing, and content development for the text, supplements, and the Pride/Ferrell Marketing Learning Center. The authors deeply appreciate the assistance of Marian Wood for providing editorial suggestions, technical assistance, and support. Melanie Drever, *University of Wyoming*, conducted research and developed boxes, cases, and other chapter content. For assistance in completing numerous tasks associated with the text and supplements, the authors express appreciation to Alexi Sherrill, Luci Vietti, Tammy Lemke, Dana Egg, Somia Qaiyum, Jonathan Wickersham, Diana Burbules, Melanie Drever, and Clarissa Means.

Special thanks to:

Linda Ferrell, *University of New Mexico*, who participated in all aspects of content and supplement development.

Daniel Sherrell, *University of Memphis*, who developed the framework used in Chapter 4 and the six major characteristics of marketing on the Internet.

Michael Hartline, *Florida State University*, who helped in the development of the marketing plan outline and the sample marketing plan as well as the career worksheets on the website.

V. Kumar, Chuck Tomkovick, Brian Jones, Todd Donavan, and John Eaton for developing supplementary modules for this edition.

Kirk Wakefield, *Baylor University*, for developing the class exercises included in the *Instructor's Resource Manual*.

John Drea, *Western Illinois University*, for developing the 'A' Student game.

Our colleagues at *Texas A&M University* and *University of New Mexico*, for their support and encouragement.

part 1

Strategic Marketing and Its Environment

Part 1 introduces the field of marketing and offers a broad perspective from which to explore and analyze various components of the marketing discipline. Chapter 1 defines *marketing* and explores some key concepts, including customers and target markets, the marketing mix, relationship marketing, the marketing concept, and value. Chapter 2 provides an overview of strategic marketing issues, such as the effect of organizational resources and opportunities on the planning process; the role of the mission statement; corporate, business-unit, and marketing strategies; and the creation of the marketing plan. These issues are profoundly affected by competitive, economic, political, legal and regulatory, technological, and sociocultural forces in the marketing environment. Chapter 3 deals with these environmental forces and with the role of social responsibility and ethics in marketing decisions.

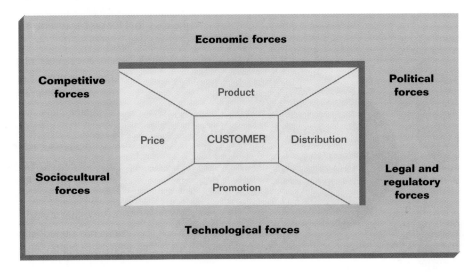

1

Customer-Driven Strategic Marketing

OBJECTIVES

1. Define marketing.

2. Understand several important marketing terms, including *target market, marketing mix, marketing exchanges,* and *marketing environment.*

3. Be aware of the marketing concept and marketing orientation.

4. Understand the importance of building customer relationships.

5. Explain the major marketing functions that are part of the marketing management process.

6. Understand the role of marketing in our society.

Consumers Reach for the Stars and Satellite Radio

XM Satellite Radio is changing the world of radio with 4 satellites, 170 channels, and more than 80 state-of-the-art performance studios in its Washington, D.C., headquarters. XM's founders believed that commuters—and anyone else traveling by car for long periods—would be willing to pay for perfect 24-hour radio reception and dozens of channel choices anywhere in the United States. After all, millions were paying for cable television, even though they could watch broadcast television for free in many geographic areas. The company started on the road to static-free radio in 1997, when it paid more than $80 million for a federal license to broadcast digital radio. Until then, AM and FM radio stations had been free to all listeners, mainly because of commercial sponsorship.

Turning the concept of digital radio into reality cost XM more than $1 billion. First, the company had to design and launch two satellites into orbit over the United States. It set up satellite dishes to beam radio signals to the satellites and erected antennas on 800 buildings in major cities to reach local listeners across the country. It also created a vast library of digital recordings and built performance studios to broadcast and record live musical performances. Another big challenge was developing the radio equipment for customers' cars. The radio had to be capable of receiving and decoding the satellite signals yet compact enough to fit in a car. After building and testing prototypes, XM began manufacturing a radio about the size of a suitcase, to be connected to an antenna on the car's roof for proper reception. Initially customers had to retrofit their cars with XM radios. In time, the company arranged for General Motors, Honda, Audi, Nissan, and several other big automakers to offer factory-installed XM radios as options in their new cars.

After a year of having the market to itself, XM gained a competitor: New York–based Sirius Satellite Radio began operating a year after XM. Like XM, Sirius paid millions for a digital radio broadcast license, launched sophisticated satellites, and created specialized programming for 120 stations. And like XM, Sirius is looking to sports and celebrities to draw in new subscribers. In addition to National Football League, National Basketball Association, and National Hockey League games, Sirius has signed "shock jock" Howard Stern, Martha Stewart, Eminem, and Pat Robertson to host shows.[1] ■

Pedagogical Features that Facilitate Learning

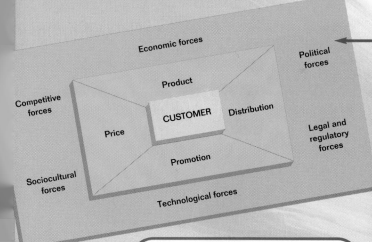

The **organizational model** provides a visual roadmap of each of the eight parts of text.

Objectives at the start of each chapter present what students are to learn as they read the chapter.

An **opening vignette** about a particular organization, brand, or marketing practice introduces the many topics and concepts for each chapter.

Numerous figures, tables, photographs, and **advertisements** throughout the text increase comprehension and stimulate interest.

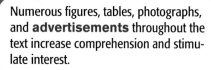

Key term definitions appear in the margin to help students build their marketing vocabulary.

Foundations of Marketing, Third Edition,

provides instructors and students of introductory marketing a concise, direct approach to the basic concepts of marketing. This program remains true to the goal helping students and professors explore the dynamic and exciting world of marketing. With a strong backing in the latest market research and compelling, contemporary ad content, this program presents marketing issues and concepts in the depth and detail needed to challenge and inform students. And with logical organization, precise definitions, and the marketing vocabulary that students need, this program's thorough coverage helps students acquire a balanced overview of the marketing discipline.

Textbook Organization

Part One: An overview of marketing; examines strategic market planning, marketing environment forces, and social responsibility and ethics.

Part Two: E-marketing, customer relationship management, and global marketing.

Part Three: Considers information systems, marketing research, and target market analysis.

Part Four: Consumer and business buying behavior.

Part Five: Conceptualization, development, and management of goods and services.

Part Six: Pricing decisions

Part Seven: Marketing channels and supply-chain management, retailing, wholesaling, and direct marketing.

Part Eight: Integrated marketing communications and promotion methods including advertising, personal selling, sales promotion, and public relations.

v

Note: Each chapter concludes with a Chapter Review, Key Concepts, Issues for Discussion and Review, Marketing Applications, and Online Exercise.

PART 3
Target-Market Selection and Research 127

6 Marketing Research and Information Systems 128

7 Target Markets: Segmentation and Evaluation 155

PART 4
Customer Behavior 181

8 Consumer Buying Behavior 182

9   Business Markets and Buying Behavior

209

PART 5

Product Decisions

231

10   Product, Branding, and Packaging Concepts

232

We are also grateful for the comments and suggestions we receive from our own students, student focus groups, and student correspondents who provide ongoing feedback through the website.

A number of talented professionals at Houghton Mifflin have contributed to the development of this book. We are especially grateful to George Hoffman, Mike Schenk, Bess Deck, Suzanna Smith, Nicole Moore, Shelley Dickerson, Rachel D'Angelo Wimberly, Susan Gilday, Katie Huha, and Marcy Kagan. Their inspiration, patience, support, and friendship are invaluable.

William M. Pride (w-pride@tamu.edu)

O.C. Ferrell (OCFerrell@mgt.unm.edu)

PART 8
Promotion Decisions   403

16 Integrated Marketing Communications   404

17 Advertising and Public Relations   431

18 Personal Selling and Sales Promotion   457

APPENDIX: Careers in Marketing   485

figure 1.1

COMPONENTS OF STRATEGIC MARKETING

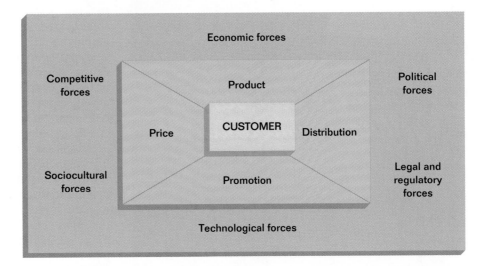

like all organizations, XM Satellite Radio must develop products that customers want, communicate useful information about them, price them appropriately, and make them available when and where customers may want to buy them. Even if it does these things well, competition from Sirius Satellite Radio and conventional radio stations, economic conditions, and other factors may affect the company's success.

This chapter introduces the strategic marketing concepts and decisions covered throughout the text. First, we develop a definition of *marketing* and explore each element of the definition in detail. Next, we introduce the marketing concept and consider several issues associated with implementing it. We also take a brief look at the management of customer relationships and then at the concept of value, which customers are demanding today more than ever before. We then explore the process of marketing management, which includes planning, organizing, implementing, and controlling marketing activities to encourage marketing exchanges. Finally, we examine the importance of marketing in our global society.

Marketing Defined

If you ask several people what *marketing* is, you are likely to hear a variety of descriptions. Although many people think marketing is advertising or selling, marketing actually encompasses many more activities than most people realize. In this book we define **marketing** as the process of creating, distributing, promoting, and pricing goods, services, and ideas to facilitate satisfying exchange relationships with customers and to develop and maintain favorable relationships with stakeholders in a dynamic environment. Our definition is consistent with that of the American Marketing Association (AMA), which defines *marketing* as "an organizational function and a set of processes for creating, communicating, and delivering value to customers and for managing customer relationships in ways that benefit the organization and its stakeholders."[2] Our definition of *marketing* guides the organization of this first chapter.

Customers Are the Focus

As the purchasers of the products that organizations develop, price, distribute, and promote, **customers** are the focal point of all marketing activities (see Figure 1.1). Organizations have to define their products not as what the companies make or

marketing The process of creating, distributing, promoting, and pricing goods, services, and ideas to facilitate satisfying exchange relationships with customers and to develop and maintain favorable relationships with stakeholders in a dynamic environment

customers The purchasers of organizations' products; the focal point of all marketing activities

Take the field without getting anywhere near it.

You're the GM and you play every advantage. ESPN Fantasy Baseball is the only place where you find all you need to make your critical decisions: a live draft, real-time scoring, player updates, and fantasy analysis and insight from the ESPN bullpen of experts.

Play Fantasy Baseball at ESPN.com/fantasybaseball

★ ESPN ★
FANTASY
BASEBALL
★ Minor League Players Need Not Apply ★

Appealing to Target Market
ESPN promotes its Fantasy Baseball primarily to men.

target market A specific group of customers on whom an organization focuses its marketing efforts

marketing mix Four marketing activities—product, pricing, distribution, and promotion—that a firm can control to meet the needs of customers within its target market

produce but as what they do to satisfy customers. The Walt Disney Company is not in the business of establishing theme parks; it is in the business of making people happy. At Disney World, customers are guests, the crowd is an audience, and employees are cast members. Customer satisfaction and enjoyment can come from anything received when buying and using a product. For instance, Procter & Gamble's Fusion razors offer a very close shave, whereas its Swiffer dusters help clean house quickly and neatly.

The essence of marketing is to develop satisfying exchanges from which both customers and marketers benefit. The customer expects to gain a reward or benefit in excess of the costs incurred in a marketing transaction. The marketer expects to gain something of value in return, generally the price charged for the product. Through buyer–seller interaction, a customer develops expectations about the seller's future behavior. To fulfill these expectations, the marketer must deliver on promises made. Over time, this interaction results in relationships between the two parties. Fast-food restaurants such as Wendy's and Burger King depend on repeat purchases from satisfied customers—many often live or work a few miles from these restaurants—whereas customer expectations revolve around tasty food, value, and dependable service.

Organizations generally focus their marketing efforts on a specific group of customers, or **target market.** Marketing managers may define a target market as a vast number of people or a relatively small group. Rolls-Royce, for example, targets its automobiles at a small, very exclusive market: wealthy people who want the ultimate in prestige in an automobile. Other companies target multiple markets, with different products, prices, distribution systems, and promotion for each one. Nike uses this strategy, marketing different types of shoes to meet specific needs of rock climbers, basketball players, aerobics enthusiasts, and other athletic-shoe buyers.

Marketing Deals with Products, Price, Distribution, and Promotion

Marketing is more than simply advertising or selling a product; it involves developing and managing a product that will satisfy customer needs. It focuses on making the product available in the right place and at a price acceptable to buyers. It also requires communicating information that helps customers determine if the product will satisfy their needs. These activities are planned, organized, implemented, and controlled to meet the needs of customers within the target market. Marketers refer to these activities—product, pricing, distribution, and promotion—as the **marketing mix** because they decide what type of each element to use and in what amounts. A primary goal of a marketing manager is to create and maintain the right mix of these elements to satisfy customers' needs for a general product type. Note in Figure 1.1 that the marketing mix is built around the customer.

Marketing managers strive to develop a marketing mix that matches the needs of customers in the target market. The marketing mix for DeWalt power tools, for example, combines rugged, high-quality products with coordinated distribution, promotion, and price appropriate for the target market of primarily professional contractors.

Red Bull Has Wings

Sleek in its blue and silver can, Red Bull is without question a huge marketing success. While established soft-drink giants struggle to revitalize stale sales, upstart Red Bull has brought new "energy" to the marketplace. Red Bull, which originated in Austria, commands 60 percent of the energy-drink market against competitors such as Hype, Rockstar, Monster, Pimp Juice, and Bong Water. Indeed, there would not even be an energy-drink market without this berry-flavored beverage featuring mysterious additives taurine and glucuronolactone. While still relatively small, the energy-drink category soared to $4.9 billion in sales in 2006. PepsiCo and Coca-Cola have even introduced their own versions. Pepsi has Mountain Dew AMP and Mountain Dew MDX, whereas Coke offers Full Throttle and Tab Energy—a twist on the 1970s soft-drink Tab, which is targeted at women.

Energy drinks have about three times the caffeine of a regular soft-drink and are loaded with sugar—an instant rush. And people are willing to pay for that buzz: from $2 for an 8-ounce can of Red Bull (double the price of a 12-ounce can of Coke) to $2.50 for a 16-ounce can of Rockstar or Monster.

Red Bull's marketing group is broken into decentralized units throughout the United States. Each marketing and salesperson is expected to take responsibility for the brand and to act like an entrepreneur, working with distributors to find retail accounts at popular venues frequented by the local "in crowd." The company grants only five accounts in an area to give the product an aura of exclusivity and encourage retailers to merchandise the brand aggressively to keep the product franchise.

Red Bull's marketing teams use a variety of techniques to create brand awareness. Beyond traditional commercials, they have used dance clubs, deejays, and even New York City cab drivers to spread the word. While others spend millions on celebrities such as Christina Aguilera, Red Bull relies on buzz from hipsters as well on as its sponsorship of approximately 500 "extreme" athletes who surf in Nova Scotia in January or jump out of planes to swim the English Channel. One of the brand's favorite targets is alternative sports venues. It's involved in national and regional events, including the Red Bull Huckfest ski and snowboard competition in Utah. Its fleet of show planes, the Flying Bulls, appears at air shows around the world. These events are naturals for reaching potential customers. The company also owns NASCAR and Formula One racing teams, as well as the New York Red Bulls soccer team.

Red Bull also uses consumer education teams, hiring hip locals in target areas to drive Red Bull cars (small sporty blue and silver vehicles with a large Red Bull can mounted on the back) and hand out samples. However, what consumers see in one city may be entirely different from what they see in another city. Red Bull's marketing philosophy is to adapt its approach to the local market. It's all part of the mystique![a]

The marketing mix for Black & Decker power tools differs from that of DeWalt—even though the two brands are owned by the same firm—with lower prices and broader distribution.[3]

Before marketers can develop a marketing mix, they must collect in-depth, up-to-date information about customer needs. Such information might include data about the age, income, ethnicity, gender, and educational level of people in the target market, their preferences for product features, their attitudes toward competitors' products, and the frequency with which they use the product. Research by Dunkin' Donuts, for example, revealed that its customers would welcome new menu items such as iced beverages, espresso drinks, and bagel breakfast sandwiches. This information helped the company refine its strategy of targeting workday on-the-go customers rather than compete directly against Starbucks.[4] Armed with market information, marketing managers are better able to develop a marketing mix that satisfies a specific target market.

Let's look more closely at the decisions and activities related to each marketing mix variable.

Product Variable   Successful marketing efforts result in products that become part of everyday life. Consider the satisfaction customers have had over the years from Coca-Cola, Levi's jeans, Visa credit cards, Tylenol pain relievers, and 3M Post-it Notes. The product variable of the marketing mix deals with researching customers' needs and wants and designing a product that satisfies them. A **product** can be a good, a service, or an idea. A *good* is a physical entity you can touch. A Toyota Yaris, an Apple iPhone, a Duracell battery, and a kitten available for adoption at an animal shelter are examples of goods. A *service* is the application of human and mechanical efforts to people or objects to provide intangible benefits to customers. Air travel, dry cleaning, haircutting, banking, medical care, and day care are examples of services. *Ideas* include concepts, philosophies, images, and issues. For instance, a marriage counselor, for a fee, gives spouses ideas to help improve their relationship. Other marketers of ideas include political parties, churches, and schools.

The product variable also involves creating or modifying brand names and packaging and may include decisions regarding warranty and repair services. Even one of the world's best basketball players is a global brand. Yao Ming, the Houston Rockets' center, has endorsed products from McDonald's, PepsiCo, and Reebok, many of which are marketed in his Chinese homeland.[5]

Product variable decisions and related activities are important because they are directly involved with creating products that address customers' needs and wants. To maintain an assortment of products that helps an organization achieve its goals, marketers must develop new products, modify existing ones, and eliminate those that no longer satisfy enough buyers or that yield unacceptable profits. In the funeral home industry, for example, some companies have developed new products such as DVD memoirs, grave markers that display photos along with a soundtrack, and caskets with drawers to hold mementos from the bereaved. To appeal to the growing number of people who prefer to be cremated, other firms are offering more cremation and memorial services.[6] We consider such product issues and many more in Chapters 10 and 11.

Price Variable   The price variable relates to decisions and actions associated with establishing pricing objectives and policies and determining product prices. Price is a critical component of the marketing mix because customers are concerned about the value obtained in an exchange. Price is often used as a competitive tool, and intense price competition sometimes leads to price wars. High prices can be used competitively to establish a product's premium image. Waterman and Mont Blanc pens, for example, have an image of high quality and high price that has given them significant status. On the other hand, some luxury goods marketers are now offering lower-priced versions of their products to appeal to middle-class consumers who want to "trade up" to prestigious brand names. Handbag maker Coach, for example, markets fabric wristlets for $78 as well as vintage leather wristlets that sell for much more.[7] We explore pricing decisions in Chapters 12 and 13.

Distribution Variable   To satisfy customers, products must be available at the right time and in convenient locations. Subway, for example, locates not only in strip malls but also inside Wal-Marts, Home Depots, laundromats, churches, and hospitals, as well as inside a Goodwill store, a car dealership, and an appliance store. There are more than 20,000 Subway restaurants in the United States, all owned by franchisees, and 22 percent of them are in nontraditional locations, such as churches, up from 13 percent ten years ago.[8] In dealing with the distribution variable, a marketing manager makes products available in the quantities desired to as

product A good, a service, or an idea

Source: 2006 Edelman Trust Barometer.

many target-market customers as possible, keeping total inventory, transportation, and storage costs as low as possible. A marketing manager also may select and motivate intermediaries (wholesalers and retailers), establish and maintain inventory control procedures, and develop and manage transportation and storage systems. The advent of the Internet and electronic commerce also has dramatically influenced the distribution variable. Companies now can make their products available throughout the world without maintaining facilities in each country. Sauce Co., a small firm in Little Rock, Arkansas, for example, sells salsa, barbecue sauce, and other sauces through its website to buyers all over the United States and as far away as London and Saudi Arabia.[9] We examine distribution issues in Chapters 14 and 15.

Promotion Variable The promotion variable relates to activities used to inform individuals or groups about the organization and its products. Promotion can aim to increase public awareness of the organization and of new or existing products. Del Monte Foods, for example, used humorous television commercials, a traveling bus tour, and a new website (SmoochablePooch.com) to introduce its new Kibbles 'n Bits Brushing Bites dog treats, which help pet owners keep their dogs' teeth clean and breath fresh.[10] Promotional activities also can educate customers about product features or urge people to take a particular stance on a political or social issue, such as smoking or drug abuse. For example, rising fuel prices prompted the U.S. Department of Energy to launch an advertising campaign featuring an Energy Hog mascot to urge the public to conserve energy, especially with regard to home heating. The campaign also used booklets, temporary tattoos for children, and two websites—one for children with games and one for adults with information about energy-saving tips and appliances.[11] Promotion can help to sustain interest in established products that have been available for decades, such as Arm & Hammer baking soda or Ivory soap. Many companies are using the Internet to communicate information about themselves and their products. Ragu's website, for example, offers Italian phrases, recipes, and a sweepstakes, whereas Southwest Airlines' website enables customers to make flight reservations. In Chapters 16 through 18 we take a detailed look at promotion activities.

The marketing-mix variables are often viewed as controllable because they can be modified. However, there are limits to how much marketing managers can alter them. Economic conditions, competitive structure, and government regulations may prevent a manager from adjusting prices frequently or significantly. Making changes in the size, shape, and design of most tangible goods is expensive; therefore, such product features cannot be altered very often. In addition, promotional campaigns and methods used to distribute products ordinarily cannot be rewritten or revamped overnight.

Marketing Builds Relationships with Customers and Other Stakeholders

Individuals and organizations engage in marketing to facilitate **exchanges**, the provision or transfer of goods, services, or ideas in return for something of value. Any product (good, service, or even idea) may be involved in a marketing exchange. We assume only that individuals and organizations expect to gain a reward in excess of the costs incurred.

For an exchange to take place, four conditions must exist. First, two or more individuals, groups, or organizations must participate, and each must possess something

exchanges The provision or transfer of goods, services, or ideas in return for something of value

figure 1.2

EXCHANGE BETWEEN BUYER AND SELLER

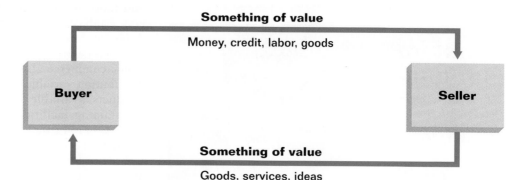

of value that the other party desires. Second, the exchange should provide a benefit or satisfaction to both parties involved in the transaction. Third, each party must have confidence in the promise of the "something of value" held by the other. If you go to a Nora Jones concert, for example, you go with the expectation of a great performance. Finally, to build trust, the parties to the exchange must meet expectations.

Figure 1.2 depicts the exchange process. The arrows indicate that the parties communicate that each has something of value available to exchange. An exchange will not necessarily take place just because these conditions exist; marketing activities can occur even without an actual transaction or sale. You may see an ad for a Sub-Zero refrigerator, for instance, but you might never buy the product. When an exchange occurs, products are traded for other products or for financial resources.

Marketing activities should attempt to create and maintain satisfying exchange relationships. To maintain an exchange relationship, buyers must be satisfied with the good, service, or idea obtained, and sellers must be satisfied with the financial reward or something else of value received. A dissatisfied customer who lacks trust in the relationship often searches for alternative organizations or products.

Marketers are concerned with building and maintaining relationships not only with customers but also with relevant stakeholders. **Stakeholders** include those constituents who have a "stake," or claim, in some aspect of a company's products, operations, markets, industry, and outcomes; these include customers, employees, investors and shareholders, suppliers, governments, communities, and many others. Developing and maintaining favorable relations with stakeholders is crucial to the long-term growth of an organization and its products.

Marketing Occurs in a Dynamic Environment

Marketing activities do not take place in a vacuum. The **marketing environment**, which includes competitive, economic, political, legal and regulatory, technological, and sociocultural forces, surrounds the customer and affects the marketing mix (see Figure 1.1). The effects of these forces on buyers and sellers can be dramatic and difficult to predict. They can create threats to marketers but also can generate opportunities for new products and new methods of reaching customers.

The forces of the marketing environment affect a marketer's ability to facilitate exchanges in three general ways. First, they influence customers by affecting their lifestyles, standards of living, and preferences and needs for products. Because a marketing manager tries to develop and adjust the marketing mix to satisfy customers, effects of environmental forces on customers also have an indirect impact on marketing-mix components. For example, rising gasoline prices and declining sales of gas-guzzling models have led many automakers, including General Motors, Ford, and DaimlerChrysler, to make improving vehicle fuel economy the highest

stakeholders Constituents who have a "stake," or claim, in some aspect of a company's products, operations, markets, industry, and outcomes

marketing environment The competitive, economic, political, legal and regulatory, technological, and sociocultural forces that surround the customer and affect the marketing mix

priority. Likewise, Hertz introduced a new service called "Green Collection" that allows customers to reserve more fuel-efficient vehicles for rent.[12] Second, marketing environment forces help to determine whether and how a marketing manager can perform certain marketing activities. Third, environmental forces may affect a marketing manager's decisions and actions by influencing buyers' reactions to the firm's marketing mix.

Marketing environment forces can fluctuate quickly and dramatically, which is one reason marketing is so interesting and challenging. Because these forces are closely interrelated, changes in one may cause changes in others. For example, evidence linking children's consumption of soft-drinks and fast foods to health issues such as obesity, diabetes, and osteoporosis has exposed marketers of such products to negative publicity and generated calls for legislation regulating the sale of soft-drinks in public schools. Some companies have responded to these concerns by voluntarily reformulating products to make them healthier or even introducing new products. PepsiCo, for example, introduced Tropicana FruitWise bars and Life cereal with yogurt and began a promotional campaign to help consumers identify healthier eating choices. The company placed a green "Smart Spot" on more than 200 products that meet nutrition criteria on limits on fat, cholesterol, sodium, and added sugar, such as Baked Lay's potato chips and Tropicana orange juice.[13] Although changes in the marketing environment produce uncertainty for marketers and at times hurt marketing efforts, they also create opportunities. Marketers who are alert to changes in environmental forces not only can adjust to and influence these changes but also can capitalize on the opportunities such changes provide.

Marketing-mix variables—product, price distribution, and promotion—are factors over which an organization has control; the forces of the environment, however, are subject to far less control. Even though marketers know that they cannot predict changes in the marketing environment with certainty, however, they must nevertheless plan for them. Because these environmental forces have such a profound effect on marketing activities, we explore each of them in considerable depth in Chapter 3.

Understanding the Marketing Concept

Some firms have sought success by buying land, building a factory, equipping it with people and machines, and then making a product they believe buyers need. However, these firms frequently fail to attract customers with what they have to offer because they defined their business as "making a product" rather than as "helping potential customers satisfy their needs and wants." For example, when CDs became more popular than vinyl records, turntable manufacturers had an opportunity to develop new products to satisfy customers' needs for home entertainment. Companies that did not pursue this opportunity, such as Dual and Empire, are no longer in business. Such organizations have failed to implement the marketing concept. Likewise, the growing popularity of MP3 technology has enabled firms such as Apple Computer to develop products like the iPod to satisfy consumers' desire to store customized music libraries. Instead of buying CDs, a consumer can download a song for 99 cents from Apple's iTunes online music store.

According to the **marketing concept**, an organization should try to provide products that satisfy customers' needs through a coordinated set of activities that also allows the organization to achieve its goals. Customer satisfaction is the major focus of the marketing concept. To implement the marketing concept, an organization strives to determine what buyers want and uses this information to develop satisfying products. It focuses on customer analysis, competitor analysis, and integration of the firm's resources to provide customer value and satisfaction, as well as generate long-term profits.[14] The firm also must continue to alter, adapt, and develop products to keep pace with customers' changing desires and preferences. Ben & Jerry's Homemade Ice Cream, for example, constantly assesses customer demand for ice cream and

marketing concept A managerial philosophy that an organization should try to satisfy customers' needs through a coordinated set of activities that also allows the organization to achieve its goals

The Marketing Concept

State Farm communicates its customer-orientation, which is part of the marketing concept. Its slogan "Like a good neighbor, State Farm is there," indicates that the organization attempts to satisfy customer needs.

sorbet. On its website it maintains a "flavor graveyard" listing combinations that were tried and ultimately failed. It also notes its top ten flavors each month. Pharmaceutical companies such as Merck and Pfizer continually strive to develop new products to fight infectious diseases, viruses, cancer, and other medical problems. Drugs that lower cholesterol, control diabetes, alleviate depression, or improve the quality of life in other ways also provide huge profits for the drug companies. When new products—such as Allegra, an allergy treatment—are developed, the companies must develop marketing activities to reach customers and communicate the products' benefits and side effects. Thus the marketing concept emphasizes that marketing begins and ends with customers. Research has found a positive association between customer satisfaction and shareholder value.[15]

The marketing concept is not a second definition of marketing. It is a management philosophy guiding an organization's overall activities. This philosophy affects all organizational activities, not just marketing. Production, finance, accounting, human resources, and marketing departments must work together.

The marketing concept is also not a philanthropic philosophy aimed at helping customers at the expense of the organization. A firm that adopts the marketing concept must satisfy not only its customers' objectives but also its own, or it will not stay in business long. The overall objectives of a business might relate to increasing profits, market share, sales, or a combination of all three. The marketing concept stresses that an organization can best achieve these objectives by being customer oriented. Thus, implementing the marketing concept should benefit the organization as well as its customers.

It is important for marketers to consider not only their current buyers' needs but also the long-term needs of society. Striving to satisfy customers' desires by

marketing
ENTREPRENEURS

Mark Zuckerberg

THE BUSINESS: Facebook

FOUNDED: In 2004 when Zuckerberg was a junior at Harvard

SUCCESS: More than 23 million registered users

Mark Zuckerberg, together with Dustin Moskovitz and Chris Hughes, started Facebook.com as a searchable online student directory that included audacious profiles, candid photos, and personal information. The social-networking site quickly expanded beyond Harvard by building communities of members from universities, colleges, and high schools all over the country. In just three years, Facebook exploded to 23 million registered users, making it the sixth most-trafficked U.S. website. Zuckerberg contends that Facebook's communities are more focused and real than those of rival MySpace partly because members are required to use their .edu e-mail addresses. Facebook continues to expand by creating new communities of users, such as military base residents.[b]

figure 1.3

THE EVOLUTION OF THE MARKETING CONCEPT

sacrificing society's long-term welfare is unacceptable. For example, while many parents want disposable diapers that are comfortable, absorbent, and safe for their babies, society in general does not want nonbiodegradable disposable diapers that create tremendous landfill problems now and in the future. Marketers are expected to act in a socially responsible manner, an idea we discuss in more detail in Chapter 3.

Evolution of the Marketing Concept

The marketing concept may seem like an obvious approach to running a business. However, businesspeople have not always believed that the best way to make sales and profits is to satisfy customers (see Figure 1.3).

The Production Orientation   During the second half of the nineteenth century, the Industrial Revolution was in full swing in the United States. Electricity, rail transportation, division of labor, assembly lines, and mass production made it possible to produce goods more efficiently. With new technology and new ways of using labor, products poured into the marketplace, where demand for manufactured goods was strong.

The Sales Orientation   In the 1920s, strong demand for products subsided, and businesses realized that they would have to "sell" products to buyers. From the mid-1920s to the early 1950s, businesses viewed sales as the major means of increasing profits, and this period came to have a sales orientation. Businesspeople believed that the most important marketing activities were personal selling, advertising, and distribution. Today, some people incorrectly equate marketing with a sales orientation.

The Marketing Orientation   By the early 1950s, some businesspeople began to recognize that efficient production and extensive promotion did not guarantee that customers would buy products. These businesses, and many others since, found that they must first determine what customers want and then produce those products rather than making the products first and then trying to persuade customers that they need them. As more organizations realized the importance of satisfying customers' needs, U.S. businesses entered the marketing era, one of marketing orientation.

A **marketing orientation** requires the "organizationwide generation of market intelligence pertaining to current and future customer needs, dissemination of the intelligence across departments, and organizationwide responsiveness to it."[16] Marketing orientation is linked to new-product innovation by developing a strategic focus to explore and develop new products to serve target markets.[17] Top management, marketing managers, nonmarketing managers (those in production, finance, human resources, and so on), and customers are all important in developing and carrying out a marketing orientation. Trust, openness, honoring promises, respect, collaboration, and recognizing the market as the raison d'être are six values required by organizations striving to become more marketing oriented.[18] Unless marketing managers provide continuous customer-focused leadership with minimal interdepartmental conflict, achieving a marketing orientation will be difficult. Nonmarketing managers must communicate with marketing managers to share information important to understanding the customer. Finally, a marketing orientation involves being responsive

marketing orientation An organizationwide commitment to researching and responding to customer needs

to ever-changing customer needs and wants. To accomplish this, Amazon.com, the online provider of books, CDs, DVDs, toys, and many other products, follows buyers' online purchases and recommends related topics. Trying to assess what customers want, which is difficult to begin with, is further complicated by the speed with which fashions and tastes can change. Today, businesses want to satisfy customers and build meaningful long-term buyer–seller relationships. Doing so helps a firm boost its own financial value.[19]

Implementing the Marketing Concept

A philosophy may sound reasonable and look good on paper, but this does not mean that it can be put into practice easily. To implement the marketing concept, a marketing-oriented organization must accept some general conditions and recognize and deal with several problems. Consequently, the marketing concept has yet to be fully accepted by all businesses.

Management must first establish an information system to discover customers' real needs and then use the information to create satisfying products. For example, Parker Brothers encouraged customers to vote online for a new Monopoly game piece (a biplane, bag of money, or piggy bank). An information system is usually expensive; management must commit money and time for its development and maintenance. Without an adequate information system, however, an organization cannot be marketing oriented.

To satisfy customers' objectives as well as its own, a company also must coordinate all its activities. This may require restructuring the internal operations and overall objectives of one or more departments. If the head of the marketing unit is not a member of the organization's top-level management, he or she should be. Some departments may have to be abolished and new ones created. Implementing the marketing concept demands the support not only of top management but also of managers and staff at all levels.

Managing Customer Relationships

Achieving the full profit potential of each customer relationship should be the fundamental goal of every marketing strategy. Marketing relationships with customers are the lifeblood of all businesses. At the most basic level, profits can be obtained through relationships in the following ways: (1) by acquiring new customers, (2) by enhancing the profitability of existing customers, and (3) by extending the duration of customer relationships. In addition to retaining customers, companies also should focus on regaining and managing relationships with customers who have abandoned the firm.[20] Implementing the marketing concept means optimizing the exchange relationship, which is the relationship between a company's financial investment in customer relationships and the return generated by customers responding to that investment.[21]

Maintaining positive relationships with customers is an important goal for marketers. The term **relationship marketing** refers to "long-term, mutually beneficial arrangements in which both the buyer and seller focus on value enhancement through the creation of more satisfying exchanges."[22] Relationship marketing continually deepens the buyer's trust in the company, and as the customer's confidence grows, this, in turn, increases the firm's understanding of the customer's needs. Successful marketers respond to customer needs and strive to increase value to buyers over time. Eventually this interaction becomes a solid relationship that allows for cooperation and mutual dependency.

To build these long-term customer relationships, marketers are increasingly turning to marketing research and information technology. **Customer relationship management (CRM)** focuses on using information about customers to create

relationship marketing
Establishing long-term, mutually satisfying buyer-seller relationships

customer relationship management (CRM) Using information about customers to create marketing strategies that develop and sustain desirable customer relationships

Customer Relationship Management

Accenture manages successful customer relationships by enhancing existing customer performance.

marketing strategies that develop and sustain desirable customer relationships. By increasing customer value over time, organizations try to retain and increase long-term profitability through customer loyalty.[23] For example, Chico's, a specialty women's retailer, offers a Passport Club that requires shoppers to spend $500 to join but confers such benefits as monthly coupons, free shipping, and 5 percent off all future purchases. Borders likewise offers Borders Rewards, a card-based system that provides incentives for frequent shoppers.[24] Borders' and Chico's initiatives create an opportunity to acquire a greater share of each customer's business.

Managing customer relationships requires identifying patterns of buying behavior and using that information to focus on the most promising and profitable customers.[25] Companies must be sensitive to customers' requirements and desires and establish communication to build their trust and loyalty. Consider that the lifetime value of a Lexus customer is about 50 times that of a Taco Bell customer, but remember, there are many more Taco Bell customers. For either organization, a customer is important. A customer's lifetime value results from his or her frequency of purchases, average value of purchases, and brand-switching patterns.[26] In general, when marketers focus on customers chosen for their lifetime value, they earn higher profits in future periods than when they focus on customers selected for other reasons.[27] Because the loss of a loyal potential lifetime customer could result in lower profits, managing customer relationships has become a major focus of strategic marketing today.

Through the use of Internet-based marketing strategies (e-marketing), companies can personalize customer relationships on a nearly one-on-one basis. A wide range of products, such as computers, jeans, golf clubs, cosmetics, and greeting cards, can be tailored for specific customers. Customer relationship management provides a strategic bridge between information technology and marketing strategies aimed at long-term relationships. This involves finding and retaining customers using information to improve customer value and satisfaction. We take a closer look at some of these e-marketing strategies in Chapter 4.

Value-Driven Marketing

Value is an important element of managing long-term customer relationships and implementing the marketing concept. We view **value** as a customer's subjective assessment of benefits relative to costs in determining the worth of a product (customer value = customer benefits − customer costs).

Customer benefits include anything a buyer receives in an exchange. Hotels and motels, for example, basically provide a room with a bed and bathroom, but each firm provides a different level of service, amenities, and atmosphere to satisfy its guests. Hampton Inns offers the minimum services necessary to maintain a quality, efficient, low-price overnight accommodation. In contrast, the Ritz-Carlton provides every imaginable service a guest might desire and strives to ensure that all service is of the highest quality. Customers judge which type of accommodation offers the best value according to the benefits they desire and their willingness and ability to pay for the costs associated with the benefits.

value A customer's subjective assessment of benefits relative to costs in determining the worth of a product

Customer costs include anything a buyer must give up to obtain the benefits the product provides. The most obvious cost is the monetary price of the product, but nonmonetary costs can be equally important in a customer's determination of value. Two nonmonetary costs are the time and effort customers expend to find and purchase desired products. To reduce time and effort, a company can increase product availability, thereby making it more convenient for buyers to purchase the firm's products. Another nonmonetary cost is risk, which can be reduced by offering good basic warranties or extended warranties for an additional charge.[28] Another risk-reduction strategy is the offer of a 100 percent satisfaction guarantee. This strategy is increasingly popular in today's catalog/telephone/Internet shopping environment. L.L. Bean, for example, uses such a guarantee to reduce the risk involved in ordering merchandise from its catalogs.

The process people use to determine the value of a product is not highly scientific. All of us tend to get a feel for the worth of products based on our own expectations and previous experience. We can, for example, compare the value of tires, batteries, and computers directly with the value of competing products. We evaluate movies, sporting events, and performances by entertainers on the more subjective basis of personal preferences and emotions. For most purchases, we do not consciously try to calculate the associated benefits and costs. It becomes an instinctive feeling that Kellogg's Corn Flakes are a good value or that McDonald's is a good place to take children for a quick lunch. The purchase of an automobile or a mountain bike may have emotional components, but more conscious decision making also may figure in the process of determining value.

In developing marketing activities, it is important to recognize that customers receive benefits based on their experiences. For example, many computer buyers consider services such as fast delivery, ease of installation, technical advice, and training assistance to be important elements of the product. Customers also derive benefits from the act of shopping and selecting products. These benefits can be affected by the atmosphere or environment of a store, such as Red Lobster's nautical/seafood theme. Even the ease of navigating a website can have a tremendous impact on perceived value. For this reason, General Motors has developed a user-friendly way to navigate its website for researching and pricing vehicles. Using the Internet to compare a Saturn with a Mercedes could result in different customers viewing each automobile as an excellent value. Owners have highly rated the Saturn as providing low-cost, reliable transportation and having dealers who provide outstanding service. A Mercedes may cost twice as much but has been rated as a better-engineered automobile that also has a higher social status than the Saturn. Different customers may view each car as being an exceptional value for their own personal satisfaction.

The marketing mix can be used to enhance perceptions of value. A product that demonstrates value usually has a feature or an enhancement that provides benefits. Promotional activities also can help to create an image and prestige characteristics that customers consider in their assessment of a product's value. In some cases value may be perceived simply as the lowest price. Many customers may not care about the quality of the paper towels they buy; they simply want the cheapest ones for use in cleaning up spills because they plan to throw them in the trash anyway. On the other hand, more people are looking for the fastest, most convenient way to achieve a goal and therefore become insensitive to pricing. For example, many busy customers are buying more prepared meals in supermarkets to take home and serve quickly, even though these meals cost considerably more than meals prepared from scratch. In such cases the products with the greatest convenience may be perceived as having the greatest value. The availability or distribution of products also can enhance their value. Taco Bell wants to have its Mexican fast-food products available at any time and any place people are thinking about consuming food. It therefore has introduced Taco Bell products into supermarkets, vending machines, college campuses, and other convenient locations. Thus the development of an effective marketing strategy requires understanding the needs and desires of customers and designing a marketing mix to satisfy them and provide the value they want.

Marketing Management

Marketing management is the process of planning, organizing, implementing, and controlling marketing activities to facilitate exchanges effectively and efficiently. Effectiveness and efficiency are important dimensions of this definition. *Effectiveness* is the degree to which an exchange helps to achieve an organization's objectives. *Efficiency* refers to minimizing the resources an organization must spend to achieve a specific level of desired exchanges. Thus the overall goal of marketing management is to facilitate highly desirable exchanges and to minimize the costs of doing so.

Planning is a systematic process of assessing opportunities and resources, determining marketing objectives, and developing a marketing strategy and plans for implementation and control. Planning determines when and how marketing activities are performed and who performs them. It forces marketing managers to think ahead, establish objectives, and consider future marketing activities and their impact on society. Effective planning also reduces or eliminates daily crises. We take a closer look at marketing strategies and plans in the next chapter.

Organizing marketing activities involves developing the internal structure of the marketing unit. The structure is the key to directing marketing activities. The marketing unit can be organized by functions, products, regions, types of customers, or a combination of all four.

Proper *implementation* of marketing plans hinges on coordination of marketing activities, motivation of marketing personnel, and effective communication within the unit. Marketing managers must motivate marketing personnel, coordinate their activities, and integrate their activities both with those in other areas of the company and with the marketing efforts of personnel in external organizations, such as advertising agencies and research firms. If McDonald's runs a promotion advertising Big Macs for 99 cents, proper implementation of this plan requires that each of the company's restaurants have enough staff and product on hand to handle the increased demand. An organization's communication system must allow the marketing manager to stay in contact with high-level management, with managers of other functional areas within the firm, and with personnel involved in marketing activities both inside and outside the organization.

The marketing *control process* consists of establishing performance standards, comparing actual performance with established standards, and reducing the difference between desired and actual performance. An effective control process has four requirements. It should ensure a rate of information flow that allows the marketing manager to detect quickly any differences between actual and planned levels of performance. It must accurately monitor various activities and be flexible enough to accommodate changes. The costs of the control process must be low relative to costs that would arise without controls. Finally, the control process should be designed so that both managers and subordinates can understand it.

The Importance of Marketing in Our Global Economy

Our definition of marketing and discussion of marketing activities reveal some of the obvious reasons the study of marketing is relevant in today's world. In this section we look at how marketing affects us as individuals and at its role in our increasingly global society.

marketing management The process of planning, organizing, implementing, and controlling marketing activities to facilitate exchanges effectively and efficiently

Marketing Costs Consume a Sizable Portion of Buyers' Dollars

Studying marketing will make you aware that many marketing activities are necessary to provide satisfying goods and services. Obviously, these activities cost money. About one-half of a buyer's dollar goes for marketing costs. If you spend $16 on a new CD, 50 to 60 percent goes toward marketing expenses, including promotion and

We don't work in the same building, but if need be, I'll help you with food and shelter.

When you help the American Red Cross, you help America. + American Red Cross

There is a place where a complete stranger will reach out to help make everything okay. That place is called America, where we look out for each other. And with your financial contribution, we can help keep it that way.

Call 1-800-RED CROSS or visit redcross.org

Marketing for Nonprofit Organizations

Red Cross uses marketing efforts to help Americans recover from disasters.

distribution, as well as profit margins. The production (pressing) of the CD represents about $1, or 6 percent of its price. A family with a monthly income of $3,000 that allocates $600 to taxes and savings spends about $2,400 for goods and services. Of this amount, $1,200 goes for marketing activities. If marketing expenses consume that much of your dollar, you should know how this money is used.

Marketing Is Used in Nonprofit Organizations

Although the term *marketing* may bring to mind advertising for Burger King, Volkswagen, and Apple, marketing is also important in organizations working to achieve goals other than ordinary business objectives such as profit. Government agencies at the federal, state, and local levels engage in marketing activities to fulfill their mission and goals. The U.S. Army, for example, uses promotion, including television advertisements and event sponsorships, to communicate the benefits of enlisting to potential recruits. The U.S. Department of Agriculture launched a promotional website with games to help teach kids about eating right according to its revised "Food Pyramid."[29] Universities and colleges engage in marketing activities to recruit new students, as well as to obtain donations from alumni and businesses.

In the private sector, nonprofit organizations also employ marketing activities to create, price, distribute, and promote programs that benefit particular segments of society. Habitat for Humanity, for example, must promote its philosophy of low-income housing to the public to raise funds and donations of supplies to build or renovate housing for low-income families who contribute "sweat equity" to the construction of their own homes. Such activities helped charitable organizations raise more than $260 billion a year in philanthropic contributions to assist them in fulfilling their missions.[30]

Marketing Is Important to Businesses

Businesses must sell products to survive and grow, and marketing activities help to sell their products. Financial resources generated from sales can be used to develop innovative products. New products allow a firm to satisfy customers' changing needs, which, in turn, enables the firm to generate more profits. Even nonprofit businesses need to "sell" to survive.

Marketing activities help to produce the profits that are essential to the survival of individual businesses. Without profits, businesses would find it difficult, if not impossible, to buy more raw materials, hire more employees, attract more capital, and create additional products that, in turn, make more profits. Without profits, marketers cannot continue to provide jobs and contribute to social causes.

Marketing Fuels Our Global Economy

Profits from marketing products contribute to the development of new products and technologies. Advances in technology, along with falling political and economic barriers and the universal desire for a higher standard of living, have made marketing across national borders commonplace while stimulating global economic growth. As a result of worldwide communications and increased international travel, many U.S. brands have achieved widespread acceptance around the world. At the same time, customers in the United States have greater choices among the products they buy because foreign brands such as Toyota (Japan), Bayer (Germany), and Nestlé (Switzerland) sell alongside U.S. brands such as General Motors, Tylenol, and Chevron. People around the world watch CNN and MTV on Toshiba and Sony televisions they purchased at Wal-Mart. Electronic commerce via the Internet now

One Planet, One IKEA

As markets fragment, it is no surprise that companies with the biggest increases in brand value operate as a single brand globally. IKEA, the Swedish home furnishings company and the world's largest furniture retailer, has shown that a well-positioned brand with a strong marketing mix travels well. It has clearly learned that a single worldwide identity is easier to manage and more cost efficient than creating new brands for each country.

While other global brands make extensive changes to fit local environments, IKEA provides a nearly identical experience in its more than 200 blue and yellow stores. IKEA stores—each the size of five football fields—feature more than 7,000 items ranging from self-assemble beds and kitchen cabinets to candlesticks and potted plants, all showcased in fully accessorized lifelike settings. The shopping experience is as much a part of the product as the products themselves.

The 1.1 million customers who visit IKEA every day enter an environment that characterizes hip Scandinavian design and simplicity. The product displays and furniture showrooms appeal to the growing global middle class that aspires to success and a comfortable living. More than just a seller of furniture, the company conveys to people all over the world that IKEA is synonymous with good taste and smart value.

While IKEA refuses to change its basic concept—a broad variety of well-designed and functional home furnishing products offered at prices low enough that as many people as possible can afford them—it does adapt to local cultures to ensure an enjoyable shopping experience for all customers. When critics suggested that Americans wouldn't assemble furniture themselves, IKEA provided better instructions and offered an assembly service. To fit Japan's small urban apartments, IKEA offered smaller versions of its products. Stores in China carry chopsticks, woks, and cleavers—essential cooking tools in that country—and there is a department dedicated to balcony furniture to accommodate the many Chinese who live in apartments with balconies. But the basic model, complete with Swedish-named products such as Leksvik and Poang and restaurants featuring IKEA's popular cinnamon rolls, remains the same. IKEA clearly recognizes that the middle class it targets has similar needs and lifestyle aspirations across the globe.[c]

enables businesses of all sizes to reach buyers around the world. We explore the international markets and opportunities for global marketing in Chapter 5.

Marketing Knowledge Enhances Consumer Awareness

Besides contributing to the well-being of our economy, marketing activities help to improve the quality of our lives. Studying marketing allows us to assess a product's value and flaws more effectively. We can determine which marketing efforts need improvement and how to attain that goal. For example, an unsatisfactory experience with a warranty may make you wish for stricter law enforcement so that sellers would fulfill their promises. You also may wish that you had more accurate information about a product before you purchased it. Understanding marketing enables us to evaluate corrective measures (such as laws, regulations, and industry guidelines) that could stop unfair, damaging, or unethical marketing practices. Thus, understanding how marketing activities work can help you to be a better consumer.

Marketing Connects People Through Technology

New technology, particularly technology related to computers and telecommunications, helps marketers to understand and satisfy more customers than ever before.

search.ebay.com /hula skirts
/portable video games
/mystery novels
/baseball tickets
/all-terrain tires
/dome tents
/stain removers

/ranch land
/hedge trimmers
/golf shoes
/video cellphones
/flip-flops
/digital sports watches
/horseshoe sets

/laptops
/swimming trunks
/digital cameras
/sprinklers
/lawnmowers
/sun hats
/artificial turf

you can get **it** on **eBay**

Marketing and the Growth of Technology

eBay uses technology to facilitate the marketing of a multitude of products.

Through toll-free telephone numbers, websites, and e-mail, customers can provide feedback about their experiences with a company's products. Even water products, such as LaCroix flavored sparkling water, provide toll-free telephone numbers and website addresses where consumers can go for questions or comments. This information can help marketers to refine and improve their products to better satisfy consumer needs. Technology also can facilitate marketing exchanges. Some restaurants, for example, are permitting customers to preorder their food and coffee products by sending text messages to the restaurants via their cell phones.

The Internet allows companies to provide tremendous amounts of information about their products to consumers and to interact with them through e-mail and blogs. A consumer shopping for a personal digital assistant, for example, can visit the websites of Blackberry and Palm to compare the features of the latest Blackberry and Treo smartphones, visit a price-comparison website to find the best price, or visit a consumer-opinion site, such as epinions, to see other consumers' reviews of the products. Although consumers are often reluctant to purchase products directly via the Internet, many value the Internet as a significant source of information for making purchasing decisions. The Internet permits marketers to target and interact with consumers in unique ways, such as through the virtual environments of Second Life, an online multiplayer game. American Apparel, for example, opened a virtual retail store in Second Life where subscribers can dress their online characters, called *avatars,* to play in the alternate reality. Shoppers who buy virtual American Apparel products get coupons for 15 percent off the same item in the real world. Other companies also have a presence in Second Life, including Adidas, Coca-Cola, Wells Fargo, and ESPN.[31] The Internet also has become a vital tool for marketing to other businesses. In fact, online sales now exceed $143 billion, accounting for about 6 percent of all retail sales.[32] Successful companies are using technology in their marketing strategies to develop profitable relationships with these customers.

Socially Responsible Marketing Can Promote the Welfare of Customers and Stakeholders

The success of our economic system depends on marketers whose values promote trust and cooperative relationships in which customers and other stakeholders are treated with respect. The public is increasingly insisting that social responsibility and ethical concerns be considered in planning and implementing marketing activities. Although some marketers' irresponsible or unethical activities end up on the front pages of *USA Today* or the *Wall Street Journal,* more firms are working to develop a responsible approach to developing long-term relationships with customers *and* society. For example, Staples, the office-supply superstore chain, has provided financial support and donated more than $400,000 worth of school supplies to the School, Home & Office Products Association (SHOPA) Kids in Need Foundation, which provides school supplies to needy children and teachers in low-income schools, through its Staples Foundation for Learning.[33] By being concerned about the impact of marketing on society, a firm can protect the interests of the general public and the natural environment.

Marketing Offers Many Exciting Career Prospects

From 25 to 33 percent of all civilian workers in the United States perform marketing activities. The marketing field offers a variety of interesting and challenging career opportunities throughout the world, such as personal selling, advertising, packaging, transportation, storage, marketing research, product development, wholesaling, and retailing. In addition, many individuals working for nonbusiness organizations engage in marketing activities to promote political, educational, cultural, church, civic, and charitable activities. Whether a person earns a living through marketing activities or performs them voluntarily for a nonprofit group, marketing knowledge and skills are valuable personal and professional assets.

...And now, back to XM Satellite Radio

While XM was getting its technology in order, it also was conducting marketing research to determine the target market's listening tastes. Based on this research, the company decided to devote most of its radio stations to specific music genres, such as country, rap, jazz, blues, rock and roll, classic rock, international pop, instrumental classical music, and movie sound-tracks. Some stations feature shows hosted by celebrities such as Bob Dylan, Snoop Dogg, and Wynton Marsalis. XM also offers news-only, sports-only, talk-only, comedy-only, and children's stations, among other special-interest stations.

Setting a price involved a delicate balancing act. On the one hand, XM wanted to build a sizable subscriber base, so its prices had to be within customers' reach. On the other hand, the company wanted to recoup some of its high startup costs and become profitable for the long haul. In the end, XM set a monthly subscription fee of $9.95 (later raised to $12.95) and priced its first radios at $300 or less. Within a year the company launched smaller, less expensive radios for the home and for listening on the go.

Today, XM Satellite Radio has nearly 8 million subscribers and expects to become profitable in the near future. Rival Sirius, in contrast, has 6 million customers. XM continues to expand and innovate. One recent innovation is a $50 radio that can be connected to a personal computer, complete with software for switching between channels. The firm also began broadcasting weather and traffic reports for the 21 largest U.S. cities to draw listeners who otherwise would have tuned into local AM or FM stations for this information. Today there are new radios capable of receiving either company's channels. XM's CEO expects to maintain his company's dominance by putting the emphasis on program content. "The technology is only the facilitator," he says. "Music connects so personally to people. We're putting the passion back into radio."

However, there may be clouds on the horizon; some analysts worry that leveling-off subscriber numbers may mean that neither XM nor Sirius will ever become profitable. Moreover, XM faces troubles with the Federal Communication Commission (FCC) because thousands of radio converters cause too much FM band interference. A key XM board member resigned in 2006, citing internal mismanagement and a possible looming financial crisis at the company. Sirius has its own problems, with 2 million subscribers tuning in to hear Howard Stern when it needs at least 3 million Stern subscribers to break even. There has been talk of a merger between Sirius and XM, and some would argue that a merger makes sense. Both companies have heavy debt, inadequate cash, and poor cash flow, perfect for an all-stock merger of equals. However, skeptics point out that the FCC probably would refuse to sign off on a merger because it would create a monopoly in satellite radio. It looks like it may be a rocky road for satellite radio to reach profitability.[34]

1. How is XM Satellite Radio differentiating its product from that of Sirius?

2. What role has price played in XM's product development and management?

3. Evaluate the marketing mix for XM.

CHAPTER REVIEW

1. Define marketing.

Marketing is the process of creating, pricing, distributing, and promoting goods, services, and ideas to facilitate satisfying exchange relationships with customers and to develop and maintain favorable relationships with stakeholders in a dynamic environment. The essence of marketing is to develop satisfying exchanges from which both customers and marketers benefit.

2. Understand several important marketing terms, including *target market, marketing mix, marketing exchanges,* and *marketing environment.*

A target market is the group of customers toward which a company directs a set of marketing efforts.

The variables—product, price, distribution, and promotion—are known as the marketing mix because marketing managers decide what type of each element to use and in what amounts. Marketing managers strive to develop a marketing mix that matches the needs of customers in the target market. Before marketers can develop a marketing mix, they must collect in-depth, up-to-date information about customer needs.

Individuals and organizations engage in marketing to facilitate exchanges—the provision or transfer of goods, services, and ideas in return for something of value. Four conditions must exist for an exchange to occur: (1) Two or more individuals, groups, or organizations must participate, and each must possess something of value that the other party desires; (2) the exchange should provide a benefit or satisfaction to both parties involved in the transaction; (3) each party must have confidence in the promise of the "something of value" held by the other; and (4) to build trust, the parties to the exchange must meet expectations. Marketing activities should attempt to create and maintain satisfying exchange relationships with all stakeholders—those constituents who have a "stake," or claim, in some aspect of a company's products, operations, markets, industry, and outcomes.

The marketing environment, which includes competitive, economic, political, legal and regulatory, technological, and sociocultural forces, surrounds the customer and the marketing mix. These forces can create threats to marketers, but they also generate opportunities for new products and new methods of reaching customers.

3. Be aware of the marketing concept and marketing orientation.

According to the marketing concept, an organization should try to provide products that satisfy customers' needs through a coordinated set of activities that also allows the organization to achieve its goals. Customer satisfaction is the marketing concept's major objective. The philosophy of the marketing concept emerged in the United States during the 1950s after the production and sales eras. Organizations that develop activities consistent with the marketing concept become marketing-oriented organizations.

4. Understand the importance of building customer relationships.

Relationship marketing involves establishing long-term, mutually satisfying buyer–seller relationships. Customer relationship management (CRM) focuses on using information about customers to create marketing strategies that develop and sustain desirable customer relationships. Managing customer relationships requires identifying patterns of buying behavior and using that information to focus on the most promising and profitable customers.

Value is a customer's subjective assessment of benefits relative to costs in determining the worth of a product. Benefits include anything a buyer receives in an exchange, whereas costs include anything a buyer must give up to obtain the benefits the product provides.

5. Explain the major marketing functions that are part of the marketing management process.

Marketing management is the process of planning, organizing, implementing, and controlling marketing activities to facilitate effective and efficient exchanges. Planning is a systematic process of assessing opportunities and resources, determining marketing objectives, developing a marketing strategy, and preparing for implementation and control. Organizing marketing activities involves developing the marketing unit's internal structure. Proper implementation of marketing plans depends on coordinating marketing activities, motivating marketing personnel, and communicating effectively within the unit. The marketing control process consists of establishing performance standards, comparing actual performance with established standards, and reducing the difference between desired and actual performance.

6. Understand the role of marketing in our society.

Marketing costs absorb about half of each buyer's dollar. Marketing activities are performed in both business and nonprofit organizations. Marketing activities help business organizations to generate profits, and they help fuel the increasingly global economy. Knowledge of marketing enhances consumer awareness. New technology improves marketers' abilities to connect with customers. Socially responsible marketing can promote the welfare of customers and society. Finally, marketing offers many exciting career opportunities.

Please visit the student website at **www.prideferrell.com** for ACE Self-Test questions that will help you prepare for exams.

KEY CONCEPTS

marketing	product	marketing concept	customer relationship
customers	exchanges	marketing orientation	management (CRM)
target market	stakeholders	relationship marketing	value
marketing mix	marketing environment		marketing management

ISSUES FOR DISCUSSION AND REVIEW

1. What is marketing? How did you define the term before you read this chapter?

2. What is the focus of all marketing activities? Why?

3. What are the four variables of the marketing mix? Why are these elements known as variables?

4. What conditions must exist before a marketing exchange can occur? Describe a recent exchange in which you participated.

5. What are the forces in the marketing environment? How much control does a marketing manager have over these forces?

6. Discuss the basic elements of the marketing concept. Which businesses in your area use this philosophy? Explain why.

7. How can an organization implement the marketing concept?

8. What is customer relationship management? Why is it so important to "manage" this relationship?

9. What is value? How can marketers use the marketing mix to enhance the perception of value?

10. What types of activities are involved in the marketing management process?

11. Why is marketing important in our society? Why should you study marketing?

MARKETING APPLICATIONS

1. Identify several businesses in your area that have not adopted the marketing concept. What characteristics of these organizations indicate nonacceptance of the marketing concept?

2. Identify possible target markets for the following products:
   a. Kellogg's Corn Flakes
   b. Wilson tennis rackets
   c. Disney World
   d. Diet Pepsi

3. Discuss the variables of the marketing mix (product, price, promotion, and distribution) as they might relate to each of the following:
   a. A trucking company
   b. A men's clothing store
   c. A skating rink
   d. A campus bookstore

Online Exercise

4. The American Marketing Association (AMA) is the marketing discipline's primary professional organization. In addition to sponsoring academic research, publishing marketing literature, and organizing meetings of local businesspeople with student members, it helps individual members to find employment in member firms. Visit the AMA website at **www.marketingpower.com.**
   a. What type of information is available on the AMA website to assist students in planning their careers and finding jobs?
   b. If you joined a student chapter of the AMA, what benefits would you receive?
   c. What marketing-mix variable does the AMA's Internet marketing effort exemplify?

globalEDGE™

Your firm is planning to develop a customer relationship management (CRM) initiative after it moves into international markets. One way to understand the similarity or dissimilarity of markets and cultures is to use Hofstede's cultural dimensions, based on scores for 56 countries. Hofstede's cultural dimensions can be found using the search term "56 countries" at **http://globaledge.msu.edu/ibrd** (and check the box "Resource Desk only") to access the Geert Hofstede Resource Center and then the link called Hofstede Scores. The Power Distance Index (PDI) can be valuable in developing a CRM strategy. What are the five countries scoring lowest on Hofstede's PDI? Are these countries on the same continent? Are they geographically close?

Video CASE

Finagle A Bagel

Finagle A Bagel, a fast-growing New England small business co-owned by Alan Litchman and Laura Trust, is at the forefront of one of the freshest concepts in the food-service business: fresh food. The 20 stores bake a new batch of bagels every hour and receive new deliveries of cheeses, vegetables, and other ingredients every day. Rather than prepackaging menu items, store employees make everything to order to satisfy the specific needs of each *guest* (Finagle A Bagel's term for a customer). Customers like this arrangement because they get fresh food prepared to their exact preferences—whether it's extra cheese on a bagel pizza or no onions in a salad—along with prompt, friendly service.

"Every sandwich, every salad is built to order, so there's a lot of communication between the customers and the cashiers, the customers and the sandwich makers, the customers and the managers," explains Trust. As a result, Finagle A Bagel's store employees have ample opportunity to build customer relationships and encourage repeat business. Many, like Mirna Hernandez of the Tremont Street store in downtown Boston, are so familiar with what certain customers order that they spring into action when regulars enter the store. "We know what they want, and we just ring it in and take care of them," she says. Some employees even know their customers by name and make conversation as they create a sandwich or fill a coffee container.

Over time, the owners have introduced a wide range of bagels, sandwiches, and salads linked to the core bagel product. Some of the most popular offerings include a breakfast bagel pizza, salads with bagel chip croutons, and BLT (bacon, lettuce, and tomato) bagel sandwiches. Round, flat, seeded, plain, crowned with cheese, or cut into croutons, bagels form the basis of every menu item at Finagle A Bagel. "So many other shops will just grab onto whatever is hot, whatever is trendy, in a 'me-too' strategy," observes Heather Robertson, director of marketing, human resources, and research and development. In contrast, she says, "We do bagels—that's what we do best. And any menu item in our stores really needs to reaffirm that as our core concept." That's the first of Finagle A Bagel's marketing rules.

To identify a new-product idea, Robertson and her colleagues conduct informal research by talking with both customers and employees. They also browse food magazines and cookbooks for ideas about out-of-the-ordinary flavors, taste combinations, and preparation methods. When developing a new bagel variety, for example, Robertson looks for ideas that are innovative yet appealing: "If someone else has a sun-dried tomato bagel, that's all the more reason for me not to do it. People look at Finagle A Bagel as kind of the trendsetter."

Once the marketing staff comes up with a promising idea, the next step is to write up a formula or recipe, walk downstairs to the dough factory, and mix up a test batch. Through trial and error, they refine the idea until they like the way the bagel or sandwich looks and tastes. Occasionally, Finagle A Bagel has to put an idea on hold until it can find just the right ingredients.

To further reinforce the brand and reward customer loyalty, Finagle A Bagel created the Frequent Finagler card. Cardholders receive one point for every dollar spent in a Finagle A Bagel store and can redeem accumulated points for coffee, juice, sandwiches, or a dozen bagels (actually a baker's dozen, meaning 13 instead of 12). To join, customers visit the company's website (**www.finagleabagel.com**) and complete a registration form asking for name, address, and other demographics. From then on, says Litchman, "It's a web-based program where customers can log on, check their points, and receive free gifts by mail. The Frequent Finagler is our big push right now to use technology as a means of generating store traffic."

Pricing is an important consideration in the competitive world of quick-serve food. This is where another of Finagle A Bagel's marketing rules comes in. Regardless of cost, the company will not compromise quality. Therefore, the first step in pricing a new product is to find the best possible ingredients and then to examine the costs and calculate an approximate retail price. After thinking about what a customer might expect to pay for such a menu item, shopping the competition, and talking with some customers, the company settles on a price that represents "a great product for a fair value," says Robertson.

Although Finagle A Bagel's rental costs vary, the owners price menu items the same in both higher-rent and lower-rent stores. "We have considered adjusting prices based upon the location of the store, but we haven't done it because it can backfire in a very significant way," owner Laura Trust explains. "People expect to be treated fairly, regardless of where they live."

Although Finagle A Bagel competes with other bagel chains in and around Boston, its competition goes well beyond restaurants in that category. "You compete with a person selling a cup of coffee; you compete with a grocery store selling a salad," Litchman notes. "People only have so many 'dining dollars,' and you need to convince them to spend those dining dollars in your store." Finagle A Bagel's competitive advantages are high-quality, fresh products, courteous and competent employees, and clean, attractive, and inviting restaurants.

Social responsibility is an integral part of Finagle A Bagel's operations. Rather than simply throwing away unsold bagels at the end of the day, the owners donate the bagels to schools, shelters, and other nonprofit organizations. When local nonprofit groups hold fundraising events, the owners contribute bagels to feed the volunteers. Over the years, Finagle A Bagel has provided bagels to bicyclists raising money for St. Jude Children's Research Hospital, to swimmers raising money for breast cancer research, and to people building community playgrounds. Also, the owners are strongly committed to being fair to their customers by offering good value and a good experience. "Something that we need to remember and instill in our people all the time," Trust emphasizes, "is that customers are coming in and your responsibility is to give them the best that you can give them."

Even with 300-plus employees, the owners find that owning a business is a nonstop proposition. "Our typical day never ends," says Trust. They are constantly visiting stores, dealing with suppliers, reviewing financial results, and planning for the future. Despite all these responsibilities, this husband-and-wife entrepreneurial team enjoys applying their educational background and business experience to build a business that satisfies thousands of customers every day.[35]

Questions for Discussion

1. Describe Finagle A Bagel's marketing mix.
2. What forces from the marketing environment provide opportunities for Finagle A Bagel? What forces might threaten the firm's marketing strategy?
3. Does Finagle A Bagel appear to be implementing the marketing concept? Explain your answer.

Planning Marketing Strategies

Ford's New Strategy: "The Way Forward"

Ford Motor Company, the world's third-largest automaker, was founded and incorporated by Henry Ford in 1903. Headquartered in Dearborn, Michigan, Ford today comprises many global brands, including Lincoln, Mercury, Jaguar, Aston Martin, Land Rover, Volvo, and Mazda, and it sells nearly 7 million vehicles around the world. Traditionally, the automaker has been one of the world's top ten corporations by revenue, and as recently as seven years ago, it ranked as one of the world's most profitable corporations. In recent years, however, Ford has not fared so well. The company has been declining in popularity for some time now, selling 4.7 percent fewer vehicles in 2005 than the previous year. In 2005 the company lost $1.6 billion (before taxes) on North American operations. Ford's share of U.S. new vehicle sales declined from 21.9 percent when Bill Ford (the founder's great-grandson) became CEO in 2001 to 16.8 percent in 2005. The firm spends an average of $2,500 per vehicle on retiree pensions and employee benefits—putting it at a sharp disadvantage relative to foreign automakers that can spend that money on such features as armrests in base models. Moreover, soaring gas prices have cut into demand for two of Ford's strongest segments: pickup trucks and sport-utility vehicles (SUVs).

In an attempt to jump-start sales, Ford Motor has embarked on a new strategy—"The Way Forward"—to reduce costs while maintaining a focus on customers as the foundation for everything the company does. The plan also includes an emphasis on cars and car-based crossover vehicles. It requires closing 16 factories and eliminating around 30,000 jobs over the course of six years. The Way Forward ultimately will reduce Ford's capacity by 1.2 million units, or 26 percent, by 2008. Ford's executives believe that refocusing its business model on customers will lead to stronger brands and products targeted more precisely for specific market segments. Ford targeted its new Fusion auto at women with a unique promotional campaign, the Fusion Studio D, a "pop-up store," that traveled to ten malls across the United States, where women could interact with the Fusion while they were being treated to beauty services, fitness training, and music, along with an opportunity to test drive the car. Ford's executives hope that this new strategy will help to propel the company into profitability and allow it to regain its foothold in U.S. and global markets.[1] ■

Copyright © Houghton Mifflin Company. All rights reserved.

OBJECTIVES

1. Describe the strategic planning process.

2. Explain how organizational resources and opportunities affect the planning process.

3. Understand the role of the mission statement in strategic planning.

4. Examine corporate, business-unit, and marketing strategies.

5. Understand the process of creating the marketing plan.

6. Describe the marketing implementation process and the major approaches to marketing implementation.

figure 2.1

COMPONENTS OF STRATEGIC PLANNING

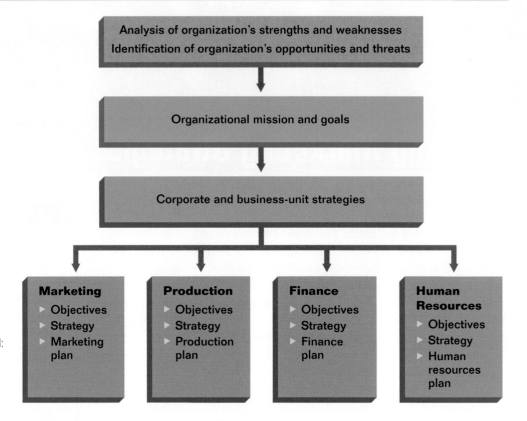

In the face of a dynamic environment, Ford Motor Company and many other companies are spending more time and resources on strategic planning, that is, on determining how to use their resources and abilities to achieve their objectives. Although most of this book deals with specific marketing decisions and strategies, this chapter focuses on the "big picture," on all the functional areas and activities—finance, production, human resources, and research and development, as well as marketing— that must be coordinated to reach organizational goals. Effectively implementing the marketing concept of satisfying customers and achieving organizational goals requires that all organizations engage in strategic planning.

We begin this chapter with an overview of the strategic planning process. Next, we examine how organizational resources and opportunities affect strategic planning and the role played by the organization's mission statement. After discussing the development of both corporate and business-unit strategy, we explore the nature of marketing strategy and creation of the marketing plan. These elements provide a framework for the development and implementation of marketing strategies, as we will see throughout the remainder of this book.

Understanding the Strategic Planning Process

strategic planning The process of establishing an organizational mission and formulating goals, corporate strategy, marketing objectives, marketing strategy, and a marketing plan

Through the process of **strategic planning,** a firm establishes an organizational mission and formulates goals, corporate strategy, marketing objectives, marketing strategy, and finally, a marketing plan.[2] A marketing orientation should guide the process of strategic planning to ensure that a concern for customer satisfaction is an integral part of the process. A marketing orientation is also important for the successful implementation of marketing strategies.[3] Figure 2.1 shows the components of strategic planning.

THE ANTIOXIDANT POWER OF POM TEA™
[POWERED BY POM$_x$]

Anti-ordinary. Anti-oxidant.

POM Tea
is no ordinary iced tea.

Thirsting for something different? Try refreshingly modern, all-natural POM Tea. It's made from the finest hand-picked, whole-leaf tea and it's gently brewed for a delicious taste with less caffeine. And it even comes in its own keepsake glass. But the most extraordinary ingredient in POM Tea is POM$_x$ – a highly concentrated blend of polyphenol antioxidants made from the same California pomegranates we use to make our POM Wonderful 100% Pomegranate Juice. It's enough to make other teas green with envy.

Enjoy the tea. Keep the glass. Reap the benefits. | pomtea.com | In produce

©2006 PomWonderful LLC. All rights reserved. POM Tea, POM, and "The antioxidant power of POM TEA" are trademarks of PomWonderful LLC.

Core Competency

Tea with pomegranate provides the advantage of antioxidants.

marketing strategy A plan of action for identifying and analyzing a target market and developing a marketing mix to meet the needs of that market

marketing plan A written document that specifies the activities to be performed to implement and control an organization's marketing activities

The process begins with a detailed analysis of the organization's strengths and weaknesses and identification of opportunities and threats within the marketing environment. Based on this analysis, the firm can establish or revise its mission and goals and then develop corporate strategies to achieve those goals. Next, each functional area of the organization (marketing, production, finance, human resources, etc.) establishes its own objectives and develops strategies to achieve them.[4] The objectives and strategies of each functional area must support the organization's overall goals and mission. The strategies of each functional area also should be coordinated with a focus on marketing orientation.

Because our focus is marketing, we are most interested, of course, in the development of marketing objectives and strategies. Marketing objectives should be designed so that their achievement will contribute to the corporate strategy and can be accomplished through efficient use of the firm's resources. To achieve its marketing objectives, an organization must develop a **marketing strategy,** which includes identifying and analyzing a target market and developing a marketing mix to satisfy individuals in that market. Thus a marketing strategy includes a plan of action for developing, distributing, promoting, and pricing products that meet the needs of the target market. Marketing strategy is best formulated when it reflects the overall direction of the organization and is coordinated with all the firm's functional areas. When properly implemented and controlled, a marketing strategy will contribute to the achievement not only of marketing objectives but also of the organization's overall goals. Consider that Apple's successful marketing strategy for its iPod line of music players helped to revitalize the computer firm's reputation for excellent design, which may transfer to other Apple products. The firm even designed its iMac G5 computer to mimic the look of an iPod with rounded corners and a translucent shell.[5]

The strategic planning process ultimately yields a marketing strategy that is the framework for a **marketing plan,** a written document that specifies the activities to be performed to implement and control the organization's marketing activities. In the remainder of this chapter we discuss the major components of the strategic planning process: organizational opportunities and resources, organizational mission and goals, corporate and business-unit strategy, marketing strategy, and the role of the marketing plan.

Assessing Organizational Resources and Opportunities

The strategic planning process begins with an analysis of the marketing environment. As we shall see in Chapter 3, competitive, economic, political, legal and regulatory, technological, and sociocultural forces can threaten an organization and influence its overall goals; they also affect the amount and type of resources the firm can acquire. However, these environmental forces can create favorable opportunities as well—opportunities that can be translated into overall organizational goals and marketing objectives.

Any strategic planning effort must assess the organization's available financial and human resources and capabilities, as well as how the level of these factors is likely to change in the future. Additional resources may be needed to achieve the organization's goals and mission.[6] Resources affect marketing and financial performance indirectly

FAMILY *Redefined.*

Enroll Today at **PETINSURANCE.COM** or **866-880-4717**

He's not just a dog. He's your baby and deserves the best medical care. VPI Pet Insurance helps pay for your pet's treatments, surgeries, lab fees, X-rays, and more. We even offer coverage for routine care, including vaccinations and prescription flea control. Plus, you're free to use any veterinarian. That's the kind of protection you need for all your family members. Call today for a free quote.

Applications subject to underwriting approval / Underwritten by Veterinary Pet Insurance Co. (CA), Brea, CA / National Casualty Co. (NAT), Madison, WI, an A+ 15-rated company / ©2006 Veterinary Pet Insurance Company

VPI PET Insurance

Market Opportunity

Because so many people are pet owners, companies such as VPI Pet Insurance have many market opportunities

by helping to create customer satisfaction and loyalty.[7] They also can include goodwill, reputation, and brand names. The reputation and well-known brand names of Rolex watches and BMW automobiles, for example, are resources that give these firms an advantage over their competitors. Such strengths also include **core competencies,** things a firm does extremely well—sometimes so well that they give the company an advantage over its competition. For example, the Chipotle Grill fast-casual restaurant chain has built an advantage over competitors such as Baja Fresh Mexican Grill and Moe's Southwest Grill through a simple menu and a fast, public food-preparation line with competitive prices.[8]

Analysis of the marketing environment involves not only an assessment of resources but also identification of opportunities in the marketplace. When the right combination of circumstances and timing permits an organization to take action to reach a particular target market, a **market opportunity** exists. For example, advances in computer technology and growth of the Internet have made it possible for real estate firms to provide prospective home buyers with databases of homes for sale all over the country. At **www.realtor.com,** the website of the National Association of Realtors, buyers have access to a wealth of online information about homes for sale, including photos, floor plans, and details about neighborhoods, schools, and shopping. The World Wide Web represents a great market opportunity for real estate firms because its visual nature is perfectly suited to the task of shopping for a home. Such opportunities are often called **strategic windows,** temporary periods of optimal fit between the key requirements of a market and the particular capabilities of a firm competing in that market.[9]

When a company matches a core competency to opportunities it has discovered in the marketplace, it is said to have a **competitive advantage.** In some cases a company may possess manufacturing, technical, or marketing skills that it can match to market opportunities to create a competitive advantage. For example, eBay pioneered the online auction and built the premier site where 212 million users around the world buy and sell products. By analyzing its customer base, eBay found an opportunity to improve growth by targeting the nearly 23 million small businesses in the United States, many of which already use the auction site to buy and sell construction, restaurant, and other business equipment. To appeal to this important market, eBay sought ways to improve customers' online shopping experience.[10]

SWOT Analysis

One tool that marketers use to assess an organization's strengths, weaknesses, opportunities, and threats is **SWOT analysis.** Strengths and weaknesses are internal factors that can influence an organization's ability to satisfy its target markets. *Strengths* refer to competitive advantages or core competencies that give the firm an advantage in meeting the needs of its target markets. John Deere, for example, promotes its service, experience, and reputation in the farm equipment business to emphasize the craftsmanship it uses in its lawn tractors and mowers for city dwellers. *Weaknesses* refer to any limitations that a company faces in developing or implementing a marketing strategy. Consider that America Online, once the leading Internet service provider, has

core competencies Things a firm does extremely well, which sometimes give it an advantage over its competition

market opportunity A combination of circumstances and timing that permits an organization to take action to reach a target market

strategic windows Temporary periods of optimal fit between the key requirements of a market and a firm's capabilities

competitive advantage The result of a company's matching a core competency to opportunities in the marketplace

SWOT analysis A tool that marketers use to assess an organization's strengths, weaknesses, opportunities, and threats

Taste versus Health: The Trans Fat War

In recent years, a great deal of press has focused on the health risks of *trans* fats, and many fast-food restaurants—major users of *trans* fat–filled oils and more—are taking notice. While many restaurant chains are replacing their *trans* fat–heavy oils with those that do not contain *trans* fats, others are sticking by the tried and true taste achieved by using *trans* fatty oils.

Wendy's, Subway, Taco Bell, Arby's, and KFC are among the companies that are in the process of replacing *trans* fatty oils with *trans* fat–free oils. Subway has long been low on *trans* fats, a fact the company is pondering advertising in 2007. Wendy's began using *trans* fat–free oils in 2006, and Taco Bell and KFC went *trans* fat–free in 2007. Arby's has promised that 75 percent of its menu will contain less than half a gram of *trans* fats by May 2007. All these restaurant chains are transitioning as a result of customer requests.

However, McDonald's, which continues to test *trans* fat–free oils, was treated to a bit of a backlash when it announced in 2002 that it would begin the move to *trans* fat–free oils. Consumers immediately began complaining about the change in taste of McDonald's french fries (cooked for years in high–*trans* fat oil)—even though the company hadn't yet begun its transition! Now the fast-food giant must struggle to balance the demands of health-conscious consumers with those of consumers who view the taste of the company's fries as forever linked with the brand itself.

Among those companies not even considering doing away with *trans* fats is the Popeyes chain, famous for its fried chicken and other Cajun delights. Unlike rival fried chicken purveyor KFC, Popeyes continues to rely on *trans* fatty oils to generate its chicken's signature inner tenderness and outer crispiness. The company has even hired an advertising agency to help promote its products, and that company, Fogarty Klein Monroe (FKM), plans to focus precisely on the unique flavors Popeyes' recipes produce. According to both Popeyes and FKM, changing the oil would change the flavor and diminish the Popeyes brand itself. Moreover, although they know it's not good for them, customers continue to fill Popeyes' restaurants, coming there for one reason—the taste of the food.

How the *trans* fats war will play out remains to be seen. Will companies committed to reducing or removing *trans* fats from their menus come out on top? Will those who stay committed to flavor and taste over health come out on top? Or will both sides win?[a]

shrunk from 30 million subscribers to fewer than 19 million, and the Time Warner unit continues to lose money.[11] Both strengths and weaknesses should be examined from a customer perspective because they are meaningful only when they help or hinder the firm in meeting customer needs. Only strengths that relate to satisfying customers should be considered true competitive advantages. Likewise, weaknesses that directly affect customer satisfaction should be considered competitive disadvantages. To boost profits, AOL has altered its marketing model, effectively ending paid subscribership in favor of advertising-driven revenues. To achieve its goals, the Internet provider will make much of its content, including e-mail, free.[12]

Opportunities and threats exist independently of the firm and therefore represent issues to be considered by all organizations, even those that do not compete with the firm. *Opportunities* refer to favorable conditions in the environment that could produce rewards for the organization if acted on properly. That is, opportunities are situations that exist but must be acted on if the firm is to benefit from them. *Threats*, on the other

It's difficult to do a side-by-side comparison when your binoculars stand alone.

Introducing the new full-size Leupold® Golden Ring® 8x42mm and 10x42mm binoculars. We've been making premium sports optics for nearly a century, and these do more than stand up to the world's best, they stand apart. The Index Matched Lens System™, with special lens coatings matched to each individual lens and lens surface, transmits vastly more usable light than other systems. Super-high reflective, phase coated prisms further assist in their magnificent light transmission, color fidelity, contrast, and clarity. You'll see the difference in the wide field of view — up to 388 feet at 1,000 yards — ideal for fast acquisition of moving game. Yet the close focus distance of a mere 5.9 feet is equally valuable, and equally bright and sharp. The unique interpupillary distance lock means one-handed use is no problem. Finally, the Leupold Golden Ring means these binoculars have been designed and assembled in our Beaverton, Oregon, factory, that they've been thoroughly tested, and are guaranteed for life to be incredibly rugged, absolutely waterproof, and fog proof in even the harshest hunting conditions. New Leupold Golden Ring binoculars...nothing else compares. Call 1-800-929-4949 for the Leupold Dealer nearest you. For a Leupold catalog, call 1-503-526-1400 or visit www.leupold.com.

© 2007 Leupold & Stevens, Inc.

LEUPOLD
AMERICA'S OPTICS AUTHORITY®

SWOT Analysis

Leupold's strength can be found in its competitive advantage of producing binoculars.

hand, refer to conditions or barriers that may prevent the firm from reaching its objectives. For example, Apple's top-selling iPod family of digital music players faces competition from cell phone makers and services that are incorporating MP3 technology into many new mobile phones. Indeed, Japanese consumers already download more songs onto their phones than onto their computers and digital players.[13] Threats must be acted on to prevent them from limiting the organization's capabilities. To counter the threat of increasing competition, Apple launched the iPhone, a cell phone with easy-to-use iTunes software, and iTunes' prices remain highly competitive.[14] Opportunities and threats can stem from many sources within the environment. When a competitor's introduction of a new product threatens a firm, a defensive strategy may be required. If the firm can develop and launch a new product that meets or exceeds the competition's offering, it can transform the threat into an opportunity.[15]

Figure 2.2 depicts a four-cell SWOT matrix that can help managers in the planning process. When an organization matches internal strengths to external opportunities, it creates competitive advantages in meeting the needs of its customers. In addition, an organization should act to convert internal weaknesses into strengths and external threats into opportunities. Ford Motor Company, for instance, converted the threats posed by rising gasoline prices and the growing acceptance of hybrid gas-electric cars from Japanese automakers into opportunities when it introduced a hybrid version of its Escape SUV. A firm that lacks adequate marketing skills can hire outside consultants to help convert a weakness into a strength.

figure 2.2

THE FOUR-CELL SWOT MATRIX

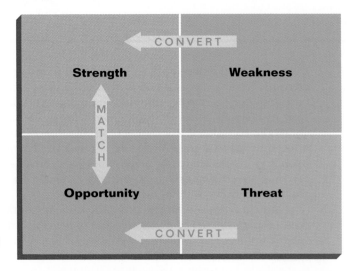

Source: Reprinted from *Market-Led Strategic Change,* by Nigel F. Piercy, p. 371, copyright © 1992 with permission from Elsevier Science.

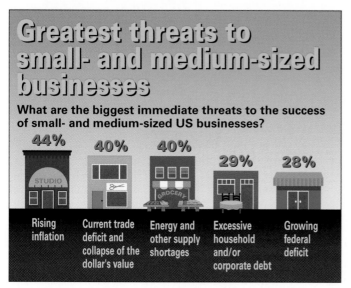

Greatest threats to small- and medium-sized businesses

What are the biggest immediate threats to the success of small- and medium-sized US businesses?

44%	40%	40%	29%	28%
Rising inflation	Current trade deficit and collapse of the dollar's value	Energy and other supply shortages	Excessive household and/or corporate debt	Growing federal deficit

Source: Data from Interland Business Barometer (www.interland.com). Margin of error: ±3 percentage points.

Establishing an Organizational Mission and Goals

Once an organization has assessed its resources and opportunities, it can begin to establish goals and strategies to take advantage of those opportunities. The goals of any organization should derive from its **mission statement,** a long-term view, or vision, of what the organization wants to become. Herbal tea marketer Celestial Seasonings, for example, says that its mission is "To create and sell healthful, naturally oriented products that nurture people's bodies and uplift their spirits."[16]

When an organization decides on its mission, it really answers two questions: Who are our customers? What is our core competency? Although these questions seem very simple, they are two of the most important questions any firm must answer. Defining customers' needs and wants gives direction to what the company must do to satisfy them. Figure 2.3 (on page 32) displays the FedEx mission that addresses customer requirements.

Companies try to develop and manage their *corporate identity*—their unique symbols, personalities, and philosophies—to support all corporate activities, including marketing. Managing identity requires broadcasting mission goals and values, sending a consistent message, and implementing visual identity with stakeholders. Mission statements, goals, and objectives must be implemented properly to achieve the desired corporate identity.[17] Johnson & Johnson, for example, has developed a credo and identity based on principles of responsibility to customers, employees, the community, and shareholders around the world.[18]

An organization's goals and objectives, derived from its mission statement, guide the remainder of its planning efforts. Goals focus on the end results that the organization seeks. Starbucks's mission statement, for example, incorporates the company's goals of striving for a high-quality product, a sound financial position, and community responsibility.

A **marketing objective** states what is to be accomplished through marketing activities. A marketing objective of Ritz-Carlton hotels, for example, is to have more than 90 percent of its customers indicate that they had a memorable experience at the hotel. Marketing objectives should be based on a careful study of the SWOT analysis and should relate to matching strengths to opportunities and/or the conversion of weaknesses or threats. These objectives can be stated in terms of product introduction, product improvement or innovation, sales volume, profitability, market share, pricing, distribution, advertising, or employee training activities.

Marketing objectives should possess certain characteristics. First, a marketing objective should be expressed in clear, simple terms so that all marketing personnel understand exactly what they are trying to achieve. Second, an objective should be written so that it can be measured accurately. This allows the organization to determine if and when the objective has been achieved. If an objective is to increase market share by 10 percent, the firm should be able to measure market share changes accurately. Third, a marketing objective should specify a time frame for its accomplishment. A firm that sets an objective of introducing a new product should state the time period in which to do this. Finally, a marketing objective should be consistent with both business-unit and corporate strategy. This ensures that the firm's mission is carried out at all levels of the organization. General Motors, for example, may have

mission statement A long-term view of what the organization wants to become

marketing objective A statement of what is to be accomplished through marketing activities

figure 2.3

FEDEX MISSION STATEMENT

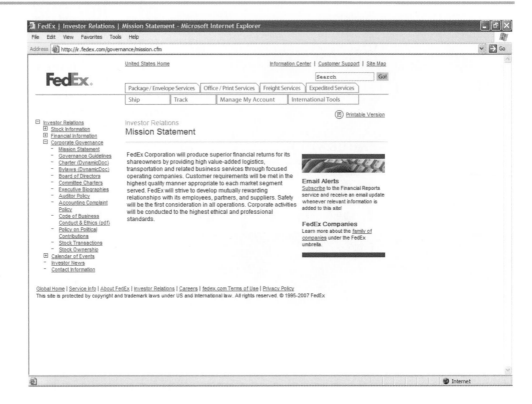

an overall marketing objective of maintaining a 25 percent share of the U.S. auto market. To achieve this objective, some GM divisions may have to increase market share while the shares of other divisions decline.

Developing Corporate, Business-Unit, and Marketing Strategies

In any organization, strategic planning begins at the corporate level and proceeds downward to the business-unit and marketing levels. Corporate strategy is the broadest of these three levels and should be developed with the organization's overall mission in mind. Business-unit strategy should be consistent with the corporate strategy, and marketing strategy should be consistent with both the business-unit and corporate strategies. Figure 2.4 shows the relationships among these planning levels.

Corporate Strategy

Corporate strategy determines the means for using resources in the functional areas of marketing, production, finance, research and development, and human resources to reach the organization's goals. A corporate strategy determines not only the scope of the business but also its resource deployment, competitive advantages, and overall coordination of functional areas. It addresses the two questions posed in the organization's mission statement: Who are our customers? What is our core competency? The term *corporate* in this context does not apply solely to corporations; corporate strategy is used by all organizations, from the smallest sole proprietorship to the largest multinational corporation.

corporate strategy A strategy that determines the means for using resources in the various functional areas to reach the organization's goals

figure 2.4

LEVELS OF STRATEGIC PLANNING

Mission statement

Corporate strategy

Business-unit strategy

Marketing strategy

Marketing mix elements
▸ Product
▸ Distribution
▸ Promotion
▸ Pricing

Corporate strategy planners are concerned with broad issues such as corporate culture, competition, differentiation, diversification, interrelationships among business units, and environmental and social issues. They attempt to match the resources of the organization with the opportunities and threats in the environment. Google, for example, purchased YouTube for $1.65 billion after recognizing that the video-sharing website's rapid growth reflected the growing popularity of viewing videos—professional and amateur—on every topic imaginable.[19] Corporate strategy planners are also concerned with defining the scope and role of the firm's business units so that they are coordinated to reach the ends desired. A firm's corporate strategy may affect its technological competence and ability to innovate.[20]

Business-Unit Strategy

After analyzing corporate operations and performance, the next step in strategic planning is to determine future business directions and develop strategies for individual business units. A **strategic business unit (SBU)** is a division, product line, or other profit center within the parent company. Borden's strategic business units, for example, consist of dairy products, snacks, pasta, niche grocery products such as ReaLemon juice and Cremora coffee creamer, and other units such as glue and paints. Each of these units sells a distinct set of products to an identifiable group of customers, and each competes with a well-defined set of competitors. The revenues, costs, investments, and strategic plans of each SBU can be separated from those of the parent company. SBUs operate in a variety of markets that have differing growth rates, opportunities, degrees of competition, and profit-making potential.

Strategic planners should recognize the different performance capabilities of each SBU and carefully allocate scarce resources among those divisions. Several tools allow a firm's portfolio of SBUs, or even individual products, to be classified and visually displayed according to the attractiveness of various markets and the business's relative market share within those markets. A **market** is a group of individuals and/or organizations that have needs for products in a product class and have the ability, willingness, and authority to purchase those products. The percentage of a market that actually buys a specific product from a particular company is referred to as that product's (or business unit's) **market share.** Hershey Foods, for example, controls 43 percent of the market for chocolate candy in the United States, whereas its rivals, Masterfoods and Nestlé, command 23 and 8 percent, respectively.[21] Product quality, order of entry into the market, and market share have been associated with SBU success.[22]

One of the most helpful tools is the **market-growth/market-share matrix,** the Boston Consulting Group (BCG) approach, which is based on the philosophy that a product's market growth rate and its market share are important considerations in determining its marketing strategy. All the firm's SBUs and products should be integrated into a single, overall matrix and evaluated to determine appropriate strategies for individual products and overall portfolio strategies. Managers can use this model to determine and classify each product's expected future cash contributions and future cash requirements. Generally, managers who use this model should examine the competitive position of a product (or SBU) and the opportunities for improving that product's contribution to profitability and cash flow.[23] The BCG analytical approach is more of a diagnostic tool than a guide for making strategy prescriptions.

Figure 2.5 (on page 34), which is based on work by the BCG, enables the strategic planner to classify a firm's products into four basic types: stars, cash cows, dogs, and

strategic business unit (SBU) A division, product line, or other profit center within a parent company

market A group of individuals and/or organizations that have needs for products in a product class and have the ability, willingness, and authority to purchase those products

market share The percentage of a market that actually buys a specific product from a particular company

market-growth/market-share matrix A strategic planning tool based on the philosophy that a product's market growth rate and market share are important in determining marketing strategy

Who advances America's power without leaving the environment behind? We do.

Innovations from Siemens can be found everywhere. From the underground substation in California to one of the world's most advanced gas turbine generators. And as a leading supplier of power and energy solutions, our focus is on developing technology that is more powerful, more efficient, more competitive and more environmentally compatible. We are constantly investing in research and development to meet the country's ever-changing energy demands and push our technology to the highest possible limits. At Siemens, our innovations have the power to make a difference in our planet's future.

automation & control • building technologies • energy & power • financial services • hearing solutions
industrial solutions • information & communication • lighting • medical solutions • transportation • water technologies

usa.siemens.com

SIEMENS

Corporate Strategy

Siemens corporate strategy focuses on its environmentally sound technology innovations.

question marks.[24] *Stars* are products with a dominant share of the market and good prospects for growth. However, they use more cash than they generate to finance growth, add capacity, and increase market share. An example of a star might be Nintendo's Wii videogame system. *Cash cows* have a dominant share of the market but low prospects for growth; typically, they generate more cash than is required to maintain market share. Bounty, the best-selling paper towels in the United States, represents a cash cow for Procter & Gamble. *Dogs* have a subordinate share of the market and low prospects for growth; these products are often found in established markets. Conventional cathode-ray tube televisions (CRTs) may be considered dogs at Sony, Toshiba, and Panasonic; the increasing popularity of flat-screen plasma and liquid-crystal display (LCD) televisions, especially high-definition televisions, has resulted in plummeting profits and market share for CRTs, and many manufacturers are implementing plans to phase them out. *Question marks,* sometimes called "problem children," have a small share of a growing market and generally require a large amount of cash to build market share. Mercedes carbon racing bikes, for example, are a question mark relative to Mercedes' automobile products.

The long-term health of an organization depends on having some products that generate cash (and provide acceptable profits) and others that use cash to support growth. Among the indicators of overall health are the size and vulnerability of the cash cows; the prospects for the stars, if any; and the number of question marks and dogs. Particular attention should be paid to products with large cash appetites. Unless the company has an abundant cash flow, it cannot afford to sponsor many such products at one time. If resources, including debt capacity, are spread too thin, the company will end up with too many marginal products and will be unable to finance promising new-product entries or acquisitions in the future.

figure 2.5

GROWTH-SHARE MATRIX DEVELOPED BY THE BOSTON CONSULTING GROUP

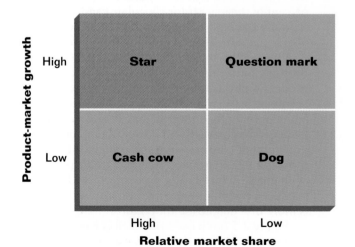

Source: Growth-Share Matrix Developed by the Boston Consulting Group, *Perspectives,* No. 66, "The Product Portfolio." Copyright © 1970. Reprinted by permission of Boston Consulting Group.

Marketing Strategy

The next phase in strategic planning is the development of sound strategies for each functional area of the organization. Corporate strategy and marketing strategy must balance and synchronize the organization's mission and goals with stakeholder relationships. This means that marketing must deliver value and be responsible in facilitating effective relationships with all relevant stakeholders.[25] An effective marketing strategy must gain the support of key stakeholders, including employees, investors, and communities, as well as channel members such as franchisees. Consider what happened when Burger King launched a $340 million advertising campaign featuring a heavy-metal band named Coq Roq. Franchisees, vital to the distribution of Burger King products, felt the marketing strategy targeted too narrow of a market—teenage males—and worried that it might alienate other desirable markets. Their dissatisfaction with the campaign and overall marketing strategy resulted in a complete communication breakdown in the Burger King national franchise organization.[26] There is a need in marketing to develop more of a stakeholder orientation to go beyond markets, competitors, and channel members to understand and address all stakeholder concerns.[27]

Within the marketing area, a strategy is typically designed around two components: (1) the selection of a target market and (2) the creation of a marketing mix that will satisfy the needs of the chosen target market. A marketing strategy articulates the best use of the firm's resources and tactics to achieve its marketing objectives. It also should match customers' desire for value with the organization's distinctive capabilities. Internal capabilities should be used to maximize external opportunities. The planning process should be guided by a marketing-oriented culture and processes in the organization.[28] A comprehensive strategy involves a thorough search for information, the analysis of many potential courses of action, and the use of specific criteria for making decisions regarding strategy development and implementation.[29] When implemented properly, a good marketing strategy also enables a company to achieve its business-unit and corporate objectives. Although corporate, business-unit, and marketing strategies all overlap to some extent, the marketing strategy is the most detailed and specific of the three.

Target Market Selection   Selecting an appropriate target market may be the most important decision a company has to make in the planning process because the target market must be chosen before the organization can adapt its marketing mix to meet this market's needs and preferences. Defining the target market and developing an appropriate marketing mix are the keys to strategic success. Toyota, for example, targeted its Yaris sedan at 18- to 34-year-olds by striving to give the compact cars a mischievous personality to complement their quirky styling and promoting them wherever Generation Y consumers could be found: MySpace and Facebook, a user-generated-content website, "mobisodes" (short mobile-phone episodes) of the television show *Prison Break*, and events such as the South X Southwest Music Festival and the Evolution Fighting Championships for videogames.[30]

Accurate target-market selection is crucial to productive marketing efforts. Products and even companies sometimes fail because marketers do not identify appropriate customer groups at whom to aim their efforts. If a company selects the wrong target market, all other marketing decisions will be a waste of time. Ford Motor, for example, experienced poor sales of its reintroduced Thunderbird in part because its $35,000 to $40,000 price tag was too steep for the retro-styled convertible's target

Target Market Selection

Dyson targets homeowners with its high-tech vacuum cleaners.

Engineered to easily navigate the most complex obstacle course ever created.

Your living room.

the ball dyson

figure 2.6

HEALTH AND WELLNESS SEGMENTS

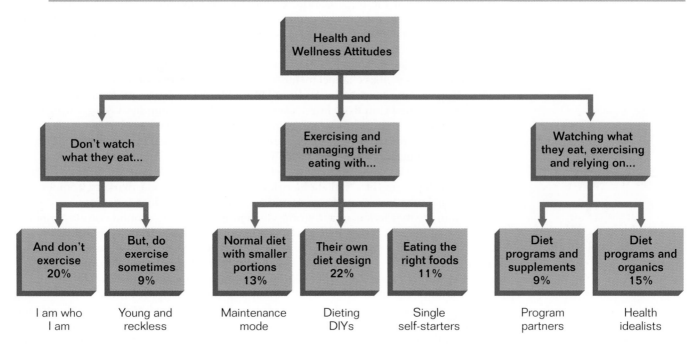

Source: ACNielsen Analytics, as reported in Joe Bucherer, Libbey Paul, and Laurie Demeritt, "The Future of Health and Wellness," *Consumer Insight,* Summer 2006, p. 9, http://us.acnielsen.com/pubs/documents/ci_q2_06_000.pdf.

market of younger baby boomers and older Generation Xers. However, the Thunderbird could not compete with luxury high-performance vehicles such as the BMW Z4 and the Audi TT, which offer greater horsepower and more features.[31] Organizations that try to be all things to all people rarely satisfy the needs of any customer group very well. An organization's management therefore should designate which customer groups the firm is trying to serve and gather adequate information about those customers. Marketers of health-food supplements and diet programs, for example, would be very interested in knowing about consumer attitudes and behaviors related to diet and exercise. A study by ACNielsen identified seven distinct segments based on information from surveys on eating habits, participation in diet plans, exercise habits, and health conditions, as well as consumers' product purchasing history for items such as fruits and vegetables; low-carb, organic, and low-fat foods; and vitamins and supplements (Figure 2.6). Identification and analysis of a target market provide a foundation on which the firm can develop a marketing mix.

When exploring possible target markets, marketing managers try to evaluate how entering them would affect the company's sales, costs, and profits. Marketing information should be organized to facilitate a focus on the chosen target customers. Accounting and information systems, for example, can be used to track revenues and costs by customer (or group of customers). In addition, managers and employees need to be rewarded for focusing on profitable customers. Teamwork skills can be developed with organizational structures that promote a customer orientation that allows quick responses to changes in the marketing environment.[32] Marketers also should assess whether the company has the resources to develop the right mix of product, price, promotion, and distribution to meet the needs of a particular target market. In addition, they determine if satisfying those needs is consistent with the firm's overall objectives and mission. When Amazon.com, the number 1 Internet bookseller, began selling electronics on its website, it made the decision that efforts to target this market would increase profits and be consistent with its objectives to be the largest online retailer. The

MMMMMMMMMMMMMORE PLEASE.
TEA CAN DO THAT.

New Lipton® Green Iced Tea is something that tastes good and is rich in naturally protective antioxidants. How's that for balance? Learn more at Lipton.com

Lipton
GREEN TEA

Creating the Marketing Mix

Lipton has targeted health-conscious consumers when determining its marketing mix.

sustainable competitive advantage An advantage that the competition cannot copy

size and number of competitors already marketing products in possible target markets are of concern as well.

Creating the Marketing Mix   The selection of a target market serves as the basis for creating a marketing mix to satisfy the needs of that market. The decisions made in creating a marketing mix are only as good as the organization's understanding of the target market. This understanding typically comes from careful, in-depth research into the characteristics of the target market. Thus, while demographic information is important, the organization also should analyze customer needs, preferences, and behavior with respect to product design, pricing, distribution, and promotion. For example, Kimberly-Clark's marketing researchers found that younger, design-conscious consumers are loath to place a run-of-the-mill box of Kleenex tissue even on top of the toilet. Kimberly-Clark therefore introduced Kleenex Oval Expressions, first as a holiday offering, in a contemporary oval package in bright colors and patterns that is stylish enough to place in more places around the house.[33]

Marketing-mix decisions should have two additional characteristics: consistency and flexibility. All marketing-mix decisions should be consistent with the business-unit and corporate strategies. Such consistency allows the organization to achieve its objectives on all three levels of planning. Flexibility, on the other hand, permits the organization to alter the marketing mix in response to changes in market conditions, competition, and customer needs. Marketing strategy flexibility has a positive influence on organizational performance. Marketing orientation and strategic flexibility complement each other to help the organization manage varying environmental conditions.[34]

The concept of the four marketing-mix variables has stood the test of time, providing marketers with a rich set of questions for the four most important decisions in strategic marketing. Consider the efforts of Harley-Davidson to improve its competitive position. The company worked to improve its product by eliminating oil leaks and other problems and set prices that customers considered fair. The firm used promotional tools to build a community of Harley riders renowned for their camaraderie. Harley-Davidson also fostered strong relationships with the dealers who distribute the company's motorcycles and related products and who reinforce the firm's promotional messages. Even the Internet has not altered the importance of finding the right marketing mix, although it has affected specific marketing-mix elements. Amazon.com, for example, has exploited information technology to facilitate sales promotion by offering product feedback from other customers to help shoppers make a purchase decision.[35]

At the marketing-mix level, a firm can detail how it will achieve a competitive advantage. To gain an advantage, the firm must do something better than its competition. In other words, its products must be of higher quality, its prices must be consistent with the level of quality (value), its distribution methods must be efficient and cost as little as possible, and its promotion must be more effective than the competition's. It is also important that the firm attempt to make these advantages sustainable. A **sustainable competitive advantage** is one that the competition cannot copy. Wal-Mart, for example, maintains a sustainable competitive advantage in groceries over supermarkets because of its very efficient and low-cost distribution system. This allows Wal-Mart to offer lower prices and helped it to gain the largest share of the supermarket business. Maintaining a sustainable competitive advantage requires flexibility in the marketing mix when facing uncertain competitive environments.[36]

Cereality Makes Breakfast Cereal Cool

Although cereal is usually purchased in supermarkets, David Roth and Rick Bacher chose to open the first all-cereal restaurant in Arizona State University's Student Union. The firm's first sit-down, café-style restaurant was opened in a retail district near the University of Pennsylvania. Why not, since more than 95 percent of all Americans like cereal! Roth and Bacher have plans for at least 26 more cafés, targeting campuses, hospitals, train stations, arenas, airports, and office buildings across the United States. Cereality: Cereal Bar and Cafe offers more than 30 varieties of brand-name hot and cold cereals plus regular, flavored, or soy milk for about $2.95 per serving. In addition, the cafés offer toppings bars with more than 30 toppings such as cherries and marshmallows, as well as made-to-order cereal, yogurt-blend smoothies ("Slurrealities"), and homemade breakfast bars. The inspiration for the concept came from the cereal-loving characters on *Seinfeld*.

How does Cereality create an "out-of-home" atmosphere and retail experience to attract customers? First, the retail cafés are designed with kitchen-style cabinets, and employees dress in pajamas and robes to enhance the retail appeal. From Corn Chex to Wheaties, Cocoa Puffs to Lucky Charms and Cap'n Crunch, customers get good fast food, high in fiber and loaded with vitamins and minerals, served in Chinese-food takeout containers. Customers can even store their custom concoctions in an onsite computer for their next visit, or they can purchase select mixes, such as "Devil Made Me Do It," consisting of Cocoa Puffs, Lucky Charms, and chocolate-milk-flavored crystals topped with malt balls. If you are perplexed as to how to combine the complex assortment of cereals and toppings, you can consult with an onsite "cereologist" who can make informed recommendations. What helps fuel Cereality's success? With 65 percent repeat customers and the financial backing of Quaker, the company expects to be profitable in two to three years. For those who are "Koo Koo for Cocoa Puffs" or any other cereal, Cereality has your scoop. Cereality illustrates the idea that a new, innovative marketing strategy can be used to sell a product as simple and traditional as cereal.[b]

Creating the Marketing Plan

marketing planning The process of assessing opportunities and resources, determining objectives, defining strategies, and establishing guidelines for implementation and control of the marketing program

A major concern in the strategic planning process is **marketing planning,** the systematic process of assessing marketing opportunities and resources, determining marketing objectives, defining marketing strategies, and establishing guidelines for implementation and control of the marketing program. The outcome of marketing planning is the development of a marketing plan. As noted earlier, a marketing plan is a written document that outlines and explains all the activities necessary to implement marketing strategies. It describes the firm's current position or situation, establishes marketing objectives for the product or product group, and specifies how the organization will attempt to achieve those objectives.

Developing a clear, well-written marketing plan, though time-consuming, is important. The plan is the basis for internal communication among employees. It covers the assignment of responsibilities and tasks, as well as schedules for implementation. It presents objectives and specifies how resources are to be allocated to achieve those objectives. Finally, it helps marketing managers monitor and evaluate the performance of a marketing strategy.

marketing
ENTREPRENEURS

Tom Szaky

THE BUSINESS: TerraCycle

FOUNDED: In 2001, when Szaky was 19

SUCCESS: $2.5 million in sales

Tom Szaky, together with his classmate John Beyer, entered TerraCycle as a business-plan competition entry when he was a freshman at Princeton. Their concept came in fourth, but Szaky couldn't let go of the idea of marketing a product made entirely from garbage. Today, TerraCycle Plant Food, a compost-tea fertilizer (made from the castings of garbage-eating worms), can be found packaged in reused soda bottles with spray tops salvaged from manufacturers that never used them. The products are shipped to 7,000 U.S. and Canadian stores such as Home Depot, Wal-Mart, Whole Foods, and Wild Oats in boxes rejected by other companies because of printing errors. TerraCycle Plant Food immediately became the top-selling natural fertilizer after it was introduced on HomeDepot.com.[c]

Marketing planning and implementation are inextricably linked in successful companies. The marketing plan provides a framework to stimulate thinking and provide strategic direction, whereas implementation occurs as an adaptive response to day-to-day issues, opportunities, and unanticipated situations—for example, increasing interest rates or an economic slowdown—that cannot be incorporated into the marketing plan. Implementation-related adaptations directly affect an organization's marketing orientation, rate of growth, and strategic effectiveness.[37]

Organizations use many different formats when devising marketing plans. Plans may be written for SBUs, product lines, individual products or brands, or specific markets. Most plans share some common ground, however, by including many of the same components. Table 2.1 describes the major parts of a typical marketing plan.

Implementing Marketing Strategies

Marketing implementation is the process of executing marketing strategies. Although implementation is often neglected in favor of strategic planning, the implementation process itself can determine whether a marketing strategy succeeds. It is also important to recognize that marketing strategies almost always turn out differently than expected. In essence, all organizations have two types of strategy: intended strategy and realized strategy.[38] The **intended strategy** is the strategy the organization decided on during the planning phase and wants to use, whereas the **realized strategy** is the strategy that actually takes place. The difference between the two is often the result of how the intended strategy is implemented. For example, Chrysler's PT Cruiser was marketed originally to young drivers, but the retro-styled vehicle ultimately proved more popular with their nostalgic baby boomer parents. Just 4 percent of the PT Cruiser's buyers were from the car's intended target market of drivers under age 25.[39] The realized strategy, though not necessarily any better or worse than the intended strategy, often does not live up to planners' expectations.

Approaches to Marketing Implementation

Just as organizations can achieve their goals by using different marketing strategies, they can implement their marketing strategies by using different approaches. In this section we discuss two general approaches to marketing implementation: internal marketing and total quality management. Both approaches represent mindsets that marketing managers may adopt when organizing and planning marketing activities. These approaches are not mutually exclusive; indeed, many companies adopt both when designing marketing activities.

Internal Marketing   **External customers** are the individuals who patronize a business—the familiar definition of customers—whereas **internal customers** are the company's employees. For implementation to succeed, the needs of both groups of customers must be addressed. If internal customers are not satisfied, it is likely that external customers will not be either. Thus, in addition to targeting marketing activities at external customers, a firm uses internal marketing to attract, motivate, and retain qualified internal customers by designing internal products (jobs) that

marketing implementation The process of putting marketing strategies into action

intended strategy The strategy the company decides on during the planning phase

realized strategy The strategy that actually takes place

external customers Individuals who patronize a business

internal customers A company's employees

table 2.1	COMPONENTS OF THE MARKETING PLAN

Plan Component	Component Summary	Highlights
Executive summary	One- to two-page synopsis of the entire marketing plan	
Environmental analysis	Information about the company's current situation with respect to the marketing environment	1. Assessment of marketing environment factors 2. Assessment of target market(s) 3. Assessment of current marketing objectives and performance
SWOT analysis	Assessment of the organization's strengths, weaknesses, opportunities, and threats	1. Strengths 2. Weaknesses 3. Opportunities 4. Threats
Marketing objectives	Specification of the firm's marketing objectives	Qualitative measures of what is to be accomplished
Marketing strategies	Outline of how the firm will achieve its objectives	1. Target market(s) 2. Marketing mix
Marketing implementation	Outline of how the firm will implement its marketing strategies	1. Marketing organization 2. Activities and responsibilities 3. Implementation timetable
Evaluation and control	Explanation of how the firm will measure and evaluate the results of the implemented plan	1. Performance standards 2. Financial controls 3. Monitoring procedures (audits)

satisfy their wants and needs. **Internal marketing** is a management philosophy that coordinates internal exchanges between the organization and its employees to achieve successful external exchanges between the organization and its customers.[40]

Generally speaking, internal marketing refers to the managerial actions necessary to make all members of the marketing organization understand and accept their respective roles in implementing the marketing strategy. Thus marketing managers need to focus internally on employees as well as externally on customers.[41] This means that everyone, from the president of the company down to the hourly workers on the shop floor, must understand the role they play in carrying out their jobs and implementing the marketing strategy. At Starbucks, all employees get training and support, including health care benefits, and this fosters an organizational culture founded on product quality and environmental concern. In short, anyone invested in the firm, both marketers and those who perform other functions, must recognize the tenet of customer orientation and service that underlies the marketing concept.

As with external marketing activities, internal marketing may involve market segmentation, product development, research, distribution, and even public relations and sales promotion.[42] For instance, an organization may sponsor sales contests to inspire sales personnel to boost their selling efforts. Motorola, for example, took its MotoZone mobile consumer promotional tour to eight corporate campuses to permit employees to tour the demo areas, experience the products, and play games for prizes.[43] Such efforts help employees (and ultimately the company) to understand customers' needs and problems, teach them valuable new skills, and heighten their enthusiasm for their regular

internal marketing Coordinating internal exchanges between the firm and its employees to achieve successful external exchanges between the firm and its customers

jobs. In addition, many companies use planning sessions, websites, workshops, letters, formal reports, and personal conversations to ensure that employees comprehend the corporate mission, the organization's goals, and the marketing strategy. The ultimate results are more satisfied employees and improved customer relations.

Total Quality Management   Quality has become a major concern in many organizations, particularly in light of intense foreign competition, more demanding customers, and poorer profit performance owing to reduced market share and higher costs. To regain a competitive edge, a number of firms have adopted a total quality management approach. **Total quality management (TQM)** is a philosophy that uniform commitment to quality in all areas of the organization will promote a culture that meets customers' perceptions of quality. Indeed, research has shown that both quality orientation and marketing orientation are sources of superior performance.[44] TQM involves coordinating efforts to improve customer satisfaction, increase employee participation and empowerment, form and strengthen supplier partnerships, and facilitate an organizational culture of continuous quality improvement. TQM requires continuous quality improvement and employee empowerment.

Continuous improvement of an organization's goods and services is built around the notion that quality is free; by contrast, *not* having high-quality goods and services can be very expensive, especially in terms of dissatisfied customers.[45] A primary tool of the continuous improvement process is **benchmarking,** the measuring and evaluating of the quality of the organization's goods, services, or processes as compared with the quality produced by the best-performing companies in the industry.[46] Benchmarking fosters organizational "learning" by helping firms to identify and enhance valuable marketing capabilities.[47] It also helps an organization to assess where it stands competitively in its industry, thus giving it a goal to aim for over time.

Ultimately, TQM succeeds or fails because of the efforts of the organization's employees. Thus employee recruitment, selection, and training are critical to the success of marketing implementation. **Empowerment** gives customer-contact employees the authority and responsibility to make marketing decisions without seeking the approval of their supervisors.[48] Although employees at any level in an organization can be empowered to make decisions, empowerment is used most often at the frontline, where employees interact daily with customers.

One characteristic of empowerment is that employees can perform their jobs the way they see fit, as long as their methods and outcomes are consistent with the organization's mission. However, empowering employees is successful only if the organization is guided by an overall corporate vision, shared goals, and a culture that supports the TQM effort.[49] For example, Ritz-Carlton hotels give each customer-contact employee permission to take care of customer needs as he or she observes issues. A great deal of time, effort, and patience are needed to develop and sustain a quality-oriented culture in an organization.

Organizing Marketing Activities

The structure and relationships of a marketing unit, including lines of authority and responsibility that connect and coordinate individuals, strongly affect marketing activities. Firms that truly adopt the marketing concept develop a distinct organizational culture: a culture based on a shared set of beliefs that makes the customer's needs the pivotal point of the firm's decisions about strategy and operations.[50] Instead of developing products in a vacuum and then trying to persuade customers to purchase them, companies using the marketing concept begin with an orientation toward their customers' needs and desires. Recreational Equipment, Inc. (REI), for example, gives customers a chance to try out sporting goods in conditions that approximate how the products actually will be used. Customers can try out hiking boots on a simulated hiking path with a variety of trail surfaces and inclines or test climbing gear on an indoor climbing wall. In addition, REI offers clinics to customers, such as "Rock Climbing Basics," "Basic Backpacking," and "REI's Outdoor School."[51]

total quality management (TQM) A philosophy that uniform commitment to quality in all areas of the organization will promote a culture that meets customers' perceptions of quality

benchmarking Comparing the quality of the firm's goods, services, or processes with that of the best-performing competitors

empowerment Giving customer-contact employees authority and responsibility to make marketing decisions on their own

If the marketing concept serves as a guiding philosophy, the marketing unit will be closely coordinated with other functional areas, such as production, finance, and human resources. Marketing must interact with other departments in a number of key areas. It needs to work with manufacturing in determining the volume and variety of the company's products. Those in charge of production rely on marketers for accurate sales forecasts. Research and development departments depend heavily on information gathered by marketers about product features and benefits consumers desire. Decisions made by the physical distribution department hinge on information about the urgency of delivery schedules and cost/service tradeoffs. Information technology is often a crucial ingredient in managing customer relationships effectively, but successful customer relationship management (CRM) programs must include every department involved in customer relations.[52]

How effectively a firm's marketing management can plan and implement marketing strategies also depends on how the marketing unit is organized. Organizing marketing activities in ways that mesh with a firm's strategic marketing approach enhances performance.[53] Effective organizational planning can give the firm a competitive advantage. The organizational structure of a marketing department establishes the authority relationships among marketing personnel and specifies who is responsible for making certain decisions and performing particular activities. This internal structure helps direct marketing activities.

One crucial decision regarding structural authority is centralization versus decentralization. In a **centralized organization,** top-level managers delegate very little authority to lower levels. In a **decentralized organization,** decision-making authority is delegated as far down the chain of command as possible. The decision to centralize or decentralize the organization directly affects marketing. Most traditional organizations are highly centralized. In these organizations, most, if not all, marketing decisions are made at the top levels. However, as organizations become more marketing oriented, centralized decision making proves somewhat ineffective. In these organizations, decentralized authority allows the company to respond to customer needs more quickly.

No single approach to organizing a marketing unit works equally well in all businesses. The best approach or approaches depends on the number and diversity of the firm's products, the characteristics and needs of the people in the target market, and many other factors. A marketing unit can be organized according to (1) functions, (2) products, (3) regions, or (4) types of customers. Firms often use some combination of these organizational approaches. Product features may dictate that the marketing unit be structured by products, whereas customer characteristics may require that it be organized by geographic region or types of customers. By using more than one type of structure, a flexible marketing unit can develop and implement marketing plans to match customers' needs precisely.

Organizing by Functions   Some marketing departments are organized by general marketing functions, such as marketing research, product development, distribution, sales, advertising, and customer relations. The personnel who direct these functions report directly to the top-level marketing executive. This structure is fairly common because it works well for some businesses with centralized marketing operations, such as Ford and General Motors. In more decentralized firms, such as grocery-store chains, functional organization can cause serious coordination problems. However, the functional approach may suit a large, centralized company whose products and customers are neither numerous nor diverse.

Organizing by Products   An organization that produces and markets diverse products may find the functional approach inadequate. The decisions and problems related to a single marketing function for one product may be quite different from those related to the same marketing function for another product. As a result, businesses that produce diverse products sometimes organize their marketing units according to product groups. Organizing by product groups gives a firm the flexibility to develop special marketing mixes for different products. Procter & Gamble, like many firms in the consumer packaged goods industry, is organized by product group. Although organizing

centralized organization A structure in which top management delegates little authority to levels below it

decentralized organization A structure in which decision-making authority is delegated as far down the chain of command as possible

Organizing by Types of Customers

Marketing is often organized according to different types of customers and their diverse needs, as seen by Business Week's digital offering.

marketing control process Establishing performance standards and trying to match actual performance to those standards

performance standard An expected level of performance

by products allows a company to remain flexible, this approach can be rather expensive unless efficient categories of products are grouped together to reduce duplication and improve coordination of product management.

Organizing by Regions   A large company that markets products nationally (or internationally) may organize its marketing activities by geographic regions. Managers of marketing functions for each region report to their regional marketing manager; all the regional marketing managers report directly to the executive marketing manager. Frito-Lay, for example, is organized into four regional divisions, allowing the company to get closer to its customers and respond more quickly and efficiently to regional competitors. This form of organization is especially effective for a firm whose customers' characteristics and needs vary greatly from one region to another. Firms that try to penetrate the national market intensively may divide regions into subregions.

Organizing by Types of Customers   Sometimes a company's marketing unit is organized according to types of customers. This form of internal organization works well for a firm that has several groups of customers whose needs and problems differ significantly. For example, Home Depot targets home builders and contractors as well as do-it-yourself customers and consumers who desire installation and service. Retailers may want more rapid delivery of small shipments and more personal selling by the producer than do either wholesalers or institutional buyers. Because the marketing decisions and activities required for these two groups of customers differ considerably, the company may find it efficient to organize its marketing unit by types of customers.

Controlling Marketing Activities

To achieve both marketing and general organizational objectives, marketing managers must control marketing efforts effectively. The **marketing control process** consists of establishing performance standards, evaluating actual performance by comparing it with established standards, and reducing the differences between desired and actual performance.

Although the control function is a fundamental management activity, it has received little attention in marketing. Organizations have both formal and informal control systems. The formal marketing control process, as mentioned before, involves performance standards, evaluation of actual performance, and corrective action to remedy shortfalls (see Figure 2.7). The informal control process involves self-control, social or group control, and cultural control through acceptance of a firm's value system. Which type of control system dominates depends on the environmental context of the firm.[54] We now discuss these steps in the formal control process and consider the major problems they involve.

Establishing Performance Standards   Planning and controlling are closely linked because plans include statements about what is to be accomplished. For purposes of control, these statements function as performance standards. A **performance standard** is an expected level of performance against which actual performance can be compared. A performance standard might be a reduction of customers' complaints by 20 percent, a monthly sales quota of $150,000, or a 10 percent increase per month in new-customer accounts. Toyota, for example, had a goal of selling 175,000 Prius hybrid-electric vehicles in the United States in 2007.[55] As stated earlier, performance standards should be tied to organizational goals.

figure 2.7

THE MARKETING CONTROL PROCESS

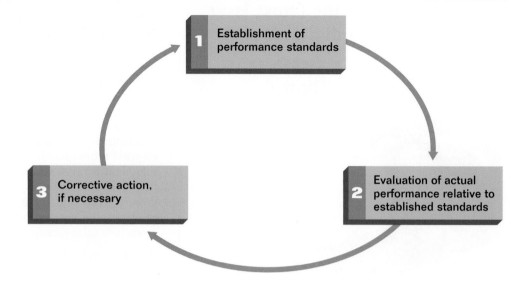

Evaluating Actual Performance   To compare actual performance with performance standards, marketing managers must know what employees within the company are doing and have information about the activities of external organizations that provide the firm with marketing assistance. For example, Saturn, like many automakers, evaluates its product and service levels by how well it ranks on the J. D. Power and Associates Customer Service Index. In 2006, Saturn ranked number 7 among all automakers, down from number 3 in 2005, behind Lexus, Buick, Cadillac, Jaguar, Lincoln, and Mercury.[56] Records of actual performance are compared with performance standards to determine whether and how much of a discrepancy exists. For example, if Toyota determines that only 162,000 Prius were sold in 2007, a discrepancy exists because its goal for the Prius was 175,000 vehicles sold annually.

Taking Corrective Action   Marketing managers have several options for reducing a discrepancy between established performance standards and actual performance. They can take steps to improve actual performance, reduce or totally change the performance standard, or do both. For example, when Motorola introduced its Q mobile phone, competition lowered the price of its products, requiring Motorola to lower the price of the Q by $100. To improve actual performance, the marketing manager may have to use better methods of motivating marketing personnel or find more effective techniques for coordinating marketing efforts.

Problems in Controlling Marketing Activities   In their efforts to control marketing activities, marketing managers frequently run into several problems. Often the information required to control marketing activities is unavailable or is available only at a high cost. Even though marketing controls should be flexible enough to allow for environmental changes, the frequency, intensity, and unpredictability of such changes may hamper control. In addition, the time lag between marketing activities and their results limits a marketing manager's ability to measure the effectiveness of specific marketing activities. This is especially true for all advertising activities.

Because marketing and other business activities overlap, marketing managers often cannot determine the precise costs of marketing activities. Without an accurate measure of marketing costs, it is difficult to know if the outcome of marketing activities is worth the expense. Finally, marketing control may be difficult because it is very hard to develop exact performance standards for marketing personnel.

...And now, back to Ford

In 2006 Ford announced the second phase of its Way Forward strategy to return the company to profitability. Bill Ford resigned as CEO (but remained chairman), and Alan Mulally, a former executive vice president of Boeing, took the reins. Although Mulally has a lot of energy, some people fret that his lack of experience in the auto industry may hamper his ability to effect a turnaround at Ford. However, he had been credited with turning around Boeing's commercial airlines unit after 9/11, and many people hope that he will be able to do the same for Ford. Since he took the helm, Mulally has made reducing capacity to match lower demand for Ford vehicles the number 1 priority. He believes that Ford has unlimited potential for savings by uniting its global operations in product development, manufacturing, and purchasing. Also, by the end of 2006, Ford was ahead of schedule and had met its target of cutting 30,000 hourly employees in the United States.

Some analysts suggest that streamlining Ford's wide range of brands in favor of the most profitable ones would be a great way to reduce costs. Toyota and BMW, for example, have only two or three brands compared with Ford's seven. These analysts contend that when there are so many brands, the ones that can't pull their weight can drain management energy and company funds. However, Ford seems to be committed to keeping all its brands, although it has taken steps in architecture sharing among them. It has focused on reducing product-development times by 6 to 12 months and on quality. In *Consumer Report*'s "New Car Preview," Ford had the best showing among domestic automakers, but it also had 12 vehicles listed among the "least reliable." By accelerating the pace of quality improvements, Ford hopes to improve customer satisfaction and thereby increase the number of people who buy its cars. Another part of the Way Forward plan is a return to clear, simple pricing—bringing its sticker prices more in line with actual transaction prices, reducing the number of rebates as it introduces new cars and trucks into the marketplace.

Whether Ford will be able to continue its aggressive Way Forward plan and implement it successfully with the help of its new leader, Alan Mulally, remains to be seen. According to former CEO Bill Ford, "We have said we intend to restore automotive profitability in North America by no later than 2008, and we remain committed to deliver on our promise." Only time will tell if Ford will succeed.[57]

1. Conduct a brief SWOT analysis for Ford.

2. What market opportunities should Ford focus on in the future?

3. Describe the target market for a Ford car or truck.

CHAPTER REVIEW

1. Describe the strategic planning process.

Through the process of strategic planning, a firm identifies or establishes its organizational mission and goals, corporate strategy, marketing goals and objectives, marketing strategy, and marketing plan. To achieve its marketing objectives, an organization must develop a marketing strategy, which includes identifying a target market and developing a plan of action for developing, distributing, promoting, and pricing products that meets the needs of customers in that target market. The strategic planning process ultimately yields the framework for a marketing plan, which is a written document that specifies the activities to be performed for implementing and controlling an organization's marketing activities.

2. Explain how organizational resources and opportunities affect the planning process.

The marketing environment, including competitive, economic, political, legal and regulatory, technological, and sociocultural forces, can affect the resources a firm can acquire and create favorable opportunities. Resources may include core competencies, which are things that a firm does extremely well, sometimes so well that it gives the company an advantage over its competition. When the right combination of circumstances and timing permits an organization to take action toward reaching a particular target market, a market opportunity exists. Strategic windows are temporary periods of optimal fit between the key requirements of a market and the particular capabilities of a firm competing in that market. When a company matches a core competency to opportunities it has discovered in the marketplace, it is said to have a competitive advantage.

3. Understand the role of the mission statement in strategic planning.

An organization's goals should be derived from its mission statement, which is a long-term view, or vision, of what the organization wants to become. A well-formulated mission statement helps to give an organization a clear purpose and direction, distinguish it from competitors, provide direction for strategic planning, and foster a focus on customers. An organization's goals and objectives, which focus on the end results sought, guide the remainder of its planning efforts.

4. Examine corporate, business-unit, and marketing strategies.

Corporate strategy determines the means for using resources in the areas of production, finance, research and development, human resources, and marketing to reach the organization's goals. Business-unit strategy focuses on strategic business units (SBUs)—divisions, product lines, or other profit centers within the parent company used to define areas for consideration in a specific strategic market plan. The Boston Consulting Group's market-growth/market-share matrix integrates a firm's products or SBUs into a single, overall matrix for evaluation to determine appropriate strategies for individual products and business units. Marketing strategies, the most detailed and specific of the three levels of strategy, are composed of two elements: selection of a target market and creation of a marketing mix that will satisfy the needs of the chosen target market. The selection of a

target market serves as the basis for creation of the marketing mix to satisfy the needs of that market. Marketing-mix decisions also should be consistent with business-unit and corporate strategies and be flexible enough to respond to changes in market conditions, competition, and customer needs. Different elements of the marketing mix can be changed to accommodate different marketing strategies.

5. Understand the process of creating the marketing plan.

The outcome of marketing planning is the development of a marketing plan, which outlines all the activities necessary to implement marketing strategies. The plan fosters communication among employees, assigns responsibilities and schedules, specifies how resources are to be allocated to achieve objectives, and helps marketing managers monitor and evaluate the performance of a marketing strategy.

6. Describe the marketing implementation process and the major approaches to marketing implementation.

Marketing implementation is the process of executing marketing strategies. Marketing strategies do not always turn out as expected. Realized marketing strategies often differ from the intended strategies because of issues related to implementation. Proper implementation requires efficient organizational structures and effective control and evaluation.

One major approach to marketing implementation is internal marketing, a management philosophy that coordinates internal exchanges between the organization and its employees to achieve successful external exchanges between the organization and its customers. For strategy implementation to be successful, the needs of both internal and external customers must be met. Another approach is total quality management (TQM), which relies heavily on the talents of employees to improve continually the quality of the organization's goods and services.

Please visit the student website at **www.prideferrell.com** for ACE Self-Test questions that will help you prepare for exams.

ACE self-test

KEY CONCEPTS

strategic planning	marketing objective	sustainable competitive advantage	total quality management (TQM)
marketing strategy	corporate strategy		
marketing plan	strategic business unit (SBU)	marketing planning	benchmarking
core competencies		marketing implementation	empowerment
market opportunity	market	intended strategy	centralized organization
strategic windows	market share	realized strategy	decentralized organization
competitive advantage	market-growth/market-share matrix	external customers	marketing control process
SWOT analysis		internal customers	performance standard
mission statement		internal marketing	

ISSUES FOR DISCUSSION AND REVIEW

1. Identify the major components of strategic planning, and explain how they are interrelated.

2. What are the two major parts of a marketing strategy?

3. What are some issues to consider in analyzing a firm's resources and opportunities? How do these issues affect marketing objectives and marketing strategy?

4. How important is SWOT analysis to the marketing planning process?

5. How should organizations set marketing objectives?

6. Explain how an organization can create a competitive advantage at the corporate, business-unit, and marketing-strategy levels.

7. Refer to question 6. How can an organization make its competitive advantages sustainable over time? How difficult is it to create sustainable competitive advantages?

8. What benefits do marketing managers gain from planning? Is planning necessary for long-run survival? Why or why not?

9. Why does an organization's intended strategy often differ from its realized strategy?

10. Why might an organization use multiple bases for organizing its marketing unit?

11. What are the major steps of the marketing control process?

MARKETING APPLICATIONS

1. Contact three organizations that appear to be successful. Talk with one of the managers or executives in the company, and ask if he or she would share with you the company's mission statement or organizational goals. Obtain as much information as possible about the statement and the organizational goals. Discuss how the statement matches the criteria outlined in the text.

2. Assume that you own a new family-style restaurant that will open for business in the coming year. Formulate a long-term goal for the company, and then develop short-term goals that will assist you in achieving the long-term goal.

3. Amazon.com identified an opportunity to capitalize on a desire of many consumers to shop at home. This strategic window gave Amazon.com a very competitive position in a new market. Consider the opportunities that may be present in your city, region, or the United States as a whole. Identify a strategic window, and discuss how a company could take advantage of this opportunity. What kind of core competencies are necessary?

4. Marketing units may be organized according to functions, products, regions, or types of customers.

Describe how you would organize the marketing units for the following:

a. Toothpaste with whitener; toothpaste with extra-strong nicotine cleaners; toothpaste with bubble-gum flavor

b. A national line offering all types of winter and summer sports clothing for men and women

c. A life insurance company that provides life, health, and disability insurance

Online Exercise

5. Internet analysts have praised Sony's website as one of the best organized and most informative on the Internet. See why by accessing **www.sony.com**.

a. Based on the information provided at the website, describe Sony's strategic business units.

b. Based on your existing knowledge of Sony as an innovative leader in the consumer electronics industry, describe the company's primary competitive advantage. How does Sony's website support this competitive advantage?

c. Assess the quality and effectiveness of Sony's website. Specifically, perform a preliminary SWOT analysis comparing Sony's website with other high-quality websites you have visited.

globalEDGE™

Rankings of the world's largest manufacturing companies provide a variety of data. Rankings by industry can be found using the search term "largest manufacturing companies" at **http://globaledge.msu.edu/ibrd** (and check the box "Resource Desk only") to access *IndustryWeek*'s IW 1000 ranking. Perform a SWOT analysis (i.e., strengths, weaknesses, opportunities, and threats) of the top five firms in the apparel industry. From the information included, which firm has the strongest market position? Analyzing all firms in the apparel industry, which five firms have the weakest positions?

Video CASE

Green Mountain Coffee Roasters Brews Up the Best Marketing Strategy

Green Mountain Coffee Roasters, Inc., is a leader in the specialty coffee industry. Founded in 1981 as a small café in Waitsfield, Vermont, Green Mountain quickly gained a reputation for its high quality, and demand for its freshly roasted coffee grew among local restaurants and inns. Incorporated in 1993, the firm today markets $162 million worth of coffee and related products through a coordinated multichannel distribution network with both wholesale and direct-to-consumer operations. This distribution network is designed to maximize brand recognition and product availability.

Green Mountain derives the majority of its revenue from more than 7,000 wholesale customer accounts located primarily in the eastern United States. The wholesale operation serves customers such as supermarkets, specialty food stores, convenience stores, food-service companies, hotels, restaurants, universities, and office coffee services. Many of these wholesale customers then resell the coffee in whole bean or ground form for home consumption or brew and sell coffee beverages at their places of business.

Green Mountain Coffee roasts 40 varieties of high-quality Arabica coffee beans and offers more than 100 selections of coffee such as single-origin, estate, and certified organic coffee, as well as proprietary blends and flavored coffees sold under the Green Mountain Coffee Roasters and Newman's Own Organics brand names. It has made a point of marketing certified Fair Trade coffees that help struggling coffee farmers earn fair market value for their efforts. It carefully selects its coffee beans and then roasts them to maximize their taste and flavor differences. Green Mountain coffee is delivered in a variety of packages, including whole bean, fractional packages, and premium one-cup coffee pods.

Green Mountain's objective is to be the leading specialty coffee company. It aims to achieve the highest market share in its target markets while maximizing company values. To meet these objectives, Green Mountain differentiates and reinforces the Green Mountain Coffee brand by distributing only the highest-quality products, providing superior customer service and distribution, stressing corporate governance and employee development, and implementing socially responsible business practices. Through these strategies, Green Mountain believes that it engenders a high degree of customer loyalty.

The company employs 600 people but has a flat organizational structure, which makes all employees responsible for implementation. Although it has functional departments that vary across the company, there are typically about four layers of hierarchy in each department. There is openness in all aspects of communication that allows employees to have regular access to all levels of the organization, including CEO Bob Stiller. The company urges each employee to voice his or her opinions and ideas. This encourages passion and commitment so that employees get to the heart of issues and challenges instead of playing office politics. In this way Green Mountain has fostered a culture that involves its workers in decision making and challenges them to find solutions to problems. Empowering employees to this degree means that the company sometimes may appear chaotic, but the communication across channels in what is sometimes termed a *constellation of communication* ensures the collaborative nature of getting things done.

In addition to growing sales and a reputation for quality, Green Mountain Coffee Roasters has been ranked among *Forbes* magazine's list of 200 Best Small Companies in America for six consecutive years. The company's commitment to social responsibility—not only to secure Fair Trade prices for coffee growers but also its support of social and environmental programs in coffee-growing regions—earned it a first place on *Business Ethics* magazine's annual list of 100 Best Corporate Citizens in 2006, up from its 2005 position of second.[58]

Questions for Discussion

1. Describe Green Mountain's marketing strategy.
2. How does Green Mountain use implementation to achieve success in a very competitive market?
3. How does empowerment work at Green Mountain?

The Marketing Environment, Social Responsibility, and Ethics

Starbucks Balances Growth and Responsibility

Starbucks was founded in 1971 by three partners, with the first store opening in Seattle's renowned Pike Place Market. Howard Schultz, then director of retail operations and marketing, recognized an opportunity to develop a coffee-bar culture in Seattle modeled after one he observed on a trip to Milan, Italy. Since then, Starbucks has been expanding across the United States, where it operates more than 8,800 stores, and around the world, with 3,600 outlets in 36 countries.

The company's objective is to establish Starbucks as the most recognized and respected brand in the world. To achieve this goal, the company intends to continue rapid expansion of its retail operations, to grow its specialty operations, and to selectively pursue other opportunities to leverage the Starbucks brand through the introduction of new products and the development of new channels of distribution. Starbucks manages its growth through careful consideration of the interests of all whom its operations affect and its corporate social responsibility.

Starbucks has gained a reputation for being a good corporate citizen. Unlike many food-service retailers, the company offers both full- and part-time employees a comprehensive benefits package that includes stock-option grants through "Bean Stock," as well as health, medical, dental, and vision benefits. It makes grants to charities and produces an annual report detailing its efforts to be socially responsible. It was one of the first major coffee-house brands to introduce "ethical" coffee in 2002, when it began offering a "Fair Trade coffee of the week." Although this was a fine gesture, many competitors have switched to 100 percent Fair Trade coffee, leaving Starbucks in a position to play catch-up in order to boost its image.

Although Starbucks has flourished, its success has attracted harsh criticism on issues such as Fair Trade coffee, genetically modified milk, Howard Shultz's alleged financial links to the Israeli government, and accusations that the company's relentless growth is forcing locally run coffee shops out of business. A survey by Global Marketing Insititute found that even Starbucks' customers view the company as "arrogant, intrusive, and self-centered." The most widespread criticism is that of Starbucks' "clustering" strategy of saturating areas with stores, which has forced many local coffee shops out of business. *Ethical Consumer* magazine researcher Ruth Rosselson says, "Starbucks operates like the supermarkets: It puts local companies out of businesses and with this policy can never be 100 percent ethical." Corporate Watch researcher Chris Grimshaw feels that Starbucks' social responsibility program is being used as a "smokescreen to create the illusion of ethics," adding that the company is committed solely to making money for shareholders.[1] ■

OBJECTIVES

1. Recognize the importance of environmental scanning and analysis.

2. Explore the effects of competitive, economic, political, legal and regulatory, technological, and sociocultural factors on marketing strategies.

3. Understand the concept and dimensions of social responsibility.

4. Differentiate between ethics and social responsibility.

Careful, the beverage you're about to enjoy is extremely...

To succeed in today's highly competitive marketplace, companies like Starbucks must respond to changes in the marketing environment, particularly changes in customer and public desires and competitors' actions. Increasingly, success also requires that marketers act responsibly and ethically. Because recognizing and responding to such changes in the marketing environment are crucial to marketing success, this chapter explores in some detail the forces that contribute to these changes.

The first half of this chapter explores the competitive, economic, political, legal and regulatory, technological, and sociocultural forces that make up the marketing environment. This discussion addresses the importance of scanning and analyzing the marketing environment, as well as how each of these forces influences marketing strategy decisions. The second half of the chapter considers the role of social responsibility and ethics. These increasingly important forces raise several issues that pose threats and opportunities to marketers, such as the natural environment and consumerism.

The Marketing Environment

The marketing environment consists of external forces that directly or indirectly influence an organization's acquisition of inputs (human, financial, natural resources and raw materials, and information) and creation of outputs (goods, services, or ideas). As indicated in Chapter 1, the marketing environment includes six such forces: competitive, economic, political, legal and regulatory, technological, and sociocultural.

Whether fluctuating rapidly or slowly, environmental forces are always dynamic. Changes in the marketing environment create uncertainty, threats, and opportunities for marketers. Consider that after uncertainty in the Middle East and the effects of hurricanes Katrina and Rita led to escalating fuel costs, many automakers saw sales of their gas-guzzling sport-utility vehicles (SUVs) plummet. For some firms, though, the situation proved fortuitous; for example, Honda, Nissan, and Toyota gained sales when many consumers switched to more fuel-efficient vehicles, such as the Toyota Prius.[2] Marketing managers who fail to recognize changes in environmental forces leave their firms unprepared to capitalize on marketing opportunities or to cope with threats created by changes in the environment. Monitoring the environment therefore is crucial to an organization's survival and to the long-term achievement of its goals.

To monitor changes in the marketing environment effectively, marketers engage in environmental scanning and analysis. **Environmental scanning** is the process of collecting information about forces in the marketing environment. Scanning involves observation; secondary sources such as business, trade, government, and Internet sources; and marketing research. The Internet has become a popular scanning tool because it makes data more accessible and allows companies to gather needed information quickly.

Environmental analysis is the process of assessing and interpreting the information gathered through environmental scanning. A manager evaluates the information for accuracy, tries to resolve inconsistencies in the data, and if warranted, assigns significance to the findings. By evaluating this information, the manager should be able to identify potential threats and opportunities linked to environmental changes.

Understanding the current state of the marketing environment and recognizing threats and opportunities arising from changes within it help companies with strategic planning. In particular, they can help marketing managers assess the performance of current marketing efforts and develop future marketing strategies.

environmental scanning The process of collecting information about forces in the marketing environment

environmental analysis The process of assessing and interpreting the information gathered through environmental scanning

Responding to the Marketing Environment

Marketing managers take two general approaches to environmental forces: accepting them as uncontrollable or attempting to influence and shape them.[3] An organization that views environmental forces as uncontrollable remains passive and reactive toward the environment. Instead of trying to influence forces in the environment,

First One To Save The Planet Wins.

We're all working for a better world. Cleaner air, a better environment and more natural resources. A worthy goal. At Toyota, we've been working on Hybrid Synergy Drive® for the past 40 years. The result? A technology that not only dramatically increases fuel economy but also creates far fewer smog-forming emissions. You'll find Hybrid Synergy Drive® on the Prius, Highlander Hybrid and, soon, the Camry Hybrid. In fact, we're working toward the day when you'll find it on all Toyota vehicles. Because we think you'll agree, better mileage and less pollution is a winning combination.

To learn more, visit toyota.com

HYBRID SYNERGY DRIVE

TOYOTA | moving forward ▶

Responding to Environmental Forces

Toyota produces hybrid cars in response to both customer demand and its own desires to exceed regulatory agency emissions standards.

competition Other firms that market products that are similar to or can be substituted for a firm's products in the same geographic area

brand competitors Firms that market products with similar features and benefits to the same customers at similar prices

product competitors Firms that compete in the same product class but market products with different features, benefits, and prices

its marketing managers adjust current marketing strategies to environmental changes. They approach with caution market opportunities discovered through environmental scanning and analysis. On the other hand, marketing managers who believe that environmental forces can be shaped adopt a more proactive approach. For example, if a market is blocked by traditional environmental constraints, proactive marketing managers may apply economic, psychological, political, and promotional skills to gain access to and operate within it. Once they identify what is blocking a market opportunity, they assess the power of the various parties involved and develop strategies to overcome the obstructing environmental forces. Microsoft, Intel, and Google, for example, have responded to political, legal, and regulatory concerns about their power in the computer industry by communicating the value of their competitive approaches to various publics. The computer giants contend that their competitive success results in superior products for their customers.

A proactive approach can be constructive and bring desired results. To exert influence on environmental forces, marketing managers seek to identify market opportunities or to extract greater benefits relative to costs from existing market opportunities. Political action is another way to affect environmental forces. The pharmaceutical industry, for example, has lobbied very effectively for fewer restrictions on prescription drug marketing. However, managers must recognize that there are limits on how much environmental forces can be shaped. Microsoft, for example, can take a proactive approach because of its financial resources and the highly visible image of its founder, Bill Gates. Although an organization may be able to influence legislation through lobbying, it is unlikely that a single organization can significantly increase the national birthrate or move the economy from recession to prosperity.

Competitive Forces

Few firms, if any, operate free of competition. In fact, for most products, customers have many alternatives from which to choose. For example, while the five best-selling soft-drinks are Coke Classic, Pepsi-Cola, Diet Coke, Mountain Dew, and Diet Pepsi, soft-drink sales in general have flattened as consumers have turned to alternatives such as bottled water, flavored water, fruit juice, and iced-tea products.[4] Thus, when marketing managers define the target market(s) their firm will serve, they simultaneously establish a set of competitors.[5] The number of firms that supply a product may affect the strength of competitors. When just one or a few firms control supply, competitive factors exert a different sort of influence on marketing activities than when many competitors exist.

Broadly speaking, all firms compete with one another for customers' dollars. More practically, however, a marketer generally defines **competition** as other firms that market products that are similar to or can be substituted for its products in the same geographic area. These competitors can be classified into one of four types. **Brand competitors** market products with similar features and benefits to the same customers at similar prices. For example, a thirsty, calorie-conscious customer may choose a diet soda such as Diet Coke or Diet Pepsi from the soda machine. However, these sodas face competition from other types of beverages. **Product competitors** compete in the same product class but market products with different features, benefits, and prices. The thirsty dieter, for instance, might purchase iced tea, juice, mineral water, or bottled

Drawn from nature.

From deep beneath the surface, filtered through ancient rock in the lush volcanic region of Auvergne. Volvic, natural spring water.

Volvic
Created by volcanoes
www.volvic-na.com

Brand Competition

Volvic bottled water has many competitors including Fiji, Evian, and Deer Park.

water instead of a soda. **Generic competitors** provide very different products that solve the same problem or satisfy the same basic customer need. Our dieter, for example, might simply have a glass of water from the kitchen tap to satisfy his or her thirst. **Total budget competitors** compete for the limited financial resources of the same customers.[6] Total budget competitors for Diet Coke, for example, might include gum, a newspaper, and bananas. Although all four types of competition can affect a firm's marketing performance, brand competitors are the most significant because buyers typically see the different products of these firms as direct substitutes for one another. Consequently, marketers tend to concentrate environmental analyses on brand competitors.

When just one or a few firms control supply, competitive factors exert a different form of influence on marketing activities than when many competitors exist. Table 3.1 presents four general types of competitive structures: monopoly, oligopoly, monopolistic competition, and pure competition. A **monopoly** exists when an organization offers a product that has no close substitutes, making that organization the sole source of supply. Because the organization has no competitors, it controls supply of the product completely and, as a single seller, can erect barriers to potential competitors. In reality, most monopolies surviving today are local utilities, which are heavily regulated by local, state, or federal agencies. An **oligopoly** exists when a few sellers control the supply of a large proportion of a prod-

generic competitors Firms that provide very different products that solve the same problem or satisfy the same basic customer need

total budget competitors Firms that compete for the limited financial resources of the same customers

monopoly A competitive structure in which an organization offers a product that has no close substitutes, making that organization the sole source of supply

oligopoly A competitive structure in which a few sellers control the supply of a large proportion of a product

table 3.1   SELECTED CHARACTERISTICS OF COMPETITIVE STRUCTURES

Type of Structure	Number of Competitors	Ease of Entry into Market	Product	Example
Monopoly	One	Many barriers	Almost no substitutes	Fort Collins (Colorado) Water Utilities
Oligopoly	Few	Some barriers	Homogeneous or differentiated (with real or perceived differences)	Toyota Motors (autos)
Monopolistic competition	Many	Few barriers	Product differentiation, with many substitutes	Levi Strauss (jeans)
Pure competition	Unlimited	No barriers	Homogeneous products	Vegetable farm (sweet corn)

uct. In this case each seller considers the reactions of other sellers to changes in marketing activities. Products facing oligopolistic competition may be homogeneous, such as aluminum, or differentiated, such as automobiles. **Monopolistic competition** exists when a firm with many potential competitors attempts to develop a marketing strategy to differentiate its product. For example, Levi Strauss has established an advantage for its blue jeans through a well-known trademark, design, advertising, and a reputation for quality. Although many competing brands of blue jeans are available, this firm has carved out a market niche by emphasizing differences in its products. **Pure competition**, if it existed at all, would entail a large number of sellers, none of which could significantly influence price or supply. The closest thing to an example of pure competition is an unregulated farmers' market, where local growers gather to sell their produce. Pure competition is an ideal at one end of the continuum; monopoly is at the other end. Most marketers function in a competitive environment somewhere between these two extremes.

Marketers need to monitor the actions of major competitors to determine what specific strategies competitors are using and how those strategies affect their own. Price is one of the marketing strategy variables that most competitors monitor. When Frontier or Southwest Airlines lowers the fare on a route, most major airlines attempt to match the price. Monitoring guides marketers in developing competitive advantages and aids them in adjusting current marketing strategies and planning new ones.

In monitoring competition, it is not enough to analyze available information; the firm must develop a system for gathering ongoing information about competitors. Understanding the market and what customers want, as well as what the competition is providing, will assist in maintaining a marketing orientation.[7] Information about competitors allows marketing managers to assess the performance of their own marketing efforts and to recognize the strengths and weaknesses in their own marketing strategies. Data about market shares, product movement, sales volume, and expenditure levels can be useful. However, accurate information on these matters is often difficult to obtain. We explore how marketers collect and organize such data in Chapter 6.

Economic Forces

Economic forces in the marketing environment influence both marketers' and customers' decisions and activities. In this section we examine the effects of buying power and willingness to spend, as well as general economic conditions.

Buying Power and Willingness to Spend.   The strength of a person's **buying power** depends on economic conditions and the size of the resources—money, goods, and services that can be traded in an exchange—that enable the individual to make purchases. The major financial sources of buying power are income, credit, and wealth.

For an individual, *income* is the amount of money received through wages, rents, investments, pensions, and subsidy payments for a given period, such as a month or a year. Normally, this money is allocated among taxes, spending for goods and services, and savings. Marketers are most interested in the amount of money left after payment of taxes because this **disposable income** is used for spending or saving. Because disposable income is a ready source of buying power, the total amount available in a nation is important to marketers. Several factors determine the size of total disposable income, including the total amount of income—which is affected by wage levels, the rate of unemployment, interest rates, and dividend rates—and the number and amount of taxes. Disposable income that is available for spending and saving after an individual has purchased the basic necessities of food, clothing, and shelter is called **discretionary income.** People use discretionary income to purchase entertainment, vacations, automobiles, education, pets, furniture, appliances, and so on. Changes in total discretionary income affect sales of these products, especially automobiles, furniture, large appliances, and other costly durable goods.

Credit is also important because it enables people to spend future income now or in the near future. However, credit increases current buying power at the expense of future

---

monopolistic competition A competitive structure in which a firm has many potential competitors and tries to develop a marketing strategy to differentiate its product

pure competition A market structure characterized by an extremely large number of sellers, none strong enough to significantly influence price or supply

buying power Resources, such as money, goods, and services, which can be traded in an exchange

disposable income After-tax income

discretionary income Disposable income available for spending and saving after an individual has purchased the basic necessities of food, clothing, and shelter

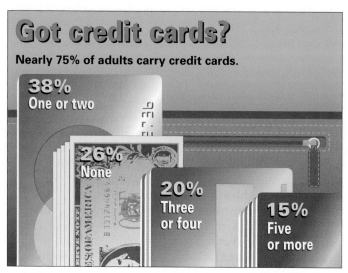

Source: Ipsos News Center.

buying power. Several factors determine whether people use or forgo credit. Interest rates affect buyers' decisions to use credit, especially for expensive purchases such as homes, appliances, and automobiles. When interest rates are low, the total cost of automobiles and houses becomes more affordable. In contrast, when interest rates are high, consumers are more likely to delay buying such expensive items. Use of credit is also affected by credit terms, such as size of the down payment and amount and number of monthly payments.

Wealth is the accumulation of past income, natural resources, and financial resources. It exists in many forms, including cash, securities, savings accounts, jewelry, and real estate. The significance of wealth to marketers is that as people become wealthier, they gain buying power in three ways: They can use their wealth to make current purchases, to generate income, and to acquire large amounts of credit.

People's **willingness to spend**—their inclination to buy because of expected satisfaction from a product—is related, to some degree, to their ability to buy. That is, people are sometimes more willing to buy if they have the buying power. However, several other elements also influence willingness to spend. Some elements affect specific products; others influence spending in general. A product's price and value influence almost all of us. Rolex watches, for example, appeal to customers who are willing to spend more for fine timepieces even when lower-priced watches are readily available. Increasingly, middle-class consumers seem more willing to splurge on high-price luxury products, such as Coach purses, BMW automobiles, and spa vacations, although they may shop for discounted groceries and other basic products at Wal-Mart and Target in order to afford the upscale products.[8] The amount of satisfaction received from a product already owned also may influence customers' desire to buy other products. Satisfaction depends not only on the quality of the currently owned product but also on numerous psychological and social forces. The American Customer Satisfaction Index, computed by the National Quality Research Center at the University of Michigan (see Figure 3.1), offers an indicator of customer satisfaction with a wide variety of businesses. Among other things, the index suggests that if customers become more dissatisfied, they may curtail their overall spending, which could stifle economic growth.[9] Other factors that affect customers' general willingness to spend are expectations about future employment, income levels, prices, family size, and general economic conditions.

Economic Conditions.   The overall state of the economy fluctuates in all countries. Changes in general economic conditions affect (and are affected by) supply and demand, buying power, willingness to spend, consumer expenditure levels, and the intensity of competitive behavior. Therefore, current economic conditions and changes in the economy have a broad impact on the success of organizations' marketing strategies.

Fluctuations in the economy follow a general pattern, often referred to as the **business cycle.** In the traditional view, the business cycle consists of four stages: prosperity, recession, depression, and recovery. During *prosperity,* unemployment is low, and total income is relatively high. Assuming a low inflation rate, this combination ensures high buying power. During a *recession,* however, unemployment rises, while total buying power declines. Pessimism accompanying a recession often stifles both consumer and business spending. A prolonged recession may become a *depression,* a period in which unemployment is extremely high, wages are very low, total disposable income is at a minimum, and consumers lack confidence in the economy. During *recovery,* the economy moves from depression or recession to prosperity. During this

willingness to spend An inclination to buy because of expected satisfaction from a product, influenced by the ability to buy and numerous psychological and social forces

business cycle A pattern of economic fluctuations that has four stages: prosperity, recession, depression, and recovery

figure 3.1

AMERICAN CUSTOMER SATISFACTION INDEX

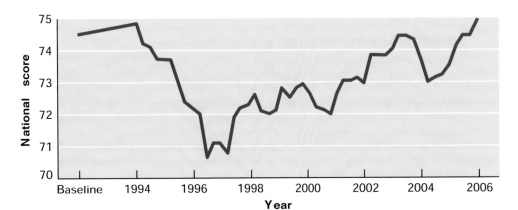

Source: "National Quarterly Scores," University of Michigan Business School, www.theacsi.org/index.php?option=com_content&task=view&id=31&Itemid=35 (accessed April 6, 2007).

period, high unemployment begins to decline, total disposable income increases, and the economic gloom that reduced consumers' willingness to buy subsides. Both the ability and willingness to buy increase.

The business cycle can enhance the success of marketing strategies. In the prosperity stage, for example, marketers may expand their product offerings to take advantage of increased buying power. They may be able to capture a larger market share by intensifying distribution and promotion efforts. In times of recession or depression, when buying power decreases, many customers may become more price conscious and seek more basic, functional products. During economic downturns, a company should focus its efforts on determining precisely what functions buyers want and ensure that these functions are available in its product offerings. Promotional efforts should emphasize value and utility. Some firms make the mistake of drastically reducing their marketing efforts during a recession, harming their ability to compete. During a recession in Mexico, the Coca-Cola Company chose to continue its marketing efforts while most of its competitors cut back or even abandoned the Mexican market. By maintaining a high level of marketing, Coca-Cola increased its share of the Mexican market by 4 to 6 percent.[10] During recovery periods, marketers should maintain as much flexibility in their marketing strategies as possible so that they can make the needed adjustments.

Political Forces

Political, legal, and regulatory forces of the marketing environment are closely interrelated. Legislation is enacted, legal decisions are interpreted by courts, and regulatory agencies are created and operated, for the most part, by elected or appointed officials. Legislation and regulations (or their lack) reflect the current political outlook. Consequently, the political forces of the marketing environment have the potential to influence marketing decisions and strategies.

Reactive marketers view political forces as beyond their control and simply adjust to conditions arising from those forces. Some firms are more proactive, however, and seek to influence the political process. In some cases organizations publicly protest the actions of legislative bodies. More often organizations help to elect to political offices individuals who regard them positively. Much of this help is in the form of campaign contributions—often in the form of "soft money," which refers to money that is donated to a political party with no specification on how the money will be spent. For example, Citigroup has made corporate donations in excess of $20 million over the last 15 years.[11] Marketers also can influence the political process through political action committees (PACs) that solicit donations from individuals and then contribute those funds to candidates running for political office.

table 3.2   MAJOR FEDERAL LAWS AFFECTING MARKETING DECISIONS

Act (Date Enacted)	Purpose
Procompetitive Legislation	
Sherman Antitrust Act (1890)	Prohibits contracts, combinations, or conspiracies to restrain trade; calls monopolizing or attempting to monopolize a misdemeanor offense.
Clayton Act (1914)	Prohibits specific practices such as price discrimination, exclusive dealer arrangements, and stock acquisitions in which the effect may notably lessen competition or tend to create a monopoly.
Federal Trade Commission Act (1914)	Created the Federal Trade Commission; also gives the FTC investigatory powers to be used in preventing unfair methods of competition.
Robinson-Patman Act (1936)	Prohibits price discrimination that lessens competition among wholesalers or retailers; prohibits producers from giving disproportionate services of facilities to large buyers.
Wheeler-Lea Act (1938)	Prohibits unfair and deceptive acts and practices, regardless of whether competition is injured; places advertising of foods and drugs under the jurisdiction of the FTC.
Celler-Kefauver Act (1950)	Prohibits any corporation engaged in commerce from acquiring the whole or any part of the stock or other share of the capital assets of another corporation when the effect substantially lessens competition or tends to create a monopoly.
Consumer Goods Pricing Act (1975)	Prohibits the use of price-maintenance agreements among manufacturers and resellers in interstate commerce.
Antitrust Improvements Act (1976)	Requires large corporations to inform federal regulators of prospective mergers or acquisitions so that they can be studied for any possible violations of the law.
Consumer Protection Legislation	
Pure Food and Drug Act (1906)	Prohibits the adulteration and mislabeling of food and drug products; established the Food and Drug Administration.
Fair Packaging and Labeling Act (1966)	Makes illegal the unfair or deceptive packaging or labeling of consumer products.
Consumer Product Safety Act (1972)	Established the Consumer Product Safety Commission; protects the public against unreasonable risk of injury and death associated with products.
Magnuson-Moss Warranty (FTC) Act (1975)	Provides for minimum disclosure standards for written consumer product warranties; defines minimum consent standards for written warranties; allows the FTC to prescribe interpretive rules in policy statements regarding unfair or deceptive practices.
Nutrition Labeling and Education Act (1990)	Prohibits exaggerated health claims and requires all processed foods to contain labels showing nutritional information.
Telephone Consumer Protection Act (1991)	Establishes procedures to avoid unwanted telephone solicitations; prohibits marketers from using automated telephone dialing system or an artificial or prerecorded voice to certain telephone lines.
Children's Online Privacy Protection Act (2000)	Regulates the online collection of personally identifiable information (name, mailing address, e-mail address, hobbies, interests, or information collected through cookies) from children under age 13.
Do Not Call Implementation Act (2003)	Directs the Federal Communications Commission (FCC) and the FTC to coordinate so that their rules are consistent regarding telemarketing call practices, including the Do Not Call Registry and other lists, as well as call abandonment.

(continued)

table 3.2   continued

Act (Date Enacted)	Purpose
Trademark and Copyright Protection Legislation	
Lanham Act (1946)	Provides protections and regulation of brand names, brand marks, trade names, and trademarks.
Trademark Law Revision Act (1988)	Amends the Lanham Act to allow brands not yet introduced to be protected through registration with the Patent and Trademark Office.
Federal Trademark Dilution Act (1995)	Gives trademark owners the right to protect trademarks and requires relinquishment of names that match or parallel existing trademarks.
Digital Millennium Copyright Act (1998)	Refines copyright laws to protect digital versions of copyrighted materials, including music and movies.

Companies also can participate in the political process through lobbying to persuade public and/or government officials to favor a particular position in decision making. Many companies concerned about the threat of legislation or regulation that may negatively affect their operations employ lobbyists to communicate their concerns to elected officials. Marketers of cigarettes, for example, spent millions on lobbyists to persuade state and local officials that their governments should not increase taxes on cigarettes, effectively raising their price.[12]

Legal and Regulatory Forces

A number of federal laws influence marketing decisions and activities. Table 3.2 lists some of the most significant pieces of legislation. Regulatory agencies and self-regulatory forces also affect marketing efforts.

Regulatory Agencies.   Federal regulatory agencies influence many marketing activities, including product development, pricing, packaging, advertising, personal selling, and distribution. Usually these bodies have the power to enforce specific laws, as well as some discretion in establishing operating rules and regulations to guide certain types of industry practices.

Of all the federal regulatory units, the **Federal Trade Commission (FTC)** influences marketing activities most. Although the FTC regulates a variety of business practices, it allocates considerable resources to curbing false advertising, misleading pricing, and deceptive packaging and labeling. When it receives a complaint or otherwise has reason to believe that a firm is violating a law, the commission issues a complaint stating that the business is in violation. For example, the FTC filed a complaint against Emerson Direct, Inc. (doing business as Council on Natural Health), for making unsubstantiated claims that its "Smoke Away" smoking-cessation product would help smokers quit easily, quickly, permanently, and without side effects. The FTC's complaint further charged that two doctors who endorsed the product did not properly use their expertise or have the claimed expertise. The company settled the charges for $1.3 million and agreed to make no more unsubstantiated claims about its product.[13] If a company continues the questionable practice, the FTC can issue a cease-and-desist order demanding that the business stop doing whatever caused the complaint. The firm can appeal to the federal courts to have the order rescinded. However, the FTC can seek civil penalties in court, up to a maximum penalty of $10,000 a day for each infraction if a cease-and-desist order is violated. The commission can require companies to run corrective advertising in response to previous ads considered misleading. The FTC also assists businesses in complying with laws, and it evaluates new marketing methods every year.

Federal Trade Commission (FTC) An agency that regulates a variety of business practices and curbs false advertising, misleading pricing, and deceptive packaging and labeling

Unlike the FTC, other regulatory units are limited to dealing with specific products, services, or business activities. For example, the Food and Drug Administration (FDA) enforces regulations prohibiting the sale and distribution of adulterated, misbranded, or hazardous food and drug products. The Consumer Product Safety Commission (CPSC) ensures compliance with the Consumer Product Safety Act and protects the public from unreasonable risk of injury from any consumer product not covered by other regulatory agencies.

In addition, all states, as well as many cities and towns, have regulatory agencies that enforce laws and regulations regarding marketing practices within their states or municipalities. State and local regulatory agencies try not to establish regulations that conflict with those of federal regulatory agencies. They generally enforce laws dealing with the production and sale of particular goods and services. Utility, insurance, financial, and liquor industries are commonly regulated by state agencies. Among these agencies' targets are misleading advertising and pricing.

Self-Regulation. In an attempt to be good corporate citizens and to prevent government intervention, some businesses try to regulate themselves. Kraft Foods, for example, stopped advertising sugary snacks and cereals to children under age 12 in response to growing concerns about childhood obesity and its effects on children's long-term health. While some competitors were astonished by the decision, Kraft executives recognized that if food product marketers did not begin to police themselves, the government could impose restrictions on advertising to children, and the industry could face potential lawsuits.[14] Several trade associations have developed self-regulatory programs. Although these programs are not a direct outgrowth of laws, many were established to stop or stall the development of laws and governmental regulatory groups that would regulate the associations' marketing practices.

Perhaps the best-known nongovernmental regulatory group is the **Better Business Bureau,** a local regulatory agency supported by local businesses. More than 140 bureaus help to settle problems between consumers and specific business firms. Each bureau also acts to preserve good business practices in a locality, although it usually lacks strong enforcement tools for dealing with firms that employ questionable practices. When a firm continues to violate what the Better Business Bureau believes to be good business practices, the bureau warns consumers through local newspapers or broadcast media. If the offending organization is a Better Business Bureau member, it may be expelled from the local bureau. For example, Cingular Wireless had its membership revoked by the Better Business Bureau of Upstate New York for having too many unresolved complaints on file.[15]

The National Advertising Division (NAD) of the Council of Better Business Bureaus operates a self-regulatory program that investigates claims regarding alleged deceptive advertising. For example, NAD asked the FTC and the FDA to investigate whether BIE Health Products' advertising for its GHR "human growth hormone 'releaser'" product misleads consumers about its ability to reverse the aging process and radically improve health.[16]

Another self-regulatory entity, the **National Advertising Review Board (NARB),** considers cases in which an advertiser challenges issues raised by the National Advertising Division about an advertisement. Cases are reviewed by panels drawn from NARB members representing advertisers, agencies, and the public. The NARB, sponsored by the Council of Better Business Bureaus and three advertising trade organizations, has no official enforcement powers. However, if a firm refuses to comply with its decision, the NARB may publicize the questionable practice and file a complaint with the FTC.

Self-regulatory programs have several advantages over governmental laws and regulatory agencies. Establishment and implementation are usually less expensive, and guidelines are generally more realistic and operational. In addition, effective self-regulatory programs reduce the need to expand government bureaucracy. However, these programs have several limitations. When a trade association creates a set of industry guidelines for its members, nonmember firms do not have to abide by them. Furthermore, many self-regulatory programs lack the tools or authority to enforce

Better Business Bureau A local, nongovernmental regulatory agency, supported by the local businesses, that helps settle problems between customers and specific business firms

National Advertising Review Board (NARB) A self-regulatory unit that considers challenges to issues raised by the National Advertising Division (an arm of the Council of Better Business Bureaus) about an advertisement

The Impact of Technology

Monster.com has changed the way people search for jobs, by allowing them to post resumes online.

technology The application of knowledge and tools to solve problems and perform tasks more efficiently

guidelines. Finally, guidelines in self-regulatory programs are often less strict than those established by government agencies.

Technological Forces

The word *technology* brings to mind scientific advances such as computers, spacecraft, DVDs, cell phones, cloning, lifestyle drugs, the Internet, radio frequency identification tags, and more. Such developments make it possible for marketers to operate ever more efficiently and to provide an exciting array of products for consumers. However, even though these innovations are outgrowths of technology, none of them *is* technology. **Technology** is the application of knowledge and tools to solve problems and perform tasks more efficiently.

Technology determines how we, as members of society, satisfy our physiologic needs. In various ways and to varying degrees, eating and drinking habits, sleeping patterns, sexual activities, health care, and work performance are all influenced by both existing technology and advances in technology. Because of the technological revolution in communications, for example, marketers can now reach vast numbers of people more efficiently through a variety of media. Electronic mail, voice mail, cell phones, personal digital assistants (PDAs), and computers help marketers to interact with customers, make appointments, and handle last-minute orders or cancellations. Consider that a growing number of U.S. households have given up their "land lines" in favor of using cell phones as their primary phones, and growth in wireless subscriptions is expected to continue at a compounded 2.9 percent through 2010.[17] The proliferation of cell phones, most with text-message capabilities, has led experts to project that 89 percent of brands will employ text and multimedia messaging on cell phones to reach their target markets. Restaurants, for example, can send their lunch specials to subscribers' cell phones.[18]

Personal computers are now in more than 65 percent of all U.S. consumers' homes, and most of them include broadband or modems for accessing the Internet. Although we enjoy the benefits of communicating through the Internet, we are increasingly concerned about protecting our privacy and intellectual property. Likewise, although health and medical research has created new drugs that save lives, cloning and genetically modified foods have become controversial issues to many segments of society. Home environments, health care, leisure, and work performance are all shaped profoundly by both current technology and advances in technology.[19]

The effects of technology relate to such characteristics as dynamics, reach, and the self-sustaining nature of technological progress. The *dynamics* of technology involve the constant change that often challenges the structures of social institutions, including social relationships, the legal system, religion, education, business, and leisure. *Reach* refers to the broad nature of technology as it moves through society. Consider the impact of cellular and wireless telephones. The ability to call from almost any location has many benefits but also has negative side effects, including increases in traffic accidents, increased noise pollution, and fears about potential health risks.[20] The *self-sustaining* nature of technology relates to the fact that technology acts as a catalyst to spur even faster development. As new innovations are introduced, they stimulate the need for more advancements to facilitate further development. For example, the Internet has created the need for ever-faster transmission of signals through broadband connections such as high-speed phone lines (DSL), satellite, and cable. Technology initiates a change process that creates new opportunities for new tech-

Technology Goes to the Dogs

Americans love their pets. A recent survey by the American Animal Hospital Association reveals that four of five pet owners consider their pets to be their children, and market trends confirm this. The pet industry has more than doubled in size in the past 10 years from $17 billion to $36 billion, making it the seventh-largest retail segment in the nation. Fueling this trend are empty nesters and young adults who are having children later and spending their time and energy with their animals. In addition, the pet industry has grown increasingly sophisticated at consumer marketing and has introduced a steady stream of new, high-tech pet products, all of which are vying for pet owners' dollars.

For example, the ThirstAlert! from JoBananas Club flashes red lights when the water level in your pet's bowl gets low. A deluxe version is scheduled for release next year that will send an e-mail or text message to let you know when your pet's bowl is empty. The Careful Clipper by Dogmatic marks the first renovation to the pet nail clipper in 20 years. It features an ergonomic handle and flexible snake light that allows you to see through almost any nail to avoid cutting the quick. The K&H Cool Bed absorbs heat from your pet and radiates the heat back into the air. And the Petmate Electronic Portion Control LeBistro is a programmable electronic dispenser that holds more than 5 pounds of food and dispenses portions of up to 3 cups at selected times in the day.

With Americans falling more in love with their pets, this industry is growing quickly and is proving to be as responsive to technology as any other market.[a]

nologies in every industry segment or personal life experience that it touches. At some point there is even a multiplier effect that causes still greater demand for more change to improve performance.[21]

It is important for firms to determine when a technology is changing an industry and to define the strategic influence of the new technology. For example, wireless devices in use today include radios, cell phones, laptop computers, TVs, pagers, and car keys. To remain competitive, companies today must keep up with and adapt to these technological advances. Through a procedure known as *technology assessment*, managers try to foresee the effects of new products and processes on their firms' operation, on other business organizations, and on society in general. With information obtained through a technology assessment, management tries to estimate whether benefits of adopting a specific technology outweigh costs to the firm and to society at large. The degree to which a business is technologically based also influences its managers' response to technology.

Sociocultural Forces

sociocultural forces The influences in a society and its culture(s) that change people's attitudes, beliefs, norms, customs, and lifestyles

Sociocultural forces are the influences in a society and its culture(s) that bring about changes in attitudes, beliefs, norms, customs, and lifestyles. Profoundly affecting how people live, these forces help to determine what, where, how, and when people buy products. Like the other environmental forces, sociocultural forces present marketers with both challenges and opportunities.

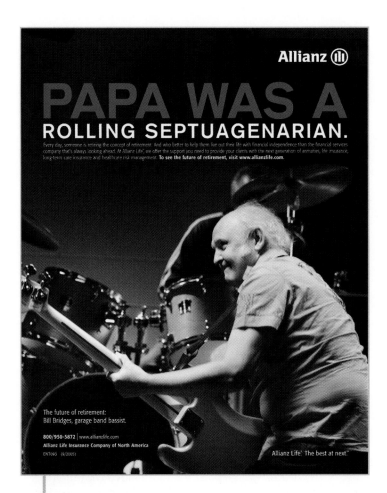

Marketing to Demographic Changes

The growing rate of older consumers has marketers focusing on that generational demographic.

Changes in a population's demographic characteristics—age, gender, race, ethnicity, marital and parental status, income, and education—have a significant bearing on relationships and individual behavior. These shifts lead to changes in how people live and ultimately in their consumption of products such as food, clothing, housing, transportation, communication, recreation, education, and health services. We look at a few of the changes in demographics and diversity that are affecting marketing activities.

One demographic change affecting the marketplace is the increasing proportion of older consumers. According to the U.S. Bureau of the Census, the number of people age 65 and older is expected to more than double by the year 2050, reaching 87 million.[22] Consequently, marketers can expect significant increases in the demand for health care services, recreation, tourism, retirement housing, and selected skin-care products.

The number of singles is also on the rise. Nearly 41 percent of U.S. adults are unmarried, and many plan to remain that way. Moreover, single men living alone comprise 11 percent of all households (up from 3.5 percent in 1970), and single women living alone make up nearly 15 percent (up from 7.3 percent in 1970).[23] Single people have quite different spending patterns than couples and families with children. They are less likely to own homes and thus buy less furniture and fewer appliances. They spend more heavily on convenience foods, restaurants, travel, entertainment, and recreation. In addition, they tend to prefer smaller packages, whereas families often buy bulk goods and products packaged in multiple servings.

The United States is entering another baby boom, with more than 81 million Americans age 19 or younger. The new baby boom represents 27.6 percent of the total population; the original baby boomers, born between 1946 and 1964, account for nearly 28 percent.[24] The children of the original baby boomers differ from one another radically in terms of race, living arrangements, and socioeconomic class. Thus the newest baby boom is much more diverse than previous generations.

Another noteworthy population trend is the increasingly multicultural nature of U.S. society. The number of immigrants into the United States has risen steadily during the last 40 years. By the turn of the twentieth century, the U.S. population had shifted from one dominated by whites to one consisting largely of three racial and ethnic groups: whites, blacks, and Hispanics. The U.S. government projects that by the year 2050, more than 102 million Hispanics, 61 million blacks, and 33 million Asians will call the United States home.[25] Figure 3.2 shows how experts believe the U.S. population will change over the next 50 years.

Changes in social and cultural values have dramatically influenced people's needs and desires for products. Although these values do not shift overnight, they do change at varying speeds. Marketers try to monitor these changes because knowing this information can equip them to predict changes in consumers' needs for products at least in the near future.

People today are more concerned about the foods they eat and thus are choosing more low-fat, organic, natural, and healthy products. Marketers have responded with a proliferation of foods, beverages, and exercise products that fit this new lifestyle. In addition to the proliferation of new organic brands, such as Earthbound Farm, Horizon Dairy, and Whole Foods' 365, many conventional marketers have introduced organic versions of their products, including Orville Redenbacher, Heinz, and even Wal-Mart.

figure 3.2

U.S. POPULATION PROJECTIONS BY RACE

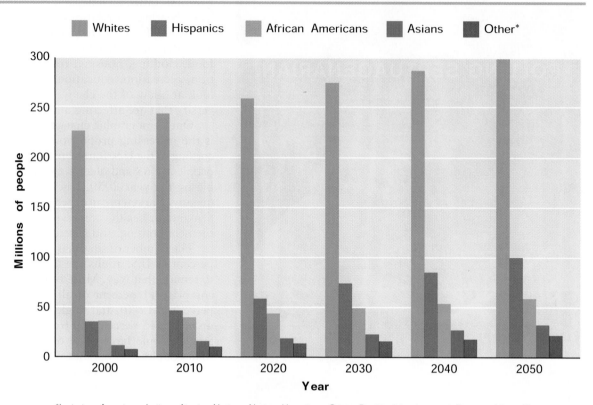

*Includes American Indian, Alaska Native, Native Hawaiian, Other Pacific Islander, and Two or More Races

Source: U.S. Census Bureau, "U.S. Interim Projections by Age, Sex, Race, and Hispanic Origin," March 18, 2004, www.census.gov/ipc/www/usinterimproj/natprojtab01a.pdf.

The major source of values is the family. Values about the permanence of marriage are changing, but children remain important. Marketers have responded with safer, up-scale baby gear and supplies, children's electronics, and family entertainment products. Marketers are also aiming more marketing efforts directly at children because children often play pivotal roles in purchasing decisions. Children and family values are also a factor in the trend toward more eat-out and takeout meals. Busy families generally want to spend less time in the kitchen and more time together enjoying themselves. Beneficiaries of this trend primarily have been fast-food and casual restaurants like McDonald's, Taco Bell, Boston Market, and Applebee's, but most supermarkets have added more ready-to-cook or ready-to-serve meal components to meet the needs of busy customers. Some, like H-E-B.'s Central Market grocery stores, also offer eat-in gourmet cafés.

Social Responsibility and Ethics in Marketing

social responsibility An organization's obligation to maximize its positive impact and minimize its negative impact on society

In marketing, **social responsibility** refers to an organization's obligation to maximize its positive impact and minimize its negative impact on society. Social responsibility thus deals with the total effect of all marketing decisions on society. In marketing, social responsibility includes the managerial processes needed to monitor, satisfy, and even exceed stakeholder expectations and needs.[26] Remember from Chapter 1 that stakeholders are groups that have a "stake," or claim, in some aspect of a company's products, operations, markets, industry, and outcomes.

figure 3.3

THE PYRAMID OF CORPORATE SOCIAL RESPONSIBILITY

RESPONSIBILITIES

Philanthropic
Be a good corporate citizen
► Contribute resources to the community; improve quality of life

Ethical
Be ethical
► Obligation to do what is right, just, and fair
► Avoid harm

Legal
Obey the law
► Law is society's codification of right and wrong
► Play by the rules of the game

Economic
Be profitable
► The foundation upon which all others rest

Source: Archie B. Carroll, "The Pyramid of Corporate Social Responsibility: Toward the Moral Management of Organizational Stakeholders," adaptation of Figure 3, p. 42. Reprinted from *Business Horizons,* July/August 1991. Copyright © 1991 by the Foundation for the School of Business at Indiana University. Reprinted with permission.

Ample evidence demonstrates that ignoring stakeholders' demands for responsible marketing can destroy customers' trust and even prompt government regulations. Irresponsible actions that anger customers, employees, or competitors not only may jeopardize a marketer's financial standing but also may have legal repercussions as well. For instance, after news reports that pharmaceutical giant Merck was aware that its arthritis-fighting drug Vioxx may cause heart problems, the firm's stock plummeted, and thousands of lawsuits were filed against the company. The company had already pulled the drug from the market.[27] In contrast, socially responsible activities can generate positive publicity and boost sales. The Breast Cancer Awareness Crusade sponsored by Avon Products, for example, has helped raised nearly $400 million to fund community-based breast cancer education and early-detection services. Hundreds of stories about Avon's efforts have appeared in major media, which contributed to an increase in company sales.[28]

Socially responsible efforts such as Avon's have a positive impact on local communities; at the same time, they indirectly help the sponsoring organization by attracting goodwill, publicity, and potential customers and employees. Thus, while social responsibility is certainly a positive concept in itself, most organizations embrace it in the expectation of indirect long-term benefits.

Socially responsible organizations strive for **marketing citizenship** by adopting a strategic focus for fulfilling the economic, legal, ethical, and philanthropic social responsibilities that their stakeholders expect of them. Companies that consider the diverse perspectives of stakeholders in their daily operations and strategic planning are said to have a *stakeholder orientation,* an important element of corporate citizenship.[29] A stakeholder orientation in marketing goes beyond customers, competitors, and regulators to include understanding and addressing the needs of all stakeholders, including communities and special-interest groups. As a result, organizations are now under pressure to undertake initiatives that demonstrate a balanced perspective on stakeholder interests.[30] Pfizer, for example, has secured stakeholder input on a number of issues, including rising health care costs and health care reform.[31] As Figure 3.3 shows, the

marketing citizenship The adoption of a strategic focus for fulfilling the economic, legal, ethical, and philanthropic social responsibilities expected by stakeholders

economic, legal, ethical, and philanthropic dimensions of social responsibility can be viewed as a pyramid.[32] The economic and legal aspects have long been acknowledged, but ethical and philanthropic issues have gained recognition more recently.

Economic Dimension

At the most basic level, all companies have an economic responsibility to be profitable so that they can provide a return on investment to their owners and investors, create jobs for the community, and contribute goods and services to the economy. How organizations relate to stockholders, employees, competitors, customers, the community, and the natural environment affects the economy.

Marketers also have an economic responsibility to compete fairly. Size frequently gives companies an advantage over others. Large firms often can generate economies of scale that allow them to put smaller firms out of business. Consequently, small companies and even whole communities may resist the efforts of firms such as Wal-Mart, Home Depot, and Best Buy to open stores in their vicinity. These firms can operate at such low costs that small, local firms often cannot compete. Such issues create concerns about social responsibility for organizations, communities, and consumers.

Legal Dimension

Marketers are also expected, of course, to obey laws and regulations. The efforts of elected representatives and special-interest groups to promote responsible corporate behavior have resulted in laws and regulations designed to keep U.S. companies' actions within the range of acceptable conduct. When marketers engage in deceptive practices to advance their own interests over those of others, charges of fraud may result. In general, fraud is any purposeful communication that deceives, manipulates, or conceals facts in order to create a false impression. It is considered a crime, and convictions may result in fines, imprisonment, or both. Fraud costs U.S. companies more than $600 billion a year; the average company loses about 6 percent of total revenues to fraud and abuses committed by its own employees.[33]

When customers, interest groups, or businesses become outraged over what they perceive as irresponsibility on the part of a marketing organization, they may urge their legislators to draft new legislation to regulate the behavior, or they may engage in litigation to force the organization to "play by the rules." Transmeta, for example, filed a lawsuit against Intel, accusing the rival chip maker of infringing on Transmeta patents that relate to controlling power consumption in computers. The suit seeks damages and a ruling banning the further sale of Intel's popular Pentium and Core lines of computer chips.[34]

Ethical Dimension

Economic and legal responsibilities are the most basic levels of social responsibility for a good reason: Failure to consider them may mean that a marketer is not around long enough to engage in ethical or philanthropic activities. Beyond these dimensions is **marketing ethics**, principles and standards that define acceptable conduct in marketing, as determined by various stakeholders, including the public, government regulators, private-interest groups, consumers, industry, and the organization itself. The most basic of these principles have been codified as laws and regulations to encourage marketers to conform to society's expectations of conduct. However, marketing ethics goes beyond legal issues. Ethical marketing decisions foster trust, which helps to build long-term marketing relationships.

Marketers should be aware of ethical standards for acceptable conduct from several viewpoints—company, industry, government, customers, special-interest groups, and society at large. When marketing activities deviate from accepted standards, the exchange process can break down, resulting in customer dissatisfaction, lack of trust, and lawsuits. In fact, 78 percent of consumers say that they avoid certain businesses or products because of negative perceptions about them.[35] Sony BMG Music Entertainment, for example, was sharply criticized for including copy-protection software on millions of CDs. Although most marketers of music have sought innovative ways

marketing ethics Principles and standards that define acceptable marketing conduct as determined by various stakeholders

Would you save this man?

Home runs can change everything in a baseball game. But save a life? Every cent you pledge during this year's Home Run Challenge goes directly toward finding a cure for prostate cancer. Pledge as little as a quarter for every home run hit in select MLB® home games from June 6th to Father's Day. Please help us turn the statistics back into human beings.
www.prostatecancerfoundation.org
Pledge now at 800.798.CURE

Cause-Related Marketing

Major League Baseball has linked pledges for this year's Home Run Challenge to finding a cure for prostate cancer.

ethical issue An identifiable problem, situation, or opportunity requiring a choice among several actions that must be evaluated as right or wrong, ethical or unethical

to stifle rampant CD piracy, many consumers felt that Sony's copy-protection software went too far because it potentially could disable computers or enable a hacker to unleash a virus if the CD was played on a Windows-based computer. Sony ultimately recalled an estimated 4.7 million CDs, at a projected cost of $2 to $4 million, but not before generating considerable consumer anger and confusion over the technology, as well as at least one class-action lawsuit. The company later settled charges by the Texas and California attorneys general that the copy-protection software violated the states' antispyware laws.[36] When managers engage in activities that deviate from accepted principles, continued marketing exchanges become difficult, if not impossible. The best time to deal with such problems is during the strategic planning process, not after major problems materialize.

An **ethical issue** is an identifiable problem, situation, or opportunity requiring an individual or organization to choose from among several actions that must be evaluated as right or wrong, ethical or unethical. Any time an activity causes marketing managers or customers in their target market to feel manipulated or cheated, a marketing ethical issue exists, regardless of the legality of that activity. For example, a Los Angeles consumer filed a lawsuit against Kraft Foods after recognizing from the label that her "guacamole" dip did not contain significant quantities of avocado. Although most consumers assume that Kraft's top-selling guacamole dip contains avocado, the product consists primarily of modified food starch, coconut and soybean oils, food coloring, and less than 2 percent avocado. Although Kraft quickly changed the labeling to "guacamole-flavored" dip, the California Avocado Commission expressed dismay at the dearth of avocado in the dip and asked its own lawyers to look at the suit.[37] Regardless of the reasons behind specific ethical issues, marketers must be able to identify these issues and decide how to resolve them. To do so requires familiarity with the many kinds of ethical issues that may arise in marketing. Research suggests that the greater the consequences associated with an issue, the more likely it will be recognized as an ethics issue, and the more important it will be to making an ethical decision.[38] Some examples of ethical issues related to product, promotion, price, and distribution (the marketing mix) appear in Table 3.3 (on page 66).

Philanthropic Dimension

At the top of the pyramid are philanthropic responsibilities. These responsibilities, which go beyond marketing ethics, are not required of a company, but they promote human welfare or goodwill, as do the economic, legal, and ethical dimensions of social responsibility. That many companies have demonstrated philanthropic responsibility is evidenced by the nearly $13.7 billion in annual corporate donations and contributions to environmental and social causes and relief efforts.[39] After hurricane Katrina killed more than 1,000 people and devastated New Orleans and parts of the Gulf Coast, many corporations—including Anheuser-Busch, BP, Capitol One, Cingular, DuPont, General Motors, Lowe's, Office Depot, Toyota, Wal-Mart, and many more—donated millions of dollars in cash, supplies, equipment, food, and medicine to help victims. Other firms matched employee donations or provided mechanisms through which customers could donate funds and supplies to help with relief efforts.[40] Even small companies participate in philanthropy through donations and volunteer support of local causes and national charities, such as the Red Cross and the United Way. Boston-based Dancing Deer

table 3.3	ETHICAL ISSUES IN MARKETING

Issue Category	Examples
Product	• Failing to disclose risks associated with a product • Failing to disclose information about a product's function, value, or use • Failing to disclose information about changes in the nature, quality, or size of a product
Distribution	• Failing to live up to the rights and responsibilities associated with specific intermediary roles • Manipulating product availability • Using coercion to force other intermediaries to behave in a certain way
Promotion	• False or misleading advertising • Using manipulative or deceptive sales promotions, tactics, and publicity • Offering or accepting bribes in personal selling situations
Pricing	• Price fixing • Predatory pricing • Failing to disclose the full price of a purchase

Baking, for example, uses environmentally friendly packaging for its scones, cookies, brownies, and cakes, and it donates 35 percent of the profits from its Sweet Home cakes to Boston nonprofits that help homeless people find jobs and housing.[41]

More companies than ever are adopting a strategic approach to corporate philanthropy. Many firms link their products to a particular social cause on an ongoing or short-term basis, a practice known as **cause-related marketing**. Target, for example, contributes significant resources to education through its Take Charge of Education program. Customers using a Target Red Card can designate a specific school to which Target donates 1 percent of their total purchase.[42] Research further indicates that such corporate support of causes generates trust in a company for 80 percent of those surveyed.[43] Some companies are beginning to extend the concept of corporate philanthropy beyond financial contributions by adopting a **strategic philanthropy** approach, the synergistic use of organizational core competencies and resources to address key stakeholders' interests and achieve both organizational and social benefits. Strategic philanthropy involves employees, organizational resources and expertise, and the ability to link these assets to the concerns of key stakeholders, including employees, customers, suppliers, and social needs. Strategic philanthropy involves both financial and nonfinancial contributions to stakeholders (employee time, goods and services, and company technology and equipment, as well as facilities), but it also benefits the company. Home Depot, for example, has been progressive in aligning its expertise and resources to address community needs. Its relationship with Habitat for Humanity gives employees a chance to improve their skills and bring direct knowledge back into the workplace to benefit customers. It also enhances Home Depot's image of expertise as the "do-it-yourself" center.[44]

Although social responsibility may seem to be an abstract ideal, managers make decisions related to social responsibility every day. To be successful, a business must determine what customers, government regulators, and competitors, as well as society in general, want or expect in terms of social responsibility. Two major categories of social responsibility issues are the natural environment and consumerism.

The Natural Environment.   One of the more common ways marketers demonstrate social responsibility is through programs designed to protect and preserve the natural environment. Most *Fortune* 500 companies now engage in recycling activities and make

cause-related marketing The practice of linking products to a particular social cause on an ongoing or short-term basis

strategic philanthropy The synergistic use of organizational core competencies and resources to address key stakeholders' interests and achieve both organizational and social benefits

marketing ENTREPRENEURS

Amy Simmons

HER BUSINESS: Amy's Ice Cream

FOUNDED: 1984

SUCCESS: $5 million in sales through 13 stores and a wholesale business

Back in 1984, Amy Simmons knew that traditional corporate life was just not for her. Having worked in an ice cream store while in college, Amy was familiar with the business, so she and a partner wrote a hot check for the first month's rent and opened Amy's Ice Cream in Austin, Texas. The store's high-quality ingredients and creative flavors, coupled with the zany antics of its behind-the-counter "scoopers," quickly gained it a loyal following and made Amy an Austin icon. Now, with 160 employees and many locations, Amy's Ice Cream eschews advertising in favor of spending money supporting local charities such as Austin public television, Candlelighter's Childhood Cancer Foundation, and Austin Partners in Education. The company's brand-new, state-of-the-art 6,000-square-foot factory, which includes numerous energy-saving devices, was recycled from an old post office.[b]

significant efforts to reduce waste and conserve energy. Many companies are making contributions to environmental protection organizations, sponsoring and participating in cleanup events, promoting recycling, retooling manufacturing processes to minimize waste and pollution, employing more environmentally friendly energy sources, and generally reevaluating the effects of their products on the natural environment.

Green marketing refers to the specific development, pricing, promotion, and distribution of products that do not harm the natural environment. Toyota, Honda, and Ford, for example, have succeeded in marketing "hybrid" cars that use electric motors to augment their internal-combustion engines, improving the vehicles' fuel economy without reducing their power. New Leaf Paper has taken a leadership role in the paper-production industry, producing paper made from 50 to 100 percent post-consumer waste instead of virgin tree pulp. The small firm's success has forced many larger competitors to introduce their own sustainable paper products. The growing trend of recycled papers is saving trees and reducing the amount of solid waste going into landfills.[45] On the other hand, some stakeholders, including customers, try to dictate companies' use of responsible suppliers and sources of products.[46] Aveda, for example, requires magazines in which it places ads for its earth-friendly personal-care products to be printed on recycled paper. The requirement has already prompted *Natural Health* to switch to recycled paper.[47]

Consumerism.   **Consumerism** consists of organized efforts by individuals, groups, and organizations seeking to protect consumers' rights. The movement's major forces are individual consumer advocates, consumer organizations and other interest groups, consumer education, and consumer laws.

To achieve their objectives, consumers and their advocates write letters or send e-mails to companies, lobby government agencies, broadcast public-service announcements, and boycott companies whose activities they deem irresponsible. Some consumers choose to boycott firms and products out of a desire to support a cause and make a difference.[48] For example, several organizations evaluate children's products for safety, often announcing dangerous products before Christmas so that parents can avoid them. Other actions by the consumer movement have resulted in seat belts and air bags in automobiles, dolphin-safe tuna, the banning of unsafe three-wheel motorized vehicles, and numerous laws regulating product safety and information.

Also of great importance to the consumer movement are four basic rights spelled out in a "consumer bill of rights" drafted by President John F. Kennedy. These rights include the right to safety, the right to be informed, the right to choose, and the right to be heard. Ensuring consumers' *right to safety* means that marketers have an obligation not to market a product that they know could harm consumers. This right can be extended to imply that all products must be safe for their intended use, include thorough and explicit instructions for proper and safe use, and have been tested to ensure reliability and quality. Consumers' *right to be informed* means that consumers should have access to and the opportunity to review all relevant information about a product before buying it. Many laws require specific labeling on product packaging to satisfy this right. In addition, labels on alcoholic and tobacco

green marketing The specific development, pricing, promotion, and distribution of products that do not harm the natural environment

consumerism Organized efforts by individuals, groups, and organizations to protect consumers' rights

Timberland: Walking in Nature's Shoes

The Timberland Company is a global leader in the design, manufacturing, and marketing of premium-quality footwear, apparel, and accessories for consumers who love the outdoors. Its iconic yellow boot with the embossed tree logo is found in department and specialty stores as well as in Timberland retail stores worldwide. Not only is Timberland known for its quality products, but it is also recognized as one of the most socially responsible corporations in the world. Recently, Timberland received the Ron Brown Award for Corporate Leadership, the only presidential award that recognizes companies for outstanding achievement in community relations. Among the company's goals are the fostering of engaged citizenship, environmental stewardship, and global human rights. To cultivate citizenship, the company created the Path of Service program, which provides 40 hours of pay to employees who engage in community service activities. Through a myriad of service events and programs, employees invest their time, skills, and energy to create a positive impact on the communities in which they live and work. Timberland employees have invested more than 278,000 hours and partnered with nonprofit organizations in 27 countries around the world. Timberland knows that being a good citizen is good for business. This civic leadership not only advances the community in which Timberland does business but also provides benefits to the company in the form of a more energetic, dedicated, and loyal work force.

Timberland also pursues a number of practices to preserve the earth's resources, such as designing its "Earthwatch" boots with natural and recycled compounds, using water-based adhesives, searching for new ways to manufacture products without having to use hazardous chemicals, and conserving energy to help combat climate change.

Through its Code of Conduct program, Timberland works to ensure that its products are made in workplaces that are fair, safe, and nondiscriminatory. The company is equally committed to improving the quality of life for its global business partners' employees. Beyond training factory management, educating factory workers, and auditing for compliance with its Code of Conduct, Timberland also partners with nongovernmental organizations and international agencies such as Verité, CARE, and Social Accountability International to ensure that its programs address current needs.

Timberland's reputation for social responsibility is well deserved. By creating programs that further its goals, the company shows that it values both people and the environment. And Timberland clearly understands that people like to do business with companies whose values they share.[c]

products inform consumers that these products may cause illness and other problems. The *right to choose* means that consumers should have access to a variety of products and services at competitive prices. They also should be assured of satisfactory quality and service at a fair price. Activities that reduce competition among businesses in an industry might jeopardize this right. The *right to be heard* ensures that consumers' interests will receive full and sympathetic consideration in the formulation of government policy. The right to be heard also promises consumers fair treatment when they complain to marketers about products. This right benefits marketers too because when consumers complain about a product, the manufacturer can use this information to modify the product and make it more satisfying.

Incorporating Social Responsibility and Ethics into Strategic Planning

Although the concepts of marketing ethics and social responsibility are often used interchangeably, it is important to distinguish between them. *Ethics* relates to individual and group decisions—judgments about what is right or wrong in a particular decision-making situation—whereas *social responsibility* deals with the total effect of marketing decisions on society. The two concepts are interrelated because a company that supports socially responsible decisions and adheres to a code of conduct is likely to have a positive effect on society. Because ethics and social responsibility programs can be profitable as well, an increasing number of companies are incorporating them into their overall strategic market planning.

Without compliance programs and uniform standards and policies regarding conduct, it is hard for a company's employees to determine what conduct is acceptable within the company. In the absence of such programs and standards, employees generally will make decisions based on their observations of how their peers and superiors behave. To improve ethics, many organizations have developed **codes of conduct** (also called *codes of ethics*) consisting of formalized rules and standards that describe what the company expects of its employees. The New York Stock Exchange now requires every member corporation to have a formal code of conduct. Codes of conduct promote ethical behavior by reducing opportunities for unethical behavior; employees know both what is expected of them and what kind of punishment they face if they violate the rules. Codes help marketers deal with ethical issues or dilemmas that develop in daily operations by prescribing or limiting specific activities. Codes of conduct often include general ethical values such as honesty and integrity, general legal compliance, discreditable or harmful acts, and obligations related to social values, as well as more marketing-specific issues such as confidentiality, responsibilities to employers and clients, obligations to the profession, independence and objectivity, and marketing-specific legal and technical compliance issues.[49]

It is important that companies consistently enforce standards and impose penalties or punishment on those who violate codes of conduct. Clear Channel Communications, for example, fired two executives and disciplined other employees for violating the firm's policies on "payola," the illegal practice of accepting payment for playing songs on the air without divulging such deals. The firm, which owns approximately 1,200 radio stations, also required station managers and programming personnel to undergo additional training on its policies.[50] In addition, a company must take reasonable steps in response to violations of standards and, as appropriate, revise the compliance program to diminish the likelihood of future misconduct. Table 3.4 lists some commonly observed types of misconduct as reported in the National Business Ethics Survey (NBES). To succeed, a compliance program must be viewed as part of the overall marketing strategy implementation. If ethics officers and other executives are not committed to the principles and initiatives of marketing ethics and social responsibility, the program's effectiveness will be in question.

Increasing evidence indicates that being ethical and socially responsible pays off. Research suggests that a relationship exists between a marketing orientation and an organizational climate that supports marketing ethics and social responsibility. This relationship implies that being ethically and socially concerned is consistent with meeting the demands of customers and other stakeholders. By encouraging their employees to understand their markets, companies can help them to respond to stakeholders' demands.[51]

There is a direct association between corporate social responsibility and customer satisfaction, profits, and market value.[52] In a survey of consumers, nearly 86 percent indicated that when quality and price are similar among competitors, they would be more likely to buy from the company associated with a particular cause. In addition, young adults aged 18 to 25 are especially likely to take a company's citizenship efforts into account when making not only purchasing but also employment and investment decisions.[53]

codes of conduct Formalized rules and standards that describe what the company expects of its employees

table 3.4   TYPES AND INCIDENCES OF OBSERVED MISCONDUCT

Type of Conduct Observed	Employees Observing It (%)
Abusive or intimidating behavior toward employees	21
Lying to employees, customers, vendors, or the public	19
A situation that places employee interests over organizational interests	18
Safety regulation violations	16
Misreporting of actual time worked	16
Discrimination on the basis of race, color, gender, age, or similar categories	12
Stealing or theft	11
Sexual harassment	9

Source: "Survey Documents State of Ethics in the Workplace," Ethics Resource Center press release, October 12, 2005, www.ethics.org/nbes/nbes2005/release.html. Reprinted by permission of Ethics Resource Center.

Thus recognition is growing that the long-term value of conducting business in a socially responsible manner far outweighs short-term costs.[54] Companies that fail to develop strategies and programs to incorporate ethics and social responsibility into their organizational culture may pay the price with poor marketing performance and the potential costs of legal violations, civil litigation, and damaging publicity when questionable activities are made public.

...And now, back to Starbucks

Starbucks has supported responsible business practices virtually since its inception, but its success has attracted criticism and increased the importance of defending its image. Starbucks created a Corporate Social Responsibility (CSR) department in 1994; the department has grown significantly in the years since and produces an annual CSR report. Starbucks is concerned about the environment and its stakeholders, including its employees, suppliers, customers, and communities. To support the natural environment, Starbucks developed an environmental mission statement to articulate more clearly how the company will interact with its environment, eventually creating an Environmental Starbucks Coffee Company Affairs Team tasked with developing environmentally responsible policies and minimizing the company's "footprint." The company is also active in using environmental purchasing guidelines, reducing waste through recycling and energy conservation, and continually educating partners through the company's "Green Team" initiatives. It ensures that it builds relationships with the farmers that supply its coffee while working with governments in the various countries in which it operates. Starbucks practices conservation as well as Starbucks' Coffee and Farmer Equity Practices (C.A.F.E.), which is a set of socially responsible coffee-buying guidelines. Starbucks also pays coffee farmers premium prices to help them make profits and support their families. The company is also involved in social development programs, investing in programs to build schools, health clinics, and other projects that benefit coffee-growing communities.

Starbucks supports causes in both the communities where stores are located and in the countries where Starbucks coffee is grown. For example, Starbucks began contributing to CARE, a worldwide relief and development foundation, as a way to give back to coffee-origin countries, in 1991. By 1995, Starbucks had become CARE's largest corporate donor, pledging more than $100,000 a year and specifying that its support go to coffee-producing countries. The company's donations helped CARE with such projects as clean-water systems, health and sanitation training, and literacy efforts. Starbucks also has partnered with Conservation International (CI), a nonprofit organization than helps to promote biodiversity in coffee-growing regions to support producers of shade-grown coffee. The results of the partnership have proven positive for both the environment and the farmers. Shade acreage increased by 220 percent, and farmers received a price premium of 65 percent above the market price and increased exports by 50 percent.

Starbucks has achieved amazing growth and financial success for its shareholders while positioning itself as a socially responsible corporation. It has built a reputation for product quality, concern for stakeholders, and a balanced approach to all its business activities. It serves as a role model for its relationship with its employees, especially in the area of benefits. However, Starbucks has suffered criticism for its ability to beat the competition and put other coffee shops out of business and for creating a uniform retail culture in many cities. One of the areas where the company faces challenges is catching up with some of its competitors who have switched to 100 percent Fair Trade coffee. Although the future looks bright for Starbucks, the company must continue to focus on a balanced stakeholder orientation along with the rapid growth that has been so key to its success.[55]

1. Why do you think Starbucks has been so concerned with social responsibility in its overall corporate strategy?

2. Is Starbucks unique in being able to provide a high level of benefits to its employees?

3. Do you think that Starbucks has grown rapidly because of its ethical and socially responsible activities or because it provides products and an environment that customers want?

CHAPTER REVIEW

1. Recognize the importance of environmental scanning and analysis.

Environmental scanning is the process of collecting information about the forces in the marketing environment; environmental analysis is the process of assessing and interpreting the information gathered through environmental scanning. This information helps marketing managers to minimize uncertainty and threats and to capitalize on opportunities presented by environmental factors.

2. Explore the effects of competitive, economic, political, legal and regulatory, technological, and sociocultural factors on marketing strategies.

Marketers need to monitor the actions of competitors to determine what strategies competitors are using and how those strategies affect their own. Economic conditions influence consumers' buying power and willingness to spend. Legislation is enacted, legal decisions are interpreted by courts, and regulatory agencies are created and operated by elected or appointed officials. Marketers also can choose to regulate themselves. Technology determines how members of society satisfy needs and wants and helps to improve the quality of life. Sociocultural forces are the influences in a society that bring about changes in attitudes, beliefs, norms, customs, and lifestyles. Changes in any of these forces can create opportunities and threats for marketers.

3. Understand the concept and dimensions of social responsibility.

Social responsibility refers to an organization's obligation to maximize its positive impact and minimize its negative impact on society. At the most basic level, companies have an economic responsibility to be profitable so that they can provide a return on investment to their stockholders, create jobs for the community, and contribute goods and services to the economy. Marketers are also expected to

obey laws and regulations. Marketing ethics refers to principles and standards that define acceptable conduct in marketing as determined by various stakeholders. Philanthropic responsibilities go beyond marketing ethics; they are not required of a company but promote human welfare or goodwill.

4. Differentiate between ethics and social responsibility.

Whereas social responsibility is achieved by balancing the interests of all stakeholders in an organization, ethics relates to acceptable standards of conduct in making individual and group decisions.

ACE self-test

Please visit the student website at **www.prideferrell.com** for ACE Self-Test questions that will help you prepare for exams.

KEY CONCEPTS

environmental scanning	oligopoly	Federal Trade Commission (FTC)	marketing citizenship
environmental analysis	monopolistic competition	Better Business Bureau	marketing ethics
competition	pure competition	National Advertising	ethical issue
brand competitors	buying power	Review Board (NARB)	cause-related marketing
product competitors	disposable income	technology	strategic philanthropy
generic competitors	discretionary income	sociocultural forces	green marketing
total budget competitors	willingness to spend	social responsibility	consumerism
monopoly	business cycle		codes of conduct

ISSUES FOR DISCUSSION AND REVIEW

1. Why are environmental scanning and analysis important to marketers?

2. What are four types of competition? Which is most important to marketers?

3. Define *income, disposable income,* and *discretionary income.* How does each type of income affect consumer buying power?

4. What factors influence a buyer's willingness to spend?

5. What are the goals of the Federal Trade Commission? List the ways in which the FTC affects marketing activities. Do you think that a single regulatory agency should have such broad jurisdiction over so many marketing practices? Why or why not?

6. Name several nongovernmental regulatory forces. Do you believe that self-regulation is more or less effective than governmental regulatory agencies? Why?

7. Discuss the impact of technology on marketing activities.

8. In what ways are cultural values changing? How are marketers responding to these changes?

9. What is social responsibility, and why is it important?

10. What are four dimensions of social responsibility? What impact do they have on marketing decisions?

11. What are some major social responsibility issues? Give an example of each.

12. Describe consumerism. Analyze some active consumer forces in your area.

13. What is the difference between ethics and social responsibility?

MARKETING APPLICATIONS

1. Assume that you are opening *one* of the following retail businesses. Identify publications at the library or online that provide information about the environmental forces likely to affect the business. Briefly summarize the information each provides.
   a. Convenience store
   b. Women's clothing store
   c. Grocery store
   d. Fast-food restaurant
   e. Furniture store

2. Identify at least one technological advancement and one sociocultural change that have affected you as a consumer. Explain the impact of each on your needs as a customer.

3. Identify an organization in your community that has a reputation for being ethical and socially responsible. What activities account for this image? Is the company successful? Why or why not?

Online Exercise

4. Business for Social Responsibility (BSR) is a nonprofit organization for companies desiring to operate responsibly and demonstrate respect for ethical values, people, communities, and the natural environment. Founded in 1992, BSR offers members practical information, research, educational programs, and technical assistance as well as the opportunity to network with peers on current social responsibility issues. Visit **http://www.bsr.org**.
   a. What types of businesses join BSR, and why?
   b. In the CSR Resources section, go to the CSR News Releases section and pick three recent articles that deal with social responsibility issues in marketing. For each article, explain how these issues relate to a concept covered in Chapter 3.
   c. In the CSR Resources section, go to the Issue Briefs section and find the white paper on ethics codes and ethics training. Using this report, list some examples of corporate codes of ethics, and describe the benefits of establishing a code of ethics.

Corporate social responsibility is an emerging area of interest for firms. As such, many companies have conducted research and developed reports on corporate social responsibility. One such report is the KPMG International Survey of Corporate Responsibility Reporting. This report can be accessed using the search term "international survey" at **http://globaledge.msu.edu/ibrd** (and check the box "Resource Desk only." In the most recent report, which category of corporate social responsibility was most widely reported, and what does it say?

Chapter CASE

PETCO: Putting Pets First Earns Loyal Customers

PETCO Animal Supplies is the nation's number 2 specialty pet supply retailer with more than 850 stores in 49 states and the District of Columbia. Its pet-related products include pet food, pet supplies, grooming products, toys, novelty items, vitamins, veterinary supplies, and small pets such as fish, birds, and hamsters. It does not sell cats or dogs, however. PETCO strives to offer customers a complete assortment of pet-related products and services at competitive prices at convenient locations and through its website, www.petco.com, with a high level of customer service.

Most PETCO stores are 12,000 to 15,000 square feet and conveniently located near local neighborhood shopping destinations, such as supermarkets, bookstores, coffee shops, dry cleaners, and video stores, where its target customers make regular weekly shopping trips. PETCO executives believe that the company is well positioned, in terms of both product offerings and location, to benefit from favorable long-term demographic trends: a growing pet population and an increasing willingness of "pet parents" to spend on their pets. Indeed, the U.S. pet population has now reached 378 million companion animals, including 143 million cats and dogs. An estimated 62 percent of all U.S. households own at least one pet, and three-quarters of those households have two or more pets. The trend to have more pets and the number of pet-owning households will continue to grow, driven by an increasing number of children under age 18 as well as a growing population of empty nesters whose pets become their new children. U.S. retail sales of pet food, supplies, small animals (excluding cats and dogs), and services grew to approximately $38.5 billion in 2006.

PETCO was founded on the principle of "connecting with the community." One of its most important missions is to promote the health, well-being, and humane treatment of animals. It strives to carry out this mission through vendor-selection programs, pet adoption programs, and partnerships with animal welfare organizations. The company is involved every year in a number of programs to raise money for local communities and local animal initiatives.

Recognizing that between 5 and 10 million pets are euthanized in the United States every year, PETCO launched an annual "Spay Today" initiative in 2000 to address the growing problem of pet overpopulation in the United States. The "Spay Today" funds come from customer donations at PETCO stores, where customers are encouraged to round up their purchases to the nearest dollar or more. In 2005, PETCO launched the "Think Adoption First" program, which supports and promotes the human–animal bond. It is a program that sets the standard for responsibility and community involvement for the industry. The "Spring a Pet" fundraiser encourages pet lovers to donate $1, $5, $10, or $20 to animal welfare causes. Donors received a personalized cutout bunny as a reminder of their generosity. In 2007, $1.7 million was raised, and each PETCO store selected an animal welfare organization to be the recipient of the money raised at its location. The Tree of Hope program encourages customers to think of animals during the Christmas season. Customers visiting PETCO during the Christmas season can purchase card orna-

ments, the proceeds of which go to animal welfare charities. The PETCO Foundation also sponsors "Kind News," a humane education program that educates children about humane treatment of companion animals and fellow human beings. It features stories about responsible pet environmental concerns and issues as well as information on all types of animals.

Like all companies, PETCO operates in an environment in which a single negative incident can influence customers' perceptions of a firm's image and reputation instantly and potentially for years afterwards. Because pets engender such strong emotional attachments, it is especially important for companies that sell pets and pet products to be able to provide a rapid response to justify or to correct activities that may arouse potentially negative perceptions. The focus should be on a commitment to make correct decisions and to continually assess and address the risks of operating the business.

All retailers are subject to criticisms and must remain vigilant to maintain internal controls that provide assurance that employees and other partners follow ethical codes. PETCO accomplishes this through an ethics office and by developing an ethical corporate culture. PETCO also has developed and implemented a comprehensive code of ethics that addresses all areas of organizational risk associated with human resources, conflicts of interests, and appropriate behavior in the workplace. The code's primary emphasis is that animals always come first—PETCO insists that the well-being of animals in its care is of paramount importance. In the case of PETCO, a desire to do the right thing and to train all organizational members to make ethical decisions ensures not only success in the marketplace but also a significant contribution to society.[56]

Questions for Discussion

1. How does PETCO's ethics program help manage the risks associated with the pet industry?
2. How can PETCO's social responsibility programs advance its marketing strategy?
3. Why is it important for PETCO to train all its employees to understand and implement its ethical policies?

part 2

Using Technology for Customer Relationships in a Global Environment

Part 2 expands the marketing environment by examining technological and global issues in greater detail. Chapter 4 explores how marketers use information technology to build long-term relationships with customers by targeting them more precisely than ever before. Both e-marketing and customer relationship management are presented in the context of building an effective marketing strategy. Chapter 5 examines factors within the global marketing environment that create challenges and opportunities in international markets. Both the environmental variables and the strategic alternatives for organizing marketing strategy are discussed.

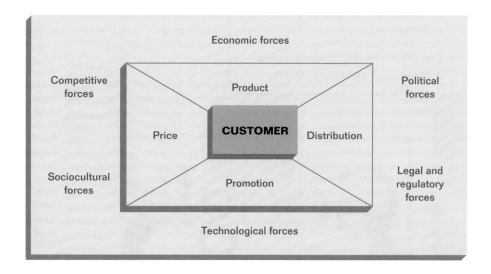

4

E-Marketing and Customer Relationship Management

OBJECTIVES

1. Define *electronic marketing* and *electronic commerce* and recognize their increasing importance in strategic planning.

2. Understand the characteristics of electronic marketing—addressability, interactivity, memory, control, accessibility, and digitalization—and how they differentiate electronic marketing from traditional marketing activities.

3. Examine how the characteristics of electronic marketing affect marketing strategy.

4. Understand how electronic marketing and information technology can facilitate customer relationship management.

5. Identify the legal and ethical considerations in electronic marketing.

Google Helps Marketers Find Answers

Google is the world's number 1 search engine, accounting for 43.5 percent of all searches in 2006 (close competitor Yahoo! had only 29 percent). Its mission is to organize the world's information and make it universally accessible and useful. The company was founded in 1996 by Larry Page and Sergey Brin, two Stanford University Ph.D. students. They believed that a search engine that analyzed the relationships between websites would produce better results than those offered by existing search engines at the time, which ranked results according to how many times the search term appeared on a page. They were proven right, and their company transformed the search landscape from one in which searches were conducted based on search words appearing on webpages to one in which the relevancy of pages became important. Google now ranks as Silicon Valley's second most valuable business (behind Microsoft), with a market value of about $163 billion and annual revenues of $6 billion, 98 percent coming from online text advertisements. Based in Mountain View, California, Google currently employs more than 9,400 employees.

Google's executives believe that the company is a global technology leader focused on improving how people connect with information. It has consistently provided a high-quality product to its consumers while refusing to allow advertisements to become annoying interruptions. The company provides objective search results and refuses to accept payment for inclusion or ranking in its results. It does include advertisements (in order to keep its search service free of charge) but strives to provide the most relevant and useful advertising and clearly identifies ads as such to its users.

Google is especially useful for people involved in marketing. The search engine can be used to conduct market and sales research, as well as company and customer research. Marketers can use it to search for potential customers, and customers can research company websites and related news articles even before calling a company. Google also can find websites such as **www.cohorts.com** and **www.claritas.com** to help with customer segmentation, and a search for market research can find results that provide reports and databases and other resources to help marketers.[1] ■

The phenomenal growth of the Internet presents exciting opportunities for companies such as Google to forge interactive relationships with consumers and business customers. The interactive nature of the Internet has made it possible to target markets more precisely and even to reach markets that previously were inaccessible. It also facilitates customer relationship management, allowing companies to network with manufacturers, wholesalers, retailers, suppliers, and outsource firms to serve customers more efficiently. Because of its ability to enhance the exchange of information between customer and marketer, the Internet has become an important component of most firms' marketing strategies.

We devote this chapter to exploring this new frontier. We begin by defining *electronic marketing* and exploring its context within marketing strategies. Next, we examine the characteristics that differentiate electronic marketing activities from traditional ones and explore how marketers are using the Internet strategically to build competitive advantage. Then we take a closer look at the role of the Internet and electronic marketing in managing customer relationships. Finally, we consider some of the ethical and legal implications that affect Internet marketing.

Marketing on the Internet

A number of terms have been coined to describe marketing activities and commercial transactions on the Internet. One of the most popular terms is **electronic commerce (or e-commerce)**, which refers to business exchanges conducted over the Internet using telecommunications tools such as webpages, e-mail, and instant or text messaging. In this chapter we focus on how the Internet, especially the World Wide Web, relates to all aspects of marketing, including strategic planning. Thus we use the term **electronic marketing (or e-marketing)** to refer to the strategic process of creating, distributing, promoting, and pricing products for targeted customers in the virtual environment of the Internet.

One of the most important benefits of e-marketing is the ability of marketers and customers to share information. Through company websites, consumers can learn about firms' products, including features, specifications, and prices. Many websites also provide feedback mechanisms through which customers can ask questions, voice complaints, indicate preferences, and otherwise communicate about their needs and desires. The Internet has changed the way marketers communicate and develop relationships not only with their customers but also with their employees and suppliers. Many companies use e-mail, groupware (software that allows people in different locations to access and work on the same file or document over the Internet), instant messaging, blogs, podcasts, videoconferencing, and other technologies to coordinate activities and communicate with employees. Because such technology facilitates and lowers the cost of communications, the Internet can contribute significantly to any industry. Indeed, adoption of the Internet as a communications channel has been found to influence business performance positively.[2]

Telecommunications technology offers additional benefits to marketers, including rapid response, expanded customer service capability (e.g., 24 hours a day, 7 days a week, or 24/7), decreased operating costs, and reduced geographic barriers. In today's fast-paced world, the ability to shop for books, clothes, jewelry, music, and other merchandise at midnight, when traditional stores are usually closed, is a benefit for both buyers and sellers. Indeed, research by comScore Networks found that 20 percent of online shopping occurs between 9 P.M. and 9 A.M.[3] Even small firms with limited resources can reach global markets. For example, Eli's Cheescake Company, a small Chicago bakery, generates 20 percent of its sales from around the world through its website.[4] Table 4.1 (on page 79) shows the most common online activities.

Despite these benefits, many companies that chose to make the Internet the core of their marketing strategies—often called *dot-coms*—failed to earn profits or acquire sufficient resources to remain in business. Many dot-coms failed because they thought the only thing that mattered was brand awareness. In reality, however, Internet

electronic commerce (or e-commerce) Business exchanges conducted over the Internet using telecommunications tools such as web pages, e-mail, and instant/text messaging

electronic marketing (or e-marketing) The strategic process of creating, distributing, promoting and pricing products for targeted customers in the virtual environment of the Internet

ADVERTISING PROMOTION

go online to
reward yourself

special offers & promotions from *Real Simple* and its advertisers

Get more from your favorite magazine by logging on to **realsimplerewards.com**.

Here *Real Simple* and its advertisers have reserved a world of rewards exclusively

for you, including special events, sweepstakes, samplings, great escapes, and

easy, everyday solutions that **make life easier**.

Electronic Marketing

Through the Internet, companies can offer customers unique services. RealSimpleRewards. com offers rewards and samples to subscribers of *Real Simple* magazine.

markets are more similar to traditional markets than they are different.[5] Thus successful e-marketing strategies, like traditional marketing strategies, depend on creating, distributing, promoting, and pricing products that customers need or want, not merely developing a brand name or reducing the costs associated with online transactions. In fact, traditional retailers continue to do quite well in some areas that many people just a few years ago thought the Internet would dominate. For example, although many marketers believed that there would be a shift to buying cars online, less than 3 percent of all new cars are sold through the Internet. Few consumers are willing to spend $30,000 online to purchase a new automobile. However, consumers are increasingly making car-buying decisions on the basis of information found at manufacturers' websites, online automotive magazine reviews, consumer review sites, and other online sources and then making their purchase at a dealership.

Indeed, e-marketing has not changed all industries, although it has had more of an impact in some industries in which the costs of business and customer transactions are very high. For example, trading stock has become significantly easier and less expensive for customers who can go online and execute their own orders. Firms such as E*Trade and Charles Schwab have been innovators in this area, and traditional brokerage firms such as Merrill Lynch, Fidelity, and T.Rowe Price had to introduce online trading for their customers to remain competitive.

Consumer-Generated Electronic Marketing

Although Internet-based marketing has generated exciting opportunities to interact with consumers, it is important to recognize that electronic marketing and related technologies are more consumer-driven than traditional markets. Two factors have caused consumer-generated information to gain importance: Consumers' desire to learn about other consumers' opinions and experiences and their increased ability to find information from other consumers' postings and to forward information about their own experiences.[6] Indeed, consumers often rely on the recommendations and suggestions of friends and family when making purchasing decisions. These informal exchanges of communication are often referred to as *word of mouth*, but online or electronic word-of-mouth practices are advancing rapidly.[7]

Today, marketers must recognize the impact of not only websites but also instant messaging, blogs, online forums, online games such as Second Life, mailing lists, and wikis, as well as text messaging via cell phones and podcasts via MP3 players. **Blogs** (short for *weblogs*) are Web-based journals in which writers can editorialize and interact with other Internet users, whereas **wikis** are software that create an interface that enables users to add or edit the content of some types of websites (also called *wikis* or *wikipages*). One of the best-known wikis is Wikipedia.com, an online encyclopedia. Marketers also must monitor websites with less than flattering names, such as **www.wakeupwalmart.com, ihatedell.net,** or **targetsucks.com** in order to gain

blogs Web-based journals in which people can editorialize and interact with other Internet users

wikis Software that create an interface that enables users to add or edit the content of some types of websites (also called *wikis* or *wikipages*)

table 4.1   LEADING INTERNET ACTIVITIES

Activity	Percent of U.S. Adults Who Have Engaged in Online Activity
Using e-mail	91
Using a search engine to find information	91
Searching for a map or driving directions	84
Looking for medical/health information	79
Researching products before making a purchase	78
Checking the weather	78
Looking for information on a hobby or interest	77
Getting travel information	73
Making online purchases	71
Getting news	67

Source: "Internet Activities," Pew Internet & Life Product, December 2006, www.pewinternet.org/trends/Internet_Activities_1.11.07.htm.

insight into public opinion about their firms. YouTube allows users to share videos—often of their own making—and some depict companies and their products in a less-than-favorable light. Social networks, such as Facebook.com, CarSpace.com, live-journal.com, and Slashdot.com, allow subscribers to blog and share anecdotes and experiences, often with pictures, audio, or even videos. For example, after Jeff Jarvis had an unhappy experience with Dell's ineffective attempts to resolve problems with his new laptop, he wrote about it on his blog. Within days, his blog became one of the most visited websites, and it triggered a surge of Dell horror stories across the Web. Soon after, when people typed "Dell" into search engines, Jarvis's blog and websites with unflattering names would appear on the first listings page.[8]

marketing
ENTREPRENEURS

Noah Glass

HIS BUSINESS: Mobo

FOUNDED: 2005, when Glass was age 24

SUCCESS: $1.8 million in revenues

Like most New Yorkers, Noah Glass got tired of waiting in long lines for his coffee, so he did something about it. His company, Mobo ("mobile order"), enables registered customers to order and pay for takeout meals at participating restaurants on their cell phones. The restaurants pay Mobo 10 percent of each sale generated by the service. Initially available only at select restaurants in Manhattan, the company is beginning to expand into Boston, Chicago, Philadelphia, Washington, Los Angeles, San Francisco, and London. Glass eventually envisions customers using his company's services to order movie tickets and taxi cabs and even to pay for parking meters.[a]

Basic Characteristics of Electronic Marketing

Although e-marketing is similar to traditional marketing, it is helpful to understand the basic characteristics that distinguish this environment from the traditional marketing environment. These characteristics include addressability, interactivity, memory, control, accessibility, and digitalization.

Addressability. The technology of the Internet makes it possible for visitors to a website to identify themselves and provide information about their product needs and wants before making a purchase. The ability of a marketer to identify customers before they make a purchase is called

Addressability

SCORE makes its website available to address the specific needs of small business owners.

addressability. Many websites encourage visitors to register to maximize their use of the site or to gain access to premium areas; some even require it. Registration forms typically ask for basic information, such as name, e-mail address, age, and occupation, from which marketers can build user profiles to enhance their marketing efforts. CD-Now (owned by Amazon.com), for example, asks music lovers to supply information about their listening tastes so that the company can recommend new releases. Some websites even offer contests and prizes to encourage users to register. Marketers also can conduct surveys to learn more about the people who access their websites, offering prizes as motivation for participation.

Addressability represents the ultimate expression of the marketing concept. With the knowledge about individual customers garnered through the Web, marketers can tailor marketing mixes more precisely to target customers with narrow interests, such as recorded blues music or golf. Addressability also facilitates tracking website visits and online buying activity, which makes it easier for marketers to accumulate data about individual customers to enhance future marketing efforts. Amazon.com, for example, stores data about customers' purchases and uses that information to make recommendations the next time they visit the site.

Some website software can store a **cookie**, an identifying string of text, on a visitor's computer. Marketers use cookies to track how often a particular user visits the website, what he or she may look at while there, and in what sequence. Cookies also permit website visitors to customize services, such as virtual shopping carts, as well as the particular content they see when they log onto a webpage. CNN, for example, allows visitors to its website to create a custom news page tailored to their particular interests. The use of cookies to store customer information can be an ethical issue, however, depending on how the data are used. If a website owner can use cookies to link a visitor's interests to a name and address, that information could be sold to advertisers and other parties without the visitor's consent or even knowledge. The potential for misuse of cookies has made many consumers wary of this technology.

addressability A marketer's ability to identify customers before they make a purchase

cookie An identifying string of text stored on a website visitor's computer

Because technology allows access to large quantities of data about customers' use of websites, companies must carefully consider how the use of such information affects individuals' privacy, as we discuss in more detail later in this chapter.

Interactivity   Another distinguishing characteristic of e-marketing is **interactivity**, which allows customers to express their needs and wants directly to a firm in response to its marketing communications. At BlueNile.com, for example, engagement ring shoppers can click on a link at any time during a search to generate a pop-up window where they can comment about their search efforts. The comments are immediately sent to the appropriate internal department to address the live feedback.[9] This characteristic means that marketers can interact with prospective customers in real time (or at least a close approximation of it). Of course, salespeople have always been able to do this, but at a much greater cost. The Web provides the advantages of a virtual sales representative with broader market coverage and at lower cost.

One implication of interactivity is that a firm's customers also can communicate with other customers (and noncustomers). For this reason, differences in the amount and type of information possessed by marketers and their customers are not as pronounced as in the past. One result is that the new- and used-car businesses have become considerably more competitive because buyers are coming into dealerships armed with more complete product and cost information obtained through comparison shopping on the Net. By providing information, ideas, and a context for interacting with other customers, e-marketers can enhance customers' interest and involvement with their products.

Interactivity enables marketers to capitalize on the concept of community to help customers derive value from the firm's products and website. **Community** refers to a sense of group membership or feeling of belonging by individual members of a group.[10] One such community is MySpace, a website where users can post and share their own personal profiles, blogs, photos, videos, and music and chat or exchange messages about topics ranging from cars and computers to health and careers. Such sites encourage visitors to "hang out" and contribute to the community (and see the website's advertising) instead of clicking elsewhere. Because such communities have well-defined demographics and common interests, they represent a valuable audience for advertisers, which typically generate the funds to maintain such sites.[11] Indeed, a few companies have created private communities where carefully recruited members interact not only with each other but also with advertisers who pay for access to the groups. Such private groups helped Kraft's Nabisco develop 100 Calorie Packs after asking the online participants of a diet group about their diet food choices.[12]

As mentioned earlier, blogs are another way to interact with customers. There are an estimated 55 million blogs on a variety of topics, including companies, brands, and products, and they can be positive—raves about Manolo shoes, for example—or negative—such as rages against Wal-Mart, Kmart, and Best Buy. When Shayne McQuade invented a backpack with solar panels that let backpackers keep their gadgets charged, a friend mentioned the product on his blog, which soon led to references and discussions on other blogs and ultimately created a positive "buzz" and orders for the new product. Companies are increasingly establishing blogs to interact with customers. General Motors, for example, hosts the GM Smallblock Engine blog, where employees and customers marvel over Corvettes and other GM vehicles.[13]

Memory.   **Memory** refers to a firm's ability to access databases or data warehouses containing individual customer profiles and past purchase histories and to use these data in real time to customize its marketing offer to a specific customer. A **database** is a collection of information arranged for easy access and retrieval. Although companies have had database systems for many years, the information these systems contain did not become available on a real-time basis until fairly recently. Current software technology allows a marketer to identify a specific visitor to its website instantaneously, locate that customer's profile in its database, and then display the customer's past purchases or suggest new products based on past purchases while he or

interactivity The ability to allow customers to express their needs and wants directly to the firm in response to the firm's marketing communications

community A sense of group membership or feeling of belonging

memory The ability to access databases or data warehouses containing individual customer profiles and past purchase histories and to use these data in real time to customize a marketing offer

database A collection of information arranged for easy access and retrieval

Building a Community: YouTube Can Do It

Whether or not you use YouTube, you've probably heard about it. Chad Hurley and Steve Chen founded the site in 2005 as a place for people to share their personal videos. Today it has become an "entertainment destination" where people can watch, browse, upload, and share more than 100 million videos per day. According to Hitwise and Nielsen NetRatings, 60 percent of all videos viewed on the Web everyday are watched on YouTube, and the free site is visited by almost 20 million unique users each month. Over time, a YouTube community has evolved, and the site has become a meeting place for those with similar interests.

With the recent success of social networking sites such as MySpace and Facebook, more major media companies such as Comcast, Verizon, Google, Yahoo! and Microsoft have been looking into the viability and ultimate profitability of sites like YouTube. Google purchased YouTube in 2006 for $1.65 billion. What makes YouTube, a company with no current profit, worth so much money?

Websites such as YouTube and MySpace are supported by advertising that, in turn, relies on *viral marketing.* This type of marketing relies on the fact that Internet users and bloggers will share the messages that they see on YouTube, for example, with other Internet users, who then will share it again and again. As the new owner of YouTube, Google now can place advertisements on webpages on which videos are viewed or perhaps even in videos themselves. Research by the Online Publishers Association indicates that watching videos with some sort of viral marketing attached often results in sales. If YouTube proves to be more than a passing phase of interest, then Google may have hit the advertising jackpot.

Although it sounds like everything is coming up dollar signs at YouTube, the company has had its share of problems—starting with the issue of copyright infringement. Many of the videos uploaded to YouTube contain copyrighted material. For example, the Japan Society for Rights of Authors sued YouTube because the site contained almost 30,000 videos with material copyrighted by the organization's members. YouTube agreed to pull those videos from the site. To avoid such lawsuits in the future, Google and YouTube have signed agreements with Universal Music Group, Sony BMG, and Warner Music Group in which they agree to share revenue in exchange for permission to post copyrighted material on the YouTube site. Some analysts suggest that this move makes an important statement for the future of YouTube and online video consumption.

While it is clear that sites such as YouTube, MySpace, and Facebook are hot right now, the question among industry analysts is, Will they stay hot? If so, those who own the sites stand to benefit tremendously.[b]

she is still visiting the site. For example, Bluefly, an online clothing retailer, asks visitors to provide their e-mail addresses, clothing preferences, brand preferences, and sizes so that it can create a customized online catalog ("My Catalog") of clothing that matches the customer's specified preferences. The firm uses customer purchase profiles to manage its merchandise buying. Whenever it adds new clothing items to its inventory, it checks them against its database of customer preferences and, if it finds a match, alerts the individual in an e-mail message. Applying memory to large numbers of customers represents a significant advantage when a firm uses it to learn more about individual customers each time they visit the firm's website.

All the music you want.
Any way you want it.

Napster® is the completely legalized way to get unlimited access to over 1,000,000 songs on your PC. Now with *Napster To Go*™, you can fill and refill any compatible MP3 player and take your music anywhere.*

Try it for free at Napster.com.

Digitalization

Napster offers music downloads of over 1 million songs.

control Customers' ability to regulate the information they view and the rate and sequence of their exposure to that information

portal A multiservice website that serves as a gateway to other websites

accessibility The ability to obtain information available on the Internet

digitalization The ability to represent a product, or at least some of its benefits, as digital bits of information

Control.   In the context of e-marketing, **control** refers to customers' ability to regulate the information they view as well as the rate and sequence of their exposure to that information. The Web is sometimes referred to as a *pull* medium because users determine what they view at websites; website operators' ability to control the content users look at and in what sequence is limited. In contrast, television can be characterized as a *push* medium because the broadcaster determines what the viewer sees once he or she has selected a particular channel. Both television and radio provide *limited exposure control* (you see or hear whatever is broadcast until you change the station).

For e-marketers, the primary implication of control is that attracting—and retaining—customers' attention is more difficult. Marketers have to work harder and more creatively to communicate the value of their websites clearly and quickly, or viewers will lose interest and click to other sites. With literally hundreds of millions of unique pages of content available to any Web surfer, simply putting a website on the Internet does not guarantee that anyone will visit it or make a purchase. Publicizing the website may require innovative promotional activities. For this reason, many firms pay millions of dollars to advertise their products or websites on high-traffic sites such as Yahoo!. Because of Yahoo!'s growing status as a **portal** (a multiservice website that serves as a gateway to other websites), firms are eager to link to it and other such sites to help draw attention to their own sites. Indeed, consumers spend most of their time online on portal sites such as MSN and Yahoo!, checking e-mail; tracking stocks; and perusing news, sports, and weather.

Accessibility.   An extraordinary amount of information is available on the Internet. The ability to obtain it is referred to as **accessibility**. Because customers can access in-depth information about competing products, prices, reviews, blog opinions, and so forth, they are much better informed about a firm's products and their relative value than ever before. Someone looking to buy a new pickup truck, for example, can go to the websites of Ford, General Motors, and Toyota to compare the features of the Ford Ranger, the GMC Canyon, and the Toyota Tacoma. The truck buyer also can access online magazines, pricing guides, and consumer review sites to get more specific information about product features, performance, and prices.

Accessibility also dramatically increases the competition for Internet users' attention. Without significant promotion, such as advertising on portals like AOL, MSN, Yahoo!, and other high-traffic sites, it is becoming increasingly difficult to attract a visitor's attention to a particular website. Consequently, e-marketers are having to become more creative and innovative to attract visitors to their sites.

Digitalization.   **Digitalization** is the ability to represent a product, or at least some of its benefits, as digital bits of information. Digitalization allows marketers to use the Internet to distribute, promote, and sell those features apart from the physical item itself. FedEx, for example, has developed Web-based software that allows consumers and business customers to track their own packages from starting point to destination. Distributed over the Web at very low cost, the online tracking system adds value to FedEx's delivery services. Digitalization can be enhanced for users who have broadband access to the Internet because broadband's faster connections allow streaming audio and video and other new technologies.

In addition to providing distribution efficiencies, digitizing part of a product's features allows new combinations of features and services to be created quickly and inexpensively. For example, a service station that keeps a customer's history of automotive oil changes in a database can e-mail that customer when the next oil change is due and at the same time suggest other types of preventive maintenance, such as tire rotations or a tune-up. Digital features are easy to mix and match to meet the demands of individual customers.

E-Marketing Strategies

Now that we have examined some distinguishing characteristics of doing business on the Internet, it is time to consider how these characteristics affect marketing strategy. Marketing strategy involves identifying and analyzing a target market and creating a marketing mix to satisfy individuals in that market regardless of whether those individuals are accessible online or through more traditional avenues. However, there are significant differences in how the marketing mix components are developed and combined into a marketing strategy in the electronic environment of the Web. As we continue this discussion, keep in mind that the Internet is a very dynamic environment, meaning that e-marketing strategies may need to be modified frequently to keep pace.

Product Considerations. The growth of the Internet presents exciting opportunities for marketing products to both consumers and organizations. Computers and computer peripherals, industrial supplies, and packaged software are the leading business purchases online. Consumer products account for a small but growing percentage of Internet transactions, with books/music/ video, toys/videogames, and consumer electronics among the fastest-growing online consumer purchases. Through e-marketing, companies can provide products, including goods, services, and ideas, that offer unique benefits and improve customer satisfaction.

The online marketing of goods such as computer hardware and software, books, DVDs, CDs, toys, automobiles, and even groceries is accelerating rapidly. Dell Computer sells more than $56 billion worth of computers and related software and hardware, about half of that amount through its website.[14] Autobytel has established an effective model for online auto sales by helping consumers find the best price on their preferred models and then arranging for local delivery. However, low profit margins owing to customized deliveries have challenged the ability of firms to deliver tangible goods.

Services may have the greatest potential for online marketing success. Many websites offer or enhance services ranging from home- and car-buying assistance to travel reservations and stock trading. At Century 21's website, consumers can search for the home of their dreams anywhere in the United States, get information about mortgages and credit and tips on buying real estate, and learn about the company's relocation services. Airlines are increasingly booking flights via their websites. Southwest Airlines, for example, now books 70 percent of its passenger revenue online.[15]

The proliferation of information on the World Wide Web has itself spawned new services. Web search engines and directories such as Google, Yahoo!, Ask.com, Excite,

E-Marketing Strategies

E-marketing has created immeasurable opportunity for service companies like Southwest Airlines. By refining its marketing message to an online community, the company has dramatically expanded its customer-base.

Your vacation is just a click away.
Book at swavacations.com and you can get all this from air, hotel, and car reservations to show tickets and attraction passes.

SOUTHWEST
VACATIONS
swavacations.com

table 4.2   TOP TEN GLOBAL WEB PROPERTIES

Property	Total Unique Visitors (000)
Microsoft sites	508,659
Google sites	494,170
Yahoo! sites	476,761
Time Warner Network	260,387
eBay	251,423
Wikipedia sites	164,675
Amazon sites	151,033
Fox Interactive Media	135,730
CNet Networks	114,940
Ask Network	113,881

Source: "comScore Networks Releases Top Web Properties Worldwide for December; Reviews Biggest Gainers for 2006," comScore Networks press release, January 31, 2007, www.comscore.com/press/release.asp?press=1139.

and Lycos are among the most heavily accessed sites on the Internet. Without these services, which track and index the vast quantity of information available on the Web, the task of finding something of interest would be tantamount to searching for the proverbial needle in a haystack. Many of these services, most notably Yahoo!, have evolved into portals by offering additional services, including news, weather, chat rooms, free e-mail accounts, and shopping. Table 4.2 lists some of the leading global Internet properties.

Even ideas have potential for success on the Internet. Web-based distance learning and educational programs are becoming increasingly popular. Corporate employee training is a $110 billion industry, and online training modules are growing rapidly. Additional ideas being marketed online include marriage and personal counseling; medical, tax, and legal advice; and even psychic services.

Distribution Considerations.   The role of distribution is to make products available at the right time at the right place in the right quantities. The Internet can be viewed as a new distribution channel. Physical distribution is especially compatible with e-marketing. The ability to process orders electronically and increase the speed of communications via the Internet reduces inefficiencies, costs, and redundancies throughout the marketing channel.

More firms are exploiting advances in information technology to synchronize the relationships between their manufacturing or product assembly and their customer contact operations. This increase in information sharing among various operations of the firm makes product customization easier to accomplish. Marketers can use their websites to query customers about their needs and then manufacture products that exactly fit those needs. Gateway, Apple, and Dell, for example, help their customers build their own computers by asking them to specify what components to include; these firms then assemble and ship the customized product directly to the customer in a few days. Imperial Sugar lets business customers place orders, check stock, and track shipments via its website, which now accounts for 10 percent of the firm's sales.[16] Now business customers even have their own search engine, ThomasNet, where they can search for goods, services, and suppliers on a local, regional, and national level.[17]

One of the most visible members of any marketing channel is the retailer, and the Internet is increasingly becoming a retail venue. Jupiter Media Metrix projects that the percentage of the population shopping online will grow to 71 percent and that online retail sales in the United States will climb to $144 billion by 2010.[18] The Internet provides an opportunity for marketers of everything from computers to travel reservations to encourage exchanges. Amazon.com, for example, sells more than $8 billion of books, CDs, DVDs, videos, toys, games, electronics, and groceries directly from its website.[19] Indeed, Amazon.com's success at marketing books online has been so

snapshot

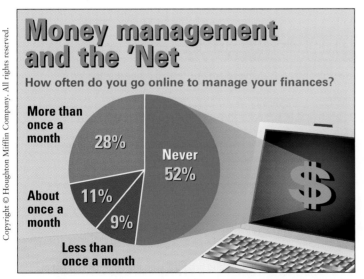

Money management and the 'Net

How often do you go online to manage your finances?

- More than once a month: 28%
- Never: 52%
- About once a month: 11%
- Less than once a month: 9%

Source: Data from Ipsos Internet Survey. Margin of error ±3 percentage points.

phenomenal that many imitators have adopted its retailing model for everything from CDs to toys. Another retailing venture is online auctioneers, such as eBay and Haggle Online, that auction everything from fine wines and golf clubs to computer goods and electronics.

Promotion Considerations.   The Internet is an interactive medium that can be used to inform, entertain, and persuade target markets to accept an organization's products. In fact, gathering information about goods and services is one of the main reasons people go online. Research indicates that many consumers view online advertisements as a source for further learning.[20] College students in particular say that they are influenced by Internet ads when buying online or just researching product purchases.[21] The accessibility and interactivity of the Internet allow marketers to complement their traditional media usage for promotional efforts. The control characteristic of e-marketing means that customers who visit a firm's website are there because they choose to be, which implies that they are interested in the firm's products and therefore can be at least somewhat involved in the message and dialog provided by the firm. For these reasons, the Internet represents a highly cost-effective communication tool for small businesses.

Many companies augment their TV and print advertising campaigns with Web-based promotions. Splenda, Kraft, and Ragu, for example, have created websites with recipes and entertaining tips to help consumers get the most out of their products. Many movie studios have set up websites at which visitors can view clips of their latest releases, and television commercials for new movies often encourage viewers to visit these sites. Some companies have even created bogus websites to entertain customers, such as Burger King's Subservient Chicken, CareerBuilder's Monk-e-mail, and Alaska Airlines' skyhighairlines.com. In addition, many companies choose to advertise their goods, services, and ideas on portals, search engines, and even other firms' websites. Table 4.3 describes the most common types of advertisements found on websites. Research indicates that the number of exposures, number of websites, and number of pages on which a customer is exposed to an ad have a positive effect on repeat purchases.[22] More than 80 percent of companies now include the Internet as an advertising medium.[23]

Many marketers are also offering buying incentives and adding value to their products online through the use of sales promotions, especially coupons. Several websites, including **www.coolsavings.com, www.valupage.com,** and **www.valpak.com,** offer online coupons for their members.

table 4.3	TYPES OF ADVERTISING ON WEBSITES
Banner Ads	Small, rectangular, static or animated ads that typically appear at the top of a webpage
Keyword ads	Ads that relate to text or subject matter specified in a Web search
Button ads	Small, square or rectangular ads bearing a corporate or brand name or logo and usually appearing at the bottom or side of a webpage
Pop-up ads	Large ads that open in a separate Web browser window on top of the website being viewed
Pop-under ads	Large ads that open in a new Web browser window underneath the website being viewed
Sponsorship ads	Ads that integrate companies' brands and products with the editorial content of certain websites.

Viral Marketing Propels Arctic Monkeys to the Top of the Charts

The Arctic Monkeys, a four-piece independent rock band from Sheffield, England, skyrocketed to fame in three short years owing in great part to viral e-marketing. About a year after the band's formation, the demo CDs the band handed out at small concert gigs were downloaded to the Internet. As loyal fans shared the music across cyberspace, people began to take notice, and the band's fan base grew tremendously. By 2004, the band had begun to attract the attention of the British press and BBC Radio 1 based on the offerings floating around the Net. In fact, some of their music is available only via download.

The Arctic Monkeys resisted the idea of signing with a record label for quite some time, even going as far as forbidding record company scouts from attending their concerts. Because the band had a large number of sold-out shows across the United Kingdom, thanks primarily to electronic word of mouth, the members weren't sure that they needed representation. Eventually, the band did sign with Domino Records' owner Laurence Bell, a representative who signs only artists whose music he personally likes. The Arctic Monkeys' debut album, *Whatever People Say I Am, That's What I'm Not,* which includes the single, "I Bet You Look Good on the Dance Floor," sold 350,000 copies in its first week of release. The album became the fastest-selling debut album in U.K. chart history, outselling all top 20 albums put together.

The band won "Best New Act" at the 2006 Brit Awards and made history yet again by being named both "Best New Band" and "Best British Band" in the same year at the 2006 NME Awards. The Arctic Monkeys' quick rise to fame has astounded those in the music business, some of whom say they haven't seen anything like it since the Beatles.[c]

The characteristics of e-marketing make promotional efforts on the Internet significantly different from those using more traditional media. First, because Internet users can control what they see, customers who visit a firm's website are there because they choose to be, which implies, as pointed out previously, that they are interested in the firm's products and therefore may be more involved in the message and dialog provided by the firm. Second, the interactivity characteristic allows marketers to enter into dialogs with customers to learn more about their interests and needs. This information then can be used to tailor promotional messages to the individual customer. Finally, addressability can make marketing efforts directed at specific customers more effective. Indeed, direct marketing combined with effective analysis of customer databases may become one of e-marketing's most valuable promotional tools.

Pricing Considerations. Pricing relates to perceptions of value and is the most flexible element of the marketing mix. Electronic marketing enables firms to charge different prices for customers purchasing through different channels, such as retail stores, catalogs, and the Internet. This ability to have multiple-channel price options can provide value to the customer and improve marketing performance.[24] Electronic marketing facilitates both price and nonprice competition because the accessibility characteristic of e-marketing gives consumers access to more information about the cost and price of products than has ever been available to them before. For example, car shoppers can access automakers' webpages, configure an ideal vehicle, and get instant feedback on its cost. They also can visit Autobytel, Edmund's, and other websites to obtain comparative pricing information on both new and used cars to help them find the best value. They can then purchase a vehicle online or at a dealership. At online auctions, price is determined by supply and demand. Research, however, suggests that consumers do not always make rational decisions in name-your-own price auctions.[25]

Customer Relationship Management

One characteristic of companies engaged in e-marketing is a renewed focus on relationship marketing by building customer loyalty and retaining customers—in other words, a focus on customer relationship management (CRM). As we noted in Chapter 1, CRM focuses on using information about customers to create marketing strategies that develop and sustain desirable long-term customer relationships. Procter & Gamble, for example, encourages Oil of Olay customers to join Club Olay, an online community with some 4 million members. In exchange for beauty tips, coupons, and special offers, the website collects some information about customers and their use of the skin-care product.[26] CRM focuses on analyzing and using databases and leveraging technologies to identify strategies and methods that will maximize the lifetime value of each desirable customer to a firm.[27]

Database Marketing

Informatica helps new customers identify and build consumer databases.

A focus on CRM is possible in e-marketing because of marketers' ability to target individual customers. This effort is enhanced over time as customers invest time and effort into "teaching" the firm what they want. This investment in the firm also increases the costs that a customer would incur by switching to another company. Once a customer has learned to trade stocks online through Charles Schwab, for example, there is a cost associated with leaving to find a new brokerage firm. Another firm may offer less service, and it may take time to find a new firm and learn a new system. Any time a marketer can learn more about its customers to strengthen the match between its marketing mix and target customers' desires and preferences, it increases the perceived costs of switching to another firm.

Electronic marketing permits companies to target customers more precisely and accurately than ever before. The addressability, interactivity, and memory characteristics of e-marketing allow marketers to identify specific customers, establish interactive dialogs with them to learn about their needs, and combine this information with their purchase histories to customize products to meet those needs. Amazon.com, for example, stores and analyzes purchase data to understand each customer's interests. This information helps the online retailer to improve its ability to satisfy individual customers and thereby increase sales of books, music, movies, and other products to each customer. The ability to identify individual customers allows marketers to shift their focus from targeting groups of similar customers to increasing their share of an individual customer's purchases. Thus the emphasis shifts from *share of market* to *share of customer*. In moving to a share-of-customer perspective,

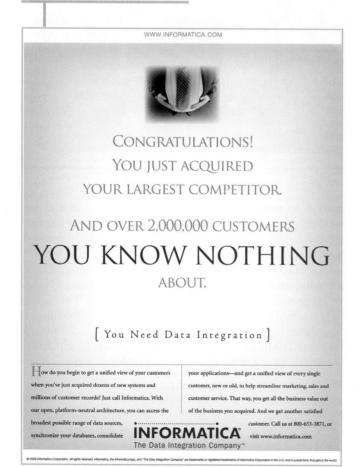

however, a firm should ensure that individual target customers have sufficient potential to justify such specialized efforts. Indeed, one benefit arising from the addressability characteristic of e-marketing is that firms can track and analyze individual customers' purchases and identify the most profitable and loyal customers. However, a firm must balance its resources between customer-acquisition efforts and customer-retention efforts in order to maximize profits.[28]

Database Marketing

CRM employs database marketing techniques to identify different types of customers and develop specific strategies for interacting with each customer. It incorporates three elements:

1. Identifying and building a database of current and potential consumers, including a wide range of demographic, lifestyle, and purchase information

2. Delivering differential messages according to each consumer's preferences and characteristics through established and new media channels

3. Tracking customer relationships to monitor the costs of retaining individual customers and the lifetime value of their purchases[29]

It is important for marketers to distinguish *active* customers—those likely to continue buying from the firm—from *inactive* customers—those who are likely to defect and those who have already defected. This information should help to (1) identify profitable inactive customers who can be reactivated, (2) remove inactive unprofitable customers from the customer database, and (3) identify active customers who should be targeted with regular marketing activities.[30] Figure 4.1 depicts some of the reasons that customers may choose to defect or take their business elsewhere.

Another aspect of CRM is supplier relationship marketing (SRM), which also uses databases to manage relationships and communications with vendors and other individuals and companies that supply goods, services, and ideas to a firm. SRM uses information technology to develop databases and measures for assessing and managing these relationships. It is necessary to monitor supplier relationships and track performance in order to assess quality and determine vendors' value to the overall operation. These systems and processes are important in creating value and effective relationships

figure 4.1

WHY CUSTOMERS DEFECT

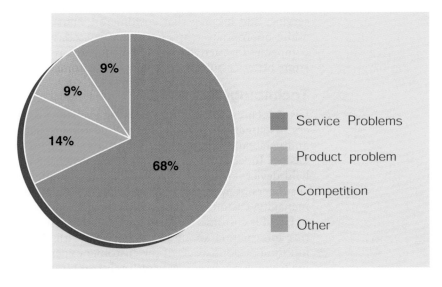

Source: "CRM," *CRM Trends,* http://crmtrends.com/crm.html (accessed January 4, 2007).

with a firm's own customers.[31] Consider that Trader Joe's Company, a specialty food retailer, had to drop award-winning Bingham Hill Cheese products from its product mix owing to frequent inventory stockouts and lost sales from lack of product availability. Bingham Hill was too small a supplier to serve a large company like Trader Joe's.[32]

Customer Lifetime Value

Focusing on share of customer requires recognizing that all customers have different needs and that all customers do not have equal value to a firm. The most basic application of this idea is the 80/20 rule: 80 percent of business profits come from 20 percent of customers. Although this idea is not new, advances in technology and data-collection techniques now permit firms to profile customers in real time. The goal is to assess the worth of individual customers and thus estimate their lifetime value to the firm. The concept of customer lifetime value (CLV) may include not only an individual's propensity to engage in purchases but also his or her strong word-of-mouth communication about the firm's products.[33] Some customers—those who require considerable handholding or who return products frequently—simply may be too expensive to retain given the low level of profits they generate. Companies can discourage these unprofitable customers by requiring them to pay higher fees for additional services. For example, many banks and brokerages charge hefty maintenance fees on small accounts. Such practices allow firms to focus their resources on developing and managing long-term relationships with more profitable customers.[34]

Thus, managing customer relationships requires allocating resources selectively to different customers based on the economic value of their relationship to the firm. CLV is a key measurement that forecasts a customer's lifetime economic contribution based on continued relationship marketing efforts. It can be calculated by taking the sum of the customer's present-value contributions to profit margins over a specific time frame. For example, the lifetime value of a Lexus customer could be predicted by how many new automobiles Lexus could sell the customer over a period of years and developing a summation of the contribution to margins across the time period. This value has been estimated at $600,000. Data from past customer behavior and other information of the effectiveness of relationship efforts could assist in this projection. While this is not an exact science, knowing a customer's potential lifetime value can help marketers to determine how best to allocate resources to marketing strategies to sustain that customer over a lifetime.

If a company truly understands each customer's lifetime value, it can maximize its own value by boosting the number, scope, and duration of value-enhancing customer relationships. To do this, managers would have to determine how much revenue each customer would generate in the future and subtract the expected costs of acquiring, serving, and keeping that customer.[35] Thus the concept of CLV helps marketers to adopt appropriate marketing activities today to increase future profitability. Indeed, companies that actively use CRM tools to precisely target their best customers demonstrate better customer service, higher customer- retention rates, and increased profits.[36]

Technology Drives CRM

CRM focuses on building satisfying exchange relationships between buyers and sellers by gathering useful data at all customer-contact points—telephone, fax, online, and personal—and analyzing those data to better understand customers' needs and desires. Indeed, the term *m-commerce* has been applied to the use of portable handheld devices—such as personal digital assistants (PDAs) and cell phones—to reach customers at every possible location.[37] Companies are increasingly automating and managing customer relationships through technology. Indeed, one fast-growing area of CRM is customer-support and call-center software, which helps companies to capture information about all interactions with customers and provides a profile of the most important aspects of the customer experience on the Web and on the phone. Using technology, marketers can analyze interactions with customers to identify performance issues and even build a library of "best practices" for customer interaction.[38]

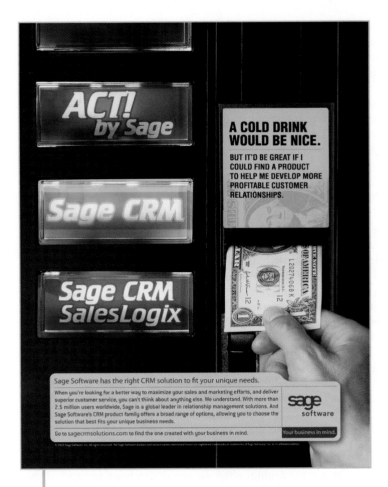

Technology as a CRM Tool

Sage designates its software for customer relationship management.

Customer-support and call-center software can focus on those aspects of customer interaction that are most relevant to performance, such as how long customers have to wait on the phone to ask a question of a service representative or how long they must wait to receive a response from an online request. This technology also can help marketers determine whether call-center personnel are missing opportunities to promote additional products or to provide better service. For example, after buying a new Saab automobile, the customer is supposed to meet a service mechanic who can answer any technical questions about the new car during the first service visit. Saab follows up this visit with a telephone survey to determine whether the new-car buyer met the Saab mechanic and to learn about the buyer's experience with the first service call.

Sales automation software can link a firm's sales force to e-marketing applications that facilitate selling and providing service to customers. Often these applications enable customers to assist themselves instead of using traditional sales and service organizations. At Cisco, for example, 83 percent of all customer-support questions can be answered online through the firm's website, yielding significant cost savings and improved customer satisfaction.[39] In addition, CRM systems can provide sales managers with information that helps provide the best product solution for customers and thus maximize service. CRM applications include software for marketing automation, sales automation, and customer support and call centers.

Customer Satisfaction Is the End Result of CRM

Although technology drives CRM and can help companies build relationships with desirable customers, it is used too often as a cost-reduction tactic or a tool for selling, with little thought toward developing and sustaining long-term relationships. Some companies spend millions to develop CRM systems yet fail to achieve the associated benefits. These companies often see themselves as sophisticated users of technology to manage customers, but they do not view customers as assets. CRM cannot be effective, however, unless it is developed as a relationship-building tool. CRM is a process of reaching out to customers and building trust, not a technology solution for customer sales.[40]

Perhaps because of the software and information technology associated with collecting information from consumers and responding to their desires, some critics view CRM as a form of manipulation. It is possible to use information about customers at their expense to obtain quick results, for example, charging higher prices whenever possible and using available data to maximize profits. However, using CRM to foster customer loyalty does not require collecting every conceivable piece of data from consumers or trying to sell customers products they don't want. Marketers should not try to control customers; they should try to develop relationships that derive from the trust gained over many transactions and that are sustained by customers' belief that the company genuinely desires their continued patronage.[41] Trust reduces the costs associated with worrying about whether expectations will be honored and simplifies the customers' buying efforts in the future.

What marketers can do with CRM technology is identify their most valuable customers so that they can make an investment in building long-term relationships with those customers.[42] Building on this information about customer preferences can permit customized offers to create a one-to-one marketing relationship.[43] To be effective, marketers must measure the effectiveness of CRM systems in terms of their progress toward developing satisfactory customer relationships. Fewer than 20 percent of companies track customer retention, but developing and assessing customer loyalty is important in managing long-term customer relationships.

The most important component of CRM is remembering that it is not about technology but about relationships with customers. CRM systems should ensure that marketers listen to customers and then respond to their needs and concerns to build long-term relationships. The Internet can provide a valuable listening post and serve as a medium to manage customer relationships.[44]

Legal and Ethical Issues in E-Marketing

How marketers use technology to gather information—both online and off—to foster long-term relationships with customers has raised numerous legal and ethical issues. The popularity and widespread use of the Internet grew so quickly that global legal systems have not been able to keep pace with advances in technology. Among the issues of concern are personal privacy, unsolicited e-mail, and the misappropriation of copyrighted intellectual property.

One of the most significant privacy issues involves the personal information companies collect from website visitors. A survey by the Progress and Freedom Foundation found that 96 percent of popular commercial websites collect personally identifying information from visitors.[45] Cookies are the most common means of obtaining such information. Some people fear that the collection of personal information from website users may violate users' privacy, especially if it is done without their knowledge.

In response to privacy concerns, some companies are cutting back on the amount of information they collect. Companies are increasingly being more transparent about how they use that information, and fewer companies are selling such information to third parties.[46] Public concerns about online privacy remain, however, and many in the industry are urging self-policing on this issue to head off potential regulation. One effort toward self-policing is the online privacy program developed by the BBBOnLine subsidiary of the Council of Better Business Bureaus (see Figure 4.2). The program awards a privacy seal to companies that clearly disclose to their website visitors what information they are collecting and how they are using it.[47]

Few laws specifically address personal privacy in the context of e-marketing, but the standards for acceptable marketing conduct implicit in other laws and regulations generally can be applied to e-marketing. Personal privacy is protected by the U.S. Constitution, various Supreme Court rulings, and laws such as the 1971 Fair Credit Reporting Act, the 1978 Right to Financial Privacy Act, and the 1974 Privacy Act, which deals with the release of government records. However, with few regulations on how businesses use information, companies can legally buy and sell information about customers to gain competitive advantage. Some have suggested that if personal data were treated as property, customers would have greater control over their use.

The most serious strides toward regulating privacy issues associated with e-marketing are emerging in Europe. The 1998 European Union Directive on Data Protection specifically requires companies that want to collect personal information to explain how the information will be used and to obtain the individual's permission. Companies must make customer data files available on request, just as

Privacy Concerns

Sharp recognizes privacy concerns in data storage and strives to protect customer security.

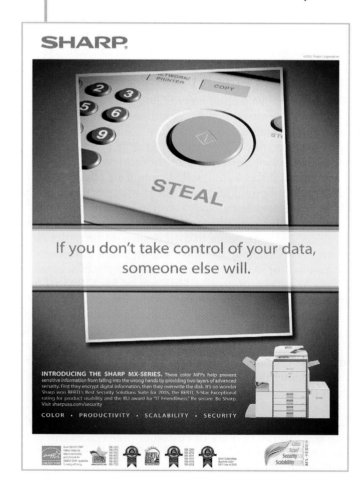

SHARP.

STEAL

If you don't take control of your data, someone else will.

INTRODUCING THE SHARP MX-SERIES. These color MFPs help prevent sensitive information from falling into the wrong hands by providing two layers of advanced security. First they encrypt digital information, then they overwrite the disk. It's no wonder Sharp won BERTL's Best Security Solutions Suite for 2005, the BERTL 5-Star Exceptional rating for product usability and the BLI award for "IT Friendliness." Be secure. Be Sharp. Visit sharpusa.com/security

COLOR · PRODUCTIVITY · SCALABILITY · SECURITY

figure 4.2

THE BBBONLINE PRIVACY SEAL AND PROGRAM EXPLANATION

U.S. credit-reporting firms must grant customers access to their personal credit histories. The law also bars website operators from selling e-mail addresses and using cookies to track visitors' movements and preferences without first obtaining permission. Because of this legislation, no company may deliver personal information about EU citizens to countries whose privacy laws do not meet EU standards.[48] The directive ultimately may establish a precedent for Internet privacy that other nations emulate.

Spam, or unsolicited commercial e-mail (UCE), has become a major source of frustration with the Internet. Many Internet users believe that spam violates their privacy and steals their resources. Many companies despise spam because it costs them nearly $22 billion a year in lost productivity, new equipment, antispam filters, and manpower. By some estimates, spam accounts for more than 75 percent of all e-mail.[49] Spam has been likened to receiving a direct-mail promotional piece with postage due. While some recipients of spam appreciate the opportunity to learn about new products (see Figure 4.3), others have become so angry that they have organized boycotts against companies that advertise in this manner. Most Internet service providers offer their subscribers the option to filter out e-mail from certain Internet addresses that generate a large volume of spam. Businesses are installing software to filter out spam from outside their networks. Some firms have filed lawsuits against spammers under the Controlling the Assault of Non-Solicited Pornography and Marketing (CAN-SPAM) Law, which bans fraudulent or deceptive unsolicited commercial e-mail and requires senders to provide information on how recipients can opt out of receiving additional messages. However, spammers appear to be ignoring the law and finding creative ways to get around spam filters. Increasingly, spam originates from outside the United States.[50]

Another issue growing in importance is *phishing*, the practice of sending fraudulent e-mails that appear to come from a trusted, legitimate source and request personal information for the purpose of committing identity theft. Phishing messages

spam Unsolicited commercial e-mail

figure 4.3

TYPES OF GOODS AND SERVICES MARKETED THROUGH SPAM

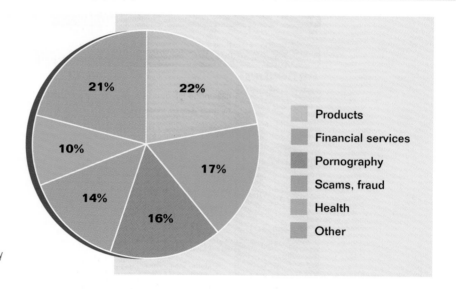

- Products
- Financial services
- Pornography
- Scams, fraud
- Health
- Other

Source: Ferris Research, in "Spam for Everyone," *The New York Times,* January 31, 2005, www.nytimes.com.

often appear to come from financial firms such as Citibank and may direct recipients to an authentic-looking website to trick them into giving personal data such as account numbers and passwords. *Consumer Reports* magazine estimated that consumers were defrauded out of $630 million in 2004 and 2005 owing to phishing scams.[51] In addition to defrauding consumers, phishing cons also harm the reputation of companies unwittingly used to dupe consumers into giving out their personal information. Phishing has spread to nonfinancial corporate websites, where the scam artists are exploiting well-known brands such as Coca-Cola to lure consumers into giving up their personal information.[52]

The Internet also has created issues associated with intellectual property, the copyrighted or trademarked ideas and creative materials developed to solve problems, carry out applications, and educate and entertain others. Intellectual property losses relate to lost revenue from the illegal copying of computer programs, movies, CDs, and books. This issue has become a global concern because of disparities in enforcement of laws throughout the world. The Business Software Alliance estimates that global losses from software piracy amount to $34 billion a year, including movies, music, and software downloaded from the Internet.[53] The Digital Millennium Copyright Act (DMCA) was passed to protect copyrighted materials on the Internet. Intellectual property rights issues have some people wondering whether fast-growing Internet video site YouTube (now owned by Google) will have to revamp its business model to avoid copyright issues. YouTube, which allows users to post short videos—often homemade ones shot with cell phones or home recording equipment—may face the prospect of litigation when fans deliberately or unwittingly post copyrighted material, such as clips from televisions shows. Viacom, which owns MTV and Comedy Central, believes that it is owed millions in copyright infringement penalties because clips pirated from its networks are watched 80,000 times a day. YouTube thus far has managed to turn litigation threats into licensing deals, but questions about the legality of many of the videos on the fast-growing website remain.[54]

Protecting trademarks also can be problematic. For example, some companies have discovered that another firm has registered a URL (website address) that duplicates or is very similar to their own trademarks. The "cybersquatter" then attempts to sell the right to use the URL to the legal trademark owner. Companies such as Taco Bell, MTC, and KFC have paid thousands of dollars to gain control of domain names that match or parallel their company trademarks.[55] To help companies address this conflict, Congress passed the Federal Trademark Dilution Act of 1995, which gives trademark owners the right to protect their trademarks, prevents the use of trademark-protected entities, and requires the relinquishment of names that duplicate or closely parallel registered trademarks.

As the Internet continues to evolve, more legal and ethical issues certainly will arise. Recognizing this, the American Marketing Association has developed a Code of Ethics for Marketing on the Internet (see Table 4.4) Such self-regulatory policies may help to head off government regulation of electronic marketing and commerce. Marketers and all other users of the Internet should make an effort to learn and abide by

table 4.4   AMERICAN MARKETING ASSOCIATION CODE OF ETHICS FOR MARKETING ON THE INTERNET PREAMBLE

The Internet, including online computer communications, has become increasingly important to marketers' activities, as they provide exchanges and access to markets worldwide. The ability to interact with stakeholders has created new marketing opportunities and risks that are not currently specifically addressed in the American Marketing Association Code of Ethics. The American Marketing Association Code of Ethics for Internet marketing provides additional guidance and direction for ethical responsibility in this dynamic area of marketing. The American Marketing Association is committed to ethical professional conduct and has adopted these principles for using the Internet, including online marketing activities utilizing network computers.

General Responsibilities

Internet marketers must assess the risks and take responsibility for the consequences of their activities. Internet marketers' professional conduct must be guided by:

1. Support of professional ethics to avoid harm by protecting the rights of privacy, ownership and access.
2. Adherence to all applicable laws and regulations with no use of Internet marketing that would be illegal, if conducted by mail, telephone, fax or other media.
3. Awareness of changes in regulations related to Internet marketing.
4. Effective communication to organizational members on risks and policies related to Internet marketing, when appropriate.
5. Organizational commitment to ethical Internet practices communicated to employees, customers and relevant stakeholders.

Privacy

Information collected from customers should be confidential and used only for expressed purposes. All data, especially confidential customer data, should be safeguarded against unauthorized access. The expressed wishes of others should be respected with regard to the receipt of unsolicited e-mail messages.

Ownership

Information obtained from the Internet sources should be properly authorized and documented. Information ownership should be safeguarded and respected. Marketers should respect the integrity and ownership of computer and network systems.

Access

Marketers should treat access to accounts, passwords and other information as confidential, and only examine or disclose content when authorized by a responsible party. The integrity of others' information systems should be respected with regard to placement of information, advertising or messages.

Source: Reprinted by permission of the American Marketing Association.

basic "netiquette" (Internet etiquette) to ensure that they get the most out of the resources available on this growing medium. Fortunately, most marketers recognize the need for mutual respect and trust when communicating in any public medium. They know that doing so will allow them to maximize the tremendous opportunities the Internet offers to foster long-term relationships with customers.

...And now, back to Google

Although Google began as a search engine, it has progressed to providing more sophisticated services for its advertisers and customers. Although the company thus far has been able to remain on the cutting edge, it needs to maintain its competitive advantage and continue to be innovative and successful.

Google's advertising service, AdWords, allows advertisers to bid to place text ads next to search results. Initially, advertisers paid Google based on the number of times their ads appeared on users' search results pages. Now, however, AdWords is offered on a cost-per-click basis, so advertisers pay only when a user clicks on one of its ads. In 2006, Google launched a new print-advertising initiative, an online marketplace that lets advertisers place bids on space in more than 50 major newspapers across the United States. It also has another program called AdSense that distributes ads for display on the websites of Google Network members. Google even has experimented with radio advertising through an online auction system similar to AdWords.

Although Google has released many new products, none has altered the Web landscape in the way that its search engine did. New products such as Picasa, a photo site, Google Finance, and Google Blog Search, as well as Gmail, Google Calendar, and Froogle, a shopping site, have yet to really compete with other available products. The company even has a website, **Labs.google.com,** where it showcases new-product ideas that aren't quite ready for mainstream use and invites users to offer feedback on the products as they are being developed.

Maintaining Google's culture of innovation is crucial as it continues to come up with new products and ways of advertising. This creative culture helps to position the firm to stay innovative in the future and to maintain its technological leadership. Although Google is growing, the company strives for a small-company feel, with pianos and lava lamps in the lobby and bicycles and large rubber exercise balls on the floors of the halls. Its offices are "high-density clusters" with three or four staffers sharing spaces with couches and dogs. Recreational facilities for employees include workout rooms, Ping-Pong tables, parking-lot roller hockey games, and free meals three times a day. All engineers are allotted 20 percent of their time to work on their own ideas, and many of these personal projects have yielded strong ideas, including a social-networking website called Orkut, as well as Google News. With its work force more than tripling in three years and new offices in diverse cities such as Beijing, Zurich, and Bangalore, Google has to work hard to continue producing new products (it has been launching a new product nearly every week), and it that believes its culture is a driving force in this innovation.[56]

1. How has Google changed the way companies advertise?

2. Is cost-per-click advertising effective?

3. What is your perception of Google's advertising? Is it intrusive? Would you click on the sponsored links?

CHAPTER REVIEW

1. Define *electronic marketing* and *electronic commerce* and recognize their increasing importance in strategic planning.

Electronic commerce (e-commerce) refers to sharing business information, maintaining business relationships, and conducting business transactions by means of telecommunications networks. Electronic marketing (e-marketing) is the strategic process of creating, distributing, promoting, and pricing products for targeted customers in the virtual environment of the Internet. The Internet has changed the way marketers communicate and develop relationships with their customers, employees, and suppliers. Telecommunications technology offers marketers potential advantages, including rapid response, expanded customer-service capability, reduced costs of operation, and reduced geographic barriers. Despite these benefits, many Internet companies have failed because they did not realize that Internet markets are more similar to traditional markets than they are different and thus require the same marketing principles.

2. Understand the characteristics of electronic marketing—addressability, interactivity, memory, control, accessibility, and digitalization—and how they differentiate electronic marketing from traditional marketing activities.

A marketer's ability to identify customers before they make a purchase is called addressability. One way websites achieve addressability is through the use of cookies, strings of text placed on a visitor's computer. Interactivity allows customers to express their needs and wants directly to a firm in response to its marketing communications. It also enables marketers to capitalize on the concept of community and customers to derive value from use of the firm's products and websites. Memory refers to a firm's ability to access collections of information in databases or data warehouses containing individual customer profiles and past purchase histories. Firms then can use these data in real time to customize their marketing offer to a specific customer. Control refers to customers' ability to regulate the information they view as well as the rate and sequence of their exposure to that information. Accessibility refers to customers' ability to obtain the vast amount of information available on the Internet. This is enhanced by the recognition value of a firm's URL, or website address. Digitalization is the representation of a product, or at least some of its benefits, as digital bits of information.

The addressability, interactivity, and memory characteristics of e-marketing enable marketers to identify specific customers, establish interactive dialogs with them to learn their needs and combine this information with their purchase histories to customize products to meet their needs. Electronic marketers thus can focus on building customer loyalty and retaining customers.

3. Examine how the characteristics of electronic marketing affect marketing strategy.

The growth of the Internet and the World Wide Web presents opportunities for marketing products (goods, services, and ideas) to both consumers and organizations. The Internet also can be viewed as a new distribution channel. The ability to process orders electronically and to increase the speed of communications via the Internet reduces inefficiencies, costs, and redundancies throughout the marketing channel. The Internet is an interactive medium that can be used to inform, entertain, and persuade target markets to accept an organization's products. The accessibility of the Internet presents marketers with an opportunity to expand and complement their traditional media promotional efforts. The Internet gives consumers access to more information about the cost and price of products than has ever been available to them before.

4. Understand how electronic marketing and information technology can facilitate customer relationship management.

One of the characteristics of companies engaged in e-marketing is a focus on customer relationship management (CRM), which employs information about customers to create marketing strategies that develop and sustain desirable long-term customer relationships. The addressability, interactivity, and memory characteristics of e-marketing allow marketers to identify specific customers, establish interactive dialogs with them to learn about their needs, and combine this information with customers' purchase histories to tailor products that meet those needs. It also permits marketers to shift their focus from share of market to share of customer. CRM employs database marketing techniques to identify different types of customers and develop specific strategies for interacting with each customer. The goal is to assess the worth of individual customers and thus estimate their customer lifetime value (CLV). Although technology drives CRM and can help companies to increase sales, CRM cannot be effective unless it is developed as a relationship-building tool.

5. Identify the legal and ethical considerations in electronic marketing.

One of the most controversial issues is personal privacy, especially the personal information that companies collect from website visitors, often through the use of cookies. Additional issues relate to spam, or unsolicited commercial e-mail, phishing, and the misappropriation of copyrighted or trademarked intellectual property. More issues are likely to emerge as the Internet and e-marketing continue to evolve.

 Please visit the student website at **www.prideferrell.com** for ACE Self-Test questions that will help you prepare for exams

ACE self-test

KEY CONCEPTS

electronic commerce
(e-commerce)
electronic marketing
(e-marketing)
blogs

wikis
addressability
cookie
interactivity

community
memory
database
control

portal
accessibility
digitalization
spam

ISSUES FOR DISCUSSION AND REVIEW

1. How does addressability differentiate e-marketing from the traditional marketing environment? How do marketers use cookies to achieve addressability?

2. Define *interactivity*, and explain its significance. How can marketers exploit this characteristic to improve relations with customers?

3. Memory gives marketers quick access to customers' purchase histories. How can a firm use this capability to customize its product offerings?

4. Explain the distinction between *push* and *pull* media. What is the significance of control in terms of using websites to market products?

5. What is the significance of digitalization?

6. How can marketers exploit the characteristics of the Internet to improve the product element of the marketing mix?

7. How do the characteristics of e-marketing affect the promotion element of the marketing mix?

8. How does e-marketing facilitate customer relationship management?

9. How can technology help marketers to improve their relationships with customers?

10. Electronic marketing has raised several ethical questions related to consumer privacy. How can cookies be misused? Should the government regulate the use of cookies by marketers?

MARKETING APPLICATIONS

Online Exercises

1. Amazon.com is one of the Web's most recognizable marketers. Visit the company's site at **www.amazon.com,** and describe how the company adds value to its customers' buying experience.

2. Some products are better suited than others to electronic marketing activity. For example, Art.com specializes in selling art prints via its online store. The ability to display a variety of prints in many different categories gives customers a convenient and efficient way to search for art. On the other hand, GE has a website displaying its appliances, but customers must visit a retailer to purchase them. Visit **www.art.com** and **www.geappliances.com,** and compare how each firm uses the electronic environment of the Internet to enhance its marketing efforts.

3. Visit the website **www.covisint.com,** and evaluate the nature of the business customers attracted. Who

is the target audience for this business marketing site? Describe the types of firms that are currently doing business through this exchange. What other types of organizations might be attracted? Is it appropriate to sell any banner advertising on a site such as this? What other industries might benefit from developing similar e-marketing exchange hubs?

4. iVillage is an example of an online community. Explore the content of this website at **www.ivillage.com.**
   a. What target market can marketers access through this community?
   b. How can marketers target this community to market their goods and services?
   c. Based on your understanding of the characteristics of e-marketing, analyze the advertisements you observe on this website.

Your firm wants to know which ten countries are most prepared for e-commerce. A ranking of the level of "e-readiness" of various markets worldwide can be accessed by using the search term "e-readiness" at **http://globaledge.msu.edu/ibrd** (and check the box "Resource Desk only"). If your firm was aiming to develop its international e-commerce competence, how can this information influence your firm's marketing strategy?

The Gnome Helps Fuel a Turnaround at Travelocity

Travelocity was launched in 1996 by Sabre Interactive, a division of AMR Corporation, which at the time owned the Sabre Reservations System and American Airlines. Today, Travelocity is the most popular travel service on the Web and the sixth-largest travel agency in the United States, with bookings of more than $7 billion. Teams of employees working in seven U.S. offices work together to bring consumers the best in airline reservations, hotel rooms, cruises, vacation packages, car rentals, and last-minute deals. Travelocity operates or powers websites in five languages across four continents. It was named the "World's Leading Travel Internet Site" for the ninth consecutive year at the World Travel Awards in 2006, and it has led all travel sites—including airline and hotel sites—in customer respect, based on a study released by the Customer Respect Group. It holds the highest possible ranking from *Consumer Reports*.

When Travelocity began in 1996, it was one of the first Internet travel websites. By 2000 and 2001, however, it had stopped growing and was fading as the pioneer brand. Travelocity executives recognized that they needed to refocus the company on more profitable products. The reality is that selling airline tickets does not make money, but selling hotels and travel packages does. Consequently, Travelocity implemented a strategy of cross-selling and up-selling to help customers get a more complete travel experience. It focused on serving as a more complete advocate for travelers by providing a more affordable and more rewarding travel experience. The result: Travelocity's package segment grew by more than 100 percent a year between 2003 and 2005.

Despite the improving outlook, executives felt that the company needed to stand behind travelers in a way that no other online travel company did. They decided to spend a year developing a Customer Bill of Rights to guarantee that everything that customers book will be right, and if it isn't, then the company will work with its partners to fix the problem. For example, if a customer books a hotel with a swimming pool but finds that the swimming pool is closed on arrival, Travelocity will, at its own expense, find a comparable or better-quality hotel and move the customer there. Travelocity maintains a 24-hour hotline open seven days a week to ensure that customers get what they want. The Travelocity Guarantee allays the concerns of Travelocity customers who may be worried about booking online. The company stood by the guarantee even when it made a mistake and sold $0 tickets to Fiji for a short time.

The company paired the new guarantee with the "Roaming Gnome Enforcer of the Travelocity Guarantee" in television and other advertising. The Roaming Gnome advertising campaign represented an effort to humanize the Travelocity brand. The character embodied the joy of travel and symbolized getting out of the garden and seeing the world with new eyes. The advertising campaign created a tremendous buzz about Travelocity and boosted revenues by 37 percent. The gnome also won the American Marketing Association Gold EFIE award for "Best Retail Advertising Campaign."

Travelocity partners with American Express Travel, AOL Travel, Yahoo! Travel, and many other firms. In this way, Travelocity has a much larger market share, and because it represents so many firms, it has more power both with consumers and with suppliers. The network partnering is especially important when it comes to marketing to customers. Travelocity can piggyback off its partners to use their tried-and-tested marketing techniques with its own customers. In this way, Travelocity and its partners gain from the synergies of their partnerships.

Travelocity is also experimenting with creative ways of marketing to its customers. It was a sponsor of the CBS series *Amazing Race*, and the competitors even had to find a gnome and carry him across the finish line. Although it was a huge investment for Travelocity, it paid off with increases in sales in only eight weeks. Executives believe that by going beyond 30-second commercials and banner ads, Travelocity is part of the complete entertainment mix of customers. Travelocity also uses search-engine marketing, spending much of its online advertising budget on paid keyword search ads. Although click-through advertising is vital, Travelocity has estimated that as many as a quarter of the people who came to Travelocity through search marketing would have come to the website anyway because Travelocity is such a well-known brand.

Travelocity also regularly tests its website for ease of use. It has seven testers in a room to find out where people are confused and where things can be improved. It has used this method to radically change its website. One of the things it realized was that people forget passwords. To counteract this problem Travelocity changed the system so that customers reentered their credit-card information, address, and e-mail address and used these things to pull up their profile rather than relying on passwords. This change resulted in an overnight increase in revenues of 10 percent. Executives realized that if you make using the website hard, then people will go elsewhere.[57]

Questions for Discussion

1. What is the role of consumer-generated information in helping Travelocity succeed?
2. Describe the marketing decisions that have helped Travelocity be so successful.
3. How did Travelocity use the Roaming Gnome as a symbol to communicate with its target market?

CHAPTER 5

Global Markets and International Marketing

Gillette: Cutting into the World Market

If you've ever used a wet razor, chances are you used a Gillette brand razor. After all, the Gillette Company, which also makes the popular Duracell battery, commands more than 70 percent of the $1.7 billion men's razor market in the United States, and it has a dominant share of the worldwide razor market as well. In 2005, Gillette merged with Procter & Gamble (P&G), a marriage of two giants spanning multiple global industries with centuries of experience and success.

Founded by King C. Gillette in 1901, the Gillette Company was one of the first great multinational organizations and, some would say, a marvel of marketing effectiveness—a trait that also has been synonymous with P&G, which was born in 1837. Just four years after founding Gillette in Boston, King Gillette opened a branch office in London, and the company quickly gained sales and profits throughout western Europe. About 20 years later, Gillette said of his safety razor, "There is no other article for individual use so universally known or widely distributed. In my travels, I have found it in the most northern town in Norway and in the heart of the Sahara Desert." From the beginning, Gillette set out to offer consumers high-quality shaving products that would satisfy their basic grooming needs at a fair price. Having gained more than half the entire razor and blades market, Gillette's manufacturing efficiency allowed it to implement marketing programs on a large scale that helped the company gain both profits and market leadership.

Today, the Gillette Company is the world leader in male grooming products, a category that includes blades, razors, and shaving preparations, and in selected female grooming products, such as wet-shaving products and hair-removal devices. In addition, the company holds the number 1 position worldwide in alkaline batteries and in manual and power toothbrushes. Gillette's manufacturing operations are conducted at 32 facilities in 15 countries, and products are distributed through wholesalers, retailers, and agents in more than 200 countries and territories.

Gillette's Mach3 and Mach3 Turbo shaving systems are the best-selling men's shavers, and its line of Venus razors leads the women's shaving market. "Gillette's blade and razor business is the single most valuable franchise in the household products and cosmetics industries," said William H. Steele, an analyst at

OBJECTIVES

1. Understand the nature of global markets and international marketing.

2. Analyze the environmental forces affecting international marketing efforts.

3. Identify several important regional trade alliances, markets, and agreements.

4. Examine methods of involvement in international marketing activities.

5. Recognize that international marketing strategies fall along a continuum from customization to globalization.

Bank of America Securities. The blade and razor segment accounts for roughly 40 percent of Gillette's sales and more than 70 percent of the company's profits. The worldwide success of the Mach3 was not a simple task, however. It took ten years, 35 patents, $200 million in research and development, $550 million in capital investments, and $300 in marketing efforts to make Mach3 successful. And all these resources were spent on an item that costs roughly $6.50 to consumers. Gillette's goal for Mach3 was a worldwide product launch, not just a domestic one. As such, the company needed to ensure that it had enough Mach3 products in the global supply chain to satisfy the likely strong global demand. Any stock-outs would be very costly to Gillette's market position and image and endanger its aggressive product launch. The successful launch paved the way for the Venus launch, which followed much the same strategy as the Mach3 launch.[1] ■

Technological advances and rapidly changing political and economic conditions are making it easier than ever for companies like Gillette and Procter & Gamble to market their products overseas as well as at home. With most of the world's population and two-thirds of total purchasing power outside the United States, international markets represent tremendous opportunities for growth. Consider that MTV now reaches 1 billion people worldwide through 100 MTV, VH1, BET, and Nickelodeon channels. The company tailors the content of each channel to match local language and culture. MTV Indonesia, for example, has a regular call to prayer for its Muslim viewers, whereas MTV Japan is very edgy and technology-oriented. Only 26 percent of MTV Network viewers live in the United States.[2]

Because of the increasingly global nature of marketing, we devote this chapter to the unique features of global markets and international marketing. We begin by considering the nature of global marketing strategy and exploring the environmental forces that create opportunities and threats for international marketers. Next, we consider several regional trade alliances, markets, and agreements. Finally, we consider the levels of commitment that U.S. firms have toward international marketing and their degree of involvement in it. These factors are significant and must be considered in any marketing plan that includes an international component.

The Nature of Global Marketing Strategy

International marketing involves developing and performing marketing activities across national boundaries. For example, Wal-Mart has 1.8 million employees and operates more than 6,600 stores in 15 countries, including the United States, Brazil, and China, whereas Starbucks serves 40 million customers a week at more than 12,000 shops in 37 countries.[3] Accessing these markets can promote innovation, whereas intensifying global competition spurs companies to market better, less expensive products.

Companies are finding that international markets provide tremendous opportunities for growth. At the same time, governments and industry leaders contend that too few firms take full advantage of international opportunities. To counter this, many countries offer significant practical assistance and valuable benchmarking research that will help their domestic firms become more competitive globally. For example, The U.S. Commercial Service, the global business solutions unit of the U.S. Department of Commerce, offers U.S. firms extensive practical knowledge about international markets and industries, a unique global network, innovative use of information technology, and a focus on small and medium-sized businesses.[4]

Traditionally, most companies—including McDonald's and KFC—have entered the global marketplace incrementally as they gained knowledge about various markets and opportunities. Beginning in the 1990s, however, some firms—such as eBay, Google, and Logitech—were founded with the knowledge and resources to expedite

international marketing
Developing and performing marketing activities across national boundaries

Honeywell wanted to lower worldwide operational costs. With Xerox as their global office document solutions provider, they will cut costs by 21%, saving millions. There's a new way to look at it.

Global Marketing Strategy

Xerox helps businesses with global office documents solutions.

their commitment and investment in the global marketplace. These *born globals*—typically small, technology-based firms earning as much as 70 percent of their sales outside the domestic home market—export their products almost immediately after being established in market niches in which they compete with larger, more established firms.[5] Whether the traditional approach, the born-global approach, or an approach that merges attributes of both is adopted to market the firm's products and services, international marketing strategy is a critical element of a firm's global operations. Today, global competition in most industries is intense and becoming increasingly fierce with the addition of newly emerging markets and firms.

Environmental Forces in International Markets

Firms that enter foreign markets often find that they must make significant adjustments in their marketing strategies. The environmental forces that affect foreign markets may differ dramatically from those affecting domestic markets. Thus a successful international marketing strategy requires a careful environmental analysis. Conducting research to understand the needs and desires of foreign customers is crucial to international marketing success. Consider that urban Mexicans, who spend an average of two hours per day on transportation, are increasingly resorting to snacks at convenience stores. Recognizing this trend has encouraged Oxxo and 7-Eleven to open thousands of new convenience stores in recent years to cater to this market.[6] Many firms have demonstrated that such efforts can generate tremendous financial rewards, increase market share, and heighten customer awareness of their products around the world. In this section we explore how differences in the sociocultural; economic; political, legal, and regulatory; social and ethical; competitive; and technological forces of the marketing environment in other countries can profoundly affect marketing activities.

Sociocultural Forces

Cultural and social differences among nations can have significant effects on marketing activities. Because marketing activities are primarily social in purpose, they are influenced by beliefs and values regarding family, religion, education, health, and recreation.

FLATHEAD RESERVATION,
HOME OF SALISH KOOTENAI COLLEGE

If I stay on the rez

*I can use my education
to help my people.*

AFTER ATTENDING A TRIBAL COLLEGE, NEARLY 80% OF NATIVE AMERICANS
TAKE JOBS TO HELP THEIR CULTURAL COMMUNITIES.

LEARN HOW THE TRIBAL COLLEGES PROVIDE QUALITY EDUCATION TO NATIVE AMERICANS. 1-800-776-FUND | COLLEGEFUND.ORG

AMERICAN INDIAN COLLEGE FUND ◊ EDUCATING THE MIND AND SPIRIT

Cultural Differences

American Indian College Fund
realizes that students are highly
influenced by cultural and family
values.

By identifying major sociocultural deviations among countries, marketers lay the groundwork for an effective adaptation of marketing strategy. In India, for instance, three-quarters of McDonald's menu was created to appeal to Indian tastes, including many vegetarian items, and it does not include pork or beef products at all. In China, however, the fast-food giant has made fewer menu adjustments and even promotes its beef burgers in a sexy ad campaign.[7] Although football is a popular sport in the United States and a major opportunity for many television advertisers, soccer is the most popular televised sport in Europe and Latin America. And, of course, marketing communications often must be translated into other languages. Sometimes, however, the true meaning of translated messages can be misinterpreted or lost. Consider some translations that went awry in foreign markets: KFC's long-running slogan, "Finger lickin' good," was translated into Spanish as "Eat your fingers off," whereas Coors' "Turn it loose" campaign was translated into Spanish as "Drink Coors and get diarrhea."[8]

It can be difficult to transfer marketing symbols, trademarks, logos, and even products to international markets, especially if these are associated with objects that have profound religious or cultural significance in a particular culture. For example, when Big Boy opened a new restaurant in Bangkok, it quickly became popular with European and American tourists, but the local Thais refused to eat there. Instead, they placed gifts of rice and incense at the feet of the Big Boy statue—a chubby boy holding a hamburger—which reminded them of Buddha.[9]

Buyers' perceptions of other countries can influence product adoption and use. Research indicates that consumer preferences for domestic products depend on both the country of origin and the product category of competing products.[10] When people are unfamiliar with products from another country, their perceptions of the country itself may affect their attitude toward the product and help determine whether they will buy it. If a country has a reputation for producing quality products and therefore has a positive image in consumers' minds, marketers of products from that country will want to make the country of origin well known. For example, a generally favorable image of Western computer technology has fueled sales of U.S.-made personal computers by Dell and Apple and software by Microsoft in Japan. On the other hand, marketers may want to dissociate themselves from a particular country. Because the world has not always viewed Mexico as producing quality products, Volkswagen may not want to advertise that some of the models it sells in the United States, including the Beetle, are made in Mexico. The extent to which a product's brand image and country of origin influence purchases is subject to considerable variation based on national culture characteristics.[11]

When products are introduced from one nation into another, acceptance is far more likely if similarities exist between the two cultures. In fact, there are many similar cultural characteristics across countries. For international marketers, cultural differences have implications for product development, advertising, packaging, and pricing. Starbucks, for example, has struggled to sell coffee products in China, a nation of tea drinkers; however, the company has been successful in targeting China's younger generations, which like the chain's made-to-order drinks, personal service, and original music. To appeal to China's "little emperors," the generation of children who resulted from China's strict one-child-per-family policy, Starbucks offers formal coffee tastings, generous samples, helpful brochures, and a comfortable, informal gathering place.[12]

iPod's Global Success: Music to Their Ears

Today, just about everyone has an iPod. Well, perhaps not everyone. But the Queen of England has one. So does the President of the United States. And the Pope. Fashion designer Karl Lagerfeldt has more than 70 of them storing his collection of more than 60,000 CDs.

From its start in 1976 with the introduction of Apple I to the more recent phenomenon of the iPod, Apple Computer, Inc., has achieved legendary status worldwide with its innovations. Whether it's the latest incarnation of the original iPod that was first introduced in October 2001 or the later additions such as the iPod shuffle or iPod nano, one of the most remarkable things about the iPod family is its almost universal appeal. It's been embraced not just by U.S. teenagers but also by people worldwide, young and old. Sit in a Starbucks in New York or San Francisco or venture out to a sidewalk café in Beijing, Melbourne, Rio de Janeiro, Stockholm, or Tokyo, and the parade of iPods seems like a universal ad for Apple. The company currently dominates the MP3 player market with its Microsoft-like 75 percent share worldwide.

Numerous companies have taken note of the phenomenal success of the iPod and are hopping on the bandwagon by developing products that go along with iPods. For example, San Francisco-based Levi Strauss is launching its Levi's RedWire DLX jeans that have a docking station in the pocket and a control panel sewn into the coin pocket. At $200 a pair, "This brings blue jeans into the 21st century. . . . The idea is to merge fashion and technology," says Levi spokeswoman Amy Jasmer.

The automobile industry is also paying close attention to the iPod. "Customers have been asking for iPod connectivity," said Randy Ewers, director of Mopar Accessories' Portfolio Team. Most carmakers now offer iPod integration. In cars made by the Chrysler Group—such as Chrysler, Jeep, and Dodge—seamless iPod integration means that drivers can listen to their iPods through their cars' audio systems. They have the traditional features of their iPods at their fingertips via the radio or steering wheel controls, and they can view selections on the radio display.

Accessories made specifically for iPod range from both upscale and lowbrow cases to Bose speaker systems. No doubt the iPod will continue to inspire new products and new marketing strategies the world over. It's time to Listen Up![a]

Economic Forces

Global marketers need to understand the international trade system, particularly the economic stability of individual nations, as well as trade barriers that may stifle marketing efforts. Economic differences among nations—differences in standards of living, credit, buying power, income distribution, national resources, exchange rates, and the like—dictate many of the adjustments that must be made in marketing abroad.

The United States and western Europe are more stable economically than many other regions of the world. In recent years, several countries, including Russia, Korea, Colombia, Argentina, and Thailand, have experienced economic problems such as recession, high unemployment, corporate bankruptcies, instability in currency markets, trade imbalances, and financial systems that need major reforms. Even more stable developing countries, such as Mexico and Brazil, tend to have greater fluctuations in their business cycles than does the United States. Economic instability can disrupt the markets for U.S. products in places that otherwise might be great marketing opportunities. On the other hand, competition from the sustained economic growth of countries such as China and India can disrupt markets for U.S. markets.

In terms of the value of all products produced by a nation, the United States has the largest gross domestic product in the world, more than $10 trillion. **Gross domestic product (GDP)** is an overall measure of a nation's economic standing; it is the market value of a nation's total output of goods and services for a given period. However, it does not take into account the concept of GDP in relation to population (GDP per capita). The United States has a GDP per capita of $41,600. Even Canada, which is comparable in size to the United States, has a lower GDP and GDP per capita.[13] Table 5.1 provides a comparative economic analysis of 15 countries, including the United States. Knowledge about per capita income, credit, and the distribution of income provides general insights into market potential.

Opportunities for international trade are not limited to countries with the highest incomes. Some nations are progressing at a much faster rate than they were a few years ago, and these countries—especially in Africa, eastern Europe, Latin America, and the Middle East—have great market potential. In Africa, for example, some cell phone service providers concede that they grossly underestimated the potential market for cell phone service in many countries because of their low GDP and low "land line" telephone use. In sub-Saharan Africa, cell phone subscriptions have risen 67 percent compared with just 10 percent in western Europe.[14] However, marketers must understand the political and legal environment before they can convert buying power of customers in these countries into actual demand for specific products.

Political, Legal, and Regulatory Forces

The political, legal, and regulatory forces of the environment are as closely intertwined in many countries as they are in the United States. Typically, legislation is enacted, legal decisions are interpreted, and regulatory agencies are operated by elected or appointed officials. A country's legal and regulatory infrastructure is a direct reflection of the political climate in the country. In some countries this political climate is determined by the people via elections, whereas in others leaders are appointed or have assumed leadership based on certain powers. While laws and regulations have direct effects on a firm's operations in a country, political forces are indirect and often not clearly known in all country markets. For example, the need to work with the government of China to enter and establish operations in the country has been a highly political process since the advent of Communist rule.

A nation's political system, laws, regulatory bodies, special-interest groups, and courts all have great impact on international marketing. A government's policies toward public and private enterprise, consumers, and foreign firms influence marketing across national boundaries. Some countries have established trade restrictions, such as tariffs. An **import tariff** is any duty levied by a nation on goods bought outside its borders and brought in. Because they raise the prices of foreign goods, tariffs impede free trade between nations. Tariffs usually are designed either to raise revenue for a country or to protect domestic products. In the United States, tariff revenues account for less than 2 percent of total federal revenues, down from about 50 percent of total federal revenues in the early 1900s.[15]

Nontariff trade restrictions include quotas and embargoes. A **quota** is a limit on the amount of goods an importing country will accept for certain product categories in a specific time period. An **embargo** is a government's suspension of trade in a particular product or with a given country. Embargoes generally are directed at specific goods or countries and are established for political, health, or religious reasons. For example, the United States forbids the importation of uncertified Iberian ham, absinthe, and any product containing dog or cat fur.[16]

Exchange controls, government restrictions on the amount of a particular currency that can be bought or sold, also may limit international trade. They can force businesspeople to buy and sell foreign products through a central agency, such as a central bank.

gross domestic product (GDP) The market value of a nation's total output of goods and services for a given period; an overall measure of economic standing

import tariff A duty levied by a nation on goods bought outside its borders and brought in

quota A limit on the amount of goods an importing country will accept for certain product categories in a specific time period

embargo A government's suspension of trade in a particular product or with a given country

exchange controls Government restrictions on the amount of a particular currency that can be bought or sold

table 5.1 COMPARATIVE ANALYSIS OF SELECTED COUNTRIES

Country	Population	GDP (US$)	Exports (US$)	Imports (US$)	Internet Users	Cell Phones	Broadcast Television Stations
Brazil	188,078,227	1.536 trillion	115 billion	78.0 billion	25.9 million	86.2 million	138
Canada	33,098,932	1.111 trillion	364.8 billion	317.7 billion	21.9 million	16.6 million	80
China	1,313,973,713	8.883 trillion	752.2 billion	631.8 billion	123 million	394.4 million	3,240
Honduras	7,326,496	20.61 billion	1.7 billion	4.2 billion	223,000	1.3 million	11
India	1,095,351,995	3.666 trillion	76.2 billion	113.1 billion	60 million	69.2 million	562
Japan	127,463,611	4.025 trillion	550.5 billion	451.1 billion	86.3 million	94.8 million	211
Jordan	5,906,760	26.85 billion	4.2 billion	8.7 billion	629,500	1.6 million	20
Kenya	34,707,817	37.89 billion	3.2 billion	5.1 billion	1.1 million	4.6 million	8
Mexico	107,449,525	1.064 trillion	213.7 billion	223.7 billion	18.6 million	47.5 million	236
Russia	142,893,540	1.584 trillion	245.0 billion	125.0 billion	23.7 million	120.0 million	7,306
South Africa	44,187,637	540.8 billion	50.9 billion	63.0 billion	5.1 million	34.0 million	556
Switzerland	7,523,934	240.9 billion	148.6 billion	135.0 billion	5.1 million	6.8 million	115
Turkey	70,413,958	584.5 billion	72.5 billion	101.2 billion	16.0 million	43.6 million	635
Thailand	64,631,595	550.2 billion	105.8 billion	107.0 billion	8.4 million	27.4 million	111
United States	298,444,215	12.31 trillion	927.5 billion	1.727 trillion	205.3 million	219.4 million	2,218

Source: CIA, *The World Fact Book,* www.cia.gov/cia/publications/factbook/index.html (accessed January 5, 2007); globalEdge Resource Desk, http://globaledge.msu.edu/ (accessed January 5, 2007); "Population Explosion!" *ClickZ Stats,* April 12, 2006, www.clickz.com/showPage.html?page=151151.

On the other hand, to promote international trade, some countries have joined together to form free trade zones—multinational economic communities that eliminate tariffs and other trade barriers. Such regional trade alliances are discussed later in this chapter. Foreign currency exchange rates also affect the prices marketers can charge in foreign markets. Fluctuations in the international monetary market can change the prices

When you do business in more than 60 countries, you learn the value of diversity.

Each day Cargill does business in food, nutrition, agriculture and supply chain management. With more than 100,000 employees in 60 countries around the world, our work in such diverse communities has made us very aware of the importance of diversity. We've learned that no one has a monopoly on good ideas and that they can come from anyone, anywhere. We're committed to employee and supplier diversity because we know it adds value to what we do for our customers... as well as promoting prosperity in communities everywhere. For more information, visit Cargill.com

Cargill
Nourishing Ideas. Nourishing People.™

www.cargill.com
©2005 Cargill, Incorporated

Global Diversity

Diversity is a value that can lead to increased competitiveness around the world.

charged across national boundaries on a daily basis. Consequently, these fluctuations must be considered in any international marketing strategy.

Countries may limit imports to maintain a favorable balance of trade. The **balance of trade** is the difference in value between a nation's exports and its imports. When a nation exports more products than it imports, a favorable balance of trade exists because money is flowing into the country. The United States has a negative balance of trade—a trade deficit—for goods and services of $765 billion.[17] A negative balance of trade is considered harmful because it means that U.S. dollars are supporting foreign economies at the expense of U.S. companies and workers.

Many nontariff barriers, such as quotas and minimum price levels set on imports, taxes, and health and safety requirements, can make it difficult for U.S. companies to export their products. For example, the collectivistic nature of Japanese culture and the high-context nature of Japanese communication make some types of direct marketing messages less effective there and may predispose many Japanese to support greater regulation of direct marketing practices.[18] A government's attitude toward importers has a direct impact on the economic feasibility of exporting to that country.

Differences in ethical values and legal standards also can affect marketing efforts. China and Vietnam, for example, have different standards regarding intellectual property than does the United States. These differences create an issue for marketers of computer software, music CDs, books, and many other products. In fact, the World Customs Organization estimates that pirated and counterfeit goods comprise as much as 5 to 7 percent of worldwide merchandise trade, particularly in China, resulting in lost sales of $512 billion a year. Among the products routinely counterfeited are consumer electronics, pharmaceuticals, cell phones, cigarettes, watches, shoes, motorcycles, and automobiles.[19] For example, several U.S. film studios—Disney, Twentieth Century Fox, Paramount Pictures, Universal Studios, and Columbia Pictures—teamed up to file a lawsuit in China against Beijing Shiji Haihong Commerce and Trade Company for allegedly selling counterfeit movies distributed by the studios.[20]

Social Responsibility and Ethics Forces[21]

When marketers travel and work abroad, they sometimes perceive that cultures in other nations have different modes of operation and different values regarding ethical conduct. Consider that many in the United States hold the perception that U.S. firms are often different from those in other countries. This implied perspective of "us" versus "them" is also widespread in other countries. Table 5.2 indicates the countries that businesspeople, risk analysts, and the general public perceived as the most and least corrupt. In marketing, the idea that "we" differ from "them" is called the *self-reference criterion* (SRC)—the unconscious reference to one's own cultural values, experiences, and knowledge. When confronted with a situation, we tend to react on the basis of knowledge we have accumulated over a lifetime, which is usually grounded in our culture of origin (and often rooted in our religious beliefs). Our reactions are based on meanings, values, and symbols that relate to our culture but may not have the same relevance to people of other cultures. However, many marketers adopt the principle of "When in Rome, do as the Romans do." They adapt to

balance of trade The difference in value between a nation's exports and its imports

table 5.2	PERCEPTIONS OF THE LEAST AND MOST CORRUPT COUNTRIES

Least Corrupt*	Most Corrupt
Finland	Haiti
Iceland	Guinea
New Zealand	Iraq
Denmark	Myanmar
Singapore	Bangladesh
Sweden	Chad
Switzerland	Congo, Democratic Republic
Norway	Sudan
Australia	Belarus
Netherlands	Cambodia
Austria	Cote d'Ivoire
Luxembourg	Equatorial Guinea
United Kingdom	Uzbekistan

*The United States is tied for twentieth least corrupt nation.
Source: Adapted from "Transparency International Corruption Perceptions Index 2006," Transparency International, November 6, 2006, www.transparency.org/content/download/10825/92857/version/1/CPI_2006_presskit_eng.pdf.

the cultural practices of the country they are working in and use that country's cultural practices to rationalize sometimes straying from their own ethical values when doing business internationally. For example, by defending the payment of bribes or "greasing the wheels of business" and other questionable practices in this fashion, some businesspeople are resorting to **cultural relativism**—the concept that morality varies from one culture to another and that business practices are therefore differentially defined as right or wrong by particular cultures.

Differences in national standards are illustrated by what the Mexicans call *la mordida,* "the bite." The use of payoffs and bribes is deeply entrenched in many governments. Because U.S. trade and corporate policy, as well as U.S. law, prohibits direct involvement in payoffs and bribes, U.S. companies may have a hard time competing with foreign firms that do engage in these practices. Some U.S. businesses that refuse to make payoffs are forced to hire local consultants, public relations firms, or advertising agencies, which results in indirect payoffs. The ultimate decision about whether to give small tips or gifts where they are customary must be based on a company's code of ethics. Under the Foreign Corrupt Practices Act of 1977, however, it is illegal for U.S. firms to attempt to make large payments or bribes to influence policy decisions of foreign governments. Nevertheless, facilitating payments, or small payments to support the performance of standard tasks, are often acceptable. The act also subjects all publicly held U.S. corporations to rigorous internal controls and recordkeeping requirements for their overseas operations.

cultural relativism The concept that morality varies from one culture to another and that business practices are therefore differentially defined as right or wrong by particular cultures

Your Business Is UNIQUE

Why feel like a big fish in a small pond?
When you can feel like the only fish in the sea.

Our people focus on applying their diverse range of knowledge and skills to earn trust and confidence. Leveraging years of proven experience, we strive to anticipate the needs of our clients and provide exceptional customer service. We develop a deep understanding of our clients' business objectives and take a personal interest in helping them achieve those goals.

We call it "Operational Empathy," and at DataPipe it's how we do business.   **DataPipe**

Silicon Valley   New York   London   Hong Kong   DataPipe.com   Managed Global IT Services

Staying Ahead of the Competition

Worldwide IT services

Because of differences in legal and ethical standards, many companies are working both individually and collectively to establish ethics programs and standards for international business conduct.[22] Levi Strauss's code of ethics, for example, bars the firm from manufacturing in countries where workers are known to be abused. Starbucks's global code of ethics strives to protect agricultural workers who harvest coffee. Many companies choose to standardize their ethical behavior across national boundaries to maintain a consistent and well-integrated corporate culture.

Competitive Forces

Competition is often viewed as a staple of the global marketplace, with customers thriving on the choices offered by competition and companies continually seeking opportunities to outmaneuver their competition. However, the increasingly interconnected international marketplace and advances in technology have resulted in competitive forces that are unique to the international marketplace. Each country has unique competitive aspects—often founded in the other environmental forces (i.e., sociocultural, technological, political, legal, regulatory, and economic forces)—that are often independent of the competitors in that country's market. The most globally competitive countries are listed in Table 5.3. Although companies drive competition, nations establish and maintain the infrastructure for the types of competition that can take place. For example, Microsoft's near monopoly over software in the United States (and in many other countries) has led the U.S. government and U.S. firms to a long-standing legal battle over the firm's competitive practices. Other countries permit monopoly structures to exist to lesser or greater degrees. In Sweden, for example, most alcohol sales are made through Systembolaget, the government store that is legally supported by the Swedish Alcohol Retail Monopoly.[23]

Beyond the types of competition (i.e., brand, product, generic, and total budget competition) and types of competitive structures (i.e., monopoly, oligopoly, monopolistic competition, and pure competition) that are discussed in Chapter 3, firms operating internationally also need to address the competitive forces in the countries

table 5.3	A RANKING OF THE MOST COMPETITIVE COUNTRIES IN THE WORLD
1. Switzerland	9. Netherlands
2. Finland	10. United Kingdom
3. Sweden	11. Hong Kong
4. Denmark	12. Norway
5. Singapore	13. Taiwan, China
6. United States	14. Iceland
7. Japan	15. Israel
8. Germany	

Source: The Global Competitiveness Report 2006–2007, *World Economic Forum.*

they target, recognize the interdependence of countries and the global competitors in those markets, and be mindful of a new breed of customers—the global customer. Until recently, customers seldom had opportunities to compare products from competitors, learn details about competing product features, and examine other options beyond the local (country or region) markets. Customers today, however, expect to be able to buy the same product in most of the world's countries, and they expect that the product they buy in their local store in Miami will have the same features as similar products sold in London or even in Beijing. If a product's quality features are more advanced in an international market, customers soon will demand that their local markets offer the same product with the same features at the same or lower prices.

Technological Forces

Advances in technology have made international marketing much easier. Voice mail, e-mail, fax, cellular phones, and the Internet make international marketing activities more affordable and convenient. Internet use has accelerated dramatically within the United States and abroad. In Japan, 86.3 million have Internet access, whereas nearly 24 million Russians, 60 million Indians, and 123 million Chinese are logging on to the Internet[24] (see Table 5.1). The majority of young adults (ages 16 to 24) in Europe prefer advertisements on the Web over any other media vehicle; these ads are more directly targeting their needs.[25]

In many developing countries that lack the level of technological infrastructure found in the United States and Japan, marketers are beginning to capitalize on opportunities to "leapfrog" existing technology. For example, cellular and wireless phone technology is reaching many countries at less expense than traditional hard-wired telephone systems. Nearly one-quarter of the world's population uses mobile phones, and growth in cell phone subscriptions has now surpassed that for fixed lines.[26] Opportunities for growth in the cell phone market remain strong in Africa, the Middle East, and Southeast Asia. One opportunity created by the rapid growth in cell phone service contracts in China is the *shouji jiayouzhan,* or "cell phone gas station," which allows consumers to recharge their phone, camera, and personal digital assistant (PDA) batteries quickly for the equivalent of 12 cents, and they can view ads during the 10-minute charging session.[27]

Regional Trade Alliances, Markets, and Agreements

Although many more firms are beginning to view the world as one huge marketplace, various regional trade alliances and specific markets affect companies engaging in international marketing. Some create opportunities; others impose constraints. In this section we examine several regional trade alliances, markets, and changing conditions affecting markets, including the North American Free Trade Agreement among the United States, Canada, and Mexico; the European Union; the Common Market of the Southern Cone; Asia-Pacific Economic Cooperation; the General Agreement on Tariffs and Trade; and the World Trade Organization.

The North American Free Trade Agreement (NAFTA)

The **North American Free Trade Agreement (NAFTA)**, implemented in 1994, effectively merged Canada, Mexico, and the United States into one market of more than 430 million consumers. NAFTA will eliminate almost all tariffs on goods produced and traded among Canada, Mexico, and the United States to create a free trade area by 2009. The estimated annual output for this trade alliance is $14 trillion.[28]

North American Free Trade Agreement (NAFTA) An alliance that merges Canada, Mexico, and the United States into a single market

OTHER AIRLINES ARE ALL OVER THE MAP.

WE'RE ALL OVER THE GLOBE.

The most international destinations of any U.S. airline.

Unlike our competitors, we continue to offer things that matter to you. And that includes service to new destinations...bringing our total to over 280 destinations in more than 45 countries. Of course, no matter where you fly with us, you can expect service that's second to none. It's yet another difference that sets us a world apart. For reservations and information, go to continental.com or call 1-800-523-FARE.

Some service operated by ExpressJet Airlines, Inc. d/b/a Continental Express.

Continental Airlines

Work Hard. Fly Right.

World Alliances

The Skyteam Alliance, with its ten member airlines, provides flexibility and a broad array of choices for international travelers.

NAFTA makes it easier for U.S. businesses to invest in Mexico and Canada, provides protection for intellectual property (of special interest to the high-technology and entertainment industries), expands trade by requiring equal treatment of U.S. firms in both countries, and simplifies country-of-origin rules, hindering Japan's use of Mexico as a staging ground for further penetration into U.S. markets. Although most tariffs on products coming to the United States will be lifted, duties on more sensitive products, such as household glassware, footware, and some fruits and vegetables, will be phased out over a 15-year period.

Canada's 33.1 million consumers are relatively affluent, with a per capita GDP of $33,900.[29] Trade between the United States and Canada totals more than $502 billion.[30] Currently, exports to Canada support approximately 1.5 million U.S. jobs. Canadian investments in U.S. companies are also increasing, and various markets, including air travel, are opening as regulatory barriers dissolve.[31] In fact, Canada is the single largest trading partner of the United States.[32]

With a per capita GDP of $10,000, Mexico's 107.4 million consumers are less affluent than Canadian consumers. However, they bought more than $120 billion worth of U.S. products last year.[33] Many U.S. companies, including Hewlett-Packard, IBM, and General Motors, have taken advantage of Mexico's low labor costs and close proximity to the United States to set up production facilities, sometimes called *maquiladoras.* Production at the *maquiladoras,* especially in the automotive, electronics, and apparel industries, has grown rapidly as companies as diverse as Ford, John Deere, Motorola, Sara Lee, Kimberly-Clark, and VF Corporation have set up facilities in north-central Mexican states. With the *maquiladoras* accounting for roughly half of Mexico's exports, Mexico has risen to become the world's twelfth-largest economy.[34]

Mexico's membership in NAFTA links the United States and Canada with other Latin American countries, providing additional opportunities to integrate trade among all the nations in the Western Hemisphere. Indeed, efforts to create a free trade agreement among the 34 nations of North and South America are underway. Like NAFTA, the *Free Trade Area of the Americas* (FTAA) will progressively eliminate trade barriers and create the world's largest free trade zone, with 800 million people. However, the negotiations to complete the agreement have been contentious, and the agreement itself has become a lightning rod for antiglobalization activists. A related trade agreement—the *Central American Dominican Republic Free Trade Agreement* (CAFTA-DR)—among Costa Rica, the Dominican Republic, El Salvador, Guatemala, Honduras, Nicaragua, and the United States also has been ratified by all those countries except Costa Rica. The United States has already begun implementing the provisions of the agreement with the countries that have ratified it. When these agreements are fully implemented, they will have great influences on trade in the region.

Mexican Coca-Cola: A Legal Alien

Coca-Cola bottled in Mexico is rapidly gaining in popularity in the United States, owing to both the growing number of Mexican immigrants living in the United States and the interest of soda connoisseurs. U.S. bottlers of Coca-Cola began to switch to high-fructose corn syrup as a sweetener in the 1980s to reduce costs. Coke bottled in Mexico, however, is still sweetened with cane sugar. Although the Coca-Cola Company insists that there is no real discrepancy between the two formulas, aficionados insist that Mexican Coke has a cleaner taste and a longer-lasting fizz. Mexican Coke also still comes in the old-fashioned glass bottles. But perhaps the most important reason many Mexican immigrants buy Mexican Coke is that the taste reminds them of home.

Erik Carvallo, owner of the Latino supermarket Las Tarascas in Lawrenceville, Georgia, sells 20 cases of Mexican Coke per week—often leaving his shelf bare—whereas the U.S. version collects dust. In many places a 20-ounce bottle of U.S.-bottled Coke sells for around $1, but Mexican Coke devotees are willing to pay as much as $1.25 per 12-ouunce bottle to drink what they call "the real thing."

As the market for imported Mexican Coke grows, the Coca-Cola Company is studying how to block

its arrival in the U.S. market. U.S. bottlers do not profit from the sale of imported Coke, which is bottled by independent Mexican companies and brought across the border by third-party distributors and retailers. Although Coca-Cola's concerns appear to relate to violations of bottling territorial rights, some suspect that the company is really worried that Americans might grow to prefer and then to demand the more costly Mexican formula. Many U.S. bottling companies are not as concerned, feeling that it makes little impact on their profits. Importing Mexican Coke is perfectly legal, but the fact that the Coca-Cola Company may produce a superior product in another country could have a negative impact on its U.S. market. In somewhat of a conundrum, the company has condemned the imports of Mexican Coke as a form of "bootlegging"; at the same time, it is now buying Coca-Cola in bottles from Mexico and importing them to Texas and southern California, two of the largest markets of Mexican immigrants in the country. Although the Coca-Cola Company has been frustrated by the importation of Mexican Coke to the United States, it is quite pleased with the product's popularity in Mexico. On average, an individual in Mexico drinks an estimated 500 bottles of Coke per year compared with the average U.S. citizen, who drinks about 410 bottles per year. Coca-Cola-branded beverages have been produced in Mexico for 80 years, and local bottlers have helped to make Coke part of Mexican culture. Regardless of the controversy surrounding Mexican Coke's importation, fans of the drink are fans for life on both sides of the border.[b]

The European Union (EU)

The **European Union (EU)**, also called the *European Community* or *Common Market*, was established in 1958 to promote trade among its members, which initially included Belgium, France, Italy, West Germany, Luxembourg, and the Netherlands. In 1991, East and West Germany united, and by 2007, the United Kingdom, Spain, Denmark, Greece, Portugal, Ireland, Austria, Finland, Sweden, Cyprus, Poland, Hungary, the Czech Republic, Slovenia Estonia, Latvia, Lithuania, Slovakia, Malta, Romania, and Bulgaria had joined as well. (Croatia and Turkey also have requested membership.[35]) Until 1993, each nation functioned as a separate market, but at that time, the members officially unified into one of the largest single world markets, which today includes nearly half a billion consumers with a combined GDP of more than $12 trillion.[36]

European Union (EU) An alliance that promotes trade among its member countries in Europe

Pitak Ploempitakkul

THE BUSINESS: Electronic Plaza Siam TV

FOUNDED: 1982, in Thailand

SUCCESS: 20 locations and millions in sales

At the age of 10, Pitak Ploempitakkul was help-ing his brother sell lottery tickets; later he opened a second-hand store, where he sold appliances he bought in pawn shops. Today, Electronic Plaza Siam TV competes head-on against large foreign retailers with ultralow prices and many choices. To build his business, Pitak sent out brochures randomly to names out of the telephone directory to build a customer database and employed a cash-only policy to keep prices low. His "lightning service" philosophy means that customers expect a TV at their doorstep by the time they get home from shopping, and they can expect fast repairs when necessary. Pitak's strategy is to work hard, build teams, and be ready to learn new things.[c]

To facilitate free trade among members, the EU is working toward standardization of business regulations and requirements, import duties, and value-added taxes; the elimination of customs checks; and the creation of a standardized currency for use by all members. Many European nations trade in a common currency, the euro; however, several EU members (e.g., Denmark, Sweden, and the United Kingdom) have rejected use of the euro in their countries. Although the common currency requires many marketers to modify their pricing strategies and will subject them to increased competition, the use of a single currency frees companies that sell goods among European countries from the nuisance of dealing with complex exchange rates.[37] The long-term goals are to eliminate all trade barriers within the EU, improve the economic efficiency of the EU nations, and stimulate economic growth, thus making the union's economy more competitive in global markets, particularly against Japan and other Pacific Rim nations and North America. Several disputes and debates still divide the member nations, however, and many barriers to completely free trade remain. Consequently, it may take many years before the EU is truly one deregulated market.

As the EU nations attempt to function as one large market, consumers in the EU may become more homogeneous in their needs and wants. Most residents of the EU strongly desire, however, to maintain their national cultures and traditions.[38] As a result, marketers may need to adjust their marketing mixes for customers within each nation to reflect their differences in tastes and preferences as well as primary language. Gathering information about these distinct tastes and preferences is likely to remain a very important factor in developing marketing mixes that satisfy the needs of European customers.

The Common Market of the Southern Cone (MERCOSUR)

The **Common Market of the Southern Cone** (also known as *Mercado Comun del Sur* or **MERCOSUR**) was established in 1991 under the Treaty of Asunción to unite Argentina, Brazil, Paraguay, and Uruguay as a free trade alliance; Venezuela joined in 2006. Bolivia, Chile, Colombia, Ecuador, and Peru are associate members. The alliance represents two-thirds of South America's population and has a combined GDP of US$1.1 trillion, making it the third-largest trading bloc behind NAFTA and the EU. Like NAFTA, MERCOSUR promotes "the free circulation of goods, services and production factors among the countries" and establishes a common external tariff and commercial policy.[39]

Asia-Pacific Economic Cooperation (APEC)

The **Asia-Pacific Economic Cooperation (APEC)**, established in 1989, promotes open trade and economic and technical cooperation among member nations, which initially included Australia, Brunei Darussalam, Canada, Indonesia, Japan, Korea, Malaysia, New Zealand, the Philippines, Singapore, Thailand, and the United States. Since then, the alliance has grown to include Chile, China, Chinese Taipei, Hong Kong, Mexico, Papua New Guinea, Peru, Russia, and Vietnam. The 21-member alliance represents 2.6 billion consumers, has a combined GDP of US$19 trillion, and accounts for nearly 47 percent of global trade. APEC differs from other international trade alliances in its commitment to facilitating business and its practice of allowing the business/private sector to participate in a wide range of APEC activities.[40]

Despite economic turmoil and a recession in Asia in recent years, companies of APEC have become increasingly competitive and sophisticated in global business in the

Common Market of the Southern Cone (MERCOSUR) An alliance that promotes the free circulation of goods, services, and production factors and has a common external tariff and commercial policy among member nations in South America

Asia-Pacific Economic Cooperation (APEC) An alliance that promotes open trade and economic and technical cooperation among member nations throughout the world

World Trade Organization (WTO) An entity that promotes free trade among member nations.

last three decades. South Korea, for example, has become the fifth-largest producer of cars and trucks in the world, exporting more than half a million vehicles to the United States. Hyundai and Kia have gained market share in the United States by expanding their product lines and improving their quality and brand image.[41] Japanese firms in particular have made tremendous inroads into world markets for automobiles, motorcycles, watches, cameras, and audio and video equipment. Products from Sony, Sanyo, Toyota, Mitsubishi, Canon, Suzuki, and Toshiba are sold all over the world and have set standards of quality by which other products are often judged. The most important emerging economic power is China, which has become one of the most productive manufacturing nations. China, which has become the second-largest trading partner of the United States, has initiated economic reforms to stimulate its economy by privatizing many industries, restructuring its banking system, and increasing public spending on infrastructure. As a result, China has become a manufacturing powerhouse, with an economy growing at a rate of 9 percent a year.[42] Nike and Adidas have shifted most of their shoe production to China, and recently, China has become a major producer of CD players, cellular phones, portable stereos, and personal computers.

The markets of APEC offer tremendous opportunities to marketers who understand them. For example, Yum! Brands, the number 2 fast-food chain after McDonald's, opened its first KFC fast-food restaurant in China in 1987 and has since opened 2,000 KFC and Pizza Hut outlets in China, as well as a new concept store called East Dawning, which serves Chinese fast food. China accounts for about 16 percent the company's profits.[43]

The World Trade Organization (WTO)

The **World Trade Organization (WTO)** is a global trade association that promotes free trade among 149 member nations. The WTO is the successor to the **General Agreement on Tariffs and Trade (GATT)**, originally signed by 23 nations in 1947, to provide a forum for tariff negotiations and a place where international trade problems could be discussed and resolved. Rounds of GATT negotiations reduced trade barriers for most products and established rules to guide international commerce, such as rules to prevent **dumping**, the selling of products at unfairly low prices.

Achieving the WTO's primary goal of free trade requires eliminating trade barriers; educating individuals, companies, and governments about trade rules around the world; and assuring global markets that no sudden changes of policy will occur. The WTO also serves as a forum for trade negotiations and dispute resolution.[44] At the heart of the WTO are agreements that provide legal ground rules for international commerce and trade policy.[45] For example, the United States, Canada, and the EU complained to the WTO that new WTO member China levies tariffs on imported car parts as if they were complete vehicles, putting foreign manufacturers of auto parts at a distinct disadvantage in China. After attempts to resolve the dispute failed, the nations asked the WTO to mediate and rule as to whether China's actions are lawful.[46]

Modes of Entry into International Markets

General Agreement on Tariffs and Trade (GATT) An agreement among nations to reduce worldwide tariffs and increase international trade

dumping Selling products at unfairly low prices

Marketers enter international markets at several levels of involvement covering a wide spectrum, as Figure 5.1 shows. Domestic marketing involves marketing strategies aimed at markets within the home country; at the other extreme, global marketing entails developing marketing strategies for major regions or for the entire world. Many firms with an international presence start as small companies serving local and regional markets and expand to national markets before considering opportunities in foreign markets. The level of commitment to international marketing is a major variable in international marketing strategies. In this section we examine importing and exporting, trading companies, licensing and franchising, contract manufacturing, joint ventures, direct ownership, and other approaches to international involvement.

figure 5.1

LEVELS OF INVOLVEMENT IN GLOBAL MARKETING

Globalized marketing
Marketing strategies are developed for the entire world
(or more than one major region), with the focus on the
similarities across regions and country markets.

Regional marketing
Marketing strategies are developed for each major region, with
the countries in the region being marketed to in the same way
based on similarities across the region's country markets.

Multinational marketing
International markets are a consideration in the marketing
strategy, with customization for the country markets based on
critical differences across regions and country markets.

Limited exporting
The firm develops no international marketing strategies, but
international distributors, foreign firms, or selected
customers purchase some of its products.

Domestic marketing
All marketing strategies focus on the market
in the country of origin.

Importing and Exporting

Importing and exporting require the least amount of effort and commitment of resources. **Importing** is the purchase of products from a foreign source. **Exporting**, the sale of products to foreign markets, enables businesses of all sizes to participate in global business. Limited exporting may occur even if a firm makes little or no effort to obtain foreign sales. Foreign buyers may seek the company and/or its products, or a distributor may discover the firm's products and export them. A firm may find an exporting intermediary to take over most marketing functions associated with selling to other countries. This approach entails minimal effort and cost. Modifications in packaging, labeling, style, or color may be the major expenses in adapting a product for the foreign market. Having sound objectives and maintaining product quality are important in attaining a competitive advantage in exporting.[47]

Export agents bring together buyers and sellers from different countries and collect a commission for arranging sales. Export houses and export merchants purchase products from different companies and then sell them abroad. They are specialists at understanding foreign customers' needs. Using exporting intermediaries involves limited risk because no direct investment in the foreign country is required.

Marketers sometimes employ a trading company, which links buyers and sellers in different countries but is not involved in manufacturing and does not own assets related to manufacturing. Trading companies buy goods in one country at the lowest price consistent with quality and sell them to buyers in another country. The best-known U.S. trading company is Sears World Trade, which specializes in

importing The purchase of products from a foreign source

exporting The sale of products to foreign markets

STREET SMART   MBA

SOME PERFECTION IS DEBATABLE.

SOME IS NOT.
Made by hand from 100% blue agave.
The world's #1 ultra-premium tequila.

SIMPLY PERFECT.
simplyperfect.com

TEQUILA
100% DE AGAVE

SILVER
PATRÓN.

Importing and Exporting
Patron has spread throughout the world as a highly desired import from Mexico.

consumer goods, light industrial items, and processed foods. Trading companies reduce the risk for firms seeking to get involved in international marketing. A trading company provides producers with information about products that meet quality and price expectations in domestic and international markets.

Licensing and Franchising

When potential markets are found across national boundaries, and when production, technical assistance, or marketing know-how is required, **licensing** is an alternative to direct investment. The licensee (the owner of the foreign operation) pays commissions or royalties on sales or supplies used in manufacturing. The licensee also may pay an initial down payment or fee when the licensing agreement is signed. Exchanges of management techniques or technical assistance are primary reasons for licensing agreements. For example, Questor Corporation owns the Spalding name but produces not a single golf club or tennis ball itself; all Spalding sporting products are licensed worldwide. Likewise, Yoplait is a French yogurt that is licensed for production in the United States; the Yoplait brand tries to maintain a French image.

Licensing is an attractive alternative to direct investment when the political stability of a foreign country is in doubt or when resources are unavailable for direct investment. Licensing also can be a valuable strategy for enhancing a firm's brand while generating additional revenue. PepsiCo has licensed many products, including T-shirts, men's and women's apparel, footwear, and accessories, under its well-known name. The company views licensing as a significant tool for building awareness of and extending the Pepsi brand.[48]

Franchising is a form of licensing in which a company (the franchiser) grants a franchisee the right to market its product using its name, logo, methods of operation, advertising, products, and other elements associated with the franchiser's business, in return for a financial commitment and an agreement to conduct business in accordance with the franchiser's standard of operations. This arrangement allows franchisers to minimize the risks of international marketing in four ways: (1) The franchiser does not have to put up a large capital investment, (2) the franchiser's revenue stream is fairly consistent because franchisees pay a fixed fee and royalties, (3) the franchiser retains control of its name and increases global penetration of its product, and (4) franchise agreements ensure a certain standard of behavior from franchisees, which protects the franchise name.[49] KFC, Wendy's, McDonald's, Holiday Inn, and Marriott are well-known franchisers with international visibility.

Contract Manufacturing

Contract manufacturing occurs when a company hires a foreign firm to produce a designated volume of the firm's product to specification, and the final product carries the domestic firm's name. The Gap, for example, relies on contract manufacturing for some of its apparel, and Reebok uses Korean contract manufacturers to manufacture many of its athletic shoes. Marketing may be handled by the contract manufacturer or by the contracting company.

licensing An alternative to direct investment requiring a licensee to pay commissions or royalties on sales or supplies used in manufacturing

franchising A form of licensing in which a franchiser, in exchange for a financial commitment, grants a franchisee the right to market its product in accordance with the franchiser's standards

contract manufacturing The practice of hiring a foreign firm to produce a designated volume of product to specification

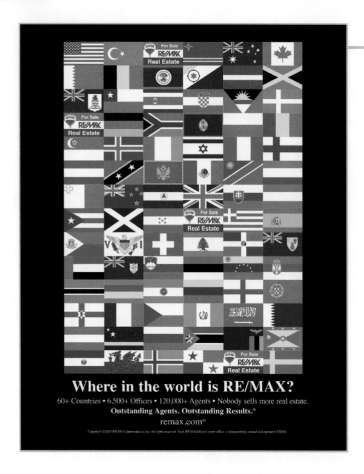

Where in the world is RE/MAX?

60+ Countries • 6,500+ Offices • 120,000+ Agents • Nobody sells more real estate.

Outstanding Agents. Outstanding Results.®

remax.com®

Copyright ©2007 RE/MAX International, Inc. All rights reserved. Each RE/MAX® real estate office is independently owned and operated. 070084

Franchising

RE/MAX has expanded its franchise throughout the world.

In recent years, outsourcing has become popular. **Outsourcing** involves contracting manufacturing or other tasks (such as customer-service help lines) to companies in countries where labor and supplies are less expensive. Consider that the majority of all footwear is now produced in China regardless of the brand on the shoe. Services also can be outsourced. Tribune, which owns daily newspapers such as *Newsday* and *The Chicago Tribune,* outsourced its customer-service operations to a firm in the Philippines in an effort to improve efficiency and boost customer service at the newspaper chain.[50] Outsourcing has been controversial however, in large part owing to the number of U.S. jobs that have been lost, as shown in Figure 5.2.

Joint Ventures

In international marketing, a **joint venture** is a partnership between a domestic firm and a foreign firm or government. Joint ventures are especially popular in industries that call for large investments, such as natural resources extraction or automobile manufacturing. Control of the joint venture may be split equally, or one party may control decision making. Joint ventures are often a political necessity because of nationalism and government restrictions on foreign ownership. eBay, for example, shuttered its troubled online auction site in China and instead entered into a joint venture with a knowledgeable Chinese firm, Tom Online, Inc.[51] Joint ventures also provide legitimacy in the eyes of the host country's citizens. Local partners have firsthand knowledge of the economic and sociopolitical environment and of distribution networks, and they may have privileged access to local resources (raw materials, labor management, and so on). Entrepreneurs in many less developed countries actively seek associations with a foreign partner as a ready means of implementing their own corporate strategy.[52]

Joint ventures are assuming greater global importance because of cost advantages and the number of inexperienced firms entering foreign markets. They may be the result of a tradeoff between a firm's desire for completely unambiguous control of an enterprise and its quest for additional resources. They may occur when acquisition or internal development is not feasible or when the risks and constraints leave no other alternative. As project sizes increase in the face of global competition and firms attempt to spread the huge costs of technological innovation, the impetus to form joint ventures is stronger.[53]

Strategic alliances, the newest form of international business structure, are partnerships formed to create competitive advantage on a worldwide basis. They are very similar to joint ventures. What distinguishes international strategic alliances from other business structures is that partners in the alliance may have been traditional rivals competing for market share in the same product class. One such collaboration is the Sky Team Alliance—involving Northwest Airlines, KLM, Aero Mexico, Air France, Alitalia, Continental Airlines, TSA Czech Airlines, Delta, and Korean Air—which is designed to improve customer service among the nine firms. Another example of such an alliance is New United Motor Manufacturing, Inc. (NUMMI), formed by Toyota and General Motors, which today manufactures the

outsourcing The practice of contracting manufacturing or other tasks to companies in countries where labor and supplies are less expensive

joint venture A partnership between a domestic firm and a foreign firm or government

strategic alliances Partnerships formed to create a competitive advantage on a worldwide basis

figure 5.2

PROJECTED U.S. JOBS MOVING OFFSHORE

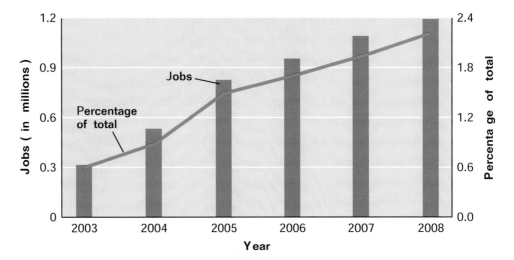

Source: "Will the New Congress Shift Gears on Free Trade?" *The Wall Street Journal,* November 18–19, 2006, p. A7.

popular Toyota Tacoma compact pickup, as well as the Toyota Corolla and Pontiac Vibe. This alliance united the quality engineering of Japanese cars with the marketing expertise and market access of General Motors.[54] Partners in international strategic alliances often retain their distinct identities, and each brings a core competency to the union.

Direct Ownership

Once a company makes a long-term commitment to marketing in a foreign nation that has a promising political and economic environment, **direct ownership** of a foreign subsidiary or division is a possibility. Liz Claiborne, Inc., for example, is opening 24 Juicy Couture retail stores and 23 Juicy Couture shops within other retail stores in China, Taiwan, Hong Kong, and throughout Southeast Asia after recognizing a favorable attitude toward U.S. fashion labels and haute couture in general.[55] Most foreign investment covers only manufacturing equipment or personnel because the expense of developing a separate foreign distribution system can be tremendous. The opening of retail stores in China, India, or Mexico can require a staggering financial investment in facilities, research, and management.

The term **multinational enterprise**, also called *multinational corporations,* refers to firms that have operations or subsidiaries in many countries. Often the parent company is based in one country and carries on production, management, and marketing activities in other countries. The firm's subsidiaries may be mostly autonomous so that they can respond to the needs of individual international markets. Table 5.4 (on page 120) lists the ten largest global corporations.

A wholly owned foreign subsidiary may be allowed to operate independently of the parent company to give its management more freedom to adjust to the local environment. Cooperative arrangements are developed to assist in marketing efforts, production, and management. A wholly owned foreign subsidiary may export products to the home country. Some U.S. automobile manufacturers, for example, import cars built by their foreign subsidiaries. A foreign subsidiary offers important tax, tariff, and other operating advantages. One of the greatest advantages is the cross-cultural approach. A subsidiary usually operates under foreign management so that it can develop a local identity. The greatest danger in such an arrangement comes from political uncertainty: A firm may lose its foreign investment.

direct ownership A situation in which a company owns subsidiaries or other facilities overseas

multinational enterprise Firms that have operations or subsidiaries in many countries

table 5.4	THE TEN LARGEST GLOBAL CORPORATIONS	
Rank Company	**Country**	**Revenues (in millions)**
1. ExxonMobil	United States	$339,938
2. Wal-Mart	United States	$315,654
3. Royal Dutch/Shell	Britain/Netherlands	$306,731
4. BP	Britain	$267,600
5. General Motors	United States	$192,604
6. Chevron	United States	$189,481
7. DaimlerChrysler	Germany	$186,106
8. Toyota Motor	Japan	$185,805
9. Ford Motor	United States	$177,210
10. ConocoPhillips	United States	$166,683

Source: "The Fortune Global 500," *Fortune,* July 24, 2006,
http://money.cnn.com/magazines/fortune/global500/2006/index.html.

Customization Versus Globalization of International Marketing Mixes

Like domestic marketers, international marketers create marketing mixes to serve specific target markets. Table 5.5 provides a sample of international issues related to product, distribution, promotion, and price. Traditionally, international marketing strategies have customized marketing mixes according to cultural, regional, and national differences. Many soap and detergent manufacturers, for example, adapt their products to local water conditions, equipment, and washing habits. Ford Motor Company has customized its F-series trucks to accommodate global differences in roads, product use, and economic conditions. The strategy has been quite successful, with millions of Ford trucks sold around the world. Ford's strategy may best be described as *mass customization,* the use of standard platforms with custom applications. This practice dissolves the oxymoron of efficiency of mass production with effectiveness of customization of a product or service.[56]

At the other end of the spectrum, **globalization** of marketing involves developing marketing strategies as though the entire world (or its major regions) were a single entity; a globalized firm approaches the world market with as much standardization in the marketing strategy as possible. Nike and Adidas shoes, for example, are standardized worldwide. Other examples of globalized products include electronic communications equipment, American clothing, movies, soft drinks, rock and alternative music CDs, cosmetics, and toothpaste. Sony televisions, Starbucks coffee, Levi jeans, and American cigarette brands post year-to-year gains in the world market. Today, technological advancement, particularly with regard to computers and telecommunications, has the potential to facilitate globalization.[57]

For many years, organizations have attempted to globalize their marketing mixes as much as possible by employing standardized products, promotion campaigns, prices, and distribution channels for all markets. The economic and competitive payoffs for globalized marketing strategies are certainly great. Brand name, product characteristics, packaging, and labeling are among the easiest marketing-mix variables to

globalization The development of marketing strategies that treat the entire world (or its major regions) as a single entity

table 5.5   INTERNATIONAL MARKETING-MIX ISSUES

	Sample International Issues
Product Element	
Core product	Is there a commonality to customers' needs across countries? How will the product be used and in what context?
Product adoption	How is awareness created for the product in various markets? How and where is the product typically bought?
Managing products	How are truly new products managed in specific international markets in relation to existing products or products that have been modified slightly?
Branding	Is the brand widely accepted around the world? Do perceptions of the home country help or hurt the brand perception of the consumer?
Distribution Element	
Marketing intermediaries	What is the role of marketing intermediaries internationally? Where is value created beyond the domestic borders of the firm?
Physical distribution	What is the most efficient movement of products from the home country to the foreign market?
Retail stores	What types of stores are available in the various countries through which to sell the product to consumers?
Retailing strategy	Where do customers typically shop in the targeted countries—downtown, suburbs, or malls?
Promotion Element	
Advertising	Consumers in some countries expect to see firm-specific advertising instead of product-specific advertising. How does this affect advertising?
Public relations	How is public relations used to manage stakeholders' interests internationally? Are the stakeholders' interests different worldwide?
Personal selling	What product types require personal selling internationally? Does it differ from how those products are sold domestically?
Sales promotion	Is coupon usage a widespread activity in the targeted international markets? What other forms of sales promotion should be used?
Pricing Element	
Core price	Is price a critical component of the value equation of the product in the targeted country markets?
Analysis of demand	Is the demand similar internationally as it is domestically? Will a change in price drastically change demand?
Demand, cost, and profit relationships	What are the costs when marketing the product internationally? Are they similar to the domestic setting?
Determination of price	How do the pricing strategy, environmental forces, business practices, and cultural values affect price?

HAMMERS DON'T TALK.
HAMMERS DON'T TRY.
HAMMERS DON'T PROMISE.
HAMMERS JUST DO.

We want to help your business stay ahead of global change. As inevitable as it is. From creating systems that help you expand faster, to implementing technology that isn't limited by geography, function, or language. And we don't want to try to do it. We want to get it done.

Like we did working with KBC, one of Belgium's largest banks, who knew that to compete in a rapidly expanding financial marketplace it needed a technology solution that worked around the world. Together we developed and implemented a solution that automated processes, integrated global offices, and cut the time it took to open a new branch in half. Helping make KBC one of the top financial institutions in the world today.

Because if you want to build a business that embraces change, think of us as your hammer. It's what we do. And we want to do it for you. www.eds.com

EDS
Let's get to work.

Customization

EDS strives for a globalized marketing strategy by standardizing its technology solutions to meet global firms' needs.

standardize; media allocation, retail outlets, and price may be more difficult. In the end, the degree of similarity among the various environmental and market conditions determines the feasibility and degree of globalization. A successful globalization strategy often depends on the extent to which a firm can implement the idea of "think globally, act locally."[58] Even takeout food lends itself to globalization: McDonald's, KFC, and Taco Bell restaurants seem to satisfy hungry customers in every hemisphere, although menus are customized to some degree to satisfy local tastes.

International marketing demands some strategic planning if a firm is to incorporate foreign sales into its overall marketing strategy. Although globalization has been viewed as a mechanism for world economic development, advances may be challenging if marketers ignore unique nation-specific factors.[59] International marketing activities often require customized marketing mixes to achieve the firm's goals. Globalization requires a total commitment to the world, regions, or multinational areas as an integral part of the firm's markets; world or regional markets become as important as domestic ones. Regardless of the extent to which a firm chooses to globalize its marketing strategy, extensive environmental analysis and marketing research are necessary to understand the needs and desires of the target market(s) and successfully implement the chosen marketing strategy. A global presence does not automatically result in a global competitive advantage. However, a global presence generates five opportunities for creating value: (1) to adapt to local market differences, (2) to exploit economies of global scale, (3) to exploit economies of global scope, (4) to mine optimal locations for activities and resources, and (5) to maximize the transfer of knowledge across locations.[60] To exploit these opportunities, marketers need to conduct marketing research, the topic of the next chapter.

...And now, back to Gillette

Gillette's current strategy in the personal-care market is to focus resources on core grooming products such as deodorants/antiperspirants and shaving preparations while providing supporting products in key markets. Another brand in Gillette's stable is Oral-B, which develops and markets a broad range of superior oral-care products worldwide in a strong and well-established partnership with dental professionals. With the acquisition of Duracell International, Gillette instantly achieved worldwide leadership in the alkaline battery market, with approximately a 40 percent share. With the company's backing, Duracell enjoys significant economies of scale and greater market penetration through P&G's worldwide distribution network. The Gillette Company also owns the Braun brand.

The merger of P&G and Gillette combined two best-in-class companies, creating what investment guru Warren Buffet described as "the greatest consumer products company in the world." Before the merger, Gillette had 5 billion-dollar brands, whereas P&G had 16; together, they have a combined portfolio of 21 billion-dollars brands and the number 1 market position in categories representing two-thirds of total sales. Both companies also had strong track records in innovation: P&G generated $5 billion in retail sales in new categories, whereas Gillette also created almost $5 billion in new sales from products launched in the past five years. The merger positioned both companies for stronger sustainable growth in the future.

Each day around the world, more than 1 billion people interact with Gillette products, whereas 3 billion times a day customers interact with P&G brands. Both Gillette and P&G have gained leadership positions through their strategies of managing their businesses with long-term global perspectives. This ability to generate long-term profitable growth in a changing global marketplace rests on several fundamental strengths, including a constantly increasing accumulation of scientific knowledge, innovative products that embody meaningful technological advances, and an immense manufacturing capability to produce billions of products every year reliably, efficiently, and cost-effectively. Gillette's and P&G's strengths have created strong and enduring consumer brand loyalty around the world.[61]

1. What environmental factors have contributed to Gillette's success in global markets? What forces may have created challenges for the company?

2. What strategy does Gillette appear to have adopted for international marketing?

3. How can Gillette continue to compete effectively in the battery and grooming markets after the merger with Procter & Gamble?

CHAPTER REVIEW

1. Understand the nature of global markets and international marketing.

International marketing involves developing and performing marketing activities across national boundaries. International markets can provide tremendous opportunities for growth.

2. Analyze the environmental forces affecting international marketing efforts.

Environmental aspects of special importance include sociocultural; economic; political, legal, and regulatory; social and ethical; competitive; and technological forces. Because marketing activities are primarily social in purpose, they are influenced by beliefs and values regarding family, religion, education, health, and recreation. Cultural differences may affect decision-making behavior, product adoption, and product use. Gross domestic product (GDP) and GDP per capita are common measures of a nation's economic standing. Political and legal forces include a nation's political and ethics systems, laws, regulatory bodies, special-interest groups, and courts. Significant trade barriers include import tariffs, quotas, embargoes, and exchange controls. In the area of ethics, cultural relativism is the concept that morality varies from one culture to another and that business practices are therefore differentially defined as right or wrong by particular cultures. In addition to considering the types of competition and the types of competitive structures that exist in other countries, marketers also need to consider the competitive forces at work and recognize the importance of the global customer who is well informed about product choices from around the world. Advances in technology have greatly facilitated international marketing.

3. Identify several important regional trade alliances, markets, and agreements.

Various regional trade alliances and specific markets, such as the North American Free Trade Agreement, the European Union, the Common Market of the Southern Cone, Asia-Pacific Economic Cooperation, the General Agreement on Tariffs and Trade, and the World Trade Organization, create both opportunities and constraints for companies engaged in international marketing.

4. Examine methods of entering international markets.

Importing (the purchase of products from a foreign source) and exporting (the sale of products to foreign markets) are the easiest and most flexible methods of entering international markets. Licensing and franchising are arrangements whereby one firm pays fees to another for the use of its name, expertise, and supplies. Contract manufacturing occurs when a company hires a foreign firm to produce a designated volume of the firm's product to specification, and the final product carries the domestic firm's name. Joint ventures are partnerships between a domestic firm and a foreign firm or a government; strategic alliances are partnerships formed to create competitive advantage on a worldwide basis. A firm also can establish its own marketing or production facilities overseas. When companies have direct ownership of facilities in many countries, they may be considered multinational enterprises.

5. Recognize that international marketing strategies fall along a continuum from customization to globalization.

Although most firms adjust their marketing mixes for differences in target markets, some firms standardize their marketing efforts worldwide. Traditional full-scale international marketing involvement is based on products customized according to cultural, regional, and national differences. Globalization, however, involves developing marketing strategies as if the entire world (or regions of it) were a single entity; a globalized firm markets standardized products in the same way everywhere. International marketing demands some strategic planning if a firm is to incorporate foreign sales into its overall marketing strategy.

ACE self-test

Please visit the student website at **www.prideferrell.com** for ACE Self-Test questions that will help you prepare for exams.

KEY CONCEPTS

international marketing
gross domestic product (GDP)
import tariff
quota
embargo
exchange controls
balance of trade
cultural relativism

North American Free Trade Agreement (NAFTA)
European Union (EU)
Common Market of the Southern Cone (MERCOSUR)
Asia-Pacific Economic Cooperation (APEC)

World Trade Organization (WTO)
General Agreement on Tariffs and Trade (GATT)
dumping
importing
exporting
licensing

franchising
contract manufacturing
outsourcing
joint venture
strategic alliances
direct ownership
multinational enterprise
globalization

ISSUES FOR DISCUSSION AND REVIEW

1. How does international marketing differ from domestic marketing?

2. What factors must marketers consider as they decide whether to become involved in international marketing?

3. Why do you think this chapter focuses on an analysis of the international marketing environment?

4. A manufacturer recently exported peanut butter with a green label to a nation in the Far East. The product failed because it was associated with jungle sickness. How could this mistake have been avoided?

5. If you were asked to provide a small tip (or bribe) to have a document approved in a foreign nation where this practice is customary, what would you do?

6. How will NAFTA affect marketing opportunities for U.S. products in North America (the United States, Mexico, and Canada)?

7. In marketing dog food to Latin America, what aspects of the marketing mix would a U.S. firm need to alter?

8. What should marketers consider as they decide whether to license or enter into a joint venture in a foreign nation?

9. Discuss the impact of strategic alliances on marketing strategies.

10. Contrast globalization with customization of marketing mixes. Is one practice better than the other? Explain.

MARKETING APPLICATIONS

1. Which environmental forces (sociocultural, economic, political/legal/regulatory, social/ethical, competitive, or technological) might a marketer need to consider when marketing the following products in the international marketplace, and why?
   a. Barbie dolls
   b. Beer
   c. Financial services
   d. Televisions

2. Which would be the best organizational approach to international marketing of the following products, and why?
   a. Construction equipment manufacturing
   b. Cosmetics
   c. Automobiles

3. Describe how a shoe manufacturer would go from domestic marketing, to limited exporting, to international marketing, and finally, to globalization of marketing. Give examples of some activities that might be involved in this process.

Online Exercise

4. Founded in 1910 as "Florists' Telegraph Delivery," FTD was the first company to offer a "flowers-by-wire" service. FTD does not itself deliver flowers but depends on local florists to provide this service. In 1994, FTD expanded its toll-free telephone-ordering service by establishing a website. Visit the site at **www.ftd.com.**
   a. Click on "International Deliveries." Select a country to which you would like to send flowers. Summarize the delivery and pricing information that would apply to that country.
   b. Determine the cost of sending fresh-cut seasonal flowers to Germany.
   c. What are the benefits of this global distribution system for sending flowers worldwide? What other consumer products could be distributed globally through the Internet?

An important element in designing your firm's internationalization strategy is to identify markets that are most similar and different culturally. Because your firm is based in the United States, one approach to determine this is to calculate the average difference in scores from the United States for each country based on Hofstede's five cultural dimensions for 56 countries. Hofstede's cultural dimensions can be found using the search term "56 countries" at **http://globaledge.msu.edu/ibrd** (and check the box "Resource Desk only"). At the Geert Hofstede Resource Center, there will be a link called "Hofstede Scores." Which five countries are most similar to the United States? Which five countries are least similar?

Video CASE

IDG: Communicating Across Cultures Is Key

International Data Group (IDG) was founded in 1964 by Patrick McGovern. Currently, more than 100 million people in 85 countries read IDG's publications, which include more than 300 newspapers and magazines internationally, such as *Computerworld, InfoWorld, Network World, PC World, Macworld,* and the CIO global publishing product lines. A true visionary in the information technology (IT) field, McGovern

is now chairman of the board of Boston-based IDG. However, it is clear that his vision is still driving the firm:

The Information technology market looks dramatically different today [in 2006] than it did when we started IDG in 1964. At that time, the United States accounted for nearly 80 percent of all IT spending. Today, with globalization accelerating, it accounts for 35 percent.

For more than 40 years, IDG has maintained and reinforced our commitment to identify and expand into new growth markets. The result is the most dynamic, most trusted worldwide family of publications, websites, research services, and events in the industry. Technology buyers throughout the world depend on IDG's timely and trusted information resources. We've taken the lead in the largest and fastest growing markets to create globally branded product lines that reach more than 120 million buyers in 85 countries representing 95 percent of worldwide IT spending.

IDG has been ranked by *Fortune* magazine as one of the "100 Best Companies to Work For" for the last several years. The magazine noted IDG's decentralized management style as a particularly impressive feature that made it a favored company for employees. "We have focused on building an organization that is a rewarding place to work and that meets customer requirements. . . . IDG operates via the corporate values of respect and dignity for each individual. . . . [W]e invest in our people, foster an action-oriented 'let's try it attitude,' and keep responsive to the marketplace," said Patrick McGovern.

This responsiveness to the global marketplace is impressive as well. In addition to newspaper and magazine publishing, IDG also produces more than 170 events in about 40 countries. It has a comprehensive portfolio of technology-focused trade shows, conferences, and events. IDG prides itself on being the premier global provider of market intelligence, advisory services, and events for the IT industries; over 775 IDG analysts in 50 countries provide global, regional, and local expertise on IT. IDG's online presence includes 400 websites in over 80 countries; these are supported by a network of more than 2,000 journalists.

IDG values proper communication around the world and thrives on communicating effectively with all its target markets in 85 countries. Managers stress the importance of proper communication, including proper translation from the home language to the preferred foreign language. At the same time, they know the value of English as the preferred business language around the world.

Patrick McGovern's founding vision for IDG is to "improve the lives of people worldwide by providing information on information technology that could make them more productive in their jobs and happier in their

lives." Given the focus on information, clear communication is perhaps the most crucial aspect of IDG regardless of which product line is the focus. IDG is responsive locally while taking advantage of global operations. Specifically, IDG employs local nationals on its editorial staff to report on stories of particular interest to its local readers. And IDG has more than 100 individual business units, each operating with a high degree of decentralized authority and autonomy (which also was noted by *Fortune* as a key aspect of why IDG is such an admired firm). At the same time, the IDG News Service, an internal newswire, links more than a thousand IDG editors and journalists. They distribute news, features, commentary, and other editorial resources, which enables IDG publications to supplement local coverage with articles of a global nature.

IDG is a part of the lives of a large number of people, many of whom do not know their involvement with the firm's products. As long as IDG provides proper communication that carries internationally, we will continue to buy their products and receive great value in return.[62]

Questions for Discussion

1. How has IDG developed a successful international marketing strategy?
2. What can other firms learn from its attention to communication style internationally?
3. Do you think IDG's global marketing strategy meets the requirements of the concept of globalization as described in this chapter?

part

3

Target-Market Selection and Research

Part 3 focuses on researching and selecting target customers. The development of a marketing strategy begins with the customer. Chapter 6 provides a foundation for analyzing customers through a discussion of marketing information systems and the basic steps in the marketing research process. Chapter 7 focuses on one of the major steps in the development of a marketing strategy: selecting and analyzing target markets.

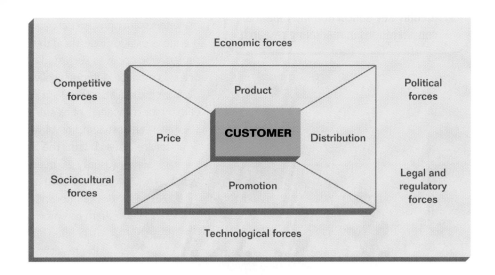

Marketing Research and Information Systems

OBJECTIVES

1. Define *marketing research* and understand its importance.

2. Describe the basic steps in conducting marketing research.

3. Explore the fundamental methods of gathering data for marketing research.

4. Describe how tools such as databases, decision support systems, and the Internet facilitate marketing information systems and research.

5. Identify key ethical and international considerations in marketing research.

Internet Research: Saving Money and Understanding Behavior

The Internet is readily accessible to hundreds of millions of people around the world and can provide nearly instantaneous information on just about every topic imaginable. As such, it is having a profound impact on the way ideas are formed and knowledge is created. Understanding how people surf the Web and identifying their website visiting and buying habits can prepare marketers for what comes next—how to translate the habits of online shoppers into real-world action. Indeed, Internet research accounts for more than $1.3 billion in research spending a year, up from $253 million in 2000.

Marketing research on the Internet can be divided into two distinct categories. The first involves using the Internet as a data-collection medium, where the marketer is not interested in understanding online behavior but merely uses the Internet as a faster and less expensive method for conducting surveys. In this category, marketers ask anyone willing to participate to take surveys online. The second category uses the Internet for passive measurement of behavior—marketers gather precise data about how consumers are using the Internet and use those data to understand their behavior online. This method relies on consumers who opt in to such studies and are ensured privacy; everything they do online is monitored through software they download.

With the wealth of software and survey tools available today, it is easy and efficient for companies of all size to learn to create and execute online surveys. They also can cost a fraction of what a large corporation might pay to retain a full-service research firm. The best type of survey for this method is a short survey (usually 20 questions or less), where only directional quantitative or qualitative data are needed. This type of survey typically does not provide the statistical data that a full-service research firm can provide. How a marketer plans to use the survey data often influences how a survey should be carried out. If the results will be used only for internal purposes and not to be presented to investors, customers, or other stakeholders, the credibility that a full-service research firm provides is not needed.[1] ■

Implementing the marketing concept requires that marketers obtain information about the characteristics, needs, and desires of target-market customers. When used effectively, such information facilitates customer relationship management by helping marketers to focus their efforts on meeting and even anticipating the needs of their customers. Marketing research and information systems that can provide practical and objective information to help firms develop and implement marketing strategies therefore are essential to effective marketing.

In this chapter we focus on how marketers gather information needed to make marketing decisions. First, we define marketing research and examine the individual steps of the marketing research process, including various methods of collecting data. Next, we look at how technology aids in collecting, organizing, and interpreting marketing research data. Finally, we consider ethical and international issues in marketing research.

The Importance of Marketing Research

Marketing research is the systematic design, collection, interpretation, and reporting of information to help marketers solve specific marketing problems or take advantage of marketing opportunities. As the word *research* implies, it is a process for gathering information not currently available to decision makers. The purpose of marketing research is to inform an organization about customers' needs and desires, marketing opportunities for particular goods and services, and changing attitudes and purchase patterns of customers. Market information increases marketers' ability to respond to customer needs, which leads to improved organizational performance.[2] Detecting shifts in buyers' behaviors and attitudes helps companies to stay in touch with the

The Value of Marketing Research

Claritas provides necessary knowledge for firms to target customers and make effective marketing decisions.

marketing research The systematic design, collection, interpretation, and reporting of information to help marketers solve specific marketing problems or take advantage of marketing opportunities

PepsiCo and Coca-Cola Research Drinks to Satisfy Every Need

Once upon a time, there were just two soft drinks—Pepsi and Coke. Next came the diet sodas, and then the flavored versions and more—all geared primarily toward satisfying the taste buds. Although PepsiCo and the Coca-Cola Company are veterans at fighting the war for taste, both companies have stepped up to meet today's challenge—working to provide the modern human with the right beverages to match his or her many "need states." What is a *need state*? Where people once drank solely to enjoy the taste of their beverages, today they drink to hydrate, boost their energy levels, become more beautiful from the inside out, relax and recreate, and yes, even refresh. The beverage companies are therefore researching and developing drinks to satisfy all these different needs, bringing the beverage industry to a new level.

Although soft drinks still account for the majority of the U.S. $100 billion beverage refreshment category, sales are down 1 to 2 percent. At the same time, sales of bottled water have grown by 22 percent, sports drinks by 23 percent, and tea by 15 percent. Euromonitor International has forecast that the health and wellness beverage industry—a major focus of the modern person's "need states"—will grow to $176 billion by 2010, up from $138 billion today. Moreover, beverage consumers interviewed for Synovate's ENation poll say that they pay more attention to a beverage's nutritional value than to anything else. According to the Synovate survey, more than 50 percent of consumers drink three or more servings of bottled water a day, whereas only a bit more than 30 percent drink three or more servings a day of soft drinks. Both Pepsi and Coca-Cola are paying attention.

In response to the growing demand for bottled water, Pepsi launched Aquafina (the number 1 bottled water brand), and Coca-Cola launched Dasani. As the nation's love for bottled water has grown, Pepsi has added Aquafina FlavorSplash (water with a hint of fruit flavor but still without calories), Propel Fitness Water, Propel Calcium, and Aquafina Alive (water with a hint of juice flavor and antioxidant vitamins). Coca-Cola, in turn, has introduced Dasani Sensations (slightly carbonated and flavored water). And this is only the water!

Over the past few years, both Pepsi and Coca-Cola have introduced a series of energy drinks; juices containing less sugar, fewer calories, more calcium, and more omega-3s; and so much more. And these companies are not alone: Ocean Spray, Cadbury Schweppes, Energy Brands, and several other firms are following the same path—working to provide consumers with drinks that suit all their "need states."[a]

ever-changing marketplace. Cell phone marketers, for example, would be very interested to know that teenagers are three times more likely than average cell phone users to use a broad range of mobile services such as shopping guides and magazine content, and they are twice as likely to use their phones to access restaurant and movie info. Fifty-seven percent of teens aged 13 to 17 already have a cell phone, and their comfort level with the mobile devices and related services forecasts a rosy future for wireless service providers.[3] Strategic planning requires marketing research to facilitate the process of assessing such opportunities or threats.

All sorts of organizations use marketing research to help them develop marketing mixes to match the needs of customers. Marketing research can help a firm better to understand market opportunities, ascertain the potential for success for new products, and determine the feasibility of a particular marketing strategy. JCPenney, for example, conducted extensive research to learn more about a core segment of shoppers who weren't being reached adequately by department stores: middle-income mothers between the ages of 35 and 54. The research involved asking 900 women about their casual clothing preferences. Later, the firm conducted in-depth interviews with 30 women about their clothing needs, feelings about fashion, and shopping experiences. The research helped the company to recognize that this "missing middle" segment of shoppers was frustrated with the choices and quality of clothing available in their price range and stressed out by the experience of shopping for clothes for themselves. Armed with this information, Penney launched two new lines of moderately priced, quality casual women's clothing, including one by designer Nicole Miller.[4] A study by SPSS, Inc., found that the most common reasons for conducting marketing research surveys included determining satisfaction (43 percent), product development (29 percent), branding (23 percent), segmentation (18 percent), business markets (11 percent), and awareness, trend tracking, and concept testing (18 percent).[5]

The real value of marketing research is measured by improvements in a marketer's ability to make decisions. Marketing research conducted for OfficeMax, for example, highlighted problems with store layout confusing shoppers and helped executives to make decisions to improve the layout. As a result, OfficeMax is replacing gridlike aisles with a less cluttered "racetrack" layout that gives shoppers a clear view all the way to the back wall and invites them to peruse expensive electronics showcased inside a main aisle that loops inside each store.[6] Marketers should treat information in the same manner as they use other resources, and they must weigh the costs of obtaining information against the benefits derived. Information should be judged worthwhile if it results in marketing activities that better satisfy the firm's target customers, leads to increased sales and profits, or helps the firm to achieve some other goal.

The Marketing Research Process

To maintain the control needed to obtain accurate information, marketers approach marketing research as a process with logical steps: (1) locating and defining issues or problems, (2) designing the research project, (3) collecting data, (4) interpreting research findings, and (5) reporting research findings (Figure 6.1). These steps should be viewed as an overall approach to conducting research rather than as a rigid set of rules to be followed in each project. In planning research projects, marketers must consider each step carefully and determine how they can best adapt them to resolve the particular issues at hand.

Locating and Defining Research Issues or Problems

The first step in launching a research study is issue or problem definition, which focuses on uncovering the nature and boundaries of a situation or question related to marketing strategy or implementation. The first sign of a problem is typically a departure from some normal function, such as failure to attain objectives. If a corporation's

figure 6.1

THE FIVE STEPS OF THE MARKETING RESEARCH PROCESS

1 Locating and defining issues or problems

2 Designing the research project

3 Collecting data

4 Interpreting research findings

5 Reporting research findings

objective is a 12 percent sales increase and the current marketing strategy resulted in a 6 percent increase, this discrepancy should be analyzed to help guide future marketing strategies. Declining sales, increasing expenses, and decreasing profits also signal problems. Armed with this knowledge, a firm could define a problem as finding a way to adjust for biases stemming from existing customers when gathering data or to develop methods for gathering information to help find new customers. Conversely, when an organization experiences a dramatic rise in sales or some other positive event, it may conduct marketing research to discover the reasons and maximize the opportunities stemming from them.

Marketing research often focuses on identifying and defining market opportunities or changes in the environment. When a firm discovers a market opportunity, it may need to conduct research to understand the situation more precisely so that it can craft an appropriate marketing strategy. For example, when General Motors saw that 42 percent of Hummer H3 buyers were women (compared with 26.3 percent of H2 buyers), it recognized an opportunity to position the smaller sport-utility vehicle to appeal to women buyers.[7] The company can use this information to focus its efforts on specific target markets and to refine its marketing strategy appropriately.

To pin down the specific boundaries of a problem or an issue through research, marketers must define the nature and scope of the situation in a way that requires probing beneath the superficial symptoms. The interaction between the marketing manager and the marketing researcher should yield a clear definition of the research need. Researchers and decision makers should remain in the issue or problem definition stage until they have determined precisely what they want from marketing research and how they will use it. Deciding how to refine a broad, indefinite issue or problem into a precise, researchable statement is a prerequisite for the next step in the research process.

Designing the Research Project

Once the problem or issue has been defined, the next step is **research design**, an overall plan for obtaining the information needed to address it. This step requires formulating a hypothesis and determining what type of research is most appropriate for testing the hypothesis to ensure that the results are reliable and valid.

Developing a Hypothesis. The objective statement of a marketing research project should include hypotheses based on both previous research and expected research findings. A **hypothesis** is an informed guess or assumption about a certain problem or set of circumstances. It is based on all the insight and knowledge available about the problem or circumstances from previous research studies and other sources. As information is gathered, a researcher can test the hypothesis. For example, a food marketer such as H. J. Heinz might propose the hypothesis that children today have considerable influence on their families' buying decisions regarding ketchup and other grocery products. A marketing researcher then would gather data, perhaps through surveys of children and their parents, and draw conclusions about whether the hypothesis is correct. Sometimes several hypotheses are developed during an actual research project; the hypotheses that are accepted or rejected become the study's chief conclusions.

Types of Research. The nature and type of research varies based on the research design and the hypotheses under investigation. Marketers may elect to conduct either exploratory research or conclusive research. While each has distinct purposes, the major differences between them are formalization and flexibility rather than the specific research methods used. Table 6.1 summarizes the differences.

Exploratory Research When marketers need more information about a problem or want to make a tentative hypothesis more specific, they may conduct **exploratory research.** The main purpose of exploratory research is to better understand a problem or situation and/or to help identify additional data needs or decision alternatives.[8] Consider that until recently there was no research available to help marketers

research design An overall plan for obtaining the information needed to address a research problem or issue

hypothesis An informed guess or assumption about a certain problem or set of circumstances

exploratory research Research conducted to gather more information about a problem or to make a tentative hypothesis more specific

understand how consumers perceive the term *clearance* versus the term *sale* in describing a discounted-price event. An exploratory study asked one group of 80 consumers to write down their thoughts about a store window sign that said "sale" and another group of 80 consumers about a store window sign that read "clearance." The results revealed that consumers expected deeper discounts when the term *clearance* was used, and they expected the quality of the clearance products to be lower than that of products on sale.[9] This exploratory research helped marketers to better understand how consumers view these terms and opened up the opportunity for additional research hypotheses about decision alternatives for retail pricing.

Conclusive Research   **Conclusive research** is designed to verify insights through an objective procedure to help marketers in making decisions. It is used when the marketer has in mind one or more alternatives and needs assistance in the final stages of decision making.[10] For example, exploratory research revealed that clearance and sale terms send different signals to consumers, but in order to make a decision, a well-defined and structured research project could be used to help marketers decide which approach is best for a specific set of products and target consumers. The study would be specific to selecting a course of action and typically quantitative using methods that can be verified. Two types of conclusive research are descriptive and experimental research.

Types of Research

Through exploratory research, firms can validate a product or concept and use that research to enhance their marketing message.

conclusive research
Research designed to verify insights through objective procedures and to help marketers in making decisions

table 6.1	DIFFERENCES BETWEEN EXPLORATORY AND CONCLUSIVE RESEARCH	
Research Project Components	**Exploratory Research**	**Conclusive Research**
Research purpose	General: to generate insights about a situation	Specific: to verify insights and aid in selecting a course of action
Data needs	Vague	Clear
Data sources	Ill-defined	Well-defined
Data collection form	Open-ended, rough	Usually structured
Sample	Relatively small; subjectively selected to maximize generalization of insights	Relatively large; objectively selected to permit generalization of findings
Data collection	Flexible; no set procedure	Rigid; well-laid-out procedure
Data analysis	Informal: typically nonquantitative	Formal; typically quantitative
Inferences/recommendations	More tentative than final	More final than tentative

Source: A. Parasuraman, Dhruv Grewal, and R. Krishnan, *Marketing Research* (Boston: Houghton Mifflin, 2007).

If marketers need to understand the characteristics of certain phenomena to solve a particular problem, **descriptive research** can aid them. Such studies may range from general surveys of customers' education, occupation, or age to specific surveys on how often teenagers eat at fast-food restaurants after school or how often customers buy new pairs of athletic shoes. For example, if Nike and Reebok want to target more young women, they might ask 15- to 35-year-old females how often they work out, how frequently they wear athletic shoes for casual use, and how many pairs of athletic shoes they buy in a year. Such descriptive research can be used to develop specific marketing strategies for the athletic shoe market. Descriptive studies generally demand much prior knowledge and assume that the issue or problem is clearly defined. Some descriptive studies require statistical analysis and predictive tools. The marketer's major task is to choose adequate methods for collecting and measuring data.

Descriptive research is limited in providing the evidence necessary to make causal inferences (i.e., that variable x causes a variable y). **Experimental research** allows marketers to make causal deductions about relationships.[11] Such experimentation requires that an independent variable (one not influenced by or dependent on other variables) be manipulated and the resulting changes in a dependent variable (one contingent on, or restricted to, one value or set of values assumed by the independent variable) be measured. For example, when Coca-Cola introduced Dasani flavored waters, managers needed to estimate sales at various potential price points. In some markets Dasani was introduced at $6.99 per six-pack. By holding variables such as advertising and shelf position constant, Coca-Cola could manipulate the price variable to study its effect on sales. If sales increased 40 percent when the price was reduced by $2, then managers could make an informed decision about the effect of price on sales. Coca-Cola also could use experimental research to manipulate other variables such as advertising or in-store shelf position to determine their effect on sales. Manipulation of the causal variable and control of other variables is what makes experimental research unique. As a result, it can provide much stronger evidence of cause and effect than data collected through descriptive research.

Research Reliability and Validity.   In designing research, marketing researchers must ensure that research techniques are both reliable and valid. A research technique has **reliability** if it produces almost identical results in repeated trials. But a reliable technique is not necessarily valid. To have **validity,** the research method must measure what it is supposed to measure, not something else. For example, although a group of customers may express the same level of satisfaction based on a rating scale, the individuals may not exhibit the same repurchase behavior because of different personal characteristics. This result might cause the researcher to question the validity of the satisfaction scale if the purpose of rating satisfaction were to estimate potential repurchase behavior.[12] A study to measure the effect of advertising on sales would be valid if advertising could be isolated from other factors or variables that affect sales. The study would be reliable if replications of it produced the same results.

Collecting Data

The next step in the marketing research process is collecting data to help prove (or disprove) the research hypothesis. The research design must specify what types of data to collect and how they will be collected.

Types of Data.   Marketing researchers have two types of data at their disposal. **Primary data** are observed and recorded or collected directly from respondents. These data must be gathered by observing phenomena or surveying people of interest. **Secondary data** are compiled both inside and outside the organization for some purpose other than the current investigation. Secondary data include general reports supplied to an enterprise by various data services and internal and online databases. Such reports might concern market share, retail inventory levels, and customers' buying behavior. Secondary data are commonly available in private or public reports or have been collected and stored by the organization itself. Given the opportunity to

descriptive research
Research conducted to clarify the characteristics of certain phenomena and thus solve a particular problem

experimental research
Research that allows marketers to make causal inferences about relationships

reliability A condition existing when a research technique produces almost identical results in repeated trials

validity A condition existing when a research method measures what it is supposed to measure

primary data Data observed and recorded or collected directly from respondents

secondary data Data compiled both inside and outside the organization for some purpose other than the current investigation

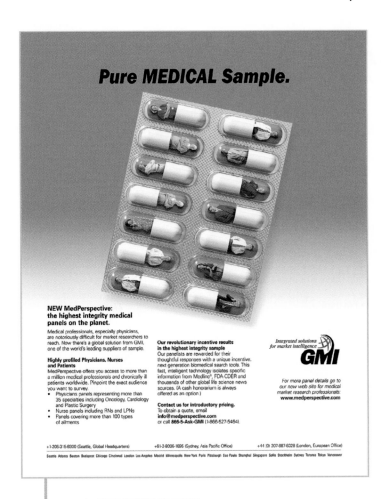

Pure MEDICAL Sample.

NEW MedPerspective:
the highest integrity medical
panels on the planet.

Medical professionals, especially physicians,
are notoriously difficult for market researchers to
reach. Now there's a global solution from GMI,
one of the world's leading suppliers of sample.

**Highly profiled Physicians, Nurses
and Patients**
MedPerspective offers you access to more than
a million medical professionals and chronically ill
patients worldwide. Pinpoint the exact audience
you want to survey.
· Physicians panels representing more than
  35 specialties including Oncology, Cardiology
  and Plastic Surgery
· Nurse panels including RNs and LPNs
· Panels covering more than 100 types
  of ailments

Our revolutionary incentive results
in the highest integrity sample
Our panelists are rewarded for their
thoughtful responses with a unique incentive.
next generation biomedical search tools. This
fast, intelligent technology isolates specific
information from Medline®, FDA CDER and
thousands of other global life science news
sources. (A cash honorarium is always
offered as an option.)

Contact us for introductory pricing.
To obtain a quote, email
info@medperspective.com
or call 866-5-Ask-GMI (1-866-527-5464).

*Integrated solutions
for market intelligence*
GMI

For more panel details go to
our new web site for medical
market research professionals:
www.medperspective.com

+1-206-315-8300 (Seattle, Global Headquarters)   +61-2-9006-1695 (Sydney, Asia Pacific Office)   +44 (0) 207-887-6028 (London, European Office)

Seattle Atlanta Boston Budapest Chicago Cincinnati London Los Angeles Madrid Minneapolis New York Paris Pittsburgh Sao Paulo Shanghai Singapore Sofia Stockholm Sydney Toronto Tokyo Vancouver

Primary Data Collection

GMI works with physicians, nurses, and patients to help pharmaceutical companies collect primary data on over 100 ailments.

obtain data via the Internet, more than half of all marketing research now comes from secondary sources.

Sources of Secondary Data.   Marketers often begin the data-collection phase of the marketing research process by gathering secondary data. They may use available reports and other information from both internal and external sources to study a marketing problem.

Internal sources of secondary data can contribute tremendously to research. An organization's own database may contain information about past marketing activities, such as sales records and research reports, that can be used to test hypotheses and pinpoint problems. From sales reports, for example, a firm may be able to determine not only which product sold best at certain times of the year but also which colors and sizes customers preferred. Such information may have been gathered using customer relationship management (CRM) tools for marketing, management or financial purposes. Table 6.2 lists some commonly available internal company information that may be useful for marketing research purposes.

Accounting records are also an excellent source of data but, strangely enough, are often overlooked. The large volume of data an accounting department collects does not automatically flow to other departments. As a result, detailed information about costs, sales, customer accounts, or profits by product category may not be easily accessible to the marketing area. This condition develops particularly in organizations that do not store marketing information on a systematic basis.

External sources of secondary data include periodicals, government publications, unpublished sources, and online databases. Periodicals such as *Business Week, The Wall Street Journal, Sales & Marketing Management, Marketing Research,* and *Industrial Marketing* publish general information that can help marketers define problems and develop hypotheses. *Survey of Buying Power,* an annual supplement to *Sales & Marketing Management,* contains sales data for major industries on a county-by-county basis. Many marketers also consult federal government publications such as the *Statistical Abstract of the United States,* the *Census of Business,* the *Census of Agriculture,* and the *Census of Population;* most of these government publications are available online. Although the government still conducts its primary census every ten years, it now surveys 250,000 households every month, providing decision makers with a more up-to-date demographic picture of the nation's population every year. Such data help Target executives make merchandising and marketing decisions as well as identify promising locations for new Target stores.[13]

In addition, companies may subscribe to services such as ACNielsen or Information Resources, Inc. (IRI), that track retail sales and other information. IRI, for

table 6.2	INTERNAL SOURCES OF SECONDARY DATA

- Sales data, which may be broken down by geographic area, product type, or even type of customer
- Accounting information, such as costs, prices, and profits, by product category
- Competitive information gathered by the sales force

table 6.3 WHY PEOPLE CHOOSE TO BLOG

Why People Choose to Blog	Percent Who Cite as Primary Reason
To express themselves creatively	52
To document their personal experiences and/or share them with others	50
To keep in touch with friends and family	37
To share their practical knowledge or skills with others	34
To motivate other people to action	29
To entertain other people	28
To store resources or information that is important to them	28
To influence the way other people think	27
To network or to meet new people	16
To make money	7

Source: Adapted from "Bloggers: A Portrait of the Internet's New Storytellers," Pew/Internet & American Life Project, July 19, 2006, www.pewinternet.org/pdfs/PIP%20Bloggers%20Report%20July%2019%202006.pdf.

example, tracks consumer purchases using in-store, scanner-based technology. Marketers can purchase information from IRI about a product category, such as frozen orange juice, as secondary data.[14] Small businesses may be unable to afford such services, but they can still find a wealth of information through industry publications and trade associations.[15]

The Internet can be especially useful to marketing researchers. As we've already seen, search engines such as Google can help marketers locate many types of secondary data or research topics of interest. Of course, companies can mine their own websites for useful information using CRM tools. Amazon.com, for example, has built a relationship with its customers by tracking the types of books, music, and other products they purchase. Each time a customer logs onto the website, the company can offer recommendations based on the customer's previous purchases. Such a marketing system helps the company track the changing desires and buying habits of its most valued customers. And marketing researchers are increasingly monitoring blogs to discover what consumers are saying about their products—both positive and negative. Some, including yogurt maker Stonyfield Farms, have even established their own blogs in order to monitor consumer dialog on issues of their choice. Table 6.3 lists the reasons people blog, whereas Table 6.4 summarizes the external sources of secondary data, excluding syndicated services.

Methods of Collecting Primary Data. The collection of primary data is a more lengthy, expensive, and complex process than the collection of secondary data. To gather primary data, researchers use sampling procedures, survey methods, and observation. These efforts can be handled in-house by the firm's own research department or contracted to a private research firm such as ACNielsen, Information Resources, Inc., IMS International, and Quality Controlled Services.

Sampling. Because the time and resources available for research are limited, it is almost impossible to investigate all the members of a target market or other population. A **population,** or "universe," includes all the elements, units, or individuals of interest

population All the elements, units, or individuals of interest to researchers for a specific study

table 6.4   EXTERNAL SOURCES OF SECONDARY DATA

Government Sources

Economic census	www.census.gov/econ/census02/index.html
Export.gov—country and industry market research	www.export.gov/mrktresearch/index.asp
National Technical Information Services	www.ntis.gov/
STAT-USA	www.stat-usa.gov/
Strategis—Canadian trade	http://strategis.ic.gc.ca/engdoc/main.html

Trade Associations and Shows

American Society of Association Executives	www.asaecenter.org/peoplegroups/content.cfm? ItemNumber=16433&navItemNumber=14962
Directory of Associations	www.marketingsource.com/associations/
Trade Show News Network	www.tsnn.com/
Tradeshow Week	www.tradeshowweek.com/

Magazines, Newspapers, Video, Audio News Programming

Blinkx	www.blinkx.com/home?safefilter=off
FindArticles.com	www.directcontactpr.com/jumpstation/
Google Video Search	http://video.google.com/
Media Jumpstation	www.directcontactpr.com/jumpstation/
News Directory	www.newsdirectory.com/magazine.php? cat=3&sub=&c=
Yahoo! Video Search	http://video.search.yahoo.com/

Corporate Information

Annual Report Service	www.annualreportservice.com/
Bitpipe	http://www.bitpipe.com/
Business Wire—press releases	http://home.businesswire.com/portal/site/home/ index.jsp?front_door=true
Hoover's Online	www.hoovers.com/free/
Open Directory Project	http://dmoz.org/
PR Newswire—press releases	www.prnewswire.com/

Source: Adapted from "Tutorial: Finding Information for Market Research," KnowThis.com, www.knowthis.com/tutorials/marketing/information-for-market-research/ (accessed January 23, 2007).

sample A limited number of units chosen to represent the characteristics of the population

sampling The process of selecting representative units from a total population

probability sampling A sampling technique in which every element in the population being studied has a known chance of being selected for study

random sampling A type of probability sampling in which all units in a population have an equal chance of appearing in a sample

to researchers for a specific study. For a Gallup poll designed to predict the results of a presidential election, all registered voters in the United States would constitute the population. By systematically choosing a limited number of units—a **sample**—to represent the characteristics of a total population, researchers can project the reactions of a total market or market segment. **Sampling** in marketing research, therefore, is the process of selecting representative units from a total population. Sampling techniques allow marketers to predict buying behavior fairly accurately on the basis of the responses from a representative portion of the population of interest. Most types of marketing research employ sampling techniques.

There are two basic types of sampling: probability sampling and nonprobability sampling. With **probability sampling,** every element in the population being studied has a known chance of being selected for study. Random sampling is a kind of probability sampling. When marketers employ **random sampling,** all the units in a population have an equal chance of appearing in the sample. The various events that can occur have an equal or known chance of taking place. For example, a specific card in a regulation

Sampling

DMS specializes in online sampling methods to develop a representative sample.

deck should have a 1/52 probability of being drawn at any one time. Sample units ordinarily are chosen by selecting from a table of random numbers statistically generated so that each digit, 0 through 9, will have an equal probability of occurring in each position in the sequence. The sequentially numbered elements of a population are sampled randomly by selecting the units whose numbers appear in the table of random numbers.

Another kind of probability sampling is **stratified sampling,** in which the population of interest is divided into groups according to a common attribute, and a random sample is then chosen within each group. The stratified sample may reduce some of the error that could occur in a simple random sample. By ensuring that each major group or segment of the population receives its proportionate share of sample units, investigators avoid including too many or too few sample units from each group. Samples are usually stratified when researchers believe that there may be variations among different types of respondents. For example, many political opinion surveys are stratified by gender, race, age, and/or geographic location.

The second type of sampling, **nonprobability sampling,** is more subjective than probability sampling because there is no way to calculate the likelihood that a specific element of the population being studied will be chosen. Quota sampling, for example, is highly judgmental because the final choice of participants is left to the researchers. In **quota sampling,** researchers divide the population into groups and then arbitrarily choose participants from each group. A study of people who wear eyeglasses, for example, may be conducted by interviewing equal numbers of men and women who wear eyeglasses. In quota sampling, there are some controls—usually limited to two or three variables, such as age, gender, or race—over the selection of participants. The controls attempt to ensure that representative categories of respondents are interviewed. Because quota samples are not probability samples, not everyone has an equal chance of being selected, and sampling error therefore cannot be measured statistically. Quota samples are used most often in exploratory studies, when hypotheses are being developed. Often a small quota sample will not be projected to the total population, although the findings may provide valuable insights into a problem. Quota samples are useful when people with some common characteristic are found and questioned about the topic of interest. A probability sample used to study people allergic to cats would be highly inefficient.

Survey Methods. Marketing researchers often employ sampling to collect primary data through mail, telephone, online, or personal-interview surveys. The results of such surveys are used to describe and analyze buying behavior. Selection of a survey method depends on the nature of the problem or issue, the data needed to test the hypothesis, and the resources, such as funding and personnel, available to the researcher. Marketers may employ more than one survey method depending on the goals of the research. The SPSS, Inc., survey of American Marketing Association members found that 43.8 percent use telephone surveys, 39.3 percent use Web-based surveys, 36.8 percent use focus groups, 19 percent use mail surveys, 11.8 percent use e-mail surveys, and 9.6 percent

stratified sampling A type of probability sampling in which the population is divided into groups according to a common attribute, and a random sample is then chosen within each group

nonprobability sampling A sampling technique in which there is no way to calculate the likelihood that a specific element of the population being studied will be chosen

quota sampling A nonprobability sampling technique in which researchers divide the population into groups and then arbitrarily choose participants from each group

table 6.5	COMPARISON OF THE FOUR BASIC SURVEY METHODS			
	Mail Surveys	**Telephone Surveys**	**Online Surveys**	**Personal Interview Surveys**
Economy	Potentially lower in cost per interview than telephone or personal surveys if there is an adequate response rate.	Avoids interviewers' travel expenses; less expensive than in-home interviews.	The least expensive method if there is an adequate response rate.	The most expensive survey method; shopping-mall and focus-group interviews have lower costs than in-home interviews.
Flexibility	Inflexible; questionnaire must be short and easy for respondents to complete.	Flexible because interviewers can ask probing questions, but observations are impossible.	Less flexible; survey must be easy for online users to receive and return; short, dichotomous, or multiple-choice questions work best.	Most flexible method; respondents can react to visual materials; demographic data are more accurate; in-depth probes are possible.
Interviewer bias	Interviewer bias is eliminated; questionnaires can returned anonymously.	Some anonymity; may be hard to develop trust in respondents.	Interviewer bias is eliminated, but e-mail address on the return eliminates anonymity.	Interviewers' personal characteristics or inability to maintain objectivity may result in bias.
Sampling and respondents' cooperation	Obtaining a complete mailing list is difficult; nonresponse is a major disadvantage.	Sample limited to respondents with telephones; devices that screen calls, busy signals, and refusals are a problem.	Sample limited to respondents with computer access; the available e-mail address list may not be a representative sample for some purposes.	Not-at-homes are a problem, which may be overcome by focus-group and shopping-mall interviewing.

mail survey A research method in which respondents answer a questionnaire sent through the mail

use in-person interviews.[16] Surveys can be quite expensive (Procter & Gamble spends about $200 million to have 600 organizations conduct surveys[17]), but small businesses can turn to sites such as SurveyMonkey.com and zoomerang.com for inexpensive or even free online surveys. Table 6.5 summarizes and compares the advantages of the various survey methods.

Gathering information through surveys is becoming increasingly difficult because fewer people are willing to participate.[18] Many people believe that responding to surveys takes up too much scarce personal time, especially as surveys become longer and more detailed. Others have concerns about how much information marketers are gathering and whether their privacy is being invaded. The unethical use of selling techniques disguised as marketing surveys also has led to decreased cooperation. These factors contribute to nonresponse rates for any type of survey. Most researchers consider nonresponse the greatest threat to valid survey research.[19]

In a **mail survey,** questionnaires are sent to respondents, who are encouraged to complete and return them. Mail surveys are used most often when the individuals in the sample are spread over a wide area and funds for the survey are limited. A mail survey is potentially the least expensive survey method as long as the response rate is high enough to produce reliable results. The main disadvantages of this method are the possibilities of a low response rate and of misleading results if respondents differ significantly from the population being sampled. Research has found that providing a monetary incentive to respond to a mail survey has a significant impact on response rates for both consumer and business samples. However, such incentives may reduce the cost-effectiveness of this survey method.[20] As a result of these issues, companies are increasingly moving to Internet surveys and automated telephone surveys, as discussed below.

In a **telephone survey,** an interviewer records respondents' answers to a questionnaire over a phone line. A telephone survey has some advantages over a mail survey. The rate of response is higher because it takes less effort to answer the telephone and talk than to fill out and return a questionnaire. If there are enough interviewers, a telephone survey can be conducted very quickly. Thus political candidates or organizations seeking an immediate reaction to an event may choose this method. In addition, a telephone survey permits interviewers to gain rapport with respondents and ask probing questions. *Automated telephone surveys,* also known as *interactive voice response surveys* or "robosurveys," rely on a recorded voice to ask questions while a computer program records respondents' answers. The primary benefit of automated surveys is the elimination of "bias" introduced by a live researcher.

However, only a small proportion of the population likes to participate in telephone surveys. Just one-third of Americans are willing to participate in telephone interviews, down from two-thirds 20 years ago.[21] This poor image can limit participation significantly and distort representation in a telephone survey. Moreover, telephone surveys are limited to oral communication; visual aids or observation cannot be included. Many households are excluded from telephone directories by choice (unlisted numbers) or because the residents moved after the directory was published. Potential respondents often use telephone answering machines, voice mail, or caller ID to screen or block calls; millions have signed up for "Do Not Call Lists." Moreover, an increasing number of younger Americans have given up their fixed phone lines in favor of wireless phones.[22] These issues have serious implications for the use of telephone samples in conducting surveys.

Online surveys are evolving as an alternative to mail and telephone surveys. In an **online survey,** questionnaires can be transmitted to respondents who have agreed to be contacted and have provided their e-mail addresses. More firms are using their websites to conduct surveys. Online surveys also can make use of online communities—such as chat rooms, Web-based forums, and newsgroups—to identify trends in interests and consumption patterns. Movies, consumer electronics, food, and computers are popular topics in many online communities.[23] Indeed, by "listening in" on these ongoing conversations, marketers may be able to identify new-product opportunities and consumer needs. Moreover, this type of online data can be gathered at little incremental cost compared with alternative data sources.[24] Evolving technology and the interactive nature of the Internet allow for considerable flexibility in designing questionnaires for online surveys.

Given the growing number of households that have computers with Internet access, marketing research is likely to rely heavily on online surveys in the future. Furthermore, as negative attitudes toward telephone surveys render that technique less representative and more expensive, the integration of e-mail, fax, and voice-mail functions into one computer-based system provides a promising alternative for survey research. E-mail surveys have especially strong potential within organizations whose employees are networked and for associations that publish members' e-mail addresses. College students in particular often are willing to provide their e-mail address and other personal information in exchange for incentives such as T-shirts and other giveaways.[25] However, there are some ethical issues to consider when using e-mail for marketing research, such as unsolicited e-mail, which could be viewed as "spam," and privacy, because some potential survey respondents fear that their personal information will be given or sold to third parties without their knowledge or permission.

telephone survey A research method in which respondents' answers to a questionnaire are recorded by interviewers on the phone

online survey A research method in which respondents answer a questionnaire via e-mail or on a website

marketing
ENTREPRENEURS

Sharon Lee and DeeDee Gordon

THE BUSINESS: Look-Look.com

FOUNDED: 1999, when Lee was 31 and Gordon was 29

SUCCESS: Have become the "go to" source on youth trends

Frustrated with the way their employer engaged in marketing research into teen trends, DeeDee Gordon and Sharon Lee struck out on their own to launch Look-Look.com, an online, real-time service that provides reliable research, news, trends, and photos about cool youths aged 14 to 30. Look-Look pays more than 35,000 handpicked, prescreened young people from all over the world to e-mail information and photos about their styles, trends, opinions, observations, and ideas. Gordon and Lee believe that truly understanding youth culture requires a constant dialog using the latest technology. They provide a growing roster with instant access to survey results and an opportunity to receive rapid access to specific research questions.[b]

In a **personal-interview survey,** participants respond to questions face to face. Various audiovisual aids—pictures, products, diagrams, or prerecorded advertising copy—can be incorporated in a personal interview. Rapport gained through direct interaction usually permits more in-depth interviewing, including probes, follow-up questions, or psychological tests. In addition, because personal interviews can be longer, they may yield more information. Finally, respondents can be selected more carefully, and reasons for nonresponse can be explored.

One such research technique is the **in-home (door-to-door) interview.** The in-home interview offers a clear advantage when thoroughness of self-disclosure and elimination of group influence are important. In an in-depth interview of 45 to 90 minutes, respondents can be probed to reveal their real motivations, feelings, behaviors, and aspirations.

The object of a **focus-group interview** is to observe group interaction when members are exposed to an idea or a concept. General Motors, for example, used focus groups consisting of celebrity athletes, actors, and musicians, including XZibit, as part of its effort to redesign the Cadillac Escalade sport-utility vehicle and CTS sedan.[26] Often these interviews are conducted informally, without a structured questionnaire, in small groups of 8 to 12 people. They allow customer attitudes, behaviors, lifestyles, needs, and desires to be explored in a flexible and creative manner. Questions are open-ended and stimulate respondents to answer in their own words. Researchers can ask probing questions to clarify something they do not fully understand or something unexpected and interesting that may help to explain buying behavior. For example, Ford Motor Company may use focus groups to determine whether to change its advertising to emphasize a vehicle's safety features rather than its style and performance. It may be necessary to use separate focus groups for each major market segment studied—men, women, and age groups—and experts recommend the use of at least two focus groups per segment in case one group is unusually idiosyncratic.[27] Focus groups have been found to be especially useful to set new-product prices.[28] However, they generally provide only qualitative, not quantitative, data and thus are best used to uncover issues that can then be explored using quantifiable marketing research techniques.

More organizations are starting **customer advisory boards,** which are small groups of actual customers who serve as sounding boards for new-product ideas and offer insights into their feelings and attitudes toward a firm's products, promotion, pricing, and other elements of marketing strategy. While these advisory boards help companies maintain strong relationships with valuable customers, they also can provide great insight into marketing research questions.[29] Yum Brands' KFC, for example, formed the KFC Moms Matter! Advisory Board to obtain insight and recommendations from mothers about its brand and products.[30]

Still another option is the **telephone depth interview,** which combines the traditional focus group's ability to probe with the confidentiality provided by telephone surveys. This type of interview is most appropriate for qualitative research projects among a small targeted group that is difficult to bring together for a traditional focus group because of members' profession, location, or lifestyle. Respondents can choose the time and day for the interview. Although this method is difficult to implement, it can yield revealing information from respondents who otherwise would be unwilling

personal-interview survey A research method in which participants respond to survey questions face to face

in-home (door-to-door) interview A personal interview that takes place in the respondent's home

focus-group interview A research method involving observation of group interaction when members are exposed to an idea or a concept

customer advisory boards Small groups of actual customers who serve as sounding boards for new-product ideas and offer insights into their feelings and attitudes toward a firm's products and other elements of marketing strategy

telephone depth interview An interview that combines the traditional focus group's ability to probe with the confidentiality provided by telephone surveys

Customer Advisory Boards

MindField helps customers develop targeted advisory boards and panels.

to participate in marketing research.[31] Similar efforts can be conducted online through WebEx meetings.

The nature of personal interviews has changed. In the past, most personal interviews, which were based on random sampling or prearranged appointments, were conducted in the respondent's home. Today, most personal interviews are conducted outside the home. **Shopping-mall intercept interviews** involve interviewing a percentage of individuals passing by certain "intercept" points in a mall. As with any face-to-face interviewing method, shopping-mall intercept interviewing has many advantages. The interviewer is in a position to recognize and react to respondents' nonverbal indications of confusion. Respondents can be shown product prototypes, videotapes of commercials, and the like and asked for their reactions. The mall environment lets the researcher deal with complex situations. For example, in taste tests, researchers know that all the respondents are reacting to the same product, which can be prepared and monitored from the mall test kitchen. In addition to the ability to conduct tests requiring bulky equipment, lower cost and greater control make shopping-mall intercept interviews popular.

Questionnaire Construction. A carefully constructed questionnaire is essential to the success of any survey. Questions must be clear, easy to understand, and directed toward a specific objective; that is, they must be designed to elicit information that meets the study's data requirements. Researchers need to define the objective before trying to develop a questionnaire because the objective determines the substance of the questions and the amount of detail. A common mistake in constructing questionnaires is to ask questions that interest the researchers but do not yield information useful in deciding whether to accept or reject a hypothesis. Finally, the most important rule in composing questions is to maintain impartiality.

The questions are usually of three kinds: open-ended, dichotomous, and multiple-choice.

Open-ended question

What is your general opinion about broadband Internet access?

_____

_____

Dichotomous question

Do you presently have broadband access at home, work, or school?

Yes _____ No _____

Multiple-choice question

What age group are you in?

Under 20 _____

20–35 _____

36 and over _____

Researchers must be very careful about questions that a respondent might consider too personal or that might require an admission of activities that other people are likely to condemn. Questions of this type should be worded to make them less offensive.

shopping-mall intercept interviews A research method that involves interviewing a percentage of persons passing by "intercept" points in a mall

In the fine art of research,
the shades of gray complete the masterpiece.

While data gives answers in black and white, it's the subtleties of the gray areas that give you the big picture. Burke understands the nuances of research. Grounded in academic principles and guided by ongoing internal research, Burke helps you determine the best research method, gather the information, and develop the best strategy for actionable results. You will have confidence in your decisions because you have the experts at Burke to support you. Visit Burke.com or call 800.688.2674 to find out more. **Burke**

The Fine Art of Marketing Research

Interpreting Research

Companies like Burke can help interpret the data collected from market research and offer insights into the areas to be investigated.

Observation Methods. In using observation methods, researchers record individuals' overt behavior, taking note of physical conditions and events. Direct contact with them is avoided; instead, their actions are examined and noted systematically. For instance, researchers might use observation methods to answer the question, "How long does the average McDonald's restaurant customer have to wait in line before being served?" Observation may include the use of ethnographic techniques, such as watching customers interact with a product in a real-world environment. Kimberly-Clark researchers employed ethnographic techniques when they asked a few consumers to wear a glasses-mounted camera so that they could observe how the consumers used Huggies baby wipes. The research revealed that parents were changing their babies on top of beds, floors, and even washing machines where they were struggling with wipe containers requiring two hands. Based on this research, the company redesigned the package so that the product can be used more easily with one hand.[32]

Observation also may be combined with interviews. For example, during a personal interview, the condition of a respondent's home or other possessions may be observed and recorded. The interviewer also can observe directly and confirm demographic information such as race, approximate age, and sex.

Data gathered through observation sometimes can be biased if the person is aware of the observation process. However, an observer can be placed in a natural market environment, such as a grocery store, without biasing or influencing shoppers' actions. If the presence of a human observer is likely to bias the outcome, or if human sensory abilities are inadequate, mechanical means may be used to record behavior. Mechanical observation devices include cameras, recorders, counting machines, scanners, and equipment that records physiologic changes. The electronic scanners used in supermarkets are very useful in marketing research. They provide accurate data on sales and customers' purchase patterns, and marketing researchers may obtain such data from the supermarkets.

Observation is straightforward and avoids a central problem of survey methods: motivating respondents to state their true feelings or opinions. However, observation tends to be descriptive. When it is the only method of data collection, it may not provide insights into causal relationships. Another drawback is that analyses based on observation are subject to the biases of the observer or the limitations of the mechanical device.

Interpreting Research Findings

After collecting data to test their hypotheses, marketers need to interpret the research findings. Interpretation of the data is easier if marketers carefully plan their data-analysis methods early in the research process. They also should allow for continual evaluation of the data during the entire collection period. They can then gain valuable insight into areas that should be probed during the formal interpretation.

The first step in drawing conclusions from most research is to display the data in table format. If marketers intend to apply the results to individual categories of the things or people being studied, cross-tabulation may be quite useful, especially in tabulating joint occurrences. For example, using the two variables gender and purchase rates of automobile tires, a cross-tabulation could show how men and women differ in purchasing automobile tires.

Mystery Shoppers Uncover Information

I n the 1940s, a number of companies began to use volunteer "mystery shoppers" to visit their retail establishments and report back on whether the stores were adhering to the companies' standards of service. These volunteer shoppers were unrecognizable to employees and often were willing to work for small fees or free items. Many companies employed mystery shoppers by the 1990s, but their use of them remained sporadic. Today there are about 500 companies in the $600 million industry that hire mystery shoppers to evaluate all kinds of goods and services for corporate clients. They are especially prevalent in the retail, banking, fast-food, and service-station sectors. Krispy Kreme Doughnuts, for example, employs mystery shoppers to evaluate its shops in England and help the firm recognize employees delivering excellent customer service.

Mystery shoppers enter establishments pretending to be regular customers. They scrutinize not only how they are treated but also how the stores appear. Some actually use digital cameras and computer equipment to document these observations. Many mystery shoppers work on a part-time basis and do so to earn free merchandise, meals, movies, and other goods. A few actually work full time. These mystery shoppers engage in meaningful observations to improve the implementation of marketing strategy. Companies rely on the information provided by mystery shoppers to ensure that employees are following company guidelines. Some companies actually base company bonuses on employee performance during mystery inspections. Although a number of companies are now using online and phone customer surveys to judge performance—a practice that costs far less than employing mystery shoppers—many companies still rely on these mystery inspections and feel that the results help them raise the bottom line—customer satisfaction.[c]

After the data are tabulated, they must be analyzed. **Statistical interpretation** focuses on what is typical or what deviates from the average. It indicates how widely responses vary and how they are distributed in relation to the variable being measured. When marketers interpret statistics, they must take into account estimates of expected error or deviation from the true values of the population. The analysis of data may lead researchers to accept or reject the hypothesis being studied.

Reporting Research Findings

The final step in the marketing research process is to report the research findings. Before preparing the report, the marketer must take a clear, objective look at the findings to see how well the gathered facts answer the research question or support or negate the initial hypotheses. In most cases it is extremely unlikely that the study can provide everything needed to answer the research question. Thus the researcher must point out the deficiencies, along with the reasons for them, in the report.

The report of research results is usually a formal, written document. Researchers must allow time for the writing task when they plan and schedule the project. Because the report is a means of communicating with the decision makers who will use the research findings, researchers need to determine beforehand how much detail and supporting data to include. They should keep in mind that corporate executives prefer reports that are short, clear, and simply expressed. Researchers often give their

statistical interpretation
Analysis of what is typical or what deviates from the average

summary and recommendations first, especially if decision makers do not have time to study how the results were obtained. A technical report allows its users to analyze data and interpret recommendations because it describes the research methods and procedures and the most important data gathered. Thus researchers must recognize the needs and expectations of the report user and adapt to them.

Using Technology to Improve Marketing Information Gathering and Analysis

Technology is making information for marketing decisions increasingly accessible. The ability of marketers to track customer buying behavior and to discern what buyers want is changing the nature of marketing. Customer relationship management is being enhanced by integrating data from all customer contacts and combining that information to improve customer retention. Information technology permits internal research and quick information gathering to understand and satisfy customers. For example, company responses to e-mail complaints, as well as to communications through mail, telephone, and fax, can be used to improve customer satisfaction, retention, and value.[33] Armed with such information, marketers can fine-tune marketing mixes to satisfy the needs of their customers.

The integration of telecommunications and computer technologies is allowing marketers to access a growing array of valuable information sources related to industry forecasts, business trends, and customer buying behavior. Electronic communication tools can be used effectively to gain accurate information with minimal customer interaction. Most marketing researchers have e-mail, voice mail, teleconferencing, and fax machines at their disposal. In fact, many firms use marketing information systems and customer relationship management technologies to network all these technologies and organize all the marketing data available to them. In this section we look at marketing information systems and specific technologies that are helping marketing researchers obtain and manage marketing research data.

Marketing Information Systems

A **marketing information system (MIS)** is a framework for the day-to-day management and structuring of information gathered regularly from sources both inside and outside an organization. An MIS provides a continuous flow of information about prices, advertising expenditures, sales, competition, and distribution expenses. Anheuser-Bush, for example, uses a system called BudNet that compiles information about past sales at individual stores, inventory, competitors' displays and prices, and a host of other information collected by distributors' sales representatives on handheld computers. BudNet allows managers to respond quickly to changes in social trends or competitors' strategies with an appropriate promotional message, package, display, or discount.[34]

The main focus of the MIS is on data storage and retrieval, as well as on computer capabilities and management's information requirements. Regular reports of sales by product or market categories, data on inventory levels, and records of salespeople's activities are examples of information that is useful in making decisions. In the MIS, the means of *gathering* data receive less attention than do the procedures for expediting the *flow* of information.

An effective MIS starts by determining the objective of the information, that is, by identifying decision needs that require certain information. The firm then can specify an information system for continuous monitoring to provide regular, pertinent information on both the external and internal environment. FedEx, for example, has developed interactive marketing systems to provide instantaneous communication between the company and its customers. Through use of the telephone and Internet, customers can track their packages and receive immediate feedback concerning delivery. The

marketing information system (MIS) A framework for the management and structuring of information gathered regularly from sources inside and outside an organization

A Web solution this **BIG** will drive even **BIGGER** results.

VISIT
http://BIG2.blackbaud.info

Shorten the distance between you and your supporters with:

Blackbaud®
NetCommunity™
Groundbreaking Web site management

- Multiple tools to help build relationships and raise funds online
- Personalized Web content and eMarketing
- Single online and offline constituent database
- Event registration and "sponsor me" fundraising
- Integrated advocacy
- True integration with The Raiser's Edge®

http://BIG2.blackbaud.info

Blackbaud

800.443.9441 • solutions@blackbaud.com

Using Technology

Blackbaud provides high-tech audience response systems to assist in data collection.

single-source data Information provided by a single marketing research firm

marketing decision support system (MDSS) Customized computer software that aids marketing managers in decision making

company's website provides valuable information about customer usage, and it allows customers to express directly what they think about company services. The evolving telecommunications and computer technology is allowing marketing information systems to cultivate one-to-one relationships with customers.

Databases

Most marketing information systems include internal databases. As we saw in Chapter 4, databases allow marketers to tap into an abundance of information useful in making marketing decisions: internal sales reports, newspaper articles, company news releases, government economic reports, bibliographies, and more, typically accessed through a computer system. Information technology has made it possible to develop databases to guide strategic planning and help improve customer services. When Pulte Homes, the nation's top homebuilder, analyzed information in its database, it realized that 80 percent of its home buyers were selecting the same countertops, carpet, fixtures, lighting, etc. The company used this information to streamline its 2,000 floorplans and reduce the number of fixtures and other home features to better match customer desires and to improve overall efficiency and decision making.[35] Many commercial websites require consumers to register and provide personal information to access the site or make a purchase. Frequent flier programs permit airlines to ask loyal customers to participate in surveys about their needs and desires, and the airlines can track their best customers' flight patterns by time of day, week, month, and year. Grocery stores gain a significant amount of data through checkout scanners tied to store discount cards. According to ACNielsen, 78 percent of U.S. households now use at least one store discount card.[36] In fact, one of the best ways to predict market behavior is the use of database information gathered through loyalty programs or other transaction-based processes.[37]

Marketing researchers also can use commercial databases developed by information research firms such as Lexis-Nexis to obtain useful information for marketing decisions. Many of these commercial databases are accessible online for a fee. They also can be obtained in printed form or on CD-ROMs. In most commercial databases, the user typically does a computer search by keyword, topic, or company, and the database service generates abstracts, articles, or reports that can be printed out. Accessing multiple reports or a complete article may cost extra.

Information provided by a single firm on household demographics, purchases, television viewing behavior, and responses to promotions such as coupons and free samples is called **single-source data**.[38] For example, Behavior Scan, offered by Information Resources, Inc., screens about 60,000 households in 26 U.S. markets. This single-source information service monitors consumer household televisions and records the programs and commercials watched. When buyers from these households shop in stores equipped with scanning registers, they present Hotline cards (similar to credit cards) to cashiers. This enables each customer's identification to be electronically coded so that the firm can track each product purchased and store the information in a database.

Marketing Decision Support Systems

A **marketing decision support system (MDSS)** is customized computer software that aids marketing managers in decision making by helping them anticipate the effects of certain decisions. Some MDSSs have a broader range and offer greater computational and modeling capabilities than spreadsheets; they let managers explore a greater number of alternatives. For example, an MDSS can determine how sales and profits might be affected by higher or lower interest rates or how sales forecasts, advertising expenditures, production levels, and the like might affect overall profits. For this reason, MDSS software often is a major component of a company's MIS. Customized decision support systems can support a customer orientation and customer satisfaction in business marketing.[39] Some MDSSs incorporate artificial intelligence and other advanced computer technologies.

Issues in Marketing Research

The Importance of Ethical Marketing Research

Marketing managers and other professionals are relying more and more on marketing research, marketing information systems, and new technologies to make better decisions. It is therefore essential that professional standards be established by which to judge the reliability of such research. Such standards are necessary because of the ethical and legal issues that develop in gathering marketing research data. In the area of online interaction, for example, consumers remain wary of how the personal information collected by marketers will be used, especially whether it will be sold to third parties. In addition, the relationships between research suppliers, such as marketing research agencies, and the marketing managers who make strategy decisions require ethical behavior. Organizations such as the Marketing Research Association have developed codes of conduct and guidelines to promote ethical marketing research. To be effective, such guidelines must instruct those who participate in marketing research on how to avoid misconduct. Table 6.6 recommends explicit steps interviewers should follow when introducing a questionnaire.

International Issues in Marketing Research

Sociocultural, economic, political, legal, and technological forces vary in different regions of the world, and these variations create challenges for organizations attempting to understand foreign customers through marketing research. The marketing research process we describe in this chapter is used globally, but to ensure

table 6.6   GUIDELINES FOR QUESTIONNAIRE INTRODUCTION

Questionnaire introduction should

- Allow interviewers to introduce themselves by name.
- State the name of the research company.
- Indicate that this questionnaire is a marketing research project.
- Explain that no sales will be involved.
- Note the general topic of discussion (if this is a problem in a "blind" study, a statement such as "consumer opinion" is acceptable).
- State the likely duration of the interview.
- Ensure the anonymity of the respondent and the confidentiality of all answers.
- State the honorarium if applicable (for many business-to-business and medical studies, this is done up front for both qualitative and quantitative studies).
- Reassure the respondent with a statement such as, "There are no right or wrong answers, so please give thoughtful and honest answers to each question" (recommended by many clients).

Source: Reprinted with permission of The Marketing Research Association, P.O. Box 230, Rocky Hill, CT 06067-0230, (860) 257-4008.

that the research is valid and reliable, data-gathering methods may have to be modified to allow for regional differences. For example, experts have found that Latin Americans do not respond well to focus groups or in-depth interviews lasting more than 90 minutes. Researchers therefore need to adjust their tactics to generate information useful for marketing products in Latin America.[40] To ensure that global and regional differences are addressed satisfactorily, many companies retain a research firm with experience in the country of interest. Most of the largest marketing research firms derive a significant share of their revenues from research conducted outside the United States. VNU, the largest marketing research firm in the world, receives 99 percent of its revenues from outside the United States.[41]

Experts recommend a two-pronged approach to international marketing research. The first phase involves a detailed search for and analysis of secondary data to gain greater understanding of a particular marketing environment and to pinpoint issues that must be taken into account in gathering primary research data. Secondary data can be particularly helpful in building a general understanding of the market, including economic, legal, cultural, and demographic issues, as well as in assessing the risks of doing business in that market and in forecasting demand.[42] Marketing researchers often begin by studying country trade reports from the U.S. Department of Commerce, as well as country-specific information from local sources, such as a country's website, and trade and general business publications such as *The Wall Street Journal*. These sources can offer insight into the marketing environment in a particular country and even can indicate untapped market opportunities abroad.

The second phase involves field research using many of the methods described earlier, including focus groups and telephone surveys, to refine a firm's understanding of specific customer needs and preferences. Specific differences among countries can have a profound influence on data gathering. For example, in-home (door-to-door) interviews are illegal in some countries. In China, few people have regular telephone lines, making telephone surveys both impractical and nonrepresentative of the total population. Primary data gathering may have a greater chance of success if the firm employs local researchers who better understand how to approach potential respondents and can do so in their own language.[43] Regardless of the specific methods used to gather primary data, whether in the United States or abroad, the goal is to understand the needs of specific target markets and thus craft the best marketing strategy to satisfy the needs of customers in each market, as we will see in the next chapter.

...And now, back to the Internet

Internet-based surveys have become the dominant mode of quantitative marketing research, and the full ramifications for the industry are now becoming apparent. The rush to accept online research has been possible because of the swift acceptance of the Internet. At least two-thirds of Americans now have access to the Internet, and there has been a declining response rate in the former dominant method of research, namely, the telephone. The Internet permits companies to conduct research faster, cheaper, and with greater interactivity with survey respondents. However, some have questioned the quality of online research. Others believe that survey respondents prefer—and are more thoughtful—in answering online surveys, whereas skeptics believe that opt-in panels do not really represent projectionable populations.

Among the major concerns about online surveys is the fact that there are so many online panels, and because it is so cost-effective to build them, research suppliers could be using the same respondents without knowing it. There is even concern about the emergence of "professional" respondents who sit at home and take a lot of surveys: How do marketers know that they are surveying who they think they are surveying? Despite these concerns, most companies are not worried about the data they collect from online surveys and plan to continue to use the Internet for collecting data in the future.

The Internet has made it easy for consumers to use search engines and shopping comparison sites to check prices and find the lowest price. After these online searches, however, as much as 90 percent of buying *actually* occurs offline. This indicates that offline retailers who are not the lowest-priced suppliers in their market need to develop a unique marketing position to ensure that they continue to survive and compete. Marketers therefore are recognizing that multichannel retailers—those with both bricks-and-mortar stores and online websites—may have an advantage. Consumers are increasingly likely to do their research online and then go to a store to view the actual product. Indeed, traffic at multichannel retail stores such as Target, Wal-Mart, and Kmart has exploded. Retailers that are solely online, such as Overstock, Amazon, and eBay, have found that their competition is no longer just online retailers; it is bricks-and-mortar stores as well. Research also has highlighted the fact that 63 percent of U.S. Internet users perform local searches online every month. Of those, 41 percent were searching for something in their home area, 47 percent visited a local merchant as a result of their search, 41 percent made offline contact, and 37 percent made contact online as a result of their search. In other words, the Internet is far more than just a way to buy products: It is also a way for consumers to research products and for marketers to research consumers.[44]

1. How reliable do you think data collected over the Internet is?

2. What advantages does the Internet have over other survey methods such as the telephone?

3. What privacy issues arise with tracking consumers online?

CHAPTER REVIEW

1. Define *marketing research* and understand its importance.

Marketing research is the systematic design, collection, interpretation, and reporting of information to help marketers solve specific marketing problems or take advantage of marketing opportunities. Marketing research can help a firm to better understand market opportunities, ascertain the potential for success for new products, and determine the feasibility of a particular marketing strategy. The value of marketing research is measured by improvements in a marketer's ability to make decisions.

2. Describe the basic steps in conducting market research.

To maintain the control needed to obtain accurate information, marketers approach marketing research as a process with logical steps: (1) defining and locating issues or problems, (2) designing the research project, (3) collecting data, (4) interpreting research findings, and (5) reporting research findings. The first step, issue or problem definition, focuses on uncovering the nature and boundaries of a situation or question related to marketing strategy or implementation. The second step involves designing a research project to obtain needed information, formulating a hypothesis, and determining what type of research to employ that will test the hypothesis so that the results are reliable and valid. Marketers conduct exploratory research when they need more information about a problem or want to make a tentative hypothesis more specific; they use conclusive research to verify insights through an objective procedure. Research is considered reliable if it produces almost identical results in successive repeated trials; it is valid if it measures what it is supposed to measure and not something else. The third step is the data-gathering phase. To apply research data to decision making, marketers must interpret and report their findings properly—the final two steps in the research process. Statistical interpretation focuses on what is typical or what deviates from the average. After interpreting the research findings, the researchers must prepare a report on the findings that the decision makers can understand and use.

3. Explore the fundamental methods of gathering data for marketing research.

For the third step in the marketing research process, two types of data are available. Primary data are observed and recorded or collected directly from subjects; secondary data are compiled inside or outside the organization for some purpose other than the current investigation. Secondary data may be collected from an organization's database and other internal sources or from periodicals, government publications, online, and unpublished sources. Methods for collecting primary data include sampling, surveys, observation, and experimentation. Sampling involves selecting representative units from a total population. In probability sampling, every element in the population being studied has a known chance of being selected for study. Nonprobability sampling is more subjective because there is no way to calculate the likelihood that a specific element of the population being studied will be chosen. Marketing researchers employ sampling to collect primary data through surveys by mail, telephone, or the Internet or through personal or group interviews. A carefully constructed questionnaire is essential to the success of any survey. In using observation methods, researchers record respondents' overt behavior and take note of physical conditions and events but avoid direct contact with respondents. In an experiment, marketing researchers attempt to maintain certain variables while measuring the effects of experimental variables.

4. Describe how tools such as databases, decision support systems, and the Internet facilitate marketing information systems and research.

Many firms use computer technology to create a marketing information system (MIS), which is a framework for gathering and managing information from sources both inside and outside the organization. A database is a collection of information arranged for easy access and retrieval. A marketing decision support system (MDSS) is customized computer software that aids marketing managers in decision making by helping them anticipate what effect certain decisions will have. The World Wide Web also enables marketers to communicate with customers and obtain information.

5. Identify key ethical and international considerations in marketing research.

Eliminating unethical marketing research practices and establishing generally acceptable procedures for conducting research are important goals of marketing research. International marketing uses the same marketing research process, but data-gathering methods may require modification to address differences.

Please visit the student website at **www.prideferrell.com** for ACE Self-Test questions that will help you prepare for exams.

ACE self-test

KEY CONCEPTS

marketing research
research design
hypothesis
exploratory research
conclusive research
descriptive research
experimental research
reliability
validity

primary data
secondary data
population
sample
sampling
probability sampling
random sampling
stratified sampling
nonprobability sampling

quota sampling
mail survey
telephone survey
online survey
personal-interview survey
in-home (door-to-door) interview
focus-group interview
customer advisory boards

telephone depth interview
shopping-mall intercept interview
statistical interpretation
marketing information system (MIS)
single-source data
marketing decision support system (MDSS)

ISSUES FOR DISCUSSION AND REVIEW

1. What is marketing research? Why is it important?

2. Describe the five steps in the marketing research process.

3. What is the difference between defining a research problem and developing a hypothesis?

4. Describe the different types of approaches to marketing research, and indicate when each should be used.

5. Where are data for marketing research obtained? Give examples of internal and external data.

6. What is the difference between probability sampling and nonprobability sampling? In what situation would it be best to use random sampling? Stratified sampling? Quota sampling?

7. Suggest some ways to encourage respondents to cooperate in mail surveys.

8. Describe some marketing problems that could be solved through information gained from observation.

9. What is a marketing information system, and what should it provide?

10. How does marketing research in other countries differ from marketing research in the United States?

MARKETING APPLICATIONS

1. After observing customers' traffic patterns, Bashas Markets repositioned the greeting card section in its stores, and card sales increased substantially. To increase sales for the following types of companies, what information might marketing researchers want to gather from customers?
   a. Furniture stores
   b. Gasoline outlets/service stations
   c. Investment companies
   d. Medical clinics

2. Choose a company in your city or town that you think might benefit from a research project. Develop a research question and outline a method to approach this question. Explain why you think the research question is relevant to the organization and why the particular methodology is suited to the question and the company.

3. Input for marketing information systems can come from internal or external sources. Indicate two firms or companies in your city or town that might benefit from internal sources and two that would benefit from external sources, and explain why they would benefit. Suggest the type of information each should gather.

4. Suppose that you were opening a health insurance brokerage firm and wanted to market your services to small businesses with fewer than 50 employees.

Determine which database for marketing information you would use in your marketing efforts, and explain why you would use it.

Online Exercise

5. The World Association of Opinion and Marketing Research Professionals [founded as the European Society for Opinion and Marketing Research (ESOMAR) in 1948] is a nonprofit association for marketing research professionals. The European organization promotes the use of opinion and marketing research to improve marketing decisions in companies worldwide and works to protect personal privacy in the research process. Visit the association's website at **www.esomar.org/**.
   a. How can ESOMAR help marketing professionals conduct research to guide marketing strategy?
   b. How can ESOMAR help marketers protect the privacy of research subjects when conducting marketing research in other countries?
   c. ESOMAR introduced the first professional code of conduct for marketing research professionals in 1948. The association continues to update the document to address new technology and other changes in the marketing environment. According to ESOMAR's code, what are the specific professional responsibilities of marketing researchers?

For a marketing research company, an important element in gathering data for a market is the level of information technology infrastructure that exists. NationMaster.com's website offers a subcategory of personal computers that can provide insight on the level of personal computer usage in a country. Use the search term "compare various statistics" at **http://globaledge.msu.edu/ibrd** (and check the box "Resource Desk only") to reach NationMaster.com, and then select the "Media" category and then the subcategory of "Personal Computers (PCs)." Give a summary of the top 15 countries as ranked by the number of PCs used. From this specified list of markets, include an assessment of the three countries with the most and least access to PCs. What conclusions can you make?

Video CASE

Research Design at LSPMA

L ake, Snell, Perry, Mermin & Associates, Inc. (LSPMA), is a national public opinion and political strategy research firm. Its expertise is conducting objective opinion polls to assess the attitudes and behaviors of important target groups that are the concern of its clients. The Washington, D.C.–based firm has become nationally recognized for its knowledge of women's, youth's, children's, and environmental political issues. Among the company's clients are the Democratic National Committee (DNC), the Democratic Governor's Association (DGA), the Sierra Club, Planned Parenthood, Human Rights Campaign, Emily's List, and the Kaiser Foundation. LSPMA also conducts regular polls for *U.S. News & World Report,* and with the Terrance Group, the Battleground Poll surveys the year's political landscape and draws attention to critical issues that Washington insiders can't afford to ignore. In 2005, LPSMA acquired the Washington, D.C.–and San Diego–based polling firm Decision Research, giving it even greater capacity to conduct research for both business and political clients.

LPSMA's primary goal is to discover what the public thinks for people who want to know. It is among the Democratic Party's leading strategists, serving as tacticians and senior advisors to dozens of political incumbents and challengers at all levels of the electoral process, as well as to a wide range of advocacy organizations, nonprofit organizations, and foundations. Its client base is split evenly among three groups: political candidates such as senators and governors; progressive-issue organizations that want research on social issues such as poverty, education, health care, and teen pregnancy; and foundations or major institutions such as the American Cancer Society.

Through research techniques, including reconnaissance and espionage, LSPMA's job is to present hard data regarding what specific segments of the public think about certain issues or candidates. LSPMA's work helps clients to identify potential problems or opportunities and to determine what strategies and messages would best help them achieve their goals and reach their target audiences. It is important to know what different segments of the population think, feel, and need so that advertising then can be targeted at the people that organizations want to target. LSPMA uses a variety of different methods, including telephone interviews, online polls, and focus groups, to create portraits of groups of people, such as "soccer moms," "waitress moms," or "NASCAR dads," so that its clients can understand those segments and what they think of and recognize as important trends.

Research allows LSMPA's clients to know what Americans are thinking and helps them to determine how to target those segments of the population who are likely to think their firm has the right product or the right candidate. It allows clients to understand where they are most vulnerable and where they have the greatest opportunities to gain more support. By knowing which people feel strongly, which are sitting on the fence, and which changed their opinion when given certain pieces of information about certain issues or characteristics, it is possible to segment people depending on what they think and how they act and behave. Once organizations know whom to target and which issues are most important to those they wish to target, they can narrow their approach down to the least expensive to accomplish their goals.

There are many reasons to segment the public; the primary one is simply because people are different. Segmentation enables marketers and pollsters to cluster like-minded people together and really trying to understand who they are. It is then possible to craft a message that precisely targets a particular audience. Markets can be segmented by age, gender, education, region of the country, income, or race to create new ways of looking at a group that tends to behave similarly.

There are pitfalls to segmentation, however. It sometimes can make people seem more diverse than they actually are. For example, women agree on 80 percent of things and have views that are similar. Segmentation can only help an individual or organization so much; the rest depends on the hottest new trends. Few groups are static or truly homogeneous, which means that continuous research is necessary to remain up to date with changes in attitudes and behaviors and to ensure that messages still reach their target audience.

Like all marketing research firms, LSPMA has a plan that details the questions that will be asked, of whom, where, and the time frame and cost. It enables the firm to know what it has to do and how to do it. All research firms are creating information for more informed understanding and decisions regardless of the client.[45]

Questions for Discussion

1. Why do political organizations need marketing research conducted by LSPMA?

2. What is the relationship between marketing research conducted by LSPMA and identifying the needs and wants of specific market segments?

3. Why would a business rely on a marketing research firm that is heavily into political polling?

CHAPTER 7

Target Markets: Segmentation and Evaluation

IKEA's Leksvik and Klippan Sofas: Coming to a Living Room Near You

For more than 60 years, the Swedish firm IKEA has marketed simple but stylish home furnishings for cost-conscious customers who don't mind assembling their purchases to save money. Ingvar Kamprad, who founded the company, came up with its name by combining his initials (I. K.) plus the first letters of Elmtaryd and Agunnaryd, the farm and village where he grew up. In addition to welcoming shoppers to its stores, IKEA invites customers to shop online and through its catalogs. While traditional furniture stores display beautiful home furnishings for high-end customers with deep pockets and little inclination to attach legs to a table or bolt together a bed frame, IKEA's strategy is "to offer a wide range of home furnishings with good design and function at prices so low that as many people as possible will be able to afford them." Its products are of wide range—from frying pans and lamps to kitchen cabinets and living room suites—and come in styles that can be coordinated easily.

To keep prices low for its thrifty customers, IKEA is relentless in looking for ways to cut costs in manufacturing, marketing, warehousing, raw materials, and sales and then pass the savings along. For example, it buys raw materials in bulk and searches the world for efficient suppliers to keep per-unit costs low. It uses a special software package to collect price quotes from suppliers and to streamline the purchasing process. For a company that buys from 1,300 suppliers in 53 countries, even small efficiencies quickly add up to significant savings. More cost savings come from shipping furniture unassembled in flat boxes and having customers assemble their purchases at home. The company first began testing the flat packages in 1956 as a measure to increase the number of items shipped in one truck, reduce storage space, reduce labor costs, and avoid transport damage. However, low costs are not the only consideration. IKEA also requires its suppliers to abide by a code of conduct that forbids child labor, sets minimum standards for working conditions, and protects the environment.

Although IKEA's customers are frugal, they want fashionable furniture that fits their personalities and lifestyles. In fact, the store's appeal cuts across demographic lines. Some customers who

OBJECTIVES

1. Learn what a market is.

2. Understand the differences among general targeting strategies.

3. Become familiar with the major segmentation variables.

4. Know what segment profiles are and how they are used.

5. Understand how to evaluate market segments.

6. Identify the factors that influence the selection of specific market segments for use as target markets.

7. Become familiar with sales forecasting methods.

can well afford to shop at the most expensive furniture stores come to IKEA because they like the combination of chic design, down-to-earth functionality, and speedy assembly. Not every item must be assembled, but those that do are accompanied by simple, step-by-step instructions that reassure even the most inexperienced do-it-yourselfer. If customers get hungry as they walk through one of IKEA's cavernous stores, they can drop into the informal store restaurant for a quick snack or a light meal of delicacies from IKEA's home country. The most popular dish is Swedish meatballs: Customers devour 150 million of these tiny meatballs every year.[1] ∎

To compete effectively, IKEA has singled out specific customer groups toward which it directs its marketing efforts. Any organization that wants to succeed must identify its customers and develop and maintain marketing mixes that satisfy the needs of those customers.

In this chapter we explore markets and market segmentation. Initially we define the term *market* and discuss the major requirements of a market. Then we examine the steps in the target-market selection process, including identifying the appropriate targeting strategy, determining which variables to use for segmenting consumer and business markets, developing market segment profiles, evaluating relevant market segments, and selecting target markets. Finally, we discuss various methods for developing sales forecasts.

What Is a Market?

In Chapter 2 we defined a *market* as a group of people who, as individuals or as organizations, have needs for products in a product class and have the ability, willingness, and authority to purchase such products. Students, for example, are part of the market for textbooks; they are also part of the markets for computers, clothes, food, music, and other products. Individuals can have the desire, the buying power, and the willingness to purchase certain products but may not have the authority to do so. For example, teenagers may have the desire, the money, and the willingness to buy liquor, but a liquor producer does not consider them a market because teenagers are prohibited by law from buying alcoholic beverages. A group of people that lacks any one of the four requirements thus does not constitute a market.

Markets fall into one of two categories: consumer markets and business markets. These categories are based on the characteristics of the individuals and groups that make up a specific market and the purposes for which they buy products. A **consumer market** consists of purchasers and household members who intend to consume or benefit from the purchased products and do not buy products for the main purpose of making a profit. Consumer markets are sometimes also referred to as *business-to-consumer* (B2C) *markets.* Each of us belongs to numerous consumer markets. The millions of individuals with the ability, willingness, and authority to buy make up a multitude of consumer markets for products such as housing, food, clothing, vehicles, personal services, appliances, furniture, recreational equipment, and so on, as we shall see in Chapter 8.

A **business market** consists of individuals or groups that purchase a specific kind of product for one of three purposes: resale, direct use in producing other products, or use in general daily operations. For example, a lamp producer that buys electrical wire to use in the production of lamps is part of a business market for electrical wire. This same firm purchases dust mops to clean its office areas. Although the mops are not used in the direct production of lamps, they are used in the operations of the firm; thus this manufacturer is part of a business market for dust mops. Business markets also may be called *business-to-business* (B2B), *industrial,* or *organizational markets.* They also can be classified into producer, reseller, government, and institutional markets, as we shall see in Chapter 9.

consumer market Purchasers and household members who intend to consume or benefit from the purchased products and do not buy products to make profits

business market Individuals or groups that purchase a specific kind of product for resale, direct use in producing other products, or use in general daily operations

Consumer and Business Markets

New Belgium Brewery aims its advertising at consumer markets with the tagline "Follow your folly."

Target-Market Selection Process

In Chapter 1 we indicated that the first of two major components for developing a marketing strategy is to select a target market. Although marketers may employ several methods for target-market selection, generally they use a five-step process. This process is shown in Figure 7.1, and we discuss it in the following sections.

Step 1: Identify the Appropriate Targeting Strategy

A target market is a group of people or organizations for which a business creates and maintains a marketing mix specifically designed to satisfy the needs of group members. The strategy used to select a target market is affected by target-market needs and characteristics, product attributes, and the organization's objectives and resources. Figure 7.2 (on page 158) illustrates the three basic targeting strategies: undifferentiated, concentrated, and differentiated.

figure 7.1

TARGET-MARKET SELECTION PROCESS

1 Identify the appropriate targeting strategy

2 Determine which segmentation variables to use

3 Develop market segment profiles

4 Evaluate relevant market segments

5 Select specific target markets

figure 7.2

TARGETING STRATEGIES

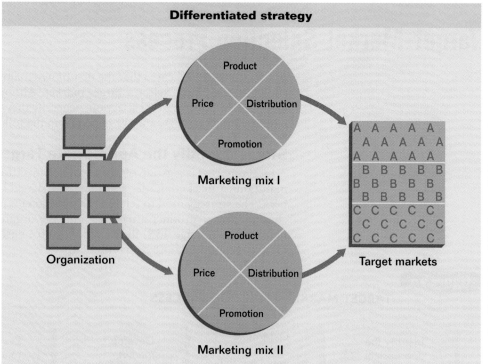

The letters in each target market represent potential customers. Customers with the same letters have similar characteristics and similar product needs.

Undifferentiated Targeting Strategy.   An organization sometimes defines an entire market for a particular product as its target market. When a company designs a single marketing mix and directs it at the entire market for a particular product, it is using an **undifferentiated targeting strategy.** As Figure 7.2 shows, the strategy assumes that all customers in the target market for a specific kind of product have similar needs, so the organization can satisfy most customers with a single marketing mix. This mix consists of one type of product with little or no variation, one price, one promotional program aimed at everybody, and one distribution system to reach most customers in the total market. Products marketed successfully through the undifferentiated strategy include commodities and staple food items, such as sugar and salt, and certain kinds of farm produce.

The undifferentiated targeting strategy is effective under two conditions. First, a large proportion of customers in a total market must have similar needs for the product, a situation termed a **homogeneous market.** A marketer using a single marketing mix for a total market of customers with a variety of needs would find that the marketing mix satisfies very few people. A "universal car" meant to satisfy everyone would satisfy very few customers' needs for cars because it would not provide the specific attributes a specific person wants. Second, the organization must be able to develop and maintain a single marketing mix that satisfies customers' needs. The company must be able to identify a set of needs common to most customers in a total market and have the resources and managerial skills to reach a sizable portion of that market.

The reality is that although customers may have similar needs for a few products, for most products their needs differ decidedly. In such instances, a company should use a concentrated or a differentiated strategy.

Concentrated Targeting Strategy Through Market Segmentation.   Markets made up of individuals or organizations with diverse product needs are called **heterogeneous markets.** Not everyone wants the same type of car, furniture, or clothes. Consider that some individuals want an economical car, whereas others desire a status symbol, and still others seek a roomy and comfortable vehicle. Thus the automobile market is heterogeneous.

For such heterogeneous markets, market segmentation is appropriate. **Market segmentation** is the process of dividing a total market into groups, or segments, consisting of people or organizations with relatively similar product needs. The purpose is to enable a marketer to design a marketing mix that more precisely matches the needs of customers in the selected market segment. A **market segment** consists of individuals, groups, or organizations with one or more similar characteristics that cause them to have relatively similar product needs. For example, the automobile market is divided into many different market segments. Toyota, for instance, aims its subcompact Yaris at the economy market segment rather than all car buyers.[2] The main rationale for segmenting heterogeneous markets is that a company can more easily develop a satisfying marketing mix for a relatively small portion of a total market than develop a mix meeting the needs of all people. Market segmentation is used widely. Fast-food chains, soft-drink companies, magazine publishers, hospitals, and banks are just a few types of organizations that employ market segmentation.

For market segmentation to succeed, five conditions must exist. First, customers' needs for the product must be heterogeneous; otherwise, there is little reason to segment the market. Second, segments must be identifiable and divisible. The company must find a characteristic or variable for effectively separating individuals in a total market into groups containing people with relatively uniform needs for the product. Third, the total market should be divided so that segments can be compared with respect to estimated sales potential, costs, and profits. Fourth, at least one segment must have enough profit potential to justify developing and maintaining a special marketing mix for that segment. Finally, the company must be able to reach the chosen segment with a particular marketing mix. Some market segments may be difficult or impossible to reach because of legal, social, or distribution constraints.

undifferentiated targeting strategy A strategy in which an organization designs a single marketing mix and directs it at the entire market for a particular product

homogeneous market A market in which a large proportion of customers have similar needs for a product

heterogeneous markets Markets made up of individuals or organizations with diverse needs for products in a specific product class

market segmentation The process of dividing a total market into groups with relatively similar product needs to design a marketing mix that matches those needs

market segment Individuals, groups, or organizations with one or more similar characteristics that cause them to have similar product needs

Concentrated Targeting Strategy

Mont Blanc employs a concentrated targeting strategy by primarily aiming writing instruments at upper end market segments.

INN●VATE

STARWALKER. THE NEW GENERATION OF WRITING INSTRUMENTS FOR A NEW GENERATION IN TIME. $355.

MONT BLANC

When an organization directs its marketing efforts toward a single market segment using one marketing mix, it is employing a **concentrated targeting strategy.** Captrust Financial Advisors, for example, targets its money and asset management services at professional and retired athletes who may need to make a few years' worth of earnings last a lifetime or fund new business ventures after their retirement from sports. With several former football-players-turned-financial-advisors on staff, Captrust is uniquely positioned to build successful relationships with professional athletes who need its financial services.[3] Notice in Figure 7.2 that the organization using the concentrated strategy is aiming its marketing mix only at "B" customers.

The chief advantage of the concentrated strategy is that it allows a firm to specialize. The firm analyzes characteristics and needs of a distinct customer group and then focuses all its energies on satisfying that group's needs. A firm may generate a large sales volume by reaching a single segment. Also, concentrating on a single segment permits a firm with limited resources to compete with larger organizations that may have overlooked smaller segments.

Specialization, however, means that a company puts all its eggs in one basket, which can be risky. If a company's sales depend on a single segment and the segment's demand for the product declines, the company's financial strength also declines. When a firm penetrates one segment and becomes well entrenched, its popularity may keep it from moving into other segments. For example, it is very unlikely that Bentley could or would want to compete with General Motors in the pickup truck and sport-utility vehicle market segment.

Differentiated Targeting Strategy Through Market Segmentation.   With a **differentiated targeting strategy,** an organization directs its marketing efforts at two or more segments by developing a marketing mix for each (see Figure 7.2). After a firm uses a concentrated strategy successfully in one market segment, it sometimes expands its efforts to include additional segments. For example, Fruit of the Loom underwear traditionally has been aimed at one segment: men. However, the company now markets underwear for women and children as well. Marketing mixes for a differentiated strategy may vary according to product features, distribution methods, promotion methods, and prices.

concentrated targeting strategy A strategy in which an organization targets a single market segment using one marketing mix

differentiated targeting strategy A strategy in which an organization targets two or more segments by developing a marketing mix for each

Whole Foods' "Whole Babies"

Whole Foods Markets is taking market segmentation to another level—it's targeting customers before they're born! Since 1980, the company has targeted customers with an interest in all-natural lifestyles. Today, it is the world's leading supermarket chain specializing in natural and organic foods. The company has sales in excess of $5 billion through more than 191 stores in the United States, Canada, and the United Kingdom.

Now Whole Foods, in partnership with *Mothering* magazine, has introduced a program called "Whole Baby" that targets expectant and new mothers. The Whole Baby program helps mothers to prepare for their growing families by providing information on proper nutritional habits and on lifestyle topics ranging from prenatal care to baby's first foods.

In developing the program, Whole Foods commissioned a survey to evaluate the attitudes and interests of expectant and new mothers. When women were asked to identify their biggest concerns about having a baby, the issues most mentioned were money (56 percent), losing pregnancy weight (47 percent), and baby's health (44 percent). When asked about natural and organic foods, the survey found that 42 percent of the women thought that eating natural or organic foods was important but that 38 percent didn't know the health advantages of those foods. Armed with this information, Whole Baby was developed to help new mothers learn about the benefits of healthier foods and lifestyles.

The program consists of free educational booklets available at Whole Foods Market stores. These guides contain money-saving coupons for the natural products that most appeal to mothers and information about parenting, as well as important nutritional information for pregnant women and new mothers. The program also includes free Whole Baby sample kits. These reusable tote bags contain product samples, information, and special offers from a variety of sponsors such as Burt's Bees, Earth's Best, Hylands, *Mothering* magazine, Seventh Generation, Stonyfield Farms, and Traditional Medicinals that can be redeemed at Whole Foods Market stores.

Whole Foods Market is also partnering with *Mothering* magazine to offer a Whole Baby lecture series in New York City, Philadelphia, Chicago, and Atlanta. These free talks provide new mothers with everything they need to know about natural foods, nourishment, raising healthy children, and breast-feeding.

Whole Foods Markets knows that the birth of a baby often gets new parents thinking about adopting healthier lifestyles. The Whole Baby program seems to be a natural for introducing this target market to Whole Foods.[a]

A firm may increase sales in the aggregate market through a differentiated strategy because its marketing mixes are aimed at more people. For example, the Gap, which established its retail clothes reputation by targeting people under age 25, now targets multiple age segments, from infants to people over age 60 with Gap, Banana Republic, and Old Navy stores, each with appropriately chosen merchandise. The company's newest retail venture, Forth & Towne, is aimed at women age 35 and up.[4] A company with excess production capacity may find a differentiated strategy advantageous because the sale of products to additional segments may absorb excess capacity. On the other hand, a differentiated strategy often demands more production processes, materials, and people. Thus production and costs may be higher than with a concentrated strategy.

Step 2: Determine Which Segmentation Variables to Use

segmentation variables
Characteristics of individuals, groups, or organizations used to divide a market into segments

Segmentation variables are the characteristics of individuals, groups, or organizations used to divide a market into segments. For example, location, age, gender, and rate of product usage all can be bases for segmenting markets. Most marketers use several variables in combination. Haggar Clothing, for example, is targeting slacks at men (gender) between the ages of 30 and 45 (age) with new products and light-hearted advertisements featuring older male models.[5]

To select a segmentation variable, several factors are considered. The segmentation variable should relate to customers' needs for, uses of, or behavior toward the product. Stereo marketers might segment the stereo market based on income and age but not based on religion because people's stereo needs do not differ due to religion. If individuals or organizations in a total market are to be classified accurately, the segmentation variable must be measurable. Age, location, and gender are measurable because such information can be obtained through observation or questioning. Segmenting a market on the basis of a variable such as intelligence, however, would be extremely difficult because this attribute is harder to measure accurately. Furthermore, a company's resources and capabilities affect the number and size of segment variables used. The type of product and degree of variation in customers' needs also dictate the number and size of segments targeted. In short, there is no best way to segment markets.

Marketers try to segment markets in ways that may help them to build and manage relationships with targeted customers. Marketing research is often necessary to acquire information about customers' preferences and interests; basic demographic information about target customers' age, income, employment status, household structure, and family roles also may be revealing. Marketers are increasingly using customer relationship management techniques to track their customers' purchases over time and to mine their databases to identify trends and develop more appropriate marketing mixes for repeat customers.

Choosing one or more segmentation variables is a critical step in targeting a market. Selecting inappropriate variables limits the chances of developing a successful marketing strategy. To help you better understand potential segmentation variables, we examine the major types of variables used to segment consumer markets and business markets.

Variables for Segmenting Consumer Markets. A marketer using segmentation to reach a consumer market can choose one or several variables from an assortment of possibilities. As Figure 7.3 shows, segmentation variables can be grouped into four categories: demographic, geographic, psychographic, and behavioristic.

Gender-Based Segmentation

When determining the marketing strategy, companies like Dial often target a gender-specific segment.

figure 7.3

SEGMENTATION VARIABLES FOR CONSUMER MARKETS

Demographic variables
- Age
- Gender
- Race
- Ethnicity
- Income
- Education
- Occupation
- Family size
- Family life cycle
- Religion
- Social class

Geographic variables
- Region
- Urban, suburban, rural
- City size
- County size
- State size
- Market density
- Climate
- Terrain

Psychographic variables
- Personality attributes
- Motives
- Lifestyles

Behavioristic variables
- Volume usage
- End use
- Benefit expectations
- Brand loyalty
- Price sensitivity

Demographic Variables. Demographic characteristics that marketers commonly use in segmenting markets include age, gender, race, ethnicity, income, education, occupation, family size, family life cycle, religion, and social class. Marketers rely on these demographic characteristics because they are often closely linked to customers' needs and purchasing behavior and can be readily measured. Like demographers, a few marketers even use mortality rates. Service Corporation International (SCI), the largest U.S. funeral services company, attempts to locate its facilities in higher-income suburban areas with high mortality rates. SCI operates more than 1,400 funeral service locations, cemeteries, and crematoriums.[6]

Age is a commonly used variable for segmentation purposes. Many products are aimed at children, and not just toys. Kimberly-Clark, for example, introduced a toilet paper product, Cottonelle Kids, that helps children learn not to waste toilet paper.[7] A trip to the shopping mall highlights the fact that many retailers, including Abercrombie & Fitch, Aeropostale, and American Eagle Outfitters, target teens and very young adults. Some of these retailers are now looking to create new marketing mixes for their customers as they age by opening new concept stores targeted at 25- to 40-year-olds, such as Ruehl No. 925, Metropark, and Martin + Osa, that offer more work clothes.[8] Marketers need to be aware of age distribution and how that distribution is changing. All age groups under 55 years are expected to decrease by the year 2025, and all age categories 55 years of age and older are expected to increase. In 1970, the average age of a U.S. citizen was 27.9 years; currently, it is about 36.2 years. As Figure 7.4 (on page 164) shows, Americans 65 years of age and older spend as much as or more on health care and entertainment than Americans in the two younger age groups.

marketing ENTREPRENEURS

Samantá Joseph

HER BUSINESS: Samantá Shoes

FOUNDED: In 2003, when Joseph was 26

SUCCESS: Her shoes sold out wherever sold and grossed more than $100,000 in the first year

Samantá Joseph has been designing shoes since she was a child in Guyana. Although she graduated from Pace University with a BS in computer information science, she decided to start Samantá Shoes with her husband Kelvin to provide women with shoes that are both stylish and comfortable. She designs shoes specifically for women's feet, using a special mold, quality materials, and extra padding. The Brazilian-made shoes and boots, which range in sizes from $5^1/_2$ to 13, never have heels higher than 3 inches to avoid future foot problems. Samantá shoes have been seen on the feet of many celebrities, including Queen Latifah and Rihanna. The company is now making shoes for men as well.[b]

figure 7.4

SPENDING LEVELS OF THREE AGE GROUPS FOR SELECTED PRODUCT CATEGORIES

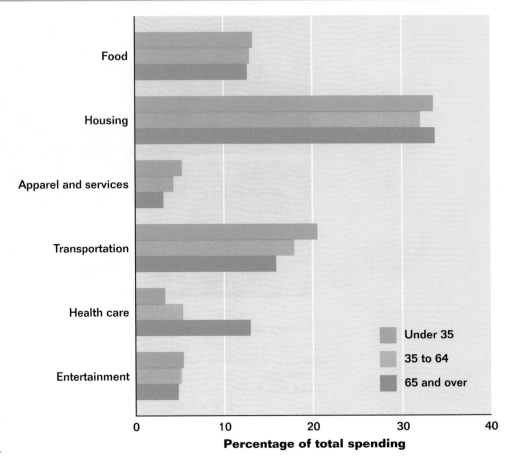

Source: "Table 3: Age of Reference Person: Average Annual Expenditures and Characteristics, Consumer Expenditure Survey 2005," U.S. Department of Labor, Bureau of Labor Statistics, 2005, www.bls.gov/cex/2005/Standard/age.pdf.

Gender is another demographic variable commonly used to segment markets, including the markets for clothing, soft drinks, nonprescription medications, toiletries, magazines, and even cigarettes. The U.S. Census Bureau reports that girls and women account for 50.7 percent and boys and men for 49.3 percent of the total U.S. population.[9] Some deodorant marketers use gender segmentation: Secret and Lady Speedstick deodorants are marketed specifically to women, whereas Old Spice and Mitchum deodorants are directed toward men.

Marketers also use race and ethnicity as variables for segmenting markets for products such as food, music, clothing, and cosmetics and for services such as banking and insurance. The U.S. Hispanic population illustrates the importance of ethnicity as a segmentation variable. Made up of people of Mexican, Cuban, Puerto Rican, and Central and South American heritage, this ethnic group is growing five times faster than the general population. Companies such as Campbell Soup, Procter & Gamble, and many others are increasingly viewing this segment as attractive because of its size and growth potential. Procter & Gamble, for example, spent some $157 million on Hispanic advertising and $52.5 million on African American advertising in 2005.[10] Asian Americans are another important subculture for many companies. Sears, for example, in an effort to better market to Asian Americans, African Americans, and Hispanics, has redesigned its apparel departments in stores located in cities with large multiethnic populations. These revisions include new in-store signage, updated merchandising displays, and new brands that appeal to an ethnically diverse audience.[11]

Se Habla Español: Banks Target Hispanics

It is estimated that more than 50 percent of the nation's 40 million Hispanics do not have checking or savings accounts. Until recently, these consumers could not cash a payroll check in a bank but had to turn instead to a check-cashing store, paying a fee of 2 to 3 percent of the check's value plus, in some cases, a transaction fee. Recognizing that the Hispanic population is growing rapidly, more financial firms are reaching out to these customers with new products.

To target Hispanics, financial companies are not just adding Spanish-speaking staff and running Spanish-language advertisements. They are increasingly offering unique products such as mortgages based on individual taxpayer ID numbers rather than Social Security numbers and intracountry fund-transfer services. Such remittance services are especially valuable for the 50 percent of Hispanic immigrants who regularly send money back to relatives in their former countries, with Mexico alone receiving nearly $20 billion annually.

Wells Fargo & Company, the nation's fourth largest bank, began targeting Hispanic customers in the nineteenth century. In addition to increasing its Spanish-speaking staff and redecorating a number of branches with Mexican themes, it also joined forces with pawn shop operator Cash America International to put check-cashing machines into grocery and convenience stores. Bank of America initiated a Spanish-language promotional campaign and introduced SafeSend, a remittance service that allows Hispanics with new Bank of America checking accounts to send money to Mexico without transfer fees.

Customers of bank-operated check-cashing stores generally report friendlier environments and lower transaction fees. By targeting an underserved market with technology and desirable products, many banks have been able to boost their profits and build relationships with more customers.[c]

Income often provides a way to divide markets because it strongly influences people's product needs. It affects their ability to buy and their desires for certain lifestyles. Product markets segmented by income include sporting goods, housing, furniture, cosmetics, clothing, jewelry, home appliances, automobiles, and electronics. While many retailers choose to target consumers with upscale incomes, some marketers are instead going after lower-income consumers with new products ranging from prepaid cell phones and debit cards to budget paper towels.[12]

Among the factors influencing household income and product needs are marital status and the presence and ages of children. These characteristics, often combined and called the *family life cycle*, affect needs for housing, appliances, food and beverages, automobiles, and recreational equipment. Family life cycles can be broken down in a number of ways. Figure 7.5 (on page 166) shows a breakdown into nine categories. The composition of the U.S. household in relation to the family life cycle has changed significantly over the last several decades. Single-parent families are on the rise, meaning that the "typical" family no longer consists of a married couple with children. Since 1970, households headed by a single mother increased from 12 to 26 percent of total family households, and that number grew from 1 to 6 percent for families headed by a single father. Another factor influencing the family life cycle is the increase in median marrying age for both women and men. The median marrying age for women has

figure 7.5

FAMILY LIFE CYCLE STAGES AS A PERCENTAGE OF ALL HOUSEHOLDS

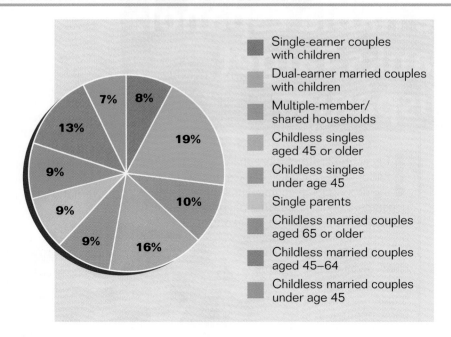

■ Single-earner couples with children

■ Dual-earner married couples with children

■ Multiple-member/ shared households

■ Childless singles aged 45 or older

■ Childless singles under age 45

■ Single parents

■ Childless married couples aged 65 or older

■ Childless married couples aged 45–64

■ Childless married couples under age 45

Source: U.S. Bureau of the Census, *Current Population Survey.*

increased from 20.8 to 25.3 years since 1970, whereas for men it increased to 27.1 from 23.2 years. More significantly, the proportion of women ages 20 to 24 years who have never been married has more than doubled over this time, and for women ages 30 to 34 years, this number has nearly tripled. Other important changes in the family life cycle include the rise in the number of people living alone and the number of unmarried couples living together.[13] Tracking these changes helps marketers to satisfy the needs of particular target markets through new marketing mixes. For example, MicroMarketing, Inc., helps companies target customers through what it calls "lifestage marketing." MicroMarketing can create a direct-mail campaign aimed at groups such as people who recently moved, soon-to-be newlyweds, recent high school and college graduates, and expectant parents. By focusing on such narrow target markets, MicroMarketing boasts a return on investments of up to 2,000 percent.[14]

Marketers also use many other demographic variables. For instance, dictionary publishing companies segment markets by education level. Some insurance companies segment markets using occupation, targeting health insurance at college students and at younger workers with small employers that do not provide health coverage.

Geographic Variables. Geographic variables—climate, terrain, city size, population density, and urban/rural areas—also influence customer product needs. Consumers in the South, for instance, rarely have need for snow tires. Markets may be divided into regions because one or more geographic variables can cause customers to differ from one region to another. A company selling products to a national market might divide the United States into the following regions: Pacific, Southwest, Central, Midwest, Southeast, Middle Atlantic, and New England. A firm operating in one or several states might regionalize its market by counties, cities, zip code areas, or other units.

City size can be an important segmentation variable. Some marketers focus efforts on cities of a certain size. For example, one franchised restaurant organization will not locate in cities of fewer than 200,000 people. It concluded that a smaller population base would result in inadequate profits. Other firms actively seek opportunities in smaller towns. A classic example is Wal-Mart, which initially located only in small towns.

Ideal for visiting
QUIET, OUT-OF-THE-WAY PLACES
like + 89° 15'50.794".

Go RVing.

Lifestyle Segmentation

GoRVing.com aims its marketing efforts at a specific lifestyle market segment.

market density The number of potential customers within a unit of land area

geodemographic segmentation Marketing segmentation that clusters people in zip code areas and smaller neighborhood units based on lifestyle and demographic information

micromarketing An approach to market segmentation in which organizations focus precise marketing efforts on very small geographic markets

Market density refers to the number of potential customers within a unit of land area, such as a square mile. Although market density relates generally to population density, the correlation is not exact. For example, in two different geographic markets of approximately equal size and population, market density for office supplies would be much higher in one area if it contained a much greater proportion of business customers than the other area. Market density may be a useful segmentation variable because low-density markets often require different sales, advertising, and distribution activities than high-density markets.

Several marketers are using geodemographic segmentation. **Geodemographic segmentation** clusters people in zip code areas and even smaller neighborhood units based on lifestyle information and especially demographic data, such as income, education, occupation, type of housing, ethnicity, family life cycle, and level of urbanization. These small, precisely described population clusters help marketers to isolate demographic units as small as neighborhoods where the demand for specific products is strongest. Geodemographic segmentation allows marketers to engage in micromarketing. **Micromarketing** is the focusing of precise marketing efforts on very small geodemographic markets, such as community and even neighborhood markets. Providers of financial and health care services, retailers, and consumer products companies use micromarketing. Special advertising campaigns, promotions, retail site-location analyses, special pricing, and unique retail product offerings are a few examples of micromarketing facilitated through geodemographic segmentation. Many retailers use micromarketing to determine the merchandise mix for individual stores. Wal-Mart is joining the micromarketing bandwagon by experimenting with tailored marketing mixes for five demographic groups: African American, affluent empty-nesters, Hispanics, suburbanites, and rural residents. The product mix for its affluent stores, for example, includes a 1,000-bottle wine department, double the organic products of its traditional stores, and an expanded home fitness equipment area—instead of a gun department.[15]

Climate is commonly used as a geographic segmentation variable because of its broad impact on people's behavior and product needs. Product markets affected by climate include air-conditioning and heating equipment, fireplace accessories, clothing, gardening equipment, recreational products, and building materials.

Psychographic Variables. Marketers sometimes use psychographic variables, such as personality characteristics, motives, and lifestyles, to segment markets. A psychographic dimension can be used by itself to segment a market or can be combined with other types of segmentation variables.

Personality characteristics can be useful for segmentation when a product resembles many competing products and consumers' needs are not significantly related to other segmentation variables. However, segmenting a market according to personality traits can be risky. Although marketing practitioners have long believed consumer choice and product use vary with personality, until recently, marketing research had indicated only weak relationships. It is hard to measure personality traits accurately, especially since most personality tests were developed for clinical use, not for segmentation purposes.

When appealing to a personality characteristic, marketers almost always select one that many people view positively. Individuals with this characteristic, as well as those who would like to have it, may be influenced to buy that marketer's brand. Marketers taking this approach do not worry about measuring how many people have the positively valued characteristic; they assume that a sizable proportion of people in the target market either have or want to have it.

When motives are used to segment a market, the market is divided according to consumers' reasons for making a purchase. Personal appearance, affiliation, status, safety, and health are examples of motives affecting the types of products purchased and the choice of stores in which they are bought. Marketing efforts based on health and fitness motives can be a point of competitive advantage. For example, Yum! Brands, Inc. (Taco Bell, Long John Silver's, Pizza Hut, KFC, and A&W Restaurants), has teamed up with Bally Total Fitness to pair a free trial membership, valued at $50, with each restaurant's better-for-you menu items. This partnership will appeal to fitness-motivated individuals and will create a link between fitness and the restaurants of Yum! Brands.[16]

Lifestyle segmentation groups individuals according to how they spend their time, the importance of things in their surroundings (homes or jobs, for example), beliefs about themselves and broad issues, and some demographic characteristics, such as income and education.[17] Lifestyle analysis provides a broad view of buyers because it encompasses numerous characteristics related to people's activities (work, hobbies, entertainment, and sports), interests (family, home, fashion, food, and technology), and opinions (politics, social issues, education, and the future). For example, home-ownership is valued by people in most income and age segments. Recent studies show, however, that 49 percent of Generation Xers (born between 1964 and 1973) own homes and account for 16.5 percent of the home furnishing market and 19.9 percent of furniture purchases. Unlike baby boomers (born 1946 to 1963), Generation X homeowners often research products for their homes on the Web and later buy those products in-store. In addition, their decisions on major home improvements are often made based on how those improvements will affect the home's resale value.[18]

One of the more popular programs studying lifestyles is conducted by the Stanford Research Institute's Value and Lifestyle Program (VALS). This program surveys U.S. consumers to select groups with identifiable values and lifestyles. Initially, VALS identified three broad consumer groups: outer-directed, inner-directed, and need-driven consumers. The current VALS classification categorizes consumers into eight basic lifestyle groups: Innovators, Thinkers, Believers, Achievers, Strivers, Experiencers, Makers, and Survivors. Figure 7.6 shows the proportion of each group that was involved in various sports activities in a recent year, according to a VALS/Mediamark Research, Inc., survey. Marketers of products related to hunting most likely would focus on the Makers, whereas marketers of products related to mountain biking most likely would target the Experiencer lifestyle segments.[19] The VALS studies have been used to create products as well as to segment markets.

Behavioristic Variables. Firms can divide a market according to some feature of consumer behavior toward a product, commonly involving some aspect of product use. For example, a market may be separated into users—classified as heavy, moderate, or light—and nonusers. To satisfy a specific group, such as heavy users, marketers may create a distinctive product, set special prices, or initiate special promotion and distribution activities. Per capita consumption data help to identify different levels of usage. For example, the Beverage Market Index shows that per capita consumption of bottled water varies from 9.0 gallons in the East Central states (Illinois, Indiana, Kentucky, Michigan, Ohio, West Virginia, and Wisconsin) to 34.5 gallons in the Southwest (Arizona, New Mexico, Oklahoma, and Texas).[20]

How customers use or apply products also may determine segmentation. To satisfy customers who use a product in a certain way, some feature—packaging, size, texture, or color—may be designed precisely to make the product easier to use, safer, or more convenient.

Benefit segmentation is the division of a market according to benefits that consumers want from the product. Although most types of market segmentation assume a relationship between the variable and customers' needs, benefit segmentation differs because the benefits customers seek *are* their product needs. For example, a customer who purchases toothpaste may be interested in cavity protection, whiter teeth, natural

benefit segmentation The division of a market according to benefits that customers want from the product

figure 7.6

VALS TYPES AND SPORTS PREFERENCES

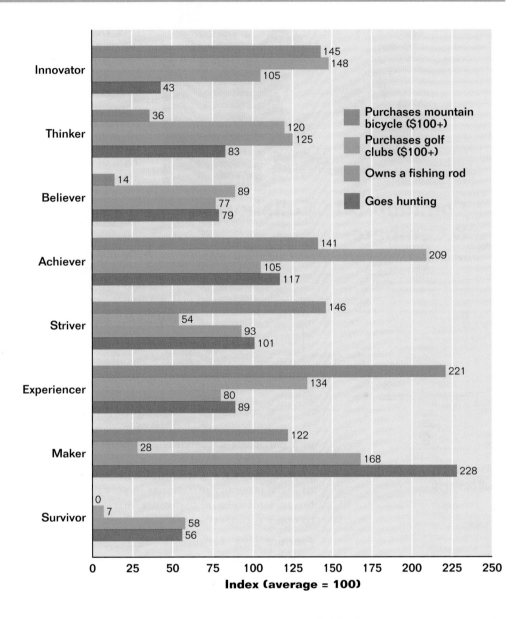

Index (average = 100)

- Purchases mountain bicycle ($100+)
- Purchases golf clubs ($100+)
- Owns a fishing rod
- Goes hunting

ingredients, or sensitive gum protection. Thus individuals are segmented directly according to their needs. By determining the desired benefits, marketers may be able to divide people into groups seeking certain sets of benefits. Dannon, for example, is targeting people who want to lose weight with its Light & Fit Crave Control probiotic yogurt.[21] The effectiveness of such segmentation depends on three conditions: The benefits sought must be identifiable; using these benefits, marketers must be able to divide people into recognizable segments; and one or more of the resulting segments must be accessible to the firm's marketing efforts. Both Timberland and Avia segment the foot apparel market based on benefits sought by purchasers.

Variables for Segmenting Business Markets.   Like consumer markets, business markets are frequently segmented, often by multiple variables in combination. Marketers segment business markets according to geographic location, type of organization, customer size, and product use.

Communicate, Collaborate & Compete

when your small business is connected by Linksys

Linksys® Small Business products provide reliable networking solutions at any stage in your company's growth. We can help you keep company data secure, connect shared storage so employees can work together, or help you save money on your phone system and phone bill.

When you're ready to grow, only Linksys offers the investment protection of the **Linksys to Cisco Trade-Up Program** – a money-back migration path to enterprise-level products.

Call Linksys now, or visit **www.Linksys.com** for more information on our business solutions, including:

• **Routing, Switching, Storage, Wireless, and Voice**
• **The Linksys One™ Integrated Data, Voice and ApplicationSolution**

To find the partner nearest you, visit **www.linksys.com/wheretobuy** or call 1-800-LINKSYS

Linksys is a registered trademark or trademark of Cisco Systems, Inc. and/or its affiliates in the U.S. and certain other countries. Copyright © 2007 Cisco Systems, Inc. All rights reserved.

CISCO.

Size Segmentation

Linksys aims a marketing mix at small business.

Geographic Location. We noted earlier that the demand for some consumer products varies considerably among geographic areas because of differences in climate, terrain, customer preferences, and similar factors. Demand for business products also varies according to geographic location. For example, producers of certain types of lumber divide their markets geographically because their customers' needs vary from region to region. Geographic segmentation may be especially appropriate for reaching industries concentrated in certain locations. Furniture and textile producers, for example, are concentrated in the Southeast.

Type of Organization. A company sometimes segments a market by types of organizations within that market. Different types of organizations often require different product features, distribution systems, price structures, and selling strategies. Given these variations, a firm may either concentrate on a single segment with one marketing mix (concentration strategy) or focus on several groups with multiple mixes (a differentiated targeting strategy). A carpet producer, for example, could segment potential customers into several groups, such as automobile makers, commercial carpet contractors (firms that carpet large commercial buildings), apartment complex developers, carpet wholesalers, and large retail carpet outlets.

Customer Size. An organization's size may affect its purchasing procedures and the types and quantities of products it wants. Size thus can be an effective variable for segmenting a business market. To reach a segment of a particular size, marketers may have to adjust one or more marketing-mix components. For example, customers who buy in extremely large quantities are sometimes offered discounts. In addition, marketers often must expand personal selling efforts to serve large organizational buyers properly. Because the needs of large and small buyers tend to be quite distinct, marketers frequently use different marketing practices to reach various customer groups.

Product Use. Certain products, especially basic raw materials such as steel, petroleum, plastics, and lumber, are used in numerous ways. How a company uses products affects the types and amounts of products purchased, as well as the purchasing method. For example, computers are used for engineering purposes, basic scientific research, and business operations such as word processing, accounting, and telecommunications. A computer maker therefore may segment the computer market by types of use because organizations' needs for computer hardware and software depend on the purpose for which products are purchased.

Step 3: Develop Market Segment Profiles

A market segment profile describes the similarities among potential customers within a segment and explains the differences among people and organizations in different segments. A profile may cover aspects such as demographic characteristics, geographic factors, product benefits sought, lifestyles, brand preferences, and usage rates. Individuals and organizations within segments should be quite similar with respect to several characteristics and product needs and differ considerably from those within other market segments. Marketers use market segment profiles to assess the degree to which the organization's possible products can match or fit potential customers' product needs. Market segment profiles help marketers to understand how a business can use its capabilities to serve potential customer groups.

The use of market segment profiles benefits marketers in several ways. Such profiles help a marketer determine which segment or segments are most attractive to the organization relative to the firm's strengths, weaknesses, objectives, and resources. While marketers initially may believe that certain segments are quite attractive, development of market segment profiles may yield information that indicates the opposite. For the market segment or segments chosen by the organization, the information included in market segment profiles can be highly useful in making marketing decisions.

Step 4: Evaluate Relevant Market Segments

After analyzing the market segment profiles, a marketer is likely to identify several relevant market segments that require further analysis and to eliminate certain other segments from consideration. To assess relevant market segments further, several important factors, including sales estimates, competition, and estimated costs associated with each segment, should be analyzed.

Sales Estimates.   Potential sales for a segment can be measured along several dimensions, including product level, geographic area, time, and level of competition.[22] With respect to product level, potential sales can be estimated for a specific product item (for example, Diet Coke) or an entire product line (for example, Coca-Cola Classic, Caffeine-Free Coke, Diet Coke, Caffeine-Free Diet Coke, Cherry Coca-Cola, Diet Cherry Coca-Cola, Vanilla Coke, and Diet Vanilla Coke). A manager also must determine the geographic area to be included in the estimate. In relation to time, sales estimates can be short range (one year or less), medium range (one to five years), or long range (longer than five years). The competitive level specifies whether sales are being estimated for a single firm or for an entire industry.

Market potential is the total amount of a product, for all firms in an industry, that customers will purchase within a specified period at a specific level of industrywide marketing activity. Market potential can be stated in terms of dollars or units. For example, with the aging of the large baby boomer generation, the market potential for medical instruments and medications to treat congestive heart failure, hypertension, and other cardiovascular conditions is estimated to reach over $20 billion by 2013.[23] A segment's market potential is affected by economic, sociocultural, and other environmental forces. Marketers must assume a certain general level of marketing effort in the industry when they estimate market potential. The specific level of marketing effort varies from one firm to another, but the sum of all firms' marketing activities equals industrywide marketing efforts. A marketing manager also must consider whether and to what extent industry marketing efforts will change.

Company sales potential is the maximum percentage of market potential that an individual firm within an industry can expect to obtain for a specific product. Several factors influence company sales potential for a market segment. First, the market potential places absolute limits on the size of the company's sales potential. Second, the magnitude of industrywide marketing activities has an indirect but definite impact on the company's sales potential. Those activities have a direct bearing on the size of the market potential. When Domino's Pizza advertises home-delivered pizza, for example, it indirectly promotes pizza in general; its commercials also may help to sell Pizza Hut's and other competitors' home-delivered pizza. Third, the intensity and effectiveness of a company's marketing activities relative to those of its competitors affect the size of the company's sales potential. If a company spends twice as much as any of its competitors on marketing efforts, and if each dollar spent is more effective in generating sales, the firm's sales potential will be quite high compared with its competitors'.

There are two general approaches to measuring company sales potential: breakdown and buildup. In the **breakdown approach,** the marketing manager first develops

market potential The total amount of a product that customers will purchase within a specified period at a specific level of industrywide marketing activity

company sales potential The maximum percentage of market potential that an individual firm can expect to obtain for a specific product

breakdown approach Measuring company sales potential based on a general economic forecast for a specific period and the market potential derived from it

a general economic forecast for a specific time period. Next, market potential is estimated on the basis of this economic forecast. The company's sales potential then is derived from the general economic forecast and estimate of market potential. In the **buildup approach,** the marketing manager begins by estimating how much of a product a potential buyer in a specific geographic area, such as a sales territory, will purchase in a given period. The manager then multiplies that amount by the total number of potential buyers in that area. The manager performs the same calculation for each geographic area in which the firm sells products and then adds the totals for each area to calculate market potential. To determine company sales potential, the manager must estimate, based on planned levels of company marketing activities, the proportion of the total market potential the company can obtain.

Competitive Assessment.   Besides obtaining sales estimates, it is crucial to assess competitors already operating in the segments being considered. Without competitive information, sales estimates may be misleading. A market segment that seems attractive based on sales estimates may prove to be much less so following a competitive assessment. Such an assessment should ask several questions about competitors: How many exist? What are their strengths and weaknesses? Do several competitors have major market shares and together dominate the segment? Can our company create a marketing mix to compete effectively against competitors' marketing mixes? Is it likely that new competitors will enter this segment? If so, how will they affect our firm's ability to compete successfully? Answers to such questions are important for proper assessment of the competition in potential market segments.

Cost Estimates.   To fulfill the needs of a target segment, an organization must develop and maintain a marketing mix that precisely meets the wants and needs of individuals and organizations in that segment. Developing and maintaining such a mix can be expensive. Distinctive product features, attractive package design, generous product warranties, extensive advertising, attractive promotional offers, competitive prices, and high-quality personal service consume considerable organizational resources. Indeed, to reach certain segments, the costs may be so high that a marketer may see the segment as inaccessible. Another cost consideration is whether the organization can reach a segment effectively at costs equal to or below competitors' costs. If the firm's costs are likely to be higher, it will be unable to compete in that segment in the long run.

Step 5: Select Specific Target Markets

An important initial issue to consider in selecting a target market is whether customers' needs differ enough to warrant the use of market segmentation. If segmentation analysis shows customer needs to be fairly homogeneous, the firm's management may decide to use the undifferentiated approach, discussed earlier. However, if customer needs are heterogeneous, which is much more likely, one or more target markets must be selected. On the other hand, marketers may decide not to enter and compete in any of the segments.

Assuming that one or more segments offer significant opportunities for the organization to achieve its objectives, marketers must decide in which segments to participate. Ordinarily, information gathered in the previous step—information about sales estimates, competitors, and cost estimates—requires careful consideration in this final step to determine long-term profit opportunities. Also, the firm's management must investigate whether the organization has the financial resources, managerial skills, employee expertise, and facilities to enter and compete effectively in selected segments. Furthermore, the requirements of some market segments may be at odds with the firm's overall objectives, and the possibility of legal problems, conflicts with stakeholders, and technological advancements could make certain segments unattractive. In addition, when prospects for long-term growth are taken into account, some segments may appear very attractive and others less desirable.

buildup approach Measuring company sales potential by estimating how much of a product a potential buyer in a specific geographic area will purchase in a given period, multiplying the estimate by the number of potential buyers, and adding the totals of all the geographic areas considered

Selecting appropriate target markets is important to an organization's adoption and use of the marketing concept philosophy. Identifying the right target market is the key to implementing a successful marketing strategy, whereas failure to do so can lead to low sales, high costs, and severe financial losses. A careful target-market analysis places an organization in a better position both to serve customers' needs and to achieve its objectives.

Developing Sales Forecasts

A **sales forecast** is the amount of a product a company actually expects to sell during a specific period at a specified level of marketing activities. The sales forecast differs from the company sales potential. It concentrates on what actual sales will be at a certain level of company marketing effort, whereas the company sales potential assesses what sales are possible at various levels of marketing activities, assuming that certain environmental conditions will exist. Businesses use the sales forecast for planning, organizing, implementing, and controlling their activities. The success of numerous activities depends on this forecast's accuracy. Common problems in companies that fail are improper planning and lack of realistic sales forecasts. Overly optimistic sales forecasts can lead to overbuying, overinvestment, and higher costs.

To forecast sales, a marketer can choose from several forecasting methods, some arbitrary and others more scientific, complex, and time-consuming. A firm's choice of method or methods depends on the costs involved, type of product, market characteristics, time span of the forecast, purposes of the forecast, stability of the historical sales data, availability of required information, managerial preferences, and forecasters' expertise and experience.[24] Common forecasting techniques fall into five categories: executive judgment, surveys, time-series analysis, regression analysis, and market tests.

Executive Judgment

At times, a company forecasts sales chiefly on the basis of **executive judgment**, the intuition of one or more executives. This approach is unscientific but expedient and inexpensive. Executive judgment may work reasonably well when product demand is relatively stable, and the forecaster has years of market-related experience. However, because intuition is swayed most heavily by recent experience, the forecast may be overly optimistic or overly pessimistic. Another drawback to intuition is that the forecaster has only past experience as a guide for deciding where to go in the future.

Surveys

Another way to forecast sales is to question customers, sales personnel, or experts regarding their expectations about future purchases. In a **customer forecasting survey,** marketers ask customers what types and quantities of products they intend to buy during a specific period. This approach may be useful to a business with relatively few customers. For example, Intel, which markets to a limited number of companies (primarily computer manufacturers), could conduct customer forecasting surveys effectively. PepsiCo, in contrast, has millions of customers and could not feasibly use a customer survey to forecast future sales.

In a **sales force forecasting survey,** the firm's salespeople estimate anticipated sales in their territories for a specified period. The forecaster combines these territorial estimates to arrive at a tentative forecast. A marketer may survey the sales staff for several reasons. The most important is that the sales staff is closer to customers on a daily basis than other company personnel and therefore should know more about customers' future product needs. When sales representatives assist in developing the forecast, they are more likely to work toward its achievement. Another advantage of this method is that forecasts can be prepared for single territories, divisions consisting of

sales forecast The amount of a product a company expects to sell during a specific period at a specified level of marketing activities

executive judgment Sales forecasting based on the intuition of one or more executives

customer forecasting survey A survey of customers regarding the types and quantities of products they intend to buy during a specific period

sales force forecasting survey A survey of a firm's sales force regarding anticipated sales in their territories for a specified period

several territories, regions made up of multiple divisions, and the total geographic market. Thus the method provides sales forecasts from the smallest geographic sales unit to the largest.

When a company wants an **expert forecasting survey,** it hires professionals to help prepare the sales forecast. These experts are usually economists, management consultants, advertising executives, college professors, or other persons outside the firm with solid experience in a specific market. Drawing on this experience and their analyses of available information about the company and the market, experts prepare and present forecasts or answer questions regarding a forecast. Using experts is expedient and relatively inexpensive. However, because they work outside the firm, these forecasters may be less motivated than company personnel to do an effective job.

A more complex form of the expert forecasting survey incorporates the Delphi technique. The **Delphi technique** is a procedure in which experts create initial forecasts, submit them to the company for averaging, and have the results returned to them so that they can make individual refined forecasts. The premise is that the experts will use the averaged results when making refined forecasts and that these forecasts will be in a narrower range. The procedure may be repeated several times until the experts, each working separately, reach a consensus on the forecasts. The ultimate goal in using the Delphi technique is to develop a highly accurate sales forecast.

Time-Series Analysis

With **time-series analysis**, the forecaster uses the firm's historical sales data to discover a pattern or patterns in the firm's sales over time. If a pattern is found, it can be used to forecast sales. This forecasting method assumes that past sales patterns will continue in the future. The accuracy, and thus usefulness, of time-series analysis hinges on the validity of this assumption.

In a time-series analysis, a forecaster usually performs four types of analyses: trend, cycle, seasonal, and random factor. **Trend analysis** focuses on aggregate sales data, such as the company's annual sales figures, covering a period of many years to determine whether annual sales are generally rising, falling, or staying about the same. Through **cycle analysis,** a forecaster analyzes sales figures (often monthly sales data) from a period of three to five years to ascertain whether sales fluctuate in a consistent, periodic manner. When performing **seasonal analysis,** the analyst studies daily, weekly, or monthly sales figures to evaluate the degree to which seasonal factors, such as climate and holiday activities, influence sales. In a **random factor analysis,** the forecaster attempts to attribute erratic sales variations to random, nonrecurrent events, such as a regional power failure, a natural disaster, or political unrest in a foreign market. After performing each of these analyses, the forecaster combines the results to develop the sales forecast. Time-series analysis is an effective forecasting method for products with reasonably stable demand, but not for products with highly erratic demand.

Regression Analysis

Like time-series analysis, regression analysis requires the use of historical sales data. In **regression analysis,** the forecaster seeks to find a relationship between past sales (the dependent variable) and one or more independent variables, such as population, per capita income, or gross domestic product. Simple regression analysis uses one independent variable, whereas multiple regression analysis includes two or more independent variables. The objective of regression analysis is to develop a mathematical formula that accurately describes a relationship between the firm's sales and one or more variables; however, the formula indicates only an association, not a causal relationship. Once an accurate formula is established, the analyst plugs

expert forecasting survey Sales forecasts prepared by experts such as economists, management consultants, advertising executives, college professors, or other persons outside the firm

Delphi technique A procedure in which experts create initial forecasts, submit them to the company for averaging, and then refine the forecasts

time-series analysis A forecasting method that uses historical sales data to discover patterns in the firm's sales over time and generally involves trend, cycle, seasonal, and random factor analyses

trend analysis An analysis that focuses on aggregate sales data over a period of many years to determine general trends in annual sales

cycle analysis An analysis of sales figures for a period of three to five years to ascertain whether sales fluctuate in a consistent, periodic manner

seasonal analysis An analysis of daily, weekly, or monthly sales figures to evaluate the degree to which seasonal factors influence sales

random factor analysis An analysis attempting to attribute erratic sales variation to random, nonrecurrent events

regression analysis A method of predicting sales based on finding a relationship between past sales and one or more variables, such as population or income

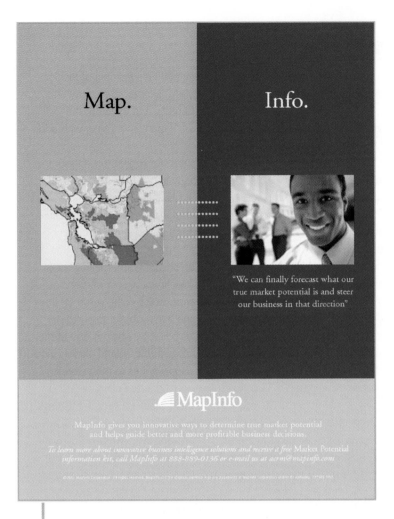

Map.

Info.

"We can finally forecast what our true market potential is and steer our business in that direction"

◢MapInfo

MapInfo gives you innovative ways to determine true market potential and helps guide better and more profitable business decisions.

To learn more about innovative business intelligence solutions and receive a free Market Potential information kit, call MapInfo at 888-889-0136 or e-mail us at acrm@mapinfo.com

Developing Sales Forecasts

A number of products are available that assist organizations in developing sales forecasts.

market test Making a product available to buyers in one or more test areas and measuring purchases and consumer responses

the necessary information into the formula to derive the sales forecast.

Regression analysis is useful when a precise association can be established. However, a forecaster seldom finds a perfect association. Furthermore, this method can be used only when available historical sales data are extensive. Thus regression analysis is futile for forecasting sales of new products.

Market Tests

A **market test** involves making a product available to buyers in one or more test areas and measuring purchases and consumer responses to distribution, promotion, and price. Test areas are often cities with populations of 200,000 to 500,000 but can be larger metropolitan areas or towns with populations of 50,000 to 200,000. For example, ACNielsen Market Decisions, a marketing research firm, conducts market tests for client firms in Boise, Tucson, Colorado Springs, Peoria, Evansville, Charleston, and Portland (Maine), in addition to custom test markets in cities chosen by clients.[25]

A market test provides information about consumers' actual, rather than intended, purchases. In addition, purchase volume can be evaluated in relation to the intensity of other marketing activities—advertising, in-store promotions, pricing, packaging, and distribution. For example, Procter & Gamble conducted market tests for new concentrated versions of its Tide, Gain, Dreft, Cheer, and Era laundry detergents in Cedar Rapids, Iowa. The company, which anticipated the new, more environmentally friendly products replacing current versions of the laundry detergent, needed to assess consumer reaction to the products, their price, and TV, instore, and online promotional efforts.[26] Forecasters base their sales estimates for larger geographic units on customer response in test areas.

Because it does not require historical sales data, a market test is effective for forecasting sales of new products or sales of existing products in new geographic areas. A market test also gives a marketer an opportunity to test various elements of the marketing mix. However, these tests are often time-consuming and expensive. In addition, a marketer cannot be certain that consumer response during a market test represents the total market response or that such a response will continue in the future.

Multiple Forecasting Methods

Although some businesses depend on a single sales forecasting method, most firms use several techniques. Sometimes a company is forced to use several methods when marketing diverse product lines, but even for a single product line, several forecasts may be needed, especially when the product is sold to different market segments. Thus a producer of automobile tires may rely on one technique to forecast tire sales for new cars and on another to forecast sales of replacement tires. Variation in the length of needed forecasts may call for several forecasting methods. A firm that employs one method for a short-range forecast may find it inappropriate for long-range forecasting. Sometimes a marketer verifies results of one method by using one or more other methods and comparing outcomes.

...And now, back to IKEA

Customers in many countries have responded enthusiastically to IKEA's formula of fashionable, affordable, and functional furniture. After expanding beyond Sweden to Norway and Denmark, the company opened stores in Europe, Australia, Canada, and in 1985, the United States. More recently, IKEA has opened stores in Russia, Japan, and China, with additional U.S. outlets on the way.

Product names such as Leksvik bookcases and Klippan sofas are known throughout the world and reflect IKEA's Swedish origins. However, the company translates its catalogs into 25 languages and distributes 160 million copies every year. It has even been suggested that the IKEA catalog has a circulation three times higher than that of the Bible. Even in its catalog, IKEA looks for ways to minimize expenses. It has all products photographed at one of Europe's largest studios and transmits the images electronically to printing facilities in the different regions where the catalogs will be distributed, saving on shipping and mailing costs. Every detail, from paper quality to type size, is scrutinized to identify new cost efficiencies.

IKEA of Sweden in Älmhult, Sweden, develops the IKEA range, which is the same for IKEA stores all over the world and consists of 9,500 articles. The route from supplier to customer must be as direct, cost-effective, and environmentally friendly as possible, which is one of the reasons IKEA tends to start in a country near ports and then moves further inland after its initial success. IKEA has 28 distribution centers in 16 countries that supply goods to IKEA stores.

IKEA's targeting strategy has helped it to become a cult global brand. Every year, 410 million people go shopping in IKEA stores. The combined annual sales of home furnishings (and restaurant meals) in all of its 226 stores is nearly $18 billion. Internet sales are slowly growing for IKEA with their website attracting more than 125 million visits worldwide. North America is one of IKEA's most important markets because it accounts for 16 percent of sales, and there are plans to have 50 new stores open by 2010. No matter how large and fast IKEA grows, its focus will remain on keeping costs low to continue satisfying its target market's need for reasonably priced, well-designed, assemble-it-yourself home furnishings.[27]

1. Whom does IKEA target?

2. Is IKEA's targeting strategy concentrated or undifferentiated? Explain your answer.

3. Which of the variables for segmenting consumer markets is IKEA using, and why are these variables appropriate?

CHAPTER REVIEW

1. Learn what a market is.

A market is a group of people who, as individuals or as organizations, have needs for products in a product class and have the ability, willingness, and authority to purchase such products.

2. Understand the differences among general targeting strategies.

The undifferentiated targeting strategy involves designing a single marketing mix directed toward the entire market for a particular product. This strategy is effective in a homogeneous market, whereas a concentrated targeting strategy or differentiated targeting strategy is more appropriate for a heterogeneous market. The concentrated strategy and differentiated strategy both divide markets into segments consisting of individuals, groups, or organizations that have one or more similar characteristics and so can be linked to similar product needs. The concentrated strategy involves targeting a single market segment with one marketing mix. The differentiated targeting strategy targets two or more market segments with marketing mixes customized for each.

3. Become familiar with the major segmentation variables.

Segmentation variables are the characteristics of individuals, groups, or organizations used to segment a total market. The variable(s) used should relate to customers' needs for, uses of, or behavior toward the product. Segmentation variables for consumer markets can be grouped into four categories: demographic (age, gender, income, ethnicity, and family life cycle), geographic (population, market density, and climate), psychographic (personality traits, motives, and lifestyles), and behavioristic (volume usage, end use, expected benefits, brand loyalty, and price sensitivity). Variables for segmenting business markets include geographic location, type of organization, customer size, and product use.

4. Know what segment profiles are and how they are used.

Segment profiles describe the similarities among potential customers within a segment and explain the differences among people and organizations in different market segments. They are used to assess the degree to which the firm's products can match potential customers' product needs.

5. Understand how to evaluate market segments.

Marketers evaluate relevant market segments by analyzing several important factors associated with each segment, such as sales estimates (including market potential and company sales potential), competitive assessments, and cost estimates.

6. Identify the factors that influence the selection of specific market segments for use as target markets.

Actual selection of specific target-market segments requires an assessment of whether customers' needs differ enough to warrant segmentation and which segments to focus on. Sales estimates, competitive assessments, and cost estimates for each potential segment and the firm's financial resources, managerial skills, employee expertise, facilities, and objectives are important factors in this decision, as are legal issues, potential conflicts with stakeholders, technological advancements, and the long-term prospects for growth.

7. Become familiar with sales forecasting methods.

A sales forecast is the amount of a product a company expects to sell during a specific period at a specified level of marketing activities. To forecast sales, marketers can choose from several techniques, including executive judgment, surveys, time-series analysis, regression analysis, and market tests. Executive judgment is based on the intuition of one or more executives. Surveys include customer, sales force, and expert forecasting surveys. Time-series analysis uses the firm's historical sales data to discover patterns in the firm's sales over time and employs four major types of analyses: trend, cycle, seasonal, and random factor. With regression analysis, forecasters attempt to find a relationship between past sales and one or more independent variables. Market testing involves making a product available to buyers in one or more test areas and measuring purchases and consumer responses to distribution, promotion, and price. Many companies employ multiple forecasting methods.

 Please visit the student website at **www.prideferrell.com** for ACE Self-Test questions that will help you prepare for exams.

ACE
self-test

KEY CONCEPTS

consumer market
business market
undifferentiated targeting
   strategy
homogeneous market
heterogeneous markets
market segmentation
market segment
concentrated targeting
   strategy

differentiated targeting
   strategy
segmentation variables
market density
geodemographic
   segmentation
micromarketing
benefit segmentation
market potential
company sales potential

breakdown approach
buildup approach
sales forecast
executive judgment
customer forecasting survey
sales force forecasting
   survey
expert forecasting survey
Delphi technique
time-series analysis

trend analysis
cycle analysis
seasonal analysis
random factor analysis
regression analysis
market test

ISSUES FOR DISCUSSION AND REVIEW

1. In your local area, identify a group of people with unsatisfied product needs who represent a market. Could this market be reached by a business organization? Why or why not?

2. Outline the five major steps in the target-market selection process.

3. What is an undifferentiated strategy? Under what conditions is it most useful? Describe a present market situation in which a company is using an undifferentiated strategy. Is the business successful? Why or why not?

4. What is market segmentation? Describe the basic conditions required for effective segmentation. Identify several firms that use market segmentation.

5. List the differences between concentrated and differentiated strategies, and describe the advantages and disadvantages of each.

6. Identify and describe four major categories of variables that can be used to segment consumer markets. Give examples of product markets that are segmented by variables in each category.

7. What dimensions are used to segment business markets?

8. What is a market segment profile? Why is it an important step in the target-market selection process?

9. Describe the important factors that marketers should analyze to evaluate market segments.

10. Why is a marketer concerned about sales potential when trying to select a target market?

11. Why is selecting appropriate target markets important to an organization that wants to adopt the marketing concept philosophy?

12. What is a sales forecast? Why is it important?

MARKETING APPLICATIONS

1. MTV Latino targets the growing Hispanic market in the United States. Identify another product marketed to a distinct target market. Describe the target market, and explain how the marketing mix appeals specifically to that group.

2. Locate an article that describes the targeting strategy of a particular organization. Describe the target market, and explain the strategy being used to reach that market.

3. The stereo market may be segmented according to income and age. Name two ways the market for each of the following products might be segmented.
   a. Candy bars
   b. Travel agency services
   c. Bicycles
   d. Hair spray

4. If you were using a time-series analysis to forecast sales for your company for the next year, how would you use the following sets of sales figures?
   a.

2000	$145,000	2005	$149,000
2001	$144,000	2006	$148,000
2002	$147,000	2007	$180,000
2003	$145,000	2008	$191,000
2004	$148,000	2009	$227,000

b.

	2007	2008	2009
Jan.	$12,000	$14,000	$16,000
Feb.	$13,000	$14,000	$15,500
Mar.	$12,000	$14,000	$17,000
Apr.	$13,000	$15,000	$17,000
May	$15,000	$17,000	$20,000
June	$18,000	$18,000	$21,000
July	$18,500	$18,000	$21,500
Aug.	$18,500	$19,000	$22,000
Sep.	$17,000	$18,000	$21,000
Oct.	$16,000	$15,000	$19,000
Nov.	$13,000	$14,000	$19,000
Dec.	$14,000	$15,000	$18,000

c. 2007 sales increased 21.2 percent (opened an additional store in 2007).
2008 sales increased 18.8 percent (opened another store in 2008).

Online Exercise

5. iExplore is an Internet company that offers a variety of travel and adventure products. Visit its website at **www.iexplore.com.**
   a. Based on the information provided at the website, what are some of iExplore's basic products?
   b. What market segments does iExplore appear to be targeting with its website? What segmentation variables are being used to segment these markets?
   c. How does iExplore appeal to comparison shoppers?

Video CASE

Jordan's Furniture: Shoppertaining Its Target Market

Samuel Tatelman began selling furniture out of the back of his truck in Waltham, Massachusetts, in 1918. Today, his grandsons, Eliot and Barry, sell more furniture per square foot at Jordan's Furniture than at any other furniture retailer in the country and attract record numbers of guests each week. With just four stores, Jordan's Furniture has grown from 15 employees 25 years ago to over 1,000 today. Now owned by Berkshire Hathaway, Jordan's Furniture is also in the process of a massive expansion and plans to double its number of both stores and employees in the next few years.

The company has broken just about all industry standards. Inventory turns over at a rate of 13 times a year, compared with an average of 1 to 2 times a year in most furniture stores. Advertising expenditures are 2 percent, whereas the industry average is 7 percent. Sales per square foot are $950, whereas most furniture stores average $150 in sales per square foot.

When the brothers took over the business in 1973, they decided to focus their efforts on the 18- to 34-year-old market segment. While most furniture stores do not target specific customers, the Tatelmans felt that people with first homes or new families would need furniture more. To bring customers, even those not currently shopping for furniture, into the stores (particularly young families), the brothers invented what they call "shoppertainment" and created stores that were imaginative, fun, and a little Disney-like. Their "shop-

pertainment" concept paid off because the stores now host more than 4,000 visitors on an average weekend.

When customers walk into a Jordan's Furniture store, they might be greeted with a welcome map, be offered freshly baked chocolate chip cookies, or receive a hearty greeting from an animatronic Elvis. "We've taken furniture shopping and given it new life by making it more of a fun experience rather than this 'God, I have to go furniture shopping' [experience]," says Tatelman. "Beantown," a re-creation of Boston made of 25 million jelly beans, stands next to an ice cream stand. Indoor fireworks and jazz music enliven a re-creation of New Orleans' famous Bourbon Street, complete with amusement rides for kids, animated characters, and snack stands. Jordan's Furniture also offers a flight simulator and trapeze lessons to adventurous customers. A 300-seat IMAX theater brings customers in for a movie, but they leave the store by walking through showrooms of furniture.

The stores are strategically laid out to make the shopping experience not only fun but also easy. Instead of arranging furniture by manufacturer, Jordan's Furniture puts all its categories together so that customers can see all the store's offerings at the same time. "If you came in looking for a bedroom set, we'll make it easy to see every bedroom set we carry," says Tatelman. The stores are also equipped with Dell workstations so that employees can quickly look up product details and pricing. Their Sleep Lab (complete with white-coated "Sleep

Technicians") offers a questionnaire that helps customers find a mattress suited for maximum personal comfort. The showrooms are also equipped with low-level lighting that dims when customers lie down on a mattress.

With so many families making Jordan's Furniture a weekend outing and school groups visiting the IMAX on field trips, Jordan's Furniture has expanded its product mix to include nursery and children's furniture. The playful displays of hanging basketballs and soccer balls are designed especially to appeal to young tastes. The youth department uses painted murals to create a fun atmosphere. A safari-themed room showcases bunk beds and lofts.

Jordan's Furniture also has added an infants' section with soft white track lights. Since each department at Jordan's Furniture has its own theme music to set the tone, soft lullabies can be heard in the nursery section.

Because of the high volume of families visiting the stores, Jordan's Furniture nursery products have been successful based on word-of-mouth alone.

By taking the focus off furniture and putting it on people, Jordan's Furniture has pulled ahead of its competitors. "A lot of people look at their business strictly from the cash register's point of view. I can stand outside and watch people leaving and coming in and see smiles on their faces. When they're walking out smiling, happy, and having a good time," says Tatelman, "I know the cash register is going to be ringing."[28]

Questions for Discussion

1. What type of targeting strategy is Jordan's Furniture using?
2. Describe and evaluate the company's target market.
3. Discuss the positioning of Jordan's Furniture's bedding products.

part 4

Customer Behavior

Part 4 continues the focus on the customer. Understanding elements that affect buying decisions enables marketers to analyze customers' needs and evaluate how specific marketing strategies can satisfy those needs. Chapter 8 examines consumer buying decision processes and factors that influence buying decisions. Chapter 9 stresses business markets, organizational buyers, the buying center, and the organizational buying decision process.

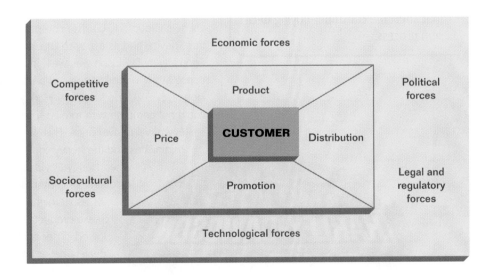

8

Consumer Buying Behavior

OBJECTIVES

1. Describe the level of involvement and types of consumer problem-solving processes.

2. Recognize the stages of the consumer buying decision process.

3. Explain how situational influences may affect the consumer buying decision process.

4. Understand the psychological influences that may affect the consumer buying decision process.

5. Be familiar with the social influences that affect the consumer buying decision process.

The Harley-Davidson Brand Roars Into Its Second Century

Harley-Davidson has roared up and down the fast track in its time. Named for its two founders, the company was born with one motorcycle built in a shed in 1903. Now Harley-Davidson sells more than 317,000 motorcycles a year across the United States, Japan, Europe, and China. During the 1970s, however, product quality suffered as Harley-Davidson expanded too quickly. The company was nearly out of business by the mid-1980s when management decided to implement new marketing strategies, reduce manufacturing output, focus on improving quality, and redesign its basic motorcycle engine. Customers noticed the difference, and sales began to accelerate.

Harley-Davidson enjoyed a monopoly in the motorcycle industry for many decades, but by the 1970s, Japanese manufacturers had flooded the market with high-quality, low-priced bikes. From 1973 to 1983, Harley's market share plummeted from 77.5 to 23.3 percent, whereas Honda achieved 44 percent of the market by 1983. Harley-Davidson refocused its marketing—including giving new Harley-Davidson owners a one-year free membership to the Harley Owners Group (HOG). The company used HOG activities as a customer relations device and as a way to showcase and demonstrate its new products. Soon Harley-Davidson was well on the road to reclaiming its market dominance in the United States and beating back competition from Yamaha, Honda, Suzuki, and Kawasaki. Harley executives realized that the company could not compete with foreign manufacturers on cost, so they developed a strategy of value over price. This was created through the development of mininiches and the heavy construction of the parts. Demand soared higher still when Harley-Davidson sold special limited-edition models to celebrate its centennial in 2003.

Despite higher demand, management was careful to increase production only slightly from year to year. This allowed closer control over quality, but it also meant that dealers never had enough inventory on hand. As a result, people had to wait 6 to 18 months for a new motorcycle, and the price for a year-old Harley was 25 to 30 percent higher than that of a new one. The shortage helped foster a must-have attitude among aficionados.[1] ∎

Marketers at successful organizations such as Harley-Davidson go to great lengths to understand their customers' needs and gain a better grasp of customers' buying behavior. A firm's ability to establish and maintain satisfying customer relationships requires an understanding of **buying behavior,** which is the decision processes and acts of people involved in buying and using products. **Consumer buying behavior** refers to the buying behavior of ultimate consumers, those who purchase products for personal or household use and not for business purposes. Marketers strive to understand buying behavior for several reasons. First, buyers' reactions to a firm's marketing strategy have a great impact on the firm's success. Second, as indicated in Chapter 1, the marketing concept stresses that a firm should create a marketing mix that satisfies customers. To find out what satisfies buyers, marketers must examine the main influences on what, where, when, and how consumers buy. Third, by gaining a better understanding of the factors that affect buying behavior, marketers are in a better position to predict how consumers will respond to marketing strategies.

In this chapter we first examine how the customer's level of involvement affects the type of problem solving employed and discuss the types of consumer problem-solving processes. Then we analyze the major stages of the consumer buying decision process, beginning with problem recognition, information search, and evaluation of alternatives and proceeding through purchase and postpurchase evaluation. Next, we examine situational influences that affect purchasing decisions: surroundings, time, purchase reason, and buyer's mood and condition. We go on to consider psychological influences on purchasing decisions: perception, motives, learning, attitudes, personality and self-concept, and lifestyles. We conclude with a discussion of social influences that affect buying behavior: roles, family, reference groups and opinion leaders, social classes, and culture and subcultures.

Level of Involvement and Consumer Problem-Solving Processes

buying behavior The decision processes and acts of people involved in buying and using products

consumer buying behavior Buying behavior of people who purchase products for personal or household use and not for business purposes

level of involvement An individual's degree of interest in a product and the importance of the product for that person

In order to acquire and maintain products that satisfy their current and future needs, consumers engage in problem solving. People engage in different types of problem-solving processes depending on the nature of the products involved. The amount of effort, both mental and physical, that buyers expend in solving problems varies considerably. A major determinant of the type of problem-solving process employed depends on the customer's **level of involvement**, the degree of interest in a product and the importance the individual places on this product. High-involvement products tend to be those that are visible to others (such as clothing, furniture, or automobiles) and expensive. Expensive bicycles, for example, are usually high-involvement products. High-importance issues, such as health care, are also associated with high levels of involvement. Low-involvement products tend to be those that are less expensive and have less associated social risk, such as many grocery items. A person's interest in a product or product category that is ongoing and long term is referred to as *enduring involvement*. In contrast, *situational involvement* is temporary and dynamic and results from a particular set of circumstances, such as the need to buy a new car after being involved in an accident. Consumer involvement may be attached to product categories (such as sports), loyalty to a specific brand, interest in a specific advertisement (e.g., a funny commercial) or a medium (such as a particular television show), or certain decisions and behaviors (e.g., a love of shopping). On the other hand, a consumer may find a particular commercial entertaining yet have little involvement with the brand advertised because of loyalty to another brand.[2] Involvement level, as well as other factors, affects a person's selection of one of three types of consumer problem

Routine Purchasing
Mountain Dew is a convenience product that requires very little search and decision effort.

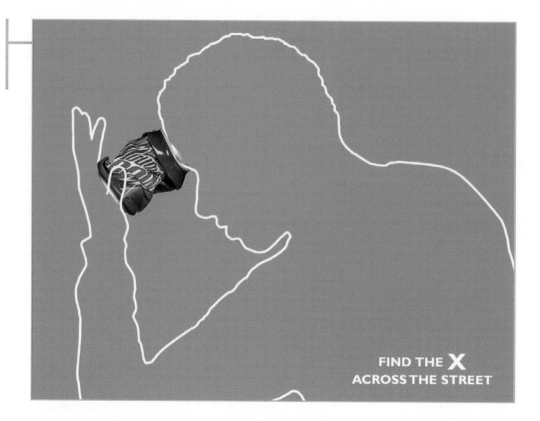

FIND THE **X** ACROSS THE STREET

routinized response behavior A type of consumer problem-solving process used when buying frequently purchased, low-cost items that require very little search and decision effort

limited problem solving A type of consumer problem-solving process that buyers use when purchasing products occasionally or when they need information about an unfamiliar brand in a familiar product category

extended problem solving A type of consumer problem-solving process employed when purchasing unfamiliar, expensive, or infrequently bought products

solving: routinized response behavior, limited problem solving, or extended problem solving (Table 8.1).

A consumer uses **routinized response behavior** when buying frequently purchased low-cost items requiring very little search and decision effort. When buying such items, a consumer may prefer a particular brand but is familiar with several brands in the product class and views more than one as being acceptable. Typically, low-involvement products are bought through routinized response behavior, that is, almost automatically. For example, most buyers spend little time or effort selecting a soft drink or a brand of cereal.

Buyers engage in **limited problem solving** when buying products occasionally or when they need to obtain information about an unfamiliar brand in a familiar product category. This type of problem solving requires a moderate amount of time for information gathering and deliberation. For example, if Procter & Gamble introduces an improved Tide laundry detergent, interested buyers will seek additional information about the new product, perhaps by asking a friend who has used it, watching a commercial about it, or visiting the company's website, before making a trial purchase.

The most complex type of problem solving, **extended problem solving,** occurs when purchasing unfamiliar, expensive, or infrequently bought products—for instance, a car, home, or a college education. The buyer uses many criteria to evaluate alternative brands or choices and spends much time seeking information and deciding on the purchase. Extended problem solving is frequently used for purchasing high-involvement products.

Purchase of a particular product does not always elicit the same type of problem-solving process. In some instances we engage in extended problem solving the first time we buy a certain product but find that limited problem solving suffices when we buy it again. If a routinely purchased, formerly satisfying brand no longer satisfies us, we may use limited or extended problem solving to switch to a new brand. Thus, if we notice that the brand of pain reliever we normally buy is no longer working, we

table 8.1   **CONSUMER PROBLEM SOLVING**

	Routinized Response	Limited	Extended
Product cost	Low	Low to moderate	High
Search effort	Little	Little to moderate	Extensive
Time spent	Short	Short to medium	Lengthy
Brand preference	More than one is acceptable, although one may be preferred	Several	Varies; usually many

may seek out a different brand through limited problem solving. Most consumers occasionally make purchases solely on impulse and not on the basis of any of these three problem-solving processes. **Impulse buying** involves no conscious planning but results from a powerful urge to buy something immediately.

Consumer Buying Decision Process

The **consumer buying decision process**, shown in Figure 8.1 (on page 186), includes five stages: problem recognition, information search, evaluation of alternatives, purchase, and postpurchase evaluation. Before we examine each stage, consider these important points. First, the act of purchasing is just one stage in the process and usually not the first stage. Second, even though we indicate that a purchase occurs, not all decision processes lead to a purchase. Individuals may end the process at any stage. Finally, not all consumer decisions include all five stages. People engaged in extended problem solving usually go through all stages of this decision process, whereas those engaged in limited problem solving and routinized response behavior may omit some stages.

Problem Recognition

Problem recognition occurs when a buyer becomes aware of a difference between a desired state and an actual condition. Consider a student who owns a nonprogrammable calculator and learns that she needs a programmable one for her math course. She recognizes that a difference exists between the desired state—having a programmable calculator—and her actual condition. She therefore decides to buy a new calculator.

The speed of consumer problem recognition can be quite rapid or rather slow. Sometimes a person has a problem or need but is unaware of it. Marketers use sales personnel, advertising, and packaging to help trigger recognition of such needs or problems. For example, a university bookstore may advertise programmable calculators in the school newspaper at the beginning of the term. Students who see the advertisement may recognize that they need these calculators for their course work.

Information Search

After recognizing the problem or need, a buyer (if continuing the decision process) searches for product information that will help resolve the problem or satisfy the need. For example, the above-mentioned student, after recognizing the need for a programmable calculator, may search for information about different types and brands of calculators. She acquires information over time from her surroundings. However, the information's impact depends on how she interprets it.

An information search has two aspects. In an **internal search,** buyers search their memories for information about products that might solve the problem. If they cannot

impulse buying An unplanned buying behavior resulting from a powerful urge to buy something immediately

consumer buying decision process A five-stage purchase decision process that includes problem recognition, information search, evaluation of alternatives, purchase, and postpurchase evaluation

internal search An information search in which buyers search their memories for information about products that might solve their problem

figure 8.1

CONSUMER BUYING DECISION PROCESS AND POSSIBLE INFLUENCES ON THE PROCESS

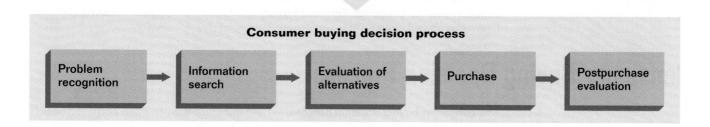

Possible influences on the decision process

Situational influences	Psychological influences	Social influences
Physical surroundings	Perception	Roles
Social surroundings	Motives	Family
Time	Learning	Reference groups
Purchase reason	Attitudes	Opinion leaders
Buyer's mood and condition	Personality and self-concept	Social classes
	Lifestyles	Culture and subcultures

Consumer buying decision process

Problem recognition → Information search → Evaluation of alternatives → Purchase → Postpurchase evaluation

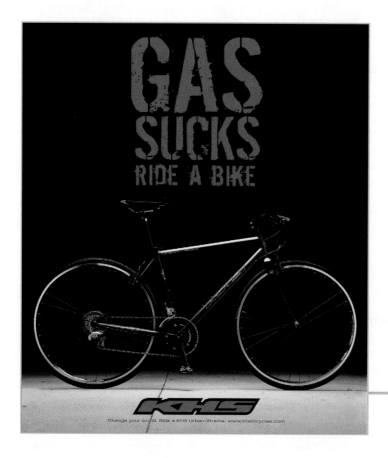

Change your world. Ride a KHS Urban-Xtreme. www.khsbicycles.com

retrieve enough information from memory to make a decision, they seek additional information from outside sources in an **external search.** The external search may focus on communication with friends or relatives, comparison of available brands and prices, marketer-dominated sources, and/or public sources. An individual's personal contacts—friends, relatives, and associates—often are influential sources of information because the person trusts and respects them. However, research suggests that consumers may overestimate friends' knowledge about products and their ability to evaluate them.[3] Using marketer-dominated sources of information, such as salespeople, advertising, websites, package labeling, and in-store demonstrations and displays, typically requires little effort on the consumer's part. Indeed, the Internet has become a major information source during the consumer buying decision process, especially for product and pricing information. Buyers also obtain information from independent sources—for instance, government reports,

Problem Recognition

KHS attempts to influence customers to recognize a problem associated with the purchase and use of gas to power cars.

news presentations, publications such as *Consumer Reports,* and reports from product-testing organizations. Consumers frequently view information from these sources as highly credible because of their factual and unbiased nature. Repetition, a technique well known to advertisers, increases consumers' learning of information. When seeing or hearing an advertising message for the first time, recipients may not grasp all its important details, but they learn more details as the message is repeated.

Evaluation of Alternatives

A successful information search yields a group of brands that a buyer views as possible alternatives—a **consideration set** (also called an *evoked set*). For example, a consideration set of programmable calculators might include those made by Texas Instruments, Hewlett-Packard, Sharp, and Casio. To assess the products in a consideration set, the buyer uses **evaluative criteria,** which are objective (such as an EPA mileage rating) and subjective (such as style) characteristics that are important to him or her. For example, one calculator buyer may want a rechargeable unit with a large display and large buttons, whereas another may have no size preferences but dislikes rechargeable calculators. The buyer also assigns a certain level of importance to each criterion; some features and characteristics carry more weight than others. Using the criteria, the buyer rates and eventually ranks brands in the consideration set. The evaluation stage may yield no brand the buyer is willing to purchase. In such a case, a further information search may be necessary.

Marketers may influence consumers' evaluations by *framing* the alternatives, that is, by describing the alternatives and their attributes in a certain manner. Framing can make a characteristic seem more important to a consumer and facilitate its recall from memory. For example, by stressing a car's superior comfort and safety features over those of a competitor's car, an automaker can direct consumers' attention toward those points of superiority. Framing probably influences the decision processes of inexperienced buyers more than those of experienced ones.

Purchase

In the purchase stage, the consumer chooses the product to be bought. Selection is based on the outcome of the evaluation stage and on other dimensions. Product availability may influence which brand is purchased. For example, if a consumer wants a black pair of Nikes and cannot find them in his size, he might buy a black pair of Reeboks.

During this stage, buyers also pick the seller from whom they will buy the product. The choice of seller may affect final product selection—and so may the terms of sale, which, if negotiable, are determined at this stage. Other issues, such as price, delivery, warranties, maintenance agreements, installation, and credit arrangements, are also settled. Finally, the actual purchase takes place during this stage, unless the consumer decides to terminate the buying decision process.

Postpurchase Evaluation

After the purchase, the buyer begins evaluating the product to ascertain if its actual performance meets expected levels. Many criteria used in evaluating alternatives are applied again during postpurchase evaluation. The outcome of this stage is either satisfaction or dissatisfaction, which influences whether the consumer complains, communicates with other possible buyers, and repurchases the product.

Shortly after purchase of an expensive product, evaluation may result in **cognitive dissonance,** doubts in the buyer's mind about whether purchasing the product was the right decision. For example, after buying a $199 iPod, a person may feel guilty about the purchase or wonder whether she purchased the right brand and quality. Cognitive dissonance is most likely to arise when a person has recently bought an expensive, high-involvement product that lacks some of the desirable features of competing brands. A buyer experiencing cognitive dissonance may attempt to return the product

external search An information search in which buyers seek information from outside sources

consideration set A group of brands that a buyer views as alternatives for possible purchase

evaluative criteria Objective and subjective characteristics that are important to a buyer

cognitive dissonance A buyer's doubts shortly after a purchase about whether the decision was the right one

or seek positive information about it to justify choosing it. Marketers sometimes attempt to reduce cognitive dissonance by having salespeople contact recent purchasers to make sure that they are satisfied with their new purchases.

As Figure 8.1 shows, three major categories of influences are believed to affect the consumer buying decision process: situational, psychological, and social. In the remainder of this chapter we focus on these influences. Although we discuss each major influence separately, their effects on the consumer decision process are interrelated.

Situational Influences on the Buying Decision Process

Situational influences result from circumstances, time, and location that affect the consumer buying decision process. For example, buying an automobile tire after noticing while washing your car that a tire is badly worn is a different experience from buying a tire right after a blowout on the highway spoils your vacation. Situational factors can influence the buyer during any stage of the consumer buying decision process and may cause the individual to shorten, lengthen, or terminate the process. Situational factors can be classified into five categories: physical surroundings, social surroundings, time perspective, reason for purchase, and the buyer's momentary mood and condition.[4]

Physical surroundings include location, store atmosphere, aromas, sounds, lighting, weather, and other factors in the physical environment in which the decision process occurs. Numerous restaurant chains, such as Olive Garden and Chili's, invest heavily in facilities, often building from the ground up, to provide special surroundings that enhance customers' dining experiences. Clearly, in some settings, dimensions, such as weather, traffic sounds, and odors, are beyond the marketers' control. Yet they must try to make customers more comfortable. General climatic conditions, for example, may influence a customer's decision to buy a specific type of vehicle (such as a sports-utility vehicle) and certain accessories (such as four-wheel drive). Current weather conditions, depending on whether they are favorable or unfavorable, may either encourage or discourage consumers to go shopping and to seek out specific products.

Social surroundings include characteristics and interactions of others, such as friends, relatives, salespeople, and other customers, who are present when a purchase decision is being made. Buyers may feel pressured to behave in a certain way because they are in public places such as restaurants, stores, or sports arenas. Thoughts about who will be around when the product is used or consumed are another dimension of the social setting. An overcrowded store or an argument between a customer and a salesperson may cause consumers to stop shopping or even leave the store.

The time dimension, such as the amount of time required to become knowledgeable about a product, to search for it, and to buy it, also influences the buying decision process in several ways. For instance, to make an informed decision at their own convenience, more men than

Situational Influences
This individual's momentary mood, characterized by anger and frustration, can influence his buying decision.

marketing ENTREPRENEURS

Marc Eckō

HIS BUSINESS: Marc Eckō Enterprises

FOUNDED: 1993, when Ecko was age 20

SUCCESS: $1 billion/year revenues

Twenty years after his birth, a graffiti artist named Marc Milecofsky started a clothing line with six hand-painted T-shirt designs. Eckō Unlimited took off when rapper Chuck D and director Spike Lee were seen in Ecko's shirts. Now, Marc Eckō Enterprises includes not only Eckō Unlimited but also G-Unit Clothing Company, Zoo York, Avirex Sportswear, *Complex* magazine, and others, with annual revenues in excess of $1 billion a year. Eckō stays up to date on what consumers want by hanging out and talking with people in social hot spots, and he focuses on point-of-sale instead of mass-media advertising in order to connect with the consumer. Eckō now offers a variety of lines and products that include gloves, hats, watches, outerwear, underwear, and shoes.[a]

ever are buying diamond engagement rings online. A high-end Internet jeweler such as Blue Nile features interactive tools on its website to help men educate themselves about diamonds and then select a unique combination from its large inventory of diamonds and settings.[5] Time plays a major role because the buyer considers the possible frequency of product use, the length of time required to use the product, and the length of the overall product life. Other time dimensions that influence purchases include time of day, day of the week or month, seasons, and holidays. The amount of time pressure a consumer is under affects how much time is devoted to purchase decisions. A customer under severe time constraints is likely either to make quick purchase decisions or to delay them.

The purchase reason raises the questions of what exactly the product purchase should accomplish and for whom. Generally, consumers purchase an item for their own use, for household use, or as a gift. For example, people who are buying a gift may buy a different product than if they were purchasing the product for themselves. If you own a Cross pen, for example, it is unlikely that you bought it for yourself.

The buyer's momentary moods (such as anger, anxiety, or contentment) or momentary conditions (such as fatigue, illness, or being flush with cash) may have a bearing on the consumer buying decision process. These moods or conditions immediately precede the current situation and are not chronic. Any of these moods or conditions can affect a person's ability and desire to search for information, receive information, or seek and evaluate alternatives. Research suggests that sad buyers are more inclined to take risks, whereas happy buyers are more likely to be risk-aversive in buying decisions.[6] Moods also can influence a consumer's postpurchase evaluation significantly.

Psychological Influences on the Buying Decision Process

situational influences Influences resulting from circumstances, time, and location that affect the consumer buying decision process

psychological influences Factors that partly determine people's general behavior, thus influencing their behavior as consumers

perception The process of selecting, organizing, and interpreting information inputs to produce meaning

information inputs Sensations received through the sense organs

Psychological influences partly determine people's general behavior and thus influence their behavior as consumers. Primary psychological influences on consumer behavior are perception, motives, learning, attitudes, personality and self-concept, and lifestyles. Even though these psychological factors operate internally, they are very much affected by social forces outside the individual.

Perception

Different people perceive the same thing at the same time in different ways. When you first look at Figure 8.2 (on page 190), do you see fish or birds? Similarly, an individual at different times may perceive the same item in a number of ways. **Perception** is the process of selecting, organizing, and interpreting information inputs to produce meaning. **Information inputs** are sensations received through sight, taste, hearing, smell, and touch. When we hear an advertisement, see a friend, smell food cooking at a nearby restaurant, or touch a product, we receive information inputs. Marketers are increasingly employing scent to help attract consumers who may be in the problem-recognition or information-search stages of the buying decision process. Some Westin Hotels, for example, use a fragrance that blends green tea, geranium, green ivy, black cedar, and freesia to evoke a sense of serenity and tranquility in their lobbies, whereas Sony uses an orange-vanilla-cedarwood scent in some SonyStyle stores to make women shoppers more comfortable.[7]

snapshot

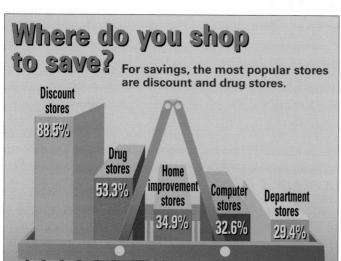

Where do you shop to save?
For savings, the most popular stores are discount and drug stores.

Discount stores
88.5%

Drug stores
53.3%

Home improvement stores
34.9%

Computer stores
32.6%

Department stores
29.4%

Source: Data from *Managing Business Risk in 2006 and Beyond*, FM Global and Harris/Interactive. Margin of error ±4 percentage points.

As the definition indicates, perception is a three-step process. Although we receive numerous pieces of information at once, only a few reach our awareness. We select some inputs and ignore others because we do not have the ability to be conscious of all inputs at one time. This phenomenon is sometimes called **selective exposure** because an individual selects which inputs will reach awareness. If you are concentrating on this paragraph, you probably are not aware that cars outside are making noise, that the room light is on, or that you are touching this page. Even though you receive these inputs, they do not reach your awareness until they are pointed out.

An individual's current set of needs affects selective exposure. Information inputs that relate to one's strongest needs at a given time are more likely to be selected to reach awareness. It is not by random chance that many fast-food commercials are aired near mealtimes. Customers are more likely to tune in to these advertisements at these times.

The selective nature of perception may result not only in selective exposure but also in two other conditions: selective distortion and selective retention. **Selective distortion** is changing or twisting currently received information; it occurs when a person receives information inconsistent with personal feelings or beliefs. For example, on seeing an advertisement promoting a disliked brand, a viewer may distort the information to make it more consistent with his or her own prior views. This distortion substantially lessens the effect of the advertisement on the individual. In **selective retention,** a person remembers information inputs that support personal feelings and beliefs and forgets inputs that do not. After hearing a sales presentation and leaving a store, a customer may forget many selling points if they contradict his or her personal beliefs.

figure 8.2

FISH OR BIRDS?

Do you see fish or birds?

figure 8.3

MASLOW'S HIERARCHY OF NEEDS

Self-actualization needs

Esteem needs

Social needs

Safety needs

Physiological needs

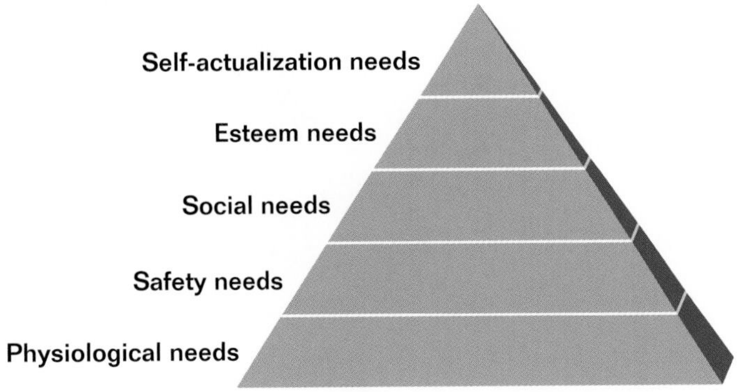

Maslow believed that people seek to fulfill five categories of needs.

The second step in the process of perception is perceptual organization. Information inputs that reach awareness are not received in an organized form. To produce meaning, an individual must mentally organize and integrate new information with what is already stored in memory. People use several methods to organize. One method, called *closure,* occurs when a person mentally fills in missing elements in a pattern or statement. In an attempt to draw attention to its brand, an advertiser will capitalize on closure by using incomplete images, sounds, or statements in its advertisements.

Interpretation, the third step in the perceptual process, is the assignment of meaning to what has been organized. A person bases interpretation on what he or she expects or what is familiar. For this reason, a manufacturer that changes a product or its package faces a major problem. When people are looking for the old, familiar product or package, they may not recognize the new one. Unless a product or package change is accompanied by a promotional program that makes people aware of the change, an organization may suffer a sales decline.

Motives

A **motive** is an internal energizing force that orients a person's activities toward satisfying needs or achieving goals. Buyers' actions are affected by a set of motives rather than by just one motive. At a single point in time, some of a person's motives are stronger than others. For example, a person's motives for having a cup of coffee are much stronger right after waking up than just before going to bed. Motives also affect the direction and intensity of behavior. Some motives may help an individual achieve his or her goals, whereas others create barriers to goal achievement.

Abraham Maslow, an American psychologist, conceived a theory of motivation based on a hierarchy of needs. According to Maslow, humans seek to satisfy five levels of needs, from most important to least important, as shown in Figure 8.3. This sequence is known as **Maslow's hierarchy of needs.** Once needs at one level are met, humans seek to fulfill needs at the next level up in the hierarchy. At the most basic level are *physiological needs,* requirements for survival such as food, water, sex, clothing, and shelter, which people try to satisfy first. Food and beverage marketers often appeal to physiological needs. At the next level are *safety needs,* which include security and freedom from physical and emotional pain and suffering. Marketers of alarm systems and insurance strive to play on people's safety needs in their promotions. Next are *social needs,* the human requirements for love and affection and a sense of belonging. Ads for cosmetics and other beauty products, jewelry, and even cars often suggest that purchasing these products will bring love. At the level of *esteem needs,* people require respect and recognition from others as well as self-esteem, a sense of

selective exposure The process of selecting inputs to be exposed to our awareness while ignoring others

selective distortion An individual's changing or twisting of information when it is inconsistent with personal feelings or beliefs

selective retention Remembering information inputs that support personal feelings and beliefs and forgetting inputs that do not

motive An internal energizing force that directs a person's behavior toward satisfying needs or achieving goals

Maslow's hierarchy of needs The five levels of needs that humans seek to satisfy, from most to least important

Learning.

The American Society for the Prevention of Cruelty to Animals attempts to change thought processes and behaviors with their advertisements.

their own worth. Owning a Lexus automobile, having a beauty makeover, or flying first class can satisfy esteem needs. At the top of the hierarchy are *self-actualization needs*. These refer to people's need to grow and develop and to become all they are capable of becoming. In its recruiting advertisements, the U.S. Army told potential enlistees to "Be all that you can be in the Army."

Motives that influence where a person purchases products on a regular basis are called **patronage motives.** A buyer may shop at a specific store because of patronage motives such as price, service, location, product variety, or friendliness of the salespeople. To capitalize on patronage motives, marketers try to determine why regular customers patronize a particular store and to emphasize these characteristics in the store's marketing mix.

patronage motives Motives that influence where a person purchases products on a regular basis

learning Changes in an individual's thought processes and behavior caused by information and experience

Learning

Learning refers to changes in a person's thought processes and behavior caused by information and experience. Consequences of behavior strongly influence the learning process. Behaviors that result in satisfying consequences tend to be repeated. For example, a consumer who buys a Snickers candy bar and enjoys the taste is more likely to buy a Snickers again. In fact, the individual probably will continue to purchase that brand until it no longer provides satisfaction. When effects of the behavior are no longer satisfying, the person may switch brands or stop eating candy bars altogether.

When making purchasing decisions, buyers process information. Individuals have differing abilities to process information. The type of information inexperienced buyers use may differ from the type used by experienced shoppers familiar with the product and purchase situation. Thus two potential purchasers of an antique desk may use different types of information in making their purchase decisions. The inexperienced buyer may judge the desk's value by price, whereas the more experienced buyer may seek information about the manufacturer, period, and place of origin to judge the desk's quality and value. Consumers lacking experience may seek information from others when making a purchase and even take along an informed "purchase pal." More experienced buyers have greater self-confidence and more knowledge about the product and can recognize which product features are reliable cues to product quality. For example, Safeway decided to launch its Safeway.com online grocery shopping service in Portland, Oregon, and Vancouver, Washington, because consumers in those two cities were already familiar with the operation and offerings of Web-based grocery stores. As a result, these consumers had the experience and knowledge and thus were more likely to understand and use Safeway.com.[8]

Marketers help customers learn about their products by helping them gain experience with them. Free samples, sometimes coupled with coupons, can successfully encourage trial and reduce purchase risk. For example, because some consumers may be wary of exotic menu items, restaurants sometimes offer free samples. In-store demonstrations foster knowledge of product uses. Test drives give potential new-car purchasers some experience with the automobile's features. Consumers also learn by experiencing products indirectly through information from salespeople, advertisements, friends, and relatives. Through sales personnel and advertisements, marketers offer information before (and sometimes after) purchases to influence what consumers learn and to create more favorable attitudes toward the product.

Attitudes

An **attitude** is an individual's enduring evaluation of, feelings about, and behavioral tendencies toward an object or idea. The objects toward which we have attitudes may be tangible or intangible, living or nonliving. For example, we have attitudes toward sex, religion, politics, and music, just as we do toward cars, football, and breakfast cereals. Although attitudes can change, they tend to remain stable and do not vary from moment to moment. However, all of a person's attitudes do not have equal impact at any one time; some are stronger than others. Individuals acquire attitudes through experience and interaction with other people.

An attitude consists of three major components: cognitive, affective, and behavioral. The cognitive component is the person's knowledge and information about the object or idea. The affective component consists of feelings and emotions toward the object or idea. The behavioral component manifests itself in the person's actions regarding the object or idea. Changes in one of these components may or may not alter the other components. Thus a consumer may become more knowledgeable about a specific brand without changing the affective or behavioral components of his or her attitude toward that brand.

Consumer attitudes toward a company and its products greatly influence success or failure of the firm's marketing strategy. When consumers have strong negative attitudes toward one or more aspects of a firm's marketing practices, they not only may stop using its products, but they also may urge relatives and friends to do likewise.

Because attitudes play such an important part in determining consumer behavior, marketers should measure consumer attitudes toward prices, package designs, brand names, advertisements, salespeople, repair services, store locations, features of existing or proposed products, and social responsibility efforts. Several methods help marketers gauge these attitudes. One of the simplest ways is to question people directly. Press Ganey Associates, in South Bend, Indiana, researches patient opinions about their hospitalization, one of the factors being hospital food. Marion General Hospital in Marion, Indiana, found satisfaction with its food service ranked in the 40th

attitude An individual's enduring evaluation of, feelings about, and behavioral tendencies toward an object or idea

Tragic Moments in Indian Country

Killed by a drunk driver.
Please don't drink and drive.

MADD Can Help
1-800-GETMADD · www.madd.org

Attempting to Change Attitudes

Mothers Against Drunk Driving works to educate about the dangers of drunk driving.

attitude scale Means of measuring consumer attitudes by gauging the intensity of individuals' reactions to adjectives, phrases, or sentences about an object

personality A set of internal traits and distinct behavioral tendencies that result in consistent patterns of behavior

self-concept Perception or view of oneself

percentile. To help increase its score, the hospital consulted with a Fort Wayne hospital whose food service ranked in the 90th percentile. Instituting several ideas from the consultation, Marion General's score rose to the 70th percentile and eventually reached a rating in the 90s.[9] Marketers also evaluate attitudes through attitude scales. An **attitude scale** usually consists of a series of adjectives, phrases, or sentences about an object. Respondents indicate the intensity of their feelings toward the object by reacting to the adjectives, phrases, or sentences in a certain way. For example, a marketer measuring people's attitudes toward shopping might ask respondents to indicate the extent to which they agree or disagree with a number of statements such as, "Shopping is more fun than watching television."

When marketers determine that a significant number of consumers have negative attitudes toward an aspect of a marketing mix, they may try to change those attitudes to make them more favorable. This task is generally lengthy, expensive, and difficult, and may require extensive promotional efforts. For example, the California Prune Growers, an organization of prune producers, has tried to use advertising to change consumers' attitudes toward prunes by presenting them as a nutritious snack high in potassium and fiber. To alter consumers' responses so that more of them buy a given brand, a firm might launch an information-focused campaign to change the cognitive component of a consumer's attitude or a persuasive (emotional) campaign to influence the affective component. Distributing free samples might help change the behavioral component. Both business and nonbusiness organizations try to change people's attitudes about many issues, from health and safety to prices and product features.

Personality and Self-Concept

Personality is a set of internal traits and distinct behavioral tendencies that result in consistent patterns of behavior in certain situations. An individual's personality arises from hereditary characteristics and personal experiences that make the person unique. Personalities typically are described as having one or more characteristics such as compulsiveness, ambition, gregariousness, dogmatism, authoritarianism, introversion, extroversion, and competitiveness. Marketing researchers look for relationships between such characteristics and buying behavior. Even though a few links between several personality traits and buyer behavior have been determined, results of many studies have been inconclusive. The weak association between personality and buying behavior may be the result of unreliable measures rather than a lack of a relationship. Some marketers are convinced that consumers' personalities do influence types and brands of products purchased. For example, the type of clothing, jewelry, or automobile a person buys may reflect one or more personality characteristics.

At times, marketers aim advertising at certain types of personalities. For example, ads for certain cigarette brands are directed toward specific personality types. Marketers focus on positively valued personality characteristics, such as security consciousness, sociability, independence, or competitiveness, rather than on negatively valued ones such as insensitivity or timidity.

A person's self-concept is closely linked to personality. **Self-concept** (sometimes called *self-image*) is a person's view or perception of himself or herself. Individuals de-

Lifestyles

Lifestyles can influence a variety of purchasing decisions.

velop and alter their self-concepts based on an interaction of psychological and social dimensions. Research shows that a buyer purchases products that reflect and enhance the self-concept and that purchase decisions are important to the development and maintenance of a stable self-concept. Consumers' self-concepts may influence whether they buy a product in a specific product category and may affect brand selection as well as where they buy. For example, home-improvement retailer Lowe's is targeting women—who make 90 percent of household decisions about home decor and home improvement—using self-concept as the basis of its advertising message. "Only Lowe's has everything and everyone to help your house tell the story about who you really are," says the company's advertising tag line.[10]

Lifestyles

As we saw in Chapter 7, many marketers attempt to segment markets by lifestyle. A **lifestyle** is an individual's pattern of living expressed through activities, interests, and opinions. Lifestyle patterns include the ways people spend time, the extent of their interaction with others, and their general outlook on life and living. People partially determine their own lifestyles, but the pattern is also affected by personality, as well as by demographic factors such as age, education, income, and social class. Lifestyles are measured through a lengthy series of questions.

Lifestyles have a strong impact on many aspects of the consumer buying decision process, from problem recognition to postpurchase evaluation. Lifestyles influence consumers' product needs, brand preferences, types of media used, and how and where they shop.

Social Influences on the Buying Decision Process

Forces that other people exert on buying behavior are called **social influences.** As Figure 8.1 shows, they are grouped into five major areas: roles, family, reference groups and opinion leaders, social classes, and culture and subcultures.

Roles

All of us occupy positions within groups, organizations, and institutions. Associated with each position is a **role,** a set of actions and activities a person in a particular position is supposed to perform based on expectations of both the individual and surrounding persons. Because people occupy numerous positions, they have many roles. For example, a man may perform the roles of son, husband, father, employee or employer, church member, civic organization member, and student in an evening college class. Thus multiple sets of expectations are placed on each person's behavior.

An individual's roles influence both general behavior and buying behavior. The demands of a person's many roles may be diverse and even inconsistent. Consider the various types of clothes that you buy and wear depending on whether you are going to class, to work, to a party, to a place of worship, or to a yoga class. You and others involved in these settings have expectations about what is acceptable clothing for

lifestyle An individual's pattern of living expressed through activities, interests, and opinions

social influences The forces other people exert on one's buying behavior

role Actions and activities that a person in a particular position is supposed to perform based on expectations of the individual and surrounding persons

Marketers Reach Out to Consumers Who Live a "Second Life"

While many of us tire of the day-to-day "business" of life and daydream about how our ideal day, week, month, year, or life might be, some people are doing more than daydreaming. These people practically live an alternate life in a virtual world called Second Life. If you've never heard of Second Life, it's a three-dimensional world completely constructed and owned by those who "live" there. Second Life is full of people, opportunities, entertainment, and much more. The people inhabiting Second Life not only interact with each other, but they also buy land; build houses and businesses; and buy, sell, and trade products. They even have their own currency—the Linden dollar. Second Life, owned by Linden Labs, went public in 2003 and is now populated by nearly 2.5 million people.

Second Life is not a game; it is more of a parallel universe of sorts. Those who choose to inhabit Second Life create "avatars" to represent themselves in the virtual world. These avatars do basically everything people do in real life, but they also can fly, walk underwater, and look like humans, animals, or pretty much anything desired. Second Life also has its own economy. Residents can purchase Linden dollars for use by their avatars at an exchange rate of about $1 to 400 Linden dollars. The site keeps track of how much money comes in and out of Second Life each day, and a recent record showed that

as much as $500,000 was changing hands on a given day.

While originally created and inhabited by people enjoying the opportunity to live in an alternate reality, Second Life has become attractive to businesses who are interested in targeting such people as well. Companies are increasingly looking at Second Life as an opportunity to test products and to interact with and entice customers. Among those opening virtual storefronts are American Apparel, Nike, Sony BMG Music Entertainment, Sun Microsystems, Nissan, Adidas/Reebok, Toyota, and Starwood Hotels. Shoe and apparel companies are marketing clothing, shoes, and accessories for avatars while also showing off their products for the real world. Entertainment companies are using Second Life to launch new artists, albums, and much more. Starwood Hotels unveiled its newest hotel design, called Aloft, in Second Life with the hope of receiving constructive feedback before launching the design in the real world. Sun Microsystems has professed excitement about being able to reach a different demographic through Second Life than it can through conventional promotional efforts. For Dell, Second Life residents can visit Dell's island to customize and buy (with Linden dollars) their own computers—and then move straight to Dell's conventional website and order the custom computer in real life. Many of Second Life's residents love buying products in the virtual world, and the idea of then replicating them in real life is exciting.

Although use of Second Life as a marketing tool is relatively new and somewhat controversial among its residents, some people believe that the entire Web is headed in the direction of Second Life. Whether Second Life's population continues to grow and remain interesting as a tool for businesses to learn about and interact with their customers remains to be seen. For now, inhabiting Second Life seems to be a win-win situation for businesses.[b]

these events. Thus the expectations of those around us affect our purchases of clothing and many other products.

Family Influences

Family influences have a very direct impact on the consumer buying decision process. Parents (and other household adults) teach children how to cope with various problems, including those dealing with purchase decisions. **Consumer socialization** is the process through which a person acquires the knowledge and skills to function as a consumer. Often children gain this knowledge and set of skills by observing parents and older siblings in purchase situations, as well as through their own purchase experiences. Children observe brand preferences and buying practices in their families and, as adults, maintain some of these brand preferences and buying practices as they establish households and raise their own families. Buying decisions made by a family are a combination of group and individual decision making.

The extent to which adult family members take part in family decision making varies among families and product categories. Traditionally, family decision-making processes have been grouped into four categories: autonomic, husband-dominant, wife-dominant, and syncratic, as shown in Table 8.2. Although female roles continue to change, women still make buying decisions related to many household items, including health-care products, laundry supplies, paper products, and foods. Indeed, research indicates that women are the primary decision makers for 80 to 85 percent of all consumer buying decisions.[11] Spouses participate jointly in the purchase of several products, especially durable goods. Owing to changes in men's roles, a significant proportion of men now are the primary grocery shoppers. Children make many purchase decisions and influence numerous household purchase decisions. Knowing that children wield considerable influence over food brand preferences, H. J. Heinz targeted them a few years ago with EZ Squirt ketchup in a squeeze bottle designed for small hands to grasp and in a rainbow of colors such as green, purple, blue, teal, pink, and orange.[12] The type of family decision making employed depends on the composition of the family as well as on the values and attitudes of family members.

When two or more family members participate in a purchase, their roles may dictate that each is responsible for performing certain purchase-related tasks, such as initiating the idea, gathering information, determining if the product is affordable,

table 8.2   TYPES OF FAMILY DECISION MAKING

Decision-Making Type	Decision Maker	Types of Products
Husband-dominant	Male head of household	Lawn mowers, hardware and tools, stereos, refrigerators, washer and dryer
Wife-dominant	Female head of household	Children's clothing, women's clothing, groceries, pots and pans, toiletries, home decoration
Autonomic	Equally likely to be made by the husband or wife but not by both	Men's clothing, luggage, toys and games, sporting equipment, cameras
Syncratic	Made jointly by husband and wife	Vacations, TVs, living-room furniture, carpets, financial planning services, family cars

consumer socialization The process through which a person acquires the knowledge and skills to function as a consumer

deciding whether to buy the product, or selecting the specific brand. The specific purchase tasks performed depend on the types of products being considered, the kind of family purchase decision process typically employed, and the amount of influence children have in the decision process. Thus different family members may play different roles in the family buying process. To develop a marketing mix that meets the needs of target-market members precisely, marketers must know not only who does the actual buying but also which other family members perform purchase-related tasks.

The family life cycle stage affects individual and joint needs of family members. (Family life cycle stages are discussed in Chapter 7.) For example, consider how the car needs of recently married twenty-somethings differ from those of the same couple when they are forty-somethings with a 13-year-old daughter and a 17-year-old son. Family life cycle changes can affect which family members are involved in purchase decisions and the types of products purchased.

Reference Groups

A **reference group** is any group that positively or negatively affects a person's values, attitudes, or behavior. Reference groups can be large or small. Most people have several reference groups, such as families, work-related groups, fraternities or sororities, civic clubs, professional organizations, or church-related groups.

In general, there are three major types of reference groups: membership, aspirational, and disassociative. A membership reference group is one to which an individual actually belongs; the individual identifies with group members strongly enough to take on the values, attitudes, and behaviors of people in that group. An aspirational reference group is a group to which one aspires to belong; one desires to be like those group members. A group that a person does not wish to be associated with is a disassociative reference group; the individual does not want to take on the values, attitudes, and behavior of group members.

A reference group may serve as an individual's point of comparison and source of information. A customer's behavior may change to be more in line with the actions and beliefs of group members. For example, a person might stop buying one brand of shirts and switch to another based on reference group members' advice. An individual also may seek information from the reference group about other factors regarding a prospective purchase, such as where to buy a certain product.

The extent to which a reference group affects a purchase decision depends on the product's conspicuousness and the individual's susceptibility to reference group influence. Generally, the more conspicuous a product, the more likely that the purchase decision will be influenced by reference groups. A product's conspicuousness is determined by whether others can see it and whether it can attract attention. Reference groups can affect whether a person does or does not buy a product at all, buys a type of product within a product category, or buys a specific brand. One way that reference groups may influence behavior is by ridiculing people who violate group norms; research has identified this practice among adolescents who admonish, haze, or even shun peers who deviate from group norms.[13] A marketer sometimes tries to use reference group influence in advertisements by suggesting that people in a specific group buy a product and are highly satisfied with it.

Opinion Leaders

In most reference groups, one or more members stand out as opinion leaders. An **opinion leader** provides information about a specific sphere that interests reference group participants who seek information. Opinion leaders are viewed by other group members as being well informed about a particular area and as easily accessible. An opinion leader is not the foremost authority on all issues, but he or she is in a position or has knowledge or expertise that makes him or her a credible source of information on one or more topics (see Table 8.3). Because such individuals know they are opinion leaders, they may feel a responsibility to remain informed about their sphere of interest and thus seek out advertisements, manufacturers' brochures, salespeople,

reference group Any group that positively or negatively affects a person's values, attitudes, or behavior

opinion leader A reference group member who provides information about a specific sphere that interests reference group participants

Big Spending on the Teen Scene

Thirty-two million teens represent a strong force in the marketplace. Teens are active consumers in terms of both the money they spend and the influence they wield among their peers and families.

It is estimated that U.S. teens spend about $190 billion a year. Favorite products of this age group include CDs, fast food, clothes, makeup, movie tickets, accessories, school supplies, books, magazines, shoes, and hair-care products. Teenage girls as well as boys like electronic gear, notably cell phones, which they use to stay in touch with each other almost constantly. Teenagers are also important sales drivers of video games and portable entertainment devices such as iPods and DVD players.

Teenagers shape their parents' consumer habits to such an extent that one industry source estimates that 37 percent of car purchases are influenced by them. Those in this age group are also strong influencers of family computer and consumer electronics purchases. Most parents wouldn't dare buy a computer or digital video recorder without consulting their techno-savvy teen.

Teenagers also influence what other teens buy. According to one economist, "Consumption is a thoroughly social activity, and what one person buys, wears, drives or eats affects the desires and behaviors of those around them." This is especially true for teenagers, who are greatly influenced by the desires and behaviors of their peer groups.

Teenagers are a diverse, growing, and crucial market group in the United States today. Their beliefs, attitudes, and behaviors do and will affect buying trends for several years.[c]

and other sources of information. An opinion leader is likely to be most influential when consumers have high product involvement but low product knowledge, when they share the opinion leader's values and attitudes, and when the product details are numerous or complicated.

Social Classes

In all societies people rank others into higher or lower positions of respect. This ranking results in social classes. A **social class** is an open group of individuals with similar social rank. A class is referred to as *open* because people can move into and out of it. Criteria for grouping people into classes vary from one society to another. In the

social class An open group of individuals with similar social rank

table 8.3	**EXAMPLES OF OPINION LEADERS AND TOPICS**
Opinion Leader	**Possible Topics**
Local religious leader	Charities to support, political ideas, lifestyle choices
Sorority president	Clothing and shoe purchases, hairstyles and stylists, nail and hair salons
"Movie buff" friend	Movies to see in theater or rent, DVDs to buy, television programs to watch
Family doctor	Prescription drugs, vitamins, health products
"Techie" acquaintance	Computer and other electronics purchases, software purchases, Internet service choices, video game purchases

United States we take into account many factors, including occupation, education, income, wealth, race, ethnic group, and possessions. A person who is ranking someone does not necessarily apply all of a society's criteria. Sometimes, too, the role of income in social class determination tends to be overemphasized. Although income does help establish social class, the other factors also play a role. Within social classes, both incomes and spending habits differ significantly among members.

Analyses of social class in the United States commonly divide people into three to seven categories. Social scientist Richard P. Coleman suggests that, for purposes of consumer analysis, the population be divided into the four major status groups shown in Table 8.4. However, he cautions marketers that considerable diversity exists in people's life situations within each status group.

To some degree, individuals within social classes develop and assume common behavioral patterns. They may have similar attitudes, values, language patterns, and possessions. Social class influences many aspects of people's lives. For example, it affects their chances of having children and their children's chances of surviving infancy. It influences their childhood training, choice of religion, access to higher education, selection of occupation, and leisure time activities. Because social class has a bearing on so many aspects of a person's life, it also affects buying decisions.

Social class influences people's spending, saving, and credit practices. It determines to some extent the type, quality, and quantity of products a person buys and

table 8.4 SOCIAL CLASS BEHAVIORAL TRAITS AND PURCHASING CHARACTERISTICS

Class (% of Population)	Behavioral Traits	Buying Characteristics
Upper (14%); includes upper-upper, lower-upper, upper-middle	Income varies among the groups, but goals are the same; various lifestyles: preppy, conventional, intellectual, etc.; neighborhood and prestigious schooling important	Prize quality merchandise; favor prestigious brands; products purchased must reflect good taste; invest in art; spend money on travel, theater, books, tennis, golf, and swimming clubs
Middle (32%)	Often in management; considered white collar; prize good schools; desire an attractive home in a nice, well-maintained neighborhood; often emulate the upper class; enjoy travel and physical activity; often very involved in children's school and sports activities	Like fashionable items; consult experts via books, articles, etc., before purchasing; spend for experiences they consider worthwhile for their children (e.g., ski trips, college education); tour packages, weekend trips; attractive home furnishings
Working (38%)	Emphasis on family, especially for economic and emotional supports (e.g., job opportunity tips, help in times of trouble); blue collar; earn good incomes; enjoy mechanical items and recreational activities; enjoy leisure time after working hard	Buy vehicles and equipment related to recreation, camping, and selected sports; strong sense of value; shop for best bargains at off-price and discount stores; purchase automotive equipment for making repairs; enjoy local travel, recreational parks
Lower (16%)	Often unemployed owing to situations beyond their control (e.g., layoffs, company takeovers); can include individuals on welfare and homeless individuals; often have strong religious beliefs; may be forced to live in less desirable neighborhoods; despite their problems, often good-hearted toward others; enjoy everyday activities when possible	Most products purchased are for survival; ability to convert good discards into usable items

Source: Adapted from Richard P. Coleman, "The Continuing Significance of Social Class to Marketing," *Journal of Consumer Research*, December 1983, pp. 265–280. Reprinted by permission of the publisher, The University of Chicago Press, and reprinted by permission of The McGraw-Hill Companies from J. Paul Peter and Jerry C. Olson, *Consumer Behavior Marketing Strategy Perspective*, p. 433. Copyright © 1987.

I DON'T NEED SWEET TALK. JUST TALK TO ME IN SPANISH.

Subculture

Products are precisely designed and aimed at people in specific subcultures.

culture The values, knowledge, beliefs, customs, objects, and concepts of a society

subculture A group of individuals whose characteristic values and behavior patterns are similar to each other and differ from those of the surrounding culture

uses. For example, it affects purchases of clothing, foods, financial and health-care services, travel, recreation, entertainment, and home furnishings. To some extent, members of lower classes attempt to emulate members of higher social classes, such as by purchasing expensive automobiles, homes, appliances, and other status symbols. Social class also affects an individual's shopping patterns and types of stores patronized. In some instances, marketers attempt to focus on certain social classes through store location and interior design, product design and features, pricing strategies, personal sales efforts, and advertising. Many companies focus on the middle and working classes because they account for such a large portion of the population. Outside the United States, the middle class is growing in India, China, Mexico, and other countries, making these consumers increasingly desirable to marketers as well. Some firms target different classes with different products. BMW, for example, introduced several models priced in the mid-$20,000 range to target middle-class consumers, although it usually targets upper-class customers with more expensive vehicles.

Culture and Subcultures

Culture is the accumulation of values, knowledge, beliefs, customs, objects, and concepts that a society uses to cope with its environment and passes on to future generations. Examples of objects are foods, furniture, buildings, clothing, and tools. Concepts include education, welfare, and laws. Culture also includes core values and the degree of acceptability of a wide range of behaviors in a specific society. For example, in our culture, customers as well as businesspeople are expected to behave ethically.

Culture influences buying behavior because it permeates our daily lives. Our culture determines what we wear and eat and where we reside and travel. Society's interest in the healthfulness of food affects food companies' approaches to developing and promoting their products. Culture also influences how we buy and use products and our satisfaction from them.

When U.S. marketers sell products in other countries, they realize the tremendous impact those cultures have on product purchases and use. Global marketers find that people in other regions of the world have different attitudes, values, and needs, which call for different methods of doing business as well as different types of marketing mixes. Some international marketers fail because they do not or cannot adjust to cultural differences.

A culture consists of various subcultures. **Subcultures** are groups of individuals whose characteristic values and behavior patterns are similar to each other and differ from those of the surrounding culture. Subcultural boundaries are usually based on geographic designations and demographic characteristics such as age, religion, race, and ethnicity. Our culture is marked by many different subcultures, among them West Coast, gay, Asian American, and college students. Within subcultures, greater similarities exist in people's attitudes, values, and actions than within the broader culture. Relative to other subcultures, individuals in one subculture may have stronger preferences for specific types of clothing, furniture, or foods. Research has shown that subcultures can play a significant role in how people respond to advertisements, particularly when pressured to make a snap judgment.[14] It is important to understand that a person can be a member of more than one subculture and that the behavioral patterns and values attributed to specific subcultures do not necessarily apply to all group members.

The percentage of the U.S. population comprising ethnic and racial subcultures is expected to grow. By 2050, about half the people of the United States will be members of racial and ethnic minorities. The Bureau of the Census reports that the three largest and fastest-growing ethnic U.S. subcultures are African Americans, Hispanics, and Asians. The population growth of these subcultures interests marketers. To target these groups more precisely, marketers are striving to become increasingly sensitive to and knowledgeable about their differences. Businesses recognize that to succeed, their marketing strategies will have to take into account the values, needs, interests, shopping patterns, and buying habits of various subcultures.

African American Subculture.   In the United States, the African American subculture represents 12.1 percent of the population.[15] Like all subcultures, African American consumers possess distinct buying patterns. For example, African American consumers spend more money on utilities, footwear, women's and children's apparel, groceries, and housing than do white consumers. The combined buying power of black consumers is projected to reach $1.1 trillion by 2011.[16]

Like many companies, Procter & Gamble has hiked up its marketing initiatives aimed at the African American community, spending $52.5 million last year.[17] By including African American actors in their ads, the company believes that it can encourage a positive response to its products, increasing sales among African American consumers while still maintaining ties with white consumers. For example, if an African American family is featured in an ad, the white consumers will see a heartwarming bond between family members. The African American viewers will note the inclusion of their race and feel a stronger connection to the product.[18]

Many other corporations are reaching out to the African American community with targeted efforts. Wal-Mart, for example, has adjusted the merchandising of 1,500 stores located in areas with large black populations to include more products favored by African American customers, such as ethnic hair-care products and a larger selection of more urban music offerings. The retailer also has included more African American actors in its advertising campaigns.[19] Another retailer, Target, launched a year-long campaign called "Dream in Color" to celebrate diversity. The campaign included numerous Martin Luther King Day events, guest appearances by poet Dr. Maya Angelou, free posters for schools, and a unique online curriculum to provide access to historical and contemporary African American poets.[20] Chrysler Group, partnering with DaimlerChrysler African American Network, organized an assortment of festivities to commemorate Black History Month. Exhibits, concerts, and guest speakers helped to increase awareness about the African American community and its vital contributions to present-day society.[21]

Hispanic Subculture.   Hispanics represent 14.5 percent of the U.S. population, and their buying power is expected to reach $1.2 trillion by 2011.[22] When considering the buying behavior of Hispanics, marketers must keep in mind that this subculture consists of nearly two dozen nationalities and ethnicities, including Cuban, Mexican, Puerto Rican, Spanish, and Dominican. Each has its own history and unique culture that affect consumer preferences and buying behavior. Marketers also should recognize that the terms *Hispanic* and *Latino* refer to an ethnic category rather than a racial distinction. Because of the group's growth and purchasing power, understanding the Hispanic subculture is critical to marketers. In general, Hispanics have strong family values, concern for product quality, and strong brand loyalty, and they will pay more for a well-known brand.[23] Like African American consumers, Hispanics spend more on housing, groceries, telephone services, and children's apparel and shoes. But they also spend more on men's apparel and appliances, whereas they spend less than average on health care, entertainment, and education.[24]

To attract this powerful subculture, marketers are taking Hispanic values and preferences into account when developing products and creating advertising and promotions. Reebok, for example, markets to young Hispanics through a website, **www.barriorbk.com,** using music and Latino celebrities. The company also has established a relationship with the Mexican soccer team, Chivas, to help market its athletic products in Mexico and the United States.[25] Kmart has launched a monthly Spanish magazine and Sunday advertising circular. Kmart has roughly one-third of its stores in urban markets.[26]

White consumers, especially between the ages of 12 and 34, continue to be influenced by minority cultures, especially in areas such as fashion, entertainment, dining, sports, and music.[27] Thanks to this increasing appeal, advertisers have made a beneficial discovery. They can target both white and Hispanic consumers by hiring famous Hispanic people to appear in their ad campaigns.[28] Pepsi put Latina pop star Shakira in its ads. Bell South hired actress Daisy Fuentes to appear in a telephone company commercial discussing the importance of friends and family. The ad was aired in both English and Spanish.[29]

Asian American Subculture.   The term *Asian American* includes people from more than 15 ethnic groups, including Filipinos, Chinese, Japanese, Asian Indians, Koreans, and Vietnamese, and they represent 4.3 percent of the U.S. population. The individual language, religion, and value system of each group influence its members' purchasing decisions. Some traits of this subculture, however, carry across ethnic divisions, including an emphasis on hard work, strong family ties, and a high value placed on education.[30] Asian Americans are the fastest-growing American subculture, and they are expected to wield $622 billion in buying power by 2011.[31]

Marketers are targeting the diverse Asian American market in many ways. Kraft, for example, learned from marketing research that its Asian American customers weren't interested in having "Asian" products from Kraft but rather in learning how to use well-known Kraft brands to create healthy Western-style dishes. Targeting immigrant mothers trying to balance between Eastern and Western cultures, the company therefore launched a new ad campaign in Chinese and Mandarin—the two most commonly spoken Asian dialects—and offered samples and demonstrations in Chinese as well as a website with recipes and healthy tips. Retailer JCPenney likewise used an advertising campaign to tout its competitive prices to Chinese and Vietnamese women, particularly during cultural holidays.[32]

...And now, back to Harley-Davidson

The motorcycle experience is central to Harley-Davidson's culture and marketing. Nearly half the company's 8,200 employees own one of the firm's motorcycles—purchased from local dealers—so they know a great deal about how their products are used. In addition, hundreds of employees attend cycling rallies around the country to mingle with customers, applying what they learn when developing new products and new marketing programs. For example, after observing how riders personalize their bikes with unusual handlebars and unique paint jobs, Harley-Davidson launched a line of custom bikes complete with special accessories. These motorcycles sell for around $25,000 and are more profitable than regular sport and touring models, which fetch $8,000 to $17,000.

To its customers, the Harley-Davidson brand represents more than just two-wheeled transportation. When they line up to buy Harley-Davidson bikes, wear branded apparel, and participate in cross-country tours benefiting charities, customers are making a lifestyle choice. Nonmotorcycle products with the Harley-Davidson brand have become so popular that they bring in revenues in excess of $10 million monthly. Customers snap up T-shirts in sizes from newborn to XXXL. They also buy leather jackets, teddy bears, blankets, drinking glasses, collectible pins, and hundreds of other branded items. In fact, some customers start out wearing Harley-Davidson clothing and then progress to buying Harley-Davidson motorcycles.

Owning a Harley-Davidson makes customers a part of a brand-oriented motorcycle community. The Harley Owners Group (HOG.)—900,000 members strong—enables enthusiasts to connect with one another and with the brand. Annual rallies such as those held at Sturgis, South Dakota, and Daytona Beach, Florida, routinely draw 100,000 or more Harley-Davidson owners. When the company threw a week-long 100th birthday bash in Milwaukee, 250,000 bikers showed up to celebrate and shop for all manner of Harley-Davidson merchandise.

Nevertheless, the company may face a bumpy ride as it searches for ways to appeal to younger customers and fend off rivals. Twenty years ago the average age of a Harley-Davidson buyer was 35; today it's 47. Moreover, high-performance models from competitors are beginning to cut into Harley's market share. In response, Harley-Davidson is introducing sleek new models with liquid-cooled engines. Some of these new models can reach speeds up to 140 miles per hour. It also has opened a new factory to keep up with demand. Through the Rider's Edge program, the company is teaching a new generation of customers how to ride and care for their motorcycles.

Harley-Davidson remains on top of the North American market and has reported record sales for more than 19 consecutive years. Harley is also riding high with foreign fans who appreciate its "all-American" powerful and free image. Fast-growing overseas markets account for more than $1 billion a year in sales, or 22.5 percent of all bikes sold. Even in Japan, Harley owns the number 1 spot for heavy-weight bikes, claiming 26 percent of the market. One of the co-founder's grandsons, Willie G. Davidson, serves as senior vice president and rides his Harley to customer gatherings. What he calls "the rebel thing" is an integral part of the brand image. Harley owners may enjoy this image when they ride, and a large number change their leathers for business suits during the workweek. To stay on the road to higher sales and profits, Harley-Davidson will have to stay attuned to its customers' perceptions of this century-old brand.[33]

1. What might Harley-Davidson's employees do to measure brand equity as they mingle with customers at motorcycle rallies?

2. Should the company continue family branding or move to individual branding for new models of motorcycles? Explain.

3. What questions should Harley-Davidson ask of an apparel company that wants to license the Harley-Davidson brand to place on its clothing?

CHAPTER REVIEW

1. Describe the level of involvement and types of consumer problem-solving processes.

An individual's level of involvement—the importance and intensity of his or her interest in a product in a particular situation—affects the type of problem-solving processes used. Enduring involvement is an ongoing interest in a product class because of personal relevance, whereas situational involvement is a temporary interest stemming from the particular circumstance or environment in which buyers find themselves. There are three kinds of consumer problem solving: routinized response behavior, limited problem solving, and extended problem solving. Consumers rely on routinized response behavior when buying frequently purchased low-cost items requiring little search and decision effort. Limited problem solving is used for products purchased occasionally or when buyers need to acquire information about an unfamiliar brand in a familiar product category. Consumers engage in extended problem solving when purchasing an unfamiliar, expensive, or infrequently bought product.

2. Recognize the stages of the consumer buying decision process.

The consumer buying decision process includes five stages: problem recognition, information search, evaluation of alternatives, purchase, and postpurchase evaluation. Not all decision processes culminate in a purchase, nor do all consumer decisions include all five stages. Problem recognition occurs when buyers become aware of a difference between a desired state and an actual condition. After recognizing the problem or need, buyers search for information about products to help resolve the problem or satisfy the need. A successful search yields a group of brands, called a *consideration set*, that a buyer views as possible alternatives. To evaluate the product in the consideration set, the buyer establishes certain criteria by which to compare, rate, and rank different products. Marketers can influence consumers' evaluation by framing alternatives. In the purchase stage, consumers select products or brands on the basis of results from the evaluation stage and other dimensions. Buyers also choose the seller from whom they will buy the product. After the purchase, buyers evaluate the product to determine if its actual performance meets expected levels.

3.   Explain how situational influences may affect the consumer buying decision process.

Situational influences are external circumstances or conditions existing when a consumer makes a purchase decision. Situational influences include surroundings, time, reason for purchase, and the buyer's mood and condition.

4.   Understand the psychological influences that may affect the consumer buying decision process.

Psychological influences partly determine people's general behavior, thus influencing their behavior as consumers. The primary psychological influences on consumer behavior are perception, motives, learning, attitudes, personality and self-concept, and lifestyles. Perception is the process of selecting, organizing, and interpreting information inputs (sensations received through sight, taste, hearing, smell, and touch) to produce meaning. The three steps in the perceptual process are selection, organization, and interpretation. An individual has numerous perceptions of packages, products, brands, and organizations, all of which affect the buying decision process. A motive is an internal energizing force that orients a person's activities toward satisfying needs or achieving goals. Learning refers to changes in a person's thought processes and behavior caused by information and experience. Marketers try to shape what consumers learn to influence what they buy. An attitude is an individual's enduring evaluation, feelings, and behavioral tendencies toward an object or idea and consists of three major components: cognitive, affective, and behavioral. Personality is the set of traits and behaviors that make a person unique. Self-concept, closely linked to personality, is a person's view of perception of himself or herself. Research indicates that a buyer purchases products that reflect and enhance self-concept. Lifestyle is an individual's pattern of living expressed through activities, interests, and opinions.

5.   Be familiar with the social influences that affect the consumer buying decision process.

Social influences are forces that other people exert on buying behavior. They include roles, family, reference groups and opinion leaders, social class, and culture and subcultures. Everyone occupies positions within groups, organizations, and institutions, and each position has a role—a set of actions and activities that a person in a particular position is supposed to perform based on expectations of both the individual and surrounding persons. In a family, children learn from parents (and other household adults) and older siblings how to make decisions, such as purchase decisions. Consumer socialization is the process through which a person acquires the knowledge and skills to function as a consumer. The consumer socialization process is partially accomplished through family influences. A reference group is any group that positively or negatively affects a person's values, attitudes, or behavior. The three major types of reference groups are membership, aspirational, and disassociative. In most reference groups, one or more members stand out as opinion leaders by furnishing requested information to reference group participants. A social class is an open group of individuals with similar social rank. Social class influences people's spending, saving, and credit practices. Culture is the accumulation of values, knowledge, beliefs, customs, objects, and concepts that a society uses to cope with its environment and passes on to future generations. A culture is made up of subcultures. A subculture is a group of individuals whose characteristics, values, and behavior patterns are similar to and differ from those of the surrounding culture. U.S. marketers focus on three major ethnic subcultures: African American, Hispanic, and Asian American.

ACE self-test

Please visit the student website at **www.prideferrell.com** for ACE Self-Test questions that will help you prepare for exams.

KEY CONCEPTS

buying behavior
consumer buying behavior
level of involvement
routinized response
   behavior
limited problem solving
extended problem solving
impulse buying
consumer buying decision
   process

internal search
external search
consideration set
evaluative criteria
cognitive dissonance
situational influences
psychological influences
perception
information inputs
selective exposure

selective distortion
selective retention
motive
Maslow's hierarchy of
   needs
patronage motives
learning
attitude
attitude scale
personality

self-concept
lifestyle
social influences
role
consumer socialization
reference group
opinion leader
social class
culture
subculture

ISSUES FOR DISCUSSION AND REVIEW

1. How does a consumer's level of involvement affect his or her choice of problem-solving process?

2. Name the types of consumer problem-solving processes. List some products you have bought using each type. Have you ever bought a product on impulse? If so, describe the circumstances.

3. What are the major stages in the consumer buying decision process? Are all these stages used in all consumer purchase decisions? Why or why not?

4. What are the categories of situational factors that influence consumer buying behavior? Explain how each of these factors influences buyers' decisions.

5. What is selective exposure? Why do people engage in it?

6. How do marketers attempt to shape consumers' learning?

7. Why are marketers concerned about consumer attitudes?

8. In what ways do lifestyles affect the consumer buying decision process?

9. How do roles affect a person's buying behavior? Provide examples.

10. What are family influences, and how do they affect buying behavior?

11. What are reference groups? How do they influence buying behavior? Name some of your own reference groups.

12. How does an opinion leader influence the buying decision process of reference group members?

13. In what ways does social class affect a person's purchase decisions?

14. What is culture? How does it affect a person's buying behavior?

15. Describe the subcultures to which you belong. Identify buying behavior that is unique to one of your subcultures.

MARKETING APPLICATIONS

1. Describe three buying experiences you have had—one for each type of problem solving—and identify which problem-solving process you used. Discuss why that particular process was appropriate.

2. Interview a classmate about the last purchase he or she made. Report the stages of the consumer buying process used and those skipped, if any.

3. Briefly describe how a beer company might alter the cognitive and affective components of consumer attitudes toward beer products and toward the company.

4. Identify two of your roles and give an example of how they have influenced your buying decisions.

5. Select five brands of toothpaste and explain how the appeals used in advertising these brands relate to Maslow's hierarchy of needs.

Online Exercises

6. Some mass-market e-commerce sites, such as Amazon.com, have extended the concept of customization to their customer base. Amazon has created an affinity group by drawing on certain users' likes and dislikes to make product recommendations to other users. Check out this pioneering online retailer at **www.amazon.com**.
   a. What might motivate some consumers to read a "top selling" list?
   b. Is the consumer's level of involvement with online book purchase likely to be high or low?
   c. Discuss the consumer buying decision process as it relates to a decision to purchase from Amazon.com.

globalEDGE™

Your firm is currently designing the next generation of mountain climbing accessories and footwear. To understand the needs and behaviors of this distinctive global market segment, you must perform market research in a variety of countries. From your own knowledge on the subject, you know that the number of Mt. Everest ascents per capita, developed by NationMaster.com, is an excellent measure of mountain climbing's popularity. To access this information, use the search term "compare various statistics" at **http://globaledge.msu.edu/ibrd** (and check the box "Resource Desk only"). Determine the top five countries in mountain climbing popularity by selecting the "Sports" category in the drop-down box to the right and the subcategory of "Mt. Everest ascents" with the most recent dates. In which three countries would you conduct focus groups to develop your new product line?

Video CASE

Want the Low Down? Consumer Reports Has It

For more than 70 years, *Consumer Reports* magazine has been helping people to make better buying decisions. A subsidiary of Consumer Union, Consumer Reports first began operations in 1936. The company is an independent, nonprofit organization whose stated mission is to strive for a fair, just, and safe marketplace for all consumers. Also, Consumer Reports attempts to empower consumers to protect themselves by teaching them about products to make better buying decisions.

The company's National Testing and Research Center in Yonkers, New York, is the largest nonprofit educational and consumer product testing center in the world. Credibility has been its key to success, and Consumer Reports works hard at maintaining its independence and impartiality by accepting no outside advertising or free samples and maintaining no other agenda than the interests of consumers. The company supports itself through the sale of information about products and services, individual contributions, and a few noncommercial grants. *Consumer Reports* magazine has about 4 million subscribers. ConsumerReports.org is the largest publication-based subscription website in the world, with more than 2 million online subscribers.

Before a product enters one of Consumer Reports' dozens of labs, it has been carefully researched as to manufacturers' claims and consumer demand in the marketplace. Products are tested not only against government and industry standards but also on how consumers use them in everyday situations. Consumer Reports employs more than 150 anonymous shoppers in 60 U.S. cities to buy the products for testing. Laboratory testing is supplemented through an annual questionnaire that is sent to subscribers that generates over 900,000 returns.

The stakes are high for Consumer Reports to be accurate in its product evaluations. In some cases the health and the lives of consumers are at stake. Consumer Reports recently investigated the multibillion-dollar nutritional supplements business and found that highly dangerous supplements were being legally sold in mainstream U.S. stores and on the Internet. Consumer Reports pointed out that a nutritional supplement's safety claims do not have to be supported scientifically and that the government does not require warning labels of potential dangers. An article profiled a consumer who suffered severe kidney damage after taking Chinese herbs. The woman had to undergo a kidney transplant and sued the therapist that recommended the products and several companies that manufactured them.

Consumer Reports also faces the risk of lawsuits. Obviously, companies are not happy when Consumer Reports disputes their claims or publishes test results that disparage their products or associated services. For example, after several fast-food chains began touting their *trans* fat–free french fries, Consumer Reports tested their fries and found that stores in one chain still served fries with measurable *trans* fats. The company also caught flak after it was forced to withdraw a report that suggested that most child safety seats were unsafe in side-impact crashes; after determining that the tests were conducted at much higher speeds that initially indicated, the company pledged to retest the child safety seats and issue a new, correct report. Although the company has been sued 15 times in its 70-year existence, it has prevailed in every case. Clearly, the nature of Consumer Reports' type of business makes Consumer Union vulnerable to lawsuits. However, its track record speaks volumes about its accuracy and integrity.

Consumer Reports has continued to keep abreast of technology and consumer buying habits. It recently announced ShopSmart, a new service designed specifically for the way people shop. ShopSmart delivers independent expert ratings, reviews, and prices on thousands of popular consumer products to subscribers over their cell phones, wherever and whenever they shop. The service is available on major cell phone carriers for a monthly fee billed to the subscriber's cell phone account.

ShopSmart will change the way people shop by supplying them with detailed product and pricing information at the point of purchase. For example, a mom out

shopping for a plasma screen TV for her family sees a sale on one of the latest models, and a salesperson assures her that it is flat-out the best TV at an unbeatable price. On an item with a price tag of $2,000, she wants to make sure that she buys the best product at the best value. By dialing ShopSmart on her cell phone, she can get a product rating, see the suggested price for the TV, and even determine if the same model is available in another store at a lower price.

"Consumer Reports ShopSmart was created with all types of shoppers in mind including the impulse buyer at the counter facing an aggressive salesperson and the researcher in the parking lot contemplating an important purchase," said the senior director and general manager of information products for Consumer Reports. "The service works for every lifestyle—from the teenager out shopping for a new MP3 player to expecting parents buying a new space heater."

Seventy years later, Consumer Reports is still helping customers to buy right.[34]

Questions for Discussion

1. What elements of the consumer buying decision process does Consumer Reports' information most affect? In what ways?
2. In what ways could information in *Consumer Reports* magazine contribute to or help reduce cognitive dissonance? Explain.
3. How can Consumer Reports help a buyer to make a better purchase decision?

Business Markets and Buying Behavior

Texas Instruments Supplies the Processing Power

Texas Instruments (TI) is often the first name evoked when people consider buying a calculator. Calculators, however, are not the only products that the Dallas, Texas–based company makes and markets. Indeed, most of the products TI makes are found inside electronic devices that other companies market under their own brand names—names such as Apple, Dell, Nokia, and Samsung. With sales of more than $13 billion, TI is the third-largest semiconductor company in the world. Texas Instruments Incorporated has manufacturing, design, or sales operations in more than 25 countries, and its largest geographic sources of revenue are Asia (excluding Japan), Europe, the United States, and Japan.

TI was founded in 1930 as Geophysical Service, Inc. (GSI), a pioneering provider of seismic exploration services. In December 1941, four GSI managers purchased the company just as the United States entered World War II. The company began manufacturing submarine detection equipment for the U.S. Navy during the war, and soon after the war, it began supplying defense systems, launching a strategy that would change the company completely. In 1951, the company changed its name to Texas Instruments to reflect the change in its business strategy. It entered the semiconductor business in 1952.

TI designed the first transistor radio in 1954, the hand-held calculator in 1967, and the single-chip microcomputer in 1971. It was assigned the first patent on a single-chip microprocessor in 1973, and it is usually given credit, with Intel, for the almost-simultaneous invention of the microprocessor, which fueled the personal computing revolution. TI also created the first commercial silicon transistor and invented the integrated circuit. It continued to manufacture equipment for use in the seismic industry, as well as providing seismic services. TI sold its GSI subsidiary to Halliburton in 1988 and in the early 1990s began a strategic process of focusing on its semiconductor business, primarily digital signal processors and analog semiconductors. Few companies can match the 75-year record of innovations from TI.

Today, TI's products continue to be used in many things that are an integral part of the products in our daily lives—from the cell phone to cable modems, home theaters, wireless Internet, digital cameras, and advanced automotive systems. TI is also working on new signal-processing innovations that will help to create cars that drive themselves and allow the blind to see and much more. Without these products, many companies could not produce their own products for business and consumer markets.[1] ∎

OBJECTIVES

1. Be able to distinguish among the various types of business markets.

2. Identify the major characteristics of business customers and transactions.

3. Understand several attributes of the demand for business products.

4. Become familiar with the major components of a buying center.

5. Understand the stages of the business buying decision process and the factors that affect this process.

6. Describe industrial classification systems and explain how they can be used to identify and analyze business markets.

erving business markets effectively requires business marketers like Texas Instruments to understand business customers. Business marketers go to considerable lengths to understand and reach their customers so that they can provide better services and develop and maintain long-term customer relationships. Like consumer marketers, business marketers are concerned about satisfying their customers.

In this chapter we look at business markets and business buying decision processes. We first discuss various kinds of business markets and the types of buyers making up these markets. Next, we explore several dimensions of business buying, such as characteristics of transactions, attributes and concerns of buyers, methods of buying, and distinctive features of demand for products sold to business purchasers. We then examine how business buying decisions are made and who makes the purchases. Finally, we consider how business markets are analyzed.

Business Markets

Serving Business Markets

Business markets can be technically complex and consist of a relatively small number of customers.

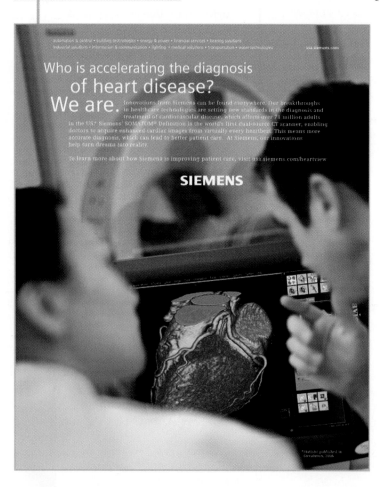

As defined in Chapter 7, a business market (also called a *business-to-business, or B2B, market*) consists of individuals, organizations, or groups that purchase a specific kind of product for resale, direct use in producing other products, or use in general daily operations. Although B2B marketing employs the same concepts as marketing to ultimate consumers, such as defining target markets, understanding buying behavior, and developing effective marketing mixes, there are structural and behavioral differences in business markets. A company marketing to business customers must recognize how its product will influence other associated firms such as wholesalers, retailers, and even other manufacturers. Business products can be technically complex, and the market often consists of sophisticated buyers. Because the business market consists of relatively smaller customer populations, a segment of the market could be as small as a few customers.[2] The market for railway equipment in the United States, for example, is limited to a few major carriers. On the other hand, a business product can be a commodity such as corn or a bolt or screw, but the quantity purchased and the buying methods differ significantly from the consumer market, as we shall see. Business marketing is often based on long-term mutually profitable relationships across members of the marketing channel. Networks of suppliers and customers recognize the importance of building strong alliances based on cooperation, trust, and collaboration.[3] Manufacturers may even co-develop new products with business customers, sharing marketing research, production, scheduling, inventory management, and information systems. Consider that when the largest distributor for independent book publishers, Consortium Book & Sales Distribution, Inc., discovered that its information technology (IT) system was outdated, the firm partnered with Integrated Knowledge Systems, Inc., to develop a new database to track book sales in real time to let publishers know which titles sell well and which should be eliminated. In this case the marketer custom-designed IT solutions with the customer to resolve its operational services and efficiency concerns.[4] Although business marketing can be based on collaborative long-term buyer-seller relationships, there are also transactions based on timely exchanges

table 9.1	NUMBER OF ESTABLISHMENTS IN INDUSTRY GROUPS	
Industry		**Number of Establishments**
Agriculture, forestry, fishing, and hunting		25,900
Mining		23,600
Construction		732,200
Manufacturing		341,800
Transportation, warehousing, and utilities		221,100
Finance, insurance, and real estate		794,200
Other services		2,513,300

Source: U.S. Bureau of the Census, *Statistical Abstract of the United States,* 2007 (Washington, DC: U.S. Government Printing Office, 2006), p. 497.

of basic products at highly competitive market prices. For most business marketers, the goal is understanding customer needs and providing a value-added exchange that shifts from attracting customers to keeping customers and developing relationships.[5]

The four categories of business markets are producer, reseller, government, and institutional. In the remainder of this section we discuss each of these types of markets.

Producer Markets

Individuals and business organizations that purchase products for the purpose of making a profit by using them to produce other products or using them in their operations are classified as **producer markets**. Producer markets include buyers of raw materials, as well as purchasers of semifinished and finished items used to produce other products. For example, manufacturers buy raw materials and component parts for direct use in product production. Supermarkets are part of producer markets for numerous support products such as paper and plastic bags, shelves, counters, and scanners. Farmers are part of producer markets for farm machinery, fertilizer, seed, and livestock. Producer markets include a broad array of industries, ranging from agriculture, forestry, fisheries, and mining to construction, transportation, communications, and utilities. As Table 9.1 indicates, the number of business establishments in national producer markets is enormous.

Manufacturers are geographically concentrated. More than half are located in just seven states: California, New York, Texas, Ohio, Illinois, Pennsylvania, and Michigan (arranged in descending order). This concentration sometimes enables businesses that sell to producer markets to serve them more efficiently. Within certain states, production in a specific industry may account for a sizable proportion of that industry's total production.

Reseller Markets

Reseller markets consist of intermediaries, such as wholesalers and retailers, who buy finished goods and resell them for profit. Aside from making minor alterations, resellers do not change the physical characteristics of the products they handle. Except for items that producers sell directly to consumers, all products sold to consumer markets are first sold to reseller markets, consisting of wholesalers and retailers. Wholesalers purchase products for resale to retailers, to other wholesalers, and to producers, governments, and institutions. Arrow Electronics, for example, buys computer chips

producer markets Individuals and business organizations that purchase products to make profits by using them to produce other products or using them in their operations

reseller markets Intermediaries who buy finished goods and resell them for profit

Naturally Potatoes? Naturally.

Naturally Potatoes was founded in the mid-1990s by a group of savvy potato farmers in Mars Hill, Aroostook County, Maine. The county's economy had long relied on potato farming, but in the 1990s, the potato market was in decline. Inspired by packaged, prewashed lettuce mixes, Rodney McCrum, Francis Fitzpatrick, and other local farmers decided to create fresh-cut potato products to fit into the preprepared produce market. McCrum put together 14 investors and set to work building a $15 million plant to process the potatoes. This move increased the company's growth by 30 percent and its sales by $20 million annually.

Naturally Potatoes sells to two markets—food service/restaurants and retailers who resell the products to ultimate consumers. Today the company is focused on the food service/restaurant end, but it plans to increase its concentration on the retail end in the future. With more consumers looking for nearly ready-to-eat food to fit their busy lifestyles, the company predicts that its packaged potatoes will be a hit in supermarkets.

With its highly automated plant, Naturally Potatoes needs just 70 employees to process 50 million potatoes annually. The machines wash, peel, and chop the potatoes. The company's mashed potatoes are cooked through, but the diced potatoes are 80 percent cooked so that chefs in restaurants or people at home can easily and quickly finish cooking them. Once processed, the potatoes are put in plastic bags and shipped in refrigerated trucks. Depending on the product, the potatoes are good for 30 to 60 days.

Naturally Potatoes faces competition from Reser's Fine Foods, which sells Potato Express, and Michael Foods, which markets Simply Potatoes. Both companies, like Naturally Potatoes, serve both the food service/restaurant and retail industries. Right now, despite a supposed decline in potato consumption, all three companies are thriving and believe that further success is ahead.[a]

and other electronics components and resells them to producers of subsystems for cell phones, computers, and automobiles. Of the 435,521 wholesalers in the United States, a large percentage are located in New York, California, Illinois, Texas, Ohio, Pennsylvania, and Florida.[6] Although some products are sold directly to end users, some manufacturers sell their products to wholesalers, who, in turn, sell the products to other firms in the distribution system. Retailers purchase products and resell them to final consumers. There are approximately 1.1 million retailers in the United States, employing more than 15 million people and generating more than $3.1 trillion in annual sales.[7] Some retailers—Home Depot, PetSmart, and Staples, for example—carry a large number of items. Supermarkets may handle as many as 50,000 different products. In small, individually owned retail stores, owners or managers make purchasing decisions.

When making purchase decisions, resellers consider several factors. They evaluate the level of demand for a product to determine in what quantity and at what prices the product can be resold. Retailers assess the amount of space required to handle a product relative to its potential profit. In fact, they sometimes evaluate products on the basis of sales per square foot of selling area. Because customers often depend on resellers to have products available when needed, resellers typically appraise a supplier's ability to provide adequate quantities when and where wanted. Resellers also take into account the ease of placing orders and the availability of technical assistance and training programs from the producer. These types of concerns distinguish reseller markets from other markets.

Government Markets

Federal, state, county, and local governments make up **government markets**. These markets spend billions of dollars annually for a variety of goods and services—ranging from office supplies and health-care services to vehicles, heavy equipment, and weapons—to support their internal operations and provide citizens with products such as highways, education, water, energy, and national defense. The federal government spends more than $530 billion annually on national defense alone. Government expenditures annually account for about 21 percent of the U.S. gross domestic product.[8] In addition to the federal government, there are 50 state governments, 3,034 county governments, and 87,525 local governments.[9] The amount spent by federal, state, and local government units over the last 30 years has increased rapidly because the total number of government units and the services they provide have both increased. Costs of providing these services also have risen.

The types and quantities of products bought by government markets reflect societal demands on various government agencies. As citizens' needs for government services change, so does the demand for products by government markets. For example, the U.S. Department of State granted Identix a contract to supply large-scale facial-recognition systems for visa processing, a capability that has become increasingly important in today's world.[10] Although it is common to hear of large corporations being awarded government contracts, in fact, businesses of all sizes market to government agencies. In recent years, the Internet has helped small businesses earn more government contracts than ever before by providing venues for small businesses to learn about and bid on government contracting opportunities. For example, VM Manufacturing, a small Holbrook, New York–based company specializing in aircraft and commercial parts, used ePublicBids to help it win contracts of up to $100,000 with defense supply centers in Philadelphia and Richmond.[11]

Because government agencies spend public funds to buy the products needed to provide services, they are accountable to the public. This accountability explains their relatively complex set of buying procedures. Some firms do not even try to sell to government buyers because they want to avoid the tangle of red tape. However, many marketers have learned to deal efficiently with government procedures and do not find them to be a stumbling block. For certain products, such as defense-related items, the government may be the only customer. The U.S. Government Printing Office publishes and distributes several documents explaining buying procedures and describing the types of products various federal agencies purchase.

Institutional Markets

Organizations with charitable, educational, community, or other nonbusiness goals constitute **institutional markets.** Members of institutional markets include churches, some hospitals, fraternities and sororities, charitable organizations, and private

Institutional Markets

Gifts In Kind International redistributes firms' excess inventory to over 50,000 nonprofit organizations worldwide. This organization is a part of an institutional market.

government markets Federal, state, county, and local governments that buy goods and services to support their internal operations and provide products to their constituencies

institutional markets Organizations with charitable, educational, community, or other nonbusiness goals

colleges. Institutions purchase millions of dollars' worth of products annually to provide goods, services, and ideas to congregations, students, patients, and others. Because institutions often have different goals and fewer resources than other types of organizations, marketers may use special marketing efforts to serve them. For example, Hussey Seating in Maine sells bleacher stadium seating to schools, colleges, churches, and other institutions, as well as to sports arenas, around the world. The family-owned business shows its support for institutional customers through assistance with school funding and reduced-cost construction of local economic development projects.[12]

Dimensions of Marketing to Business Customers

Having considered different types of business customers, we now look at several dimensions of marketing to them, including transaction characteristics, attributes of business customers, primary concerns of business customers, buying methods, major types of purchases, and the characteristics of demand for business products.

Characteristics of Transactions with Business Customers

Transactions between businesses differ from consumer sales in several ways. Orders by business customers tend to be much larger than individual consumer sales. Consider that Ireland's RyanAir, the largest discount airline in Europe, placed an order for 32 Boeing 737-800 passenger jet aircraft at an estimated cost of $2.25 billion to add to its fleet of 281 Boeing 737 aircraft.[13] Suppliers often must sell products in large quantities to make profits; consequently, they prefer not to sell to customers who place small orders. Some business purchases involve expensive items, such as computer systems. Other products, such as raw materials and component items, are used continuously in production, and the supply may need frequent replenishing. The contract regarding terms of sale of these items is likely to be a long-term agreement.

Discussions and negotiations associated with business purchases can require considerable marketing effort. Purchasing decisions often are made by committee. Orders frequently are large and expensive. Products may be custom-built. Several people or departments in the purchasing organization may be involved.

One practice unique to business markets is **reciprocity,** an arrangement in which two organizations agree to buy from each other. Reciprocal agreements that threaten competition are illegal. The Federal Trade Commission and the Justice Department take actions to stop anticompetitive reciprocal practices. Nonetheless, a certain amount of reciprocal activity occurs among small businesses and, to a lesser extent, among larger companies. Because reciprocity influences purchasing agents to deal only with certain suppliers, it can lower morale among agents and lead to less than optimal purchases.

Attributes of Business Customers

Business customers differ from consumers in their purchasing behavior because they are better informed about the products they purchase. They typically demand detailed information about products' functional features and technical specifications to ensure that the products meet the organization's needs. Personal goals, however, also may influence business buying behavior. Most purchasing agents seek the psychological satisfaction that comes with organizational advancement and financial rewards. Agents who consistently exhibit rational business buying behavior are likely to attain these personal goals because they help their firms achieve organizational objectives. Today, many suppliers and their customers build and maintain mutually beneficial relationships, sometimes called *partnerships*. Researchers have found that even in a partnership between a small vendor and a large corporate buyer, a strong partnership exists because high levels of interpersonal trust can lead to higher levels of commitment to the partnership by both organizations.[14]

reciprocity An arrangement unique to business marketing in which two organizations agree to buy from each other

Primary Concerns of Business Customers

Cargill focuses on providing quality products that meet customers' product specifications.

CREATING BETTER PARMESAN TAKES DISCRIMINATING TASTE. PARTICULARLY ON THE PART OF THE COW.

Italian cheese makers take pride in Parmigiano Reggiano, a cheese so distinctive that law dictates it come only from select provinces. Parmesan makers wanted more productivity while maintaining this legendary quality. Cargill brought animal nutrition experts into the process, who understood that dairy cows fed certain foods give milk with better yields of Parmesan. We created special feeds and a supply chain that ensures traceability of the milk furnished by producers to the Parmesan makers. Now there's more of the famed cheese for all to enjoy. This is how Cargill works with customers.

collaborate > create > succeed

Cargill
Nourishing Ideas. Nourishing People.

Primary Concerns of Business Customers

When making purchasing decisions, business customers take into account a variety of factors. Among their chief considerations are price, product quality, service, and supplier relationships. Obviously, price matters greatly to business customers because it influences operating costs and costs of goods sold, which, in turn, affect selling price, profit margin, and ultimately, the ability to compete. When purchasing major equipment, a business customer views price as the amount of investment necessary to obtain a certain level of return or savings. A business customer is likely to compare the price of a product with the benefits the product will provide to the organization, often over a period of years.

Most business customers try to achieve and maintain a specific level of quality in the products they buy. To achieve this goal, most firms establish standards (usually stated as a percentage of defects allowed) for these products and buy them on the basis of a set of expressed characteristics, commonly called *specifications*. A customer evaluates the quality of the products being considered to determine whether they meet specifications. If a product fails to meet specifications or malfunctions for the ultimate consumer, the customer may drop that product's supplier and switch to a different supplier. On the other hand, business customers are ordinarily cautious about buying products that exceed specifications because such products often cost more, thus increasing the organization's overall costs. Specifications are designed to meet a customer's wants, and anything that does not contribute to meeting those wants may be considered wasteful.

marketing ENTREPRENEURS

Venus McNabb decided to start 1-800-GeeksOnTime after her Internet startup's computer broke down and she couldn't find a reasonable and fast repair service. Her new venture is a national repair service that relies on on-call contract technicians to repair systems for business and residential customers in all 50 states. The service, which has a 24-hour guarantee, serves as a sort of "help desk" for both consumers and businesses too small for their own IT department. The working mom started 1-800-GeeksOnTime in Phoenix with just $5,000 and has grown the business primarily through strong word-of-mouth promotion from satisfied customers.[b]

Venus McNabb

HER BUSINESS: 1-800-GeeksOnTime

FOUNDED: 1999, when McNabb was age 22

SUCCESS: Revenues of more than $2 million

Business buyers value service. Services offered by suppliers directly and indirectly influence customers' costs, sales, and profits. In some instances the mix of customer services is the major means by which marketers gain a competitive advantage. Procter & Gamble, for example, provided Wendy's International with customized videos and laminated guides to show Wendy's employees how to use its industrial cleaning supplies to clean every part of each restaurant.[15] Typical services desired by customers are market information, inventory maintenance, on-time delivery, repair services, and online communication capabilities. Business buyers are likely to need technical product information, data regarding demand, information about general economic conditions, or supply and delivery information. Maintaining adequate inventory is critical because it helps to make products accessible when a customer needs them and reduces customer inventory requirements and costs. Because business customers are usually responsible for ensuring that products are on hand and ready for use when needed, on-time delivery is crucial. Furthermore, reliable, on-time delivery saves business customers money because it enables them to carry less inventory. Purchasers of machinery are especially concerned about obtaining repair services and replacement parts quickly because inoperable equipment is costly. Caterpillar, Inc., manufacturer of earth-moving, construction, and materials-handling machinery, has built an international reputation, as well as a competitive advantage, by providing prompt service and replacement parts for its products around the world. Business customers are likely to resist a supplier's effort to implement a new technology if there are questions about the technology's compatibility, reliability, or other factors that could cause the supplier to fail to deliver on promises.[16]

Communication channels that allow customers to ask questions, voice complaints, submit orders, and trace shipments are indispensable components of service. Marketers should strive for uniformity of service, simplicity, truthfulness, and accuracy. Marketers should develop customer service objectives and monitor customer service programs. Firms can monitor service by formally surveying customers or informally calling on customers and asking questions about the quality of the services they receive. Expending the time and effort to ensure that customers are happy can greatly benefit marketers by increasing customer retention.

Finally, business customers are concerned about the costs of developing and maintaining relationships with their suppliers. By developing relationships and building trust with a particular supplier, buyers can reduce their search effort and uncertainty about monetary price.[17] Business customers have to keep in mind the overall fit of a purchase, including its potential to reduce inventory and carrying costs, as well as to increase inventory turnover and ability to move the right products to the right place at the right time. The entire business can be affected by a single supplier failing to be a good partner.[18]

Methods of Business Buying

Although no two business buyers do their jobs the same way, most use one or more of the following purchase methods: description, inspection, sampling, and negotiation. When products are standardized according to certain characteristics (such as size, shape, weight, and color) and graded using such standards, a business buyer may be able to purchase simply by describing or specifying quantity, grade, and other attributes. Agricultural products often fall into this category. Sometimes buyers specify a particular brand or its equivalent when describing the desired product. Purchases on the basis of description are especially common between a buyer and seller with an ongoing relationship built on trust.

Certain products, such as industrial equipment, used vehicles, and buildings, have unique characteristics and may vary with regard to condition. For example, a particular used truck may have a bad transmission. Consequently, business buyers of such products must base purchase decisions on inspection.

Sampling entails taking a specimen of the product from the lot and evaluating it on the assumption that its characteristics represent the entire lot. This method is

The Focus Is on Service at IBM

IBM provides technology and support services to help companies operate. Based on earnings, IBM is number 1 in IT services, hardware, and financing; it is number 2 in software. Over the years, IBM has transferred its focus from computer hardware to computer services.

In 2003, IBM made some big changes and refined its business model. The company sold its personal computer division to Lenovo, a Chinese firm, and phased out its presence in creating and selling hard disk drives, memory chips, and networking hardware. Instead, the company decided to focus on forming and maintaining collaborative relationships and providing services to solve the information management needs of its business customers. Some of the major shifts IBM has made are the restructuring of its business skills, assets, and delivery capabilities to meet the needs of customers wanting to blend IT with business operations. IBM is always moving forward and reinventing its focus through effective customer relationship strategies.

Today, IBM continues to make its business more tangible, flexible, and innovative. The company vows to create a global reach and use the talent available worldwide by giving authority and resources to those working in close contact with its clients. IBM's target customers include companies such as General Motors, which is outsourcing $15 billion worth of IT contracts. To satisfy the auto giant, IBM will have to adjust to GM's demands for smaller contracts and standardized ways of doing things. In addition, it will need to develop a close partnership and craft the right value proposition to a company that is attempting to restructure in the highly competitive automotive market. IBM also must compete with EDS, Hewlett-Packard, and CapGemini, as well as other IT firms, to get its share of GM's business. With IBM's new focus, every new customer represents a challenge to craft precisely the right service.[c]

appropriate when the product is homogeneous—for instance, grain—and examining the entire lot is not physically or economically feasible.

Some purchases by businesses are based on negotiated contracts. In certain instances, buyers describe exactly what they need and ask sellers to submit bids. They then negotiate with the suppliers who submit the most attractive bids. This approach may be used when acquiring commercial vehicles, for example. In other cases, the buyer may be unable to identify specifically what is to be purchased but can provide only a general description, such as might be the case for a piece of custom-made equipment. A buyer and seller might negotiate a contract that specifies a base price and provides for the payment of additional costs and fees. These contracts are used most commonly for one-time projects such as buildings, custom-made equipment, and special projects.

Types of Business Purchases

Most business purchases are one of three types: new-task, straight-rebuy, or modified-rebuy purchase. Each type is subject to different influences and thus requires business marketers to modify their selling approach appropriately.[19] In a **new-task purchase**, an organization makes an initial purchase of an item to be used to perform a new job or solve a new problem. A new-task purchase may require development of product specifications, vendor specifications, and procedures for future purchases of that product. To make the initial purchase, the business buyer usually needs much information. For

new-task purchase An initial purchase by an organization of an item to be used to perform a new job or solve a new problem

MORE FOR YOUR MONEY.

IT'S WHAT YOU GET WITH A MORE PRODUCTIVE IC DESIGN FLOW

You have to deliver more chips faster, but tighter engineering resources, increasing design sizes and the growing challenges of nanometer process technologies make it harder and more costly to get your ICs to market. A design system that concurrently analyzes and optimizes your IC for timing, area, power, signal integrity and yield is what you need. And that's what Magma provides. Our integrated RTL-to-GDSII design system lets you get your next chip out on time, on budget and on spec – with the engineering resources you already have.

For more on how Magma lets you get a higher return on investment in your chip designs, visit **www.magma-da.com/4ROI**. Find out why the world's top chip companies rely on Magma software to design their most critical ICs.

MAGMA.

© 2005 Magma Design Automation, Inc. All rights reserved. Magma and the Magma logo are registered trademarks of Magma Design Automation, Inc.

Derived Demand

In response to the growing consumer demand for technological precision, Magma creates and markets its chip design system to customers trying to produce chips according to market specifications.

example, if Heineken were introducing a salty, spicy beer-flavored snack and were purchasing automated packaging equipment, that would be a new-task purchase.

A **straight-rebuy purchase** occurs when buyers purchase the same products routinely under approximately the same terms of sale. Buyers require little information for these routine purchase decisions and tend to use familiar suppliers that have provided satisfactory service and products in the past. These suppliers try to set up automatic reordering systems to make reordering easy and convenient for business buyers. For example, Degussa Construction Chemicals Operations, Inc., a chemical manufacturer, contracts with freight carrier DistTech to manage and deliver its products with real-time shipment tracking.[20]

In a **modified-rebuy purchase**, a new-task purchase is changed the second or third time it is ordered, or requirements associated with a straight-rebuy purchase are modified. A business buyer might seek faster delivery, lower prices, or a different quality level of product specifications. A modified-rebuy situation may cause regular suppliers to become more competitive to keep the account because other suppliers could obtain the business. When a firm changes the terms of a service contract, such as for telecommunication services, it has made a modified purchase. Gateway Computer Systems is expanding its commercial business by focusing on small businesses by offering on-site help and online educational resources. This effort may give Gateway a competitive advantage in serving small firms making modified-rebuy purchases.[21]

Demand for Business Products

Unlike consumer demand, demand for business products (also called *industrial demand*) can be characterized as (1) derived, (2) inelastic, (3) joint, or (4) fluctuating.

Derived Demand.   Because business customers, especially producers, buy products for direct or indirect use in the production of goods and services to satisfy consumers' needs, the demand for business products derives from the demand for consumer products. It is therefore called **derived demand.** In the long run, no demand for business products is totally unrelated to the demand for consumer products. The derived nature of demand is usually multilevel. Business marketers at different levels are affected by a change in consumer demand for a particular product. For instance, consumers have become concerned with health and good nutrition and as a result are purchasing more products with less fat, cholesterol, and sodium. When consumers reduced their purchases of high-fat foods, a change occurred in the demand for products marketed by food processors, equipment manufacturers, and suppliers of raw materials associated with these products. When consumer demand for a product changes, it sets in motion a wave that affects demand for all firms involved in the production of that product.

Inelastic Demand.   **Inelastic demand** means that a price increase or decrease will not significantly alter demand for a business product. Because some business products

straight-rebuy purchase A routine purchase of the same products under approximately the same terms of sale by a business buyer

modified-rebuy purchase A new-task purchase that is changed on subsequent orders or when the requirements of a straight-rebuy purchase are modified

derived demand Demand for industrial products that stems from demand for consumer products

inelastic demand Demand that is not significantly altered by a price increase or decrease

joint demand Demand involving the use of two or more items in combination to produce a product

contain a number of parts, price increases affecting only one or two parts may yield only a slightly higher per-unit production cost. When a sizable price increase for a component represents a large proportion of the product's cost, demand may become more elastic because the price increase in the component causes the price at the consumer level to rise sharply. For example, if aircraft engine manufacturers substantially increase the price of engines, forcing Boeing to raise the prices of the aircraft it manufactures, the demand for airliners may become more elastic as airlines reconsider whether they can afford to buy new aircraft. An increase in the price of windshields, however, is unlikely to affect greatly either the price of or the demand for airliners.

Inelasticity applies only to industry demand for business products, not to the demand curve that an individual firm faces. Suppose that a spark plug producer increases the price of spark plugs sold to small-engine manufacturers, but its competitors continue to maintain lower prices. The spark plug company probably will experience reduced unit sales because most small-engine producers will switch to lower-priced brands. A specific firm is vulnerable to elastic demand, even though industry demand for a specific business product is inelastic. We will take another look at price elasticity in Chapter 12.

Joint Demand.   Demand for certain business products, especially raw materials and components, is subject to joint demand. **Joint demand** occurs when two or more items are used in combination to produce a product. For example, a firm that manufactures axes needs the same number of ax handles as it does ax blades. These two products thus are demanded jointly. If a shortage of ax handles exists, the producer buys fewer ax blades. Understanding the effects of joint demand is particularly important for a marketer selling multiple jointly demanded items. Such a marketer realizes that when a customer begins purchasing one of the jointly demanded items, a good opportunity exists to sell related products.

Fluctuating Demand.   Because the demand for business products is derived from consumer demand, it may fluctuate enormously. In general, when particular consumer products are in high demand, their producers buy large quantities of raw materials and components to ensure meeting long-run production requirements. In addition, these producers may expand production capacity, which entails acquiring new equipment and machinery, more workers, and more raw materials and component parts. Conversely, a decline in demand for certain consumer goods significantly reduces demand for business products used to produce those goods. Sometimes price changes lead to surprising temporary changes in demand. A price increase for a business product initially may cause business customers to buy more of the item because they expect the price to rise further. Similarly, demand for a business product may be significantly lower following a price cut because buyers are waiting for further price reductions. Fluctuations in demand can be substantial in industries in which prices change frequently.

Business Buying Decisions

business (organizational) buying behavior The purchase behavior of producers, government units, institutions, and resellers

buying center The people within an organization, including users, influencers, buyers, deciders, and gatekeepers, who make business purchase decisions

Business (organizational) buying behavior refers to the purchase behavior of producers, government units, institutions, and resellers. Although several factors affecting consumer buying behavior (discussed in Chapter 8) also influence business buying behavior, several factors are unique to the latter. We first analyze the buying center to learn who participates in business purchase decisions. We then focus on the stages of the buying decision process and the factors affecting it.

The Buying Center

Relatively few business purchase decisions are made by just one person; often they are made through a buying center. A **buying center** is a group of people within an organization who make business purchase decisions. They include users, influencers, buyers, deciders, and gatekeepers.[22] One person may perform several roles.

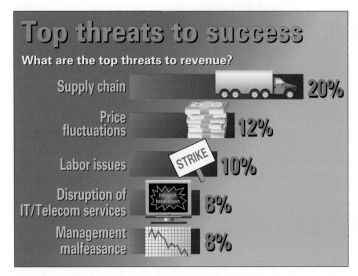

Top threats to success

What are the top threats to revenue?

Supply chain	20%
Price fluctuations	12%
Labor issues	10%
Disruption of IT/Telecom services	8%
Management malfeasance	8%

Source: Data from *Managing Business Risk in 2006 and Beyond*, FM Global and Harris/Interactive. Margin of error ±4 percentage points.

Tired of paying for incoming calls?

Sprint Free Incoming Call Plans give you free incoming calls from all phones, all networks, all the time. AT&T plans don't. So your small business can cut wireless costs and still take every client's call. It's another reason why twice as many businesses choose Sprint over AT&T for their wireless needs.

1-8SPRINT-BIZ   sprint.com/business   **Sprint**   **POWER UP**
Together with NEXTEL

Users are the organization members who actually use the product being acquired. They frequently initiate the purchase process and/or generate purchase specifications. After the purchase, they evaluate product performance relative to the specifications. Influencers are often technical personnel, such as engineers, who help develop the specifications and evaluate alternative products. Technical personnel are especially important influencers when products being considered involve new, advanced technology. Buyers select suppliers and negotiate terms of purchase. They also may become involved in developing specifications. Buyers are sometimes called *purchasing agents* or *purchasing managers.* Their choices of vendors and products, especially for new-task purchases, are heavily influenced by people occupying other roles in the buying center. Deciders actually choose the products. Although buyers may be deciders, it is not unusual for different people to occupy these roles. For routinely purchased items, buyers are commonly deciders. However, a buyer may not be authorized to make purchases exceeding a certain dollar limit, in which case higher-level management personnel are deciders. Gatekeepers, such as secretaries and technical personnel, control the flow of information to and among people occupying other roles in the buying center. Buyers who deal directly with vendors also may be gatekeepers because they can control information flows.

The number and structure of an organization's buying centers are affected by the organization's size and market position, the volume and types of products being purchased, and the firm's overall managerial philosophy regarding exactly who should be involved in purchase decisions. The size of a buying center is influenced by the stage of the buying decision process and the type of purchase (new task, straight rebuy, or modified rebuy).[23] For example, when Siebel Systems (now owned by Oracle) began talking with Fleetwood Enterprises about purchasing Siebel's customer relationship management software—a new-task buy—Siebel personnel had to consider the needs and influence of the executives who would make the final buying decision, as well as those of the influencers (including Fleetwood's IT experts) and the actual users (Fleetwood's marketing, sales, and customer-service personnel).[24]

A marketer attempting to sell to a business customer should determine who is in the buying center, the types of decisions each individual makes, and which individuals are most influential in the decision process. Because in some instances many people make up the buying center, marketers cannot feasibly contact all participants. Instead, they must be certain to contact a few of the most influential participants.

Problem Recognition

Sprint tries to help owners of small businesses to recognize that they may have a problem—paying for incoming calls.

figure 9.1

BUSINESS (ORGANIZATIONAL) BUYING DECISION PROCESS AND FACTORS THAT MAY INFLUENCE IT

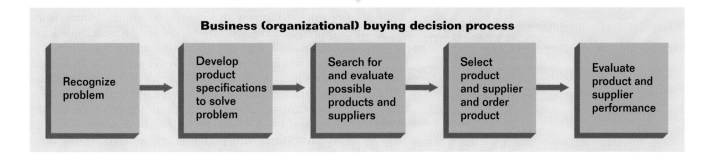

Possible influences on the decision process

Environmental
▸ Competitive factors
▸ Economic factors
▸ Political forces
▸ Legal and regulatory forces
▸ Technological changes
▸ Sociocultural issues

Organizational
▸ Objectives
▸ Purchasing policies
▸ Resources
▸ Buying center structure

Interpersonal
▸ Cooperation
▸ Conflict
▸ Power relationships

Individual
▸ Age
▸ Education level
▸ Personality
▸ Tenure
▸ Position in organization

Business (organizational) buying decision process

Recognize problem → Develop product specifications to solve problem → Search for and evaluate possible products and suppliers → Select product and supplier and order product → Evaluate product and supplier performance

Stages of the Business Buying Decision Process

Like consumers, businesses follow a buying decision process. This process is summarized in the lower portion of Figure 9.1. In the first stage, one or more individuals recognize that a problem or need exists. Problem recognition may arise under a variety of circumstances—for instance, when machines malfunction or a firm modifies an existing product or introduces a new one. Individuals in the buying center, such as users, influencers, or buyers, may be involved in problem recognition, but it may be stimulated by external sources, such as sales representatives or advertisements.

The second stage of the process, development of product specifications, requires that buying center participants assess the problem or need and determine what is necessary to resolve or satisfy it. During this stage, users and influencers, such as engineers, often provide information and advice for developing product specifications. By assessing and describing needs, the organization should be able to establish product specifications.

Searching for and evaluating potential products and suppliers constitute the third stage in the decision process. Search activities may involve looking in company files and trade directories, contacting suppliers for information, soliciting proposals from known vendors, and examining websites, catalogs, and trade publications. To facilitate vendor searches, some organizations, such as Wal-Mart, advertise their desire to build partnerships with specific types of vendors, such as those owned by women or by minorities. During this stage, some organizations engage in **value analysis,** an evaluation of each component of a potential purchase. Value analysis examines quality, design, materials, and possibly item reduction or deletion to acquire the product in the most cost-effective way. Products are evaluated to make sure that they meet or exceed product specifications developed in the second stage. Usually suppliers are judged according to multiple criteria. A number of firms employ **vendor analysis,** a formal,

value analysis An evaluation of each component of a potential purchase

vendor analysis A formal, systematic evaluation of current and potential vendors

AfricanAmerican
AsianAmerican
HispanicAmerican
NativeAmerican
AmericanAirlines®

We believe success comes from diversity. At American, we take pride in working with companies who offer quality products and services through our Diversified Supplier Program. If you are a diversified supplier and would like to explore opportunities with us, we'd like to hear from you. Send information on your product or services and a copy of your minority/women-owned or small business certification to American Airlines, Inc., P.O. Box 619616, MD 5223, DFW Airport, TX 75261-9616. Visit our Web site at www.aa.com/supplierdiversity, or e-mail Luis Gomez, Manager of our Diversified Supplier Program at supplierdiversity@aa.com.

We know why you fly.
AmericanAirlines®
American Eagle

Dedicated to the growth of minority/women-owned and small businesses.

Supplier Diversity

American Airlines focuses on supplier diversity.

multiple sourcing An organization's decision to use several suppliers

sole sourcing An organization's decision to use only one supplier

systematic evaluation of current and potential vendors focusing on characteristics such as price, product quality, delivery service, product availability, and overall reliability. Some vendors may be deemed unacceptable because they lack the resources to supply needed quantities. Others may be excluded because of poor delivery and service records. Sometimes the product is not available from any existing vendor, and the buyer must find an innovative company such as 3M to design and make the product.

Results of deliberations and assessments in the third stage are used during the fourth stage to select the product to be purchased and the supplier from which to buy it. In some cases the buyer selects and uses several suppliers, a process known as **multiple sourcing.** In others, only one supplier is selected, a situation known as **sole sourcing.** For example, Best Buy and UPS recently agreed to an exclusive shipping relationship that resulted in greater savings, efficiencies, and customer loyalty for both companies.[25] Firms with federal government contracts are required to have several sources for an item. Sole sourcing traditionally has been discouraged, except when a product is available from only one company. Sole sourcing is much more common today, however, partly because such an arrangement means better communications between buyer and supplier, stability and higher profits for suppliers, and often lower prices for buyers. However, many organizations still prefer multiple sourcing because this approach lessens the possibility of disruption caused by strikes, shortages, or bankruptcies. The actual product is ordered in this fourth stage, and specific details regarding terms, credit arrangements, delivery dates and methods, and technical assistance are finalized.

During the fifth stage, the product's performance is evaluated by comparing it with specifications. Sometimes the product meets the specifications, but its performance does not solve the problem adequately or satisfy the need recognized in the first stage. In such a case, product specifications must be adjusted. The supplier's performance also is evaluated during this stage. If supplier performance is inadequate, the business purchaser seeks corrective action from the supplier or searches for a new supplier. Results of the evaluation become feedback for the other stages in future business purchase decisions.

This business buying decision process is used in its entirety primarily for new-task purchases. Several stages, but not necessarily all, are used for modified-rebuy and straight-rebuy situations.

Influences on the Business Buying Decision Process

Figure 9.1 also lists four major categories of factors that influence business buying decisions: environmental, organizational, interpersonal, and individual.

Environmental factors include competitive and economic factors, political forces, legal and regulatory forces, technological changes, and sociocultural issues. These factors generate considerable uncertainty for an organization, which can make individuals in the buying center apprehensive about certain types of purchases. Changes in one or more environmental forces can create new purchasing opportunities and threats. For example, changes in competition and technology can make buying decisions difficult in the case of such products as software, computers, and telecommunications equipment. On the other hand, many business marketers believe that the Internet can reduce their customer service costs and allow firms to improve relationships with business customers.[26]

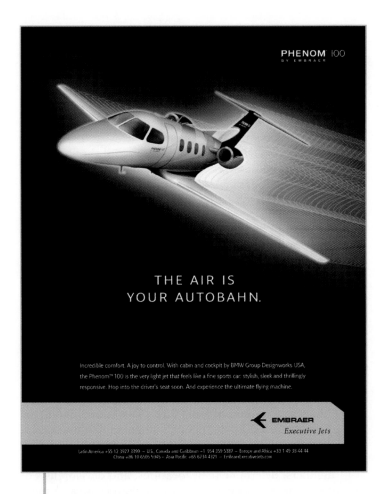

PHENOM 100
BY EMBRAER

THE AIR IS
YOUR AUTOBAHN.

Incredible comfort. A joy to control. With cabin and cockpit by BMW Group Designworks USA, the Phenom™ 100 is the very light jet that feels like a fine sports car: stylish, sleek and thrillingly responsive. Hop into the driver's seat soon. And experience the ultimate flying machine.

EMBRAER
Executive Jets

Latin America +55 12 3927 3399 – U.S., Canada and Caribbean +1 954 359 5387 – Europe and Africa +33 1 49 38 44 44
China +86 10 6505 5045 – Asia Pacific +65 6734 4321 – Embraer.executivejets.com

Influences on the Business Buying Decision Process

A variety of factors may influence the purchase of a corporate aircraft.

Organizational factors influencing the buying decision process include the company's objectives, purchasing policies, and resources, as well as the size and composition of its buying center. An organization may have certain buying policies to which buying center participants must conform. For instance, a firm's policies may mandate unusually long- or short-term contracts, perhaps longer or shorter than most sellers desire. General Motors, for example, limits technology contracts to five years even though the industry standard is seven- or ten-year contracts. The company also has imposed strict standardized sets of operating rules governing its awarding of contracts. These rules give GM greater flexibility and control but create additional challenges for firms marketing to the auto giant.[27] An organization's financial resources may require special credit arrangements. Any of these conditions could affect purchase decisions.

Interpersonal factors are the relationships among people in the buying center. Trust among all members of collaborative partnerships is crucial, particularly in purchases involving customized products.[28] Use of power and level of conflict among buying center participants influence business buying decisions. Certain individuals in the buying center may be better communicators than others and may be more persuasive. Often these interpersonal dynamics are hidden, making them difficult for marketers to assess.

Individual factors are personal characteristics of participants in the buying center, such as age, education, personality, and tenure and position in the organization. For example, a 55-year-old manager who has been in the organization for 25 years may affect decisions made by the buying center differently than a 30-year-old person employed only 2 years. How influential these factors are depends on the buying situation, the type of product being purchased, and whether the purchase is new task, modified rebuy, or straight rebuy. Negotiating styles of people vary within an organization and from one organization to another. To be effective, marketers must know customers well enough to be aware of these individual factors and the effects they may have on purchase decisions.

Industrial Classification Systems

Marketers have access to a considerable amount of information about potential business customers because much of this information is available through government and industry publications and websites. Marketers use this information to identify potential business customers and to estimate their purchase potential.

Much information about business customers is based on industrial classification systems. In the United States, marketers traditionally have relied on the *Standard Industrial Classification (SIC) System*, which the federal government developed to classify selected economic characteristics of industrial, commercial, financial, and service organizations. However, the SIC System has been replaced by a new industry classification system called the **North American Industry Classification System (NAICS)**. NAICS is a single-industry classification system used by the United States, Canada, and Mexico to generate comparable statistics among the three partners of the North American Free Trade Agreement (NAFTA). The NAICS classification is based on the types of production activities performed. NAICS is similar to the International

North American Industry Classification System (NAICS) An industry classification system that will generate comparable statistics among the United States, Canada, and Mexico

table 9.2   NAICS INDUSTRIAL SECTORS

Code	NAICS Sectors
11	Agriculture, forestry, fishing, and hunting
21	Mining
22	Utilities
23	Construction
31–33	Manufacturing
42	Wholesale trade
44, 45	Retail trade
48, 49	Transportation and warehousing
51	Information
52	Finance and insurance
53	Real estate and rental and leasing
54	Professional, scientific, and technical services
55	Management of companies and enterprises
56	Administrative support, waste management, and remediation services
61	Educational services
62	Health care and social assistance
71	Arts, entertainment, and recreation
72	Accommodation and food services
81	Other services (except public administration)
92	Public administration

Source: *History of NAICS,* NAICS Association, www.naics.com/info.htm (accessed May 24, 2007).

Standard Industrial Classification (ISIC) System used in Europe and many other parts of the world. Whereas the SIC System divides industrial activity into 10 divisions, NAICS divides it into 20 sectors (Table 9.2). NAICS contains 1,172 industry classifications compared with 1,004 in the SIC System. NAICS is more comprehensive and more up to date and provides considerably more information about service industries and high-tech products.[29] Over the next few years, all three NAFTA countries will convert from previously used industrial classification systems to NAICS.

Industrial classification systems are ready-made tools that help marketers to categorize organizations into groups based mainly on the types of goods and services provided. Although an industrial classification system is a vehicle for segmentation, it is used most appropriately in conjunction with other types of data to determine exactly how many and which customers a marketer can reach.

A marketer can take several approaches to determine the identities and locations of organizations in specific industrial classification groups. One approach is to use state directories or commercial industrial directories, such as *Standard & Poor's Register* and Dun & Bradstreet's *Million Dollar Directory*. These sources contain information about a firm, such as its name, industrial classification, address, phone number, and annual sales. By referring to one or more of these sources, marketers isolate business customers with industrial classification numbers, determine their locations, and develop lists of potential customers by desired geographic area. A more expedient, although more expensive, approach is to use a commercial data service. Dun & Bradstreet, for example, can provide a list of organizations that fall into a particular industrial classification group. For each company on the list, Dun & Bradstreet gives the name, location, sales volume, number of employees, types of products handled, names of chief executives, and other pertinent information. Either method can effectively identify and locate a group of potential customers. However, a marketer probably cannot pursue all organizations on the list. Because some companies have greater purchasing potential than others, marketers must determine which customer or customer group to pursue.

To estimate the purchase potential of business customers or groups of customers, a marketer must find a relationship between the size of potential customers' purchases and a variable available in industrial classification data, such as the number of employees. For example, a paint manufacturer might attempt to determine the average number of gallons purchased by a specific type of potential customer relative to the number of employees. A marketer with no previous experience in this market segment probably will have to survey a random sample of potential customers to establish a relationship between purchase sizes and numbers of employees. Once this relationship is established, it can be applied to potential customer groups to estimate their purchases. After deriving these estimates, the marketer is in a position to select the customer groups with the most sales and profit potential.

Despite their usefulness, industrial classification data pose several problems. First, a few industries do not have specific designations. Second, because a transfer of products from one establishment to another is counted as part of total shipments, double counting may occur when products are shipped between two establishments within the same firm. Third, because the U.S. Bureau of the Census is prohibited from providing data that identify specific business organizations, some data, such as value of total shipments, may be understated. Finally, because government agencies provide industrial classification data, a significant lag usually exists between data-collection time and the time the information is released.

...And now, back to Texas Instruments

TI is organized into three separate business segments: (1) semiconductors, which accounts for about 85 percent of its revenue, (2) sensors and controls, with about 10 percent of revenue, and (3) educational and productivity solutions, with about 5 percent of revenue. The company's vision is world leadership in digital solutions for the networked society. It intends to fulfill this through excellence in everything it does, by supplying products and technologies that differentiate it—and its customers—from the competition, by competing in high-growth markets, and by providing consistently good financial performance. About 75 percent of semiconductor revenue comes from its core products—analog semiconductors and digital signal processors (DSPs). These products enhance, and often make possible, a variety of applications that serve the communications, computer, consumer, automotive, and industrial markets. TI believes that virtually all of today's digital electronic equipment requires some form of analog or digital signal processing.

Although TI primarily markets to businesses, it had one of the hottest brands in techdom back in 1982. Its digital watches and calculators were everywhere, as were its ads with TV icon Bill Crosby promoting its home computers. But the company retreated from mass marketing when its PC business folded in 1984. At that time, TI recognized that it needed to re-align its marketing strategy and reaffirm its focus. The company decided to focus on its semiconductor business and became one of the defense industry's top suppliers.

During the early 2000s, TI launched a major marketing blitz, including ads on the Super Bowl broadcast, to reintroduce itself to consumers and spur sales of flat-screen TVs that employ its digital light-processing (DLP) microchips. The DLP technology includes chips filled with millions of mirrors that direct the light toward a TV's screen. The technology comes closer than any other display solution to reproducing the exact mirror image of its source material, enabling the delivery of precise, sharp, lifelike images with virtually no pixelization. With a 2006 federal mandate requiring all televisions produced after 2009 to be digital, TI's DLP technology likely will remain popular among TV manufacturers such as Samsung, Mitsubishi, and Toshiba.

Some people worry that because TI is the number 1 supplier of microchips for cell phones, it is too closely tied to the market for cell phones, which seems to be maturing. However, the booming popularity of flat-screen TVs, along with the mandate for digital television, gives TI access to a growing market that should maintain strong derived demand for its chips. Although TI's name rarely appears on the products in which its chips are major components, its advertising campaign is aimed at increasing awareness of the brand, much as Intel did with its "Intel Inside" campaign. Even if the campaign does not boost consumer awareness significantly, many companies are very familiar with TI's products and value its long history of innovation and creativity.[30]

1. Why is TI advertising its DLP chips?

2. What kind of demand does TI have for its DLP chips?

3. Do you think TI's advertising campaign has been successful?

CHAPTER REVIEW

1. Be able to distinguish among the various types of business markets.

Business (B2B) markets consist of individuals and groups that purchase a specific kind of product for resale, direct use in producing other products, or use in day-to-day operations. Producer markets include those individuals and business organizations purchasing products for the purpose of making a profit by using them to produce other products or as part of their operations. Intermediaries that buy finished products and resell them to make a profit are classified as reseller markets. Government markets consist of federal, state, county, and local governments, which spend billions of dollars annually for goods and services to support internal operations and to provide citizens with services. Organizations with charitable, educational, community, or other nonprofit goals constitute institutional markets.

2. Identify the major characteristics of business customers and transactions.

Transactions involving business customers differ from consumer transactions in several ways. Such transactions tend to be larger, and negotiations occur less frequently, although they are often lengthy when they do occur. They often involve more than one person or department in the purchasing organization. They also may involve reciprocity, an arrangement in which two organizations agree to buy from each other. Business customers are usually better informed than ultimate consumers and more likely to seek information about a product's features and technical specifications.

3. Understand several attributes of demand for business products.

Business customers are particularly concerned about quality, service, price, and supplier relationships. Quality is important because it directly affects the quality of products the buyer's firm produces. To achieve an exact level of quality, organizations often buy products on the basis of a set of expressed characteristics, called *specifications*. Because services have such a direct influence on a firm's costs, sales, and profits, matters such as market information, on-time delivery, availability of parts, and communication capabilities are crucial to a business buyer. Although business customers do not depend solely on price to decide which products to buy, price is of prime concern because it directly influences profitability.

Business buyers use several purchasing methods, including description, inspection, sampling, and negotiation. Most organizational purchases are new task, straight rebuy, or modified rebuy. In a new-task purchase, an organization makes an initial purchase of items to be used to perform new jobs or to solve new problems. A straight-rebuy purchase occurs when a buyer purchases the same products routinely under approximately the same terms

of sale. In a modified-rebuy purchase, a new-task purchase is changed the second or third time it is ordered, or requirements associated with a straight-rebuy purchase are modified.

Industrial demand differs from consumer demand along several dimensions. Industrial demand derives from demand for consumer products. At the industry level, industrial demand is inelastic. Some business products are subject to joint demand, which occurs when two or more items are used in combination to make a product. Finally, because organizational demand derives from consumer demand, the demand for business products can fluctuate widely.

4. Become familiar with the major components of a buying center.

Business purchase decisions are made through a buying center, the group of people involved in making such purchase decisions. Users are those in the organization who actually use the product. Influencers help to develop specifications and evaluate alternative products for possible use. Buyers select suppliers and negotiate purchase terms. Deciders choose the products. Gatekeepers control the flow of information to and among individuals occupying other roles in the buying center.

5. Understand the stages of the business buying decision process and the factors that affect this process.

The stages of the business buying decision process are problem recognition, development of product specifications to solve problems, search for and evaluation of products and suppliers, selection and ordering of the most appropriate product, and evaluation of the product's and supplier's performance.

Four categories of factors influence business buying decisions. Environmental factors include competitive forces, economic conditions, political forces, laws and regulations, technological changes, and sociocultural factors. Organizational factors include the company's objectives, purchasing policies, and resources, as well as the size and composition of its buying center. Interpersonal factors are the relationships among people in the buying center. Individual factors are personal characteristics of members of the buying center, such as age, education, personality, tenure, and position in the organization.

6. Describe industrial classification systems and explain how they can be used to identify and analyze business markets.

An industrial classification system—such as the North American Industry Classification System (NAICS) used by the United States, Canada, and Mexico—provides marketers with information needed to identify business customer groups. It is best used for this purpose in conjunction with other information. After identifying target industries, a marketer can obtain the names and locations of potential customers by using government and commercial data sources. Marketers then must estimate potential purchases of business customers by finding a relationship between a potential customer's purchases and a variable available in industrial classification data.

ACE self-test

Please visit the student website at **www.prideferrell.com** for ACE Self-Test questions that will help you prepare for exams.

KEY CONCEPTS

producer markets
reseller markets
government markets
institutional markets
reciprocity
new-task purchase

straight-rebuy purchase
modified-rebuy purchase
derived demand
inelastic demand
joint demand

business (organizational) buying behavior
buying center
value analysis
vendor analysis

multiple sourcing
sole sourcing
North American Industry Classification System (NAICS)

ISSUES FOR DISCUSSION AND REVIEW

1. Identify, describe, and give examples of the four major types of business markets.

2. Regarding purchasing behavior, why might business customers generally be considered more rational than ultimate consumers?

3. What are the primary concerns of business customers?

4. List several characteristics that differentiate transactions involving business customers from consumer transactions.

5. What are the commonly used methods of business buying?

6. Why do buyers involved in a straight-rebuy purchase require less information than those making a new-task purchase?

7. How does demand for business products differ from consumer demand?

8. What are the major components of a firm's buying center?

9. Identify the stages of the business buying decision process. How is this decision process used when making straight rebuys?

10. How do environmental, business, interpersonal, and individual factors affect business purchases?

11. What function does an industrial classification system help marketers perform?

12. List some sources that a business marketer can use to determine the names and addresses of potential customers.

MARKETING APPLICATIONS

1. Identify organizations in your area that fit each business market category—producer, reseller, government, and institutional. Explain your classifications.

2. Indicate the method of buying (description, inspection, sampling, or negotiation) an organization would be most likely to use when purchasing each of the following items. Defend your selection.
   a. A building for the home office of a light bulb manufacturer
   b. Wool for a clothing manufacturer
   c. An Alaskan cruise for a company retreat, assuming a regular travel agency is used
   d. One-inch nails for a building contractor

3. Categorize the following purchase decisions as new task, modified rebuy, or straight rebuy and explain your choice.
   a. Bob has purchased toothpicks from Smith Restaurant Supply for 25 years and recently

placed an order for yellow toothpicks rather than the usual white ones.
   b. Jill's investment company has been purchasing envelopes from AAA Office Supply for a year and now needs to purchase boxes to mail year-end portfolio summaries to clients. Jill calls AAA to purchase these boxes.
   c. Reliance Insurance has been supplying its salespeople with small personal computers to assist in their sales efforts. The company recently agreed to begin supplying them with faster, more sophisticated computers.

4. Identifying qualified customers is important to the survival of any organization. NAICS provides helpful information about many different businesses. Find the NAICS manual at the library and identify the NAICS code for the following items.
   a. Chocolate candy bars

b. Automobile tires

c. Men's running shoes

Online Exercise

5. General Electric Company is a highly diversified, global corporation with many divisions. GE Plastics (recently purchased by SABIC) is the online site for GE's resins and plastics business. Visit the site at **http://order. geplastics.com/ordna/servlet/ public?pageId=logon.HomePage.**

a. At what type of business markets are GE's resin products targeted?

b. How does GE Plastics' (SABIC) website address some of the concerns of business customers?

c. What environmental factors do you think affect the demand for GE resin products?

globalEDGE™

Part of your firm's evaluation of a supplier's performance is based on the degree to which it seamlessly delivers goods and materials. A recent complication for global suppliers is an initiative to enhance shipping container security for international trade and transport. A report concerning container security for international trade and transportation can be found using the search term "international trade and transport" at **http://globaledge.msu.edu/ibrd** (and check the box "Resource Desk only"). At the United Nations Conference on Trade and Development (UNCTAD) website, click on the "Transport & Trade Logistics" link, go to the Documents section, and look for a report on container security. What are the four parts of this program? Based on this, do you think that your firm should change its evaluation of supplier performance?

Video CASE

Lextant Corporation: Design Research at Its Best

These days, competition is fierce. It's no longer possible just to make a product and hope that it sells; products must be designed with end users in mind. Lextant Corporation provides design research for its business customers, including PepsiCo, Procter & Gamble, Motorola, Goodyear, Whirlpool, Microsoft, and Hard Rock Café. Its name comes from the word *lexicon* meaning a "vocabulary or language"—in this case, a language of consumers. The privately held Columbus, Ohio–based company strives to translate this language into actionable insights, equipping its clients to design for the motivations, behaviors, and desires of their customers.

Lextant was founded with one fundamental goal—to help companies achieve a sustainable competitive advantage by understanding their end users and by designing products to satisfy them. To achieve this goal, Lextant examines what motivates and drives people and presents this information to its clients so that they can make informed decisions about the products they are designing. Lextant brings together teams of experts in psychology, sociology, anthropology, human factors, industrial design, and interaction design, and it combines ethnographic, participatory, marketing, behavioral, and usability research techniques to provide tools to make products better. Then researchers learn from consumers by following them in everything they do in their environment. Finally, researchers design systems that will yield the desired results for the firm's clients.

Lextant researchers discover what end users want by getting a broad view of people and trying to know and understand them, often by observing them in their own environment. They understand the importance of observing people actually using the products being studied in their place of use. It is important in this process to really listen to end users when they explain what matters to them. Lextant has two approaches for collecting data. The first is qualitative—through the context and environment of the user. The second is quantitative—based on what the client wants. The quantitative approach involves presenting prototypes of a product to a sample of end users. These clients then use the sample product and give feedback on what they like and don't like about the product, as well as suggestions on how the product could be improved.

In some cases, Lextant uses focus groups to discover information for its clients. Researchers bring people together at a central facility to use and test the product and provide feedback about its design, color, and ease of use. This method is especially useful when budget or time is limited because it permits researchers to gather information at a central location in a short time and results in instant feedback.

Once researchers have collected the data from various sources, they are often confronted with an overwhelming amount of data. They must analyze the data to find the patterns and recognize anomalies that occur in only a few cases. Researchers use affinity diagrams and Post-it Notes stuck to the wall to help the process flow. By having Post-it Notes labeled with each important characteristic, it is easy to move the parts around until the relevant story becomes clear. By having many pictures of the users and the environments in which a product is used, it is possible for any person in the organization to come into the room and understand the consumers: their personas, attitudes, and motivations.

Employees at Lextant immerse themselves in the information that they gather to evaluate which information is relevant while at the same time discarding useless information. It is then possible to see where people say similar things and to focus on those and find out what is wrong with certain products.

Clients of Lextant are often surprised by the findings of the Lextant team, especially when it comes to identifying ways that they can modify their existing products to better satisfy end users. For example, Lextant helped Hard Rock Café to answer the question, "Is our website experience helping or hurting our brand?" Indeed, its website was challenging to navigate and was sapping online sales. Lextant helped the restaurant chain develop an easy-to-use, compelling website to help rejuvenate the legendary brand. Lextant researchers examined the Hard Rock website from the customers' perspective, documented the user goals and ideal experiences, and then developed an architecture that facilitated desired activity flows. The research firm created a complete prototype featuring an intuitive café locator, personalization features, and a streamlined shopping process. This enabled Hard Rock to corroborate and refine site concepts before making significant investments in implementation.

Lextant provides a business product that has a derived demand from producing products that delight consumers. Design research is not about the *what* but rather the *why*. If you understand why people do not like an existing design, then it is possible to design a new solution.[31]

Questions for Discussion

1. Why is the Lextant product a derived-demand business product?
2. What types of business markets does Lextant serve?
3. When purchasing Lextant services, what type of buying method would be used: description, sampling, inspection, or negotiation?

part **5**

Product Decisions

We are now prepared to analyze the decisions and activities associated with developing and maintaining effective marketing mixes. In Parts 5 through 8 we focus on the major components of the marketing mix: product, pricing, distribution, and promotion. Part 5 explores the product ingredient of the marketing mix. Chapter 10 focuses on basic product concepts and on branding and packaging decisions. Chapter 11 analyzes various dimensions regarding product management, including line extensions and product modification, new-product development, product deletions, and the management of services as products.

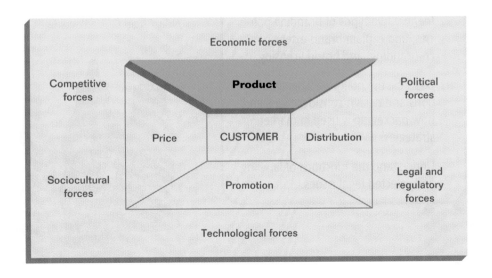

231

10

Product, Branding, and Packaging Concepts

OBJECTIVES

1. Understand the concept of a product and how products are classified.

2. Explain the concepts of product item, product line, and product mix, and understand how they are connected.

3. Understand the product life cycle and its impact on marketing strategies.

4. Describe the product adoption process.

5. Explain the value of branding and the major components of brand equity.

6. Recognize the types of brands and how they are selected and protected.

7. Identify two types of branding policies, and explain brand extensions, co-branding, and brand licensing.

8. Describe the major packaging functions and design considerations and how packaging is used in marketing strategies.

9. Understand the functions of labeling and selected legal issues.

Heinz Brand Thrives with Innovative Products and Creative Labels

The Heinz Company was founded in 1869 by Henry John Heinz in Sharpsburg, Pennsylvania. Heinz started by delivering processed condiments to local grocers via horse-drawn wagon. The company's first product was horseradish, followed by pickles, sauerkraut, and vinegar. The company was forced into bankruptcy during the banking panic of 1875, but with his brother John and cousin Frederick, Henry started over in 1875. The new company introduced a new product—tomato ketchup—and red and green pepper sauce soon followed. In 1886, Heinz sailed with his family to England, where he called on Fortnum & Mason, England's leading food purveyor, whose buyer tasted the seven products and accepted all seven for distribution.

In 1896, Heinz noticed an advertisement for "21 styles of shoes" and decided that his own products were not styles but varieties. Although Heinz had many more than 57 foods in production at the time, the numbers 5 and 7 held a special significance for him and his wife, so he adopted the slogan "57 Varieties." Thus a new advertising campaign was launched for Heinz 57 Varieties.

The Heinz Company today is an enterprise with over 110 major locations worldwide, with leading brands on six continents. Heinz brand names—such as Ore-Ida, Smart Ones, Bagel Bites, Plasmon, Wattie's San Marco, Farley's, Bio

Dieterba, DeRuijter, Olivine, and Pudinski—appear on thousands of different products worldwide. Heinz is popular for different products in other countries. In the United Kingdom, for example, Heinz is popular not just for its ketchup but also for its baked beans. Its advertising slogan in the United Kingdom, "Beanz Meanz Heinz," was recently acknowledged as the most memorable television commercial slogan of all time, even though many people in the United States do not even know that Heinz does beans.

Although Heinz sells many traditional food products that people have bought for a long time, the company must understand the needs of its consumers and continue to innovate and create new products. Some of the products the company has tried over the years include green ketchup, Ez Squeeze ketchup bottles, and reduced-sugar ketchup. In 2006, Heinz zeroed in on innovation and promised to launch 100 new products. Heinz' commitment to innovation and attentiveness to trends in health and wellness have resulted in new varieties such as Organic, Reduced Sugar, and No Salt Ketchup and Hot and Spicy Ketchup Kick'rs that, combined with novel packaging, have helped increase ketchup sales in the United States at an annual rate of 7 percent over the past three years. Heinz is also bringing out new products for its other lines, such as Ore-Ida chilled mashed and au gratin potatoes and macaroni and cheese; Ore-Ida roasted potatoes; expanded varieties of Classico sauce, including new organic varieties; and new varieties of Weight Watchers Smart Ones meals for breakfast, lunch, dinner, and snacking occasions.[1] ■

Products are an important variable in the marketing mix. The mix of products offered by a company such as Heinz can be a firm's most important competitive tool. If a company's products do not meet customers' desires and needs, the company will fail unless it makes adjustments. Developing successful products like Dell personal computers requires knowledge of fundamental product concepts.

In this chapter we first define a product and discuss how products are classified. Next, we examine the concepts of product line and product mix. We then explore the stages of the product life cycle and the effect of each life cycle stage on marketing strategies. Next, we outline the product adoption process. Then we discuss branding, its value to customers and marketers, brand loyalty, and brand equity. Next, we examine the various types of brands. We then consider how companies choose and protect brands, the various branding policies employed, brand extensions, co-branding, and brand licensing. We look at the critical role packaging plays as part of the product. We then explore the functions of packaging, issues to consider in packaging design, and how the package can be a major element in marketing strategy. We conclude with a discussion of labeling.

What Is a Product?

As defined in Chapter 1, a *product* is a good, a service, or an idea received in an exchange. It can be either tangible or intangible and includes functional, social, and psychological utilities or benefits. It also includes supporting services, such as installation, guarantees, product information, and promises of repair or maintenance. Thus the four-year/50,000-mile warranty that covers some new automobiles is part of the product itself. A **good** is a tangible physical entity, such as a Dell personal computer or a Big Mac. A **service,** in contrast, is intangible; it is the result of the application of human and mechanical efforts to people or objects. Examples of services include a performance by Beyonce, online travel agencies, medical examinations, child day care, real estate services, and martial arts lessons. An **idea** is a concept, philosophy, image, or issue. Ideas provide the psychological stimulation that aids in solving problems or adjusting to the environment. For example, Mothers Against Drunk Driving (MADD) promotes safe consumption of alcohol and stricter enforcement of laws against drunk driving.

good A tangible physical entity

service An intangible result of the application of human and mechanical efforts to people or objects

idea A concept, philosophy, image, or issue

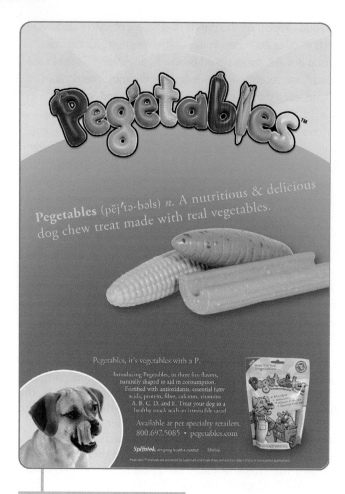

What is a Product?

Pegetables is a product that has been developed for pet owners who are concerned about the well-being of their pets.

It is helpful to think of a total product offering as having three interdependent elements: the core product itself, its supplemental features, and its symbolic or experiential benefits (see Figure 10.1). Consider that some people buy new tires for their basic utility (e.g., Sears' Guardsman III), whereas some look for safety (e.g., Michelin), and others buy on the basis of brand name or exemplary performance (e.g., Pirelli). The core product consists of a product's fundamental utility or main benefit and usually addresses a fundamental need of the consumer. Broadband Internet services, for instance, offer speedy Internet access, but some buyers want additional features, such as wireless connectivity anywhere they go. Supplemental features provide added value or attributes in addition to the core utility or benefit. Supplemental products also can provide installation, delivery, training, and financing. These supplemental attributes are not required to make the core product function effectively, but they help to differentiate one product brand from another. Blockbuster, for example, offers an extra feature—it lets customers return rented DVDs to its stores; rival Netflix customers must return their rentals by mail.[2] Finally, customers also receive benefits based on their experiences with the product. In addition, many products have symbolic meaning for buyers. For some consumers, the simple act of shopping gives symbolic value and improves their attitudes. Some stores capitalize on this value by striving to create a special experience for customers. For example, you can buy stuffed toys at many retailers, but at Build-a-Bear you can choose the type of animal, stuff it yourself, give it a heart, create a name complete with a birth certificate, and give the toy a bath and clothe and accessorize it. The atmosphere and decor of a retail store, the variety and depth of product choices, the customer support, and even the sounds and smells all contribute to the experiential element.

figure 10.1

THE TOTAL PRODUCT

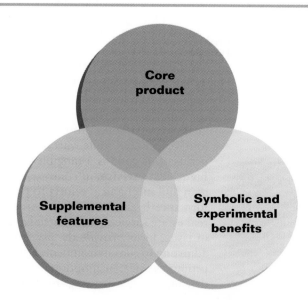

marketing ENTREPRENEURS

Arielle Eckstut, Jonah Shaw, and Jason Dorf

THEIR BUSINESS: LittleMissMatched

FOUNDED: 2003

SUCCESS: 600,000 socks now in 600 stores

While pondering the great mystery of socks disappearing in the laundry, Arielle Eckstut, Johan Shaw, and Jason Dorf recognized an opportunity to market socks that don't match. They targeted young girls ages 8 to 12 with their LittleMissMatched brand socks. A package of just one sock goes for $2, a package with three unmatched socks goes for $5, and a package with seven mixed socks goes for $10. Customers then use their imaginations to pair the socks (into 19,900 possible combinations) according to color, design, or their own sense of style. Today, LittleMissMatched has expanded its concept to sheets, flip-flops, pajamas, and other garments that can be mismatched for fun and fashion for adults and toddlers as well as for preteens.[a]

When buyers purchase a product, they are really buying the benefits and satisfaction they think the product will provide. A Rolex watch, for example, is often purchased to make a statement of success, not just for telling time. Services in particular are purchased on the basis of expectations. Expectations, suggested by images, promises, and symbols, as well as processes and delivery, help consumers to make judgments about tangible and intangible products. Products are formed by the activities and processes that help to satisfy expectations. For instance, Starbucks did not originate the coffee shop, but it did make high-quality coffee beverages readily available around the world with standardized service and in stylish, inviting stores. Often symbols and cues are used to make intangible products more tangible, or real, to the consumer. Allstate Insurance Company, for example, uses giant hands to symbolize security, strength, and friendliness.

Classifying Products

Products fall into one of two general categories. Products purchased to satisfy personal and family needs are **consumer products.** Those bought to use in a firm's operations, to resell, or to make other products are **business products.** Consumers buy products to satisfy their personal wants, whereas business buyers seek to satisfy the goals of their organizations. Product classifications are important because they may influence pricing, distribution, and promotion decisions. In this section we examine the characteristics of consumer and business products and explore the marketing activities associated with some of these products.

Consumer Products

The most widely accepted approach to classifying consumer products is based on characteristics of consumer buying behavior. It divides products into four categories: convenience, shopping, specialty, and unsought products. However, not all buyers behave in the same way when purchasing a specific type of product. Thus a single product can fit into several categories. To minimize this problem, marketers think in terms of how buyers *generally* behave when purchasing a specific item. Examining the four traditional categories of consumer products can provide further insight.

Convenience Products.   **Convenience products** are relatively inexpensive, frequently purchased items for which buyers exert only minimal purchasing effort. They range from bread, soft drinks, and chewing gum to gasoline and newspapers. The buyer spends little time planning the purchase or comparing available brands or sellers. Even a buyer who prefers a specific brand will readily choose a substitute if the preferred brand is not conveniently available. A convenience product is normally marketed through many retail outlets, such as 7-Eleven, Exxon Mobil, and Starbucks. Starbucks, for example, has opened locations inside airports, hotels, and grocery stores, and half its company-owned stores now have drive-through lanes to ensure that customers can get coffee whenever or wherever the desire strikes.[3] Because sellers experience high inventory turnover, per-unit gross margins can be relatively low. Producers of convenience

consumer products Products purchased to satisfy personal and family needs

business products Products bought to use in an organization's operations, to resell, or to make other products

convenience products Relatively inexpensive, frequently purchased items for which buyers exert minimal purchasing effort

Specialty Products

Seven Cycles makes custom bikes - a specialty product.

The average cyclist doesn't need a custom bike...

Then again, who's average?

There are those who say that the average cyclist doesn't need a custom bike. Well we say that's the type of thinking that produces average bikes. Because when it comes right down to it, **average is just another word for compromise**. So while other companies build bikes for the "the average cyclist", we build yours.

seven cycles

www.sevencycles.com   telephone 617.923.7774   email info@sevencycles.com   One Bike. Yours.

products, such as Altoid mints, expect little promotional effort at the retail level and thus must provide it themselves with advertising and sales promotion. Packaging is also important because many convenience items are available only on a self-service basis at the retail level, and thus the package plays a major role in selling the product.

Shopping Products.   **Shopping products** are items for which buyers are willing to expend considerable effort in planning and making the purchase. Buyers spend much time comparing stores and brands with respect to prices, product features, qualities, services, and perhaps warranties. Department stores such as Macy's carry shopping products and often are found in the same shopping centers with competitors so that consumers can shop and compare products and prices. Appliances, bicycles, furniture, stereos, cameras, and shoes exemplify shopping products. These products are expected to last a fairly long time and thus are purchased less frequently than convenience items. Even though shopping products are more expensive than convenience products, few buyers of shopping products are particularly brand-loyal. If they were, they would be unwilling to shop and compare among brands. Shopping products require fewer retail outlets than convenience products. Because shopping products are purchased less frequently, inventory turnover is lower, and marketing channel members expect to receive higher gross margins. In certain situations, both shopping products and convenience products may be marketed in the same location. H-E-B, a privately held Texas grocery chain, recently implemented a new store concept called H-E-B Plus. These stores carry everything from toys and home entertainment products to area rugs and high-end televisions, as well as the traditional groceries and ethnic foods in which H-E-B excels.[4]

Specialty Products.   **Specialty products** possess one or more unique characteristics, and generally buyers are willing to expend considerable effort to obtain them. Buyers actually plan the purchase of a specialty product; they know exactly what they want and will not accept a substitute. Examples of specialty products include a Mont Blanc pen and a one-of-a-kind piece of baseball memorabilia, such as a ball signed by Babe Ruth. When searching for specialty products, buyers do not compare alternatives. They are concerned primarily with finding an outlet that has the preselected product available. Tag Heuer, for example, issued a special Indy 500 watch designed especially for racing fans. Specialty products are often distributed through a limited number of retail outlets. Like shopping products, they are purchased infrequently, causing lower inventory turnover and thus requiring relatively high gross margins.

shopping products Items for which buyers are willing to expend considerable effort in planning and making purchases

specialty products Items with unique characteristics that buyers are willing to expend considerable effort to obtain

Unsought Products.   **Unsought products** are products purchased when a sudden problem must be solved, products of which customers are unaware, and products that people do not necessarily think of purchasing. Emergency medical services and automobile repairs are examples of products needed quickly to solve a problem. A consumer who is sick or injured has little time to plan to go to an emergency medical center or hospital. Likewise, in the event of a broken fan belt on the highway, a consumer likely will seek the nearest auto repair facility to get back on the road as quickly as possible. In such cases, speed and problem resolution are far more important than price and other features buyers might normally consider if they had more time for making decisions. Companies such as ServiceMaster, which markets emergency services such as disaster recovery and plumbing repair, are making the purchases of these unsought products more bearable by building trust with consumers through recognizable brands (ServiceMaster Clean and Rescue Rooter) and superior functional performance.

Business Products

Business products are usually purchased on the basis of an organization's goals and objectives. Generally, the functional aspects of the product are more important than the psychological rewards sometimes associated with consumer products. Business products can be classified into seven categories according to their characteristics and intended uses: installations; accessory equipment; raw materials; component parts; process materials; maintenance, repair, and operating (MRO) supplies; and business services.

Installations.   **Installations** include facilities, such as office buildings, factories, and warehouses, and major equipment that are nonportable, such as production lines and very large machines. Normally, installations are expensive and intended to be used for a considerable length of time. Because they are so expensive and typically involve a long-term investment of capital, purchase decisions often are made by high-level management. Marketers of installations frequently must provide a variety of services, including training, repairs, maintenance assistance, and even aid in financing such purchases.

Accessory Equipment.   **Accessory equipment** does not become part of the final physical product but is used in production or office activities. Examples include file cabinets, fractional-horsepower motors, calculators, and tools. Compared with major equipment, accessory items usually are much cheaper, purchased routinely with less negotiation, and treated as expense items rather than capital items because they are not expected to last as long. More outlets are required for distributing accessory equipment than for installations, but sellers do not have to provide the multitude of services expected of installations marketers.

Raw Materials.   **Raw materials** are the basic natural materials that actually become part of a physical product. They include minerals, chemicals, agricultural products, and materials from forests and oceans. Corn, for example, is a raw material found in many different products, including food, beverages (as corn syrup), and even fuel (ethanol). Indeed, the growing popularity of ethanol as an alternative fuel has caused corn prices to soar.[5] Raw materials are usually bought and sold according to grades and specifications and in relatively large quantities.

Component Parts.   **Component parts** become part of the physical product and are either finished items ready for assembly or products that need little processing before assembly. Although they become part of a larger product, component parts often can be identified and distinguished easily. Spark plugs, tires, clocks, brakes, and switchers are all component parts of the automobile. German-based Robert Bosch GmbH, the world's largest auto parts maker, supplies 30 percent of the 46 million antilock brakes installed in vehicles worldwide.[6] Buyers purchase such items according to their own specifications or industry standards. They expect the parts to be of specified quality and delivered on time so that production is not slowed or stopped. Producers

unsought products Products purchased to solve a sudden problem, products of which customers are unaware, and products that people do not necessarily think about buying

installations Facilities and nonportable major equipment

accessory equipment Equipment that does not become part of the final physical product but is used in production or office activities

raw materials Basic natural materials that become part of a physical product

component parts Items that become part of the physical product and are either finished items ready for assembly or products that need little processing before assembly

Product Line

All-natural salad dressing is one of Newman's Own product lines.

that are primarily assemblers, such as most lawn mower and computer manufacturers, depend heavily on suppliers of component parts.

Process Materials.   **Process materials** are used directly in the production of other products. Unlike component parts, however, process materials are not readily identifiable. For example, a salad dressing manufacturer includes vinegar in its salad dressing. The vinegar is a process material because it is included in the salad dressing but is not identifiable. As with component parts, process materials are purchased according to industry standards or the purchaser's specifications.

MRO Supplies.   **MRO supplies** are maintenance, repair, and operating items that facilitate production and operations but do not become part of the finished product. Paper, pencils, oils, cleaning agents, and paints are in this category. Although you might be familiar with Tide, Downy, and Febreze as consumer products, to restaurants and hotels, they are MRO supplies needed to wash dishes and launder sheets and towels. Procter & Gamble is increasingly targeting business customers in the $3.2 billion market for janitorial and housekeeping products.[7] MRO supplies are commonly sold through numerous outlets and are purchased routinely. To ensure supplies are available when needed, buyers often deal with more than one seller.

Business Services.   **Business services** are the intangible products that many organizations use in their operations. They include financial, legal, marketing research, information technology, and janitorial services. Firms must decide whether to provide their own services internally or obtain them from outside the organization. This decision depends on the costs associated with each alternative and how frequently the services are needed. For example, few firms have the resources to provide global overnight delivery services efficiently, so most companies rely on FedEx, UPS, DHL, and other service providers.

Product Line and Product Mix

process materials Materials that are used directly in the production of other products but are not readily identifiable

MRO supplies Maintenance, repair, and operating items that facilitate production and operations but do not become part of the finished product

business services The intangible products that many organizations use in their operations

Marketers must understand the relationships among all the products of their organization to coordinate the marketing of the total group of products. The following concepts help to describe the relationships among an organization's products. A **product item** is a specific version of a product that can be designated as a distinct offering among an organization's products. A Gillette M3 Power Nitro razor represents a product item. A **product line** is a group of closely related product items that are considered to be a unit because of marketing, technical, or end-use considerations. For example, Procter & Gamble, with the acquisition of Gillette, has hundreds of brands that fall into one of 22 product lines ranging from deodorants to paper products.[8] The exact boundaries of a product line (although sometimes blurred) are usually indicated by using descriptive terms such as *frozen dessert* product line or *shampoo* product line. To develop the optimal product line, marketers must understand buyers' goals. Specific product items in a product line usually reflect the desires of different target markets or the different needs of consumers.

A **product mix** is the composite, or total, group of products that an organization makes available to customers. For example, all the health-care, beauty-care, laundry

figure 10.2   THE CONCEPTS OF PRODUCT MIX WIDTH AND DEPTH APPLIED
TO SELECTED U.S. PROCTER & GAMBLE PRODUCTS

Laundry detergents	Toothpastes	Bar soaps	Deodorants	Shampoos	Tissue/Towel
Ivory Snow 1930	Gleem 1952	Ivory 1879	Old Spice 1948	Pantene 1947	Charmin 1928
Dreft 1933	Crest 1955	Camay 1926	Secret 1956	Head & Shoulders 1961	Puffs 1960
Tide 1946		Zest 1952	Sure 1972	Vidal Sassoon 1974	Bounty 1965
Cheer 1950		Safeguard 1963		Pert Plus 1979	
Bold 1965		Oil of Olay 1993		Ivory 1983	
Gain 1966				Infusium 23 1986	
Era 1972				Physique 2000	
Febreze Clean Wash 2000				Herbal Essence 2001	

(Vertical axis label: Depth; horizontal axis label: Width)

Source: © The Procter & Gamble Company. Used by permission.

and cleaning, food and beverage, paper, cosmetic, and fragrance products that Procter & Gamble manufactures constitute its product mix. The **width of product mix** is measured by the number of product lines a company offers. Robert Bosch GmbH, for example, offers multiple product lines, including automotive technology components such as brakes and stability control systems, consumer products such as household appliances, and business products such as packaging machines.[9] The **depth of product mix** is the average number of different product items offered in each product line. Figure 10.2 shows the width and depth of part of Procter & Gamble's product mix.

Product Life Cycles and Marketing Strategies

Just as biological cycles progress from birth through growth and decline, so do product life cycles. As Figure 10.3 (on page 240) shows, a **product life cycle** has four major stages: introduction, growth, maturity, and decline. As a product moves through its cycle, the strategies relating to competition, pricing, distribution, promotion, and market information must be evaluated periodically and possibly changed. Astute marketing managers use the life cycle concept to make sure that the introduction, alteration, and deletion of a product are timed and executed properly. By understanding the typical life cycle pattern, marketers can maintain profitable product mixes.

Introduction

The **introduction stage** of the product life cycle begins at a product's first appearance in the marketplace, when sales start at zero and profits are negative. Profits are below zero because initial revenues are low, and the company generally must cover large expenses for product development, promotion, and distribution. Notice in Figure 10.3 how sales should move upward from zero, and profits also should move upward from a position in which they are negative because of high expenses.

Potential buyers must be made aware of new-product features, uses, and advantages. Efforts to highlight a new product's value can create a foundation for building brand loyalty and customer relationships.[10] Two difficulties may arise at this point. First, sellers may lack the resources, technological knowledge, and marketing know-how to launch the product successfully. Entrepreneurs without large budgets still can attract attention, however, by giving away free samples, as Essence of Vali does with its aromatherapy products. Another technique is to gain visibility through media

product item A specific version of a product that can be designated as a distinct offering among a firm's products

product line A group of closely related product items viewed as a unit because of marketing, technical, or end-use considerations

product mix The total group of products that an organization makes available to customers

width of product mix The number of product lines a company offers

depth of product mix The average number of different product items offered in each product line

figure 10.3

THE FOUR STAGES OF THE PRODUCT LIFE CYCLE

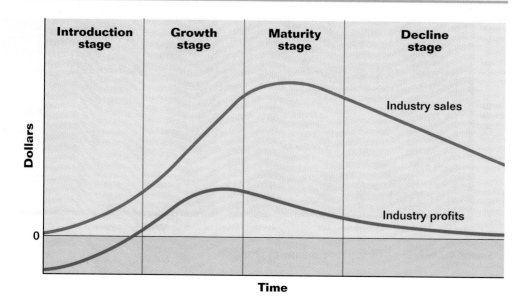

appearances. Dave Dettman, also known as Dr. Gadget, specializes in promoting new products on television news and talk programs. Companies such as Sony, Disney, Warner Bros., and others have hired Dr. Gadget to help with the introduction of new products.[11] Second, the initial product price may have to be high to recoup expensive marketing research or development costs. Given these difficulties, it is not surprising that many products never get beyond the introduction stage.

Most new products start off slowly and seldom generate enough sales to bring immediate profits. As buyers learn about the new product, marketers should be alert for product weaknesses and make corrections quickly to prevent the product's early demise. As the sales curve moves upward, the breakeven point is reached, and competitors enter the market, the growth stage begins.

Growth

During the **growth stage,** sales rise rapidly; and profits reach a peak and then start to decline (see Figure 10.3). The growth stage is critical to a product's survival because competitive reactions to the product's success during this period will affect the product's life expectancy. When Splenda, a sugar substitute, was introduced, sales rose quickly as consumers switched from other low-calorie sweetners. Sales rose even more quickly when restaurants such as McDonald's began offering Splenda in single-serving packets.[12] Profits begin to decline late in the growth stage as more competitors enter the market, driving prices down.

As sales increase, management must support the momentum by adjusting the marketing strategy. The goal is to establish and fortify the product's market position by encouraging brand loyalty. To achieve greater market penetration, segmentation may have to be used more intensely. This requires developing product variations to satisfy the needs of people in several different market segments. Apple, for example, introduced variations on its wildly popular iPod MP3 player, including the slimmer, colorful mini, the affordable shuffle, the smaller nano, and the iPod Video, with a larger screen for viewing downloaded videos; all these variations helped to expand Apple's market penetration in the competitive MP3 player industry. Marketers also should analyze the competing brands' product positions relative to their own brands and take corrective actions, if needed.

product life cycle The progression of a product through four stages: introduction, growth, maturity, and decline

introduction stage The initial stage of a product's life cycle—its first appearance in the marketplace—when sales start at zero and profits are negative

growth stage The stage of a product's life cycle when sales rise rapidly and profits reach a peak and then start to decline

Introduction Stage

Product introduction usually involves new packaging.

maturity stage The stage of a product's life cycle when the sales curve peaks and starts to decline as profits continue to fall

As sales volume increases, efficiencies in production may result in lower costs, thus providing an opportunity for lower prices. For example, when flat-panel televisions were introduced, the price was $5,000 or more. As demand soared, manufacturers of both liquid crystal display (LCD) and plasma technologies were able to take advantage of economies of scale to reduce production costs and lower prices to less than $1,000 within several years. If price cuts are feasible, they can help a brand gain market share and discourage new competitors from entering the market. Gaps in geographic market coverage should be filled during the growth period. As a product gains market acceptance, new distribution outlets usually become easier to obtain. Promotion expenditures may be slightly lower than during the introductory stage but are still quite substantial. As sales increase, promotion costs should drop as a percentage of total sales. The advertising messages should stress brand benefits. Coupons and samples may be used to increase market share.

Maturity

During the **maturity stage,** the sales curve peaks and starts to decline, and profits continue to fall (see Figure 10.3). This stage is characterized by intense competition because many brands are now in the market. Competitors emphasize improvements and differences in their versions of the product. As a result, during the maturity stage, weaker competitors are squeezed out of the market. The producers who remain in the market are likely to change their promotional and distribution efforts. Advertising and dealer-oriented promotions are typical during this stage of the product life cycle. Marketers also must take into account that as the product reaches maturity, buyers' knowledge of it attains a high level. Consumers are no longer inexperienced generalists. Instead, they are experienced specialists. Marketers of mature products sometimes expand distribution into global markets. Often the products have to be adapted to fit differing needs of global customers more precisely.

Because many products are in the maturity stage of their life cycles, marketers must know how to deal with these products and be prepared to adjust their marketing strategies. Consider that traditional truck-based sport-utility vehicles, such as the Ford Explorer and GMC Tahoe, have reached maturity, and their sales are beginning to decline. Facing rising gasoline costs, consumers became interested in "crossovers," car-based utility vehicles (SUVs) such as the Honda Pilot, BMW X3, Porsche Cayenne, and Saturn Vue, which generally have better fuel economy and more carlike handling. Automakers responded to this interest with more models and features. With their improved ride, handling, and fuel economy, crossovers are in a rapid sales growth stage at the expense of traditional SUVs.[13] There are many approaches to altering marketing strategies during the maturity stage. To increase the sales of mature products, marketers may suggest new uses for them. Arm & Hammer has boosted demand for its baking soda by this method.

During the maturity stage, three objectives are sometimes pursued, including generating cash flow, maintaining share of market, and increasing share of customer. Generating cash flow is essential for recouping the initial investment and generating excess cash to support new products. For example, General Motors, after years of

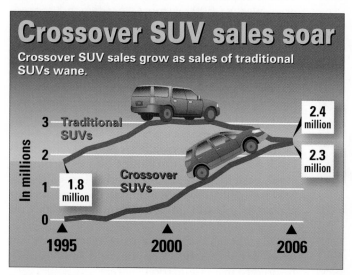

Source: Ford Motor.

declining sales in a mature market, is focused on cash flow to support its global operations. Some firms, such as Coca-Cola, simply strive to maintain their current market shares through aggressive promotions and new-product introductions. Companies with marginal market shares must decide whether they have a reasonable chance to improve their position or whether they should drop out. Companies also can focus on boosting their share of their individual customer's purchases, as Wells Fargo has done by striving to get customers to take advantage of as many of its product offerings (checking accounts, savings accounts, certificates of deposit, brokerage services, and so on) as possible.

A greater mixture of pricing strategies is used during the maturity stage. Strong price competition is likely and may ignite price wars. Firms also compete in other ways besides price, such as through product quality or services. In addition, marketers develop price flexibility to differentiate offerings in product lines. Markdowns and price incentives are common. Prices may have to be increased, however, if distribution and production costs rise.

During the maturity stage, marketers go to great lengths to serve dealers and to provide incentives for selling their brands. Maintaining market share during the maturity stage requires moderate, and sometimes large, promotion expenditures. Advertising messages focus on differentiating a brand from the field of competitors, and sales promotion efforts may be aimed at both consumers and resellers.

Decline

During the **decline stage,** sales fall rapidly (see Figure 10.3). When this happens, the marketer considers pruning items from the product line to eliminate those not earning a profit. The marketer also may cut promotion efforts, eliminate marginal distributors, and finally, plan to phase out the product. For example, although Procter & Gamble's Sure deodorant had been around for nearly three decades, sharply declining sales led the company to sell the well-known brand to Innovative Brands LLC, which had earlier purchased Procter & Gamble's Pert shampoo brand.[14]

In the decline stage, marketers must determine whether to eliminate the product or try to reposition it to extend its life. Usually a declining product has lost its distinctiveness because similar competing products have been introduced. Competition engenders increased substitution and brand switching as buyers become insensitive to minor product differences. For these reasons, marketers do little to change a product's style, design, or other attributes during its decline. New technology or social trends, product substitutes, or environmental considerations also may indicate that the time has come to delete the product.

During a product's decline, outlets with strong sales volumes are maintained, and unprofitable outlets are weeded out. An entire marketing channel may be eliminated if it does not contribute adequately to profits. An outlet not used previously, such as a factory outlet or Internet retailer, sometimes will be used to liquidate remaining inventory of an obsolete product. As sales decline, the product becomes more inaccessible, but loyal buyers seek out dealers who still carry it. Spending on promotion efforts is usually reduced considerably. Advertising of special offers may slow the rate of decline. Sales promotions, such as coupons and premiums, may regain buyers' attention temporarily. As the product continues to decline, the sales staff shifts its emphasis to more profitable products.

decline stage The stage of a product's life cycle when sales fall rapidly

Product Adoption Process

Acceptance of new products—especially new-to-the-world products—usually doesn't happen overnight. In fact, it can take a very long time. People are sometimes cautious or even skeptical about adopting new products, as indicated by some of the remarks quoted in Table 10.1. Customers who eventually accept a new product do so through an adoption process. The stages of the **product adoption process** are as follows:

1. *Awareness.* The buyer becomes aware of the product.

2. *Interest.* The buyer seeks information and is receptive to learning about the product.

3. *Evaluation.* The buyer considers the product's benefits and decides whether to try it.

4. *Trial.* The buyer examines, tests, or tries the product to determine if it meets his or her needs.

5. *Adoption.* The buyer purchases the product and can be expected to use it again whenever the need for this general type of product arises.[15]

In the first stage, when individuals become aware that the product exists, they have little information about it and are not concerned about obtaining more. Consumers enter the interest stage when they are motivated to get information about the product's features, uses, advantages, disadvantages, price, or location. During the evaluation stage, individuals consider whether the product will satisfy certain criteria that are crucial to meeting their specific needs. In the trial stage, they use or experience the product for the first time, possibly by purchasing a small quantity, taking advantage of free

---

table 10.1   **MOST NEW IDEAS HAVE THEIR SKEPTICS**

"I think there is a world market for maybe five computers."

–Thomas Watson, chairman of IBM, 1943

"This 'telephone' has too many shortcomings to be seriously considered as a means of communication. The device is inherently of no value to us."

–Western Union internal memo, 1876

"The wireless music box has no imaginable commercial value. Who would pay for a message sent to nobody in particular?"

–David Sarnoff's associates in response to his urgings for investment in the radio in the 1920s

"The concept is interesting and well-formed, but in order to earn better than a 'C,' the idea must be feasible."

–A Yale University management professor in response to Fred Smith's paper proposing reliable overnight delivery service (Smith went on to found Federal Express Corp.)

"Who the hell wants to hear actors talk?"

–H. M. Warner, Warner Brothers, 1927

"A cookie store is a bad idea. Besides, the market research reports say America likes crispy cookies, not soft and chewy cookies like you make."

–Banker's response to Debbie Fields's idea of starting Mrs. Fields' Cookies

"We don't like their sound, and guitar music is on the way out."

–Decca Recording Company rejecting the Beatles, 1962

---

product adoption process
The stages buyers go through in accepting a product

DISTRIBUTION OF PRODUCT ADOPTER CATEGORIES

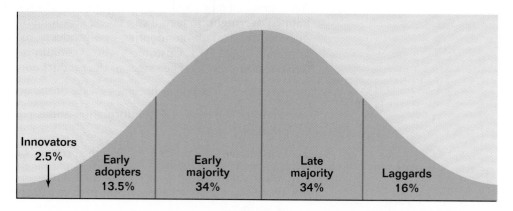

Innovators
2.5%

Early adopters 13.5%

Early majority 34%

Late majority 34%

Laggards 16%

samples, or borrowing the product from someone. Individuals move into the adoption stage by choosing a specific product when they need a product of that general type. Entering the adoption process does not mean that the person will eventually adopt the new product. Rejection may occur at any stage, including the adoption stage. Both product adoption and product rejection can be temporary or permanent.

When an organization introduces a new product, people do not begin the adoption process at the same time, nor do they move through the process at the same speed. Of those who eventually adopt the product, some enter the adoption process rather quickly, whereas others start considerably later. For most products, there is also a group of nonadopters who never begin the process.

Depending on the length of time it takes them to adopt a new product, consumers fall into one of five major adopter categories: innovators, early adopters, early majority, late majority, and laggards.[16] Figure 10.4 illustrates each adopter category and the percentage of total adopters it typically represents. **Innovators** are the first to adopt a new product; they enjoy trying new products and tend to be venturesome. **Early adopters** choose new products carefully and are viewed as "the people to check with" by those in the remaining adopter categories. People in the **early majority** adopt just prior to the average person; they are deliberate and cautious in trying new products. Individuals in the **late majority** are quite skeptical of new products but eventually adopt them because of economic necessity or social pressure. **Laggards,** the last to adopt a new product, are oriented toward the past. They are suspicious of new products, and when they finally adopt the innovation, it may already have been replaced by a new product.

Branding

Marketers must make many decisions about products, including choices about brands, brand names, brand marks, trademarks, and trade names. A **brand** is a name, term, design, symbol, or any other feature that identifies one marketer's product as distinct from those of other marketers. A brand may identify a single item, a family of items, or all items of that seller.[17] Some have defined a brand as not just the physical good, name, color, logo, or ad campaign but everything associated with the product, including its symbolism and experiences.[18] A **brand name** is the part of a brand that can be spoken—including letters, words, and numbers—such as 7Up. A brand name is often a product's only distinguishing characteristic. Without the brand name, a firm could not differentiate its products. To consumers, a brand name is as fundamental as the product itself. Indeed, many brand names have become

innovators First adopters of new products

early adopters Careful choosers of new products

early majority Those adopting new products just before the average person

Find your influences and then find theirs.

Get a free 7-day trial at napster.com   **Find Your** napster.

© 2007 Napster, LLC. Napster and the Napster logo are trademarks of Napster, LLC.

Brand Mark

Napster's brand mark—the headphone wearing cat—has become readily recognizable.

late majority Skeptics who adopt new products when they feel it is necessary

laggards The last adopters, who distrust new products

brand A name, term, design, symbol, or any other feature that identifies one marketer's product as distinct from those of other marketers

brand name The part of a brand that can be spoken

brand mark The part of a brand not made up of words

trademark A legal designation of exclusive use of a brand

trade name Full legal name of an organization

synonymous with the product, such as Scotch Tape and Xerox copiers. Through promotional activities, the owners of these brand names try to protect them from being used as generic names for tape and photocopiers.

The element of a brand that is not made up of words—often a symbol or design—is a **brand mark.** Examples of brand marks include McDonald's Golden Arches, Nike's "swoosh," and the stylized silhouette of Apple's iPod. A **trademark** is a legal designation indicating that the owner has exclusive use of a brand or a part of a brand and that others are prohibited by law from using it. To protect a brand name or brand mark in the United States, an organization must register it as a trademark with the U.S. Patent and Trademark Office. In a typical year, the Patent and Trademark Office registers about 150,000 new trademarks.[19] Finally, a **trade name** is the full and legal name of an organization, such as Ford Motor Company, rather than the name of a specific product.

Value of Branding

Both buyers and sellers benefit from branding. Brands help buyers to identify specific products that they do and do not like, which, in turn, facilitates the purchase of items that satisfy their needs and reduces the time required to purchase the product. Without brands, product selection would be quite random because buyers could have no assurance that they were purchasing what they preferred. The purchase of certain brands can be a form of self-expression. For example, clothing brand names are important to many consumers. Names such as Tommy Hilfiger, Polo, Champion, Nike, and Guess? give manufacturers an advantage in the marketplace. Especially when a customer is unable to judge a product's quality, a brand may symbolize a certain quality level to the customer, and in turn, the person lets that perception of quality represent the quality of the item. A brand helps to reduce a buyer's perceived risk of purchase. In addition, a psychological reward may come from owning a brand that symbolizes status. The Mercedes-Benz brand in the United States is an example.

Sellers benefit from branding because each company's brands identify its products, which makes repeat purchasing easier for customers. Branding helps a firm to introduce a new product that carries the name of one or more of its existing products because buyers are already familiar with the firm's existing brands. It facilitates promotional efforts because the promotion of each branded product indirectly promotes all other similarly branded products. Branding also fosters brand loyalty. To the extent that buyers become loyal to a specific brand, the company's market share for that product achieves a certain level of stability, allowing the firm to use its resources more efficiently. Once a firm develops some degree of customer loyalty for a brand, it can maintain a fairly consistent price rather than continually cutting the price to attract customers.

There is a cultural dimension to branding. Most brand experiences are individual, and each consumer confers his or her own social meaning onto brands. A brand's appeal is largely at an emotional level based on its symbolic image and key associations.[20] For some brands, such as Harley-Davidson, Google, and Apple, this can result in an almost cultlike following. These brands often develop a community of loyal customers that communicate through get-togethers, online forums, blogs, podcasts,

The Mets and Citigroup Brand Together

In November 2006, the New York Mets and Citigroup broke ground not only on a new stadium for the Mets baseball team but on a new type of partnership between a major league sports team and a corporation. The two entered into a 20-year sponsorship deal that will do much more than put Citigroup's name on the new stadium. Although corporate presence in sports is nothing new, the Mets' stadium is going to be the first belonging to a major team in New York to be named after a corporate sponsor, and feelings are mixed.

The Mets' management estimates that its investment into the new stadium, due to open in 2009, will come to more than $600 million. By joining forces with Citigroup, the Mets will receive $20 million per year for the lifetime of the partnership.

What does Citigroup get out of the deal? First, the partnership gives Citigroup naming rights to the stadium—slated to be called Citi Field—as well as brand presence throughout the park. Citigroup also gets to be incorporated into Mets television, print, radio, and online media campaigns and onto the new outdoor marquees at the field. A large number of promotional programs are being developed to maximize the partnership. Citigroup also has agreed to purchase time on SportsNet New York, the Mets' year-round TV home, which will include brand spots, billboards, special programming features, and promotions in about 125 regular-season Mets game broadcasts. Citigroup also will have a presence throughout the other broadcasts on the station.

In addition, Citigroup and the Mets—both of which are heavily involved in their communities already—plan to band together to create new outreach programs throughout New York. Their first joint project is to be the Jackie Robinson rotunda at the new stadium, which will honor the first African American baseball player to enter the major leagues in 1947 and promote the nine values he embodied: courage, integrity, determination, persistence, citizenship, justice, commitment, teamwork, and excellence. Citigroup and the Mets also have agreed to assist in the creation of the Jackie Robinson Foundation Museum and Education Center and to support programs such as leadership development and scholarships for students who carry on Robinson's humanitarian spirit.

Some analysts argue that hard-core fans may object to losing Shea Stadium, where the Mets have played since 1964, to a corporate sponsor and feel that the wholesomeness of baseball is being corrupted by money. Others argue that sports fans are used to the commercialization of sports. While it's true that many Mets fans will be sorry to see the old stadium go, the new stadium boasts plenty of upgrades that may help them to feel that the constant sighting of the Citigroup logo is well worth it.[b]

and other means. These brands even may help consumers to develop their identity and self-concept and serve as a form of self-expression. In fact, the term *cultural branding* has been used to explain how a brand conveys a powerful myth that consumers find useful in cementing their identities.[21] It is also important to recognize that because a brand exists independently in the consumer's mind, it is not controlled directly by the marketer. Every aspect of a brand is subject to a consumer's emotional involvement, interpretation, and memory. By understanding how branding influences purchases, marketers can foster customer loyalty.[22]

Stimulating Brand Associations
Quaker oats uses its trademarked Quaker character to stimulate favorable brand associations.

Brand Equity

A well-managed brand is an asset to an organization. The value of this asset is often referred to as brand equity. **Brand equity** is the marketing and financial value associated with a brand's strength in a market. Besides the actual proprietary brand assets, such as patents and trademarks, four major elements underlie brand equity: brand name awareness, brand loyalty, perceived brand quality, and brand associations[23] (see Figure 10.5 on page 248).

Being aware of a brand leads to brand familiarity, which, in turn, results in a level of comfort with the brand. A familiar brand is more likely to be selected than an unfamiliar brand because the familiar brand often is viewed as more reliable and of more acceptable quality. The familiar brand is likely to be in a customer's consideration set, whereas the unfamiliar brand is not.

Brand loyalty is a customer's favorable attitude toward a specific brand. If brand loyalty is strong enough, customers may purchase this brand consistently when they need a product in that product category. Customer satisfaction with a brand is the most common reason for loyalty to that brand.[24] Development of brand loyalty in a customer reduces his or her risks and shortens the time spent buying the product. However, the degree of brand loyalty for products varies from one product category to another. It is challenging to develop brand loyalty for some products, such as bananas, because customers can readily judge the quality of these products and do not need to refer to a brand as an indicator of quality. Brand loyalty also varies by country. Customers in France, Germany, and the United Kingdom tend to be less brand-loyal than U.S. customers.

There are three degrees of brand loyalty: recognition, preference, and insistence. **Brand recognition** occurs when a customer is aware that the brand exists and views it as an alternative purchase if the preferred brand is unavailable or if the other available brands are unfamiliar. This is the mildest form of brand loyalty. The term *loyalty* clearly is being used very loosely here. **Brand preference** is a stronger degree of brand loyalty. A customer definitely prefers one brand over competitive offerings and will purchase this brand if it is available. However, if the brand is not available, the customer will accept a substitute brand rather than expending additional effort finding and purchasing the preferred brand. When **brand insistence** occurs, a customer strongly prefers a specific brand, will accept no substitute, and is willing to spend a great deal of time and effort to acquire that brand. If a brand-insistent customer goes to a store and finds the brand unavailable, he or she will seek the brand elsewhere rather than purchase a substitute brand. Brand insistence also can apply to service products such as Hilton Hotels or sports teams such as the Chicago Bears or the Dallas Cowboys. Brand insistence is the strongest degree of brand loyalty; it is a brander's dream. However, it is the least common type of brand loyalty.

Brand loyalty is an important component of brand equity because it reduces a brand's vulnerability to competitors' actions. It allows an organization to keep its existing customers and avoid spending significant resources to gain new ones. Loyal

brand equity The marketing and financial value associated with a brand's strength in a market

brand loyalty A customer's favorable attitude toward a specific brand

brand recognition A customer's awareness that the brand exists and is an alternative purchase

brand preference The degree of brand loyalty in which a customer prefers one brand over competitive offerings

brand insistence The degree of brand loyalty in which a customer strongly prefers a specific brand and will accept no substitute

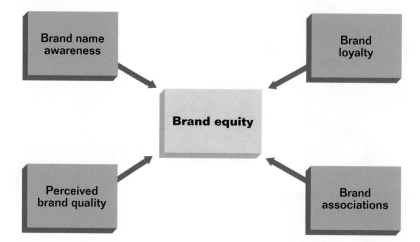

figure 10.5

MAJOR ELEMENTS OF BRAND EQUITY

Source: Adapted with the permission of The Free Press, a division of Simon & Schuster Adult Publishing Group, from *Managing Brand Equity: Capitalizing on the Value of a Brand Name* by David A. Aaker. Copyright © 1991 by David A. Aaker. All rights reserved.

customers provide brand visibility and reassurance to potential new customers. And because customers expect their brands to be available when and where they shop, retailers strive to carry the brands known for their strong customer following.

Customers associate a particular brand with a certain level of overall quality. A brand name may be used as a substitute for actual judgment of quality. In many cases, customers can't actually judge the quality of the product for themselves and instead must rely on the brand as a quality indicator. Perceived high brand quality helps to support a premium price, allowing a marketer to avoid severe price competition. Also, favorable perceived brand quality can ease the introduction of brand extensions because the high regard for the brand likely will translate into high regard for the related products.

The set of associations linked to a brand is another key component of brand equity. At times, a marketer works to connect a particular lifestyle or, in some instances, a certain personality type with a specific brand. For example, customers associate Michelin tires with protecting family members; a De Beers diamond with a loving, long-lasting relationship ("A Diamond Is Forever"); and Dr Pepper with a unique taste. These types of brand associations contribute significantly to the brand's equity. Brand associations sometimes are facilitated by using trade characters, such as the Jolly Green Giant, the Pillsbury Dough Boy, and Charlie the Tuna. Placing these trade characters in advertisements and on packages helps consumers to link the ads and packages with the brands.

Although difficult to measure, brand equity represents the value of a brand to an organization. Table 10.2 lists the top ten brands with the highest economic value. Any company that owns a brand listed in Table 10.2 would agree that the economic value of that brand is likely to be the greatest single asset in the organization's possession.

table 10.2 TOP TEN MOST VALUABLE BRANDS IN THE WORLD

Brand	Brand Value (in billion $)
Coca-Cola	67.0
Microsoft	56.9
IBM	56.2
GE	48.9
Intel	32.3
Nokia	30.1
Toyota	27.9
Disney	27.8
McDonald's	27.5
Mercedes-Benz	21.8

Source: "The 100 Top Brands, 2006," *BusinessWeek,* http://bwnt.businessweek.com/brand/2006/ (accessed June 15, 2007). The brand valuations draw on publicly available information that has not been investigated independently by Interbrand. Data: Interbrand Corp., J. P. Morgan Chase & Company, Citigroup, Morgan Stanley, and *BusinessWeek.*

Types of Brands

There are three categories of brands: manufacturer, private distributor, and generic. **Manufacturer brands** are initiated by producers and ensure that producers are identified with their

The Rise and Fall of Bingham Hill Cheese Company

Tom and Kristi Johnson, inspired by the fact that many artisan cheeses widely available in Europe were not available in the United States, decided to start the Bingham Hill Cheese Company in 1999. Observing the success of local microbreweries such as New Belgium (creator of Fat Tire ale) and O'Dell's (creator of 90 Schilling), the Johnsons began talking with the microbrewery owners, who proved to be most helpful in providing advice on starting a specialty business, as well as on equipment and supplies. They ultimately chose to model Bingham Hill after the microbreweries, even calling it a "microcheesery." Bingham Hill's first batch of Rustic Blue was an instant hit, winning first place in the blue cheese class of the American Cheese Society's annual competition. The Johnsons sent samples of Rustic Blue to a number of stores, and the orders flooded in.

One thing that made the Bingham Hill brand stand out is the handmade artisan cheese. The cheese was stirred, cut, ladled, turned, and inspected daily by the owners and their employees. Even in the midst of growth, the Johnsons intend to continue hand making the cheese. They have become well known for making spreadable cheeses, which are not aged, cutting down on costs for space and time. The Johnsons also created new products made from goat's milk and sheep's milk as well as cow's milk.

The Johnsons continued to experiment and learn about the craft of cheese making. In 2005, Bingham Hill cheeses won 10 medals at the annual World Cheese Awards in London. The company became one of just three national specialty cheese makers, and its products were regularly requested by top restaurants and chefs.

One important early customer of Bingham Hill was the California specialty foods retailer Trader Joe's. However, the cheese proved to be so popular that Bingham Hill simply could not supply its 200 stores with enough cheese. Although the Johnsons made significant investments to expand to accommodate Trade Joe's and other hoped-for large accounts, the small firm could not keep up with demand. Trader Joe's eventually eliminated the brand. Facing a huge bill for the expansion, rising costs, and the loss of a major customer, the company closed its doors in 2006. The state of Wisconsin offered the Johnsons financial incentives to move the firm to Wisconsin, but the owners were unwilling to move so far from family and friends.[c]

manufacturer brands Brands initiated by producers

private distributor brands Brands initiated and owned by resellers

products at the point of purchase—for example, Green Giant, Dell, Starbucks, and Levi's jeans. A manufacturer brand usually requires a producer to become involved in distribution, promotion, and to some extent, pricing decisions.

Private distributor brands (also called *private brands, store brands,* or *dealer brands*) are initiated and owned by resellers—wholesalers or retailers. The major characteristic of private brands is that the manufacturers are not identified on the products. Retailers and wholesalers use private distributor brands to develop more efficient promotion, generate higher gross margins, and change store image. Familiar retailer brand names include Sears' Kenmore and JCPenney's Arizona. Some successful private brands, such as Kenmore, are distributed nationally. Sometimes retailers with successful private distributor brands start manufacturing their own products to gain more control over product costs, quality, and design with the hope of increasing profits. Sales of private labels are now growing at more than twice the rate of brand names and account for 15 percent of packaged goods revenues in supermarkets. Some private

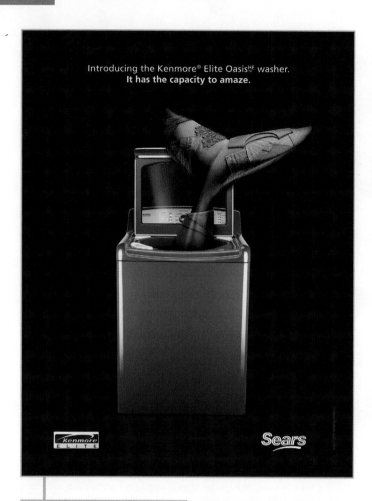

Introducing the Kenmore® Elite Oasis^{HE} washer.
It has the capacity to amaze.

Kenmore
ELITE

Sears

Private Brands

Sears' Kenmore, as a private brand, is as well known as most manufacturer brands.

brands have even gone upscale, such as Whole Food's 365 line of organic goods and Safeway's Rancher's Reserve premium beef.[25]

Some marketers of traditionally branded products have embarked on a policy of not branding, often called *generic branding.* **Generic brands** indicate only the product category (such as aluminum foil) and do not include the company name or other identifying terms. Generic brands usually are sold at lower prices than comparable branded items. Although at one time generic brands may have represented as much as 10 percent of all retail grocery sales, today they account for less than a half of a percent.

Selecting a Brand Name

Marketers consider several factors in selecting a brand name. First, the name should be easy for customers (including foreign buyers if the firm intends to market its products in other countries) to say, spell, and recall. Short, one-syllable names, such as Cheer, often satisfy this requirement. Second, the brand name should indicate the product's major benefits and, if possible, should suggest in a positive way the product's uses and special characteristics; negative or offensive references should be avoided. For example, the brand names of household cleaning products such as Ajax dishwashing liquid, Vanish toilet bowl cleaner, Formula 409 multipurpose cleaner, Cascade dishwasher detergent, and Wisk laundry detergent connote strength and effectiveness. Research suggests that consumers are more likely to recall and to evaluate favorably names that convey positive attributes or benefits.[26] Third, to set it apart from competing brands, the brand should be distinctive. If a marketer intends to use a brand for a product line, that brand must be compatible with all products in the line. AT&T, for example, renamed its Cingular wireless service AT&T so that all the company's products would have the same brand name.[27] Finally, a brand should be designed so that it can be used and recognized in all types of media. Finding the right brand name has become a challenging task because many obvious product names have already been used.

How are brand names devised? Brand names can be created from single or multiple words—for example, Dodge Nitro. Letters and numbers are used to create brands such as Volvo's S60 sedan or Motorola's RAZR V3 phone. Words, numbers, and letters are combined to yield brand names such as Apple's iPhone or BMW's Z4 Roadster. To avoid terms that have negative connotations, marketers sometimes use fabricated words that have absolutely no meaning when created—for example, Kodak and Exxon. Starwood Hotels & Resorts named its new Westin extended-stay suite hotels ELEMENT after months of brainstorming among employees. The company wanted the new chain brand to have a simple, modern name that would stand out against competitors' names.[28]

Who actually creates brand names? Brand names can be created internally by the organization. At Del Monte, a team of executives brainstormed 27 ideas for new cat food offerings with names such as "paté," "souffle," and "crème brulee."[29] Sometimes a name is suggested by individuals who are close to the development of the product. Some organizations have committees that participate in brand name creation and approval. Large companies that introduce numerous new products annually are likely to have a department that develops brand names. At times, outside consultants and companies that specialize in brand name development are used.

generic brands Brands indicating only the product category

Protecting a Brand

A marketer also should design a brand so that it can be protected easily through registration. A series of court decisions has created a broad hierarchy of protection based on brand type. From most protectable to least protectable, these brand types are fanciful (Exxon), arbitrary (Dr Pepper), suggestive (Spray 'n Wash), descriptive (Minute Rice), and generic (aluminum foil). Generic brands are not protectable. Surnames and descriptive, geographic, or functional names are difficult to protect.[30] However, research shows that overall, consumers prefer descriptive and suggestive brand names and find them easier to recall compared with fanciful and arbitrary brand names.[31] Because of their designs, some brands can be legally infringed on more easily than others. Although registration protects trademarks domestically for ten years, and trademarks can be renewed indefinitely, a firm should develop a system for ensuring that its trademarks are renewed as needed.

To protect its exclusive rights to a brand, a company must ensure that the brand is not likely to be considered an infringement on any brand already registered with the U.S. Patent and Trademark Office. Consider that after Apple launched the iPhone to much fanfare, it was sued by Cisco, which owns the trademark name iPhone, after the two companies failed to reach agreement on Apple's use of the name. This task may be complex because infringement is determined by the courts, which base their decisions on whether a brand causes consumers to be confused, mistaken, or deceived about the source of the product. McDonald's is one company that aggressively protects its trademarks against infringement; it has brought charges against a number of companies with *Mc* names because it fears that use of the prefix will give consumers the impression that these companies are associated with or owned by McDonald's.

A marketer should guard against allowing a brand name to become a generic term used to refer to a general product category. Generic terms cannot be protected as exclusive brand names. For example, *aspirin, escalator,* and *shredded wheat*—all brand names at one time—eventually were declared generic terms that refer to product classes. Thus they could no longer be protected. To keep a brand name from becoming a generic term, the firm should spell the name with a capital letter and use it as an adjective to modify the name of the general product class, as in Kool-Aid Brand Soft Drink Mix.[32] Including the word *brand* just after the brand name is also helpful. An organization can deal with this problem directly by advertising that its brand is a trademark and should not be used generically. The firm also can indicate that the brand is a registered trademark by using the symbol ®.

A U.S. firm that tries to protect a brand in a foreign country frequently encounters problems. In many countries, brand registration is not possible; the first firm to use a brand in such a country automatically has the rights to it. In some instances, U.S. companies actually have had to buy their own brand rights from a firm in a foreign country because the foreign firm was the first user in that country. Consider the decade-long dispute over Havana Club rum, which is marketed in 183 countries by Pernod Ricard, a French company, in a joint venture with the Cuban government, which nationalized the brand in 1960. However, Bacardi purchased the rights and original recipe from the brand's Cuban originators with the intention of producing it for distribution in the United States. Pernod Ricard sued Bacardi for violating its agreement, but Bacardi insists that the Cuban registration of the trademark in the United States is no longer valid. The dispute has involved U.S. courts and the World Trade Organization.[33]

Marketers trying to protect their brands also must contend with brand counterfeiting. In the United States, for instance, one can purchase counterfeit General Motors parts, Cartier watches, Louis Vuitton handbags, Walt Disney character dolls, Warner Brothers clothing, Mont Blanc pens, and a host of other products illegally marketed by manufacturers that do not own the brands. Losses caused by counterfeit products are estimated to be between $250 billion and $350 billion annually.

In the interest of strengthening trademark protection, Congress enacted the Trademark Law Revision Act in 1988, the only major federal trademark legislation since the Lanham Act of 1946. The purpose of this more recent legislation is to increase the value of the federal registration system for U.S. firms relative to foreign competitors and to protect the public from counterfeiting, confusion, and deception.[34]

Branding Policies

Before establishing branding policies, a firm must decide whether to brand its products at all. If a company's product is homogeneous and is similar to competitors' products, it may be difficult to brand in a way that will generate brand loyalty. Raw materials such as coal, sand, and farm produce are hard to brand because of the homogeneity of such products and their physical characteristics.

If a firm chooses to brand its products, it may use individual branding, family branding, or a combination. **Individual branding** is a policy of naming each product differently. Sara Lee uses individual branding among its many divisions, which include Hanes underwear, L'eggs pantyhose, Champion sportswear, Bali, Jimmy Dean, Ball Park, and other vastly different brands. A major advantage of individual branding is that if an organization introduces an inferior product, the negative images associated with it do not contaminate the company's other products. An individual branding policy also may facilitate market segmentation when a firm wishes to enter many segments of the same market. Separate, unrelated names can be used, and each brand can be aimed at a specific segment.

When using **family branding**, all of a firm's products are branded with the same name or at least part of the name, such as Kellogg's Frosted Flakes, Kellogg's Rice Krispies, and Kellogg's Corn Flakes. In some cases, a company's name is combined with other words to brand items. Arm & Hammer uses its name on all its products, along with a general description of the item, such as Arm & Hammer Heavy Duty Detergent, Arm & Hammer Pure Baking Soda, and Arm & Hammer Carpet Deodorizer. Unlike individual branding, family branding means that the promotion of one item with the family brand promotes the firm's other products. Examples of other companies that use family branding include Mitsubishi, Heinz, and Sony.

An organization is not limited to a single branding policy. A company that uses primarily individual branding for many of its products also may use family branding for a specific product line. Branding policy is influenced by the number of products and product lines the company produces, the characteristics of its target markets, the number and types of competing products available, and the size of the firm's resources.

Brand Extensions

A **brand extension** occurs when an organization uses one of its existing brands to brand a new product in a different product category. For example, Kellogg employed a brand extension when it gave its Special K cereal brand name to a new protein water product and a calorie-counting watch.[35] Another example is when Bic, the maker of disposable pens, introduced Bic disposable razors and Bic lighters. A brand extension should not be confused with a line extension. A line extension refers to using an existing brand on a new product in the same product category, such as new flavors or sizes. For example, when the maker of Tylenol, McNeil Consumer Products, introduced Extra Strength Tylenol P.M., the new product was a line extension because it was in the same category.

Marketers share a common concern that if a brand is extended too many times or extended too far outside its original product category, the brand can be weakened significantly. For example, the Nabisco Snackwell brand initially appeared only on crackers, cookies, and snack bars, all of which fall into the baked-snack category. However, extending the brand to yogurts and gelatin mixes goes further afield. Although some experts might caution Nabisco against extending the Snackwell brand to

individual branding A policy of naming each product differently

family branding Branding all of a firm's products with the same name

brand extension Using an existing brand to brand a new product in a different product category

this degree, some evidence suggests that brands can be extended successfully to less closely related product categories through the use of advertisements that extend customers' perceptions of the original product category. For example, Waterford, an upscale Irish brand of crystal, extended its name to writing instruments when seeking sales growth beyond closely related product categories such as china, cutlery, and table linens.[36] Research has found that a line extension into premium categories can be an effective strategy to revitalize a brand, but the line extension needs to be closely linked to the core brand.[37] Other research, however, suggests that diluting a brand by extending it into dissimilar product categories could have the potential to suppress consumer consideration and choice for the original brand.[38]

Co-Branding

Co-branding is the use of two or more brands on one product. Marketers employ co-branding to capitalize on the brand equity of multiple brands. Co-branding is popular in several processed-food categories and in the credit card industry. The brands used for co-branding can be owned by the same company. For example, Kraft's Lunchables product teams the Kraft cheese brand with Oscar Mayer lunchmeats, another Kraft-owned brand. The brands also may be owned by different companies. Credit card companies such as American Express, Visa, and MasterCard, for instance, team

Co-Branding
Many credit card companies, like Visa and Citi, offer co-branded cards with such organizations as airlines and universities to enhance the benefits to the cardholder.

up with other brands such as General Motors, AT&T, and many airlines. Effective co-branding capitalizes on the trust and confidence customers have in the brands involved. The brands should not lose their identities, and it should be clear to customers which brand is the main brand. For example, it is fairly obvious that Kellogg owns the brand and is the main brander of Kellogg's Healthy Choice Cereal. It is important for marketers to understand that when a co-branded product is unsuccessful, both brands are implicated in the product failure. To gain customer acceptance, the brands involved must represent a complementary fit in the minds of buyers. Trying to link a brand such as Harley-Davidson with a brand such as Healthy Choice will not achieve co-branding objectives because customers are not likely to perceive these brands as compatible.

Brand Licensing

A popular branding strategy involves **brand licensing**, an agreement in which a company permits another organization to use its brand on other products for a licensing fee. Royalties may be as low as 2 percent of wholesale revenues or higher than 10 percent. Kohl's, for example, licensed the Tony Hawk brand for use on a line of casual footwear.[39] The licensee is responsible for all manufacturing, selling, and advertising functions and bears the costs if the licensed product fails. The advantages of licensing range from extra revenues and low-cost or free publicity to new images and trademark protection. The major disadvantages are a lack of manufacturing control, which could hurt the company's name, and bombarding consumers with too many unrelated products bearing the same name.

co-branding Using two or more brands on one product

brand licensing An agreement whereby a company permits another organization to use its brand on other products for a licensing fee

Packaging

Packaging involves the development of a container and a graphic design for a product. A package can be a vital part of a product, making it more versatile, safer, and easier to use. Like a brand name, a package can influence customers' attitudes toward a product and so affect their purchase decisions. For example, several producers of jellies, sauces, and ketchups have packaged their products in squeezable plastic containers to make use and storage more convenient, whereas several paint manufacturers have introduced easy-to-open and -pour paint cans. Package characteristics help to shape buyers' impressions of a product at the time of purchase or during use. In this section we examine the main functions of packaging and consider several major packaging decisions. We also analyze the role of the package in a marketing strategy.

Packaging Functions

Effective packaging involves more than simply putting products in containers and covering them with wrappers. First, packaging materials serve the basic purpose of protecting the product and maintaining its functional form. Fluids such as milk and orange juice need packages that preserve and protect them. The packaging should prevent damage that could affect the product's usefulness and thus lead to higher costs. Since product tampering has become a problem, several packaging techniques have been developed to counter this danger. Some packages are also designed to deter shoplifting.

Another function of packaging is to offer convenience to consumers. For example, small, aseptic packages—individual-size boxes or plastic bags that contain liquids and do not require refrigeration—strongly appeal to children and young adults with active lifestyles. The size or shape of a package may relate to the product's storage, convenience of use, or replacement rate. Small, single-serving cans of vegetables, for instance, may prevent waste and make storage easier. A third function of packaging is to promote a product by communicating its features, uses, benefits, and image. Sometimes a reusable package is developed to make the product more desirable. For example, the Cool Whip package doubles as a food-storage container.

Major Packaging Considerations

As they develop packages, marketers must take many factors into account. Obviously, one major consideration is cost. Although a number of different packaging materials, processes, and designs are available, costs vary greatly. In recent years, buyers have shown a willingness to pay more for improved packaging, but there are limits. Research by Nestlé reveals that hard-to-open packages are among consumers' top complaints.[40]

Marketers should consider how much consistency is desirable among an organization's package designs. No consistency may be the best policy, especially if a firm's products are unrelated or aimed at vastly different target markets. To promote an overall company image, a firm may decide that all packages should be similar or include one major element of the design. This approach is called **family packaging**. Sometimes it is used only for lines of products, as with Campbell's soups, Weight Watcher's foods, and Planter's nuts.

A package's promotional role is an important consideration. Through verbal and nonverbal symbols, the package can inform potential buyers about the product's content, features, uses, advantages, and hazards. A firm can create desirable images and associations by its choice of color, design, shape, and texture. Many cosmetics manufacturers, for example, design their packages to create impressions of richness, luxury, and exclusiveness. To develop a package that has a definite promotional value, a designer must consider size, shape, texture, color, and graphics. Beyond the obvious limitation that the package must be large enough to hold the product, a package can be designed to appear taller or shorter. Light-colored packaging may make a package appear larger, whereas darker colors may minimize the perceived size.

family packaging Using similar packaging for all of a firm's products or packaging that has one common design element

Colors on packages are often chosen to attract attention, and color can positively influence customers' emotions. People often associate specific colors with certain feelings and experiences. Blue is soothing; it is also associated with wealth, trust, and security. Gray is associated with strength, exclusivity, and success. Orange can stand for low cost. Red connotes excitement and stimulation. Purple is associated with dignity and stateliness. Yellow connotes cheerfulness and joy. Black is associated with being strong and masterful.[41] When opting for color on packaging, marketers must judge whether a particular color will evoke positive or negative feelings when linked to a specific product. Rarely, for example, do processors package meat or bread in green materials because customers may associate green with mold. Marketers also must determine whether a specific target market will respond favorably or unfavorably to a particular color. Packages designed to appeal to children often use primary colors and bold designs.

Packaging also must meet the needs of resellers. Wholesalers and retailers consider whether a package facilitates transportation, storage, and handling. Resellers may refuse to carry certain products if their packages are cumbersome. Concentrated versions of laundry detergents and fabric softeners aid retailers in offering more product diversity within the existing shelf space.

Packaging and Marketing Strategy

Packaging can be a major component of a marketing strategy. A new cap or closure, a better box or wrapper, or a more convenient container may give a product a competitive advantage. The developers of the SpinBrush, a $5 electric toothbrush, had this in mind when they created packaging that allowed shoppers to turn the brush on in the store to see how it worked. This bold strategy helped SpinBrush sell over 10 million units in its first year on the shelves.[42] The right type of package for a new product can help it to gain market recognition very quickly. In the case of existing brands, marketers should reevaluate packages periodically. Marketers should view packaging as a major strategic tool, especially for consumer convenience products. For instance, in the food industry, jumbo and large package sizes for products such as hot dogs, pizzas, English muffins, frozen dinners, and biscuits have been very successful. When considering the strategic uses of packaging, marketers also must analyze the cost of packaging and package changes. In this section we examine several ways in which packaging can be used strategically.

Altering the Package.   At times, a marketer changes a package because the existing design is no longer in style, especially when compared with the packaging of competitive products. Arm & Hammer now markets a refillable plastic shaker for its baking soda. Quaker Oats hired a package design company to redesign its Rice-A-Roni package to give the product the appearance of having evolved with the times while retaining its traditional taste appeal. A package may be redesigned because new product features need to be highlighted or because new packaging materials have become available. An organization may decide to change a product's packaging to make the product safer or more convenient to use. The J.M. Smucker Company introduced Crisco vegetable oil in its new Simple Measures container, which includes a cap that doubles as a measuring cup. After measuring out the desired amount of oil and replacing the cap, any unused oil falls back into the bottle.[43]

Secondary-Use Packaging.   A secondary-use package is one that can be reused for purposes other than its initial function. For example, a margarine container can be reused to store leftovers, and a jelly container can serve as a drinking glass. Customers often view secondary-use packaging as adding value to products, in which case its use should stimulate unit sales.

Category-Consistent Packaging.   With category-consistent packaging, the product is packaged in line with the packaging practices associated with a particular product category. Some product categories—for example, mayonnaise, mustard, ketchup,

Count yourself lucky.

Introducing Pringles® 100 Calorie Packs. With zero trans fat, zero cholesterol and all that great Pringles taste, it adds up to one smart snack.

Packaging Strategies

Pringles incorporates the multiple packaging strategy to increase demand. By providing a select amount of product at the time of consumption, they can more specifically meet customer needs.

and peanut butter—have traditional package shapes. Other product categories are characterized by recognizable color combinations, such as red and white for soup and red, white, and blue for Ritz-like crackers. When an organization introduces a brand in one of these product categories, marketers often will use traditional package shapes and color combinations to ensure that customers will recognize the new product as being in that specific product category.

Innovative Packaging. Sometimes a marketer employs a unique cap, design, applicator, or other feature to make a product distinctive. Such packaging can be effective when the innovation makes the product safer or easier to use or provides better protection for the product. Nestlé, for example, introduced its new Country Creamery ice cream in an innovative package that included a plastic lid that's easy to remove even when the product is frozen and ribbed carton corners that make it easier to grip while scooping.[44] In some instances, marketers use innovative or unique packages that are inconsistent with traditional packaging practices to make the brand stand out from its competitors. Unusual packaging sometimes requires spending considerable resources not only on package design but also on making customers aware of the unique package and its benefits. Moreover, the findings of a recent study suggest that uniquely shaped packages that attract attention are more likely to be perceived as containing a higher volume of product.[45]

Multiple Packaging. Rather than packaging a single unit of a product, marketers sometimes use twin-packs, tri-packs, six-packs, or other forms of multiple packaging. For certain types of products, multiple packaging may increase demand because it increases the amount of the product available at the point of consumption (in one's house, for example). It also may increase consumer acceptance of the product by encouraging the buyer to try the product several times. Multiple packaging can make products easier to handle and store, as in the case of six-packs for soft drinks.

Handling-Improved Packaging. A product's packaging may be changed to make it easier to handle in the distribution channel—for example, by changing the outer carton or using special bundling, shrink-wrapping, or pallets. In some cases, the shape of the package is changed. Outer containers for products are sometimes changed so that they will proceed more easily through automated warehousing systems.

Labeling

labeling Providing identifying, promotional, or other information on package labels

Labeling is very closely interrelated with packaging and is used for identification, promotional, and informational, and legal purposes. Labels can be small or large relative to the size of the product and carry varying amounts of information. The sticker on a Chiquita banana, for example, is quite small and displays only the brand name of the fruit and perhaps a stock-keeping unit number. A label can be part of the package itself or a separate feature attached to the package. The label on a can of Coke is actually part of the can, whereas the label on a two-liter bottle of Coke is separate and can be removed. Information presented on a label may include the brand name and mark, the registered trademark symbol, package size and content, product features, nutritional information, potential presence of allergens, type and style of the product, number of servings, care instructions, directions for use and safety precautions, the name and address of the manufacturer, expiration dates, seals of approval, and other facts.

Labels can facilitate the identification of a product by displaying the brand name in combination with a unique graphic design. For example, Heinz ketchup is easy to identify on a supermarket shelf because the brand name is easy to read, and the label has a distinctive, crownlike shape. By drawing attention to products and their benefits, labels can strengthen an organization's promotional efforts. Labels may contain promotional messages such as the offer of a discount or a larger package size at the same price or information about a new or improved product feature.

Several federal laws and regulations specify information that must be included on the labels of certain products. Garments must be labeled with the name of the manufacturer, country of manufacture, fabric content, and cleaning instructions. Labels on nonedible items such as shampoos and detergents must include both safety precautions and directions for use. The Nutrition Labeling Act of 1990 requires the Food and Drug Administration (FDA) to review food labeling and packaging, focusing on nutrition content, label format, ingredient labeling, food descriptions, and health messages. This act regulates much of the labeling on more than 250,000 products made by 26,000 U.S. companies. Any food product for which a nutritional claim is made must have nutrition labeling that follows a standard format. Food product labels must state the number of servings per container, serving size, number of calories per serving, number of calories derived from fat, number of carbohydrates, and amounts of specific nutrients such as vitamins. In addition, new nutritional labeling requirements focus on the amounts of *trans*-fatty acids in food products.

The use of new technology in the production and processing of food has led to additional food labeling issues. The FDA now requires that a specific irradiation logo be used when labeling irradiated food products. In addition, the FDA has issued voluntary guidelines for food marketers to follow if they opt to label foods as being free of genetically modified organisms or to promote their biotech ingredients.

Of concern to many manufacturers are the Federal Trade Commission's (FTC) guidelines regarding "Made in U.S.A." labels, a growing problem owing to the increasingly global nature of manufacturing. The FTC requires that "all or virtually all" of a product's components be made in the United States if the label says "Made in U.S.A." Table 10.3 provides insight into just how important the "Made in USA" label can be for both Americans and western Europeans. It includes assessments of both quality and value for USA-, Japan-, Korea-, and Chinese-origin labels.

table 10.3   PERCEIVED QUALITY AND VALUE OF PRODUCTS BASED ON COUNTRY OF ORIGIN*

	"Made in USA"		"Made in Japan"		"Made in Korea"		"Made in China"	
	Value	Quality	Value	Quality	Value	Quality	Value	Quality
U.S. adults	4.0	4.2	3.2	3.2	2.6	2.4	2.8	2.4
Western Europeans	3.3	3.4	3.5	3.5	2.8	2.4	2.9	2.4

*On a scale of 1 (low) to 5 (high).
Source: "American Demographics 2006 Consumer Perception Survey," *Advertising Age,* January 2, 2006, p. 9. Data by Synovate.

...And now, back to Heinz

In order to remain competitive in the increasingly crowded supermarket aisle, Heinz must continue to come up with strong products and unique advertising. The long-time American favorite recently partnered with Hasbro for a Trivial Pursuit online holiday promotion to help recapture the nostalgic spirit of the ketchup brand and its iconic place in American pop culture. More than 200 million ketchup packets at select restaurants, schools, stadiums, and hospitals featured questions and answers from the new Trivial Pursuit Totally '80s Edition. The packets were intended to drive consumers to HeinzTrivialPursuit.com, where they could register the name and location of the restaurant where they found the special-edition ketchup packet in an attempt to win $2,500 in cash; in addition, hundreds of runners up won Trivial Pursuit games. The website also featured ketchup TV ads from the 1980s.

Heinz marketers also recognized another place to make their products stand out—the humble product label. In the late 1990s, the company began putting witty phrases, such as "Taller than mayonnaise," on its ketchup bottles. After discerning that consumers really enjoyed the catchy quips on Heinz labels, Heinz gave them a chance to "Create Your Own" labels by visiting **www.myheinz.com.** There, consumers could devise their own clever, sentimental, or celebratory message to create their own customized Heinz Ketchup bottle for the ultimate unique party favor or personalized gift for $4 to $6.50. Heinz is offering three sizes of customizable Ketchup bottles, the 14-ounce glass, the 20-ounce Top-Down, and the special "mini" 2.25-ounce Ketchup bottles. The myheinz site also features a special promotional section that will include an assortment of fun, specially designed seasonal and themed labels that also can be customized.

Heinz continually tries to come up with new packaging ideas such as the refrigerator door large-sized bottle that is convenient, easy to pour, and easy to store. The icon needs to continue to be innovative in its advertising and products to remain competitive and to maintain its position as the leading ketchup brand. Although the brand is over 125 years old, it is still popular among children and adults alike, and Heinz wants to keep it that way.[46]

1. As a consumer product, how can Heinz ketchup be classified?

2. Identify the product life cycle stage that Heinz ketchup is in.

3. Do you believe that the talking-labels campaign will be successful? How about the customizable ketchup bottles?

CHAPTER REVIEW

1. Understand the concept of a product and how products are classified.

A product is a good, a service, an idea, or any combination of the three received in an exchange. It can be either tangible or intangible and includes functional, social, and psychological utilities or benefits. When consumers purchase a product, they are buying the benefits and satisfaction they think the product will provide.

Products can be classified on the basis of the buyer's intentions. Consumer products are those purchased to satisfy personal and family needs. Business products are purchased for use in a firm's operations, to resell, or to make other products. Consumer products can be subdivided into convenience, shopping, specialty, and unsought products. Business products can be classified as installations, accessory equipment, raw materials, component parts, process materials, MRO supplies, and business services.

2. Explain the concepts of product item, product line, and product mix, and understand how they are connected.

A product item is a specific version of a product that can be designated as a distinct offering among an organization's products. A product line is a group of closely related product items that are considered a unit because of marketing, technical, or end-use considerations. The composite, or total, group of products that an organization makes available to customers is called the product mix. The width of the product mix is measured by the number of product lines the company offers. The depth of the product mix is the average number of different products offered in each product line.

3. Understand the product life cycle and its impact on marketing strategies.

The product life cycle describes how product items in an industry move through four stages: introduction, growth, maturity, and decline. The sales curve is at zero at introduction, rises at an increasing rate during growth, peaks during the maturity stage, and then declines. Profits peak toward the end of the growth stage of the product life cycle.

4. Describe the product adoption process.

When customers accept a new product, they usually do so through a five-stage adoption process. The first stage is awareness, when buyers become aware that a product exists. Interest, the second stage, occurs when buyers seek information and are receptive to learning about the product. The third stage is evaluation; buyers consider the product's benefits and decide whether to try it. The fourth stage is trial; during this stage, buyers examine, test, or try the product to determine if it meets their needs. The last stage is adoption, when buyers actually purchase the product and use it whenever a need for this general type of product arises.

5. Explain the value of branding and the major components of brand equity.

A brand is a name, term, design, symbol, or any other feature that identifies one seller's good or service and distinguishes it from those of other sellers. Branding helps buyers to identify and evaluate products, helps sellers to facilitate product introduction and repeat purchasing, and fosters brand loyalty. Brand equity is the marketing and financial value associated with a brand's strength. It represents the value of a brand to an organization. The four major elements underlying brand equity include brand name awareness, brand loyalty, perceived brand quality, and brand associations.

6. Recognize the types of brands and how they are selected and protected.

A manufacturer brand is initiated by a producer. A private distributor brand is initiated and owned by a reseller, sometimes taking on the name of the store or distributor. A generic brand indicates only the product category and does not include the company name or other identifying terms. When selecting a brand name, a marketer should choose one that is easy to say, spell, and recall and that alludes to the product's uses, benefits, or special characteristics.

Brand names can be devised from words, letters, numbers, nonsense words, or a combination of these. Companies protect ownership of their brands through registration with the U.S. Patent and Trademark Office.

7. Identify two types of branding policies, and explain brand extensions, co-branding, and brand licensing.

Individual branding designates a unique name for each of a company's products. Family branding identifies all of a firm's products with a single name. A brand extension is the use of an existing name on a new or improved product in a different product category. Co-branding is the use of two or more brands on one product. Through a licensing agreement and for a licensing fee, a firm may permit another organization to use its brand on other products. Brand licensing enables producers to earn extra revenue, receive low-cost or free publicity, and protect their trademarks.

8. Describe the major packaging functions and design considerations and how packaging is used in marketing strategies.

Packaging involves the development of a container and a graphic design for a product. Effective packaging offers protection, economy, safety, and convenience. It can influence a customer's purchase decision by promoting features, uses, benefits, and image. When developing a package, marketers must consider the value to the customer of efficient and effective packaging, offset by the price the customer is willing to pay. Other considerations include how to make the package tamper resistant, whether to use multiple packaging and family packaging, how to design the package as an effective promotional tool, and how best to accommodate resellers. Packaging can be an important part of an overall marketing strategy and can be used to target certain market segments. Modifications in packaging can revive a mature product and extend its product life cycle. Producers alter packages to convey new features or to make them safer or more convenient. If a package has a secondary use, the product's value to the consumer may increase. Category-consistent packaging makes products more easily recognized by consumers. Innovative packaging enhances a product's distinctiveness.

9. Understand the functions of labeling and selected legal issues.

Labeling is closely interrelated with packaging and is used for identification, promotional, and informational and legal purposes. Various federal laws and regulations require that certain products be labeled or marked with warnings, instructions, nutritional information, manufacturer's identification, and perhaps other information.

Please visit the student website at **www.prideferrell.com** for ACE Self-Test questions that will help you prepare for exams.

ACE self-test

KEY CONCEPTS

good	process materials	product adoption process	brand recognition
service	MRO supplies	innovators	brand preference
idea	business services	early adopters	brand insistence
consumer products	product item	early majority	manufacturer brands
business products	product line	late majority	private distributor brands
convenience products	product mix	laggards	generic brands
shopping products	width of product mix	brand	individual branding
specialty products	depth of product mix	brand name	family branding
unsought products	product life cycle	brand mark	brand extension
installations	introduction stage	trademark	co-branding
accessory equipment	growth stage	trade name	brand licensing
raw materials	maturity stage	brand equity	family packaging
component parts	decline stage	brand loyalty	labeling

ISSUES FOR DISCUSSION AND REVIEW

1. Is a personal computer sold at a retail store a consumer product or a business product? Defend your answer.

2. How do convenience products and shopping products differ? What are the distinguishing characteristics of each type of product?

3. How does an organization's product mix relate to its development of a product line? When should an enterprise add depth to its product line rather than width to its product mix?

4. How do industry profits change as a product moves through the four stages of its life cycle?

5. What are the stages in the product adoption process, and how do they affect the commercialization phase?

6. How does branding benefit consumers and marketers?

7. What is brand equity? Identify and explain the major elements of brand equity.

8. What are the three major degrees of brand loyalty?

9. Compare and contrast manufacturer brands, private distributor brands, and generic brands.

10. Identify the factors a marketer should consider in selecting a brand name.

11. What is co-branding? What major issues should be considered when using co-branding?

12. Describe the functions a package can perform. Which function is most important? Why?

13. What are the main factors a marketer should consider when developing a package?

14. In what ways can packaging be used as a strategic tool?

15. What are the major functions of labeling?

MARKETING APPLICATIONS

1. Choose a familiar clothing store. Describe its product mix, including its depth and width. Evaluate the mix and make suggestions to the owner.

2. Tabasco pepper sauce is a product that has entered the maturity stage of the product life cycle. Name products that would fit into each of the four stages (introduction, growth, maturity, and decline). Describe each product and explain why it fits in that stage.

3. Generally, buyers go through a product adoption process before becoming loyal customers. Describe your experience in adopting a product you now use consistently. Did you go through all the stages?

4. Identify two brands for which you are brand insistent. How did you begin using these brands? Why do you no longer use other brands?

5. General Motors introduced the subcompact Geo with a name that appeals to a world market. Invent a brand name for a line of luxury sports cars that also would appeal to an international market. Suggest a name that implies quality, luxury, and value.

6. For each of the following product categories, choose an existing brand. Then, for each selected brand, suggest a co-brand and explain why the co-brand would be effective.
   a. Cookies   c. Long-distance telephone service
   b. Pizza   d. A sports drink

7. Identify a package that you believe to be inferior. Explain why you think the package is inferior, and discuss your recommendations for improving it.

Online Exercise

8. In addition to providing information about the company's products, Goodyear's website helps consumers find the exact products they want and even directs them to the nearest Goodyear retailer. Visit the Goodyear site at **www.goodyear.com.**

a. How does Goodyear use its website to communicate information about the quality of its tires?
b. How does Goodyear's website demonstrate product and design features?
c. Based on what you learned at the website, describe what Goodyear has done to position its tires.

Brands are no longer a domestic phenomenon. In fact, many consumers now associate global brands with higher degrees of quality or prestige than more localized or even regionalized brands. Find data on this topic at *BusinessWeek*'s Global Brands section by using the search term "global brands" at **http://globaledge.msu.edu/ibrd** (and check the box "Resource Desk only"). Once there, click on the "Top 100 Brands Interactive Scoreboard." What are the top ten brands worldwide? Which countries are represented? Which brands from the overall study are from Germany? Summarize three German brands and compare each with a competing brand.

Video CASE

New Belgium Brewing Company

The idea for New Belgium Brewing Company (NBB) began with a bicycling trip through Belgium, where some of the world's finest ales have been brewed for centuries. As Jeff Lebesch, a U.S. electrical engineer, cruised around the country on a fat-tired mountain bike, he wondered if he could produce such high-quality ales in his home state of Colorado. After returning home, Lebesch began to experiment in his Fort Collins basement. When his home-brewed experiments earned rave reviews from friends, Lebesch and his wife, Kim Jordan, decided to open the New Belgium Brewing Company in 1991. They named their first brew Fat Tire Amber Ale in honor of Lebesch's Belgian biking adventure.

Today, New Belgium markets a variety of permanent and seasonal ales and pilsners. The standard line includes Sunshine Wheat, Blue Paddle Pilsner, Abbey Ale, Trippel Ale, and 1554 Black Ale, as well as the firm's number one seller, the original Fat Tire Amber Ale. NBB also markets seasonal beers, such as Frambozen and Abbey Grand Cru, released at Thanksgiving, and Christmas and Farmhouse Ale, sold during the early fall months. The firm also occasionally offers one-time-only brews—such as 2° Below, a winter ale—that are sold only until the batch runs out. Bottle label designs employ "good ol' days" nostalgia. The Fat Tire label, for example, features an old-style cruiser bike with wide tires, a padded seat, and a basket hanging from the handlebars. All the label and packaging designs were created by the same watercolor artist, Jeff Lebesch's next-door neighbor.

New Belgium beers are priced to reflect their quality at about $7 per six-pack. This pricing strategy conveys the message that the products are special and of consistently higher quality than macrobrews, such as Budweiser and Coors, but also keeps them competitive with other microbrews, such as Pete's Wicked Ale, Pyramid Pale Ale, and Sierra Nevada. To demonstrate its appreciation for its retailers and business partners, New Belgium does not sell beer to consumers on-site at the brewhouse for less than the retailers charge.

Although Fat Tire was sold initially only in Fort Collins, distribution quickly expanded throughout the rest of Colorado. Customers now can find Fat Tire and other New Belgium offerings in 16 western states, including Washington, Montana, Texas, New Mexico, and Arizona. The brewery regularly receives e-mails and telephone inquiries as to when New Belgium beers will be available elsewhere.

Since its founding, NBB's most effective promotion has been via word-of-mouth advertising by customers devoted to the brand. The company initially avoided mass advertising, relying instead on small-scale, local promotions, such as print advertisements in alternative magazines, participation in local festivals, and sponsorship of alternative sports events. Through event sponsorships, such as the Tour de Fat and Ride the Rockies, NBB has raised thousands of dollars for various environmental, social, and cycling nonprofit organizations.

With expanding distribution, however, the brewery recognized a need to increase its opportunities for reaching its far-flung customers. It consulted with Dr. David Holt, an Oxford professor and branding expert. After studying the young company, Holt, together with Marketing Director Greg Owsley, drafted a 70-page "manifesto" describing the brand's attributes, character, cultural relevancy, and promise. In particular, Holt identified in New Belgium an ethos of pursuing creative activities simply for the joy of doing them well and in harmony with the natural environment. With the brand thus defined, New Belgium went in search of an advertising agency to help communicate that brand identity; it soon found Amalgamated, an equally young, independent New York advertising agency. Amalgamated created a $10 million advertising campaign for New Belgium that targets high-end beer drinkers, men ages 25 to 44, and highlights the brewery's image as being down to earth. The grainy ads focus on a man rebuilding a cruiser bike out of used parts and then riding it along pastoral country roads. The product appears in just five seconds of each ad between the tag lines, "Follow Your Folly . . . Ours Is Beer." The ads helped to position the growing brand as whimsical, thoughtful, and reflective. In addition to the ad campaign, the company maintained its strategy of promotion through event sponsorships.

NBB's marketing strategy has always involved pairing the brand with a concern for how the company's activities affect the natural environment. The brewery looks for cost-efficient, energy-saving alternatives to conducting business and reducing its impact on the environment. Thus the company's employee-owners unanimously agreed to invest in a wind turbine, making NBB the first fully wind-powered brewery in the United States. The company further reduces its energy use with a steam condenser that captures and reuses the hot water from boiling the barley and hops in the production process to start the next brew; the steam is redirected to heat the floor tiles and deice the loading docks in cold weather. NBB also strives to recycle as many supplies as possible, including cardboard boxes, keg caps, office materials, and the amber glass used in bottling. The brewery stores spent barley and hop grains in an on-premise silo and invites local farmers to pick up the grains, free of charge, to feed their pigs. Another way NBB conserves energy is through the use of "sun tubes," which provide natural daytime lighting throughout the brewhouse all year long. NBB also encourages employees to reduce air pollution through alternative transportation. As an incentive, NBB gives each employee a "cruiser bike"—just like the one on the Fat Tire Amber Ale label and in the television ads—after one year of employment to encourage biking to work.

Beyond its use of environment-friendly technologies and innovations, New Belgium Brewing Company strives to improve communities and enhance lives through corporate giving, event sponsorship, and philanthropic involvement. The company donates $1 per barrel of beer sold to various cultural, social, environmental, and drug and alcohol awareness programs across the 15 western states in which it distributes beer. Typical grants range from $2,500 to $5,000. Involvement is spread equally among the 15 states, unless a special need requires greater participation or funding. The brewhouse also maintains a community board where organizations can post community involvement activities and proposals. This board allows tourists and employees to see opportunities to help out the community and provides nonprofit organizations with a forum for making their needs known. Organizations also can apply for grants through the New Belgium Brewing Company website, which has a link designated for this purpose.

New Belgium's commitment to quality, the environment, and its employees and customers is clearly expressed in its stated purpose: "To operate a profitable brewery which makes our love and talent manifest." This dedication has been well rewarded with loyal customers and industry awards.

From cutting-edge environmental programs and high-tech industry advancements to employee-ownership programs and a strong belief in giving back to the community, New Belgium demonstrates its desire to create a living, learning community. According to David Edgar, director of the Institute for Brewing Studies, "They've created a very positive image for their company in the beer-consuming public with smart decision making." Although some members of society do not believe a brewery can be socially responsible, New Belgium has set out to prove that for those who make the choice to drink responsibly, the company can do everything possible to contribute to society.[47]

Questions for Discussion

1. How does New Belgium Brewing Company's social responsibility initiatives help to build its brand?
2. Describe New Belgium's branding policy. How does it use packaging to further its brand image?
3. Assess New Belgium's brand equity.

Developing and Managing Goods and Services

Crayola Finds Toys Are Fun with No Mess

Joseph Binney and his cousin, C. Harold Smith, took over Binney's father's pigment company in 1885 and started producing red oxide pigment used in barn paint and carbon black for car tires. Their company, Binney & Smith, began producing slate school pencils in 1900 and introduced the first dustless chalk in 1902. Perhaps it was no surprise, therefore, that Binney & Smith invented the Crayola Crayon after recognizing the need for safe, quality, affordable wax crayons. Binney's wife Alice combined *craie,* the French word for "chalk," and *ola* from the word *oleaginous,* meaning "oily," to come up with the word *Crayola.* In 1903, the first box of Binney & Smith crayons sold for a nickel and contained eight colors: red, orange, yellow, green, blue, violet, brown, and black. The company added to the product line in the 1920s with lines Crayola Rubens (fat, oversized coloring sticks) and perma-pressed fine-art crayons, as well as a separate line of paints. In 1979, Binney & Smith introduced a new corporate logo and began a program to consolidate a range of individual brand names that it had developed or acquired under the Crayola brand name.

Since its creation, the Crayola brand has grown into one of the most respected and recognizable names in the consumer marketplace. The company has continued to innovate with new colors, new color names, and creative packaging; it equates the brand with color, fun, quality, and development. Binney & Smith has continued to expand the Crayola brand to include crayons, colored pencils, paints, markers, modeling compounds, and craft and activity products. Today, the Hallmark Company subsidiary sells $500 million worth of Crayola products—including more than 100 different crayon colors—as well as an array of materials to stimulate children's creative development.

In 1977, Binney & Smith acquired the rights to Silly Putty—a failed experiment to create a synthetic rubber compound—which became a toy classic much like Crayola Crayons. Today, Silly Putty brand products come in more than 15 different colors in the unmistakable egg-shaped packaging. Kids today continue to discover and marvel over Silly Putty's unique properties that allow it to be bounced, stretched, and molded into a multitude of shapes. Silly Putty still can be bought in its original color, as well as colors that change color when held in the hand. The company introduced a metallic version in 2000 for Silly Putty's fiftieth anniversary.[1] ■

OBJECTIVES

1. Understand how companies manage existing products through line extensions and product modifications.

2. Describe how businesses develop a product idea into a commercial product.

3. Know the importance of product differentiation and the elements that differentiate one product from another.

4. Explain product positioning and repositioning.

5. Understand how product deletion is used to improve product mixes.

6. Understand the characteristics of services and how these characteristics present challenges when developing marketing mixes for service products.

7. Be familiar with organizational structures used for managing products.

To compete effectively and achieve their goals, organizations such as Binney & Smith must be able to adjust their product mixes in response to changes in customers' needs. A firm often has to introduce new products, modify existing products, or delete products that were successful perhaps only a few years ago. To provide products that satisfy target markets and achieve the organization's objectives, a marketer must develop, alter, and maintain an effective product mix. An organization's product mix may need several types of adjustments. Because customers' attitudes and product preferences change over time, their desire for certain products may wane.

In this chapter we examine several ways to improve an organization's product mix. First, we discuss managing existing products through effective line extension and product modification. Next, we examine the stages of new-product development. Then we go on to discuss the ways companies differentiate their products in the marketplace and follow with a discussion of product positioning and repositioning. Next, we examine the importance of deleting weak products and the methods companies use to eliminate them. Then we explore the characteristics of services as products and how these services' characteristics affect the development of marketing mixes for services. Finally, we look at the organizational structures used to manage products.

Managing Existing Products

An organization can benefit by capitalizing on its existing products. By assessing the composition of the current product mix, a marketer can identify weaknesses and gaps. This analysis then can lead to improvement of the product mix through line extensions and product modifications.

Line Extensions

A **line extension** is the development of a product closely related to one or more products in the existing product line but designed specifically to meet somewhat different customer needs. Kellogg, for example, created a line extension for its Special K cereal with a successful new flavor, Special K Red Berries.[2]

Many of the so-called new products introduced each year are in fact line extensions. Line extensions are more common than new products because they are a less expensive, lower-risk alternative for increasing sales. A line extension may focus on a different market segment or may be an attempt to increase sales within the same market segment by more precisely satisfying the needs of people in that segment. Hormel, for example, extended the Spam line of processed meat with new flavors such as Stinky French Garlic, as well as single-serve packets.[3] Line extensions are also used to take market share from competitors. The bottled water category leader, Nestlé, released its own four-flavor line of water called Pure Life Splash in direct response to Coca-Cola and Pepsi's latest bottled-water line extensions.[4] However, one side effect of employing a line extension is that it may result in a less positive evaluation of the core product if customers are less satisfied with the line extension.

Product Modifications

Product modification means changing one or more characteristics of a product. A product modification differs from a line extension because the original product does not remain in the line. For example, automakers use product modifications annually when they create new models of the same brand. Once the new models are introduced, the manufacturers stop producing last year's model. Like line extensions, product modifications entail less risk than developing new products.

Product modification can indeed improve a firm's product mix, but only under certain conditions. First, the product must be modifiable. Second, customers must be able to perceive that a modification has been made. Third, the modification should make the product more consistent with customers' desires so that it provides greater satis-

line extension Development of a product that is closely related to existing products in the line but meets different customer needs

product modification Change in one or more characteristics of a product

Four wholesome grains.
One great-tasting snack.

New TOSTITOS® Multigrain Tortilla Chips are made with the wholesome goodness of four grains. They're a fun, great-tasting snack that your family will love and a perfect companion to 100% all-natural TOSTITOS® Salsa.
MEET ME AT THE TOSTITOS BRAND

TOSTITOS, TOSTITOS Logo and MEET ME AT THE TOSTITOS are trademarks used by Frito-Lay. ©2006 Frito-Lay North America, Inc.

Line Extensions

Tostitos multigrain chips is a line extension.

faction. One drawback to modifying a successful product is that the consumer who had experience with the original version of the product may view a modified version as a riskier purchase.[5] There are three major ways to modify products: quality, functional, and aesthetic modifications.

Quality Modifications. **Quality modifications** are changes relating to a product's dependability and durability. The changes usually are executed by altering the materials or the production process. For example, Energizer increased its product's durability by using better materials—a larger cathode and anode interface—that make batteries last longer. For a service, such as a sporting event or air travel, quality modifications may involve enhancing the emotional experience that makes the consumer passionate and loyal to the brand.

Reducing a product's quality may allow an organization to lower its price and direct the item at a different target market. In contrast, increasing the quality of a product may give a firm an advantage over competing brands. Higher quality may enable a company to charge a higher price by creating customer loyalty and lowering customer sensitivity to price. However, higher quality may require the use of more expensive components and processes, thus forcing the organization to cut costs in other areas. Some firms, such as Caterpillar, are finding ways to increase quality while reducing costs.

Functional Modifications. Changes that affect a product's versatility, effectiveness, convenience, or safety are called **functional modifications;** they usually require that the product be redesigned. Product categories that have undergone considerable functional modification include office and farm equipment, appliances, cleaning products, and consumer electronics. Functional modifications can make a product useful to more people and thus enlarge its market. They can place a product in a favorable competitive position by providing benefits that competing brands do not offer. For example, Lexus introduced the LS 460 sedan with an Advanced Parking Guidance System that essentially parallel parks the vehicle with little effort by the driver. The parking system comes as part of an options package that includes a navigation system, voice-activated Bluetooth, and XM satellite radio.[6] They also can help an organization achieve and maintain a progressive image. Finally, functional modifications are sometimes made to reduce the possibility of product liability lawsuits.

Aesthetic Modifications. **Aesthetic modifications** change the sensory appeal of a product by altering its taste, texture, sound, smell, or appearance. A buyer making a purchase decision is swayed by how a product looks, smells, tastes, feels, or sounds. Cadbury Schweppes, for example, added a new cherry vanilla flavor to its Dr Pepper soft-drink product line. An aesthetic modification may strongly affect purchases. Automobile makers have relied on both quality and aesthetic modifications. For example, the Acura MDX sport-utility vehicle (SUV) was redesigned to give it a sportier and more stylish look.[7]

Through aesthetic modifications, a firm can differentiate its product from competing brands and thus gain a sizable market share. Eastern Spice & Flavors, for example, localizes its spice blends to match the tastes of various regional markets around the world.[8] The major drawback in using aesthetic modifications is that their value is determined subjectively. Although a firm may strive to improve the product's sensory appeal, customers actually may find the modified product less attractive.

quality modifications
Changes relating to a product's dependability and durability

functional modifications
Changes affecting a product's versatility, effectiveness, convenience, or safety

aesthetic modifications
Changes to the sensory appeal of a product

Developing New Products

Example of a New Product
M&M's introduces dark chocolate.

A firm develops new products as a means of enhancing its product mix. Developing and introducing new products is frequently expensive and risky. For example, Hormel's managers pulled the plug on the four ethnic-themed varieties of its Refrigerated Entrees line after two years on the market when they finally recognized that most consumers were dubious that the producer of Spam could produce restaurant-quality ethnic meals.[9] Although introducing new products is risky, failure to introduce new products is also risky. Both Ford Motor Company and General Motors have lost market share to Japanese and Korean automakers in recent years as sales of some of their most profitable models have declined. Chrysler, however, has maintained market share with successful new products.[10]

The term *new product* can have more than one meaning. A genuinely new product offers innovative benefits. Envigo, a green-tea product offered by a joint venture of Coca-Cola and Nestlé, purports to be "calorie deficient" in order to help consumers burn fewer calories.[11] But products that are different and distinctly better are often viewed as new. Cascade Lacrosse, for example, introduced a new sports helmet that reduces shock sustained by the brain by 40 percent. Since 40 percent of pro hockey players get at least one concussion a year, this represents a significant new product.[12] The following items are product innovations of the last 30 years: Post-it Notes, fax machines, cell phones, personal computers, personal digital assistants (PDAs), digital music players, satellite radio, and digital video recorders. A new product can be an innovative product that has never been sold by any organization, such as the digital camera when it was introduced for the first time. A radically new product involves a complex developmental process, including an extensive business analysis to determine the possibility of success.[13] A new product also can be one that a specific firm is currently launching even though other firms are already producing and marketing similar products. Finally, a product can be viewed as new when it is brought to one or more markets from another market. For example, making the Saturn VUE SUV available in Japan is viewed as a new-product introduction in Japan.

Before a product is introduced, it goes through the seven phases of the **new-product development process** shown in Figure 11.1: (1) idea generation, (2) screening, (3) concept testing, (4) business analysis, (5) product development, (6) test marketing, and (7) commercialization. A product may be dropped—and many are—at any stage of development. In this section we look at the process through which products are developed from idea inception to fully commercialized product.

Idea Generation

Businesses and other organizations seek product ideas that will help them to achieve their objectives. This activity is **idea generation.** The fact that only a few ideas are good enough to be successful commercially underscores the challenge of the task. Although some organizations get their ideas almost by chance, firms that try to manage their product mixes effectively usually develop systematic approaches for generating new-product ideas. Indeed, there is a relationship between the amount of market information gathered and the number of ideas generated by work groups in organizations.[14] At the heart of innovation is a purposeful, focused effort to identify new ways to serve a market.

new-product development process A seven-phase process for introducing products

idea generation Seeking product ideas to achieve objectives

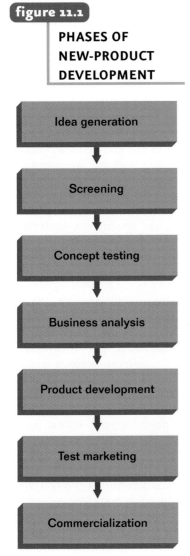

New-product ideas can come from several sources. They may come from internal sources—marketing managers, researchers, sales personnel, engineers, or other organizational personnel. Brainstorming and incentives or rewards for good ideas are typical intrafirm devices for stimulating development of ideas. For example, the idea for 3M Post-it Notes came from an employee. As a church choir member, he used slips of paper to mark songs in his hymnal. Because the pieces of paper fell out, he suggested developing an adhesive-backed note. In the restaurant industry, ideas may come from franchisees. At McDonald's, for example, franchise owners invented the Big Mac and the Egg McMuffin. Today, new McDonald's product ideas often come from corporate chef Dan Coudreaut, who developed the fast-food giant's new snack wrap.[15]

New-product ideas also may arise from sources outside the firm, such as customers, competitors, advertising agencies, management consultants, and research organizations. Procter & Gamble gets 35 percent of its ideas from inventors and outside consultants.[16] Consultants are often used as sources for stimulating new-product ideas. Home Depot got the idea for its new Orange Works architect-designed fire extinguisher from Arnell Group, a marketing and design company; Arnell Group's founder once worked for architect Michael Graves, who provided ideas and designs for many new products at retail giant Target.[17] Another consulting firm, Fahrenheit 212, serves as an "idea factory" that provides ready-to-go product ideas including market potential analysis.[18] When outsourcing new-product development activities to outside organizations, the best results are achieved from spelling out the specific tasks with detailed contractual specifications.[19] A significant portion of this money is used to assess customers' needs. Asking customers what they want from products and organizations has helped many firms become successful and remain competitive.

Screening

In the process of **screening,** the ideas with the greatest potential are selected for further review. During screening, product ideas are analyzed to determine whether or not they match the organization's objectives and resources. If a product idea results in a product similar to the firm's existing products, marketers must assess the degree to which the new product could cannibalize the sales of current products. The company's overall abilities to produce and market the product are also analyzed. Other aspects of an idea to be weighed are the nature and wants of buyers and possible environmental changes. At times, a checklist of new-product requirements is used when making screening decisions. This practice encourages evaluators to be systematic and thus reduces the chances of overlooking some pertinent fact. Compared with other phases, the greatest number of new-product ideas are rejected during the screening phase.

Concept Testing

To evaluate ideas properly, it may be necessary to test product concepts. In **concept testing,** a small sample of potential buyers is presented with a product idea through a written or oral description (and perhaps a few drawings) to determine their attitudes and initial buying intentions regarding the product. For a single product idea, an organization can test one or several concepts of the same product. Concept testing is a low-cost procedure that allows a company to determine customers' initial reactions to a product idea before it invests considerable resources in research and development. Input from online communities also may be beneficial in the product development process.[20] The results of concept testing can help product development personnel better understand which product attributes and benefits are most important to potential customers.

During concept testing, the concept is described briefly, and then a series of questions is presented. The questions vary considerably depending on the type of product being tested. Typical questions are: In general, do you find this proposed product

screening Choosing the most promising ideas for further review

concept testing Seeking potential buyers' responses to a product idea

attractive? Which benefits are especially attractive to you? Which features are of little or no interest to you? Do you feel that this proposed product would work better for you than the product you currently use? Compared with your current product, what are the primary advantages of the proposed product? If this product were available at an appropriate price, would you buy it? How often would you buy this product? How could this proposed product be improved?

Business Analysis

During the **business analysis** stage, the product idea is evaluated to determine its potential contribution to the firm's sales, costs, and profits. In the course of a business analysis, evaluators ask various questions: Does the product fit with the organization's existing product mix? Is demand strong enough to justify entering the market, and will the demand endure? What types of environmental and competitive changes can be expected, and how will these changes affect the product's future sales, costs, and profits? Are the organization's research, development, engineering, and production capabilities adequate to develop the product? If new facilities must be constructed, how quickly can they be built, and how much will they cost? Is the necessary financing for development and commercialization on hand or obtainable at terms consistent with a favorable return on investment?

In the business analysis stage, firms seek market information. The results of consumer polls, along with secondary data, supply the specifics needed to estimate potential sales, costs, and profits. For many products in this stage (when they are still just product ideas), forecasting sales accurately is difficult. This is especially true for innovative and completely new products. Organizations sometimes employ breakeven analysis to determine how many units they would have to sell to begin making a profit. At times, an organization also uses payback analysis, in which marketers compute the time period required to recover the funds that would be invested in developing the new product. Because breakeven and payback analyses are based on estimates, they are usually viewed as useful but not particularly precise tools.

Product Development

Product development is the phase in which the organization determines if it is technically feasible to produce the product and if it can be produced at costs low enough to make the final price reasonable. To test its acceptability, the idea or concept is converted into a prototype, or working model. The prototype should reveal tangible and intangible attributes associated with the product in consumers' minds. The product's design, mechanical features, and intangible aspects must be linked to wants in the marketplace. Through marketing research and concept testing, product attributes that are important to buyers are identified. These characteristics must be communicated to customers through the design of the product. Honda, for example, developed a prototype minivan that targets Japan's growing population of pet owners with pet-friendly features, such as paneled floors and seats that convert to a holding pen. Displayed at the Tokyo Auto Show, the prototype helped Honda assess interest in the concept.[21]

After a prototype is developed, its overall functioning must be tested. Its performance, safety, convenience, and other functional qualities are tested both in a laboratory and in the field. Functional testing should be rigorous and lengthy enough to test the product thoroughly. Manufacturing issues that come to light at this stage may require adjustments. When Cadbury Schweppes was developing its Trident Splash gum, production problems necessitated changes in the ingredients. One combination resulted in a too-soft gum that jammed machines; another combination resulted in the gum's liquid center leaking during trial deliveries. Finding just the right recipe required months.[22]

A crucial question that arises during product development is how much quality to build into the product. For example, a major dimension of quality is durability. Higher quality often calls for better materials and more expensive processing, which

business analysis Evaluating the potential contribution of a product idea to the firm's sales, costs, and profits

product development Determining if producing a product is technically feasible and cost effective

marketing
ENTREPRENEURS

Alex Fisher and Stew Maloney

THEIR BUSINESS: Planet Dog

FOUNDED: 1997

SUCCESS: Nearly 850 products sold through 2,000 stores around the world

Add Alex Fisher and Stew Maloney to the ranks of business founders who sketched their business plan on a napkin. Their plan for Planet Dog has grown into a successful dog-centric retailer based in Portland, Maine. It markets dog-tested toys, bones, leashes, beds, and other products through a website, catalog, and national retailers such as PetSmart and PETCO. From the beginning, Fisher and Maloney focused on designing products to please dogs and infused their small business with a fun, free-thinking philosophy where "there's no such thing as a bad idea." The fast-growing company sets aside 10 percent of profits for its charitable foundation. There's also a Planet Cat and a company store in Portland.[a]

increase production costs and, ultimately, the product's price. In determining the specific level of quality, a marketer must ascertain approximately what price the target market views as acceptable. In addition, a marketer usually tries to set a quality level consistent with that of the firm's other products. Obviously, the quality of competing brands is also a consideration.

The development phase of a new product is frequently lengthy and expensive; thus a relatively small number of product ideas are put into development. If the product appears sufficiently successful during this stage to merit test marketing, then, during the latter part of the development stage, marketers begin to make decisions regarding branding, packaging, labeling, pricing, and promotion for use in the test marketing stage.

Test Marketing

A limited introduction of a product in geographic areas chosen to represent the intended market is called **test marketing.** Heineken, for example, test marketed Heineken Premium Light in Providence, Tampa, Phoenix, and Dallas for several months before rolling out the product.[23] Its aim is to determine the extent to which potential customers will buy the product. Test marketing is not an extension of the development stage; it is a sample launching of the entire marketing mix. Test marketing should be conducted only after the product has gone through development and initial plans regarding the other marketing-mix variables. Companies use test marketing to lessen the risk of product failure. The dangers of introducing an untested product include undercutting already profitable products and, should the new product fail, loss of credibility with distributors and customers.

Selection of appropriate test areas is very important because the validity of test market results depends heavily on selecting test sites that provide accurate representation of the intended target market. The top ten most often used U.S. test market cities appear in Table 11.1.

The criteria used for choosing test cities depend on the product's attributes, the target market's characteristics, and the firm's objectives and resources. Test marketing provides several benefits. It lets marketers expose a product in a natural marketing environment to measure its sales performance. While the product is being marketed in a limited area, the company can strive to identify weaknesses in the product or in other parts of the marketing mix. A product weakness discovered after a nationwide introduction can be expensive to correct. If consumers' early reactions are negative, marketers may be unable to persuade consumers to try the product again. Thus, making adjustments after test marketing can be crucial to the success of a new product. On the other hand, testing results may be positive enough to accelerate introduction of the new product. Test marketing also allows marketers to experiment with variations in advertising, pricing, and packaging in different test areas and to measure the extent of brand awareness, brand switching, and repeat purchases resulting from these alterations in the marketing mix.

table 11.1	TOP TEN U.S. TEST MARKET CITIES

Rank	City
1	Albany, NY
2	Rochester, NY
3	Greensboro, NC
4	Birmingham, AL
5	Syracuse, NY
6	Charlotte, NC
7	Nashville, TN
8	Eugene, OR
9	Wichita, KS
10	Richmond, VA

Source: "Which American City Provides the Best Consumer Test Market?" *Business Wire,* May 24, 2004.

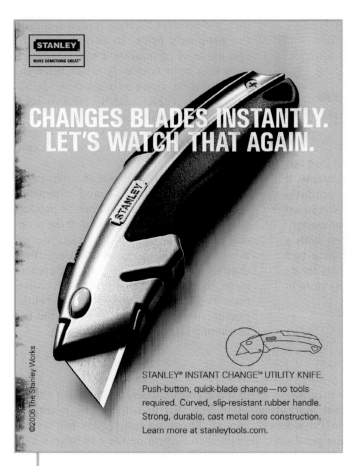

CHANGES BLADES INSTANTLY.
LET'S WATCH THAT AGAIN.

STANLEY® INSTANT CHANGE™ UTILITY KNIFE.
Push-button, quick-blade change—no tools
required. Curved, slip-resistant rubber handle.
Strong, durable, cast metal core construction.
Learn more at stanleytools.com.

Commercialization

Stanley successfully develops
innovative products and rolls
them out nationally.

test marketing Introducing a
product on a limited basis to
measure the extent to which
potential customers will actually
buy it

commercialization Deciding
on full-scale manufacturing and
marketing plans and preparing
budgets

Test marketing is not without risks. It is expensive, and competitors may try to interfere. A competitor may attempt to "jam" the test program by increasing its own advertising or promotions, lowering prices, and offering special incentives, all to combat the recognition and purchase of the new brand. Any such tactics can invalidate test results. Sometimes, too, competitors copy the product in the testing stage and rush to introduce a similar product. This is the time to conduct research to identify issues that might drive potential customers to market-leading competitors instead.[24] It is desirable to move to the commercialization phase as soon as possible after successful testing. On the other hand, some firms have been known to promote new products heavily long before they are ready for the market to discourage competitors from developing similar new products.

Because of these risks, many companies use alternative methods to measure customer preferences. One such method is simulated test marketing. Typically, consumers at shopping centers are asked to view an advertisement for a new product and are given a free sample to take home. These consumers are interviewed subsequently over the phone and asked to rate the product. The major advantages of simulated test marketing are greater speed, lower costs, and tighter security, which reduce the flow of information to competitors and reduce jamming. Several marketing research firms, such as ACNielsen Company, offer test marketing services to help provide independent assessment of proposed products.

Clearly, not all products that are test marketed are launched. At times, problems discovered during test marketing cannot be resolved. Procter & Gamble, for example, test marketed a new plastic wrap product called Impress in Grand Junction, CO, but decided not to launch the brand nationally.[25]

Commercialization

During the **commercialization** phase, plans for full-scale manufacturing and marketing must be refined and settled and budgets for the project prepared. Early in the commercialization phase, marketing management analyzes the results of test marketing to find out what changes in the marketing mix are needed before the product is introduced. The results of test marketing may tell marketers to change one or more of the product's physical attributes, modify the distribution plans to include more retail outlets, alter promotional efforts, or change the product's price. However, as more and more changes are made based on test marketing findings, the test marketing projections may become less valid.

During the early part of this stage, marketers not only must gear up for larger-scale production but also must make decisions about warranties, repairs, and replacement parts. The type of warranty a firm provides can be a critical issue for buyers, especially when expensive, technically complex products are involved. Establishing an effective system for providing repair services and replacement parts is necessary to maintain favorable customer relationships. Although the producer may furnish these services directly to buyers, it is more common for the producer to provide such services through regional service centers. Regardless of how services are provided, it is important to customers that they be performed quickly and correctly.

The product enters the market during the commercialization phase. When introducing a product, a firm may spend enormous sums for advertising, personal selling, and other types of promotion, as well as for plant and equipment. Such expenditures may not be recovered for several years. Smaller firms may find this process difficult, but even so, they may use press releases, blogs, podcasts, and other tools to capture quick feedback as well as promote the new product. Another low-cost promotional tool is product reviews in newspapers and magazines, which can be especially helpful when they are positive and target the same customers.

Products are not usually launched nationwide overnight but are introduced through a process called a *rollout*. Through a rollout, a product is introduced in stages, starting in one geographic area and gradually expanding into adjacent areas. It may take several years to market the product nationally. Sometimes the test cities are used as initial marketing areas, and introduction of the product becomes a natural extension of test marketing. A product test marketed in Albany, NY, Birmingham, AL, Eugene, OR, and Wichita, KS, as the map in Figure 11.2 shows, could be introduced first in those cities. After the stage 1 introduction is complete, stage 2 could include market coverage of the states where the test cities are located. In stage 3, marketing efforts might be extended into adjacent states. All remaining states then would be covered in stage 4. Gradual product introductions do not always occur state by state; other geographic combinations, such as groups of counties that cross state borders, are sometimes used. Products destined for multinational markets also may be rolled out one country or region at a time. After Heineken test marketed its Heineken Premium Light beer in several cities in the United States, it gradually rolled out the product's distribution nationally.[26]

Gradual product introduction is desirable for several reasons. It reduces the risks of introducing a new product. If the product fails, the firm will experience smaller losses if it introduced the item in only a few geographic areas than if it marketed the product nationally. Furthermore, a company cannot introduce a product nationwide overnight because a system of wholesalers and retailers necessary to distribute the product cannot be established so quickly. The development of a distribution network may take considerable time. Also, the number of units needed to satisfy national demand for a successful product can be enormous, and a firm usually cannot produce the required quantities in a short time. Finally, gradual introduction allows for fine-tuning of the marketing mix to better satisfy target customers. Procter & Gamble, for example, originally conceived of Febreze deodorizer as a fabric-care product, but over

figure 11.2

STAGES OF EXPANSION INTO A NATIONAL MARKET DURING COMMERCIALIZATION

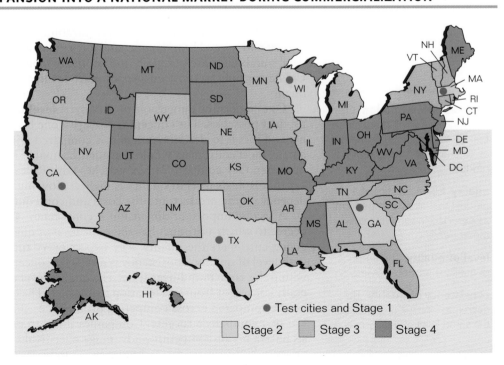

time, the company's view of the highly successful brand evolved into an air-freshening line because that's how consumers indicated they were using it.[27]

Despite the good reasons for introducing a product gradually, marketers realize that this approach creates some competitive problems. A gradual introduction allows competitors to observe what the firm is doing and to monitor results, just as the firm's own marketers are doing. If competitors see that the newly introduced product is successful, they may quickly enter the same target market with similar products. In addition, as a product is introduced region by region, competitors may expand their marketing efforts to offset promotion of the new product.

Product Differentiation Through Quality, Design, and Support Services

Some of the most important characteristics of products are the elements that distinguish them from one another. **Product differentiation** is the process of creating and designing products so that customers perceive them as different from competing products. Customer perception is critical in differentiating products. Perceived differences might include quality, features, styling, price, and image. A crucial element used to differentiate one product from another is the brand. In this section we examine three aspects of product differentiation that companies must consider when creating and offering products for sale: product quality, product design and features, and product support services. These aspects involve the company's attempt to create real differences among products. Later in this chapter we discuss how companies position their products in the marketplace based on these three aspects.

Product Quality

Quality refers to the overall characteristics of a product that allow it to perform *as expected* in satisfying customer needs. The words *as expected* are very important to this definition because quality usually means different things to different customers. For some, durability signifies quality. For other customers, a product's ease of use may indicate quality.

The concept of quality also varies between consumer and business markets. According to one study, U.S. consumers consider high-quality products to have these characteristics (in order): reliability, durability, ease of maintenance, ease of use, a known and trusted brand name, and a reasonable price.[28] For business markets, technical suitability, ease of repair, and company reputation are important characteristics. Unlike consumers, most businesses place far less emphasis on price than on product quality.

One important dimension of quality is **level of quality,** the amount of quality a product possesses. The concept is a relative one because the quality level of one product is difficult to describe unless it is compared with that of other products. For example, most consumers would consider the quality level of Timex watches to be good, but when they compare Timex watches with Rolex watches, most consumers would say that Rolex's level of quality is higher. How high should the level of quality be? It depends on the product and the costs and consequences of a product failure.

A second important dimension is consistency. **Consistency of quality** refers to the degree to which a product has the same level of quality over time. Consistency means giving customers the quality they expect every time they purchase the product. As with level of quality, consistency is a relative concept. It implies a quality comparison within the same brand over time. The quality level of McDonald's french fries is generally consistent from one location to another. The consistency of product quality also can be compared across competing products. At this stage, consistency becomes critical to a company's success. Companies that can provide quality on a consistent basis have a major competitive advantage over rivals.

product differentiation Creating and designing products so that customers perceive them as different from competing products

quality Characteristics of a product that allow it to perform as expected in satisfying customer needs

level of quality The amount of quality a product possesses

consistency of quality The degree to which a product has the same level of quality over time

EQUAL EXCHANGE FAIRLY TRADED GOURMET COFFEE

Quality
Coffee
Starts with Farmers

At Equal Exchange, we believe a good cup of coffee starts with the farmers that grow the beans. Since 1986, we have worked directly with small-scale coffee farmers to ensure the highest quality for our customers, while guaranteeing above market premiums for our farmer partners.

Now that's quality everyone can enjoy!

To learn more about Equal Exchange, our farmer partners and how to brew the best possible cup of coffee, visit **www.equalexchange.com**

All Equal Exchange products are Fair Trade Certified™ by TransFair USA

Product Quality

Fair trade supports market premiums for small farmers to ensure the highest quality.

Product Design and Features

Product design refers to how a product is conceived, planned, and produced. Design is a very complex topic because it involves the total sum of all the product's physical characteristics. Many companies are known for the outstanding designs of their products: Sony for personal electronics, Hewlett-Packard for printers, Apple for computers and music players, and JanSport for backpacks. Good design is one of the best competitive advantages any brand can possess.

One component of design is **styling,** or the physical appearance of the product. The style of a product is one design feature that can allow certain products to sell very rapidly. Good design, however, means more than just appearance; it also involves a product's functioning and usefulness. For example, a pair of jeans may look great, but if they fall apart after three washes, clearly the design was poor. Most consumers seek products that both look good and function well.

Product features are specific design characteristics that allow a product to perform certain tasks. By adding or subtracting features, a company can differentiate its products from those of the competition. Chrysler promotes its line of minivans as having more features related to passenger safety—dual air bags, steel-reinforced doors, and integrated child safety seats—than any other auto company. Product features also can be used to differentiate products within the same company. For example, Nike offers both a walking shoe and a run-walk shoe for specific consumer needs. In these cases, the company's products are sold with a wide range of features, from low-priced "base" or "stripped-down" versions to high-priced, prestigious, "feature-packed" ones. The automotive industry regularly sells products with a wide range of features. In general, the more features a product has, the higher is its price, and often, the higher is the perceived quality. For a brand to have a sustainable competitive advantage, marketers must determine the product designs and features that customers desire. Information from marketing research efforts and from databases can help in assessing customers' product design and feature preferences. Being able to meet customers' desires for product design and features at prices they can afford is crucial to a product's long-term success.

Product Support Services

Many companies differentiate their product offerings by providing support services. Usually referred to as **customer services,** these services include any human or

product design How a product is conceived, planned, and produced

styling The physical appearance of a product

product features Specific design characteristics that allow a product to perform certain tasks

customer services Human or mechanical efforts or activities that add value to a product

mechanical efforts or activities a company provides that add value to a product.[29] Examples of customer services include delivery and installation, financing arrangements, customer training, warranties and guarantees, repairs, layaway plans, convenient hours of operation, adequate parking, and information through toll-free numbers and websites. For example, Zappos, an online shoe retailer, has earned a reputation for excellent customer service in part owing to its 24-hour service and free, fast returns.[30]

Whether as a major or minor part of the total product offering, all marketers of goods sell customer services. Providing good customer service may be the only way that a company can differentiate its products when all products in a market have essentially the same quality, design, and features. This is especially true in the computer industry. When buying a laptop computer, for example, some customers are more concerned about fast delivery, technical support, warranties, and price than about product quality and design. Through research, a company can discover the types of services customers want and need. The level of customer service a company provides can profoundly affect customer satisfaction.

Product Positioning and Repositioning

Product positioning refers to the decisions and activities intended to create and maintain a certain concept of the firm's product (relative to competitive brands) in customers' minds. When marketers introduce a product, they try to position it so that it appears to have the characteristics that the target market most desires. PepsiCo positioned its new Fuelosophy protein drinks as being from a small entrepreneurial company so that it would better appeal to shoppers at Whole Foods, where the new drinks are sold. The drinks' packaging and website bear no hint as to their corporate parentage.[31] This projected image is crucial. Crest is positioned as a fluoride toothpaste that fights cavities, and Close-Up is positioned as a whitening toothpaste that enhances the user's sex appeal.

Perceptual Mapping

A product's position is the result of customers' perceptions of the product's attributes relative to those of competitive brands. Buyers make numerous purchase decisions on a regular basis. To avoid a continuous reevaluation of numerous products, buyers tend to group, or "position," products in their minds to simplify buying decisions. Rather than allowing customers to position products independently, marketers often try to influence and shape consumers' concepts or perceptions of products through advertising. Marketers sometimes analyze product positions by developing perceptual maps, as shown in Figure 11.3. Perceptual maps are created by questioning a sample of consumers about their perceptions of products, brands, and organizations with respect to two or more dimensions. To develop a perceptual map like the one in Figure 11.3, respondents would be asked how they perceive selected pain relievers in regard to price and type of pain for which the products are used. Also, respondents would be asked about their preferences for product features to establish "ideal points" or "ideal clusters," which represent a consensus about what a specific group of customers' desires in terms of product features. Then marketers can see how their brand is perceived compared with the ideal points.

Bases for Positioning

Marketers can use several bases for product positioning. A common basis for positioning products is to use competitors. A firm can position a product to compete head-on with another brand, as PepsiCo has done against Coca-Cola, or to avoid competition, as 7Up has done relative to other soft-drink producers. Head-to-head competition may be a marketer's positioning objective if the product's performance

product positioning Creating and maintaining a certain concept of a product in customers' minds

figure 11.3

HYPOTHETICAL PERCEPTUAL MAP FOR PAIN RELIEVERS

Expensive

Excedrin ●

● Bufferin

Aleve ●   ● Nuprin

Orudis KT ●

● Advil

● Anacin

● Extra Strength Tylenol

Tylenol ●

For headaches   **For body aches**

Motrin ●

● Bayer

St. Joseph's ●   ● Norwich

Inexpensive

Price as a Basis for Positioning

Geico positions its insurance based on price.

characteristics are at least equal to those of competitive brands and if the product is priced lower. Head-to-head positioning may be appropriate even when the price is higher if the product's performance characteristics are superior. For example, Ford has positioned its Fusion sedan head-to-head against the Honda Accord and Toyota Camry through advertisements that highlight the results of a *Car and Driver* magazine driving challenge in which the Fusion earned the top ratings.[32] Conversely, positioning to avoid competition may be best when the product's performance characteristics do not differ significantly from those of competing brands. Moreover, positioning a brand to avoid competition may be appropriate when that brand has unique characteristics that are important to some buyers. Volvo, for example, has for years positioned itself away from competitors by focusing on the safety characteristics of its cars. Whereas some auto companies mention safety issues in their advertisements, many are more likely to focus on style, fuel efficiency, performance, or terms of sale. Avoiding competition is critical when a firm introduces a brand into a market in which the company already has one or more brands. Marketers usually want to avoid cannibalizing sales of their existing brands unless the new brand generates substantially larger profits.

A product's position can be based on specific product attributes or features. For example, the Apple's iPhone is positioned based on product attributes such as its unique shape, its easy-to-use touchscreen, and its access to iTunes. If a product has been planned properly, its features will give it the distinct appeal needed. Style, shape, construction, and color help to create the image and the appeal. If buyers can easily identify the benefits, they are, of course, more likely to purchase the product. When the new product does not offer certain preferred attributes, there is room for another new product.

Other bases for product positioning include price, quality level, and benefits provided by the product. For example, Era laundry detergent provides stain treatment and stain removal. Also, the target market can be a positioning basis caused by marketing. This type of positioning relies heavily on promoting the types of people who use the product.

Repositioning

Positioning decisions are not just for new products. Evaluating the positions of existing products is important because a brand's market share and profitability may be strengthened by product repositioning. For example, several years ago Kraft was on the verge of discontinuing Cheez Whiz because its sales had declined considerably. After Kraft marketers repositioned Cheez Whiz as a fast, convenient, microwavable cheese sauce, its sales rebounded to new heights. When introducing a new product into a product line, one or more existing brands may have to be repositioned to minimize cannibalization of established brands and thus ensure a favorable position for the new brand.

Repositioning can be accomplished by physically changing the product, its price, or its distribution. Rather than making any of these changes, marketers sometimes reposition a product by changing its image through promotional efforts. Burgerville USA, for example, repositioned itself as being an environmentally friendly and more healthful alternative to McDonald's and Wendy's. The chain, which has half of its 40 stores in Portland, Oregon, heavily promoted its corporate citizenship, sustainable agriculture, and healthy food.[33] Finally, a marketer may reposition a product by aiming it at a different target market.

Product Deletion

Generally, a product cannot satisfy target market customers and contribute to the achievement of an organization's overall goals indefinitely. **Product deletion** is the process of eliminating a product from the product mix, usually because it no longer satisfies a sufficient number of customers. Nikon, for example, discontinued seven film camera models, leaving the Japanese firm with just two film camera models on the market, in order to focus on digital cameras.[34] A declining product reduces an organization's profitability and drains resources that could be used to modify other products or develop new ones. A marginal product may require shorter production runs, which can increase per-unit production costs. Finally, when a dying product completely loses favor with customers, the negative feelings may transfer to some of the company's other products.

Most organizations find it difficult to delete a product. A decision to drop a product may be opposed by managers and other employees who believe that the product is necessary to the product mix. Salespeople who still have some loyal customers are especially upset when a product is dropped. Considerable resources and effort are sometimes spent trying to change a slipping product's marketing mix to improve its sales and thus avoid having to eliminate it.

Some organizations delete products only after the products have become heavy financial burdens. Delta Airlines, for example, eliminated its Song discount airline subsidiary after entering bankruptcy proceedings.[35] A better approach is some form of systematic review in which each product is evaluated periodically to determine its impact on the overall effectiveness of the firm's product mix. Such a review should analyze the product's contribution to the firm's sales for a given period, as well as estimate future sales, costs, and profits associated with the product. It also should gauge the value of making changes in the marketing strategy to improve the product's performance. A systematic review allows an organization to improve product performance and ascertain when to delete products. M&M Mars, for example,

product deletion Eliminating a product from the product mix

figure 11.4

PRODUCT DELETION PROCESS

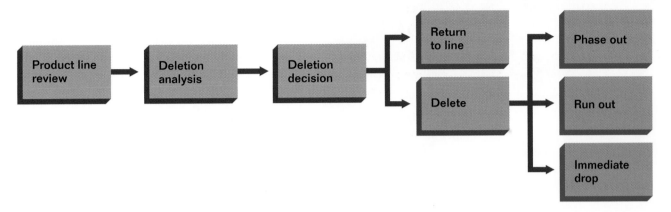

Source: Martin L. Bell, *Marketing: Concepts and Strategy,* 3rd ed., p. 267; copyright 1979, Houghton Mifflin Company; used by permission of Marcellette Bell Chapman.

discontinued all but one variety of its M-Azing candy bar with embedded M&M candies after two years of disappointing performance. However, the company intends to rebrand the remaining M-Azing Crunchy Singles bar.[36]

There are three basic ways to delete a product: phase it out, run it out, or drop it immediately (see Figure 11.4). A *phase-out* allows the product to decline without a change in the marketing strategy; no attempt is made to give the product new life. Nikon, for example, simply allowed sales of its discontinued film cameras to continue until their supplies ran out.[37] A *run-out* exploits any strengths left in the product. Intensifying marketing efforts in core markets or eliminating some marketing expenditures, such as advertising, may cause a sudden jump in profits. This approach is commonly taken for technologically obsolete products, such as older models of computers and calculators. Often the price is reduced to get a sales spurt. The third alternative, an *immediate drop* of an unprofitable product, is the best strategy when losses are too great to prolong the product's life.

Managing Services as Products

Many products are services rather than tangible goods. The organizations that market service products include for-profit firms, such as those offering financial, personal, and professional services, and nonprofit organizations, such as educational institutions, churches, charities, and governments. In this section we focus initially on the growing importance of service industries in our economy. Then we address the unique characteristics of services. Finally, we deal with the challenges these characteristics pose in developing and managing marketing mixes for services.

Nature and Importance of Services

All products, whether goods, services, or ideas, are to some extent intangible. Services are usually provided through the application of human and/or mechanical efforts directed at people or objects. For example, a service such as education involves the efforts of service providers (teachers) directed at people (students), whereas janitorial and interior decorating services direct their efforts at objects. Ruckus Network is a service that allows college students to download ad-supported movies and music for free.[38] Services also can involve the use of mechanical efforts directed at people (air or mass transportation) or objects (freight transportation). A wide variety of services,

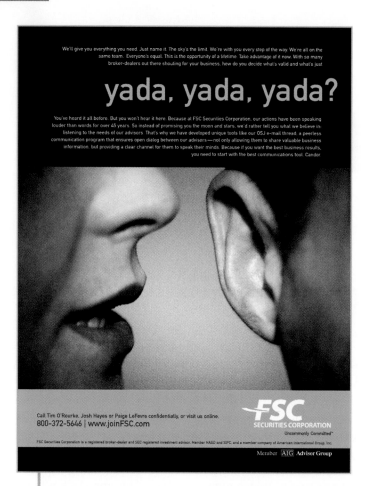

yada, yada, yada?

Characteristics of Services

FSC Securities recognizes the inseparability between production and consumption.

such as health care and landscaping, involve both human and mechanical efforts. Although many services entail the use of tangibles such as tools and machinery, the primary difference between a service and a good is that a service is dominated by the intangible portion of the total product. Services, as products, should not be confused with the related topic of customer services. While customer service is part of the marketing of goods, service marketers also provide customer services.

The increasing importance of services in the U.S. economy has led many people to call the United States the world's first service economy. In most developed countries, including Germany, Japan, Australia, and Canada, services account for about 70 percent of the country's gross domestic product (GDP). More than half of new businesses are service businesses, and service employment is expected to continue to grow. These industries have absorbed much of the influx of women and minorities into the work force. In the United States, some customer-contact jobs, especially call centers, have been outsourced—into the homes of U.S. workers, especially women. JetBlue, for example, has 1,400 reservation agents who work from their homes.[39]

Characteristics of Services

The issues associated with marketing service products are not exactly the same as those associated with marketing goods. To understand these differences, it is first necessary to understand the distinguishing characteristics of services. Services have six basic characteristics: intangibility, inseparability of production and consumption, perishability, heterogeneity, client-based relationships, and customer contact.[40]

Intangibility. As already noted, the major characteristic that distinguishes a service from a good is intangibility. **Intangibility** means a service is not physical and therefore cannot be touched. For example, it is impossible to touch the education that students derive from attending classes; the intangible benefit is becoming more knowledgeable. In addition, services cannot be physically possessed. Products range from pure goods (tangible) to pure services (intangible). Pure goods, if they exist at all, are rare because practically all marketers of goods also provide customer services. Intangible, service-dominant products such as education and health care are clearly service products. Of course, some products, such as a restaurant meal or a hotel stay, have both tangible and intangible dimensions.

Inseparability of Production and Consumption. Another important characteristic of services that creates challenges for marketers is **inseparability,** which refers to the fact that the production of a service cannot be separated from its consumption by customers. For example, air passenger service is produced and consumed simultaneously. In other words, services are often produced, sold, and consumed at the same time. In goods marketing, a customer can purchase a good, take it home, and store it until he or she is ready to use it. The manufacturer of the good may never see an actual customer. Customers, however, often must be present at the production of a service (such as marriage counseling or surgery) and cannot take the service home. For instance, customers who use coin-counting machines in their local supermarkets must pour in their coins and then wait until all the change is tallied. Inseparability implies a shared responsibility between the customer and service provider. As a result, training programs for employees should stress the customer's role in the service experience to elevate their perceptions of shared responsibility and positive feelings.[41]

intangibility A service that is not physical and cannot be touched

inseparability Being produced and consumed at the same time

The Marketing of "Wicked"

It's hard to develop a successful Broadway musical and harder still to create a true "hit." About 80 percent of Broadway shows close without breaking even. But "Wicked," a musical "prequel" to Frank Baum's *Wizard of Oz* tales, broke even after 14 months and now grosses about $1.3 million a week.

The $14 million production is based on Gregory Maguire's novel and explores the teenage friendship between Glinda, the "Good Witch," and Elphaba, the "Wicked Witch," from *The Wizard of Oz.* The show's two strong, nonromantic female leads have made it especially appealing to teenage girls. In addition to the show itself, there are related products, including a 192-page coffee-table book, *Wicked,* T-shirts, golfballs, and themed necklaces.

"Wicked" was one of the first Broadway shows to break the $100 per ticket ceiling. After garnering mixed reviews when the show debuted, producers discounted tickets by as much as 30 percent through mail offerings to draw people in. The strategy worked: Within months, strong word-of-mouth promotion helped the show, and it began to sell out. The first performances debuted at the Gershwin Theater, but clones of the show have since opened in Chicago, Los Angeles, and London, where they broke attendance records. Additionally, the Broadway show also went on a 30-city tour in the United States and Canada.

In addition to traditional advertising, the show was promoted through websites and chat rooms, licensing deals, and karaoke contests, but strong word-of-mouth promotion really helped the show find its following. Nancy Coyne, who runs Serino Coyne, Broadway's largest advertising/marketing agency, says the show spent a great deal of money on billboard advertising because it is "such a powerful title and image. You don't need to convince people to see 'Wicked.' You need to remind them that they can."

With a successful and flexible marketing strategy, "Wicked" has become the number 1 show on Broadway. It won three Tony Awards for best scenic design, best actress in a musical, and best costume design, as well as seven Drama Desk Awards.[b]

Perishability.   Services are characterized by **perishability** because the unused service capacity of one time period cannot be stored for future use. For example, empty seats on an air flight today cannot be stored and sold to passengers at a later date. Other examples of service perishability include unsold basketball tickets, unscheduled dentists' appointment times, and empty hotel rooms. Although some goods, such as meat, milk, and produce, are perishable, goods generally are less perishable than services. If a pair of jeans has been sitting on a department store shelf for a week, someone still can buy them the next day. Goods marketers can handle the supply-demand problem through production scheduling and inventory techniques. Service marketers do not have the same advantage, and they face several hurdles in trying to balance supply and demand. They can, however, plan for demand that fluctuates according to day of the week, time of day, or season.

Heterogeneity.   Services delivered by people are susceptible to **heterogeneity,** or variation in quality. Quality of manufactured goods is easier to control with standardized procedures, and mistakes are easier to isolate and correct. Because of the nature of human behavior, however, it is very difficult for service providers to maintain a consistent quality of service delivery. This variation in quality can occur from one organization to another, from one service person to another within the same service facility, and from

perishability The inability of unused service capacity to be stored for future use

heterogeneity Variation in quality

Characteristics of Services

Hair stylists develop close client-based relationships.

one service facility to another within the same organization. For example, the retail clerks in one bookstore may be more knowledgeable and therefore more helpful than those in another bookstore owned by the same chain. Heterogeneity usually increases as the degree of labor intensiveness increases. Many services, such as auto repair, education, and hairstyling, rely heavily on human labor. Other services, such as telecommunications, health clubs, and public transportation, are more equipment-intensive. People-based services are often prone to fluctuations in quality from one time period to the next. For example, the fact that a hairstylist gives a customer a good haircut today does not guarantee that customer a haircut of equal quality from the same hairstylist at a later date. Equipment-based services, in contrast, suffer from this problem to a lesser degree than people-based services. For instance, automated teller machines have reduced inconsistency in the quality of teller services at banks, and bar-code scanning has improved the accuracy of service at the checkout counters in grocery stores.

Client-Based Relationships.   The success of many services depends on creating and maintaining **client-based relationships,** interactions with customers that result in satisfied customers who use a service repeatedly over time.[42] In fact, some service providers, such as lawyers, accountants, and financial advisers, call their customers *clients* and often develop and maintain close long-term relationships with them. For such service providers, it is not enough to attract customers. They are successful only to the degree to which they can maintain a group of clients who use their services on an ongoing basis. For example, an accountant may serve a family in his or her area for decades. If the members of this family like the quality of the accountant's services, they are likely to recommend the accountant to other families. If several families repeat this positive word-of-mouth communication, the accountant likely will acquire a long list of satisfied clients. This process is the key to creating and maintaining client-based relationships. To ensure that it actually occurs, the service provider must take steps to build trust, demonstrate customer commitment, and satisfy customers so well that they become very loyal to the provider and unlikely to switch to competitors.

Customer Contact.   Not all services require a high degree of customer contact, but many do. **Customer contact** refers to the level of interaction between the service provider and the customer that is necessary to deliver the service. High-contact services include health-care, real estate, legal, and hair-care services. Examples of low-contact services are tax preparation, auto repair, and dry cleaning. Some service-oriented businesses are reducing their level of customer contact through technology. Alamo Rent-A-Car, for example, introduced self-service check-in kiosks, where customers can print out their rental agreement and then head straight to the rental vehicle.[43] Note that high-contact services generally involve actions directed toward people, who must be present during production. A hairstylist's customer, for exam-

client-based relationships Interactions that result in satisfied customers who use a service repeatedly over time

customer contact The level of interaction between provider and customer needed to deliver the service

ple, must be present during the styling process. When the customer must be present, the process of production may be just as important as its final outcome. Although it is sometimes possible for the service provider to go to the customer, high-contact services typically require that the customer go to the production facility. Thus the physical appearance of the facility may be a major component of the customer's overall evaluation of the service. For example, when the physical setting fosters customer-to-customer interactions, it can lead to greater loyalty to an establishment and positive word-of-mouth communications.[44]

Employees of high-contact service providers are part of a very important ingredient in creating satisfied customers. A fundamental precept of customer contact is that satisfied employees lead to satisfied customers. In fact, research indicates that employee satisfaction is the single most important factor in providing high service quality. Thus, to minimize the problems that customer contact can create, service organizations must take steps to understand and meet the needs of employees by training them adequately, empowering them to make more decisions, and rewarding them for customer-oriented behavior.[45] To provide the quality of customer service that has made it the fastest-growing coffee retailer in the world, Starbucks provides extensive employee training. Employees receive about 24 hours of initial training, which includes memorizing recipes and learning the differences among a variety of coffees, proper coffee-making techniques, and many other skills that stress Starbucks' dedication to customer service.[46]

Creating Marketing Mixes for Services

The characteristics of services create a number of challenges for service marketers (see Table 11.2 on page 282). These challenges are especially evident in the development and management of marketing mixes for services. Although such mixes contain the four major marketing-mix variables—product, price, distribution, and promotion—the characteristics of services require that marketers consider additional issues.

Development of Services.   A service offered by an organization generally is a package, or bundle, of services consisting of a core service and one or more supplementary services. A *core service* is the basic service experience or commodity that a customer expects to receive. A *supplementary service* is a supportive one related to the core service that is used to differentiate the service bundle from that of competitors. For example, Hampton Inns provides a room as a core service. Bundled with the room are supplementary services such as free local phone calls, cable television, and a complimentary continental breakfast.

As discussed earlier, heterogeneity results in variability in service quality and makes it difficult to standardize services. However, heterogeneity provides one advantage to service marketers: It allows them to customize their services to match the specific needs of individual customers. Health care is an example of an extremely customized service; the services provided differ from one patient to the next. Such customized services can be expensive for both provider and customer, and some service marketers therefore face a dilemma: how to provide service at an acceptable level of quality in an efficient and economic manner and still satisfy individual customer needs. To cope with this problem, some service marketers offer standardized packages. For example, a lawyer may offer a divorce package at a specified price for an uncontested divorce. When service bundles are standardized, the specific actions and activities of the service provider usually are highly specified. Automobile quick-lube providers frequently offer a service bundle for a single price; the specific actions to be taken are quite detailed about what will be done to a customer's car. Various other equipment-based services are also often standardized into packages. For instance, cable television providers frequently offer several packages, such as "Basic," "Standard," "Premier," and "Hollywood."

The characteristic of intangibility makes it difficult for customers to evaluate a service prior to purchase. Intangibility requires service marketers, such as hairstylists, to market promises to customers. The customer is forced to place some degree of trust in the service provider to perform the service in a manner that meets or exceeds those promises. Service marketers must guard against making promises that raise customer

table 11.2   SERVICE CHARACTERISTICS AND MARKETING CHALLENGES

Service Characteristics	Resulting Marketing Challenges
Intangibility	Difficult for customer to evaluate Customer does not take physical possession Difficult to advertise and display Difficult to set and justify prices Service process usually not protectable by patents
Inseparability of production and consumption	Service provider cannot mass produce services Customer must participate in production Other consumers affect service outcomes Services are difficult to distribute
Perishability	Services cannot be stored Balancing supply and demand is very difficult Unused capacity is lost forever Demand may be very time-sensitive
Heterogeneity	Service quality is difficult to control Service delivery is difficult to standardize
Client-based relationships	Success depends on satisfying and keeping customers over the long term Generating repeat business is challenging Relationship marketing becomes critical
Customer contact	Service providers are critical to delivery Requires high levels of service employee training and motivation Changing a high-contact service into a low-contact service to achieve lower costs without reducing customer satisfaction

Sources: K. Douglas Hoffman and John E. G. Bateson, *Essentials of Services Marketing* (Mason, OH: South-Western, 2001); Valarie A. Zeithaml, A. Parasuraman, and Leonard L. Berry, *Delivering Quality Service: Balancing Customer Perceptions and Expectations* (New York: Free Press, 1990); Leonard L. Berry and A. Parasuraman, *Marketing Services: Competing through Quality* (New York: Free Press, 1991), p. 5.

expectations beyond what they can provide. To cope with the problem of intangibility, marketers employ tangible cues, such as well-groomed, professional-appearing contact personnel and clean, attractive physical facilities, to help assure customers about the quality of the service. Most service providers uniform at least some of their high-contact employees. Uniforms help to make the service experience more tangible, and they serve as physical evidence to signal quality, create consistency, and send cues to suggest a desired image.[47] Consider the professionalism, experience, and competence conveyed by an airline pilot's uniform. Life insurance companies sometimes try to make the quality of their policies more tangible by putting them on very-high-quality paper and enclosing them in leather sheaths.

The inseparability of production and consumption and the level of customer contact also influence the development and management of services. The fact that customers are present during the production of a service means that other customers can affect the outcome of the service. For instance, if a nonsmoker dines in a restaurant without a no-smoking section, the overall quality of service experienced by the nonsmoking customer declines. Service marketers can reduce these problems by encour-

Service Quality and Consistency in the Hotel Industry

Over the past seven years, many hotels across the country have been changing ownership/brand name with astonishing speed. In some cases guests have actually gone to sleep one night in a hotel with one name and awakened the next morning to find themselves in a hotel with an entirely different name. These changes have confused and sometimes even upset travelers. At the same time, they have spurred hotel companies to take a closer look at both brand consistency and customer service.

It is important to hotel guests, particularly business travelers, that they be able to count on a hotel brand to offer the same services and amenities regardless of a particular location. Hotel chains are getting more aggressive in ensuring that this is happening. Hyatt, for example, plans to send undercover inspectors to each of its 215 properties to ensure that the company's policies are being followed. This includes details such as making sure that each room sports an alarm clock with an iPod docking station. The Marriott hotel chain is now getting as specific as insisting that all properties carry the same types of cereal on their breakfast menus. One might wonder why hotel chains are going to such lengths, but to some extent, without consistency, a brand really isn't a brand.

Interestingly, a large number of hotels are not actually owned by the company whose brand name appears on the building. A hotel owner can enter a franchise agreement to pay a hotel chain a sum in order to use its brand name in exchange for adhering to the brand standards. If the hotel standards mandate upgrades of, for example, televisions, owners then have a certain amount of time to follow through. Because this time frame is usually a long one, a traveler may find that not all hotels have completed the updates in a given travel period. Having a number of different owners running hotels under one brand name certainly can make consistency more challenging to attain.

Hotel consistency is particularly important to business travelers. According to the *Wall Street Journal*, on any night, about 40 percent of Hilton's guests are members of the chain's loyalty program, which gives business travelers the same types of benefits that belonging to a frequent flyer program would. Frequent travelers are often loyal to a hotel brand because it offers certain standards or amenities. If the company's properties are not consistent in offering those expected standards, that traveler may take his or her business—and loyalty—elsewhere.

Along with consistency, many hotels are focusing on upgrading their services now that the rate of consumer travel is growing. A major focus of this upgrade is on employee training. Hotels are now striving to build their own unique cultures—something they feel will help to create consumer loyalty. Hotel chains such as Starwood and Choice have hired full-time employee trainers. Park Hyatt, based in Chicago, actually hired a local theater group to train its staff in acting techniques meant to help employees read body language, sustain small talk, and think spontaneously. And the Omni Hotel in Austin, Texas, recently sent a number of its employees to a local Whole Foods Market (known for its excellent customer service) to pick up some skills. Although it's too soon to say what kinds of effects these efforts are going to have on the hotel industry at large, with all the efforts being made to improve the quality of a guest's stay, we can at least hope that hotel travel will be more pleasant in the future.[c]

aging customers to share the responsibility of maintaining an environment that allows all participants to receive the intended benefits of the service.

Pricing of Services.   Services should be priced so as to reflect consumer price sensitivity, the nature of the transaction, and its costs.[48] Prices for services can be established on several different bases. The prices of pest-control services, dry cleaning, carpet cleaning, and a physician's consultation usually are based on the performance of specific tasks. Other service prices are based on time. For example, attorneys, consultants, counselors, piano teachers, and plumbers often charge by the hour or day.

Some services use demand-based pricing. When demand for a service is high, the price is also high; when demand for a service is low, so is the price. The perishability of services means that when demand is low, the unused capacity cannot be stored and is therefore lost forever. Every empty seat on an airline flight or in a movie theater represents lost revenue. Some services are very time-sensitive because a significant number of customers desire the service at a particular time. This point in time is called *peak demand*. A provider of time-sensitive services brings in most of its revenue during peak demand. For an airline, peak demand is usually early and late in the day. Providers of time-sensitive services often use demand-based pricing to manage the problem of balancing supply and demand. They charge top prices during peak demand and lower prices during off-peak demand to encourage more customers to use the service. This is why the price of a matinee movie is often half the price of the same movie shown at night.

When services are offered to customers in a bundle, marketers must decide whether to offer the services at one price, price them separately, or use a combination of the two methods. For example, some hotels offer a package of services at one price, whereas others charge separately for the room, phone service, and breakfast. Some service providers offer a one-price option for a specific bundle of services and make add-on bundles available at additional charges. For example, telephone services, such as call waiting and caller ID, frequently are bundled and sold as a package for one price.

Because of the intangible nature of services, customers rely heavily at times on price as an indicator of quality. If customers perceive the available services in a service category as being similar in quality, and if the quality of such services is difficult to judge even after these services are purchased, customers may seek out the lowest-priced provider. For example, many customers seek auto insurance providers with the lowest rates. If the quality of different service providers is likely to vary, customers may rely heavily on the price-quality association. For example, if you have to have an appendectomy, will you choose the surgeon who charges an average price of $1,500 or the surgeon who will take your appendix out for $399?

Distribution of Services. Marketers deliver services in various ways. In some instances customers go to a service provider's facility. For example, most health-care, dry-cleaning, and spa services are delivered at the service providers' facilities. Some services are provided at the customer's home or business. Lawn care, air-conditioning and heating repair, and carpet cleaning are examples. Some services are delivered primarily at "arm's length," meaning that no face-to-face contact occurs between the customer and the service provider. Several equipment-based services are delivered at arm's length, including electric, Internet, cable television, and telephone services. Providing high-quality customer service at arm's length can be costly but essential in keeping customers satisfied and maintaining market share. For example, many airlines, although trying to cut costs, are also increasing spending on overhauling their websites to better serve customers. Companies such as United and American Airlines are working on user-friendly websites as a way to draw customers to their online services rather than going through an online travel agent such as Orbitz or Travelocity.[49]

Marketing channels for services usually are short and direct, meaning that the producer delivers the service directly to the end user. Some services, however, use intermediaries. For example, travel agents facilitate the delivery of airline services, independent insurance agents participate in the marketing of various insurance policies, and financial planners market investment services.

Service marketers are less concerned with warehousing and transportation than are goods marketers. They are very concerned, however, about inventory management, especially balancing supply and demand for services. The service characteristics of inseparability and level of customer contact contribute to the challenges of demand management. In some instances service marketers use appointments and reservations as approaches for scheduling the delivery of services. Health-care providers, attorneys, accountants, auto mechanics, and restaurants often use reservations or ap-

Promotion of Services.

The distribution of a web hosting service occurs over the Internet.

Web hosting with spice.

The PowWeb OnePlan
- 300 GB of Disk Space for Your Files
- 3000 GB of Monthly Data Transfer
- Unlimited E-Mail Accounts
- Free Domain Name*
- 75 MySQL Databases
- Host Unlimited Domains
- 24/7 Friendly Customer Support

Call us today 1.877.4.POWWEB
www.powweb.com/spice

*Free one-year domain name available with one- and two-year plans.

pointments to plan and pace the delivery of their services. To increase the supply of a service, marketers use multiple service sites and also increase the number of contact service providers at each site. National and regional eye-care and hair-care services are examples.

To make delivery more accessible to customers and to increase the supply of a service, as well as reduce labor costs, some service providers have decreased the use of contact personnel and replaced them with equipment. In other words, they have changed a high-contact service into a low-contact one. The banking industry is an example. By installing ATMs, banks have increased production capacity and reduced customer contact. In addition, numerous automated banking services are now available by telephone 24 hours a day. Such services have helped to lower costs by reducing the need for customer-service representatives. Changing the delivery of services from human to equipment has created some problems, however.

Promotion of Services.   The intangibility of services results in several promotion-related challenges to service marketers. Because it may not be possible to depict the actual performance of a service in an advertisement or to display it in a store, explaining a service to customers can be a difficult task. Promotion of services typically includes tangible cues that symbolize the service. For example, Trans America uses its pyramid-shaped building to symbolize strength, security, and reliability, important features associated with insurance and other financial services. Similarly, the hands Allstate uses in its ads symbolize personalized service and trustworthy, caring representatives. Although these symbols have nothing to do with the actual services, they make it much easier for customers to understand the intangible attributes associated with insurance services. To make a service more tangible, advertisements for services often show pictures of facilities, equipment, and service personnel.

Compared with goods marketers, service providers are more likely to promote price, guarantees, performance documentation, availability, and training and certification of contact personnel. The International Smart Tan Network, a trade association for indoor tanning salons, offers a certification course in professional standards for tanning facility operators. The association encourages salons to promote their "Smart Tan Certification" in advertising and throughout the salon as a measure of quality training.[50] When preparing advertisements, service marketers are careful to use concrete, specific language to help make services more tangible in the minds of customers. Bear Stearns, for example, advertises that it was voted "America's most admired securities company." Service companies are also careful not to promise too much regarding their services so that customer expectations do not rise to unattainable levels.

Through their actions, service contact personnel can be directly or indirectly involved in the personal selling of services. Personal selling is often important because personal influence can help the customer visualize the benefits of a given service. Because service contact personnel may engage in personal selling, some companies invest heavily in training. Best Buy, for example, spends 5 percent of its payroll on employee training. On a salesperson's first day on the job, he or she gets a four-hour classroom session to learn how to fit into the company's sales force and the basics for giving the customer a happy experience.[51]

Because of the heterogeneity and intangibility of services, word-of-mouth communication is important in service promotion. What other people say about a service provider can have a tremendous impact on whether an individual decides to use that provider. Some service marketers attempt to stimulate positive word-of-mouth communication by asking satisfied customers to tell their friends and associates about the service and may even provide incentives for doing so.

Organizing to Develop and Manage Products

After reviewing the concepts of product line and mix, life cycles, positioning, and repositioning, it should be obvious that managing products is a complex task. Often the traditional functional form of organization, in which managers specialize in business functions such as advertising, sales, and distribution, does not fit a company's needs. In this case management must find an organizational approach that accomplishes the tasks necessary to develop and manage products. Alternatives to functional organization include the product or brand manager approach, the market manager approach, and the venture team approach.

A **product manager** is responsible for a product, a product line, or several distinct products that make up an interrelated group within a multiproduct organization. A **brand manager** is responsible for a single brand. General Foods, for example, has one brand manager for Maxim coffee and one for Maxwell House coffee. Both product and brand managers operate cross-functionally to coordinate the activities, information, and strategies involved in marketing an assigned product. Product managers and brand managers plan marketing activities to achieve objectives by coordinating a mix of distribution, promotion (especially sales promotion and advertising), and price. They must consider packaging and branding decisions and work closely with personnel in research and development, engineering, and production. Marketing research helps product managers understand consumers and find target markets. Because luxury brands such as Mercedes-Benz and Jaguar can have their brand image reduced by association with their producers' other mass-market brands, brand managers must balance their brands' independent image with associated brands of the firm.[52] The product or brand manager approach to organization is used by many large, multiple-product companies.

A **market manager** is responsible for managing the marketing activities that serve a particular group of customers. This organizational approach is particularly effective when a firm engages in different types of marketing activities to provide products to diverse customer groups. A company might have one market manager for business markets and another for consumer markets. These broad market categories might be broken down into more limited market responsibilities.

A **venture team** creates entirely new products that may be aimed at new markets. Unlike a product or market manager, a venture team is responsible for all aspects of developing a product: research and development, production and engineering, finance and accounting, and marketing. Venture team members are brought together from different functional areas of the organization. In working outside established divisions, venture teams have greater flexibility to apply inventive

product manager The person within an organization responsible for a product, a product line, or several distinct products that make up a group

brand manager The person responsible for a single brand

market manager The person responsible for managing the marketing activities that serve a particular group of customers

venture team A cross-functional group that creates entirely new products that may be aimed at new markets

approaches to develop new products that can take advantage of opportunities in highly segmented markets. Companies are increasingly using such cross-functional teams for product development in an effort to boost product quality. Quality may be positively related to information integration within the team, customers' influence on the product development process, and a quality orientation within the firm.[53] When a new product has demonstrated commercial potential, team members may return to their functional areas, or they may join a new or existing division to manage the product.

...And now, back to Crayola

In 2007, Binney & Smith executives decided to reinvent the company and change its name to Crayola, in part because many consumers didn't recognize the company's true name—indeed, some thought Binney & Smith was a law firm or doctors' practice. The renamed Crayola also launched a blitz of new products in an initiative to rid the company of its stodgy, buck-a-pack image. New products include a $15 monster-face pencil sharpener that belches when sharpening is complete; a range of scented crayons, markers, and pencils called Booger Buster, Soda Burp, and Alien Armpit; and children's drinks such as Screamin' Green and Purple Pizzazz vitamin-infused drinks. So serious is the company's effort to reinvent itself as a toymaker that sales of Crayola toys and crafts may surpass those of its core line of crayons and drawing products by the end of the decade. Crayola is also getting in the holiday spirit. Rather than bet everything on back-to-school time, Crayola launched a range of $20 gifts in time for the 2006 holiday season. The new toys include a messless sprayer—an an airbrush that sprays out a colorless mist yet works like spray paint on Color Wonder paper; the Color Explosion Spinner, a messless spinner that reveals color patterns when kids drip a clear solution on special paper; and a battery-powered cutting tool that cuts any shape from the center of a page. All three of the products were so popular that they sold out before the holiday season actually began.

Crayola also introduced new outdoor products for the summer, such as the Color Cyclone, a motorized machine filled with colorful, washable Sidewalk Paint that can create patterns by adjusting the speed. Another product, the Grand Canvas, is a 3- by 4-foot easel that comes with washable paint, chalk, stencils, oversized brush, rollers, and holders that can be washed and reused all summer long. The Chalk Stomperz turns a sidewalk into a giant stamp pad with oversized chalk pods that can be used to create letters, numbers, and shapes.

Crayola executives believe that the key to changing a brand's position is to morph toward products that only you can make. A brand equity study revealed that while customers trust the Crayola name, many were bored with its products. Crayola's new products therefore are innovative, not me-too products. The company is also well positioned to exploit the fact that while the $22 billion toy industry in general is slowing, the $1.6 billion arts and crafts category is growing. Through research and development, the company learned that what moms dislike the most about arts and crafts is the associated mess. Crayola listened and began developing mess-free products. One potential new hit, a messless "clear" paintbrush, was so popular in focus groups that panelists tried to steal the samples. Time will tell whether these new products will be as successful as Crayola's renowned crayons or Silly Putty and whether they will help the company in its quest to become a serious toymaker.[54]

1. How has Crayola managed to remain successful?

2. How does Crayola differentiate itself from its competition?

3. What advantages and disadvantages will Crayola face as a toy maker?

CHAPTER REVIEW

1. Understand how companies manage existing products through line extensions and product modifications.

Organizations must be able to adjust their product mixes to compete effectively and achieve their goals. Using existing products, a product mix can be improved through line extension and through product modification. A line extension is the development of a product closely related to one or more products in the existing line but designed specifically to meet different customer needs. Product modification is the changing of one or more characteristics of a product. This approach can be achieved through quality modifications, functional modifications, and aesthetic modifications.

2. Describe how businesses develop a product idea into a commercial product.

Before a product is introduced, it goes through a seven-phase new-product development process. In the idea-generation phase, new-product ideas may come from internal or external sources. In the process of screening, ideas are evaluated to determine whether they are consistent with the firm's overall objectives and resources. Concept testing, the third phase, involves having a small sample of potential customers review a brief description of the product idea to determine their initial perceptions of the proposed product and their early buying intentions. During the business analysis stage, the product idea is evaluated to determine its potential contribution to the firm's sales, costs, and profits. In the product development stage, the organization determines if it is technically feasible to produce the product and if it can be produced at a cost low enough to make the final price reasonable. Test marketing is a limited introduction of a product in areas chosen to represent the intended market. Finally, in the commercialization phase, full-scale production of the product begins, and a complete marketing strategy is developed.

3. Know the importance of product differentiation and the elements that differentiate one product from another.

Product differentiation is the process of creating and designing products so that customers perceive them as different from competing products. Product quality, product design and features, and product support services are three dimensions of product differentiation that companies consider when creating and marketing products.

4. Explain product positioning and repositioning.

Product positioning refers to the decisions and activities that create and maintain a certain concept of the firm's product in the customer's mind. Organizations can position a product to compete head to head with another brand if the product's performance is at least equal to the competitive brand's and if the product is priced lower. When a brand possesses unique characteristics that are important to some buyers, positioning it to avoid competition is appropriate. Companies also increase an existing brand's market share and profitability through product repositioning.

5. Understand how product deletion is used to improve product mixes.

Product deletion is the process of eliminating a product that no longer satisfies a sufficient number of customers. Although a firm's personnel may oppose product deletion, weak products are unprofitable, consume too much time and effort, may require shorter production runs, and can create an unfavorable impression of the firm's other products. A product mix should be systematically reviewed to determine when to delete products. Products to be deleted can be phased out, run out, or dropped immediately.

6. Understand the characteristics of services and how these characteristics present challenges when developing marketing mixes for service products.

Services are intangible products involving deeds, performances, or efforts that cannot be physically possessed. They have six fundamental characteristics: intangibility, inseparability of production and consumption, perishability, heterogeneity, client-based relationships, and customer contact. Intangibility means that a service cannot be seen, touched, tasted, or smelled. Inseparability refers to the fact that the production of a service cannot be separated from its consumption. Perishability means that unused service capacity of one time period cannot be stored for future use. Heterogeneity is variation in service quality. Client-based relationships are interactions with customers that lead to the repeated use of a service over time. Customer contact is the interaction needed to deliver a service between providers and customers.

7. Be familiar with organizational structures used for managing products.

Often the traditional functional form or organization does not lend itself to the complex task of developing and managing products. Alternative organizational forms include the product or brand manager approach, the market manager approach, and the venture team approach. A product manager is responsible for a product, a product line, or several distinct products that make up an interrelated group within a multiproduct organization. A brand manager is a product manager who is responsible for a single brand. A market manager is responsible for managing the marketing activities that serve a particular group or class of customers. A venture team is sometimes used to create entirely new products that may be aimed at new markets.

ACE self-test

Please visit the student website at **www.prideferrell.com** for ACE Self-Test questions that will help you prepare for exams.

KEY CONCEPTS

line extension
product modification
quality modifications
functional modifications
aesthetic modifications
new-product development
 process
idea generation
screening

concept testing
business analysis
product development
test marketing
commercialization
product differentiation
quality
level of quality
consistency of quality

product design
styling
product features
customer services
product positioning
product deletion
intangibility
inseparability
perishability

heterogeneity
client-based relationships
customer contact
product manager
brand manager
market manager
venture team

ISSUES FOR DISCUSSION AND REVIEW

1. What is a line extension, and how does it differ from a product modification?

2. Compare and contrast the three major approaches to modifying a product.

3. Identify and briefly explain the seven major phases of the new-product development process.

4. Do small companies that manufacture just a few products need to be concerned about developing and managing products? Why or why not?

5. Why is product development a cross-functional activity within an organization? That is, why must finance, engineering, manufacturing, and other functional areas be involved?

6. What is the major purpose of concept testing, and how is it accomplished?

7. What are the benefits and disadvantages of test marketing?

8. Why can the process of commercialization take a considerable amount of time?

9. What is product differentiation, and how can it be achieved?

10. Explain how the term *quality* has been used to differentiate products in the automobile industry in recent years. What are some makes and models of automobiles that come to mind when you hear the terms *high quality* and *poor quality*?

11. What is product positioning? Under what conditions would head-to-head product positioning be appropriate? When should head-to-head positioning be avoided?

12. What types of problems does a weak product cause in a product mix? Describe the most effective approach for avoiding such problems.

13. How important are services in the U.S. economy?

14. Identify and discuss the major service characteristics.

15. For each marketing-mix element, which service characteristics are most likely to have an impact?

16. What type of organization might use a venture team to develop new products? What are the advantages and disadvantages of such a team?

MARKETING APPLICATIONS

1. A company often test markets a proposed product in a specific area or location. Suppose that you wish to test market your new revolutionary SuperWax car wax, which requires only one application for a lifetime finish. Where and how would you test market your new product?

2. Select an organization that you think should reposition itself in the consumer's eye. Identify where it is currently positioned, and make recommendations for repositioning. Explain and defend your suggestions.

3. Identify a familiar product that recently was modified, categorize the modification (quality, functional,

or aesthetic), and describe how you would have modified it differently.

4. The characteristics of services affect the development of marketing mixes for services. Choose a specific service and explain how each marketing-mix element could be affected by these service characteristics.

5. Identify three service organizations you see in outdoor, television, or magazine advertising. What symbols are used to represent their services? What message do the symbols convey to potential customers?

6. Visit a retail store in your area, and ask the manager what products he or she has had to discontinue in the recent past. Find out what factors influenced the decision to delete the product and who was involved in the decision. Ask the manager to identify any products that should be but have not been deleted, and try to ascertain the reason.

Online Exercise

7. Merck, a leading global pharmaceutical company, develops, manufactures, and markets a broad range of health-care products. In addition, the firm's Merck-Medco Managed Care Division manages pharmacy benefits for more than 40 million Americans. The company has established a website to serve as an educational and informational resource for Internet users around the world. Visit Merck at **www.merck.com**.

a. What products has Merck developed and introduced recently?

b. What role does research play in Merck's success? How does research facilitate new-product development at Merck?

c. Find Merck's mission statement. Is Merck's focus on research consistent with the firm's mission and values?

A firm's ability to innovate and develop new-product concepts is usually determined by the level of inventiveness and adeptness to adjust to market demands. As a result, successful firms generally benefit from an increase in revenue and publicity in magazines devoted to business innovation. *Business 2.0* annually ranks the fastest-growing companies, which often have the greatest rates of innovation. The ranking can be accessed by using the search term "business innovation" at **http://globaledge.msu.edu/ibrd** (and check the box "Resource Desk only"). Once you reach the CNN/Money website, click on "Rankings," and then choose the "Fastest-Growing Companies" option. Based on the "List of Fastest-Growing Companies," what are the top ten fastest-growing companies? Which industry appears currently to have the most successful commercial innovativeness? Why do you think this industry is thriving?

Video CASE

Starbucks' Products Create a Unique Coffee Experience

Starbucks was founded in 1971 by three partners in Seattle's renowned open-air Pike Place Market and was named after the first mate in Herman Melville's *Moby Dick*. Howard Schultz joined Starbucks in 1982 as director of retail operations and marketing. Returning from a trip to Milan, Italy, with its 1,500 coffee bars, Schultz recognized an opportunity to develop a similar retail coffee-bar culture in Seattle. In 1985, the company tested the first downtown Seattle coffeehouse, served the first Starbucks Café latté, and introduced its Christmas blend. Since then, Starbucks has been expanding across the United States and around the globe and now operates 12,440 locations in 36 countries. It opens about three new stores a day and serves more than 30 million customers a week.

Starbucks purchases and roasts high-quality whole coffee beans and resells them, along with fresh brewed coffees, Italian-style espresso beverages, cold blended beverages, bottled water, complementary food items, coffee-related accessories and equipment, premium teas, and a line of CDs, primarily through company-operated retail stores. It also sells coffee and tea products and licenses its trademark through other channels, and through some of its partners, Starbucks produces and sells bottled Frappuccino coffee drinks, Starbucks DoubleShot espresso drinks, and a line of superpremium ice cream.

Starbucks locates its walk-in stores in high-traffic, high-visibility locations. While Starbucks can be found in a few shopping malls, the company generally focuses on locations that provide convenient access for pedestrians and drivers. The stores are designed to provide an inviting coffee-bar environment that is an important part of the Starbucks product and experience. Because the company is flexible with regard to size and format, it can locate stores in or near a variety of settings, including downtown and suburban retail centers, office buildings, and university campuses. It also can situate retail stores in select rural and off-highway locations to serve a broader array of customers outside major metropolitan markets and further expand brand awareness. To provide a greater degree of access and convenience for nonpedestrian customers, the company has increased development of stores with drive-thru lanes.

Starbucks constantly strives to update its products and introduce new drinks with each season. At Christmastime, drinks such as eggnog lattés, peppermint mochas, and gingerbread lattés helped boost earnings. Starbucks also tries hard to keep up with consumer desires and needs, for example, introducing a low-calorie version of its popular frappuccino, which has about 30 to 40 percent fewer calories than the original. The low-cal frappucino has been very successful. The company also introduced breakfast and lunch sandwiches and a new line of coffee-flavored liquors. Through a joint venture with PepsiCo, Starbucks is introducing Starbucks vending machines.

Although Starbucks is always developing new products, a few drinks have fallen flat. In 2006 Starbucks pulled Chantico, its "drinkable dessert," from the menu. Chantico was marketed to resemble the thick, sweet hot-chocolate drinks found in European cafés, but it was available without any variations in a 6-ounce size. The size limitation proved fatal: Customers are used to dictating not only the size of their lattés but also whether they want them regular or decaf and with non-fat, whole, or soy milk; sugar-free or regular flavor shots; and extras such as whipped cream and caramel. However, Starbucks will try to replace the failed Chantico with a similar product with more available variations.

Starbucks' executives believe that the experience customers have in its stores should be the same in any country. The company tries to foster brand loyalty by increasing repeat business. One of the ways it has done so is through the Starbucks Card, a reloadable stored-value card that was introduced in 2001. It has exceeded $2 billion in total activations and reloads, and more than 100 million cards have been activated to date. The typical Starbucks customer visits Starbucks about 18 times a month.

Starbucks has been ranked on *Fortune*'s "100 Best Companies to Work" for list for eight years and in 2006 ranked twenty-ninth. The company offers both full- and part-time employees a comprehensive benefits package that includes stock-option grants through *Bean Stock,* as well as health, medical, dental, and vision benefits. It also embraces diversity as an essential component of doing business. The company has 91,056 employees with 11,444 outside the United States. Of these, 28 percent are minorities and 64 percent are women. However, being a great employer does take its toll on Starbucks. In 2005, Starbucks spent more on health insurance for its employees than on raw materials required to brew its coffee. The company, which provides health-care coverage to employees who work at least 20 hours a week, has faced double-digit increases in insurance costs each of the last four years. Nonetheless, the Starbucks' benefits policy is a key reason that it has notably low employee turnover and high productivity.

In the process of trying to establish Starbucks as the most recognized and respected brand of coffee in the world, the company also has built an excellent reputation for social responsibility and business ethics. Starbucks pays coffee farmers premium prices to help them make profits and support their families. It is also involved in social development initiatives that invest in programs to build schools, health clinics, and other projects that benefit coffee-growing communities. It collaborates with farmers through the Farmer Support Center, located in Costa Rica, to provide technical support and training that promotes high-quality coffee for the future. It strives to buy conservation and certified coffees, including Fair Trade Certified, shade grown, and certified organic coffee, to promote responsible environmental and economic efforts. In 2006, Starbucks ranked seventeenth on *Business Ethics'* "100 Best Corporate Citizens" list, up from its 2005 position of forty-second. Starbucks' sense of social responsibility, fair trade, and support for the environment are a part of the total product it markets for consumers who are concerned about these social issues.[55]

Questions for Discussion

1. What is the total product that Starbucks markets?
2. What is the role of the development of new products in Starbucks' success?
3. Why do you think some new Starbucks products succeed and others, like Chantico, fail?

Pricing Decisions

If an organization is to provide a satisfying marketing mix, the price must be acceptable to target-market members. Pricing decisions can have numerous effects on other parts of the marketing mix. For example, price can influence how customers perceive the product, what types of marketing institutions are used to distribute the product, and how the product is promoted. Chapter 12 discusses the importance of price and looks at some characteristics of price and nonprice competition. It explores fundamental concepts such as demand, elasticity, marginal analysis, and breakeven analysis. Then it examines the major factors that affect marketers' pricing decisions. Chapter 13 discusses six major stages in the process marketers use to establish prices.

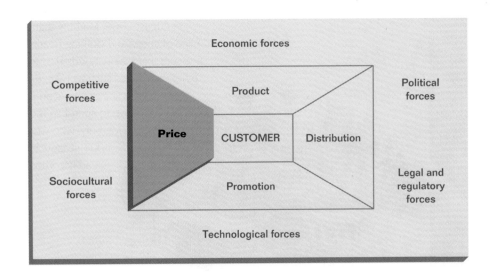

12

Pricing Fundamentals

1. Understand the role of price.

2. Identify the characteristics of price and nonprice competition.

3. Be familiar with demand curves and the price elasticity of demand.

4. Understand the relationships among demand, costs, and profits.

5. Describe key factors that may influence marketers' pricing decisions.

6. Be familiar with the major issues that affect the pricing of products for business markets.

The Starbury One Scores with Low-Price Strategy

Most star-named basketball shoes cost more than $100, but a pair of Starbury Ones—named for and endorsed by NBA All-Star Stephon Marbury—cost just $14.97. Marbury, who plays point guard with the New York Knicks, was born and raised on Coney Island, the sixth of seven children. During his teenage years, when he earned the nickname "Starbury," he was often heralded as the next great New York City point guard. His four brothers all played NCAA basketball, and like them, he wears the number 3.

In 1995, Marbury was recruited by every major university, named a McDonalds All-American, listed as one of the top five recruits in the country, and heavily pursued by Georgia Tech, which he eventually joined. After a very successful year there, Marbury was selected fourth overall by the Milawkee Bucks in the 1996 NBA Draft. He later played for the Minnesota Timberwolves, whom he helped lead to the NBA playoffs in 1997 and 1998, the New Jersey Jets, the Phoenix Suns, and finally, the New York Knicks in 2004. He made an immediate impact, leading the Knicks to the playoffs on the strength of his performances, and in December 2006, Marbury became the ninety-eighth player to score 15,000 points in NBA history. Known for his quickness, ball handling, and inside scoring, he stands as only the second player in NBA history to have career averages of at least 20 points and 8 assists per game.

In August 2006, Marbury teamed up with retailer Steve & Barry's to launch a line of shoes and clothing bearing his nickname "Starbury." Understanding the pressure that inner-city kids face to spend $150 to $200 on footwear sold by other companies such as Nike, Reebok, and Adidas, Marbury believed it crucial that his line of shoes be priced at $14.97. He says, "Kids shouldn't have to spend so much to feel good about the way they look." Marbury, who wore the shoes on court for the entire 2006 to 2007 season, is not being paid to endorse the shoes but instead is compensated based on how well they sell.[1] ■

ike Starbury and Steve & Barry's, many firms use pricing as a tool to compete against major competitors. However, their rivals also may employ pricing as a major competitive tool. In some industries, firms are very successful even if they don't have the lowest prices. The best price is not always the lowest price.

In this chapter we focus first on the role of price. We then consider some characteristics of price and nonprice competition. Next, we discuss several pricing-related concepts such as demand, elasticity, and breakeven analysis. Then we examine in some detail the numerous factors that can influence pricing decisions. Finally, we discuss selected issues related to the pricing of products for business markets.

The Role of Price

The purpose of marketing is to facilitate satisfying exchange relationships between buyer and seller. **Price** is the value exchanged for products in a marketing transaction. Many factors may influence the assessment of value, including time constraints, price levels, perceived quality, and motivations to use available information about prices.[2] However, price does not always take the form of money paid. In fact, trading of products, or **barter,** is the oldest form of exchange. Money may or may not be involved. Barter among businesses accounts for about $9 billion in annual U.S. sales. Websites such as SwapThing.com and BarterYourServices.com may help facilitate business-to-business (B2B) bartering.[3]

Buyers' interest in price stems from their expectations about the usefulness of a product or the satisfaction they may derive from it. Because consumers have limited resources, they must allocate those resources to obtain the products they most desire. They must decide whether the utility gained in an exchange is worth the buying power sacrificed. Almost anything of value—ideas, services, rights, and goods—can be assessed by a price. In our society, financial price is the measurement of value commonly used in exchanges. The purpose of price is to quantify and express the value of the items in marketing exchanges.

As pointed out in Chapter 11, developing a product may be a lengthy process. It takes time to plan promotion and to communicate benefits. Distribution usually requires a long-term commitment to dealers who will handle the product. Often price is the only thing a marketer can change quickly to respond to changes in demand or to actions of competitors. Under certain circumstances, however, the price variable may be relatively inflexible.

Price is a key element in the marketing mix because it relates directly to the generation of total revenue. The following equation is an important one for the entire organization:

$$\text{Profit} = \text{total revenue} - \text{total costs}$$

or

$$\text{Profits} = (\text{price} \times \text{quantity sold}) - \text{total costs}$$

Prices affect an organization's profits in several ways because price is a key component of the profit equation and can be a major determinant of the quantities sold. For example, price is a top priority for Hewlett-Packard in gaining market share and improving financial performance.[4] Furthermore, total costs are influenced by quantities sold.

Because price has a psychological impact on customers, marketers can use it symbolically. By pricing high, they can emphasize the quality of a product and try to increase the prestige associated with its ownership. By lowering a price, marketers can emphasize a bargain and attract customers who go out of their way to save a small amount of money. Thus, as this chapter details, price can have strong effects on a firm's sales and profitability.

price Value exchanged for products in a marketing transaction

barter The trading of products

Price and Nonprice Competition

The competitive environment strongly influences the marketing-mix decisions associated with a product. Pricing decisions often are made according to the price or nonprice competitive situation in a particular market. Price competition exists when consumers have difficulty distinguishing competitive offerings, and marketers emphasize low prices. Nonprice competition involves a focus on marketing-mix elements other than price.

Price Competition

When engaging in **price competition,** a marketer emphasizes price as an issue and matches or beats the prices of competitors. To compete effectively on a price basis, a firm should be the low-cost seller of the product. If all firms producing the same product charge the same price for it, the firm with the lowest costs is the most profitable. Firms that stress low price as a key marketing-mix element tend to market standardized products. A seller competing on price may change prices frequently or at least must be willing and able to do so. Consider that when Southwest Airlines moved into the Denver market, where Frontier Airlines is headquartered, Frontier's stock price fell 28 percent. Frontier had to cut fares 20 percent to compete with Southwest's introductory $59 and up one-way fare. However, Frontier's nonfuel costs are lower than Southwest's, and it offers passengers Direct TV and roomier seats. So far Frontier's flights remain near capacity.[5] Whenever competitors change their prices, the seller usually responds quickly and aggressively.

Price competition gives a marketer flexibility. Prices can be altered to account for changes in the firm's costs or in demand for the product. If competitors try to gain market share by cutting prices, an organization competing on a price basis can react quickly to such efforts. However, a major drawback of price competition is that competitors also have the flexibility to adjust prices. If they quickly match or beat a company's price cuts, a price war may ensue. For example, a price war has developed in the market for some generic pharmaceuticals. After Wal-Mart announced that it would offer approximately 300 generic medicines for $4 in some markets, rival Target announced that it would offer $4 generics at every U.S. Target store with a pharmacy.[6] Chronic price wars can weaken organizations substantially.

Nonprice Competition

Nonprice competition occurs when a seller decides not to focus on price and instead emphasizes distinctive product features, service, product quality, promotion, packaging, or other factors to distinguish its product from competing brands. Thus nonprice competition allows a company to increase its brand's unit sales through means other than changing the brand's price. Mars, for example, markets not only Snickers and M&Ms but also has an upscale candy line called Ethel's Chocolate. With the tagline, "No mystery middles," Ethel's Chocolates competes on the basis of taste,

Price Competition

The maker of Purex engages in price competition.

The maker of Purex competes on the basis of price

Cleans the pocket that holds the wallet that holds the money you'll save.

Purex® gets clothes clean and smelling fresh for about half the price of more expensive brands. Don't waste money on dirt.

Purex

21 | 1

Netflix Survives Price Competition

Netflix, founded in 1997, is currently the top online DVD subscription service in the United States. Its most popular service gives customers unlimited DVD rentals for $17.99 a month—although they may have only three DVDs at any particular time. Once finished with a DVD, the customer sends it back through the mail, and a new DVD from his or her stored list is shipped to replace it. Netflix charges no late fees, and there are no time limits on how long a person takes to watch a DVD.

When Wal-Mart and Blockbuster entered the online DVD rental business, each offered the service at lower prices than Netflix. After a time, Wal-Mart developed a joint venture with Netflix, and now the companies

promote each other's services. Blockbuster, which originally offered its online rental service for $14.99 a month, is expected to raise its price by $3 a month. Nonetheless, Netflix added a $5.99 per month subscription tier for customers willing to rent just one DVD at a time. While a recent ForeSee Results' survey ranked Netflix number 1 in customer satisfaction, the key seems to be inventory. Netflix currently offers more than 70,000 DVD titles—far exceeding any video rental store and most online sites.

In addition to remaining responsive to price, Netflix continues to delve into new areas of the online rental business. The company's Friends Network, for example, allows a customer's friends to view the movies on his or her stored list and to read his or her movie reviews. The company is also experimenting with allowing customers to download movies directly to their computers. Netflix's highly personalized website enables the firm to cut down on employee costs. In 2005, the company had more than 3 million customers but just 43 customer-service representatives.[a]

attractive appearance, and hip packaging and thus has little need to engage in price competition.[7] A major advantage of nonprice competition is that a firm can build customer loyalty toward its brand. If customers prefer a brand because of nonprice factors, they may not be easily lured away by competing firms and brands. In contrast, when price is the primary reason customers buy a particular brand, a competitor is often able to attract these customers through price cuts. However, surveys show that a relatively small number of customers use price as the sole factor when making purchase decisions.[8]

Nonprice competition is effective only under certain conditions. A company must be able to distinguish its brand through unique product features, higher product quality, promotion, packaging, or excellent customer service. Vermont Pure, a New England bottled-water company, used superior service and the addition of a customer-oriented delivery service to compete against the bottled-water behemoths Coca-Cola, PepsiCo, and Nestlé. As a result of an increased focus on the service aspect of bottled water, Vermont Pure expected sales to rise about 15 percent.[9] Buyers not only must be able to perceive these distinguishing characteristics, but they also must view them as important. The distinguishing features that set a particular brand apart from competitors should be difficult, if not impossible, for competitors to imitate. Finally, the organization must extensively promote the distinguishing characteristics of the brand to establish its superiority and set it apart from competitors in the minds of buyers.

Even a marketer that is competing on a nonprice basis cannot ignore competitors' prices. It must be aware of them and sometimes be prepared to price its brand near or slightly above competing brands. Therefore, price remains a crucial marketing-mix component even in environments that call for nonprice competition.

price competition Emphasizing price and matching or beating competitors' prices

nonprice competition Emphasizing factors other than price to distinguish a product from competing brands

Analysis of Demand

Determining the demand for a product is the responsibility of marketing managers, who are aided in this task by marketing researchers and forecasters. Marketing research and forecasting techniques yield estimates of sales potential, or the quantity of a product that could be sold during a specific period. These estimates are helpful in establishing the relationship between a product's price and the quantity demanded.

The Demand Curve

For most products, the quantity demanded goes up as the price goes down, and as the price goes up, the quantity demanded goes down. Intel, for example, knows that lowering prices boosts demand for its processors. Thus an inverse relationship exists between price and quantity demanded. As long as the marketing environment and buyers' needs, ability (purchasing power), willingness, and authority to buy remain stable, this fundamental inverse relationship holds.

Figure 12.1 illustrates the effect of one variable—price—on the quantity demanded. The classic **demand curve** (D_1) is a graph of the quantity of products expected to be sold at various prices if other factors remain constant.[10] It illustrates that as price falls, the quantity demanded usually rises. Demand depends on other factors in the marketing mix, including product quality, promotion, and distribution. An improvement in any of these factors may cause a shift to, say, demand curve D_2. In such a case, an increased quantity (Q_2) will be sold at the same price (P).

There are many types of demand, and not all conform to the classic demand curve shown in Figure 12.1. Prestige products, such as select perfumes and jewelry, seem to sell better at high prices than at low ones. These products are desirable partly because their expense makes buyers feel elite. If the price fell drastically and many people owned these products, they would lose some of their appeal.

The demand curve in Figure 12.2 (on page 300) shows the relationship between price and quantity demanded for prestige products. Quantity demanded is greater, not less, at higher prices. For a certain price range—from P_1 to P_2—the quantity demanded (Q_1) goes up to Q_2. After a certain point, however, raising the price backfires. If the price goes too high, the quantity demanded goes down. The figure shows that if the price is raised from P_2 to P_3, the quantity demanded goes back down from Q_2 to Q_1.

Demand Fluctuations

Changes in buyers' needs, variations in the effectiveness of other marketing-mix variables, the presence of substitutes, and dynamic environmental factors can influence demand. Restaurants and utility companies experience large fluctuations in demand daily. Toy manufacturers, fireworks suppliers, and air-conditioning and heating contractors also face demand fluctuations because of the seasonal nature of their products. The demand for broadband services, beef, and flat-screen TVs has changed over the last few years. In the case of the flat-screen plasma and LCD TVs, demand accelerated as prices dropped by as much as 50 percent.[11] In some cases demand fluctuations are predictable. It is no surprise to restaurants and utility

Prestige Products

Rolex is an example of a classic prestige product.

marketing ENTREPRENEURS

Elliott Breece, Joshua Boltuch, and Elias Roman

THEIR BUSINESS: Amie Street

FOUNDED: Founded in 2006 when they all were 22

SUCCESS: 6,000 users in just one month

After graduating from Brown University, Elliott Breece, Joshua Boltuch, and Elias Roman decided to create a new model for marketing music on-line. At Amie Street, unlike most other online music services, all songs start out free for the download. As a particular song gains in popularity—as determined by the number of times it has been downloaded—its price increases to as much as 98 cents per download. Site users can make music recommendations, and they earn free downloads when music they've recommended does well. The site focuses primarily on independent and unknown artists who have yet to develop a following; the artists keep 70 percent of the revenues from their downloaded tracks.[b]

company managers that demand fluctuates. However, changes in demand for other products may be less predictable, and this leads to problems for some companies. Other organizations anticipate demand fluctuations and develop new products and prices to meet consumers' changing needs.

Assessing Price Elasticity of Demand

Up to this point, we have seen how marketers identify the target market's evaluation of price and its ability to purchase and how they examine demand to learn whether price is related inversely or directly to quantity. The next step is to assess price elasticity of demand. **Price elasticity of demand** provides a measure of the sensitivity of demand to changes in price. It is formally defined as the percentage change in quantity demanded relative to a given percentage change in price[12] (see Figure 12.3 on page 300). The percentage change in quantity demanded caused by a percentage change in price is much greater for elastic demand than for inelastic demand. For a product such as electricity, demand is relatively inelastic: When its price increases, say, from P_1 to P_2, quantity demanded goes down only a little, from Q_1 to Q_2. For products such as recreational vehicles, demand is relatively elastic: When price rises sharply, from P_1 to P_2, quantity demanded goes down a great deal, from Q_1 to Q_2.

If marketers can determine the price elasticity of demand, setting a price is much easier. By analyzing total revenues as prices change, marketers can determine whether a product is price elastic. Total revenue is price times quantity; thus 10,000 rolls of wallpaper sold in one year at a price of $10 per roll equals $100,000 of total revenue. If demand is elastic, a change in price causes an opposite change in total revenue; an

---

figure 12.1

DEMAND CURVE ILLUSTRATING THE PRICE-QUANTITY RELATIONSHIP AND INCREASE IN DEMAND

demand curve A graph of the quantity of products expected to be sold at various prices if other factors remain constant

price elasticity of demand A measure of the sensitivity of demand to changes in price

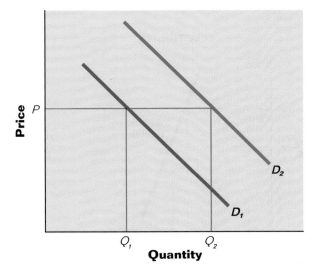

figure 12.2

DEMAND CURVE ILLUSTRATING THE RELATIONSHIP BETWEEN PRICE AND QUANTITY FOR PRESTIGE PRODUCTS

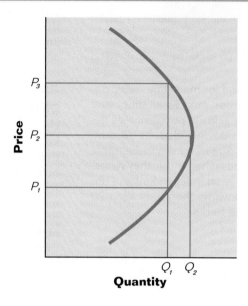

increase in price will decrease total revenue, and a decrease in price will increase to-tal revenue. Inelastic demand results in a change in the same direction in total revenue. An increase in price will increase total revenue, and a decrease in price will decrease total revenue. The following formula determines the price elasticity of demand:

$$\text{Price elasticity of demand} = \frac{(\% \text{ change in quantity demanded})}{(\% \text{ change in price})}$$

For example, if demand falls by 8 percent when a seller raises the price by 2 per-cent, the price elasticity of demand is −4 (the negative sign indicating the inverse rela-tionship between price and demand). If demand falls by 2 percent when price is increased by 4 percent, elasticity is −0.5. The less elastic the demand, the more bene-ficial it is for the seller to raise the price. Products without readily available substitutes

figure 12.3

ELASTICITY OF DEMAND

ELECTRICITY

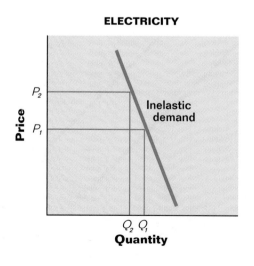

RECREATIONAL VEHICLES

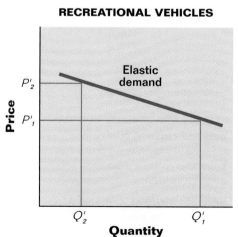

and for which consumers have strong needs, such as electricity or appendectomies, usually have inelastic demand.

Marketers cannot base prices solely on elasticity considerations. They also must examine the costs associated with different sales volumes and evaluate what happens to profits.

Demand, Cost, and Profit Relationships

The analysis of demand, cost, and profit is important because customers are becoming less tolerant of price increases, forcing manufacturers to find new ways to control costs. In the past, many customers desired premium brands and were willing to pay extra for these products. Today, customers pass up certain brand names if they can pay less without sacrificing quality. To stay in business, a company has to set prices that not only cover its costs but also meet customers' expectations. In this section we explore two approaches to understanding demand, cost, and profit relationships: marginal analysis and breakeven analysis.

Marginal Analysis

Marginal analysis examines what happens to a firm's costs and revenues when production (or sales volume) changes by one unit. Both production costs and revenues must be evaluated. To determine the costs of production, it is necessary to distinguish among several types of costs. **Fixed costs** do not vary with changes in the number of units produced or sold. For example, an airplane manufacturer's cost of renting a building for use as a production facility does not change because of increased production of airplanes in this facility. Rent may go up when the lease is renewed but not because the factory has increased production or revenue. **Average fixed cost** is the fixed cost per unit produced and is calculated by dividing fixed costs by the number of units produced.

Variable costs vary directly with changes in the number of units produced or sold. The wages for a second shift and the cost of more materials are extra costs that occur when production is increased. **Average variable cost,** the variable cost per unit produced, is calculated by dividing the variable costs by the number of units produced.

Total cost is the sum of average fixed costs and average variable costs times the quantity produced. The **average total cost** is the sum of the average fixed cost and the average variable cost. **Marginal cost (MC)** is the extra cost a firm incurs when it produces one more unit of a product.

Table 12.1 illustrates various costs and their relationships. Notice that average fixed cost declines as output increases. Average variable cost follows a U shape, as does average total cost. Because average total cost continues to fall after average variable cost begins to rise, its lowest point is at a higher level of output than that of average variable cost. Average total cost is lowest at 5 units at a cost of $22.00, whereas average variable cost is lowest at 3 units at a cost of $10.67. As Figure 12.4 (on page 302) shows, marginal cost equals average total cost at the latter's lowest level. In Table 12.1 this occurs at between 5 and 6 units of production. Average total cost decreases as long as marginal cost is less than average total cost, and it increases when marginal cost rises above average total cost.

Marginal revenue (MR) is the change in total revenue that occurs when a firm sells an additional unit of a product. Figure 12.5 depicts marginal revenue and a demand curve. Most firms in the United States face downward-sloping demand curves for their products. They must lower their prices to sell additional units. This situation means that each additional unit of product sold provides the firm with less revenue than the previous unit sold. MR then becomes less than average revenue, as Figure 12.5 (on page 303) shows. Eventually, MR reaches zero, and the sale of additional units actually hurts the firm.

fixed costs Costs that do not vary with changes in the number of units produced or sold

average fixed cost The fixed cost per unit produced

variable costs Costs that vary directly with changes in the number of units produced or sold

average variable cost The variable cost per unit produced

total cost The sum of average fixed and average variable costs times the quantity produced

average total cost The sum of the average fixed cost and the average variable cost

marginal cost (MC) The extra cost a firm incurs by producing one more unit of a product

marginal revenue (MR) The change in total revenue resulting from the sale of an additional unit of a product

table 12.1   COSTS AND THEIR RELATIONSHIPS

1 Quantity	2 Fixed Cost	3 Average Fixed Cost (2) ÷ (1)	4 Average Variable Cost	5 Average Total Cost (3) + (4)	6 Total Cost (5) × (1)	Marginal Cost
1	$40	$40.00	$20.00	$60.00	$ 60	
						$10
2	40	20.00	15.00	35.00	70	
						2
3	40	13.33	10.67	24.00	72	
						18
4	40	10.00	12.50	22.50	90	
						20
5	40	8.00	14.00	22.00	110	
						30
6	40	6.67	16.67	23.33	140	
						40
7	40	5.71	20.00	25.71	180	

Before the firm can determine whether a unit makes a profit, it must know its cost, as well as its revenue, because profit equals revenue minus cost. If MR is a unit's addition to revenue and MC is a unit's addition to cost, MR minus MC tells us whether the unit is profitable. Table 12.2 illustrates the relationships among price, quantity sold, total revenue, marginal revenue, marginal cost, total cost, and profit for various combinations of price and quantity. Notice that the total cost and the marginal cost figures in Table 12.2 are calculated and appear in Table 12.1.

figure 12.4

TYPICAL MARGINAL COST AND AVERAGE TOTAL COST RELATIONSHIP

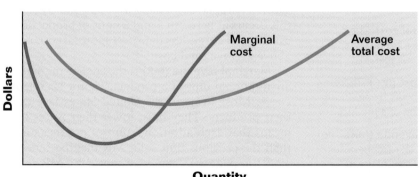

figure 12.5

TYPICAL MARGINAL REVENUE AND AVERAGE REVENUE RELATIONSHIP

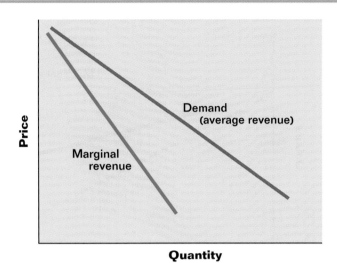

Profit is the highest where MC = MR (see Table 12.2). In this table, note that at a quantity of 4 units, profit is the highest, and MR − MC = 0. The best price is $33, and the profit is $42. Up to this point, the additional revenue generated from an extra unit sold exceeds the additional cost of producing it. Beyond this point, the additional cost of producing another unit exceeds the additional revenue generated, and profits decrease. If the price were based on minimum average total cost—$22 (see Table 12.1)—it would result in a lower profit of $40 (see Table 12.2) for 5 units priced at $30 versus a profit of $42 for 4 units priced at $33.

Graphically combining Figures 12.4 and 12.5 into Figure 12.6 (on page 304) shows that any unit for which MR exceeds MC adds to a firm's profits, and any unit

table 12.2   MARGINAL ANALYSIS METHOD FOR DETERMINING THE MOST PROFITABLE PRICE

1	2	3	4	5	6	7
Price	Quantity Sold	Total Revenue (1) × (2)	Marginal Revenue	Marginal Cost	Total Cost	Profit (3) − (6)
$57	1	$ 57	$ 57	$ 60	$ 60	−$ 3
50	2	100	43	10	70	30
38	3	114	14	2	72	42
33*	**4**	**132**	**18**	**18**	**90**	**42**
30	5	150	18	20	110	40
27	6	162	12	30	140	22
25	7	175	13	40	180	−5

*Boldface indicates the best price-profit combination.

figure 12.6

COMBINING THE MARGINAL COST AND MARGINAL REVENUE CONCEPTS FOR OPTIMAL PROFIT

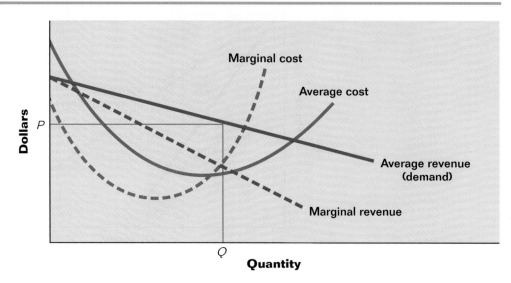

for which MC exceeds MR subtracts from profits. The firm should produce at the point where MR equals MC because this is the most profitable level of production.

This discussion of marginal analysis may give the false impression that pricing can be highly precise. If revenue (demand) and cost (supply) remained constant, prices could be set for maximum profits. In practice, however, cost and revenue change frequently. The competitive tactics of other firms or government action can quickly undermine a company's expectations of revenue. Thus marginal analysis is only a model from which to work. It offers little help in pricing new products before costs and revenues are established. On the other hand, in setting prices of existing products, especially in competitive situations, most marketers can benefit by understanding the relationship between marginal cost and marginal revenue.

Breakeven Analysis

The point at which the costs of producing a product equal the revenue made from selling the product is the **breakeven point.** If a wallpaper manufacturer has total annual costs of $100,000 and sells $100,000 worth of wallpaper in the same year, the company has broken even.

Figure 12.7 (on page 306) illustrates the relationships among costs, revenue, profits, and losses involved in determining the breakeven point. Knowing the number of units necessary to break even is important in setting the price. If a product priced at $100 per unit has an average variable cost of $60 per unit, the contribution to fixed costs is $40. If total fixed costs are $120,000, the breakeven point in units is determined as follows:

$$\text{Breakeven point} = \frac{\text{fixed costs}}{\text{per-unit contribution to fixed costs}}$$

$$= \frac{\text{fixed costs}}{\text{price-variable costs}}$$

$$= \frac{\$120,000}{\$40}$$

$$= 3,000 \text{ units}$$

breakeven point The point at which the costs of producing a product equal the revenue made from selling the product

To calculate the breakeven point in terms of dollar sales volume, multiply the breakeven point in units by the price per unit. In the preceding example, the breakeven point in terms of dollar sales volume is 3,000 (units) times $100, or $300,000.

Airlines Struggle to Balance Demand, Costs

Airlines often struggle to balance costs and demand for air travel. Consider that more than half of major U.S. airline companies were operating under Chapter 11 bankruptcy protection in 2005. Two of them, United and US Airways, were directly affected by the terrorist attacks on 9/11 when United had two planes hijacked, and US Airways was not able to fly out of Washington Reagan National Airport, one of its main hubs, for a considerable time. Delta and Northwest, which both filed for Chapter 11 in September 2005, suffered from a failure to keep up with low-cost airlines, lower fares, and rising fuel prices after several

hurricanes devastated the Gulf Coast. Although the major U.S. air carriers have all undergone major downsizings, the cyclic nature of the airline business continues to make cost management crucial to survival.

Delta and Northwest, along with many of the other long-standing airlines, have made little effort to adapt to compete with the new low-fare carriers that have popped up in recent years, such as Southwest, Frontier, and JetBlue. Some experts believe that the major carriers didn't think the discounters would last, but in fact, most appear to be thriving. The discount airlines have been able to maintain a 1- to 3-cent advantage per seat mile (the cost of flying one passenger one mile) over the traditional airlines.

To continue flying while dealing with bankruptcy and intense competition, both United Airlines and US Airways had to reduce their "flying capacity" by around 15 percent. United also slashed employee pay, benefits, and pensions. Delta and Northwest likely will have to make similar changes, such as fare increases, limitations on cities to which the airlines will fly, use of aircraft types, and the amount/quality of inflight service.

One way many airlines plan to boost revenues is by adding more international flights. Delta, for example, intends to increase its flights to Europe and Latin America. There is great demand for flights to Asia. Currently, only Continental and United are flying "ultralong-haul"—nonstop international—flights, although these flights represent a small portion of their overall flights. Although U.S. airlines are looking to international travel as a way out of financial woes, few can afford to get into the ultralong-haul market. However, all the companies currently operating under Chapter 11 plan to continue with flights for the foreseeable future and hope to come through the process intact. Both United and US Airways emerged from bankruptcy protection in 2006.[c]

To use breakeven analysis effectively, a marketer should determine the breakeven point for each of several alternative prices. This determination allows the marketer to compare the effects on total revenue, total costs, and the breakeven point for each price under consideration. Although this comparative analysis may not tell the marketer exactly what price to charge, it will identify highly undesirable price alternatives that definitely should be avoided.

Breakeven analysis is simple and straightforward. It does assume, however, that the quantity demanded is basically fixed (inelastic) and that the major task in setting prices is to recover costs. It focuses more on how to break even than on how to achieve a pricing objective, such as percentage of market share or return on investment. Nonetheless, marketing managers can use this concept to determine whether a product will achieve at least a breakeven volume.

figure 12.7

DETERMINING THE BREAKEVEN POINT

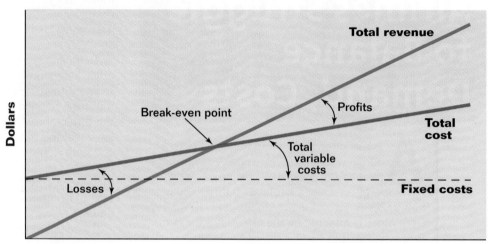

Factors Affecting Pricing Decisions

Pricing decisions can be complex because of the number of factors to be considered. Frequently, there is considerable uncertainty about the reactions to price among buyers, distribution channel members, and competitors. Price is also an important consideration in marketing planning, market analysis, and sales forecasting. It is a major issue when assessing a brand's position relative to competing brands. Most factors that affect pricing decisions can be grouped into one of the eight categories shown in Figure 12.8. In this section we explore how each of these eight groups of factors enters into price decision making.

Organizational and Marketing Objectives

Marketers should set prices that are consistent with the organization's goals and mission. For example, a retailer trying to position itself as value-oriented may wish to set prices that are quite reasonable relative to product quality. In this case a marketer would not want to set premium prices on products but would strive to price products in line with this overall organizational goal.

Pricing decisions also should be compatible with the organization's marketing objectives. For instance, suppose that one of a producer's marketing objectives is a 12 percent increase in unit sales by the end of the next year. Assuming that buyers are price-sensitive, increasing the price or setting a price above the average market price would not be in line with this objective.

Marketing Objectives

One of the marketing objectives at American Ironhorse is to provide a product and product image focused on high quality, which is supported by the company's pricing structure.

figure 12.8

FACTORS THAT AFFECT PRICING DECISIONS

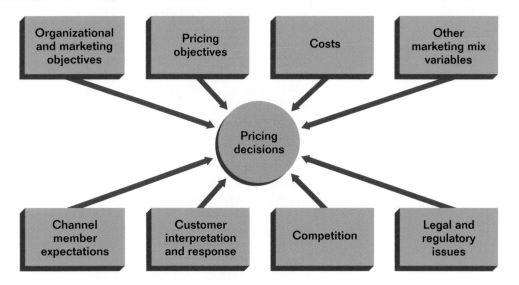

Types of Pricing Objectives

The types of pricing objectives a marketer uses obviously have considerable bearing on the determination of prices. For example, an organization that uses pricing to increase its market share likely would set the brand's price below those of competing brands of similar quality to attract competitors' customers. A marketer sometimes uses temporary price reductions in the hope of gaining market share. If a business needs to raise cash quickly, it likely will use temporary price reductions such as sales, rebates, and special discounts. We examine pricing objectives in more detail in the next chapter.

Costs

Clearly, costs must be an issue when establishing price. A firm temporarily may sell products below cost to match competition, to generate cash flow, or even to increase market share, but in the long run it cannot survive by selling its products below cost. Even when a firm has a high-volume business, it cannot survive if each item is sold slightly below what it costs. A marketer should be careful to analyze all costs so that they can be included in the total cost associated with a product.

To maintain market share and revenue in an increasingly price-sensitive market, many marketers have concentrated on reducing costs. In the highly competitive computer industry, for example, Sun Microsystems constantly looks for ways to lower the cost of developing, producing, and marketing computers, software, and related products. As a cost-cutting move, the company recently laid off 3,700 employees and shrunk its real estate holdings.[13] Labor-saving technologies, a focus on quality, and efficient manufacturing processes have brought productivity gains that translate into reduced costs and lower prices for customers.

Besides considering the costs associated with a particular product, marketers must take into account the costs that the product shares with others in the product line. Products often share some costs, particularly the costs of research and development, production, and distribution. Most marketers view a product's cost as a minimum, or floor, below which the product cannot be priced.

Other Marketing-Mix Variables

All marketing-mix variables are highly interrelated. Pricing decisions can influence decisions and activities associated with product, distribution, and promotion variables. A product's price frequently affects the demand for that item. A high price, for instance, may result in low unit sales, which, in turn, may lead to higher production costs per unit. Conversely, lower per-unit production costs may result from a low price. For many products, buyers associate better product quality with a high price and poorer product quality with a low price. This perceived price–quality relationship influences customers' overall image of products or brands. Sony, for example, prices its televisions higher than average to help communicate that Sony televisions are high-quality electronic products. Consumers recognize the Sony brand name, its reputation for quality, and the prestige associated with buying Sony products. Individuals who associate quality with a high price are likely to purchase products with well-established and recognizable brand names.[14]

The price of a product is linked to several dimensions of its distribution. Premium-priced products—a Bentley or a Rolls Royce automobile, for example—are often marketed through selective or exclusive distribution. Lower-priced products in the same product category may be sold through intensive distribution. For example, Cross pens are distributed through selective distribution and Bic pens through intensive distribution. Moreover, an increase in physical distribution costs, such as shipping, may have to be passed on to customers. After fuel prices soared in 2005 and 2006, many firms were forced to pass the cost onto their customers in the form of higher prices or fuel surcharges. Big Sky Airlines, for example, had to increase fares by 25 to 40 percent, whereas Briggs Distributing Company had to levy a fuel surcharge of $3 on every delivery of beer and other beverages to its retail customers.[15] When setting a price, the profit margins of marketing channel members, such as wholesalers and retailers, must be considered. Channel members must be compensated adequately for the functions they perform.

Price may determine how a product is promoted. Bargain prices are often included in advertisements. Premium prices are less likely to be advertised, although they are sometimes included in advertisements for upscale items such as luxury cars or fine jewelry. Higher-priced products are more likely than lower-priced ones to require personal selling. Furthermore, the price structure can affect a salesperson's relationship with customers. A complex pricing structure takes longer to explain to customers, is more likely to confuse potential buyers, and may cause misunderstandings that result in long-term customer dissatisfaction. For example, the pricing structures of many airlines are complex and frequently confuse ticket sales agents and travelers alike.

Channel Member Expectations

When making price decisions, a producer must consider what members of the distribution channel expect. A channel member certainly expects to receive a profit for the functions it performs. The amount of profit expected depends on what the intermediary could make if it were handling a competing product instead. Also, the amount of time and the resources required to carry the product influence intermediaries' expectations.

Channel members often expect producers to give discounts for large orders and prompt payment. At times, resellers expect producers to provide several support activities such as sales training, service training, repair advisory service, cooperative advertising, sales promotions, and perhaps a program for returning unsold merchandise to the producer. These support activities clearly have associated costs that a producer must consider when determining prices.

Customer Interpretation and Response

When making pricing decisions, marketers should be concerned with a vital question: How will our customers inter-

Premium Pricing Affects Advertising
Duracell compares its quality to its direct competitors and justifies its price

Why do you think they're so cheap?

You know the saying: You get what you pay for.

In this case, what you're getting are zinc batteries that rely on different, less powerful technology. That's why Duracell® will last up to 4 times longer than one of these so-called "Heavy Duty" batteries.

DURACELL®

TRUSTED EVERYWHERE™

HAWKER 400XP

Tired of dropping
money on fuel?

AVERAGE FUEL COST PER HOUR*	
Competition:	**$1,150**
Avantair:	$255

Fuel numbers based on Dec. 2006 fractional industry fuel costs.

Avantair will not only line your pockets with the extra 78% of the money you have been spending on fuel, we'll do it without compromising anything. Surprised? Actually the Avanti P.180 offers more comfort than the Hawker 400XP, with a cabin that is over a foot taller and wider. The P.180 is the perfect combination of safety, performance, fuel efficiency, comfort and value. — Call today to experience for yourself what our competition doesn't want you to find out about — Avantair, in a class all our own.

avantair®

AVANTAIR P.180

AVANTAIR FRACTIONAL OWNERSHIP | 877.289.7180 | AVANTAIR.COM

Value Conscious Customers

By emphasizing both quality and cost savings, Avantair aims its Avanti jet at value-conscious consumers.

internal reference price A price developed in the buyer's mind through experience with the product

external reference price A comparison price provided by others

pret our prices and respond to them? *Interpretation* in this context refers to what the price means or what it communicates to customers. Does the price mean "high quality," "low quality," or "great deal," "fair price," or "rip-off"? Customer *response* refers to whether the price will move customers closer to the purchase of the product and the degree to which the price enhances their satisfaction with the purchase experience and with the product after purchase.

Customers' interpretation of and response to a price are determined to some degree by their assessment of value, or what they receive compared with what they give up to make the purchase. In evaluating what they receive, customers will consider product attributes, benefits, advantages, disadvantages, the probability of using the product, and possibly the status associated with the product. In assessing the cost of the product, customers likely will consider its price, the amount of time and effort required to obtain it, and perhaps the resources required to maintain it after purchase. Consider that research shows that an increasing number of investors with at least $500,000 of investable assets are using full-service brokers, which suggests that these customers view the costs of full-service brokerage services as more acceptable, given the return on their investments.[16]

At times, customers interpret a higher price as an indication of higher product quality. They are especially likely to make this price–quality association when they cannot judge the quality of the product themselves. This is not always the case, however. Whether price is equated with quality depends on the types of customers and products involved. Obviously, marketers who rely on customers making a price–quality association and who provide moderate- or low-quality products at high prices will be unable to build long-term customer relationships.

When interpreting and responding to prices, how do customers determine if the price is too high, too low, or about right? In general, they compare prices with internal or external reference prices. An **internal reference price** is a price developed in the buyer's mind through experience with the product. It is a belief that a product should cost approximately a certain amount. To arrive at an internal reference price, consumers may consider one or more values, including what they think the product "ought" to cost, the price usually charged for it, the last price they paid, the highest and lowest amounts they would be willing to pay, the price of the brand they usually buy, the average price of similar products, the expected future price, and the typical discounted price.[17] As consumers, our experiences have given each of us internal reference prices for several products. For example, most of us have a reasonable idea of how much to pay for a six-pack of soft drinks, a loaf of bread, or a gallon of milk. For the product categories with which we have less experience, we rely more heavily on external reference prices. An **external reference price** is a comparison price provided by others, such as retailers or producers. For example, a retailer in an advertisement might state "while this product is sold for $100 elsewhere, our price is only $39.95." When attempting to establish a reference price in customers' minds by advertising a higher price against which to compare the company's real price, a marketer must make sure that the higher price is realistic because if it is not, customers will not use this price when establishing or altering their reference prices.[18] Customers' perceptions of prices are also influenced by their expectations about future price increases, by what they paid for the product recently, and by what they would like to

What is a fair price?

What people in industrial nations said would be a "fair price" for a gallon of gas.

UK $5.16
Germany $4.87
South Korea $4.11
France $4.08
Spain $3.32
Australia $2.94
Canada $2.72
United States $1.99

Source: Data from Ipsos-Public Affairs polls. Margin of error is ±3.1 to 3.2 percentage points.

pay for the product. Other factors affecting customers' perception of whether the price is right include time or financial constraints, the costs associated with searching for lower-priced products, and expectations that products will go on sale.

Buyers' perceptions of a product relative to competing products may allow the firm to set a price that differs significantly from rivals' prices. If the product is deemed superior to most of the competition, a premium price may be feasible. However, even products with superior quality can be overpriced. Strong brand loyalty sometimes provides the opportunity to charge a premium price. On the other hand, if buyers view a product less than favorably (although not extremely negatively), a lower price may generate sales.

In the context of price, buyers can be characterized according to their degree of value consciousness, price consciousness, and prestige sensitivity. Marketers who understand these characteristics are better able to set pricing objectives and policies. **Value-conscious** consumers are concerned about both price and quality of a product.[19] To appeal to the value-conscious consumer, Apple Computer introduced the Mac Mini and iPod Shuffle, more compact versions of their respective counterparts offered at discount prices.[20] **Price-conscious** individuals strive to pay low prices.[21] A price-conscious pet food buyer, for example, probably would purchase Wal-Mart's Ol' Roy brand because it is the lowest-priced dog food and satisfies a basic need. **Prestige-sensitive** buyers focus on purchasing products that signify prominence and status.[22] For example, the limited-edition Vertu Signature Cobra, one of the highest-priced mobile phones ever marketed, is studded with diamonds and rubies and sells for $310,000; the less expensive Vertu Python is priced at $115,000. Prestige-sensitive buyers also can talk on designer phones from Bang & Olufsen, Dolce & Gabbana, Diane von Furstenberg, Juicy Couture, or Mister Cartoon.[23] It is important to recognize that some consumers vary in their degree of value, price, and prestige consciousness. In some segments, moreover, consumers are increasingly "trading up" to higher-status products in categories such as automobiles, home appliances, restaurants, and even pet food; yet they remain price conscious regarding cleaning and grocery products. This trend has benefited marketers such as Starbucks, Sub-Zero, BMW, Whole Foods, and Petco, which can charge premium prices for high-quality, prestige products, as well as Sam's Club and Costco, which offer basic household products at everyday low prices.[24]

Competition

A marketer needs to know competitors' prices so that it can adjust its own prices accordingly. This does not mean that a company will necessarily match competitors' prices; it may set its price above or below theirs. For some organizations, however, matching competitors' prices is an important strategy for survival.

When adjusting prices, a marketer must assess how competitors will respond. Will competitors change their prices, and if so, will they raise or lower them? In Chapter 3 we described several types of competitive market structures. The structure that characterizes the industry to which a firm belongs affects the flexibility of price setting. For example, because of reduced pricing regulation, firms in the telecommunications industry have moved from a monopolistic market structure to an oligopolistic one, which has resulted in significant price competition.

When an organization operates as a monopoly and is unregulated, it can set whatever prices the market will bear. However, the company may not price the product at

value-conscious Concerned about price and quality of a product

price-conscious Striving to pay low prices

prestige-sensitive Drawn to products that signify prominence and status

the highest possible level to avoid government regulation or to penetrate a market by using a lower price. If the monopoly is regulated, it normally has less pricing flexibility; the regulatory body lets it set prices that generate a reasonable, but not excessive, return. A government-owned monopoly may price products below cost to make them accessible to people who otherwise could not afford them. Transit systems, for example, sometimes operate this way. However, government-owned monopolies sometimes charge higher prices to control demand. In some states with state-owned liquor stores, the price of liquor is higher than in states where liquor stores are not owned by a government body.

The automotive and airline industries exemplify oligopolies, in which there are only a few sellers and the barriers to competitive entry are high. Companies in such industries can raise their prices, hoping competitors will do the same. When an organization cuts its price to gain a competitive edge, other companies are likely to follow suit. Thus very little advantage is gained through price cuts in an oligopolistic market structure.

A monopolistic competition market structure consists of numerous sellers with product offerings that are differentiated by physical characteristics, features, quality, and brand images. The distinguishing characteristics of its product may allow a company to set a different price than its competitors. However, firms in a monopolistic competitive market structure are likely to practice nonprice competition, discussed earlier in this chapter.

Under conditions of perfect competition, many sellers exist. Buyers view all sellers' products as the same. All firms sell their products at the going market price, and buyers will not pay more than that. Thus this type of market structure gives a marketer no flexibility in setting prices. Farming, as an industry, has some characteristics of perfect competition. Farmers sell their products at the going market price. At times, for example, corn, soybean, and wheat growers have had bumper crops and been forced to sell them at depressed market prices.

Legal and Regulatory Issues

Legal and regulatory issues influence pricing decisions. To curb inflation, the federal government can invoke price controls, freeze prices at certain levels, or determine the rates at which prices may be increased. In some states, regulatory agencies set prices on products such as insurance, dairy products, and liquor.

Many regulations and laws affect pricing decisions and activities. The Sherman Antitrust Act prohibits conspiracies to control prices, and in interpreting the act, courts have ruled that price fixing among firms in an industry is illegal. Marketers must refrain from fixing prices by developing independent pricing policies and setting prices in ways that do not even suggest collusion. Both the Federal Trade Commission Act and the Wheeler-Lea Act prohibit deceptive pricing. Some other nations and trade agreements have similar prohibitions. The European Commission, for example, fined six rubber producers—Royal Dutch Shell PLC, Eni SpA, Dow Chemical Company, Unipetrol AS, and Trade-Stomil—a combined $682 million for fixing the price of rubber products. Bayer AG had been found guilty of the same charges but escaped a fine after blowing the whistle on the other companies to the European Union's trade watchdog.[25] In establishing prices, marketers must guard against deceiving customers.

The Robinson-Patman Act has had a strong impact on pricing decisions. For various reasons, marketers may wish to sell the same type of product at different prices. Provisions in the Robinson-Patman Act, as well as those in the Clayton Act, limit the use of such price differentials. The practice of providing price differentials that tend to injure competition by giving one or more buyers a competitive advantage over other buyers is called **price discrimination** and is prohibited by law. However, not all price differentials are discriminatory. A marketer can use price differentials if they do not hinder competition, if they result from differences in the costs of selling or transportation to various customers, or if they arise because the firm has had to cut its price to a particular buyer to meet competitors' prices. Airlines, for example, may charge different

price discrimination Providing price differentials that injure competition by giving one or more buyers a competitive advantage

customers different prices for the same flights based on the availability of seats at the time of purchase. As a result, fliers sitting in adjacent seats may have paid vastly different fares because one passenger booked weeks ahead, whereas the other booked on the spur of the moment a few days before, when only a few seats remained on the flight.

Pricing for Business Markets

Business markets consist of individuals and organizations that purchase products for resale, for use in their own operations, or for producing other products. Establishing prices for this category of buyers sometimes differs from setting prices for consumers. Differences in the size of purchases, geographic factors, and transportation considerations require sellers to adjust prices. In this section we discuss several issues unique to the pricing of business products, including discounts, geographic pricing, and transfer pricing.

Price Discounting

Producers commonly provide intermediaries with discounts, or reductions, from list prices. Although there are many types of discounts, they usually fall into one of five categories: trade, quantity, cash, seasonal, and allowance. Table 12.3 summarizes

table 12.3   DISCOUNTS USED FOR BUSINESS MARKETS

Type	Reasons for Use	Examples
Trade (functional)	To attract and keep effective resellers by compensating them for performing certain functions, such as transportation, warehousing, selling, and providing credit	A college bookstore pays about one-third less for a new textbook than the retail price a student pays.
Quantity	To encourage customers to buy large quantities when making purchases and, in the case of cumulative discounts, to encourage customer loyalty	Large department store chains purchase some women's apparel at lower prices than do individually owned specialty stores.
Cash	To reduce expenses associated with accounts receivable and collection by encouraging prompt payment of accounts	Numerous companies serving business markets allow a 2 percent discount if an account is paid within ten days.
Seasonal	To allow a marketer to use resources more efficiently by stimulating sales during off-peak periods	Florida hotels provide companies holding national and regional sales meetings with deeply discounted accommodations during the summer months.
Allowance	In the case of a trade-in allowance, to assist the buyer in making the purchase and potentially earn a profit on the resale of used equipment; in the case of a promotional allowance, to ensure that dealers participate in advertising and sales support programs	A farm equipment dealer takes a farmer's used tractor as a trade-in on a new one. Nabisco pays a promotional allowance to a supermarket for setting up and maintaining a large end-of-aisle display for a two-week period.

some reasons to use each type of discount and provides examples. Such discounts can be a significant element in a marketing strategy. Consider that Simmons, the mattress manufacturer, had $95 million in allowances, incentives, and cash discounts, or more than 11 percent of its wholesale shipment volume, in 2005.[26]

Trade Discounts.   A reduction off the list price given by a producer to an intermediary for performing certain functions is called a **trade,** or **functional, discount.** A trade discount is usually stated in terms of a percentage or series of percentages off the list price. Intermediaries are given trade discounts as compensation for performing various functions, such as selling, transporting, storing, final processing, and perhaps providing credit services. Although certain trade discounts are often a standard practice within an industry, discounts vary considerably among industries. It is important that a manufacturer provide a trade discount large enough to offset the intermediary's costs, plus a reasonable profit, to entice the reseller to carry the product.

Quantity Discounts.   Deductions from list price that reflect the economies of purchasing in large quantities are called **quantity discounts.** Quantity discounts are used in many industries and pass on to the buyer cost savings gained through economies of scale.

Quantity discounts can be either cumulative or noncumulative. **Cumulative discounts** are quantity discounts aggregated over a stated time period. Purchases totaling $10,000 in a three-month period, for example, might entitle the buyer to a 5 percent, or $500, rebate. Such discounts are supposed to reflect economies in selling and to encourage the buyer to purchase from one seller. **Noncumulative discounts** are one-time reductions in prices based on the number of units purchased, the dollar value of the order, or the product mix purchased. Like cumulative discounts, these discounts should reflect some economies in selling or trade functions.

Cash Discounts.   A **cash discount,** or price reduction, is given to a buyer for prompt payment or cash payment. Accounts receivable are an expense and a collection problem for many organizations. A policy to encourage prompt payment is a popular practice and sometimes a major concern in setting prices.

Discounts are based on cash payments or cash paid within a stated time. For example, "2/10 net 30" means that a 2 percent discount will be allowed if the account is paid within ten days. If the buyer does not make payment within the ten-day period, the entire balance is due within 30 days without a discount. If the account is not paid within 30 days, interest may be charged.

Seasonal Discounts.   A price reduction to buyers who purchase goods or services out of season is a **seasonal discount.** These discounts let the seller maintain steadier production during the year. For example, automobile rental agencies offer seasonal discounts in winter and early spring to encourage firms to use automobiles during the slow months of the automobile rental business.

Allowances.   Another type of reduction from the list price is an **allowance,** or a concession in price to achieve a desired goal. Trade-in allowances, for example, are price reductions granted for turning in a used item when purchasing a new one. Allowances help to make the buyer better able to make the new purchase. This type of discount is popular in the aircraft industry. Another example is a *promotional allowance,* a price reduction granted to dealers for participating in advertising and sales support programs intended to increase sales of a particular item.

Geographic Pricing

Geographic pricing involves reductions for transportation costs or other costs associated with the physical distance between buyer and seller. Prices may be quoted as F.O.B. (free-on-board) factory or destination. An **F.O.B. factory** price indicates the price of the merchandise at the factory, before it is loaded onto the carrier, and thus excludes transportation costs. The buyer must pay for shipping. For example,

---

trade (functional) discount Also known as functional discount; a reduction off the list price given by a producer to an intermediary for performing certain functions

quantity discounts Deductions from list price for purchasing large quantities

cumulative discounts Quantity discounts aggregated over a stated period

noncumulative discounts One-time reductions in price based on specific factors

cash discount A price reduction given to buyers for prompt payment or cash payment

seasonal discount A price reduction given to buyers for purchasing goods or services out of season

allowance A concession in price to achieve a desired goal

geographic pricing Reductions for transportation and other costs related to the physical distance between buyer and seller

F.O.B. factory The price of the merchandise at the factory, before shipment

Tesco, the British supermarket chain, negotiates factory-based prices for its goods and then arranges to transport them using its own fleet of trucks.[27] An **F.O.B. destination** price means that the producer absorbs the costs of shipping the merchandise to the customer. This policy may be used to attract distant customers. Although F.O.B. pricing is an easy way to price products, it is sometimes difficult for marketers to administer, especially when a firm has a wide product mix or when customers are widely dispersed. Because customers will want to know about the most economical method of shipping, the seller must be informed about shipping rates.

To avoid the problems involved in charging different prices to each customer, **uniform geographic pricing**, sometimes called *postage-stamp pricing*, may be used. The same price is charged to all customers regardless of geographic location, and the price is based on average shipping costs for all customers. Paper products and office equipment are often priced on a uniform basis.

Zone pricing sets uniform prices for each of several major geographic zones; as the transportation costs across zones increase, so do the prices. For example, a Florida manufacturer's prices may be higher for buyers on the Pacific Coast and in Canada than for buyers in Georgia.

Base-point pricing is a geographic pricing policy that includes the price at the factory plus freight charges from the base point nearest the buyer. This approach to pricing has virtually been abandoned because of its questionable legal status. The policy resulted in all buyers paying freight charges from one location, such as Detroit or Pittsburgh, regardless of where the product was manufactured.

When the seller absorbs all or part of the actual freight costs, **freight absorption pricing** is being used. The seller might choose this method because it wishes to do business with a particular customer or to get more business; more business will cause the average cost to fall and counterbalance the extra freight cost. This strategy is used to improve market penetration and to retain a hold in an increasingly competitive market.

Transfer Pricing

Transfer pricing occurs when one unit in an organization sells a product to another unit. The price is determined by one of several methods. *Actual full cost* is calculated by dividing all fixed and variable expenses for a period into the number of units produced. *Standard full cost* is computed based on what it would cost to produce the goods at full plant capacity. *Cost plus investment* is full cost plus the cost of a portion of the selling unit's assets used for internal needs. *Market-based cost* is the market price less a small discount to reflect the lack of sales effort and other expenses. The choice of transfer-pricing method depends on the company's management strategy and the nature of the units' interaction. An organization also must ensure that transfer pricing is fair to all units involved in the purchases.

F.O.B. destination A price indicating the producer is absorbing shipping costs

uniform geographic pricing Charging all customers the same price, regardless of geographic location

zone pricing Pricing based on transportation costs within major geographic zones

base-point pricing Geographic pricing combining factory price and freight charges from the base point nearest the buyer

freight absorption pricing Absorption of all or part of actual freight costs by the seller

transfer pricing Prices charged in sales between an organization's units

...And now, back to Starbury One

Teenage boys are famous for yearning for expensive toys: $600 PlayStation 3s, $350 video iPods, $200 Motorola RAZR V3 cell phones, and of course, expensive basketball shoes. However, the Starbury One shoe, which is priced at less than $15, has been flying off shelves since its introduction in 2006. More than 3 million of the shoes sold in the first six months, and Steve & Barry's, the hip retailer, has been having trouble keeping the shoes in stock. The first run of the shoes sold out in three days.

The Starbury collection features a variety of lifestyle and athletic footwear, including the Starbury One—a high-performance basketball shoe that comes in a variety of colors—and the Starbury Crossover—a low-top, stylish casual sneaker that comes in white, black, and cocoa/tan. Like many of the high-end basketball shoes produced and marketed by other top brands and retailers, the Starbury collection is produced in China. The shoes and merchandise are currently available only in Steve & Barry's 130 stores, a retail chain that is renowned for its low-cost products. The retailer makes it a top priority to offer high-quality merchandise at low prices, which it achieves through tight cost-control measures throughout the company and by purchasing in bulk and selling in higher volumes than other retailers in the industry. Steve & Barry's also does not sell merchandise online.

Mark Cuban, the billionaire owner of the Dallas Mavericks, praised Marbury for having the best business idea of 2006. According to Cuban, "you would be hard-pressed to name anyone else in the business world, forget sports, who created a business that could create more cultural change than Steph. The concept of $15 shoes that are cool and hip for kids to wear could have more of an impact on family finances and [the] culture of consumption in many households than anything that has happened in years."

Many kids love the fact that they can actually buy a pair of Starbury Ones with their own money and don't have to ask their parents for money. Parents like the fact that the brand is cool and cheap. But is it just a fad, or will it have a lasting impact on the $16.5 billion branded athletic shoe market? Strong competitors such as Nike have been trying to enter the low-cost shoe market (sneakers under $50), which has grown nearly 9 percent over the past two years and now accounts for more than half the market. But Nike's cheap sneakers haven't been able to get much traction against low-cost entrants such as the $35 Amp runner, a creation from Payless ShoeSource, and the Starbury One. However, Nike continues to dominate the basketball sneaker market and currently sells 95 percent of $100-plus shoes, such as the Converse Dwayne Wade sneaker endorsed by the Miami Heat guard. While the $100 athletic shoe isn't likely to fade away, the success of Starbury One means that there's plenty of room in the market for some new players.[28]

1. Why is the Starbury One so popular?

2. How can selling a sneaker for $14.97 be profitable?

3. What are the issues involved in pricing a product so low?

CHAPTER REVIEW

1. Understand the role of price.

Price is the value exchanged for products in marketing transactions. Price is not always money paid; barter, the trading of products, is the oldest form of exchange. Price is a key element in the marketing mix because it relates directly to the generation of total revenue. The profit factor can be determined mathematically by multiplying price by quantity sold to get total revenue and then subtracting total costs. Price is the marketing-mix variable that usually can be adjusted quickly and easily to respond to changes in the external environment.

2. Identify the characteristics of price and nonprice competition.

Price competition emphasizes price as the major product differential. Prices fluctuate frequently, and price competition among sellers is aggressive. Nonprice competition emphasizes product differentiation through distinctive features, services, product quality, or other factors. Establishing brand loyalty by using nonprice competition works best when the product can be physically differentiated and the customer can recognize these differences.

3. Be familiar with demand curves and the price elasticity of demand.

The classic demand curve is a graph of the quantity of products expected to be sold at various prices if other factors hold constant. It illustrates that as price falls, the quantity demanded usually increases. For prestige products, however, there is a direct positive relationship between price and quantity demanded; demand increases as price increases. Price elasticity of demand—the percentage change in quantity demanded relative to a given percentage change in price—must be determined. If demand is elastic, a change in price causes an opposite change in total revenue. Inelastic demand results in a parallel change in total revenue when a product's price is changed.

4. Understand the relationships among demand, costs, and profits.

Analysis of demand, cost, and profit relationships can be accomplished through marginal analysis or breakeven analysis. Marginal analysis examines what happens to a firm's costs and revenues when production (or sales volume) is changed by one unit. Marginal analysis combines the demand curve with the firm's costs to develop a price that yields maximum profit. Fixed costs do not vary with changes in the number of units produced or sold; average fixed cost is the fixed cost per unit produced. Variable costs vary directly with changes in the number of units produced or sold. Average variable cost is the variable cost per unit produced. Total cost is the sum of average fixed cost and average variable costs times the quantity produced. The optimal price is the point at which marginal cost (the cost associated with producing one more unit of the product) equals marginal revenue (the change in total revenue that occurs when one additional unit of the product is sold).

Breakeven analysis—determining the number of units that must be sold to break even—is important in setting prices. The point at which the cost of production equals the revenue from selling the product is the breakeven point. To use breakeven analysis effectively, a marketer should determine the breakeven point for each of several alternative prices. This determination makes it possible to compare the effects on total revenue, total costs, and the breakeven point for each price under consideration.

5. Describe key factors that may influence marketers' pricing decisions.

Eight factors affect price decision making: organizational and marketing objectives, pricing objectives, costs, other marketing-mix variables, channel member expectations, customer interpretation and response, competition, and legal and regulatory issues. When setting prices, marketers should make decisions consistent with the organization's goals and mission. Pricing objectives heavily influence price-setting decisions. Most marketers view a product's cost as the floor below which a product cannot be priced. Because of the interrelation among the marketing-mix variables, price can affect product, promotion, and distribution decisions. The revenue that channel members expect for their functions also should be considered when making price decisions. Buyers' perceptions of price vary. Some consumer segments are sensitive to price, but others may not be. Knowledge of the prices charged for competing brands is essential so that the firm can adjust its prices relative to competitors. Government regulations and legislation influence pricing decisions.

6. Be familiar with the major issues that affect the pricing of products for business markets.

The categories of discounts offered to business customers include trade, quantity, cash, seasonal, and allowance. A trade discount is a price reduction for performing functions such as storing, transporting, final processing, or providing credit services. If an intermediary purchases in large enough quantities, the producer gives a quantity discount, which can be either cumulative or noncumulative. A cash discount is a price reduction for prompt payment or payment in cash. Buyers who purchase goods or services out of season may be granted a seasonal discount. A final type of reduction from the list price is an allowance, such as a trade-in allowance.

Geographic pricing involves reductions for transportation costs or other costs associated with the physical distance between buyer and seller. A price quoted as F.O.B. factory means that the buyer pays for shipping from the factory. An F.O.B. destination price means that the producer pays for shipping. This is the easiest way to price products, but it is difficult for marketers to administer. When the seller charges a fixed average cost for transportation, it is using uniform geographic pricing. Zone prices are uniform within major geographic zones; they increase by zone as the transportation costs increase. With base-point pricing, prices are adjusted for shipping expenses incurred by the seller from the base point nearest the buyer. Freight absorption pricing occurs when a seller absorbs all or part of the freight costs.

Transfer pricing occurs when a unit in an organization sells products to another unit in the same organization. Methods used for transfer pricing include actual full cost, standard full cost, cost plus investment, and market-based cost.

ACE self-test

Please visit the student website at **www.prideferrell.com** for ACE Self-Test questions that will help you prepare for exams.

KEY CONCEPTS

price	price elasticity of demand	total cost	internal reference price
barter	fixed costs	average total cost	external reference price
price competition	average fixed cost	marginal cost (MC)	value-conscious
nonprice competition	variable costs	marginal revenue (MR)	price-conscious
demand curve	average variable cost	breakeven point	prestige-sensitive

price discrimination	noncumulative discounts	geographic pricing	zone pricing
trade (functional) discount	cash discount	F.O.B. factory	base-point pricing
quantity discounts	seasonal discount	F.O.B. destination	freight absorption pricing
cumulative discounts	allowance	uniform geographic pricing	transfer pricing

ISSUES FOR DISCUSSION AND REVIEW

1. Why are pricing decisions important to an organization?

2. Compare and contrast price and nonprice competition. Describe the conditions under which each form works best.

3. Why do most demand curves demonstrate an inverse relationship between price and quantity?

4. List the characteristics of products that have inelastic demand, and give several examples of such products.

5. Explain why optimal profits should occur when marginal cost equals marginal revenue.

6. Chambers Company has just gathered estimates for conducting a breakeven analysis for a new product. Variable costs are $7 a unit. The additional plant will cost $48,000. The new product will be charged $18,000 a year for its share of general overhead.

Advertising expenditures will be $80,000, and $55,000 will be spent on distribution. If the product sells for $12, what is the breakeven point in units? What is the breakeven point in dollar sales volume?

7. In what ways do other marketing-mix variables affect pricing decisions?

8. What types of expectations may channel members have about producers' prices? How might these expectations affect pricing decisions?

9. How do legal and regulatory forces influence pricing decisions?

10. Compare and contrast a trade discount and a quantity discount.

11. What is the reason for using the term *F.O.B.?*

12. What are the major methods used for transfer pricing?

MARKETING APPLICATIONS

1. Price competition is intense in the fast-food, air travel, and personal computer industries. Discuss a recent situation in which companies had to meet or beat a competitor's price in a price-competitive industry. Did you benefit from this situation? Did it change your perception of the companies and/or their products?

2. Customers' interpretations and responses regarding a product and its price are an important influence on marketers' pricing decisions. Perceptions of price are affected by the degree to which customers are value conscious, price conscious, or prestige sensitive. Discuss how these factors influence the buying decision process for the following products:
   a. A new house
   b. Weekly groceries for a family of five
   c. An airline ticket
   d. A soft-drink from a vending machine

Online Exercise

3. Autosite offers car buyers a free, comprehensive website to find the invoice prices for almost all car models. The browser also can access a listing of all the latest new-car rebates and incentives. Visit this site at **www.autosite.com.**
   a. Which Lexus dealer is closest to you? Find the lowest-priced Lexus available today, and examine its features.
   b. If you wanted to purchase this Lexus, what are the lowest monthly payments you could make over the longest time period?
   c. Is this free site more credible than a "pay" site? Why or why not?

Business strategists and economists sometimes use a consumer price index (CPI) in their decision models. In fact, some organizations perform a comparison across countries to inform the public of consumer pricing trends. A report entitled "Consumer Price Indices (CPIs) for OECD Countries" should prove helpful in answering this question. Access this report by using the search term "comparison across countries" at **http://globaledge.msu.edu/ibrd** (and check the box "Resource Desk only"). Once you reach the OECD webpage, click on "View Long Abstract" for the link for "Consumer Price Indices (CPI) for OECD Countries." What is a CPI generally used to measure?

Video CASE

Low-Fare JetBlue Competes on More Than Price

Can JetBlue Airways stay in the black over the long term? Founded by David Neeleman, a savvy entrepreneur who sold his regional airline to Southwest Airlines in 1994, JetBlue sent its first flight into the skies in 2000. The airline quickly attained profitability and built a loyal customer base on the winning combination of customer-friendly service and low airfares. In recent years, however, JetBlue's high-flying profitability has lost a little altitude owing to high fuel costs and sagging revenues.

CEO Neeleman knows that price is one of the top considerations for travelers. Major carriers typically quote dozens of fares between two locations depending on time of day and other factors. By comparison, JetBlue's everyday pricing structure is far simpler and avoids complicated requirements such as Saturday night stayovers. The CEO says that the fares are based on demand and that JetBlue uses pricing to equalize the loads on the flights so that no jet takes off empty while another is completely full. Thus fares for Sunday night flights tend to be higher because of higher demand, whereas Tuesday night flights may be priced lower owing to lower demand. Still, JetBlue's highest fare generally undercuts the lowest fare of its competitors. Promotional fares are even lower, such as the unusually low one-way price of $79 for nonstop flights from New York to California.

Price is not the only way that JetBlue sets itself apart from competitors. Whereas many new carriers buy used jets, JetBlue flies new Airbus A320 and Embraer 190 jets with seat-back video screens showing satellite television programming. Rather than squeeze in the maximum 180 seats that A320s can hold, JetBlue flies with only 156, giving passengers more legroom. In addition, the jets are outfitted with roomier leather seats, which cost twice as much as ordinary seats but last twice as long and make passengers feel pampered.

Another advantage of new jets is higher fuel efficiency. A320s can operate on 60 percent of the amount of fuel burned by an equivalent jet built decades before. Even so, JetBlue's profit margin was squeezed as fuel costs skyrocketed from 81 cents per gallon to more than $1.50, pushing annual operating costs above $2.5 million. Nonetheless, the airline's total costs of 6.5 cents per mile remain well below the per-mile costs of most major competitors. In part, this is so because JetBlue's technicians work on only two types of jets, which means that they gain proficiency at maintenance tasks and therefore save the airline time and money. Also, new jets come with a five-year warranty, so JetBlue need not budget for major repairs.

Why base a low-fare airline in New York City? CEO Neeleman made this decision for two main reasons. First, he knew that New York travelers departing from nearby LaGuardia Airport faced crowds and delays unless they were willing to venture eight miles farther to fly from John F. Kennedy International Airport. Second, unlike some metropolitan airports, JFK was not a regional hub for major airlines or for low-fare carriers such as Southwest. Seizing an opportunity to trade off a slightly less convenient location for lower competition and better on-time performance, Neeleman secured more than 70 takeoff and landing slots at JFK Airport, enough to accommodate JetBlue's growth for years to come.

From its first day of operation, JetBlue has relied on Internet bookings to minimize sales costs. Travelers who buy tickets directly through the company's website (**www.jetblue.com**) get a special discount and are also eligible for online specials such as "Get It Together" fares designed for two people traveling together. JetBlue books about half its fares on the Web and saves about $5 in transaction costs for each ticket booked online.

The CEO's flight plan is to have JetBlue flying nearly 300 jets by 2010, transforming what was once a tiny startup into one of the largest airlines in the United States. The biggest question mark in JetBlue's future is the effect of competition. Not only does the airline compete with low-cost carriers such as Southwest and Air-Tran, but it also must deal with low-fare airline brands established by United and Delta. An airfare price war in Atlanta became so intense not long ago that JetBlue pulled out of the market to concentrate on expanding into western states. Now, as Neeleman adds one new jet every three weeks and hires 1,700 new employees per year, he must keep JetBlue's prices competitive without grounding profits.[29]

Questions for Discussion

1. In an industry in which pricing has driven many firms out of business or into bankruptcy protection, why does JetBlue compete so successfully on the basis of price?
2. How does JetBlue use pricing to deal with demand fluctuations?
3. Is a businessperson's demand for air travel likely to be relatively elastic or inelastic? Is a vacationer's demand for air travel likely to be relatively elastic or inelastic?
4. What other factors related to pricing are most important to JetBlue's management when making pricing decisions?

Pricing Management

Napster 2.0: The Cat Is Back

Napster was the brainchild of Shawn Fanning, a 17-year-old freshman at Northeastern University who left college to develop a technology to trade music over the Internet. He commercialized the technology through Napster, which allowed computer users to share high-quality digital recordings (MP3s) of music via the Internet using its proprietary MusicShare software. Napster didn't actually store the recordings on its own computers; rather, it provided an index of all the songs available on the computers of members who were logged on to the service. In other words, Napster functioned as a sort of clearinghouse through which members could search by artist or song title, identify MP3s of interest, and download their choices from other members' hard drives. From its 1999 launch, Napster quickly became one of the most popular sites on the Internet, claiming some 15 million users in little more than a year. Indeed, so many college students were downloading songs from Napster that many universities were forced to block the site from their systems to regain bandwidth.

From the beginning, Napster's free service was as controversial as it was popular. Barely a year after its launch, Napster was sued by the Recording Industry Association of America (RIAA), which represents major recording companies such as Universal Music, BMG, Sony Music, Warner Music Group, and EMI. The RIAA claimed that Napster's service violated copyright laws by allowing users to swap music recordings for free. The RIAA also sought an injunction to stop the downloading of copyrighted songs and damages for lost revenue. The RIAA argued that song swapping via Napster and similar firms had cost the music industry more than $300 million in lost sales.

Napster ultimately was found guilty of direct copyright infringement of RIAA members' musical recordings, and the ruling was upheld on appeal. The District Court of Appeals ordered the company to stop allowing its millions of users to download and share copyrighted material without properly compensating the owners of that material. Napster agreed to pay $26 million for past distribution of unauthorized music and made a proposal that would let songwriters and musicians distribute their music on Napster for a fee. This settlement would have covered as many as 700,000 songs, but Napster still needed an agreement before it could legally distribute the music. However, after several failed attempts to reach a suitable compromise with the recording industry, and with litigation expenses mounting, the

OBJECTIVES

1. Understand the six major stages of the process used to establish prices.

2. Know the issues that are related to developing pricing objectives.

3. Understand the importance of identifying the target market's evaluation of price.

4. Describe how marketers analyze competitive prices.

5. Be familiar with the bases used for setting prices.

6. Explain the different types of pricing strategies.

7. Understand how a final, specific price is determined.

company entered Chapter 11 bankruptcy proceedings in 2002. The final nail in the coffin for Napster came when a Delaware bankruptcy judge blocked the sale of the company to Bertelsmann AG, ruling that negotiations with the German media company had not been made at arm's length and in good faith. Bertelsmann had agreed to pay creditors $8 million for Napster's assets. Shortly after the judge's ruling, Napster laid off nearly all of its 42-person staff and proceeded to convert its Chapter 11 reorganization into a Chapter 7 liquidation. At the time, Napster appeared to be doomed.[1] ■

apster, like most companies, has developed a specific approach to pricing in order to attract and retain customers. Selecting pricing strategies is one of the fundamental steps in the process of setting prices. Indeed, some firms have developed products, especially software, to help client companies set the best price for their own products. One such firm is Zilliant, which assists airlines and hotels in establishing optimal prices.[2]

In this chapter we examine six stages of a process marketers can use when setting prices (Figure 13.1). Stage 1 is the development of a pricing objective that is compatible with the organization's overall objectives and its marketing objectives. Stage 2 entails assessing the target market's evaluation of price. Stage 3 involves evaluating competitors' prices, which helps to determine the role of price in the marketing strategy. Stage 4 involves choosing a basis for setting prices. Stage 5 is the selection of a pricing strategy, or the guidelines for using price in the marketing mix. Stage 6, determining the final price, depends on environmental forces and marketers' understanding and use of a systematic approach to establishing prices. These stages are not rigid steps that all marketers must follow; rather, they are guidelines that provide a logical sequence for establishing prices.

Development of Pricing Objectives

The first step in setting prices is developing **pricing objectives,** goals that describe what a firm wants to achieve through pricing. Developing pricing objectives is an important task because pricing objectives form the basis for decisions about other stages of pricing. Thus pricing objectives must be stated explicitly, and the statement should include the time frame for accomplishing them.

pricing objectives Goals that describe what a firm wants to achieve through pricing

figure 13.1

STAGES FOR ESTABLISHING PRICES

1 Development of pricing objectives

2 Assessment of target market's evaluation of price

3 Evaluation of competitors' prices

4 Selection of a basis for pricing

5 Selection of a pricing strategy

6 Determination of a specific price

Marketers must make sure that the pricing objectives are consistent with the organization's marketing objectives and with its overall objectives because pricing objectives influence decisions in many functional areas, including finance, accounting, and production. A marketer can use both short- and long-term pricing objectives and can employ one or multiple pricing objectives. For instance, a firm may wish to increase market share by 18 percent over the next three years, achieve a 15 percent return on investment, and promote an image of quality in the marketplace. In this section we examine some of the pricing objectives that companies might set for themselves (Table 13.1).

Survival

A fundamental pricing objective is survival. Most organizations will tolerate problems such as short-run losses and internal upheaval if necessary for survival. Because price is a flexible variable, it is sometimes used to keep a company afloat by increasing sales volume to levels that match expenses. For example, a women's apparel retailer may run a three-day 60-percent-off sale to generate enough cash to pay creditors, employees, and rent.

Profit

Although a business may claim that its objective is to maximize profits for its owners, the objective of profit maximization is rarely operational because its achievement is difficult to measure. Because of this difficulty, profit objectives tend to be set at levels that the owners and top-level decision makers view as satisfactory. Specific profit objectives may be stated in terms of actual dollar amounts or in terms of a percentage of sales revenues. For example, when Procter & Gamble introduced the Gillette Fusion five-blade razor, it set a price 30 percent higher than its Mach 3 three-blade products. With an overall 72 percent market share, P&G hopes that the Fusion family of shaving products will help to boost profits.[3]

Return on Investment

Pricing to attain a specified rate of return on the company's investment is a profit-related pricing objective. Most pricing objectives based on return on investment (ROI) are achieved by trial and error because not all cost and revenue data needed to project

table 13.1	PRICING OBJECTIVES AND TYPICAL ACTIONS TAKEN TO ACHIEVE THEM
Objective	**Possible Action**
Survival	Adjust price levels so that the firm can increase sales volume to match organizational expenses
Profit	Identify price and cost levels that allow the firm to maximize profit
Return on investment	Identify price levels that enable the firm to yield targeted return on investment
Market share	Adjust price levels so that the firm can maintain or increase sales relative to competitors' sales
Cash flow	Set price levels to encourage rapid sales
Status quo	Identify price levels that help stabilize demand and sales
Product quality	Set prices to recover research and development expenditures and establish a high-quality image

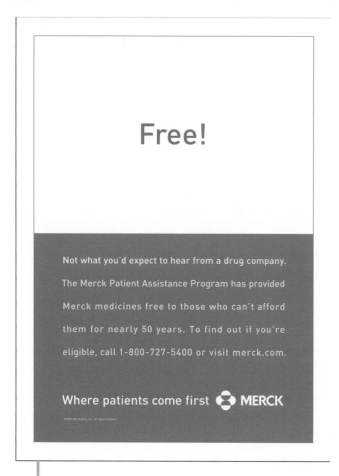

Not what you'd expect to hear from a drug company.

The Merck Patient Assistance Program has provided

Merck medicines free to those who can't afford

them for nearly 50 years. To find out if you're

eligible, call 1-800-727-5400 or visit merck.com.

Where patients come first   MERCK

Market Share

Merck has attempted to achieve its market share pricing objective by using socially responsible pricing.

the ROI are available when prices are set. General Motors uses ROI pricing objectives. Many pharmaceutical companies also use ROI pricing objectives because of their great investment in research and development.

Market Share

Many firms establish pricing objectives to maintain or increase market share, a product's sales in relation to total industry sales. Toyota priced its Prius, a hybrid, at a reasonable price, which allowed more consumers to afford this car and, in turn, built a strong market share in the hybrid category.[4] Many firms recognize that high relative market shares often translate into higher profits. The Profit Impact of Market Strategies (PIMS) studies, conducted over the last 30 years, have shown that both market share and product quality heavily influence profitability. Thus marketers often use an increase in market share as a primary pricing objective.

Maintaining or increasing market share need not depend on growth in industry sales. Remember that an organization can increase its market share even if sales for the total industry are flat or decreasing. On the other hand, a firm's sales volume may increase while its market share decreases if total industry sales are growing.

Cash Flow

Some companies set prices so that they can recover cash as quickly as possible. Financial managers understandably seek to quickly recover capital spent to develop products. This objective may have the support of a marketing manager who anticipates a short product life cycle.

Although it may be acceptable in some situations, the use of cash flow and recovery as an objective oversimplifies the value of price in contributing to profits. If this pricing objective results in high prices, competitors with lower prices may gain a large share of the market.

Status Quo

In some cases an organization is in a favorable position and, desiring nothing more, may set an objective of status quo. Status quo objectives can focus on several dimensions, such as maintaining a certain market share, meeting (but not beating) competitors' prices, achieving price stability, and maintaining a favorable public image. A status quo pricing objective can reduce a firm's risks by helping to stabilize demand for its products. The use of status quo pricing objectives sometimes minimizes pricing as a competitive tool, leading to a climate of nonprice competition in an industry.

Product Quality

A company may have the objective of leading its industry in product quality. This goal normally dictates a high price to cover the high product quality and, in some instances, the high cost of research and development. For example, Bentley Motors uses premium prices to help signal the quality of its hand-made cars, which can cost from $190,000 to well over $260,000 depending on accessories and options.[5] As mentioned previously, the PIMS studies have shown that both product quality and market share are good indicators of profitability. The products and brands that customers perceive to be of high quality are more likely to survive in a competitive marketplace. High quality usually enables a marketer to charge higher prices for the product.

Product Quality as a Pricing Objective

Porsche produces high-quality vehicles, like the Cayenne, that are priced to communicate the level of quality.

When do you tell it that it's not a sports car?

The new Cayenne. Starting at $43,400.

Levi's High-End Low Riders

Levi Strauss & Co., well known for its 501 blue jeans and affordable prices, is trying to break in to the premium denim jean market. The company, which has been making jeans since the 1800s, wants a part of the fast-growing $1 billion market for upscale denim. The premium jean market is dominated by brands such as Earl Jeans, Seven for All Mankind, Citizens of Humanity, and True Religion. Levi's is entering the market with its Levi's Premium collection, selling for between $110 and $180 a pair. Eco, its new upscale line of environmentally friendly jeans, made from organic cotton, is priced at about $250.

People in the fashion industry feel that Levi's reputation as a long-standing, reliable, inexpensive department store brand may jeopardize its chances in the upscale market. To compete, Levi's must prove that its Premium line has the quality and style comparable with those of other high-end brands.

Levi's joined with the Warhol Foundation to create a 2006 Premium collection based on the art of Andy Warhol, a lover of Levi's jeans. The company also threw an "underground" party to promote its Ultimate boot-cut jeans with the help of cast members from the hit TV show *Desperate Housewives.* In addition, the company planned to open two new Levi's stores in Beverly Hills and Georgetown (Washington, DC) to market both the company's popular Red Tab jeans collection and the Premium collection.

Levi's Premium collection may contribute a small portion of the company's revenue, but right now it is driving the company's innovation. After seeing losses for several years, the company is seeing positive sales results in the premium market in Europe and Asia. Overall premium sales saw more than a 100 percent increase in 2004.[a]

Assessment of the Target Market's Evaluation of Price

After developing pricing objectives, marketers next need to assess the target market's evaluation of price. Despite the general assumption that price is a major issue for buyers, the importance of price depends on the type of product, the type of target market, and the purchase situation. For example, buyers are probably more sensitive to gasoline prices than to luggage prices. With respect to the type of target market, adults may have to pay more than children for certain products. The purchase situation also affects the buyer's view of price. In other situations, most moviegoers would never pay the prices charged for soft drinks, popcorn, and candy at movie concession stands. By assessing the target market's evaluation of price, a marketer is in a better position to know how much emphasis to put on price in the overall marketing strategy. Information about the target market's price evaluation also may help a marketer to determine how far above the competition the firm can set its prices.

Because some consumers today are seeking less expensive products and shopping more selectively, some manufacturers and retailers are focusing on the value of their products. Value combines a product's price and quality attributes, which customers use to differentiate among competing brands. Consumers are looking for good deals on products that provide better value for their money. They also may view products that have highly desirable attributes, such as organic content or time-saving features, as having great value. Companies that offer both low prices and high quality, such as Target and Best Buy, have altered consumers' expectations about how much quality they must sacrifice for low prices.[6] Even retail atmospherics can influence consumers' perceptions of price; the use of soft lights and colors has been found to have a positive influence on perception of price fairness.[7] Understanding the importance of a product to customers, as well as their expectations about quality and value, helps marketers to correctly assess the target market's evaluation of price.

Evaluation of Competitors' Prices

In most cases marketers are in a better position to establish prices when they know the prices charged for competing brands, the third step in establishing prices. Discovering competitors' prices may be a regular function of marketing research. Some grocery and department stores, for example, have full-time comparative shoppers who systematically collect data on prices. However, uncovering competitors' prices is not always easy, especially in producer and reseller markets. Competitors' price lists are often closely guarded. Even if a marketer has access to competitors' price lists, these lists may not reflect the actual prices at which competitive products are sold because those prices may be established through negotiation.

Knowing the prices of competing brands can be very important for a marketer. Competitors' prices and the marketing-mix variables they emphasize partly determine how important price will be to customers. A marketer in an industry in which price competition prevails needs competitive price information to ensure that its prices are the same as, or lower than, competitors' prices. In some instances an organization's prices are designed to be slightly above competitors' prices to give its products an exclusive image. In contrast, another company may use price as a competitive tool and price its products below those of competitors. "Category killers" like Staples and Home Depot have acquired large market shares through highly competitive pricing.[8]

Selection of a Basis for Pricing

The fourth step involves selecting a basis for pricing: cost, demand, and/or competition. The choice of the basis to use is affected by the type of product, the market structure of the industry, the brand's market share position relative to competing

snapshot

Airline fares soar with rising fuel prices

$1.51
2005

$1.12
2004

$.84
2003

Domestic airline fuel prices in dollars per gallon

$.70
2002

$.76
2001

Source: Data from Bureau of Transportation Statistics.

brands, and customer characteristics. Although we discuss each basis separately in this section, an organization generally considers two or all three of these dimensions, even though one may be the primary dimension on which it bases prices. For example, if a company is using cost as a basis for setting prices, marketers in that firm are also aware of and concerned about competitors' prices. If a company is using demand as a basis for pricing, those making pricing decisions still must consider costs and competitors' prices. Indeed, cost is a factor in every pricing decision because it establishes a price minimum below which the firm will not be able to recoup its production and other costs; demand likewise sets an effective price maximum above which customers are unlikely to buy the product. In setting prices for its 44,000 products, Fairchild Semiconductor uses software to assess all three dimensions, as well as buying behavior, manufacturing capacity, inventories, and product life cycles.[9]

Cost-Based Pricing

With **cost-based pricing,** a dollar amount or percentage is added to the cost of the product. This approach thus involves calculations of desired profit margins. Cost-based pricing does not necessarily take into account the economic aspects of supply and demand, nor must it relate to just one pricing strategy or pricing objective. Cost-based pricing is straightforward and easy to implement. Two common forms of cost-based pricing are cost-plus and markup pricing.

Cost-Plus Pricing. In **cost-plus pricing,** the seller's costs are determined (usually during a project or after a project is completed), and then a specified dollar amount or percentage of the cost is added to the seller's cost to establish the price. Cost-plus pricing and competition-based pricing are in fact the most common bases for pricing services.[10] When production costs are difficult to predict, cost-plus pricing is appropriate. Projects involving custom-made equipment and commercial construction are often priced by this technique. The government frequently uses such cost-based pricing in granting defense contracts. One pitfall for the buyer is that the seller may increase costs to establish a larger profit base. Furthermore, some costs, such as overhead, may be difficult to determine. In periods of rapid inflation, cost-plus pricing is popular, especially when the producer must use raw materials that are fluctuating in price.

Markup Pricing. A common pricing approach among retailers is **markup pricing,** in which a product's price is derived by adding a predetermined percentage of the cost, called *markup,* to the cost of the product. Although the percentage markup in a retail store varies from one category of goods to another—35 percent of cost for hardware items and 100 percent of cost for greeting cards, for example—the same percentage often is used to determine the price on items within a single product category, and the percentage markup may be largely standardized across an industry at the retail level. Using a standard percentage markup for a specific product category reduces pricing to a routine task that can be performed quickly. This is one of the major reasons that many retailers use markup pricing.

Markup can be stated as a percentage of the cost or as a percentage of the selling price. The following example illustrates how percentage markups are determined and points out the differences in the two methods. Assume that a retailer purchases a can

cost-based pricing Adding a dollar amount or percentage to the cost of the product

cost-plus pricing Adding a specified dollar amount or percentage to the seller's cost

markup pricing Adding to the cost of the product a predetermined percentage of that cost

of tuna at 45 cents, adds 15 cents to the cost, and then prices the tuna at 60 cents. Here are the figures:

$$\text{Markup as percentage of cost} = \frac{\text{markup}}{\text{cost}}$$

$$= \frac{15}{45}$$

$$= 33.3 \text{ percent}$$

$$\text{Markup as percentage of selling price} = \frac{\text{markup}}{\text{selling price}}$$

$$= \frac{15}{60}$$

$$= 25.0 \text{ percent}$$

Obviously, when discussing a percentage markup, it is important to know whether the markup is based on cost or selling price.

Demand-Based Pricing

Marketers sometimes base prices on the level of demand for the product. When **demand-based pricing** is used, customers pay a higher price when demand for the product is strong and a lower price when demand is weak. For example, hotels that otherwise attract numerous travelers often offer reduced rates during lower-demand periods. The Taxi Driver's Association in Berlin arranged to discount cab fares by 50 percent during the early evening, a period of lower demand. If the discount succeeds in attracting more passengers, the taxis will continue to offer it on a regular basis.[11] Some long-distance telephone companies, such as Sprint and Verizon, also use demand-based pricing by charging peak and off-peak rates or offering free cell phone minutes during off-peak times. To use this pricing basis, a marketer must be able to estimate the amounts of a product consumers will demand at different prices. The marketer then chooses the price that generates the highest total revenue. Obviously, the effectiveness of demand-based pricing depends on the marketer's ability to estimate demand accurately. Compared with cost-based pricing, demand-based pricing places a firm in a better position to reach higher profit levels, assuming that buyers value the product at levels sufficiently above the product's cost.

Competition-Based Pricing

In **competition-based pricing,** an organization considers costs as secondary to competitors' prices. The importance of this method increases when competing products are relatively homogeneous, and the organization is serving markets in which price is a key purchase consideration. A firm that uses competition-based pricing may choose to price below competitors' prices, above competitors' prices, or at the same level. Airlines use competition-based pricing, often charging identical fares on the same routes. Also, online travel services such as Orbitz, Expedia, and Priceline.com employ competition-based pricing.

Although not all introductory marketing texts have exactly the same price, they

marketing ENTREPRENEURS

Amy Mayer and Ellen Navarro

THEIR BUSINESS: Express Drop

FOUNDED: in 2004, when both were 23

SUCCESS: $1.4 million in annual sales

Lots of people have stuff lying around but are reluctant to list it on eBay for a variety of reasons. Folks in Chicago can take their no-longer-wanted stuff to Express Drop, a modern-day consignment shop. After assessing the items, Express Drop auctions them on eBay and pockets a 32 percent commission on the first $500 (25 percent after that) for items that sell. The customer receives a check after Express Drop has deducted the cost of shipping the item to the winning bidder. Mayer and Navarro, who met while working at a clothing boutique, both wanted to start their own business. Although they are younger than most of their customers, they have built a strong reputation for personal service and professionalism.[b]

Demand-Based Pricing

Woodstock Inn & Resort uses demand-based pricing to reflect seasonal needs for its resort property.

do have similar prices. The price the bookstore paid to the publishing company for this textbook was determined on the basis of competitors' prices. Competition-based pricing can help a firm achieve the pricing objective of increasing sales or market share. Competition-based pricing may necessitate frequent price adjustments. For example, for many competitive airline routes, fares are adjusted often.

Selection of a Pricing Strategy

The next step after choosing a basis for pricing is to select a pricing strategy, an approach or a course of action designed to achieve pricing and marketing objectives. Generally, pricing strategies help marketers to solve the practical problems of establishing prices. Table 13.2 (on page 330) lists the most common pricing strategies, which we discuss in this section.

Differential Pricing

An important issue in pricing decisions is whether to use a single price or different prices for the same product. Using a single price has several benefits. A primary advantage is simplicity. A single price is easily understood by both employees and customers, and since many salespeople and customers do not like having to negotiate a price, it reduces the chance of an adversarial relationship developing between marketer and customer. The use of a single price does create some challenges, however. If the single price is too high, some potential customers may be unable to afford the product. If it is too low, the firm loses revenue from customers who would have paid more if the price had been higher.

Differential pricing means charging different prices to different buyers for the same quality and quantity of product. For differential pricing to be effective, the market must consist of multiple segments with different price sensitivities, and the method should be used in a way that avoids confusing or antagonizing customers. Customers paying the lower prices should not be able to resell the product to the individuals and organizations paying higher prices, unless that is the intention of the seller. Differential pricing

demand-based pricing Pricing based on the level of demand for the product

competition-based pricing Pricing influenced primarily by competitors' prices

differential pricing Charging different prices to different buyers for the same quality and quantity of product

table 13.2 COMMON PRICING STRATEGIES

Differential Pricing Negotiated pricing Secondary-market pricing Periodic discounting Random discounting	**Psychological Pricing** Reference pricing Bundle pricing Multiple-unit pricing Everyday low prices Odd-even pricing Customary pricing Prestige pricing
New-Product Pricing Price skimming Penetration pricing	**Professional Pricing**
Product-Line Pricing Captive pricing Premium pricing Bait pricing Price lining	**Promotional Pricing** Price Leaders Special-event pricing Comparison discounting

can occur in several ways, including negotiated pricing, secondary-market discounting, periodic discounting, and random discounting.

Negotiated Pricing. **Negotiated pricing** occurs when the final price is established through bargaining between seller and customer. If you buy a house, for example, you are likely to negotiate the final price with the seller. Negotiated pricing occurs in numerous industries and at all levels of distribution. Cutler-Hammon/Eaton has streamlined its contract-negotiations process for more than 90,000 products by reducing quote response times and implementing automatic acceptance of offers.[12] Even when there is a predetermined stated price or a price list, manufacturers, wholesalers, and retailers still may negotiate to establish the final sales price. Consumers commonly negotiate prices for houses, cars, and used equipment.

Secondary-Market Pricing. **Secondary-market pricing** means setting one price for the primary target market and a different price for another market. Often the price charged in the secondary market is lower. However, when the costs of serving a secondary market are higher than normal, secondary-market customers may have to pay a higher price. Examples of secondary markets include a geographically isolated domestic market, a market in a foreign country, and a segment willing to purchase a product during off-peak times. For example, some restaurants offer special "early bird" prices during the early evening hours, movie theaters offer senior-citizen discounts, and some textbooks and pharmaceutical products are sold for considerably less in certain foreign countries than in the United States. Secondary markets give an organization an opportunity to use excess capacity and to stabilize the allocation of resources.

Periodic Discounting. **Periodic discounting** is the temporary reduction of prices on a patterned or systematic basis. For example, most retailers have annual holiday sales. Automobile dealers regularly discount prices on current models when the next year's models are introduced. From the marketer's point of view, a major problem with periodic discounting is that because the discounts follow a pattern, customers can predict when the reductions will occur and may delay their purchases until they can take advantage of the lower prices.

Random Discounting. To alleviate the problem of customers knowing when discounting will occur, some organizations employ **random discounting;** that is, they temporarily reduce their prices on an unsystematic basis. When price reductions of a product occur randomly, current users of that brand are likely to be unable to predict

negotiated pricing Establishing a final price through bargaining

secondary-market pricing Setting one price for the primary target market and a different price for another market

periodic discounting Temporary reduction of prices on a patterned or systematic basis

random discounting Temporary reduction of prices on an unsystematic basis

when the reductions will occur and so will not delay their purchases. However, in the automobile industry, with its increasing dependence on sales, rebates, and incentives such as 0 percent financing, random discounting has become nearly continuous discounting, and some analysts have warned that automakers will find it increasingly difficult to cease generous incentives that consumers have come to expect. Marketers also use random discounting to attract new customers.

Regardless of whether periodic discounting or random discounting is used, retailers often employ tensile pricing when putting products on sale. *Tensile pricing* refers to a broad statement about price reductions as opposed to detailing specific price discounts. Examples of tensile pricing would be statements such as "20 to 50 percent off," "up to 75 percent off," and "save 10 percent or more." Generally, using and advertising the tensile price that mentions only the maximum reduction (such as "up to 50 percent off") generates the highest customer response.[13]

New-Product Pricing

Setting the base price for a new product is a necessary part of formulating a marketing strategy. The base price is easily adjusted (in the absence of government price controls), and its establishment is one of the most fundamental decisions in the marketing mix. When a marketer sets base prices, it also considers how quickly competitors will enter the market, whether they will mount a strong campaign on entry, and what effect their entry will have on the development of primary demand. Two strategies used in new-product pricing are price skimming and penetration pricing.

Price Skimming.   **Price skimming** is charging the highest possible price that buyers who most desire the product will pay. The Apple iPhone, for example, was introduced through AT&T with a starting price of $599 for a smartphone with 8 gigabytes of memory, $200 more than the next most expensive phone offered by AT&T.[14] This approach provides the most flexible introductory base price. Price skimming can provide several benefits, especially when a product is in the introductory stage of its life cycle. A skimming policy can generate much-needed initial cash flows to help offset sizable developmental costs. When introducing a new pharmaceutical, most drug makers such as Merck and Pfizer often use a skimming price to defray large research and development costs and to help fund further research and development into other drugs. Price skimming protects the marketer from problems that arise when the price is set too low to cover costs. When a firm introduces a product, its production capacity may be limited. A skimming price can help to keep demand consistent with the firm's production capabilities. The use of a skimming price may attract competition into an industry because the high price makes that type of business appear to be quite lucrative.

Penetration Pricing.   In **penetration pricing,** prices are set below those of competing brands to penetrate a market and gain a large market share quickly. Perhaps the ultimate penetration-pricing strategy was implemented by the Arctic Monkeys. The U.K. rock band handed out free CDs of its music at early performances, and fans e-mailed the music to friends. The resulting viral effort led to a recording contract for the band, which has the fastest-selling debut album in British music history.[15] This approach is less flexible for a marketer than price skimming because it is more difficult to raise a penetration price than to lower or discount a skimming price. It is not unusual for a firm to use a penetration price after having skimmed the market with a higher price.

Penetration pricing can be especially beneficial when a marketer suspects that competitors could enter the market easily. If penetration pricing allows the marketer to gain a large market share quickly, competitors may be discouraged from entering the market. In addition, because the lower per-unit penetration price results in lower per-unit profit, the market may not appear to be especially lucrative to potential new entrants. Apple prices its iPod digital music players at penetration prices. Although retailers such as Best Buy and Circuit City earn very little profit on

price skimming Charging the highest possible price that buyers who most desire the product will pay

penetration pricing Setting prices below those of competing brands to penetrate a market and gain a significant market share quickly

Penetration Pricing

1&1 competes with other business domain providers by using penetration pricing.

iPods, they benefit from selling iPod accessories. Many iPod buyers purchase at least two accessories, and the market for accessories such as speakers and covers is expected to double. Moreover, 40 percent of vehicles sold in the United States now offer some sort of iPod integration.[16]

Product-Line Pricing

Rather than considering products on an item-by-item basis when determining pricing strategies, some marketers employ product-line pricing. **Product-line pricing** means establishing and adjusting the prices of multiple products within a product line. When marketers use product-line pricing, their goal is to maximize profits for an entire product line rather than focusing on the profitability of an individual product. Product-line pricing can provide marketers with flexibility in price setting. For example, marketers can set prices so that one product is quite profitable, while another increases market share by virtue of having a lower price than competing products. When marketers employ product-line pricing, they have several strategies from which to choose, including captive pricing, premium pricing, bait pricing, and price lining.

Captive Pricing. With **captive pricing,** the basic product in a product line is priced low, whereas the price on the items required to operate or enhance it may be higher. Printer companies such as Hewlett-Packard and Canon have used this pricing strategy, providing relatively low-cost, low-margin printers and selling ink cartridges to generate significant profits. Likewise, Sony set an introduction price for its PlayStation 3 videogame console at $599—$240 below cost—with the anticipation of selling accessories and games to generate profits.[17]

Premium Pricing. **Premium pricing** is often used when a product line contains several versions of the same product; the highest-quality products or those with the most versatility are given the highest prices. Other products in the line are priced to appeal to price-sensitive shoppers or to those who seek product-specific features. Marketers who use a premium strategy often realize a significant portion of their profits from premium-priced products. Examples of product categories that commonly use premium pricing are small kitchen appliances, beer, ice cream, and cable television service.

product-line pricing Establishing and adjusting prices of multiple products within a product line

captive pricing Pricing the basic product in a produce line low while pricing related items at a higher level

premium pricing Pricing the highest-quality or most versatile products higher than other models in the product line

Why Did Microsoft Price the Xbox 360 Below Cost?

Microsoft raised eyebrows when it used captive pricing for its Xbox 360 videogame system. According to an iSuppli survey, the parts used to make the Xbox cost the company $470 prior to factoring in assembly; however, each Xbox retails for $399—a $71 loss. Factoring in additional items such as power supply, cables, and controllers boosts the loss for each Xbox to $126. Microsoft has said that it may break even on the unit in 2007 with the help of sales on games for the Xbox 360, of which it expected to sell 10 million units by 2007. In 2005, Microsoft's home entertainment division lost $391 million on sales of $3.3 billion. So why is the company producing a product on which it looses money?

For one thing, the cost of each game for the Xbox 360 has increased by $10 over the previous version. Also, multiplayer game functions cost $70 a year. Xbox users who network receive lots of online offers to buy more Microsoft products such as games and game add-ons. It appears that Microsoft expects to profit not only from game software and networking access but also from additional software buys. Users may want to make their Xboxes part of their home entertainment systems. The new Xbox system connects to a television and allows users to view photographs, play music, and more as well as playing games. Microsoft assumes that all the extra operating products will be purchased after the Xbox is purchased.

Although Bill Gates and the Microsoft team feel that the Xbox will begin to help Microsoft turn a profit, the reality of this feeling is still up in the air—only time will tell. In any case, Sony followed Microsoft's captive strategy for its own PlayStation 3.[c]

bait pricing Pricing an item in the product line low with the intention of selling a higher-priced item in the line

price lining Setting a limited number of prices for selected groups or lines of merchandise

Bait Pricing. To attract customers, marketers may put a low price on one item in a product line, with the intention of selling a higher-priced item in the line; this strategy is known as **bait pricing.** For example, a computer retailer might advertise its lowest-priced computer model, hoping that when customers come to the store, they will purchase a higher-priced one. This strategy can facilitate sales of a line's higher-priced products. As long as a retailer has sufficient quantities of the advertised low-priced model available for sale, this strategy is considered acceptable. However, *bait and switch* is an activity in which retailers have no intention of selling the bait product; they use the low price merely to entice customers into the store to sell them higher-priced products. Bait and switch is considered unethical, and in some states it is illegal as well.

Price Lining. When an organization sets a limited number of prices for selected groups or lines of merchandise, it is using **price lining**. A retailer may have various styles and brands of similar-quality men's shirts that sell for $15 and another line of higher-quality shirts that sell for $22. Microsoft set different prices for different versions of its Vista operating system depending on features: the barebones Windows Vista Home Basic for $199; Windows Vista Home Premium, $239; Windows Vista

Premium Pricing

Kohler uses unique adervtising to sell its higher-end products.

Business, $299; and the feature-packed Windows Vista Ultimate, $399.[18] Price lining simplifies customers' decision making by holding constant one key variable in the final selection of style and brand within a line. Another type of pricing lining is subscription services. Cable or satellite TV subscribers choose different packages or groupings of channels with different prices. Likewise, subscribers to subscription DVD rental services such as Netflix can choose a membership price based on the number of DVDs they want to receive at one time.

The basic assumption in price lining is that the demand for various groups or sets of products is inelastic. If the prices are attractive, customers will concentrate their purchases without responding to slight changes in price. Thus a women's dress shop that carries dresses priced at $85, $55, and $35 may not attract many more sales with a drop to, say, $83, $53, and $33. The "space" between the price of $85 and $55, however, can stir changes in consumer response.

Psychological Pricing

Learning the price of a product is not always a pleasant experience for customers. It can sometimes be surprising (as at a movie concession stand) and sometimes downright horrifying. Most of us have been afflicted with "sticker shock." Research indicates that consumers are likely to have negative reactions to incomplete or unclear pricing information, especially when conveyed through misleading communications.[19] **Psychological pricing** attempts to influence a customer's perception of price to make a product's price more attractive. In this section we consider several forms of psychological pricing: reference pricing, bundle pricing, multiple-unit pricing, everyday low prices (EDLP), odd-even pricing, customary pricing, and prestige pricing.

Reference Pricing. **Reference pricing** means pricing a product at a moderate level and displaying it next to a more expensive model or brand in the hope that the customer will use the higher price as an external reference price (i.e., a comparison price). Because of the comparison, the customer is expected to view the moderate price favorably. Reference pricing is based on the "isolation effect," meaning an alternative is less attractive when viewed by itself than when compared with other alternatives. When you go to Best Buy to buy a DVD player, a moderately priced DVD player may appear especially attractive because it offers most of the important attributes of the more expensive alternatives on display and at a lower price. It is not unusual for an organization's moderately priced private brands to be positioned alongside more expensive, better-known manufacturer brands. On the other hand, some retailers of private store brands are raising prices to improve the image of these products.[20]

Bundle Pricing. **Bundle pricing** is packaging together two or more products, usually complementary ones, to be sold for a single price. Many fast-food restaurants, for example, offer combination meals at a price that is lower than the combined prices of each item priced separately. Most telephone and cable television providers bundle local telephone service, broadband Internet access, and digital cable or satellite television for

psychological pricing Pricing that attempts to influence a customer's perception of price to make a product's price more attractive

reference pricing Pricing a product at a moderate level and displaying it next to a more expensive model or brand

bundle pricing Packaging together two or more complementary products and selling them for a single price

one monthly fee. To attract customers, the single price is usually considerably less than the sum of the prices of the individual products. Some marketing studies suggest that marketers can develop bundles of products with optimal prices for different market segments.[21] Bundle pricing facilitates customer satisfaction and, when slow-moving products are bundled with products with higher turnover, can help a company stimulate sales and increase revenues. It also may help to foster customer loyalty and improve customer retention. Selling products as a package rather than individually also may result in cost savings. Bundle pricing is commonly used for banking and travel services, computers, and automobiles with option packages.

Some organizations, however, are unbundling in favor of a more itemized approach sometimes called *à la carte pricing*. This provides customers with the opportunity to pick and choose the products they want without having to purchase bundles that may not be the right mix for their purposes.[22] For example, some television viewers would prefer to subscribe only to their favorite channels rather than a predetermined package of channels.[23] Furthermore, with the help of the Internet, comparison shopping has become more convenient than ever, allowing customers to price items and create their own mixes. Nevertheless, bundle pricing continues to appeal to customers who prefer the convenience of a package.[24]

Multiple-Unit Pricing.   **Multiple-unit pricing** occurs when two or more identical products are packaged together and sold for a single price. This normally results in a lower per-unit price than the one regularly charged. Multiple-unit pricing is used commonly for twin-packs of potato chips, four-packs of light bulbs, and six- and twelve-packs of soft drinks. Customers benefit from the cost saving and convenience this pricing strategy affords. A company may use multiple-unit pricing to attract new customers to its brand and, in some instances, to increase consumption of its brands. When customers buy in larger quantities, their consumption of the product may increase. For example, multiple-unit pricing may encourage a customer to buy larger quantities of snacks, which are likely to be consumed in higher volume at the point of consumption simply because they are available. However, this is not true for all products. For instance, greater availability at the point of consumption of light bulbs, bar soap, and table salt is not likely to increase usage.

Discount stores and especially warehouse clubs, such as Sam's Club and Costco, are major users of multiple-unit pricing. For certain products in these stores, customers receive significant per-unit price reductions when they buy packages containing multiple units of the same product, such as an eight-pack of canned tuna fish.

Everyday Low Prices (EDLP).   To reduce or eliminate the use of frequent short-term price reductions, some organizations use an approach referred to as **everyday low prices (EDLP).** With EDLP, a marketer sets a low price for its products on a consistent basis rather than setting higher prices and frequently discounting them. Everyday low prices, though not deeply discounted, are set far enough below competitors' prices to make customers feel confident they are receiving a fair price. EDLP is employed by retailers such as Wal-Mart. Indeed, Wal-Mart, which has already trademarked the phrase, "Always Low Prices. Always," sought to trademark the acronym EDLP because of its extensive use of the practice. Vociferous opposition from the National Grocers Association and Supervalue, a supermarket chain, as well as other firms, may prevent the retail giant from registering the term, however.[25] A company that uses EDLP benefits from reduced losses from frequent markdowns, greater stability in sales, and reduced promotional costs. The furniture industry, where consumers' greatest concern seems to be price relative to quality, has taken a cue from Wal-Mart. Traditionally dominated by U.S. manufacturing, even long-standing U.S. companies such as Timberlake are now offering lower-priced furniture made overseas to compete more effectively.[26]

A major problem with EDLP is that customers have mixed responses to it. Over the last several years, many marketers have "trained" customers to seek and expect deeply discounted prices. In some product categories, such as apparel, finding the

multiple-unit pricing
Packaging together two or more identical products and selling them for a single price

everyday low prices (EDLP)
Setting a low price for products on a consistent basis

Prestige Pricing

Dorfman Sterling Jewelry uses prestige pricing.

odd-even pricing Ending the price with certain numbers to influence buyers' perceptions of the price or product

customary pricing Pricing on the basis of tradition

prestige pricing Setting prices at an artificially high level to convey prestige or a quality image

deepest discount has become almost a national consumer sport. Thus failure to provide deep discounts can be a problem for certain marketers. In some instances customers simply don't believe that everyday low prices are what marketers claim they are but are instead a marketing gimmick.

Odd-Even Pricing. Through **odd-even pricing—** ending the price with certain numbers—marketers try to influence buyers' perceptions of the price or the product. Odd pricing assumes that more of a product will be sold at $99.95 than at $100. Theoretically, customers will think, or at least tell friends, that the product is a bargain—not $100, but $99 and change. Also, customers will supposedly think that the store could have charged $100 but instead cut the price to the last cent, to $99.95. Some claim, too, that certain types of customers are more attracted by odd prices than by even ones. However, research on the effect of odd-even prices has demonstrated conflicting results; one recent study found that odd prices ending in 5, 8, or 9 failed to trigger the threshold of consumer response.[27] Another study, however, found that consumers favor prices ending in 0 or 5 in investment decisions.[28] Nonetheless, odd prices are far more common today than even prices.

Even prices are often used to give a product an exclusive or upscale image. An even price supposedly will influence a customer to view the product as being a high-quality premium brand. A shirt maker, for example, may print on a premium shirt package a suggested retail price of $42.00 instead of $41.95; the even price of the shirt is used to enhance its upscale image.

Customary Pricing. In **customary pricing,** certain goods are priced primarily on the basis of tradition. Recent economic uncertainties have made most prices fluctuate fairly widely, but the classic example of the customary, or traditional, price is the price of a candy bar. For years, a candy bar cost 5 cents. A new candy bar would have had to be something very special to sell for more than a nickel. This price was so sacred that rather than change it, manufacturers increased or decreased the size of the candy bar itself as chocolate prices fluctuated. Today, of course, the nickel candy bar has disappeared. Yet most candy bars still sell at a consistent, but obviously higher, price. Thus customary pricing remains the standard for this market.

Prestige Pricing. In **prestige pricing,** prices are set at an artificially high level to convey prestige or a quality image. Prestige pricing is used especially when buyers associate a higher price with higher quality. Pharmacists report that some consumers complain when a prescription does not cost enough; apparently some consumers associate a drug's price with its potency. Typical product categories in which selected products are prestige priced include perfumes, liquor, jewelry, and cars. Although traditionally appliances have not been prestige priced, upscale appliances have appeared in recent years to capitalize on the willingness of some consumer segments to "trade up" for high-quality products. These consumers do not mind paying extra for a Sub-Zero refrigerator, a Viking commercial range, or a Whirlpool Duet washer and dryer because these products offer high quality as well as a level of prestige. If producers who use prestige pricing lowered their prices dramatically, the new prices would be inconsistent with the perceived high-quality images of their products.

Professional Pricing

Professional pricing is used by people who have great skill or experience in a particular field. Professionals often believe their fees (prices) should not relate directly to the time and effort spent in specific cases; rather, a standard fee is charged regardless of the problems involved in performing the job. Some doctors' and lawyers' fees are prime examples: $75 for a checkup, $1,500 for an appendectomy, and $399 for a divorce. Other professionals set prices in other ways. Like other marketers, professionals have costs associated with facilities, labor, insurance, equipment, and supplies. Certainly, costs are considered when setting professional prices.

The concept of professional pricing carries the idea that professionals have an ethical responsibility not to overcharge customers. In some situations a seller can charge customers a high price and continue to sell many units of the product. If a diabetic requires one insulin treatment per day to survive, the individual probably will buy that treatment whether its price is $1 or $10. In fact, the patient surely would purchase the treatment even if the price went higher. In these situations, sellers could charge exorbitant fees.

Promotional Pricing

As an ingredient in the marketing mix, price is often coordinated with promotion. The two variables sometimes are so interrelated that the pricing policy is promotion-oriented. Types of promotional pricing include price leaders, special-event pricing, and comparison discounting.

Price Leaders.   Sometimes a firm prices a few products below the usual markup, near cost, or below cost, which results in prices known as **price leaders.** This type of pricing is used most often in supermarkets and restaurants to attract customers by giving them especially low prices on a few items. In the United Kingdom, for example, the discount store chain ASDA uses packaged food and beverage price leaders to compete more effectively with supermarket chains such as Sainsbury and Tesco.[29] Management hopes that sales of regularly priced products will more than offset the reduced revenues from the price leaders.

Special-Event Pricing.   To increase sales volume, many organizations coordinate price with advertising or sales promotions for seasonal or special situations. **Special-event pricing** involves advertised sales or price cutting linked to a holiday, season, or event. If the pricing objective is survival, special sales events may be designed to generate the necessary operating capital. Special-event pricing entails coordination of production, scheduling, storage, and physical distribution. Whenever a sales lag occurs, special-event pricing is an alternative that marketers should consider.

Comparison Discounting.   **Comparison discounting** sets the price of a product at a specific level and simultaneously compares it with a higher price. The higher price may be the product's previous price, the price of a competing brand, the product's price at another retail outlet, or a manufacturer's suggested retail price. Customers may find comparative discounting informative, and it can have a significant impact on their purchases. However, overuse of comparison pricing may reduce customers' internal reference prices, meaning that they no longer believe that the higher price is the regular or normal price.[30]

Because this pricing strategy has on occasion led to deceptive pricing practices, the Federal Trade Commission has established guidelines for comparison discounting. If the higher price against which the comparison is made is the price formerly charged for the product, the seller must have made the previous price available to customers for a reasonable period of time. If the seller presents the higher price as the one charged by other retailers in the same trade area, it must be able to demonstrate that this claim is true. When the seller presents the higher price as the manufacturer's suggested retail price, the higher price must be similar to the price at which a reasonable

professional pricing Fees set by people with great skill or experience in a particular field

price leaders Product priced below the usual markup, near cost, or below cost

special-event pricing Advertised sales or price cutting linked to a holiday, season, or event

comparison discounting Setting a price at a specific level and comparing it with a higher price

proportion of the product was sold. Some manufacturers' suggested retail prices are so high that very few products are actually sold at those prices. In such cases, comparison discounting would be deceptive.

Determination of a Specific Price

A pricing strategy will yield a certain price. However, this price may need refinement to make it consistent with circumstances as well as pricing practices in a particular market or industry. When Blockbuster eliminated late fees for movie rentals, it probably did not anticipate that revenue would fall by nearly 10 percent. Given increasing competition from online movie rental and pay-per-view services, the company will need to evaluate its overall approach to pricing in light of decreased profitability.[31]

In the absence of government price controls, pricing remains a flexible and convenient way to adjust the marketing mix. The online brokerage arm of American Express (Amex), for example, sets prices on a sliding scale depending on how much service support each customer uses. Customers who conduct all their securities trades without going through Amex employees pay lower prices than those who work with the firm's financial advisers to complete trades. As a result, American Express can provide the exact services each customer requires at an appropriate price.[32] In many situations, prices can be adjusted quickly—in a matter of minutes or over a few days. Such flexibility is unique to this component of the marketing mix.

To set the final price, it is important for marketers to establish pricing objectives, have considerable knowledge about target-market customers, and determine demand, price elasticity, costs, and competitive factors.

...And now, back to Napster

Napster's name and assets were purchased in late 2002 by Roxio, a company known for its CD "burning" software. Roxio introduced Napster 2.0 on October 29, 2003, as a fee-based service offering 1 million songs for download at 99 cents per track or $9.95 per album. Members also could pay $9.95 per month for unlimited music streaming to their desktops. Perhaps most important, Napster's revival came with the blessing of five major record labels. Napster also developed a number of partnerships with Microsoft, Gateway, Yahoo!, and Samsung that gave it an advantage during its rebirth. Napster's partnership with Samsung led to the creation of the Samsung YP-910GS, a 20-gigabyte digital audio player that was fully integrated with Napster 2.0. The device allowed users to transfer songs from Napster directly to the unit via a USB connection. The player also boasted an integrated FM transmitter that allowed users to broadcast MP3 playback through their home or car stereo systems.

Although the reborn Napster currently offers a huge catalog of songs, it faces stiff competition from a growing number of firms, particularly iTunes, Rhapsody, and MusicMatch. Apple's iTunes poses the biggest threat with more than 3.5 million songs and thousands more added weekly. It also offers a wide selection of audio books, music videos, and television show episodes as well as movies and iPod games. The popularity of Apple's iPod MP3 player and the introduction of the iTunes-compatible iPhone confer on Apple a distinct advantage: The iPod provides customers with a perfect vehicle to get the music they desire.

Walmart.com also entered the online music business—with 88-cents-per-song downloads. Even Microsoft jumped on the bandwagon and launched a service of its own to compete with iTunes. Other competitors include the thousands of offline and online music record stores that offer CDs and other merchandise, as well as satellite radio and music downloads via mobile phones. Moreover, there are still websites from which music can be downloaded free of charge, albeit illegally. Some potential customers would rather risk getting caught than pay for the music.

Today, Napster gives music lovers the power to listen on-demand to a massive catalog of songs from major and independent labels—legally and for free. They can listen to any of the more than 3 million songs up to three times before they have to purchase them or become a Napster subscriber. The Napster music subscription service also offers a premium experience that includes unlimited access to CD-quality music, while Napster To Go subscribers enjoy unlimited transfer of music to an MP3 player. In 2007, Napster acquired AOL's Music Now service as well as Virgin Digital. Analysts have long thought that Napster needed to boost its user base to better amortize its fixed costs and perhaps attract more advertising dollars. Given the competition, it is imperative that Napster continue to grow its customer base and exploit new avenues for distributing music, such as mobile phones.[33]

1. Evaluate Napster's pricing strategy of charging 99 cents per song. Under what circumstances should the company consider changing this strategy?

2. What factors seem to have the greatest influence on Napster 2.0's pricing decisions? Explain.

3. Assess the level of price competition in the music industry as a whole and within the online music distribution business specifically.

CHAPTER REVIEW

1. Understand the six major stages of the process used to establish prices.

The six stages in the process of setting prices are (1) developing pricing objectives, (2) assessing the target market's evaluation of price, (3) evaluating competitors' prices, (4) choosing a basis for pricing, (5) selecting a pricing strategy, and (6) determining a specific price.

2. Know the issues that are related to developing pricing objectives.

Setting pricing objectives is critical because pricing objectives form a foundation on which the decisions of subsequent stages are based. Organizations may use numerous pricing objectives, including short- and long-term ones, and different ones for different products and market segments. Pricing objectives are overall goals that describe the role of price in a firm's long-range plans. There are several major types of pricing objectives. The most fundamental pricing objective is the organization's survival. Price usually can be easily adjusted to increase sales volume or combat competition to help the organization stay

alive. Profit objectives, which are usually stated in terms of sales dollar volume or percentage change, are normally set at a satisfactory level rather than at a level designed for profit maximization. A sales growth objective focuses on increasing the profit base by increasing sales volume. Pricing for return on investment (ROI) has a specified profit as its objective. A pricing objective to maintain or increase market share implies that market position is linked to success. Other types of pricing objectives include cash flow, status quo, and product quality.

3. Understand the importance of identifying the target market's evaluation of price.

Assessing the target market's evaluation of price tells the marketer how much emphasis to place on price and may help to determine how far above the competition the firm can set its prices. Understanding how important a product is to customers relative to other products, as well as customers' expectations of quality, helps marketers to correctly assess the target market's evaluation of price.

4. Describe how marketers analyze competitive prices.

A marketer needs to be aware of the prices charged for competing brands. This allows the firm to keep its prices in line with competitors' prices when nonprice competition is used. If a company uses price as a competitive tool, it can price its brand below competing brands.

5. Be familiar with the bases used for setting prices.

The three major dimensions on which prices can be based are cost, demand, and competition. When using cost-based pricing, the firm determines price by adding a dollar amount or percentage to the cost of the product. Two common cost-based pricing methods are cost-plus and markup pricing. Demand-based pricing is based on the level of demand for the product. To use this method, a marketer must be able to estimate the amounts of a product that buyers will demand at different prices. Demand-based pricing results in a high price when demand for a product is strong and a low price when demand is weak. In the case of competition-based pricing, costs and revenues are secondary to competitors' prices.

6. Explain the different types of pricing strategies.

A pricing strategy is an approach or a course of action designed to achieve pricing and marketing objectives. The major categories of pricing strategies are differential pricing, new-product pricing, product-line pricing, psychological pricing, professional pricing, and promotional pricing. When marketers employ differential pricing, they charge different buyers different prices for the same quality and quantity of products. Negotiated pricing, secondary-market discounting, periodic discounting, and random discounting are forms of differential pricing. Two strategies used in new-product pricing are price skimming and penetration pricing. With price skimming, the organization charges the highest price that buyers who most desire the product will pay. A penetration price is a low price designed to penetrate a market and gain a significant market share quickly. Product-line pricing establishes and adjusts the prices of multiple products within a product line. This category of strategies includes captive pricing, premium pricing, bait pricing, and price lining. Psychological pricing attempts to influence customer's perceptions of price to make a product's price more attractive. Psychological pricing strategies include reference pricing, bundle pricing, multiple-unit pricing, everyday low prices, odd-even pricing, customary pricing, and prestige pricing. Professional pricing is used by people who have great skill or experience in a particular field, therefore allowing them to set the price. This concept carries the idea that professionals have an ethical responsibility not to overcharge customers. As an ingredient in the marketing mix, price is often coordinated with promotion. The two variables are sometimes so interrelated that the pricing policy is promotion-oriented. Promotional pricing includes price leaders, special-event pricing, and comparison discounting. Price leaders are products that are priced below the usual markup, near cost, or below cost. Special-event pricing involves advertised sales or price-cutting linked to a holiday, season, or event. Marketers who use a comparison discounting strategy to price a product at a specific level and compare it with a higher price.

7. Understand how a final, specific price is determined.

Once a price is determined by using one or more pricing strategies, it will need to be refined to a final price consistent with the pricing practices in a particular market or industry. Using pricing strategies helps in setting a final price. The way that pricing is used in the marketing mix affects the final price. Because pricing is flexible, it is a convenient way to adjust the marketing mix.

ACE self-test

Please visit the student website at **www.prideferrell.com** for ACE Self-Test questions that will help you prepare for exams.

KEY CONCEPTS

pricing objectives
cost-based pricing
cost-plus pricing
markup pricing
demand-based pricing
competition-based pricing
differential pricing
negotiated pricing

secondary-market pricing
periodic discounting
random discounting
price skimming
penetration pricing
product-line pricing
captive pricing
premium pricing

bait pricing
price lining
psychological pricing
reference pricing
bundle pricing
multiple-unit pricing
everyday low prices
  (EDLP)

odd-even pricing
customary pricing
prestige pricing
professional pricing
price leaders
special-event pricing
comparison discounting

ISSUES FOR DISCUSSION AND REVIEW

1. Identify the six stages involved in the process of establishing prices.

2. How does a return on investment pricing objective differ from an objective of increasing market share?

3. Why must marketing objectives and pricing objectives be considered when making pricing decisions?

4. Why should a marketer be aware of competitors' prices?

5. What are the benefits of cost-based pricing?

6. Under what conditions is cost-plus pricing most appropriate?

7. A retailer purchases a can of soup for 24 cents and sells it for 36 cents. Calculate the markup as a percentage of cost and as a percentage of selling price.

8. What is differential pricing? In what ways can it be achieved?

9. For what types of products would price skimming be most appropriate? For what types of products would penetration pricing be more effective?

10. Describe bundle pricing, and give three examples using different industries.

11. What are the advantages and disadvantages of using everyday low prices?

12. Why do customers associate price with quality? When should prestige pricing be used?

13. Are price leaders a realistic approach to pricing? Explain your answer.

MARKETING APPLICATIONS

1. Which strategy—price skimming or penetration pricing—is more appropriate for the following products? Explain.
   a. Short airline flights between cities in Florida
   b. A DVD player
   c. A backpack or book bag with a lifetime warranty
   d. Season tickets for a newly franchised NBA team

2. Visit a few local retail stores to find examples of price lining. For what types of products and stores is this practice most common? For what products and stores is price lining not typical or usable?

3. Find examples (advertisements, personal contacts) that reflect a professional-pricing policy. How is the price established? Are there any restrictions on the services performed at that price?

4. Locate an organization that uses several pricing objectives, and discuss how this approach influences the company's marketing-mix decisions. Are some objectives oriented toward the short term and others toward the long term? How does the marketing environment influence these objectives?

Online Exercise

5. T-Mobile has attempted to position itself as a low-cost cell phone service provider. A person can purchase a calling plan, a cellular phone, and phone accessories at its website. Visit the T-Mobile website at **www.t-mobile.com**.
   a. Determine the various nationwide rates available in your area.
   b. How many different calling plans are available in your area?
   c. What type of pricing strategy is T-Mobile using on its rate plans for your area?

globalEDGE™

Your firm may purchase raw materials from the Czech Republic. Initial estimates put the cost of your first shipment at 1 billion Czech koruna. Find out how much this is in U.S. dollars by using the search term "foreign exchange markets" at **http://globaledge .msu.edu/ibrd** (and check the box "Resource desk only"). Once you reach the FX Street webpage, click on the "Currency Converter." Using your abilities to navigate foreign exchange markets, how much is this amount in U.S. dollars?

How New Balance Runs Its Pricing Strategy

When marketers at New Balance race to develop a new product, they have a particular price in mind from the start. New Balance makes high-quality, high-performance athletic shoes. The brand is, as company ads proclaim, "endorsed by no one," yet the century-old company regularly racks up $1.5 billion in annual worldwide sales and currently trails only Nike and Reebok in the U.S. market.

Major competitors keep labor costs down by manufacturing their shoes outside the United States, mainly in the Far East. In contrast, New Balance produces 25 percent of its shoes in five company-owned New England factories: one in Boston, one in Lawrence, Massachusetts, and three in Maine. How can New Balance remain competitive while balancing "made in America" and "the price is right"?

New Balance marketers strive to satisfy customers in a variety of segments by designing, making, and marketing shoes that fit properly, perform properly, and look good. They begin by studying customer needs in a specific category—for instance, running— and ask questions such as: For what type of runner will the shoe be designed? How many miles is that person likely to run every day or week? What is the runner's body makeup?

Although costs and prices are not the key factors in marketing athletic shoes, they are very important. In the first stage of development, New Balance hires an outside firm to prepare a marketing brief. This gives marketers detailed information about the target customer, outlines the special features that the shoe should have, and identifies the target price that will yield adequate profits.

Members of New Balance's design, development, and marketing teams consider costs an integral part of the marketing strategy. They look at material costs, labor costs, and overhead costs, as well as any special treatments the shoe design may include, such as specially molded pieces, labels, or embroidery. As product development progresses, the teams create a rough cost estimate that will be a major factor in the retail price.

Material costs are a key factor in any athletic shoe product. Upscale high-performance shoes may contain more expensive materials and technology and thus sell for higher prices. Lower-end products may employ less technology and use different materials that perform at a different level. By varying both materials and technology, New Balance can offer a variety of products at different price points for various segments in each sports category, such as running shoes or basketball sneakers. Still, most New Balance shoes are priced at $60 and above, reinforcing the brand's high-performance positioning.

Competitors' prices are also an important part of New Balance's pricing strategy. When New Balance is developing an $80 cushioning shoe, for example, its marketers examine $80 cushioning shoes from competitors, comparing features as well as appearance and color. They often purchase competing shoes to see what else is on the market and how New Balance products match up to the competition.

After designing a new shoe, New Balance will either make a prototype in New England or, if the shoe is to be manufactured abroad, have one of the overseas factories make a prototype. This part of the process gives marketers a more realistic picture of material costs, labor costs, and the costs of any extras needed in actually making the product. Then New Balance makes final adjustments to materials, manufacturing, and design in line with the new product's expected price and costs.

New Balance's decision to maintain production facilities in the United States is proving to be a smart competitive move for two reasons. First, the company has modernized and reorganized its U.S. factories to cut the production cycle from eight days to just eight hours. This means that it can get by with much less inventory. More important, it can start production immediately when retailers order merchandise. Second, New Balance has the manufacturing flexibility to fill special orders for unusual sizes and widths quickly, which strengthens its relationships with retail partners.

Other pressures also affect the way New Balance runs its pricing strategy. Retailers continue to use bargain prices to attract shoppers, a trend that is pushing down the average price of athletic shoes at the cash register. In addition, New Balance must consider how fluctuations in the value of the U.S. dollar against the value of foreign currencies affect its costs and export pricing. Every day brings new challenges and opportunities for New Balance to refine its pricing strategy even more.[34]

Questions for Discussion

1. What pricing objectives does New Balance seem to employ?
2. What type of pricing strategy is New Balance using?
3. What other pricing tools does New Balance employ?

part 7

Distribution Decisions

Developing products that satisfy customers is important, but it is not enough to guarantee successful marketing strategies. Products also must be available in adequate quantities in accessible locations at the times when customers desire them. Part 7 deals with the distribution of products and the marketing channels and institutions that help to make products available. Chapter 14 discusses the structure and functions of marketing channels, as well as the decisions and activities associated with the physical distribution of products, such as order processing, materials handling, warehousing, inventory management, and transportation. Chapter 15 explores retailing and wholesaling, including types of retailers and wholesalers, direct marketing and selling, and strategic retailing issues.

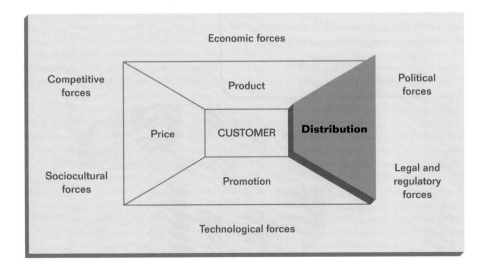

CHAPTER

14

Marketing Channels and Supply-Chain Management

OBJECTIVES

1. Describe the nature and functions of marketing channels.

2. Identify the types of marketing channels.

3. Explore the concepts of leadership, cooperation, and conflict in channel relationships.

4. Recognize common strategies for integrating marketing channels.

5. Examine the major levels of marketing coverage.

6. Recognize the importance of the role of physical distribution activities in supply-chain management and overall marketing strategies.

7. Examine the major physical distribution functions of order processing, inventory management, materials handling, warehousing, and transportation.

FedEx Packages Marketing for Overnight Success

Federal Express Corporation was founded in 1973 by Frederick W. Smith with part of an $8 million inheritance. At the time, the U.S. Postal Service and United Parcel Service (UPS) provided the only means of delivering packages, and they often took several days or more to get packages to their destinations. While a student at Yale in 1965, Smith had studied topology, a mathematical discipline dedicated to geometric configurations. He applied these principles to a business plan that envisioned a hub system from which packages could be delivered across the globe. Smith wrote a paper proposing an independent overnight delivery service. Although he received only a C on the paper, Smith never lost sight of his vision. He believed that many businesses would be willing to pay more to get letters, documents, and packages delivered overnight. He was right.

Federal Express began shipping packages overnight from Memphis, Tennessee, on April 17, 1973. On that first night of operations, the company handled six packages, one of which was a birthday present sent by Smith himself. Today, FedEx Corporation handles more than 3 million overnight packages and documents a day and sends more than 6 million shipments a day around the world, including India, China, and Brazil. It controls more than 50 percent of the overnight delivery market, with an astounding $32 billion in total revenue. FedEx does not view itself as being in the package and document transport business; rather, it describes its business as delivering "certainty." The firm delivers this certainty by connecting the global economy with a wide range of transportation, information, and supply-chain services.

Each package—whether it is dropped off at one of more than 42,000 drop boxes or 715 world service centers or picked up by FedEx courier— is taken to a local FedEx office, where it is trucked to the nearest airport. The package is flown to one of the company's distribution "hubs" for sorting and then flown to the airport nearest its destination. The package is then trucked to another FedEx office, where a courier picks it up and hand delivers it to the correct business or residential recipient. All this takes place overnight, with many packages delivered before 8:00 a.m. the following day. FedEx confirms that roughly 99 percent of its deliveries are made on time.[1] ■

FedEx helps companies make decisions regarding the **distribution** component of the marketing mix, which focuses on the decisions and activities involved in making products available to customers when and where they want to purchase them. Choosing marketing channels and managing supply chains are major issues in the development of competitive marketing strategies.

In this chapter we focus on marketing channels and supply-chain management. First, we discuss the nature of marketing channels and supply-chain management, including the need for intermediaries. Next, we outline the types of marketing channels and consider supply-chain management, including behavioral patterns within marketing channels. We also explore ways to integrate marketing channels and how marketers determine the appropriate intensity of market coverage for a product. Finally, we look at the role of physical distribution within the supply chain, including its objectives and basic functions.

Marketing Channels and Supply-Chain Management

A **marketing channel** (also called a *channel of distribution* or *distribution channel*) is a group of individuals and organizations that directs the flow of products from producers to customers. The major role of marketing channels is to make products available at the right time, at the right place, and in the right quantities. Providing customer satisfaction should be the driving force behind marketing-channel decisions. Buyers' needs and behavior are therefore important concerns of channel members.

Some marketing channels are direct, meaning that the product goes directly from the producer to customer. For example, when a customer orders a laptop from Dell,

Technology Facilitates Supply Chain Management

Technology-based tools help supply chain managers improve efficiency and coordination.

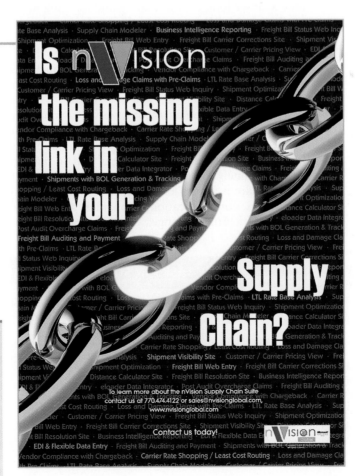

distribution The decisions and activities that make products available to customers when and where they want to purchase them

marketing channel A group of individuals and organizations directing the flow of products from producers to customers

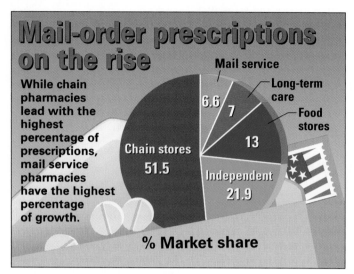

Source: IMS Health, October 2005

this product is sent from the manufacturer to the customer. Most channels, however, have marketing intermediaries. A **marketing intermediary** (or *middleman*) links producers to other intermediaries or to ultimate consumers through contractual arrangements or through the purchase and reselling of products. Marketing intermediaries can perform most marketing activities. They also play key roles in customer relationship management not only through their distribution activities but also by maintaining databases and information systems to help all members of the marketing channel maintain effective customer relationships. For example, eBay serves as a marketing intermediary between Internet sellers and buyers. The online auction site not only provides a forum for these exchanges, but it also keeps an extensive database of members' rankings to facilitate relationships among eBay channel members.[2]

Wholesalers and retailers are examples of intermediaries. Wholesalers buy and resell products to other wholesalers, to retailers, and to industrial customers. Retailers purchase products and resell them to ultimate consumers. For example, your local supermarket probably purchased the Tylenol or Advil on its shelves from a wholesaler, which purchased that product, along with other over-the-counter drugs, from manufacturers such as McNeil Consumer Labs and Whitehall-Robins. We'll take a closer look at wholesaling and retailing in Chapter 15.

An important function of the marketing channel is the joint effort of all channel members to create a supply chain, a total distribution system that serves customers and creates a competitive advantage. **Supply-chain management** refers to long-term partnerships among marketing-channel members that reduce inefficiencies, costs, and redundancies in the marketing channel and develop innovative approaches to satisfy customers.

Supply-chain management involves manufacturing, research, sales, advertising, shipping, and most of all, cooperation and understanding of tradeoffs throughout the whole channel to achieve the optimal level of efficiency and service. Table 14.1 outlines the key tasks involved in supply-chain management. Whereas traditional marketing channels tend to focus on producers, wholesalers, retailers, and customers, the supply chain is a broader concept that includes facilitating agencies such as shipping companies, communication companies, and other organizations that indirectly take part in marketing exchanges. Thus the supply chain includes all entities that facilitate

marketing intermediary A middleman linking producers to other middlemen or ultimate consumers through contractual arrangements or through the purchase and resale of products

supply-chain management Long-term partnerships among marketing-channel members that reduce inefficiencies, costs, and redundancies and develop innovative approaches to satisfy customers

table 14.1	KEY TASKS IN SUPPLY-CHAIN MANAGEMENT
Planning	Organizational and systemwide coordination of marketing-channel partnerships to meet customers' product needs.
Sourcing	Purchasing of necessary resources, goods, and services from suppliers to support all supply-chain members.
Facilitating delivery	All activities designed to move the product through the marketing channel to the end user.
Building relationships	All marketing activities related to sales, service, and the development of long-term customer relationships.

Partnering Helps Drive Toyota to the Top

To do a better job of reaching and satisfying customers through improved channel efficiencies, companies and channel members must choose their partners carefully, communicate clearly, and agree on the expectations and obligations of both sides.

Excelling at channel partnerships is one of the many reasons that Toyota is one of the world's leading makers of automobiles. Toyota has long been praised for its production system that focuses on standardized processes and tooling. But the company believes in continual improvement, both for Toyota and for its suppliers. Toyota's channel partnerships are based on the principle that product knowledge is intellectual property, but process knowledge is shared. Toyota offers process-improvement lessons to its suppliers, disseminating information across Toyota's channel. The company even developed the Bluegrass Automotive Manufacturers Association in the United States, which provides information on the best practices in the industry to all members.

Toyota also works with suppliers to help them develop more efficient practices, which brings the benefit of standardization beyond production and into supply-chain management. Toyota believes that unless every partner is working together to lower costs and raise efficiency, the goal will never be met. However, despite evidence of the importance of working with channel partners, only 6 percent of businesses that responded to a recent survey said that they standardize with supply-channel partners.

Companies that do business globally face the challenge of partnering with hundreds or thousands of channel members, sometimes across vast distances. Toyota famously tackled this challenge by creating multiple short channels. Toyota has built 52 plants in 27 markets outside Japan to reduce costs by shortening the supply channel. Avoiding the high cost of importing has improved Toyota's profits. In fact, as American car companies move overseas, Toyota is building more factories in the United States, including a strategically located truck factory in Texas.

Through partnering with suppliers, Toyota hopes to increase efficiencies to ensure its ability to remain highly competitive in the global automotive business.[a]

product distribution and benefit from cooperative efforts. Consider that Intel, the computer chip maker, spends $3 billion to build a new semiconductor facility, and it loses $1 million a day if an assembly line goes down owing to system failures or part shortages. Consequently, Intel requires its equipment suppliers to respond to failures within 15 minutes.[3]

Supply chains start with the customer and require the cooperation of channel members to satisfy customer requirements. All members should focus on cooperation to reduce the costs of all channel members and thereby improve profits. When the buyer, the seller, marketing intermediaries, and facilitating agencies work together, the cooperative relationship results in compromise and adjustments that meet customers' needs regarding delivery, scheduling, packaging, or other requirements.

Technology has improved supply-chain management capabilities on a global basis dramatically. Information technology in particular has created an almost seamless distribution process for matching inventory needs to customers' requirements. With integrated information sharing among channel members, costs can be reduced, service can be improved, and value provided to the customer can be enhanced. Indeed, information is crucial in operating global supply chains efficiently and effectively. Each marketing channel member requires information from other channel members. For example, suppliers need order and forecast information from the manufacturer; they also may need availability information from their own suppliers. Companies must be able to identify changes in the supply chain, assess their potential impact, and respond to these changes rapidly.[4] Customer relationship management (CRM) systems exploit the information from supply-chain partners' database and information systems to help all channel members make marketing strategy decisions that develop and sustain desirable customer relationships. Thus, managing relationships with supply-chain partners is crucial to satisfying customers. CRM is gaining popularity, with big companies such as Hewlett-Packard and Amazon.com spending large sums of money on implementation and support for data mining and CRM analytical applications. By 2008, companies that supply CRM technology, such as Siebel, SAS, and NetlQ, are expected to bring in over $11 billion in revenue.[5]

The Significance of Marketing Channels

Although distribution decisions need not precede other marketing decisions, they are a powerful influence on the rest of the marketing mix. Channel decisions are critical because they determine a product's market presence and buyers' accessibility to the product. Consider that small businesses are more likely to purchase computers from office-supply stores such as Office Depot or warehouse clubs such as Sam's, putting computer companies without distribution through these outlets at a disadvantage. Channel decisions have additional strategic significance because they generally entail long-term commitments. Thus it is usually easier to change prices or promotional strategies than to change marketing channels.

Marketing channels serve many functions, including creating utility and facilitating exchange efficiencies. Although some of these functions may be performed by a single channel member, most functions are accomplished through both independent and joint efforts of channel members. When managed effectively, the relationships among channel members also can form supply chains that benefit all members of the channel, including the ultimate consumer.

Marketing Channels Create Utility. Marketing channels create three types of utility: time, place, and possession. *Time utility* is having products available when the customer wants them. *Place utility* is created by making products available in locations where customers wish to purchase them. *Possession utility* means that the customer has access to the product to use or to store for future use. Possession utility can occur through ownership or through arrangements that give the customer the right to use the product, such as a lease or rental agreement. Channel members sometimes create *form utility* by assembling, preparing, or otherwise refining the product to suit individual customer needs.

Marketing Channels Facilitate Exchange Efficiencies. Marketing intermediaries can reduce the costs of exchanges by performing certain services or functions efficiently. Even if producers and buyers are located in the same city, there are costs associated with exchanges. As Figure 14.1 shows, when four buyers seek products from four producers, 16 transactions are possible. If one intermediary serves both producers and buyers, the number of transactions can be reduced to 8. Intermediaries are specialists in facilitating exchanges. They provide valuable assistance because of their access to and control over important resources used in the proper functioning of marketing channels.

Nevertheless, the press, consumers, public officials, and even other marketers freely criticize intermediaries, especially wholesalers. Critics accuse wholesalers of being inefficient and parasitic. Buyers often wish to make the distribution channel as short as possible, assuming the fewer the intermediaries, the lower the price will be.

Critics who suggest that eliminating wholesalers would lower customer prices fail to recognize that this would not eliminate the need for the services that wholesalers

EFFICIENCY IN EXCHANGES PROVIDED BY AN INTERMEDIARY

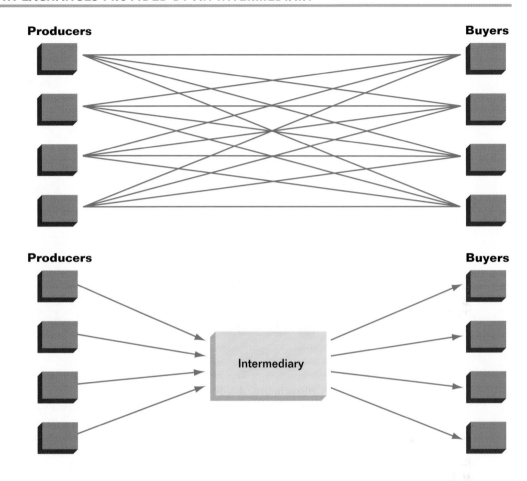

provide. Although wholesalers can be eliminated, their functions cannot. Other channel members would have to perform those functions, and customers still would have to pay for them. In addition, all producers would have to deal directly with retailers or customers, meaning that every producer would have to keep voluminous records and hire enough personnel to deal with a multitude of customers. Customers might end up paying a great deal more for products because prices would reflect the costs of less efficient channel members.

Because suggestions to eliminate wholesalers come from both ends of the marketing channel, wholesalers must be careful to perform only those marketing activities that are truly desired. To survive, they must be more efficient and more customer-focused than other marketing institutions. Indeed, research suggests that lower wholesale prices may result in higher sales volume when combined with low retailing costs at discount firms such as Wal-Mart.[6]

Types of Marketing Channels

Because marketing channels appropriate for one product may be less suitable for others, many different distribution paths have been developed. The various marketing channels can be classified generally as channels for consumer products and channels for business products.

Channels for Consumer Products.   Figure 14.2 (on page 350) illustrates several channels used in the distribution of consumer products. Channel A depicts the direct

figure 14.2

TYPICAL MARKETING CHANNELS FOR CONSUMER PRODUCTS

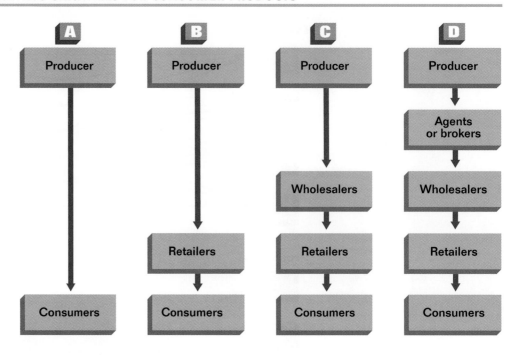

movement of goods from producer to consumers. For example, the legal advice given by attorneys moves through channel A. Producers that sell goods directly from their factories to end users are using direct marketing channels, as are companies that sell their own products over the Internet, such as Dell Computer. In fact, the Internet has become an important component of many companies' distribution strategies. Although direct marketing channels are the simplest, they are not necessarily the most effective distribution method. Faced with the strategic choice of going directly to the customer or using intermediaries, a firm must evaluate the benefits to customers of going direct versus the transaction costs involved in using intermediaries.

Channel B, which moves goods from the producer to a retailer and then to customers, is a frequent choice of large retailers because it allows them to buy in quantity from manufacturers. Retailers such as Target and Wal-Mart sell clothing, stereos, and many other items purchased directly from producers. New automobiles and new college textbooks are also sold through this type of marketing channel. Primarily nonstore retailers, such as L.L. Bean and J. Crew, also use this type of channel.

A long-standing distribution channel, especially for consumer products, channel C takes goods from the producer to a wholesaler, then to a retailer, and finally, to consumers. This is a practical option for producers that sell to hundreds of

marketing ENTREPRENEURS

David Ansel

HIS BUSINESS: The Soup Peddler

FOUNDED: 2002, when Ansel was 28

SUCCESS: Has grown from 17 "Soupies" to more than 2,000

David Ansel, a software developer, followed his girlfriend to Austin, Texas; there, neither the relationship nor the job prospects panned out. To make ends meet, Ansel began making soup and selling it to his neighbors, delivering it in a cooler he pulled behind his yellow bicycle. After he outgrew his own kitchen, he leased space in a local Thai restaurant after hours. His delicious homemade soups quickly gained a following well beyond his south Austin neighborhood. Today, the Soup Peddler has his own production facility and a crew of eight, and he delivers soup all over Austin in two orange refrigerated trucks (although some soup is still delivered by bike in his home neighborhood).[b]

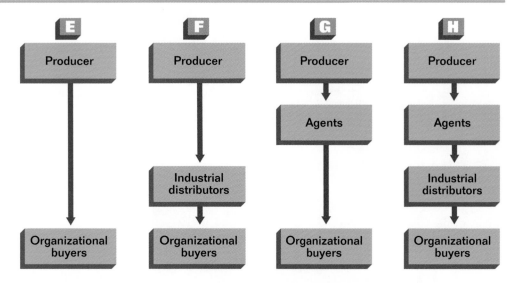

figure 14.3

TYPICAL MARKETING CHANNELS FOR BUSINESS PRODUCTS

Channels for Business Products

The Internet allows many organizations to facilitate the distribution of their products directly to business channels.

thousands of customers through thousands of retailers. A single producer finds it hard to do business directly with thousands of retailers. Consider the number of retailers marketing Wrigley's chewing gum. It would be extremely difficult, if not impossible, for Wrigley to deal directly with each retailer that sells its brand of gum. Manufacturers of tobacco products, some home appliances, hardware, and many convenience goods sell their products to wholesalers, which then sell to retailers, which, in turn, do business with individual consumers.

Channel D, through which goods pass from producer to agents to wholesalers to retailers and then to consumers, is used frequently for products intended for mass distribution, such as processed foods. For example, to place its cracker line in specific retail outlets, a food processor may hire an agent (or a food broker) to sell the crackers to wholesalers. Wholesalers then sell the crackers to supermarkets, vending-machine operators, and other retail outlets.

Contrary to popular opinion, a long channel may be the most efficient distribution channel for some consumer goods. When several channel intermediaries perform specialized functions, costs may be lower than when one channel member tries to perform them all.

Channels for Business Products. Figure 14.3 shows four of the most common channels for business products. As with consumer products, manufacturers of business products sometimes work with more than one level of wholesalers.

Channel E illustrates the direct channel for business products. In contrast to consumer goods, more than half of all business products, especially expensive equipment, is sold through direct channels.

Problems no longer
keep you up at night.
Solutions do.

att.com/OnwardSmallBiz

You are the small business owner. Always thinking, planning and solving. Introducing a program that's uniquely yours. An online resource rich with inspiration. Where relevant content comes to you, based on your industry or interest. With online courses, one-on-one consulting, and constructive news to help keep you at the forefront of your world. Get ready to engage, exchange and excel. Log on, and it's onward, business. **att.com/OnwardSmallBiz**

The new **at&t**
Your world. Delivered.™

© 2007 AT&T Knowledge Ventures. All rights reserved. AT&T and the AT&T logo are trademarks of AT&T Knowledge Ventures.

Business customers like to communicate directly with producers, especially when expensive or technically complex products are involved. For this reason, business buyers prefer to purchase expensive and highly complex mainframe computers directly from IBM, Cray, and other mainframe producers. Intel has established direct marketing channels for selling its microprocessor chips to computer manufacturers. In these circumstances, a customer wants the technical assistance and personal assurances that only a producer can provide.

In the second business products channel, channel F, an industrial distributor facilitates exchanges between the producer and the customer. An **industrial distributor** is an independent business that takes title to products and carries inventories. Industrial distributors usually sell standardized items such as maintenance supplies, production tools, and small operating equipment. Some industrial distributors carry a wide variety of product lines. W.W. Grainger, for example, sells more than $6 billion of power and hand tools, pumps, janitorial supplies, and many other products to producer, government, and institutional markets around the world.[7] Other industrial distributors specialize in one or a small number of lines. Industrial distributors are carrying an increasing percentage of business products. They can be used most effectively when a product has broad market appeal, is easily stocked and serviced, is sold in small quantities, and is needed on demand to avoid high losses.

Using Multiple Marketing Channels

Many products—including Millstone Coffee—are marketed through multiple distribution channels.

The third channel for business products, channel G, employs a manufacturers' agent, an independent businessperson who sells complementary products of several producers in assigned territories and is compensated through commissions. Unlike an industrial distributor, a manufacturers' agent does not acquire title to the products and usually does not take possession. Acting as a salesperson on behalf of the producers, a manufacturers' agent has little or no latitude in negotiating prices or sales terms.

Finally, channel H includes both a manufacturers' agent and an industrial distributor. This channel may be appropriate when the producer wishes to cover a large geographic area but maintains no sales force because of highly seasonal demand or because it cannot afford a sales force. This type of channel also can be useful for a business marketer that wants to enter a new geographic market without expanding its existing sales force.

Multiple Marketing Channels and Channel Alliances.   To reach diverse target markets, manufacturers may use several marketing channels simultaneously, with each channel involving a different group of intermediaries. For example, when Del Monte markets ketchup for household use, it is sold to supermarkets through grocery wholesalers or, in some cases, directly to retailers, whereas ketchup going to restaurants or institutions follows a different distribution channel. In some instances a producer may prefer **dual distribution,** the use of two or more marketing channels to distribute the same products to the same target market. An example of dual distribution is a firm that sells products through retail outlets and its own mail-order catalog or website. For example, Kellogg sells its cereals directly to large retail grocery chains (channel B) and to food wholesalers that, in turn, sell them to retailers (channel C). Another example of dual distribution is a firm that sells products through retail

industrial distributor An independent business that takes title to business products and carries inventories

dual distribution The use of two or more channels to distribute the same product to the same target market

outlets and its own mail-order catalog or website. Dual distribution can cause dissatisfaction among wholesalers and smaller retailers when they must compete with large retail grocery chains that make direct purchases from manufacturers such as Kellogg. The practice of dual distribution has been challenged as being anticompetitive.

A **strategic channel alliance** exists when the products of one organization are distributed through the marketing channels of another. The products of the two firms are often similar with respect to target markets or uses, but they are not direct competitors. For example, a brand of bottled water might be distributed through a marketing channel for soft drinks, or a domestic cereal producer might form a strategic channel alliance with a European food processor. Ocean Spray and PepsiCo formed such an alliance, whereby Pepsi manufactured, bottled, and distributed single-serve cranberry juice products under the Ocean Spray name.[8] Alliances can provide benefits for both the organization that owns the marketing channel and the company whose brand is being distributed through the channel.

Selecting Marketing Channels

Selecting appropriate marketing channels is important. While the process varies across organizations, channel-selection decisions usually are significantly affected by one or more of the following factors: customer characteristics, product attributes, type of organization, competition, marketing environmental forces, and characteristics of intermediaries (see Figure 14.4).

Customer Characteristics.   Marketing managers must consider the characteristics of target-market members in channel selection. As we have discussed, the channels appropriate for consumers are different from those for business customers. A different

strategic channel alliance
An agreement whereby the products of one organization are distributed through the marketing channels of another

figure 14.4

SELECTING MARKETING CHANNELS

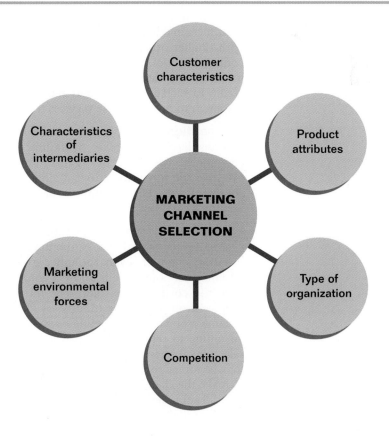

marketing channel will be required for business customers purchasing carpet for commercial buildings compared with consumers purchasing carpet for their homes. As already mentioned, business customers often prefer to deal directly with producers (or very knowledgeable channel intermediaries such as industrial distributors), especially for highly technical or expensive products such as mainframe computers, jet airplanes, and large mining machines. Moreover, business customers are more likely to buy complex products requiring strict specifications and technical assistance and/or to buy in considerable quantities.

Consumers, on the other hand, generally buy limited quantities of a product, purchase from retailers, and often do not mind limited customer service. Additionally, when customers are concentrated in a small geographic area, a more direct channel may be ideal, but when many customers are spread across an entire state or nation, distribution through multiple intermediaries is likely to be more efficient.

Product Attributes.   The attributes of the product can have a strong influence on the choice of marketing channels. Marketers of complex and expensive products such as automobiles likely will employ short channels, as will marketers of perishable products such as dairy and produce. Less expensive, more standardized products such as soft drinks and canned goods can employ longer channels with many intermediaries. In addition, channel decisions may be affected by a product's sturdiness: Fragile products that require special handling are more likely to be distributed through shorter channels to minimize the risk of damage. Firms that desire to convey an exclusive image for their products may wish to limit the number of outlets available.

Type of Organization.   Clearly, the characteristics of the organization will have a great impact on the distribution channels chosen. Owing to their sheer size, larger firms may be better able to negotiate better deals with vendors or other channel members. Compared with small firms, they may be in better positions to have more distribution centers, which may reduce delivery times to customers. A smaller regional company using regional or local channel members may be in a position to better serve customers in that region compared with a larger, less flexible organization. Compared with smaller organizations, large companies can use an extensive product mix as a competitive tool. Smaller firms may not have the resources to develop their own sales force, to ship their products long distances, to store or own products, or to extend credit. In such cases, they may have to include other channel members that have the resources to provide these services to customers efficiently and cost-effectively.

Competition.   Competition is another important factor for supply-chain managers to consider. The success or failure of a competitor's marketing channel may encourage or dissuade an organization from considering a similar approach. A firm also may be forced to adopt a similar strategy to remain competitive. In a highly competitive market, it is important for a company to keep its costs low so that it can underprice its competitors if necessary.

Marketing Environment Forces.   Environmental forces also can play a role in channel selection. Adverse economic conditions might force an organization to use a low-cost channel, even though customer satisfaction is reduced. In contrast, a booming economy might allow a company to choose a channel that previously had been too costly to consider. The introduction of new technology might cause an organization to add or modify its channel strategy. For instance, as the Internet became a powerful marketing communication tool, many companies were forced to go online to remain competitive. Government regulations also can affect channel selection. As new labor and environmental regulations are passed, an organization may be forced to modify its existing distribution channel structure. Firms may choose to make the changes before regulations are passed in order to appear compliant or to avoid legal issues. Governmental regulations also can include trade agreements with other countries that complicate the supply chain.

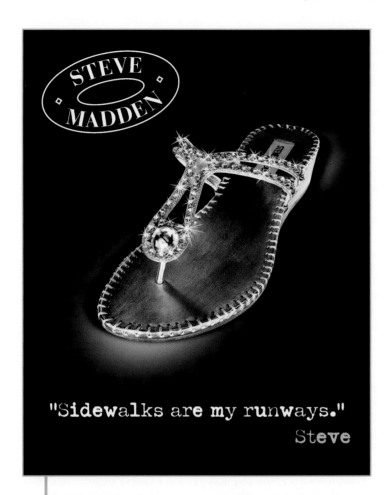

"Sidewalks are my runways."
Steve

Channel Leadership

Steve Madden Shoes provides channel leadership in the distribution of its products.

channel power The ability of one channel member to influence another member's goal achievement

Characteristics of Intermediaries. When an organization believes that a current intermediary is not promoting the organization's products adequately, it may reconsider its channel choices. In these instances the company may choose another channel member to handle its products, or it may choose to eliminate intermediaries altogether and perform the eliminated intermediaries' functions itself. Alternatively, an existing intermediary may not offer an appropriate mix of services, forcing an organization to change to another intermediary.

Channel Leadership, Cooperation, and Conflict

Each channel member performs a different role in the system and agrees (implicitly or explicitly) to accept certain rights, responsibilities, rewards, and sanctions for nonconformity. Each channel member also holds certain expectations of other channel members. Retailers, for instance, expect wholesalers to maintain adequate inventories and deliver goods on time. Wholesalers expect retailers to honor payment agreements and keep them informed of inventory needs.

Channel partnerships facilitate effective supply-chain management when partners agree on objectives, policies, and procedures for physical distribution efforts associated with the supplier's products. Such partnerships eliminate redundancies and reassign tasks for maximum systemwide efficiency. One of the best-known partnerships is that between Wal-Mart and Procter & Gamble. Procter & Gamble locates some of its staff near Wal-Mart's purchasing department in Bentonville, Arkansas, to establish and maintain the supply chain. Sharing information through a cooperative computer system, Procter & Gamble monitors Wal-Mart's inventory and additional data to determine production and distribution plans for its products. The results are increased efficiency, decreased inventory costs, and greater satisfaction for the customers of both companies. In this section we discuss channel member behavior, including leadership, cooperation, and conflict, that marketers must understand to make effective channel decisions.

Many marketing-channel decisions are determined by consensus. Producers and intermediaries coordinate efforts for mutual benefit. Some marketing channels, however, are organized and controlled by a single channel leader, or *channel captain.* The channel captain may be a producer, a wholesaler, or a retailer. Channel captains may establish channel policies and coordinate development of the marketing mix. Wal-Mart, for example, dominates the supply chain for its retail stores by virtue of the magnitude of its resources (especially information management) and strong, nationwide customer base. To become a captain, a channel member must want to influence overall channel performance. To attain desired objectives, the captain must possess **channel power,** the ability to influence another channel member's goal achievement. The member that becomes the channel captain will accept the responsibilities and exercise the power associated with this role.

Channel cooperation is vital if each member is to gain something from other members. By cooperating, retailers, wholesalers, and suppliers can speed up inventory replenishment, improve customer service, and cut the costs of bringing products to the consumer.[9] Without cooperation, neither overall channel goals nor member goals can be realized. All channel members must recognize and understand that the success of one firm in the channel depends, in part, on other member firms. Thus marketing channel members should make a coordinated effort to satisfy market requirements. Channel cooperation leads to greater trust among channel members and improves the overall functioning of the channel. It also leads to more satisfying relationships among channel members.

Although all channel members work toward the same general goal—distributing products profitably and efficiently—members sometimes may disagree about the best methods for attaining this goal. However, if self-interest creates misunderstanding about role expectations, the end result is frustration and conflict for the whole channel. Consider what happened when the New England–based Hannaford Brothers supermarket chain introduced a new system that rated the nutritional content of every single product on the stores' shelves for the benefit of consumers looking for the healthiest products. Although Hannaford Brothers' executives insisted that they simply wanted to offer confused shoppers more guidance on finding healthful choices, many of its suppliers grumbled when the supermarket gave their products a lower than expected rating, especially those marketing products touted as "healthy" but with significant salt or sugar content.[10] For individual organizations to function together, each channel member must clearly communicate and understand role expectations. Communication difficulties are a potential form of channel conflict because ineffective communication leads to frustration, misunderstandings, and ill-coordinated strategies, jeopardizing further coordination.

The increased use of multiple channels of distribution, driven partly by new technology, has increased the potential for conflict between manufacturers and intermediaries. Hewlett-Packard, for example, makes products available directly to consumers through its website, thereby directly competing with existing distributors and retailers, such as Best Buy and CompUSA. Channel conflicts also arise when intermediaries overemphasize competing products or diversify into product lines traditionally handled by other intermediaries. Sometimes conflict develops because producers strive to increase efficiency by circumventing intermediaries. Such conflict is occurring in marketing channels for computer software. A number of software-only stores are establishing direct relationships with software producers, bypassing whole-sale distributors altogether.

There are several ways to improve channel cooperation. If a marketing channel is viewed as a unified supply chain competing with other systems, individual members will be less likely to take actions that create disadvantages for other members. Similarly, channel members should agree to direct efforts toward common objectives so that channel roles can be structured for maximum marketing effectiveness, which, in turn, can help members achieve individual objectives. A critical component in co-operation is a precise definition of each channel member's tasks. A precise definition provides a basis for reviewing the intermediaries' performance and helps to reduce conflicts because each channel member knows exactly what is expected of it.

Channel Integration

Channel members can either combine and control most activities or pass them on to another channel member. Channel functions may be transferred between intermediaries and to producers and even customers. However, a channel member cannot eliminate functions; unless buyers themselves perform the functions, they must pay for the labor and resources needed to perform the functions.

Various channel stages may be combined under the management of a channel captain either horizontally or vertically. Such integration may stabilize supply, reduce costs, and increase coordination of channel members.

vertical channel integration
Combining two or more stages of the marketing channel under one management

Vertical Channel Integration.   **Vertical channel integration** combines two or more stages of the channel under one management. This may occur when one member of a marketing channel purchases the operations of another member or simply performs the functions of another member, eliminating the need for that

Radio Shack Faces Channel Challenge

Radio Shack believes in channel integration and cooperation. The Fort Worth–based electronics specialty retailer operates 4,972 company-owned stores, 1,702 dealer and franchisee outlets, more than 700 wireless phone kiosks, regional distribution centers, and a shopping website. Its retail stores sell everything from high-end electronic products such as HDTVs, digital cameras, cell phones, and satellite navigational devices to low-end items such as batteries, plugs, and connectors. And Radio Shack is the largest U.S. seller of mobile phones and accessories, which account for about a third of its sales.

The company faces competition from discounters such as Wal-Mart and Target, as well as a growing range of stores owned by wireless service providers such as Verizon, Cingular, and T-Mobile. To maintain its position in wireless, where it has about 10 percent of the U.S. market, Radio Shack has agreements to operate cell phone kiosks in 542 Sam's Warehouse Club locations and a growing network of Sprint- and Cingular-branded kiosks in shopping malls.

Under the agreements, the Radio Shack name will not be used at these kiosk locations, and there will be no brand tie-in with the retail stores. Nonetheless, Radio Shack sees benefits in the arrangements. For one, Radio Shack's marketers believe that the company will make incremental sales and profits through these partnerships that it would not have otherwise made because these customers were not shopping at Radio Shack stores.

In general, then, Radio Shack's company-owned stores, dealerships, and franchisee stores compete among each other as well as with Sam's Club and the Sprint and Cingular kiosks that Radio Shack manages. When you consider that the company's website is in competition with all these retail outlets, it is easy to see why maintaining marketing-channel harmony may be challenging to Radio Shack.[c]

intermediary. For example, Smithfield Foods, a leading U.S. food processor, acquired Premium Standard Farms, Inc., the number 2 U.S. hog farmer. Although the purchase may trigger antitrust concerns, it reflects a trend among large meat processors to grow and slaughter their own livestock instead of obtaining them from independent farmers.[11] Unlike conventional channel systems, participants in vertical channel integration coordinate efforts to reach a desired target market. In this more progressive approach to distribution, channel members regard other members as extensions of their own operations. Vertically integrated channels are often more effective against competition because of increased bargaining power and the sharing of information and responsibilities. At one end of a vertically integrated channel, a manufacturer might provide advertising and training assistance, and the retailer at the other end might buy the manufacturer's products in large quantities and actively promote them.

Integration has been institutionalized successfully in marketing channels called **vertical marketing systems (VMSs),** in which a single channel member coordinates or manages channel activities to achieve efficient, low-cost distribution aimed at satisfying target-market customers. Vertical integration brings most or all stages of the marketing channel under common control or ownership. The Limited, a retail clothing chain, uses a wholly owned subsidiary, Mast Industries, as its primary supply source. Radio Shack operates as a VMS, encompassing both wholesale and retail functions.

vertical marketing systems (VMSs) A marketing channel managed by a single channel member

Because efforts of individual channel members are combined in a VMS, marketing activities can be coordinated for maximum effectiveness and economy without duplication of services. VMSs are competitive, accounting for a share of retail sales in consumer goods.

Most VMSs take one of three forms: corporate, administered, or contractual. A *corporate VMS* combines all stages of the marketing channel, from producers to consumers, under a single owner. Supermarket chains that own food-processing plants and large retailers that purchase wholesaling and production facilities are examples of corporate VMSs. In an *administered VMS,* channel members are independent, but a high level of interorganizational management is achieved through informal coordination. Although individual channel members maintain autonomy, as in conventional marketing channels, one channel member (such as a producer or large retailer) dominates the administered VMS so that distribution decisions take the whole system into account. Under a *contractual VMS,* the most popular type of VMS, channel members are linked by legal agreements spelling out each member's rights and obligations. Franchise organizations, such as McDonald's and KFC, are contractual VMSs. Other contractual VMSs include wholesaler-sponsored groups, such as Independent Grocers' Alliance (IGA) stores, and retailer-sponsored cooperatives, which own and operate their own wholesalers.

Horizontal Channel Integration.   Combining organizations at the same level of operation under one management constitutes **horizontal channel integration.** An organization may integrate horizontally by merging with other organizations at the same level in the marketing channel. The owner of a dry-cleaning firm, for example, might buy and combine several other existing dry-cleaning establishments. Japan Tobacco, the world's third largest cigarette maker, acquired Britain's Gallaher Group PLC, which owns several upscale cigarette brands and has a strong presence in Russia and Eastern Europe, for about $14.7 billion. The purchase boosted Japan Tobacco's global market share from 3 to 11 percent.[12] Horizontal integration may enable a firm to generate sufficient sales revenue to integrate vertically as well.

Although horizontal integration permits efficiencies and economies of scale in purchasing, marketing research, advertising, and specialized personnel, it is not always the most effective method of improving distribution. Problems of size often follow, resulting in decreased flexibility, difficulties in coordination, and the need for additional marketing research and large-scale planning. Unless distribution functions for the various units can be performed more efficiently under unified management than under the previously separate managements, horizontal integration will neither reduce costs nor improve the competitive position of the integrating firm.

Intensity of Market Coverage

In addition to deciding how to organize marketing channels for distributing a product, marketers must determine the intensity of coverage that a product should get, that is, the number and kinds of outlets in which it will be sold. This decision depends on the characteristics of the product and the target market. To achieve the desired intensity of market coverage, distribution must correspond to behavior patterns of buyers. In considering products for purchase, consumers take into account replacement rate, product adjustment (services), duration of consumption, time required to find the product, and similar factors.[13] These variables directly affect the intensity of market coverage. Three major levels of market coverage are intensive, selective, and exclusive distribution.

Intensive distribution uses all available outlets for distributing a product. Intensive distribution is appropriate for convenience products such as bread, chewing gum, soft drinks, and newspapers. Convenience products have a high replacement rate and require almost no service. To meet these demands, intensive distribution is necessary, and multiple channels may be used to sell through all possible outlets. For example, soft drinks, snacks, laundry detergent, and aspirin are available at convenience stores,

horizontal channel integration Combining organizations at the same level of operation under one management

intensive distribution Using all available outlets to distribute a product

Intensive Distribution

Chewing gum, such as Extra, is distributed through intensive distribution.

NEW MOUTHWATERINGLY
COOL WATERMELON
REMARKABLY LONG LASTING

service stations, supermarkets, discount stores, and other types of retailers. To consumers, availability means that a store is located nearby and minimum time is necessary to search for the product at the store. Sales may have a direct relationship to product availability.

Selective distribution uses only some available outlets in an area to distribute a product. Selective distribution is appropriate for shopping products; durable goods such as televisions, stereos, and home computers usually fall into this category. These products are more expensive than convenience goods, and consumers are willing to spend more time visiting several retail outlets to compare prices, designs, styles, and other features. Selective distribution is desirable when a special effort, such as customer service from a channel member, is important. Shopping products require differentiation at the point of purchase. Many business products are sold on a selective basis to maintain some control over the distribution process.

Exclusive distribution uses only one outlet in a relatively large geographic area. Exclusive distribution is suitable for products purchased infrequently, consumed over a long period of time, or requiring service or information to fit them to buyers' needs. It is also used for expensive, high-quality products, such as Porsche, Bentley, and Rolls-Royce automobiles. It is not appropriate for convenience products and many shopping products.

Physical Distribution in Supply-Chain Management

selective distribution Using only some available outlets to distribute a product

exclusive distribution Using a single outlet in a fairly large geographic area to distribute a product

physical distribution Activities used to move products from producers to consumers and other end users

outsourcing The contracting of physical distribution tasks to third parties who do not have managerial authority within the marketing channel

Physical distribution, also known as *logistics,* refers to the activities used to move products from producers to consumers and other end users. Physical distribution systems must meet the needs of both the supply chain and customers. Distribution activities are thus an important part of supply-chain planning and require the cooperation of all partners. Often one channel member manages physical distribution for all channel members.

Within the marketing channel, physical distribution activities may be performed by a producer, a wholesaler, or a retailer, or they may be outsourced. In the context of distribution, **outsourcing** is the contracting of physical distribution tasks to third parties that do not have managerial authority within the marketing channel. Most physical distribution activities can be outsourced to third-party firms that have special expertise in areas such as warehousing, transportation, inventory management, and information technology. Some manufacturing firms, for example, outsource delivery services to Penske Truck Leasing, a joint venture between General Electric and Penske Corp. Penske Truck, in turn, has outsourced some of its own activities, including some scheduling, billing, and invoicing services, to employees and contractors in Mexico and India. Outsourcing has saved Penske $15 million and helped the company to improve efficiency and customer service.[14] Cooperative relationships

Reducing Distribution Costs

Distribution-related organizations, such as Data2Logistics, help companies improve efficiencies and reduce costs.

with third-party organizations, such as trucking companies, warehouses, and data-service providers, can help to reduce marketing-channel costs and boost service and customer satisfaction for all supply-chain partners. For example, several e-businesses, as well as some traditional bricks-and-mortar ones, have outsourced physical distribution activities, including shipping and warehousing, to build a supply chain of strategic partners to maximize customer service. Such relationships are increasingly being integrated in the supply chain to achieve physical distribution objectives. When choosing companies through which to outsource, marketers must be cautious and use efficient firms that help the outsourcing company provide excellent customer service.

Planning an efficient physical distribution system is crucial to developing an effective marketing strategy because it can decrease costs and increase customer satisfaction. Speed of delivery, service, and dependability are often as important to customers as costs. Companies that have the right goods, in the right place, at the right time, in the right quantity, and with the right support services are able to sell more than competitors that do not. A construction equipment dealer with a low inventory of replacement parts requires fast, dependable service from component suppliers when it needs parts not in stock. Even when the demand for products is unpredictable, suppliers must be able to respond quickly to inventory needs. In such cases, physical distribution costs may be a minor consideration when compared with service, dependability, and timeliness.

As mentioned earlier, CRM systems exploit the information from supply-chain partners' database and information systems to facilitate marketing strategy decisions. This information can help logistics managers identify and root out inefficiencies in the supply chain for the benefit of all marketing-channel members—from the producer to the ultimate consumer. Indeed, technology is playing a larger and larger role in physical distribution within marketing channels. The Internet, in particular, has transformed physical distribution by facilitating just-in-time delivery, precise inventory visibility, and instant shipment tracking capabilities, which help companies to avoid expensive mistakes, reduce costs, and even generate revenues. Web-based information technology brings visibility to the supply chain by allowing all marketing-channel members to see precisely where an item is within the supply chain at any time.[15] For example, Landstar Logistics, which provides transportation services throughout North America, introduced a new Web-based tracking service that enables customers to track the status of their shipments at any time through their office or laptop computers or their cell phones or pagers.[16]

Although physical distribution managers try to minimize the costs associated with order processing, inventory management, materials handling, warehousing, and transportation, decreasing the costs in one area often raises them in another. Figure 14.5 shows the percentage of total costs that physical distribution functions represent. A total-cost approach to physical distribution enables managers to view physical distribution as a system rather than a collection of unrelated activities. This approach shifts the emphasis from lowering the separate costs of individual activities to minimizing overall distribution costs.

Physical distribution managers must be sensitive to the issue of cost tradeoffs. Higher costs in one functional area of a distribution system may be necessary to

figure 14.5   PROPORTIONAL COST OF EACH PHYSICAL DISTRIBUTION FUNCTION AS A PERCENTAGE OF TOTAL DISTRIBUTION COSTS

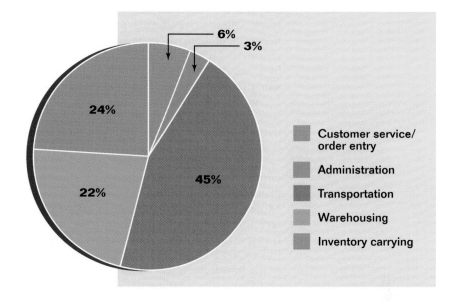

Source: From Davis Database, 2005. Reprinted by permission of Establish, Inc./Herbert W. Davis and Company.

achieve lower costs in another. Tradeoffs are strategic decisions to combine (and recombine) resources for greatest cost-effectiveness. When distribution managers regard the system as a network of integrated functions, tradeoffs become useful tools in implementing a unified, cost-effective distribution strategy.

Another important goal of physical distribution involves reducing **cycle time,** the time needed to complete a process. Doing so can reduce costs and/or increase customer service. Many companies, particularly overnight delivery firms, major news media, and publishers of books of current interest, are using cycle-time reduction to gain a competitive advantage. FedEx believes so strongly in this concept that, in the interest of being the fastest provider of overnight delivery, it conducts research on reducing cycle time and identifying new management techniques and procedures for its employees. Seattle's Boeing Company is considering the construction of a plant to be run by two major suppliers and built next to Boeing's proposed 7E7 assembly plant. The plant would assemble about 75 percent of the 7E7's fuselage and deliver it to Boeing's final assembly plant next door. Not only would this arrangement reduce cycle time, but it also would save transportation costs on large pieces.[17]

In the rest of this chapter we take a closer look at physical distribution activities, which include order processing, inventory management, materials handling, warehousing, and transportation.

Order Processing

Order processing is the receipt and transmission of sales-order information. Although management sometimes overlooks the importance of these activities, efficient order processing facilitates product flow. Computerized order processing provides a database for all supply-chain members to increase their productivity. When carried out quickly and accurately, order processing contributes to customer satisfaction, decreased costs and cycle time, and increased profits.

Order processing entails three main tasks: order entry, order handling, and order delivery. Order entry begins when customers or salespeople place purchase orders via telephone, mail, e-mail, or website. Electronic ordering is less time-consuming than a manual, paper-based ordering system and reduces costs. In some companies, sales

cycle time The time needed to complete a process

order processing The receipt and transmission of sales-order information

representatives receive and enter orders personally and also handle complaints, prepare progress reports, and forward sales order information.

Order handling involves several tasks. Once an order is entered, it is transmitted to a warehouse, where product availability is verified, and to the credit department, where prices, terms, and the customer's credit rating are checked. If the credit department approves the purchase, warehouse personnel (sometimes assisted by automated equipment) pick and assemble the order. If the requested product is not in stock, a production order is sent to the factory, or the customer is offered a substitute.

When the order has been assembled and packed for shipment, the warehouse schedules delivery with an appropriate carrier. If the customer pays for rush service, overnight delivery by FedEx, UPS, or another overnight carrier is used. The customer is sent an invoice, inventory records are adjusted, and the order is delivered.

Whether to use a manual or an electronic order-processing system depends on which method provides the greater speed and accuracy within cost limits. Manual processing suffices for small-volume orders and is more flexible in certain situations. Most companies, however, use **electronic data interchange (EDI)**, which uses computer technology to integrate order processing with production, inventory, accounting, and transportation. Within the supply chain, EDI functions as an information system that links marketing-channel members and outsourcing firms together. It reduces paperwork for all members of the supply chain and allows them to share information on invoices, orders, payments, inquiries, and scheduling. Consequently, many companies have pushed their suppliers toward EDI to reduce distribution costs and cycle times. Krispy Kreme, for example, uses EDI to automate supply-chain and financial activities with both suppliers and wholesale customers such as supermarkets and convenience stores. The system helped the company to save money and time and improve information flows across its supply chain.[18]

Inventory Management

Inventory management involves developing and maintaining adequate assortments of products to meet customers' needs. Because a firm's investment in inventory usually represents a significant portion of its total assets, inventory decisions have a major impact on physical distribution costs and the level of customer service provided. When too few products are carried in inventory, the result is *stock-outs,* or shortages of products, which, in turn, result in brand switching, lower sales, and loss of customers. When too many products (or too many slow-moving products) are carried, costs increase, as do risks of product obsolescence, pilferage, and damage. The objective of inventory management is to minimize inventory costs while maintaining an adequate supply of goods to satisfy customers. To achieve this objective, marketers focus on two major issues: when to order and how much to order.

To determine when to order, a marketer calculates the *reorder point,* the inventory level that signals the need to place a new order. To calculate the reorder point, the marketer must know the order lead time, the usage rate, and the amount of safety stock required. The *order lead time* refers to the average time lapse between placing the order and receiving it. The *usage rate* is the rate at which a product's inventory is used or sold during a specific time period. *Safety stock* is the amount of extra inventory a firm keeps to guard against stockouts resulting from above-average usage rates and/or longer-than-expected lead times. The reorder point can be calculated using the following formula:

$$\text{Reorder point} = (\text{order lead time} \times \text{usage rate}) + \text{safety stock}$$

Thus, if order lead time is 10 days, usage rate is 3 units per day, and safety stock is 20 units, the reorder point is 50 units.

Efficient inventory management with accurate reorder points is crucial for firms that use a **just-in-time (JIT)** approach, in which supplies arrive just as they are needed for use in production or for resale. When using JIT, companies maintain low

electronic data interchange (EDI) A computerized means of integrating order processing with production, inventory, accounting, and transportation

inventory management Developing and maintaining adequate assortments of products to meet customers' needs

just-in-time (JIT) An inventory-management approach in which supplies arrive just when needed for production or resale

YOU NAME IT

We'll Customize A Supply Chain Solution For It
Whatever you manufacture or wherever you store and distribute your products, Ryder's end-to-end supply chain solutions are designed to fit perfectly with your company's unique needs. Unmatched experience, flexibility and innovative thinking. This is what we offer to hundreds of companies around the world, from electronics and car makers to consumer product and aircraft manufacturers. We can do the same for you. Call 1-888-88-RYDER or visit www.ryder.com.

Ryder

SUPPLY CHAIN, WAREHOUSING, TRANSPORTATION & FLEET MANAGEMENT SOLUTIONS
©2006 Ryder System, Inc. All rights reserved.

Handling and Warehousing

Among its supply chain functions, Ryder provides customized solutions to improve transportation and warehousing.

materials handling Physical handling of tangible goods, supplies, and resources

warehousing The design and operation of facilities for storing and moving goods

inventory levels and purchase products and materials in small quantities whenever they need them. Usually there is no safety stock, and suppliers are expected to provide consistently high-quality products. JIT inventory management requires a high level of coordination between producers and suppliers, but it eliminates waste and reduces inventory costs significantly. This approach has been used successfully by many well-known firms, including DaimlerChrysler, Harley-Davidson, and Dell Computer, to reduce costs and boost customer satisfaction. When a JIT approach is used in a supply chain, suppliers often move close to their customers.

Materials Handling

Materials handling, the physical handling of tangible goods, supplies, and resources, is an important factor in warehouse operations, as well as in transportation from points of production to points of consumption. Efficient procedures and techniques for materials handling minimize inventory management costs, reduce the number of times a good is handled, improve customer service, and increase customer satisfaction. Systems for packaging, labeling, loading, and movement must be coordinated to maximize cost reduction and customer satisfaction. A growing number of firms are turning to radio waves to track materials tagged with radiofrequency ID (RFID) through every phase of handling. Starbucks, for example, is using RFID to track perishable foods being delivered to its shops to ensure that they remain at the correct temperatures during transportation.[19]

Product characteristics often determine handling. For example, the characteristics of bulk liquids and gases determine how they can be moved and stored. Internal packaging is also an important consideration in materials handling; goods must be packaged correctly to prevent damage or breakage during handling and transportation. Most companies employ packaging consultants during the product design process to help them decide which packaging materials and methods will result in the most efficient handling.

Unit loading and containerization are two common methods used in materials handling. With *unit loading,* one or more boxes are placed on a pallet or skid; these units then can be loaded efficiently by mechanical means such as forklifts, trucks, or conveyer systems. *Containerization* is the consolidation of many items into a single, large container that is sealed at its point of origin and opened at its destination. Containers are usually 8 feet wide, 8 feet high, and 10 to 40 feet long. They can be conveniently stacked and shipped via train, barge, or ship. Once containers reach their destinations, wheel assemblies can be added to make them suitable for ground transportation. Because individual items are not handled in transit, containerization greatly increases efficiency and security in shipping.

Warehousing

Warehousing, the design and operation of facilities for storing and moving goods, is another important physical distribution function. Warehousing provides time utility by enabling firms to compensate for dissimilar production and consumption rates. When mass production creates a greater stock of goods than can be sold immediately, companies may warehouse the surplus until customers are ready to buy. Warehousing also helps to stabilize prices and the availability of seasonal items.

The choice of warehouse facilities is an important strategic consideration. The right type of warehouse allows a company to reduce transportation and inventory costs or improve service to customers. The wrong type of warehouse may drain company resources. Beyond deciding how many facilities to operate and where to locate them, a company must determine which type of warehouse is most appropriate. Warehouses fall into two general categories: private and public. In many cases a combination of private and public facilities provides the most flexible warehousing approach.

Companies operate **private warehouses** for shipping and storing their own products. A firm usually leases or purchases a private warehouse when its warehousing needs in a given geographic market are substantial and stable enough to warrant a long-term commitment to a fixed facility. Private warehouses are also appropriate for firms that require special handling and storage and that want control of warehouse design and operation. Retailers such as Sears, Radio Shack, and Kmart find it economical to integrate private warehousing with purchasing and distribution for their retail outlets. When sales volumes are fairly stable, ownership and control of a private warehouse may provide benefits such as property appreciation. Private warehouses, however, face fixed costs such as insurance, taxes, maintenance, and debt expense. They also limit flexibility when firms wish to move inventories to more strategic locations. Many private warehouses are being eliminated by direct links between producers and customers, reduced cycle times, and outsourcing to public warehouses.

Public warehouses lease storage space and related physical distribution facilities to other companies. They sometimes provide distribution services such as receiving, unloading, inspecting, and reshipping products; filling orders; providing financing; displaying products; and coordinating shipments. ODW, for example, offers a wide range of such services through its 3 million square feet of warehouse space at 11 facilities.[20] Public warehouses are especially useful to firms that have seasonal production or low-volume storage needs, have inventories that must be maintained in many locations, are testing or entering new markets, or own private warehouses but occasionally require additional storage space. Public warehouses also serve as collection points during product-recall programs. Whereas private warehouses have fixed costs, public warehouses offer variable (and often lower) costs because users rent space and purchase warehousing services only as needed.

Many public warehouses furnish security for products being used as collateral for loans, a service provided at either the warehouse or the site of the owner's inventory. *Field public warehouses* are established by public warehouses at the owner's inventory location. The warehouser becomes custodian of the products and issues a receipt that can be used as collateral for a loan. Public warehouses also provide *bonded storage,* a warehousing arrangement in which imported or taxable products are not released until the products' owners pay U.S. customs duties, taxes, or other fees. Bonded warehouses enable firms to defer tax payments on such items until they are delivered to customers.

Distribution centers are large, centralized warehouses that receive goods from factories and suppliers, regroup them into orders, and ship them to customers quickly, the focus being on movement of goods rather than storage.[21] Distribution centers are specially designed for rapid flow of products. They are usually one-story buildings (to eliminate elevators) with access to transportation networks such as major highways and/or railway lines. Many distribution centers are highly automated, with computer-directed robots, forklifts, and hoists that collect and move products to loading docks. Overstock.com, for example, operates a 350,000-square-foot distribution center in Salt Lake City to process all the name-brand housewares, electronics, toys, sporting goods, and gifts it markets through a website. Efficiency in distribution operations helps the firm to offer deep discounts and stay on top of busy holiday seasons.[22] Although some public warehouses offer such specialized services, most distribution centers are privately owned. They serve customers in regional markets and, in some cases, function as consolidation points for a company's branch warehouses.

private warehouses Company-operated facilities for storing and shipping products

public warehouses Businesses that lease storage space and related physical distribution facilities to other firms

distribution centers Large, centralized warehouses that focus on moving rather than storing goods

table 14.2	CHARACTERISTICS AND RELATIVE RATINGS OF TRANSPORTATION MODES BY SELECTION CRITERIA				
	Railroads	**Trucks**	**Pipelines**	**Waterways**	**Airplanes**
Selection criteria					
Cost	Moderate	High	Low	Very low	Very high
Speed	Average	Fast	Slow	Very slow	Very fast
Dependability	Average	High	High	Average	High
Load flexibility	High	Average	Very low	Very high	Low
Accessibility	High	Very high	Very limited	Limited	Average
Frequency	Low	High	Very high	Very low	Average
% Ton-miles transported	36.8	29.0	19.9	13.9	0.3
Products carried	Coal, grain, lumber, heavy equipment, paper and pulp products, chemicals	Clothing, computers, books, groceries and produce, livestock	Oil, processed coal, natural gas	Chemicals, bauxite, grain, motor vehicles, agricultural implements	Flowers, food (highly perishable), technical instruments, emergency parts and equipment, overnight mail

Source: U.S. Bureau of Transportation Statistics, *National Transportation Statistics 2006* (Washington, DC: U.S. Government Printing Office), February 2007, www.bts.gov/publications/national_transportation_statistics/2006/pdf/entire.pdf.

Transportation

Transportation, the movement of products from where they are made to intermediaries and end users, is the most expensive physical distribution function. Because product availability and timely deliveries depend on transportation functions, transportation decisions directly affect customer service. A firm even may build its distribution and marketing strategy around a unique transportation system if that system can ensure on-time deliveries and thereby give the firm a competitive edge. Companies may build their own transportation fleets (private carriers) or outsource the transportation function to a common or contract carrier.

Transportation Modes.   There are five basic transportation modes for moving physical goods: railroads, trucks, waterways, airways, and pipelines. Each mode offers distinct advantages. Many companies adopt physical handling procedures that facilitate the use of two or more modes in combination. Table 14.2 indicates the percentage of intercity freight carried by each transportation mode.

Railroads such as Union Pacific and Canadian National carry heavy, bulky freight that must be shipped long distances over land. Railroads commonly haul minerals, sand, lumber, chemicals, and farm products, as well as low-value manufactured goods and an increasing number of automobiles. They are especially efficient for transporting full carloads, which can be shipped at lower rates than smaller quantities because they require less handling. Many companies locate factories or warehouses near rail lines for convenient loading and unloading.

Trucks provide the most flexible schedules and routes of all major transportation modes because they can go almost anywhere. Because trucks have a unique ability to

transportation The movement of products from where they are made to intermediaries and end users

move goods directly from factory or warehouse to customer, they are often used in conjunction with other forms of transport that cannot provide door-to-door deliveries. Although trucks usually travel much faster than trains, they are more expensive and somewhat more vulnerable to bad weather. They are also subject to size and weight restrictions on the products they carry. Trucks are sometimes criticized for high levels of loss and damage to freight and for delays caused by the rehandling of small shipments. In response, the trucking industry has turned to computerized tracking of shipments and the development of new equipment to speed loading and unloading. Marten Transport, Ltd., in Wisconsin, charges its customers for the time drivers have to wait and rewards clients that help keep things moving. Using a satellite tracking system, the company can track when a driver arrives at a site and how long it takes to load and unload freight. The data are shared with customers, and Marten and its customers work together to eliminate wasteful practices. Marten has lost customers but has also reduced rates to others who have expedited loading and unloading.[23]

Waterways are the cheapest method of shipping heavy, low-value, nonperishable goods such as ore, coal, grain, and petroleum products. Water carriers offer considerable capacity. Powered by tugboats and towboats, barges that travel along intracoastal canals, inland rivers, and navigation systems can haul at least ten times the weight of one rail car, and ocean-going vessels can haul thousands of containers. More than 95 percent of international cargo is transported by water. However, many markets are inaccessible by water transportation unless supplemented by rail or truck. Droughts and floods also may create difficulties for users of inland waterway transportation. Nevertheless, the extreme fuel efficiency of water transportation and the continuing globalization of marketing likely will increase its use in the future.

Air transportation is the fastest but most expensive form of shipping. It is used most often for perishable goods; for high-value, low-bulk items; and for products requiring quick delivery over long distances, such as emergency shipments. Some air carriers transport combinations of passengers, freight, and mail. Despite its expense, air transit can reduce warehousing and packaging costs and losses from theft and damage, thus helping to lower total costs (but truck transportation needed for pickup and final delivery adds to cost and transit time). Although air transport accounts for less than 1 percent of total ton-miles carried, its importance as a mode of transportation is growing. In fact, the success of many businesses is now based on the availability of overnight air delivery service provided by organizations such as UPS, FedEx, DHL, RPS Air, and the U.S. Postal Service. Amazon.com, for example, ships many products ordered online via UPS within a day of order.

Pipelines, the most automated transportation mode, usually belong to the shipper and carry the shipper's products. Most pipelines carry petroleum products or chemicals. The Trans-Alaska Pipeline, owned and operated by a consortium of oil companies that includes ExxonMobil and BP-Amoco, transports crude oil from remote oil-drilling sites in central Alaska to shipping terminals on the coast. Slurry pipelines carry pulverized coal, grain, or wood chips suspended in water. Pipelines move products slowly but continuously and at relatively low cost. They are dependable and minimize the problems of product damage and theft. However, contents are subject to as much as 1 percent shrinkage, usually from evaporation. Pipelines also have been a concern to environmentalists, who fear installation and leaks could harm plants and animals.

Choosing Transportation Modes.   Logistics managers select a transportation mode based on the combination of cost, speed, dependability, load flexibility, accessibility, and frequency that is most appropriate for their products and generates the desired level of customer service. Table 14.2 shows relative ratings of each transportation mode by these selection criteria.

Marketers compare alternative transportation modes to determine whether benefits from a more expensive mode are worth higher costs. Companies such as Accuship can assist marketers in analyzing various transportation options. This Internet firm's

intermodal transportation
Two or more transportation modes used in combination

freight forwarders Organizations that consolidate shipments from several firms into efficient lot sizes

megacarriers Freight transportation firms that provide several modes of shipment

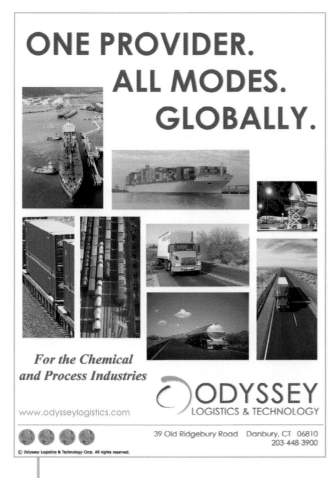

ONE PROVIDER.
ALL MODES.
GLOBALLY.

For the Chemical
and Process Industries

ODYSSEY
LOGISTICS & TECHNOLOGY

www.odysseylogistics.com

39 Old Ridgebury Road   Danbury, CT 06810
203-448-3900

© Odyssey Logistics & Technology Corp. All rights reserved.

Intermodal Transportation.

Odyssey offers intermodal transportation capabilities.

software gives corporate users, such as Coca-Cola and the Home Shopping Network, information about the speed and cost of different transportation modes and allows them to order shipping and then track shipments online. Accuship processes almost a million shipments every day.[24]

Coordinating Transportation.   To take advantage of the benefits offered by various transportation modes and compensate for deficiencies, marketers often combine and coordinate two or more modes. In recent years, **intermodal transportation,** as this integrated approach is sometimes called, has become easier because of new developments within the transportation industry.

Several kinds of intermodal shipping are available. All combine the flexibility of trucking with the low cost or speed of other forms of transport. Containerization facilitates intermodal transportation by consolidating shipments into sealed containers for transport by *piggyback* (shipping that uses both truck trailers and railway flatcars), *fishyback* (truck trailers and water carriers), and *birdyback* (truck trailers and air carriers). As transportation costs have increased, intermodal shipping has gained popularity.

Specialized outsource agencies provide other forms of transport coordination. Known as **freight forwarders,** these firms combine shipments from several organizations into -efficient lot sizes. Small loads (less than 500 pounds) are much more expensive to ship than full carloads or truckloads, which frequently require consolidation. Freight forwarders take small loads from various marketers, buy transport space from carriers, and arrange for goods to be delivered to buyers. Freight forwarders' profits come from the margin between the higher, less-than-carload rates they charge each marketer and the lower carload rates they themselves pay. Because large shipments require less handling, use of freight forwarders can speed delivery. Freight forwarders also can determine the most efficient carriers and routes and are useful for shipping goods to foreign markets. Some companies prefer to outsource their shipping to freight forwarders because the latter provide door-to-door service.

Another transportation innovation is the development of **megacarriers,** freight transportation companies that offer several shipment methods, including rail, truck, and air service. CSX, for example, has trains, barges, container ships, trucks, and pipelines, thus offering a multitude of transportation services. In addition, air carriers have increased their ground-transportation services. As they expand the range of transportation alternatives, carriers too put greater stress on customer service.

. . . And now, back to FedEx

To achieve its highly successful delivery rate, FedEx maintains an impressive infrastructure of equipment and processes. The company owns more than 70,000 vehicles, and its 677 aircraft fly more than 500,000 miles every day. It even operates its own weather forecasting service, which helps to ensure that most of its flights arrive within 15 minutes of schedule. The hub envisioned by Smith in college is located in Memphis, Tennessee. FedEx takes over control of Memphis International Airport at roughly 11:00 each night. For an hour every night, FedEx planes begin to arrive in Memphis and land side by side on parallel runways every minute. After the packages are sorted, all FedEx planes take off in time to reach their destinations. Beginning at 2:48 a.m. every Monday through Friday, FedEx dispatches 8 to12 aircraft every 6 minutes. By 4:12 a.m., FedEx has launched about 150 aircraft to more than 136 domestic and international destinations. Not all packages are shipped via air; whenever possible, FedEx uses ground transportation to save on expenses.

In 2004, FedEx acquired Kinko's to provide new business services and expand shipping options through Kinko's nationwide stores. Kinko's, which operated in 11 countries, helped FedEx to reach new customers and expand in Asia and Europe.

One of the most important keys to success for FedEx is its flexibility to be ready to deal with the unexpected or the uncontrollable. Natural disasters are a major obstacle in the shipping business. In 2004 and 2005, FedEx had to rely on contingency plans to successfully navigate the 57 tropical storms that threatened to interrupt its business. Every day, some part of the globe visited by FedEx is experiencing some type of political or natural unrest. This is the reason FedEx has implemented disaster drills covering everything from bioterrorism to typhoons. Each night eight planes sit in Memphis with fuel, supplies, and communications gear ready to deploy to a FedEx facility in need. Also, five cargoless planes roam the skies, ready to help out in cases of unexpected volume, air emergencies, or broken-down planes.

Many analysts still argue that the overnight delivery market eventually could lose as much as 30 percent of its letter business to electronic document delivery, especially e-mail. This trend may be balanced by the enormous growth of online businesses that rely on shipping services to deliver merchandise. This boom of clicking, buying, and shipping led to a record-breaking holiday season for FedEx recently. The company experienced all-time highs in business and broke its own records with 9.8 million packages handled in a single day.

FedEx has been successful for many reasons. First, FedEx tries to stay focused on its mission statement. A second reason is the company's enviable corporate culture and work force. Because employees are critical to the company's success, FedEx strives to hire the best people and offers them the best training and compensation in the industry. A third reason for FedEx's success is its technology and customer relationship management. A final reason for FedEx's success is its highly effective marketing. FedEx is a master at recognizing untapped customer needs and building relationships. After 30 years of success, there is little doubt that Fred Smith's C paper has become an indispensable part of the business world.[25]

1. What role does FedEx play in the supply chain of some companies?

2. What characteristics might dictate the inclusion of FedEx into a company's marketing channel?

3. How can FedEx facilitate inventory management and cycle-time reduction?

CHAPTER REVIEW

1. Describe the nature and functions of marketing channels.

A marketing channel, or channel of distribution, is a group of individuals and organizations that directs the flow of products from producers to customers. The major role of marketing channels is to make products available at the right time, at the right place, and in the right amounts. In most channels of distribution, producers and consumers are linked by marketing intermediaries, usually wholesalers and/or retailers. Marketing channels also form a supply chain, which refers to long-term partnerships among channel members working together to reduce inefficiencies, costs, and redundancies. Marketing channels create time, place, and possession utility by making products available when and where customers want them and providing customers with access to product use through sale or rental. Marketing intermediaries facilitate exchange efficiencies by reducing the total number of transactions that otherwise would be required to move products from producer to ultimate users.

2. Identify the types of marketing channels.

Marketing channels are broadly classified as channels for consumer products and channels for business products. Although consumer goods can move directly from producer to consumers, consumer product channels that include wholesalers and retailers are usually more economical and efficient. For business products, direct distribution channels are common. Business channels often include industrial distributors, manufacturers' agents, or a combination of agents and distributors. Most producers employ multiple or dual channels so that they can adapt the distribution system for various target markets. To determine which channel is most appropriate, managers must think about customer characteristics, product attributes, the type of organization, competition, environmental forces, and the availability and characteristics of intermediaries.

3. Explore the concepts of leadership, cooperation, and conflict in channel relationships.

Each channel member performs a different role in the supply chain and agrees to accept certain rights, responsibilities, and rewards, as well as sanctions for nonconformance. Although marketing channels may be determined by consensus, many are organized and controlled by a single leader, or channel captain. A channel leader may be a producer, wholesaler, or retailer. Channels function most effectively when members cooperate; when they deviate from their roles, channel conflict can arise.

4. Recognize common strategies for integrating marketing channels.

Vertical integration combines two or more stages of the marketing channel under one management. The vertical marketing system (VMS) is managed centrally for the mutual benefit of all channel members. Vertical marketing systems may be corporate, administered, or contractual. Horizontal integration combines institutions at the same level of channel operation under a single management.

5. Examine the major levels of marketing coverage.

A marketing channel is managed so that products receive appropriate market coverage. Intensive distribution makes a product available to all possible dealers. In selective distribution, only some outlets in an area are chosen to distribute a product. Exclusive distribution usually gives one dealer exclusive right to sell a product in a large geographic area.

6. Recognize the importance of the role of physical distribution activities in supply-chain management and overall marketing strategies.

Physical distribution, or logistics, refers to the activities used to move products from producers to customers and other end users. These activities include order processing, inventory management, materials handling, warehousing, and transportation. An efficient physical distribution system is an important component of an overall marketing strategy because it can decrease costs and increase customer satisfaction. Within the marketing channel, physical distribution activities are often performed by a wholesaler, but they also may be performed by a producer or retailer or outsourced to a third party. Efficient physical distribution systems can decrease costs and transit time while increasing customer service.

7. Examine the major physical distribution functions of order processing, inventory management, materials handling, warehousing, and transportation.

Order processing is the receipt and transmission of sales-order information. It consists of three main tasks—order entry, order handling, and order delivery—which may be done manually but are more often handled through electronic data interchange systems. Inventory management involves developing and maintaining adequate assortments of products to meet customers' needs. Logistics managers must strive to find the optimal level of inventory to satisfy customer needs while keeping costs down. Materials handling, the physical handling of products, is a crucial element in warehousing and transporting products. Warehousing involves the design and operation of facilities for storing and moving goods; such facilities may be privately owned or public. Transportation, the movement of products from where they are made to where they are purchased and used, is the most expensive physical distribution function. The basic modes of transporting goods include railroads, trucks, waterways, airways, and pipelines.

ACE self-test

Please visit the student website at **www.prideferrell.com** for ACE Self-Test questions that will help you prepare for exams.

KEY CONCEPTS

distribution
marketing channel
marketing intermediary
supply-chain management

industrial distributor
dual distribution
strategic channel alliance
channel power

vertical channel integration
vertical marketing systems
  (VMSs)

horizontal channel
  integration
intensive distribution
selective distribution

exclusive distribution
physical distribution
outsourcing
cycle time
order processing

electronic data interchange
   (EDI)
inventory management
just-in-time (JIT)
materials handling

warehousing
private warehouses
public warehouses
distribution centers
transportation

intermodal transportation
freight forwarders
megacarriers

ISSUES FOR DISCUSSION AND REVIEW

1. Describe the major functions of marketing channels. Why are these functions better accomplished through the combined efforts of channel members?

2. Compare and contrast the four major types of marketing channels for consumer products. Through which type of channel is each of the following products most likely to be distributed?
   a. New automobiles
   b. Saltine crackers
   c. Cut-your-own Christmas trees
   d. New textbooks
   e. Sofas
   f. Soft drinks

3. Outline the four most common channels for business products. Describe the products or situations that lead marketers to choose each channel.

4. "Channel cooperation requires that members support the overall channel goals to achieve individual goals." Comment on this statement.

5. Explain the major characteristics of each of the three types of vertical marketing systems: corporate, administered, and contractual.

6. Explain the differences among intensive, selective, and exclusive methods of distribution.

7. Discuss the cost and service tradeoffs involved in developing a physical distribution system.

8. What are the main tasks involved in order processing?

9. Explain the tradeoffs inventory managers face when reordering products or supplies. How is the reorder point computed?

10. Explain the major differences between private and public warehouses. How do they differ from a distribution center?

11. Compare and contrast the five major transportation modes in terms of cost, speed, and dependability.

MARKETING APPLICATIONS

1. Select one of the following companies and explain how supply-chain management could increase marketing productivity.
   a. Dell Computer
   b. FedEx
   c. Nike
   d. Taco Bell

2. Find an article in a newspaper or on the Internet that describes a strategic channel alliance. Briefly summarize the article and indicate the benefits each organization expects to gain.

3. Indicate the intensity level—intensive, selective, or exclusive—best suited for the following products, and explain why it is appropriate.
   a. Personal computer
   b. Deodorant
   c. Collector baseball autographed by Mark McGwire
   d. Windows XP computer software

4. Assume that you are responsible for the physical distribution of computers at a Web-based company. What would you do to ensure product availability, timely delivery, and quality service for your customers?

Online Exercise

5. FedEx has become a critical link in the distribution network of both small and large firms. With its efficient and strategically located superhub in Memphis, FedEx has truly revolutionized the shipping industry. View the company's website at **www.fedex.com.**
   a. Comment on how the website's overall design reflects the services the site promotes.
   b. Why does FedEx so prominently display a "News" area on its website?
   c. Does FedEx differentiate between small and large customers on its website? Why or why not?

globalEDGE™

Like many firms in your industry, your firm sources materials from abroad. The shipment of materials vital to the manufacturing process of a new line of high-quality, water-resistant winter sweaters is currently missing. You had expected the shipment four weeks ago, but the tracking information you have is outdated. To determine whether your shipment entered the United States, you must consult with the Global Statistics website, which can be accessed by using the search term "global statistics" at **http://globaledge.msu.edu/** (and check the box "Resource Desk only"). Once you reach the Global Statistics website, click on the "Charts" link at the top right. Using this information, find the largest domestic container ports and seaports. This will direct your search and help you to resolve the impending manufacturing emergency. Where will you be traveling to begin your investigation?

Video CASE

Coca-Cola Stuffs the Channel to Make the Numbers

The Coca-Cola Company, founded in the late 1800s, is the largest beverage company in the world, with customers in more than 200 countries. The company's brands are many of the most recognized; they include Coca-Cola, Diet Coke, Fanta, Sprite, Powerade, Minute Maid, and Dasani bottled water. Although Coca-Cola focused primarily on customers in the United States in its early years, it has since recognized and relentlessly pursued international opportunities. By the late 1990s, Coca-Cola dominated its market with more than 50 percent of international soft-drink sales. The company has always maintained a strong focus on bringing in, satisfying, and keeping loyal customers. Strategic, recognizable designs on bottles and cans and well-liked global advertising have contributed to the strong reputation the company holds. Coca-Cola consistently is rated the most valuable brand in the world.

Over the last ten years, Coca-Cola has focused on traditional soft drinks, whereas archrival PepsiCo has gained a strong foothold on new-age drinks, formed a partnership with Starbucks, and expanded rapidly into the snack business. PepsiCo's Frito-Lay division has 60 percent of the U.S. snack-food market. Ten years ago, Coca-Cola's market value was more than three times greater than PepsiCo's. By 2006, PepsiCo had a market capitalization greater than Coca-Cola.

Coca-Cola has long focused on social responsibility issues. It makes donations to several foundations that focus on education and community improvement. Coca-Cola is also involved in issuing grants and scholarships both in the United States and internationally. It is also concerned with preserving the environment and helping stem the AIDS/HIV crisis in Africa. All these

contributions help Coca-Cola develop an emotional, trusting relationship with its customers. In 2005, Coca-Cola issued a 50-page report on corporate responsibility in Great Britain. Key accomplishments include supplier compliance and audits, recycling, open work environment, community investment, and an environmental advisory board. Coca-Cola has always prided itself on its strong reputation. The Harris Interactive and the Reputation Institute (creating reputation quotients for companies by measuring 20 perceived attributes) ranked Coca-Cola second in overall reputation in 1999. The company had long been featured on *Fortune* magazine's "America's Most Admired Companies" list. However, the company failed to make the 2000 *Fortune* list owing to problems with performance and leadership in 1999. It also was eliminated from *Business Ethics* magazine's "100 Best Corporate Citizens" list in 2001. The 2005 *Business Ethics* "100 Best Corporate Citizens" list also did not include Coca-Cola.

Coca-Cola's problems in 1999 began with a contamination scare that had a negative effect on its European

reputation. That year also brought a racial discrimination lawsuit by about 2,000 current and former African American employees against the company. The company settled the suit by paying $193 million. And then-CEO Doug Invester raised concentrate prices—a strategy that did not go over well with the company's bottlers. Overall, it was thought that the company did not handle these crises well. In addition to reflecting poorly on Coca-Cola's reputation, these crises had a negative impact on the firm's bottlers, distributors, suppliers, and other related third parties.

A major problem that Coca-Cola faced during this period was accusations of channel stuffing. Channel stuffing is the practice of shipping extra inventory to wholesalers and retailers at an excessive rate, typically before the end of a quarter. Essentially, a company counts the shipments as sales, although the products often remain in warehouses or are later returned to the manufacturer. Channel stuffing tends to create the appearance of strong demand (or conceals declining demand) for a product, which may result in inflated financial statement earnings, misleading investors. Accusations of channel stuffing have been made recently against companies such as Krispy Kreme Donuts, Harley-Davidson, Clear One Communications, Symbol Technologies, Network Associates, Bristol-Myers, Taser International, and Intel.

In Coca-Cola's case, the company was accused of sending extra concentrate to Japanese bottlers from 1997 through 1999 in an effort to inflate its profit. The company was already under investigation after a former employee filed a lawsuit in 2000 accusing the company of fraud and improper business practices. In 2004, former finance officials for Coca-Cola reported finding statements of inflated earnings owing to the company shipping extra concentrate to Japan. Although the company settled the allegations, the Securities and Exchange Commission (SEC) did find that channel stuffing had occurred. However, what Coca-Cola had done was to pressure bottlers into buying additional concentrate in exchange for extended credit. Therefore, the sales were technically considered legitimate.

To settle with the SEC, Coke agreed to avoid engaging in channel stuffing in the future. The company also created an ethics and compliance office and is required to verify each financial quarter that it has not altered the terms of payment or extended special credit. The company further agreed to work to reduce the amount of concentrate held by international bottlers. Although the company settled with the SEC and the Justice Department, it still faces a shareholder lawsuit regarding channel stuffing in Japan, North America, Europe, and South Africa.

Despite a solid focus on building and maintaining a strong, positive reputation and a firm dedication to social responsibility, Coca-Cola has had major problems in competing with its rival PepsiCo. The use of channel stuffing and other questionable practices has not been the answer to making the numbers.[26]

Questions for Discussion

1. How could channel stuffing at Coca-Cola affect its relationships with channel members such as bottlers?
2. In what ways could channel stuffing impact Coke's own customer-service standards?
3. Why would Coca-Cola risk its reputation by engaging in channel stuffing?

Retailing, Direct Marketing, and Wholesaling

The Hard Rock Joins the Undefeated—the Seminole Nation

Every year, 30 million customers around the world and high in the sky enjoy the Hard Rock Café's casual American meals and rock-and-roll theme. The first Hard Rock Café opened in London in 1971. Today, Hard Rock Café International operates more than 138 restaurants in 42 countries, including dozens of cities worldwide, from Boston and Bangkok to Berlin and Beiruit, as well as hotels, casinos, and a website (**www.hardrock.com**). The company also sells sandwiches and salads on United Airlines flights. "We saw this as an opportunity to put our food and product in front of business and leisure travelers," explains Hard Rock's CEO. "Some of them may have never been to one of our restaurants."

Along with burgers and beer, Hard Rock Cafés offer branded merchandise, live and recorded music, and rock music memorabilia. Arranging for branded merchandise to be shipped to every restaurant in the right quantities and at the right times is a complex undertaking. The company has hired outside experts to help with supplier contacts, inventory management, transportation, and storage. As a result of this effort, the company expects that it will require 44 percent less warehouse space in the United States and be able to cut its operational costs by 20 percent.

The company also has an unparalleled memorabilia collection with more than 70,000 pieces that are rotated from restaurant to restaurant. The collection includes classic guitars, gold and platinum LPs, one of Madonna's bustiers, and even John Lennon's handwritten lyrics to "Help." The company arranges to rotate its $32 million collection of rock music artifacts between restaurants to draw repeat business. In addition, each restaurant's design reflects the local music scene, enhanced by the ever-changing memorabilia. On the stage of the Detroit café, for example, a garage door stands as a tribute to garage-band music. The original London café has showcased guitars from Eric Clapton and Pete Townsend, among other British rock artists. Other cafés display costumes, instruments, posters, and photos of Eminem, Elvis Presley, Jimi Hendrix, the Goo Goo Dolls, and hundreds of other rockers.

Hard Rock Café International is also proceeding with plans to open a $400 million, 140-acre rock 'n' roll theme park in Myrtle Beach, South Carolina, in 2008. The park will feature six custom-designed zones that feature elements from rock music. The park, which is expected to draw an estimated 30,000 visitors per day and to create more than 3,000 jobs, is being billed as a totally immersive full-day attraction, appealing to visitors of all generations. It will have more than 40 attractions, including a multipurpose amphitheater, roller coasters, restaurants, cafés, retail stores, children's play areas, and a Hard Rock Hotel.[1] ■

OBJECTIVES

1. Understand the purpose and function of retailers in the marketing channel.

2. Identify the major types of retailers.

3. Explore strategic issues in retailing.

4. Recognize the various forms of direct marketing and selling.

5. Examine franchising and its benefits and weaknesses.

6. Understand the nature and functions of wholesalers.

7. Understand how wholesalers are classified.

etailers such as the Hard Rock Café are the most visible and accessible marketing-channel members to consumers. They are an important link in the marketing channel because they are both marketers for and customers of producers and wholesalers. They perform many supply-chain functions, such as buying, selling, grading, risk taking, and developing and maintaining information databases about customers. Retailers are in a strategic position to develop relationships with consumers and partnerships with producers and intermediaries in the marketing channel.

In this chapter we examine the nature of retailing, direct marketing, and wholesaling and their importance in supplying consumers with goods and services. First, we explore the major types of retail stores and consider strategic issues in retailing: location, retail positioning, store image, scrambled merchandising, and the wheel of retailing. Next, we discuss direct marketing, including catalog marketing, direct response marketing, telemarketing, television home shopping, online retailing, and direct selling. Then we look at franchising, a retailing form that continues to grow in popularity. Finally, we examine the importance of wholesalers in marketing channels, including their functions and classifications.

Retailing

retailing All transactions in which the buyer intends to consume the product through personal, family, or household use

retailer An organization that purchases products for the purpose of reselling them to ultimate consumers

Retailing includes all transactions in which the buyer intends to consume the product through personal, family, or household use. Buyers in retail transactions are therefore the ultimate consumers. A **retailer** is an organization that purchases products for the purpose of reselling them to ultimate consumers. Although most retailers' sales are made directly to the consumer, nonretail transactions occur occasionally when retailers sell products to other businesses. Retailing often takes place in stores or service establishments, but it also occurs through direct selling, direct marketing, and vending machines outside stores.

Retailing is important to the national economy. Approximately 1.1 million retailers operate in the United States.[2] This number has remained relatively constant for the past 25 years, but sales volume has increased more than fourfold. Most personal income is spent in retail stores, and nearly one of every eight people employed in the United States works in a retail operation.

Retailers add value, provide services, and assist in making product selections. They can enhance the value of products by making buyers' shopping experiences more convenient, as in home shopping. Through their locations, retailers can facilitate comparison shopping; for example, car dealerships often cluster in the same general vicinity, as do furniture stores. Product value is also enhanced when retailers offer services, such as technical advice, delivery, credit, and repair. Finally, retail sales personnel can demonstrate to customers how products can satisfy their needs or solve problems.

The value added by retailers is significant for both producers and ultimate consumers. Retailers are the critical link between producers and ultimate consumers because they provide the environment in which exchanges with ultimate consumers occur. Ultimate consumers benefit through retailers' performance of marketing functions that result in the availability of broader arrays of products. Retailers play a major role in creating time, place, and possession utility and, in some cases, form utility.

Leading retailers such as Wal-Mart, Home Depot, Macy's, Staples, and Best Buy offer consumers a place to browse and compare merchandise to find just what they need. However, such traditional retailing is being challenged by direct marketing channels that provide home shopping through catalogs, television, and the Internet. "Bricks and mortar" retailers are responding to this change in the retail environment in various ways. Wal-Mart, for example, is offering more upscale merchandise such as plasma TVs and more fashionable apparel as well as more extended warranties on merchandise.[3] It also has established a website for online shopping and joined forces

Department Stores

Department stores like JCPenney offer a host of product lines.

with fast-food giants McDonald's and KFC to attract consumers and offer them the added convenience of eating where they shop.

New store formats and advances in information technology are making the retail environment highly dynamic and competitive. Instant-messaging technology is enabling online retailers to converse in real time with customers so that they don't click away to another site. For example, shoppers on the Lands' End website can click to chat, via keyboard, directly with a customer-service representative about sizes, colors, or other product details. The key to success in retailing is to have a strong customer focus with a retail strategy that provides the level of service, product quality, and innovation that consumers desire. Partnerships among noncompeting retailers and other marketing-channel members are providing new opportunities for retailers. For example, airports are leasing space to retailers such as Sharper Image, McDonald's, Sunglass Hut, and The Body Shop. Kroger and Nordstrom have developed joint cobranded credit cards that offer rebates to customers at participating stores.

Retailers are also finding global opportunities. For example, both McDonald's and The Gap, Inc., are now opening more international stores than domestic ones, a trend that is likely to continue for the foreseeable future. Starbucks has opened hundreds of stores in Japan and Southeast Asia. Increasingly, retailers from abroad, such as IKEA, Zara, and BP, are opening stores in the United States.

Major Types of Retail Stores

Many types of retail stores exist. One way to classify them is by the breadth of products offered. Two general categories include general merchandise retailers and specialty retailers.

General Merchandise Retailers.   A retail establishment that offers a variety of product lines stocked in considerable depth is referred to as a **general merchandise retailer.** The types of product offerings, mixes of customer services, and operating styles of retailers in this category vary considerably. The primary types of general merchandise retailers are department stores, discount stores, convenience stores, supermarkets, superstores, hypermarkets, warehouse clubs, and warehouse showrooms (see Table 15.1 on page 376).

general merchandise retailer A retail establishment that offers a variety of product lines that are stocked in considerable depth

table 15.1   GENERAL MERCHANDISE RETAILERS

Type of Retailer	Description	Examples
Department store	Large organization offering wide product mix and organized into separate departments	Macy's, Sears, JCPenney
Discount store	Self-service general merchandise store offering brand name and private brand products at low prices	Wal-Mart, Target, Kmart
Convenience store	Small self-service store offering narrow product assortment in convenient locations	7-Eleven, Circle K, Stripes
Supermarket	Self-service store offering complete line of food products and some nonfood products	Kroger, Albertson's, Winn-Dixie
Superstore	Giant outlet offering all food and nonfood products found in supermarkets, as well as most routinely purchased products	Wal-Mart Supercenters
Hypermarket	Combination supermarket and discount store; larger than a superstore	Carrefour
Warehouse club	Large-scale members-only establishments combining cash-and-carry wholesaling with discount retailing	Sam's Club, Costco
Warehouse showroom	Facility in a large, low-cost building with large on-premises inventories and minimal service	IKEA

Department Stores. **Department stores** are large retail organizations characterized by wide product mixes and organized into separate departments, such as cosmetics, housewares, apparel, home furnishings, and appliances, to facilitate marketing and internal management. Often each department functions as a self-contained business, and buyers for individual departments are fairly autonomous. Typical department stores, such as Macy's, Sears, Dillard's, and Neiman Marcus, obtain a large proportion of sales from apparel, accessories, and cosmetics. Other products that these stores carry include gift items, luggage, electronics, home accessories, and sports equipment. Some department stores offer services such as automobile insurance, hair care, income tax preparation, and travel and optical services. In some cases, space for these specialized services is leased out, with proprietors managing their own operations and paying rent to the department store. Many department stores also sell products through their websites.

Department stores are somewhat service-oriented. Their total product may include credit, delivery, personal assistance, merchandise returns, and a pleasant atmosphere. Although some so-called department stores are actually large, departmentalized specialty stores, most department stores are shopping stores. Consumers can compare price, quality, and service at one store with those at competing stores. Along with large discount stores, department stores are often considered retailing leaders in a community and are found in most places with populations of more than 50,000.

Discount Stores. In recent years, department stores have been losing market share to discount stores.[4] **Discount stores** are self-service general merchandise outlets that regularly offer brand name and private brand products at low prices. Discounters accept lower margins than conventional retailers in exchange for high sales volume. To keep inventory turnover high, they carry a wide but carefully selected assortment of products, from appliances to housewares and clothing. Major discount establishments also offer food products, toys, automotive services, garden supplies, and sports equipment. Wal-Mart and Target are the two largest discount stores. Wal-Mart has grown

department stores Large retail organizations characterized by wide product mixes and organized into separate departments to facilitate marketing and internal management

discount stores Self-service, general merchandise stores offering brand name and private brand products at low prices

Discount Stores

Target is a successful discount store.

to 6,400 stores worldwide and brings in more than $315 billion in sales annually.[5] When Kmart Holding Corporation agreed to buy Sears, it introduced a smaller version of the Sears department store, called Sears Essentials, to compete with Target and Wal-Mart.[6] Some discounters such as Meijer, Inc., are regional organizations. Most operate in large (50,000 to 80,000 square feet), no-frills facilities. Discount stores usually offer everyday low prices rather than relying on sales events.

Convenience Stores. A **convenience store** is a small self-service store that is open long hours and carries a narrow assortment of products, usually convenience items such as soft drinks and other beverages, snacks, newspapers, tobacco, and gasoline, as well as services such as automatic teller machines. The primary product offered by the "corner store" is convenience. 7-Eleven's director of processed foods says, "When consumers visit a 7-Eleven, they seek something that will solve their immediate need. They are in the mood for a consumable product and want it right now, and expect the convenience store to deliver it."[7] According to the National Association of Convenience Stores, there are 140,655 convenience stores in the United States with 1.5 million employees. They are typically less than 5,000 square feet; open 24 hours a day, 7 days a week, and stock about 500 items. In addition to many national chains, there are many family-owned independent convenience stores in operation.[8] The convenience store concept was developed in 1927 when Southland Ice in Dallas began stocking milk, eggs, and other products for customers replenishing their "ice boxes." Southland eventually evolved into 7-Eleven, which now has 5,300 stores in the United States. Gasoline sales account for just one-third of the chain's total sales, which increasingly include upscale merchandise such as wine and high-end sandwiches and snacks.[9]

Supermarkets. **Supermarkets** are large self-service stores that carry a complete line of food products, as well as some nonfood products such as cosmetics and nonprescription drugs. Supermarkets are arranged in departments for maximum efficiency in stocking and handling products but have central checkout facilities. They offer

convenience store A small self-service store that is open long hours and carries a narrow assortment of products, usually convenience items

supermarkets Large, self-service stores that carry a complete line of food products, along with some nonfood products

lower prices than smaller neighborhood grocery stores, usually provide free parking, and also may cash checks. Today, consumers make more than three-quarters of all grocery purchases in supermarkets. Even so, supermarkets' total share of the food market is declining because consumers now have widely varying food preferences and buying habits, and in many communities, shoppers can choose from several convenience stores, discount stores, and specialty food stores, as well as a wide variety of restaurants. Wal-Mart, for example, expects to generate in its "supermarket-type" stores more revenue than the top three U.S. supermarket chains—Kroger, Albertson's, and Safeway—combined. To attract more customers, Albertson's plans to make grocery shopping quick and easy with new technology that will eliminate checkout lines.[10]

Superstores. **Superstores**, which originated in Europe, are giant retail outlets that carry not only food and nonfood products ordinarily found in supermarkets but also routinely purchased consumer products. Superstores combine features of discount stores and supermarkets. Examples include Wal-Mart Supercenters and some Kroger stores. Besides a complete food line, superstores sell housewares, hardware, small appliances, clothing, personal-care products, garden products, and tires—about four times as many items as supermarkets. Services available at superstores include dry cleaning, automotive repair, check cashing, bill paying, and snack bars. To cut handling and inventory costs, they use sophisticated operating techniques and often have tall shelving that displays entire assortments of products. Superstores can have an area of as much as 200,000 square feet (compared with 20,000 square feet in traditional supermarkets). Sales volume is two to three times that of supermarkets partly because locations near good transportation networks help to generate the in-store traffic needed for profitability.

Hypermarkets. **Hypermarkets** combine supermarket and discount store shopping in one location. Larger than superstores, they range from 225,000 to 325,000 square feet and offer 45,000 to 60,000 different types of low-priced products. They commonly allocate 40 to 50 percent of their space to grocery products and the remainder to general merchandise, including athletic shoes, designer jeans, and other apparel; refrigerators, televisions, and other appliances; housewares; cameras; toys; jewelry; hardware; and automotive supplies. Many lease space to noncompeting businesses such as banks, optical shops, and fast-food restaurants. All hypermarkets focus on low prices and vast selections. Although Kmart, Wal-Mart, and Carrefour (a French retailer) have operated hypermarkets in the United States, most of these stores were unsuccessful and closed. Such stores may be too big for time-constrained U.S. shoppers. However, hypermarkets are more successful in Europe, South America, and Mexico. For example, the hypermarket has become such a success in Mexico that the leading chains are currently waging a retail war. Wal-Mart de Mexico is leading the battle with annual sales of $11.7 billion, but competitors such as Soriana, with annual sales of $3.2 billion, are taking risks and fighting back.[11]

Warehouse Clubs. **Warehouse clubs,** a rapidly growing form of mass merchandising, are large-scale members-only selling operations combining cash-and-carry wholesaling with discount retailing. Sometimes called *buying clubs,* warehouse clubs offer the same types of products as discount stores but in a limited range of sizes and styles. Whereas most discount stores carry around 40,000 items, a warehouse club handles only 3,500 to 5,000 products, usually acknowledged brand leaders. Sam's Club stores, for example, stock about 4,000 items, with 1,400 available most of the time and the rest being one-time buys. Costco leads the warehouse club industry with sales of $60.2 billion. Sam's Club is second with nearly $40 billion in store sales. A third company, BJ's Wholesale Club, which operates in the Northeast and Florida, has a much smaller market.[12] All these establishments offer a broad product mix, including food, beverages, books, appliances, housewares, automotive parts, hardware, and furniture.

superstores Giant retail outlets that carry food and nonfood products found in supermarkets, as well as most routinely purchased consumer products

hypermarkets Stores that combine supermarket and discount store shopping in one location

warehouse clubs Large-scale members-only establishments that combine features of cash-and-carry wholesaling with discount retailing

To keep prices lower than those of supermarkets and discount stores, warehouse clubs provide few services. They generally do not advertise, except through direct mail. Their facilities, often located in industrial areas, have concrete floors and aisles wide enough for forklifts. Merchandise is stacked on pallets or displayed on pipe racks. Customers must transport purchases themselves. Warehouse clubs appeal to many price-conscious consumers and small retailers unable to obtain wholesaling services from large distributors. The average warehouse club shopper has more education, a higher income, and a larger household than the average supermarket shopper.

Warehouse Showrooms. **Warehouse showrooms** are retail facilities with five basic characteristics: large, low-cost buildings; warehouse materials-handling technology; vertical merchandise displays; large on-premises inventories; and minimal services. IKEA, a Swedish company, sells furniture, household goods, and kitchen accessories in warehouse showrooms and through catalogs around the world, including China and Russia. These high-volume, low-overhead operations stress fewer personnel and services. Lower costs are possible because some marketing functions have been shifted to consumers, who must transport, finance, and perhaps store larger quantites of products. Most consumers carry away purchases in the manufacturer's carton, although stores will deliver for a fee.

Specialty Retailers.   In contrast to general merchandise retailers with their broad product mixes, specialty retailers emphasize narrow and deep assortments. Despite their name, specialty retailers do not sell specialty items (except when specialty goods complement the overall product mix). Instead, they offer substantial assortments in a few product lines. We examine three types of specialty retailers: traditional specialty retailers, category killers, and off-price retailers.

Traditional specialty retailers are stores that carry a narrow product mix with deep product lines. Sometimes called *limited-line retailers*, they may be referred to as *single-line retailers* if they carry unusual depth in one main product category. Traditional specialty retailers commonly sell shopping products such as apparel, jewelry, sporting goods, fabrics, computers, toys, and pet supplies. The Limited, Radio Shack, Hickory Farms, The Gap, and Foot Locker are examples of retailers offering limited product lines but great depth within those lines. Many traditional specialty retailers are small businesses with just one or a few outlets.

Because they are usually small, specialty stores may have high costs in proportion to sales, and satisfying customers may require carrying some products with low turnover rates. However, these stores sometimes obtain lower prices from suppliers by purchasing limited lines of merchandise in large quantities. Successful traditional specialty stores understand their customer types and know what products to carry, thus reducing the risk of unsold merchandise. Traditional specialty stores usually offer better selections and more sales expertise than department stores, their main competitors. By capitalizing on fashion, service, personnel, atmosphere, and location, these retailers position themselves strategically to attract customers in specific market segments.

Over the last 15 years, a new breed of specialty retailer, the category killer, has evolved. A **category killer** is a very large specialty store that concentrates on a major product category and competes on the basis of low prices and enormous product availability. These stores are referred to as category killers because they expand rapidly and gain sizable market shares, taking business away from smaller, high-cost retail outlets. Examples of category killers include Home Depot and Lowe's (home-improvement chains); Staples, Office Depot, and OfficeMax (office-supply chains); Borders and Barnes & Noble (booksellers); Petco and PetSmart (pet-supply chains); and Best Buy and Circuit City (consumer electronics).

Off-price retailers are stores that buy manufacturers' seconds, overruns, returns, and off-season production runs at below-wholesale prices for resale to consumers at deep discounts. Unlike true discount stores, which pay regular wholesale prices for goods and usually carry second-line brand names, off-price retailers offer limited lines

warehouse showrooms Retail facilities in large, low-cost buildings with large on-premises inventories and minimal services

traditional specialty retailers Stores that carry a narrow product mix with deep product lines

category killer A very large specialty store concentrating on a major product category and competing on the basis of low prices and product availability

off-price retailers Stores that buy manufacturers' seconds, overruns, returns, and off-season merchandise for resale to consumers at deep discounts

Fashion meets flora.

Visit Lowe's Garden Center today for our abundant selection of planters and accessories in styles ranging from classic to contemporary.

LOWE'S
Let's Build Something Together™

Items shown are metal with a copper finish: 16.5" Vase (227361), 6" Urn (227364), 11" Planter (227306).   © 2006 by Lowe's. All rights reserved. Lowe's and the gable design are registered trademarks of LF, LLC.

Category Killers

Some stores, like Lowe's, are referred to as category killers because of their enormous product mixes and low prices.

of national-brand and designer merchandise, usually clothing, shoes, or housewares. The number of off-price retailers such as T.J. Maxx, Marshalls, Stein Mart, and Burlington Coat Factory has grown since the mid-1980s. Off-price stores charge 20 to 50 percent less than do department stores for comparable merchandise but offer few customer services. They often feature community dressing rooms and central checkout counters. Some of these stores do not take returns or allow exchanges. Off-price stores may or may not sell goods with the original labels intact. They turn over their inventory nine to twelve times a year, three times as often as traditional specialty stores. They compete with department stores for the same customers: price-conscious customers who are knowledgeable about brand names.

Strategic Issues in Retailing

Whereas most business purchases are based on economic planning and necessity, consumer purchases may result from social and psychological influences. Because consumers shop for various reasons—to search for specific items, escape boredom, or learn about something new—retailers must do more than simply fill space with merchandise. They must make desired products available, create stimulating shopping environments, and develop marketing strategies that increase store patronage. In this section we discuss how store location, retail positioning, store image, category management, scrambled merchandising, and the wheel of retailing affect retailing objectives.

Location, Location, Location.   Location, the least flexible of the strategic retailing issues, is one of the most important because location dictates the limited geographic trading area from which a store draws its customers. Retailers consider various factors when evaluating potential locations, including location of the firm's target market within the trading area, kinds of products being sold, availability of public transportation, customer characteristics, and competitors' locations. In choosing a location, a retailer evaluates the relative ease of movement to and from the site, including factors such as pedestrian and vehicular traffic, parking, and transportation. Retailers also evaluate the characteristics of the site itself: types of stores in the area; size, shape, and visibility of the lot or building under consideration; and rental, leasing, or ownership terms. Retailers look for compatibility with nearby retailers because stores that complement one another draw more customers for everyone.

Many retailers choose to locate in downtown central business districts, whereas others prefer sites within various types of planned shopping centers. Some retailers, including Toys 'R' Us, Wal-Mart, Home Depot, and many fast-food restaurants, opt for freestanding structures that are not connected to other buildings, but many chain stores are found in planned shopping centers and malls. Some retailers choose to locate in less orthodox settings. McDonald's, for example, has opened several stores inside hospitals, whereas Subway has franchise locations inside churches, laundromats, and hospitals.[13] Although shopping centers have been very popular over the last three decades, today's time-challenged consumers are increasingly turning to freestanding specialty and discount stores where they can park nearby, grab exactly what they want, and check out quickly.[14] Planned shopping centers include neighborhood, community, regional, superregional, lifestyle, and power shopping centers.

Retail Location

The location of a retail store is crucial. There are a number of organizations that assist retailers to make retail site location decisions.

neighborhood shopping centers Shopping centers usually consisting of several small convenience and specialty stores

community shopping centers Shopping centers with one or two department stores, some specialty stores, and convenience stores

regional shopping centers A type of shopping center with the largest department stores, the widest product mix, and the deepest product lines of all shopping centers

superregional shopping centers A type of shopping center with the widest and deepest product mixes that attracts customers from many miles away

Neighborhood shopping centers usually consist of several small convenience and specialty stores, such as small grocery stores, gas stations, and fast-food restaurants. Many of these retailers consider their target markets to be consumers who live within two to three miles of their stores, or ten minutes' driving time. Because most purchases are based on convenience or personal contact, there is usually little coordination of selling efforts within a neighborhood shopping center. Generally, product mixes consist of essential products, and depth of the product lines is limited.

Community shopping centers include one or two department stores and some specialty stores, as well as convenience stores. They draw consumers looking for shopping and specialty products not available in neighborhood shopping centers. Because these centers serve larger geographic areas, consumers must drive longer distances to community shopping centers than to neighborhood centers. Community shopping centers are planned and coordinated to attract shoppers. Special events, such as art exhibits, automobile shows, and sidewalk sales, stimulate traffic. Managers of community shopping centers look for tenants that complement the centers' total assortment of products. Such centers have wide product mixes and deep product lines.

Regional shopping centers usually have the largest department stores, the widest product mixes, and the deepest product lines of all shopping centers. Many shopping malls are regional shopping centers, although some are community shopping centers. With 150,000 or more consumers in their target market, regional shopping centers must have well-coordinated management and marketing activities. Target markets may include consumers traveling from a distance to find products and prices not available in their hometowns. Because of the expense of leasing space in regional shopping centers, tenants are more likely to be national chains than small, independent stores. Large centers usually advertise, have special events, furnish transportation to some consumer groups, maintain their own security forces, and carefully select the mix of stores. The largest of these centers, sometimes called **superregional**

Shopping Centers

Wrentham Village Premium Outlets in Massachusetts is one of the country's largest outlet centers and features many designer brands in an outdoor village setting.

lifestyle shopping centers A type of shopping center that is typically open air and features upscale specialty, dining, and entertainment stores

power shopping centers A type of shopping center that combines off-price stores with category killers

retail positioning Identifying an unserved or underserved market segment and serving it through a strategy that distinguishes the retailer from others in the minds of consumers in that segment

shopping centers, have the widest and deepest product mixes and attract customers from many miles away. Superregional centers often have special attractions beyond stores, such as skating rinks, amusement centers, or upscale restaurants. Mall of America, in the Minneapolis area, is the largest shopping mall in the United States with 520 stores, including Nordstrom and Bloomingdale's, and 50 restaurants. The shopping center also includes a walk-through aquarium, museum, theme parks, 14-screen movie theater, hotels, and many special events.[15]

With traditional mall sales declining, some shopping center developers are looking to new formats that differ significantly from traditional shopping centers. A **lifestyle shopping center** is typically an open-air shopping center that features upscale specialty, dining, and entertainment stores, usually owned by national chains. They are often located near affluent neighborhoods and may have fountains, benches, and other amenities that encourage "casual browsing." Indeed, architectural design is an important aspect of these "minicities," which may include urban streets or parks, and is intended to encourage consumer loyalty by creating a sense of place. Some lifestyle centers are designed to resemble traditional "Main Street" shopping centers or may have a central theme evidenced by architecture.[16]

Some shopping center developers are bypassing the traditional department store anchor and combining off-price stores and small stores with category killers in **power shopping center** formats. These centers may be anchored by a store such as The Gap, Toys 'R' Us, Circuit City, PetSmart, and Home Depot. The number of power shopping centers is growing, resulting in a variety of formats vying for the same retail dollar.

Factory outlet malls feature discount and factory outlet stores carrying traditional manufacturer brands, such as Quicksilver, Liz Claiborne, Reebok, and Le Creuset. Some outlet centers feature upscale products. Manufacturers own these stores and make a special effort to avoid conflict with traditional retailers of their products. Manufacturers claim that their stores are in noncompetitive locations; indeed, most factory outlet centers are located outside metropolitan areas. Not all factory outlets stock closeouts and irregulars, but most avoid comparison with discount houses. Factory outlet centers attract value-conscious customers seeking quality and major brand names. They operate in much the same way as regional shopping centers but usually draw customers, some of which may be tourists, from a larger shopping radius. Promotional activity is at the heart of these shopping centers. Craft and antique shows, contests, and special events attract a great deal of traffic.

Retail Positioning.   The large variety of shopping centers and the expansion of product offerings by traditional stores have intensified retailing competition. Retail positioning is therefore an important consideration. **Retail positioning** involves identifying an unserved or underserved market segment and serving it through a strategy that distinguishes the retailer from others in the minds of those customers. For example, Payless ShoeSource, a specialty store chain, has built a reputation for providing a wide variety of low-price shoes in a warehouse-like environment. The retailer is attempting to reposition itself as a purveyor of stylish and trendy shoes with a wider price range (going as high as $60) by expanding its merchandise mix and sprucing up its 4,500 stores. Targeting more women interested as much in fashion as in low prices, Payless has even opened a New York design office to focus on original styles and has

A Wild Place to Eat and Shop: The Rainforest Café

Back when the Rainforest Café opened its doors in the mammoth Mall of America in 1994, themed restaurants were all the rage. Hungry customers sometimes had to wait as long as two hours to get a table at the Minneapolis-based eatery. A year later, the Rainforest Café became a publicly traded company, and its stock soared, only to plummet a short time later. By 2000, the restaurant's owners, still struggling to remain one of the last independently owned themed restaurants, finally gave in and agreed to be acquired by Landry's Restaurants, Inc. Although the restaurant fought to hold on as an independent chain, being acquired by Landry's turned the eatery around, and today it is a thriving chain with 34 restaurants in the United States and around the world.

A number of things set the Rainforest Café apart from other trendy themed restaurants such as Planet Hollywood and Fashion Café that opened in the 1990s—and have since closed. While places like Planet Hollywood struggled with oversaturated markets and the failure to bring in repeat customers, the Rainforest Café has always been able to draw customers through its doors. Its problems lay in the area of operational expenses, an area where Landry's Restaurants excels.

If you've never been to a Rainforest Café, it is an entertaining experience. The restaurants boast canopies of Banyan trees, animatronic jungle animals, aquariums, rainstorms complete with thunder and lightning, and much more. The company calls servers safari guides; hosts/hostesses, tour guides; and cooks, trailblazers. The Rainforest Café also has its own line of characters, geared toward children. Landry's has continued to build on the restaurant's fun factor, recently adding the Rainforest River Adventure Ride to its location in Galveston, Texas.

The Rainforest Café is more than a place to eat and enjoy the jungle theme. It's also a retail operation. All customers walk by café merchandise as they enter the restaurant, and many have good views of this merchandise while they eat. It's difficult to leave without purchasing at least a small souvenir.

The Rainforest Café is the only themed restaurant located in all the Disneyland parks (with the exception of Hong Kong). Over the years, Landry's has worked to improve on the original Rainforest Café concept, and this work has paid off. Among its accolades, the Rainforest Café has received the "Best Themed Restaurant Award" and been named the number 1 themed restaurant by *Restaurant Hospitality*.[a]

introduced a line of shoes designed by Laura Poretzky.[17] Many discount and specialty store chains are positioning themselves to appeal to time- and cash-strapped consumers with convenient locations and layouts as well as low prices. This strategy has helped discount and specialty stores gain market share at the expense of large department stores.[18]

Store Image.   To attract customers, a retail store must project an image—a functional and psychological picture in the consumer's mind—that appeals to its target market. Store environment, merchandise quality, and service quality are key determinants of store image.

Atmospherics, the physical elements in a store's design that appeal to consumers' emotions and encourage buying, help to create an image and position a retailer.

atmospherics The physical elements in a store's design that appeal to consumers' emotions and encourage buying

Atmospherics

Stores like Pier 1 Imports use atmospheric elements such as lighting and elaborate floor displays to encourage purchasing.

category management A retail strategy of managing groups of similar, often substitutable products produced by different manufacturers

scrambled merchandising The addition of unrelated products and product lines to an existing product mix, particularly fast-moving items that can be sold in volume

wheel of retailing A hypothesis holding that new retailers usually enter the market as low-status, low-margin, low-price operators but eventually evolve into high-cost, high-price merchants

Barnes & Noble, for example, uses murals of authors and framed pictures of classic book covers to convey a literary image. Studies show that retailers can use different elements—music, color, and complexity of layout and merchandise presentation—to influence customer arousal based on their shopping motivation. Supermarkets, for example, should use cooler colors and simple layout and presentations because their customers tend to be task-motivated, whereas specialty retailers may be able to use more complex layouts and brighter colors to stimulate their more recreationally motivated customers.[19]

Exterior atmospheric elements include the appearance of the storefront, display windows, store entrances, and degree of traffic congestion. Exterior atmospherics are particularly important to new customers, who tend to judge an unfamiliar store by its outside appearance and may not enter if they feel intimidated by the building or inconvenienced by the parking lot. Interior atmospheric elements include aesthetic considerations such as lighting, wall and floor coverings, dressing facilities, and store fixtures. Interior sensory elements contribute significantly to atmosphere. Color can attract shoppers to a retail display. Many fast-food restaurants use bright colors, such as red and yellow, because these have been shown to make customers feel hungrier and eat faster, which increases turnover. Sound is another important sensory component of atmosphere and may range from silence to subdued background music. Pottery Barn, for example, plays 1950s cocktail bar music, whereas JCPenney varies the music in its stores—even within departments—based on local demographics.[20] Many retailers employ scent, especially food aromas, to attract customers. Research suggests that consumer evaluations of a product are affected by scent, but only when the scent employed is congruent with the product.[21] In one study, 90 percent of surveyed consumers ranked cleanliness—particularly in supermarkets—as the most important atmospheric element in choosing a shopping destination. Lighting, temperature, and aisle width also were ranked highly. Active elements such as in-store televisions were rated among the least influential.[22]

Category Management   **Category management** is a retail strategy of managing groups of similar, often substitutable products produced by different manufacturers. For example, supermarkets such as Safeway use category management to determine space for products such as cosmetics, cereals, and soups. An assortment of merchandise is both customer and strategically driven to improve performance. Category management developed in the food industry because supermarkets were concerned about highly competitive behavior among manufacturers. Category management is a move toward a collaborative supply-chain initiative to enhance customer value. Successful category management requires the acquisition, analysis, and sharing of sales and consumer information between the retailer and manufacturer. Wal-Mart, for example, has developed strong supplier relationships with manufacturers such as Procter & Gamble. The development of information about demand, consumer behavior, and optimal allocations of products should be available from one source. Firms such as SAS provide software to manage data associated with each step of the category management decision cycle. The key is cooperative interaction between the manufacturers of category products and the retailer to create maximum success for all parties in the supply chain.

Scrambled Merchandising.   When retailers add unrelated products and product lines—particularly fast-moving items that can be sold in volume—to an existing product mix, they are practicing **scrambled merchandising.** Retailers adopting this strategy hope to accomplish one or more of the following: (1) convert stores into one-stop shopping centers, (2) generate more traffic, (3) realize higher profit margins, and (4) increase impulse purchases. In scrambled merchandising, retailers must deal with diverse marketing channels. Scrambled merchandising also can blur a store's image in consumers' minds, making it more difficult for a retailer to succeed in today's highly competitive, saturated markets. Finally, scrambled merchandising intensifies competition among traditionally distinct types of stores and forces suppliers to adjust distribution systems to accommodate new channel members.

The Wheel of Retailing.   As new types of retail businesses come into being, they strive to fill niches in a dynamic retailing environment. One hypothesis regarding the evolution and development of new types of retail stores is the **wheel of retailing.** According to this theory, new retailers enter the marketplace with low prices, margins, and status. Their low prices are usually the result of innovative cost-cutting procedures and soon attract imitators. Gradually, as these businesses attempt to broaden their customer base and increase sales, their operations and facilities become more elaborate and more expensive. They may move to more desirable locations, begin to carry higher-quality merchandise, or add services. Eventually, they emerge at the high end of the price, cost, and service scales, competing with newer discount retailers following the same evolutionary process.[23]

Consider the evolution of department stores, discount stores, warehouse clubs, category killers, and online retailers. Department stores such as Sears started out as high-volume, low-cost merchants competing with general stores and other small retailers. Discount stores developed later in response to rising expenses of services in department stores. Many discount outlets now appear to be following the wheel of retailing by offering more services, better locations, quality inventories, and therefore higher prices. Some discount stores, such as Kohl's, are almost indistinguishable from department stores. In response have emerged category killers, such as PetSmart and Office Depot, which concentrate on a major product category and offer enormous product depth, in many cases at lower prices than discount stores. Yet even these retailers seem to be following the wheel. Lowe's, a home-improvement retailer, has added big-ticket items and more upscale brands, such as Laura Ashley. Consumers have less time to shop and greater access to more sophisticated technology, so such retailing venues as catalog retailing, television home shopping, and online retailing will take on greater importance. New retailers will evolve to capitalize on these opportunities, whereas those that cannot adapt will not survive.

Direct Marketing and Direct Selling

Although retailers are the most visible members of the supply chain, many products are sold outside the confines of a retail store. Direct selling and direct marketing account for an increasing percentage of product sales. Products also may be sold in automatic vending machines, but these account for less than 2 percent of all retail sales.

Direct Marketing

direct marketing The use of telecommunications and nonpersonal media to introduce products to consumers, who then can purchase them via mail, telephone, or the Internet

Direct marketing is the use of telecommunications and nonpersonal media to communicate product and organizational information to customers, who then can purchase products via mail, telephone, or the Internet. Direct marketing can occur through catalog marketing, direct response marketing, telemarketing, television home shopping, and online retailing.

catalog marketing A type of marketing in which an organization provides a catalog from which customers make selections and place orders by mail, telephone, or the Internet

Catalog Marketing.   In **catalog marketing,** an organization provides a catalog from which customers make selections and place orders by mail, telephone, or the Internet.

Successful Email Marketing is Not Just a Science, But an Art.

First Campaign is FREE
(Up to 50,000 messages)

What good is a creative, well-targeted Email campaign if the messages never get delivered?

Email marketing is one of the most effective methods for contacting customers and prospects today. The benefits are enormous: it is more cost effective than traditional direct marketing, it provides instant feedback as to the effectiveness, it allows your customers to make immediate buying decisions, and it gives greater flexibility when it comes to targeting specific messages to specific groups of people.

However, none of this matters if your Emails are not delivered. That's where we come in. We ensure the highest delivery rates for you and your customers by providing years of industry experience along with state-of-the-art technology. Delivering Emails is a mix of art (experience) and science (technology). DirectoryNETMail combines both of these, along with strict SPAM and abuse policies, to ensure the highest delivery rates possible.

The DirectoryNET*Mail* **Suite of Products Includes:**

• Email Distribution
• Email Append
• Data Enhancement
• Best Practices Consulting

Contact us today and your first campaign is **FREE** (Up to 50,000 messages).

800-733-1212
CustomerService@DirectoryNET.com

The Choice for Business Intelligence Solutions.

DirectoryNET Mail™

© Copyright 2005, DirectoryNET, LLC. All rights reserved.

Direct Marketing

Companies like DirectoryNET Mail sometimes are used to help catalog marketers reach their target markets.

direct response marketing
A type of marketing that occurs when a retailer advertises a product and makes it available through mail or telephone orders

telemarketing The performance of marketing-related activities by telephone

Catalog marketing began in 1872, when Montgomery Ward issued its first catalog to rural families. Today there are more than 7,000 catalog marketing companies in the United States, as well as several retail stores, such as JCPenney, that engage in catalog marketing. Some organizations, including Spiegel and JCPenney, offer a broad array of products spread over multiple product lines. Catalog companies such as Lands' End, Pottery Barn, and J. Crew offer considerable depth in one major line of products. Still other catalog companies specialize in only a few products within a single line. Some catalog retailers—for instance, Crate and Barrel and The Sharper Image—have stores in major metropolitan areas.

The advantages of catalog retailing include efficiency and convenience for customers. The retailer benefits by being able to locate in remote, low-cost areas; save on expensive store fixtures; and reduce both personal selling and store operating expenses. On the other hand, catalog retailing is inflexible, provides limited service, and is most effective for a selected set of products.

Direct Response Marketing. Direct response marketing occurs when a retailer advertises a product and makes it available through mail or telephone orders. Generally, a purchaser may use a credit card, but other forms of payment are acceptable. Examples of direct response marketing include a television commercial offering a recording artist's musical collection available through a toll-free number, a newspaper or magazine advertisement for a series of children's books available by filling out the form in the ad or calling a toll-free number, and even a billboard promoting floral services available by calling 1-800-Flowers. Direct response marketing is also conducted by sending letters, samples, brochures, or booklets to prospects on a mailing list and asking that they order the advertised products by mail or telephone. In general, products must be priced above $20 to justify the advertising and distribution costs associated with direct response marketing.

Telemarketing. A number of organizations use the telephone to strengthen the effectiveness of traditional marketing methods. **Telemarketing** is the performance of marketing-related activities by telephone. Some organizations use a prescreened list of prospective clients. Telemarketing can help to generate sales leads, improve customer service, speed up payments on past-due accounts, raise funds for nonprofit organizations, and gather marketing data.

Currently, the laws and regulations regarding telemarketing, while in a state of flux, are becoming more restrictive. Many states have established do-not-call lists of customers who do not want to receive telemarketing calls from companies operating in their state. The U.S. Congress implemented the national do-not-call registry for consumers who do not wish to receive telemarketing calls in 2003. By the end of 2003, nearly one-third of the 166 million residential phone numbers in the United States had been listed on the registry. Companies are subject to a fine of up to $12,000 for each call made to a consumer listed on the national do-not-call registry.[24] The national registry is enforced by the Federal Trade Commission and the Federal Communications Commission.[25] Certain exceptions apply to do-not-call lists. A company still can use telemarketing to communicate with existing customers. In addition, charitable, political, and telephone survey organizations are not restricted by the national registry.

L.L. Bean Is Coming Out of the Woods

.L. Bean, the well-known seller of outdoor clothing and equipment, is facing another hurdle in its successful history—how to change its way of doing business without changing its image. Leon Leonwood Bean founded his company in Freeport, Maine, in 1912, the year after he made the first rubber-bottomed hunting boot. He sold his boots through a four-page mailer that he sent to hunters in Maine and out-of-staters who held Maine hunting licenses. The business prospered as the company expanded its product line to outdoor clothing and hunting and fishing gear.

Today, the company is a global organization with annual sales in excess of $1.5 billion. About 40 percent of its merchandise is sold through catalogs, 40 percent over the Internet, and 20 percent through 7 retail stores and 14 factory stores in or near Maine. L.L. Bean's success has been due primarily to its high-quality, dependable products and a carefully constructed image of a Maine-based company that embraces the region's old-fashioned values of integrity, frugality, and quality.

In recent years, the marketplace has changed owing to the emergence of savvy and aggressive competitors, three of whom are each approaching annual sales of $1 billion. Eddie Bauer has more than 400 locations across the United States. Eastern Mountain Sports has 100, and Gander Mountain has 98 stores. For the most part, these competitors have built their businesses through retail sales outlets.

L.L. Bean plans to open more retail stores across the country to compete more effectively and grow long term. The challenge is to expand to new areas while maintaining its rustic Maine image. According to the current CEO, the important goal for the future is to convince people that the company still stands for the same things it did 40 years ago: outdoors, service, and quality products.[b]

television home shopping A form of selling in which products are presented to television viewers, who can buy them by calling a toll-free number and paying with a credit card

Television Home Shopping.   **Television home shopping** presents products to television viewers, encouraging them to order through toll-free numbers and pay with credit cards. The Home Shopping Network in Florida originated and popularized this format. The most popular products sold through television home shopping are jewelry (40 percent of total sales), clothing, housewares, and electronics. Home shopping channels have grown so rapidly in recent years that more than 60 percent of U.S. households have access to home shopping programs. Home Shopping Network and QVC are two of the largest home shopping networks. Approximately 60 percent of home shopping sales revenues come from repeat purchasers.

The television home shopping format offers several benefits. Products can be demonstrated easily, and an adequate amount of time can be spent showing the product so that viewers are well informed. The length of time a product is shown depends not only on the time required for doing demonstrations but also on whether the product is selling. Once the calls peak and begin to decline, a new product is shown. Other benefits are that customers can shop at their convenience and from the comfort of their homes.

Benefits of online marketing

Researchers report that the four major advantages of online marketing are increased revenue, greater visibility, cost savings, and reaching new customers.

Increased revenue 73%

Greater visibility 58%

Cost savings 56%

Reaching new customers 54%

Search [   ] GO   Clothing Footwear Accessories Home

Source: Multichannel Marketing 2005 Report, DMA.

Online Retailing. **Online retailing** makes products available to buyers through computer connections. The phenomenal growth of Internet use and online information services such as AOL has created new retailing opportunities. Many retailers have set up websites to disseminate information about their companies and products. Although most retailers with websites use them primarily to promote products, a number of companies, including Barnes & Noble, REI, Lands' End, and Office-Max, sell goods online. Consumers can purchase hard-to-find items, such as Pez candy dispensers and Elvis memorabilia, on eBay. They can buy upscale items for their dogs at SitStay.com, a Web retailer specializing in high-end dog supplies that carries a carefully screened selection of 1,500 products. Banks and brokerage firms have established websites to give customers direct access to manage their accounts and enable them to trade online. Jupiter Media Metrix projects that online retail sales in the United States will climb to $144 billion by 2010.[26] With advances in computer technology continuing and consumers ever more pressed for time, online retailing will continue to escalate.

Although online retailing represents a major retailing venue, security remains an issue. In a recent survey conducted by the Business Software Alliance, about 75 percent of Internet users expressed concerns about shopping online. The major issues are identity theft and credit card theft.

Direct Selling

Direct selling is the marketing of products to ultimate consumers through face-to-face sales presentations at home or in the workplace. Traditionally called *door-to-door selling,* direct selling in the United States began with peddlers more than a century ago and has since grown into a sizable industry of several hundred firms. Although direct sellers historically used a cold-canvass, door-to-door approach for finding prospects, many companies today, such as Kirby, Amway, Mary Kay, and Avon, use other approaches. They initially identify customers through the mail, telephone, Internet, or shopping-mall intercepts and then set up appointments.

While the majority of direct selling takes place on an individual, or person-to-person, basis, it sometimes also includes the use of a group, or "party," plan. With a party plan, a consumer acts as a host and invites friends and associates to view merchandise in a group setting, where a salesperson demonstrates products. The congenial party atmosphere helps to overcome customers' reluctance and encourages them to buy. Tupperware and

Excited. Can't sleep. Mind racing. Is it love, or vacation?

Bring on the goose bumps and the night before giddiness. It's time to begin the countdown to not being here. This is your pre-vacation, and you've got to make the most of it. So overpack the suitcase, assemble your tiny toiletry team and butter up those neighbors to collect all your newspapers and mail. It's time to embrace travel like a long lost friend.

Expedia.com
enjoy your trip.

Online Retailing

Expedia is an online retailer of travel-related services.

marketing
ENTREPRENEURS

Jacquelyn Tran

HER BUSINESS: Perfume Bay

FOUNDED: 1999, when Tran was 22

SUCCESS: More than 800 brands of beauty products generate $9 million in sales

Jacquelyn Tran was just three years old when her parents emigrated from Vietnam. She grew up working in her parents' small Los Angeles cosmetics/perfume store, and she helped run their wholesale business after college. Recognizing the influence of the rapidly growing Internet, Tran educated herself about websites and e-commerce and then launched Perfume Bay as a classy website marketing beauty and skin-care products as well as perfumes and colognes. Tran admits that she made a lot of mistakes at first, but the business grew steadily. Perfume Bay, which describes some products rather like a sommelier describes a wine, has gained an excellent reputation for selection service, earning a "Gold Honoree" designation by BizRate, the online retail watchdog.[c]

Mary Kay were the pioneers of this selling technique, paving the way for companies such as Pampered Chef to grow from a basement business into a corporation that brings in over $700 million in revenues annually.[27]

Direct selling has both benefits and limitations. It gives the marketer an opportunity to demonstrate the product in an environment—usually customers' homes—where it most likely would be used. The door-to-door seller can give the customer personal attention, and the product can be presented to the customer at a convenient time and location. Personal attention to the customer is the foundation on which some direct sellers, such as Mary Kay, have built their businesses. Because commissions for salespeople are so high, ranging from 30 to 50 percent of the sales price, and great effort is required to isolate promising prospects, overall costs of direct selling make it the most expensive form of retailing. Furthermore, some customers view direct selling negatively, owing to unscrupulous and fraudulent practices used by some direct sellers in the past. Some communities even have local ordinances that control or, in some cases, prohibit direct selling. Despite these negative views held by some individuals, direct selling is still alive and well, bringing in revenues of $30 billion a year.[28]

Franchising

online retailing Retailing that makes products available to buyers through computer connections

direct selling The marketing of products to ultimate consumers through face-to-face sales presentations at home or in the workplace

franchising An arrangement in which a supplier (franchiser) grants a dealer (franchisee) the right to sell products in exchange for some type of consideration

Franchising is an arrangement in which a supplier, or franchiser, grants a dealer, or franchisee, the right to sell products in exchange for some type of consideration. The franchiser may receive some percentage of total sales in exchange for furnishing equipment, buildings, management know-how, and marketing assistance to the franchisee. The franchisee supplies labor and capital, operates the franchised business, and agrees to abide by the provisions of the franchise agreement. Table 15.2 (on page 390) lists the leading U.S. franchises, types of products, and startup costs.

Because of changes in the international marketplace, shifting employment options in the United States, the expanding U.S. service economy, and corporate interest in more joint-venture activity, franchising is increasing rapidly. Franchising companies and their franchisees account for an estimated $1.5 trillion in annual U.S. retail sales from 767,483 franchised small businesses in 75 industries. Franchising accounts for more than 40 percent of all U.S. retail sales and employ nearly 10 million people.[29]

Franchising offers advantages to both the franchisee and the franchiser. It enables a franchisee to start a business with limited capital and benefit from the business experience of others. Moreover, nationally advertised franchises, such as ServiceMaster and Burger King, are often assured of customers as soon as they open. If business problems arise, the franchisee can obtain guidance and advice from the franchiser at little or no cost. Franchised outlets are generally more successful than independently owned businesses. Fewer than 10 percent of franchised retail businesses fail during the first two years of operation compared with approximately 50 percent of independent retail businesses. Also, the franchisee receives materials to use in local advertising and can benefit from national promotional campaigns sponsored by the franchiser.

No Nights, No Weekends, No Holidays—and that's just the beginning. When you become a Merry Maids franchise owner you'll also **gain the freedom of being your own boss.**

Learn how to own, manage and develop your business through **continuous support and guidance** from the industry leaders.

For a business that provides you time to live, **call 1-800-798-8000** or visit merrymaids.com for more information.

Own a franchise with the name people know and trust.

merry maids
Relax. It's Done.

Franchising

Merry Maids entices franchisees by marketing the perks of owning a business.

Through franchise arrangements, the franchiser gains fast and selective product distribution without incurring the high cost of constructing and operating its own outlets. The franchiser therefore has more capital for expanding production and advertising. It also can ensure, through the franchise agreement, that outlets are maintained and operated according to its own standards. The franchiser benefits from the fact that the franchisee, being a sole proprietor in most cases, is likely to be very highly motivated to succeed. Success of the franchise means more sales, which translate into higher income for the franchiser.

Franchise arrangements also have several drawbacks. The franchiser can dictate many aspects of the business: decor, design of employees' uniforms, types of signs, and numerous details of business operations. In addition, franchisees must pay to use the franchiser's name, products, and assistance. Usually there is a one-time franchise fee and continuing royalty and advertising fees, often collected as a percentage of sales. Franchisees often must work very hard, putting in 10- to 12-hour days, six or seven days a week. In some cases, franchise agreements are not uniform; one franchisee may pay more than another for the same services. Finally, the franchiser gives up a certain amount of control when entering into a franchise agreement. Consequently, individual establishments may not be operated exactly according to the franchiser's standards.

table 15.2 **TOP U.S. FRANCHISERS AND THEIR STARTUP COSTS**

Rank*	Franchise	Description	No. of Franchise Outlets Worldwide	Startup Costs
1	Subway	Sandwiches, salads	26,197	$74,900–$222,800
2	Dunkin' Donuts	Doughnuts, baked goods	6,892	$179,000–$1.6 million
3	Jackson-Hewitt Tax Service	Tax preparation services	5,379	$48,600–$91,800
4	7-Eleven	Convenience stores	27,161	Varies
5	UPS Store/Mail Boxes Etc.	Postal, business, communications services	5,760	$153,950–$266,800
6	Domino's Pizza	Pizza, breadsticks, buffalo wings	7,652	$141,400–$415,100
7	Jiffy Lube	Fast oil change	1,946	$214,000–$273,000
8	Sonic Drive-In	Drive-in restaurants	2,495	$861,300
9	McDonald's	Hamburgers, chicken, salads	22,554	$506,000–$1.6 million
10	Papa John's	Pizza	2,405	$250,000

*Ranking is based primarily on financial strength and stability, growth rate, size of the system, number of years in business, startup costs, litigation, percentage of terminations, and whether the company provides financing.

Source: "Franchise 500® 2007 Rankings," www.entrepreneur.com/franchises/rankings/franchise500-115608/2007,.html (accessed February 13, 2007).

Wholesaling

Wholesaling refers to all transactions in which products are bought for resale, for making other products, or for general business operations. It does not include exchanges with ultimate consumers. A **wholesaler** is an individual or organization that sells products that are bought for resale, for making other products, or for general business operations. In other words, wholesalers buy products and resell them to reseller, government, and institutional users. For example, Sysco, the nation's number 1 food-service distributor, supplies restaurants, hotels, schools, industrial caterers, and hospitals with everything from frozen and fresh food and paper products to medical and cleaning supplies. Wholesaling activities are not limited to goods; service companies, such as financial institutions, also use active wholesale networks. For example, some banks buy loans in bulk from other financial institutions, as well as making loans to their own retail customers. There are more than 453,000 wholesaling establishments in the United States,[30] and more than half of all products sold in this country pass through these firms.

Wholesalers may engage in many supply-chain management activities, including warehousing, shipping and product handling, inventory control, information system management and data processing, risk taking, financing, budgeting, and even marketing research and promotion. Regardless of whether there is a wholesaling firm involved in the supply chain, all product distribution requires the performance of these activities. In addition to bearing the primary responsibility for the physical distribution of products from manufacturers to retailers, wholesalers may establish information systems that help producers and retailers better manage the supply chain from producer to customer. Many wholesalers are using information technology and the Internet to allow their employees, customers, and suppliers to share information between intermediaries and facilitating agencies such as trucking companies and warehouse firms. Other firms are making their databases and marketing information systems available to their supply-chain partners to facilitate order processing, shipping, and product development and to share information about changing market conditions and customer desires. As a result, some wholesalers play a key role in supply-chain management decisions.

Services Provided by Wholesalers

Wholesalers provide essential services to both producers and retailers. By initiating sales contacts with a producer and selling diverse products to retailers, wholesalers serve as an extension of the producer's sales force. Wholesalers also provide financial assistance. They often pay for transporting goods; they reduce a producer's warehousing expenses and inventory investment by holding goods in inventory; they extend credit and assume losses from buyers who turn out to be poor credit risks; and when they buy a producer's entire output and pay promptly or in cash, they are a source of working capital. Wholesalers also serve as conduits for information within the marketing channel, keeping producers up to date on market developments and passing along the manufacturers' promotional plans to other intermediaries. Using wholesalers therefore gives producers a distinct advantage because the specialized services wholesalers perform allow producers to concentrate on developing and manufacturing products that match customers' needs and wants.

Wholesalers support retailers by assisting with marketing strategy, especially the distribution component. Wholesalers also help retailers to select inventory. They are often specialists on market conditions and experts at negotiating final purchases. In industries in which obtaining supplies is important, skilled buying is indispensable. For example, Atlanta-based Genuine Parts Company (GPC), the nation's top automotive parts wholesaler, has more than 70 years of experience in the auto parts business, which helps it serve its customers effectively. GPC supplies more than 300,000 replacement parts (from 150 different suppliers) to 6,000 NAPA Auto Parts stores.[31] Effective wholesalers make an effort to understand the businesses of their customers.

wholesaling Transactions in which products are bought for resale, for making other products, or for general business operations

wholesaler An individual or organization that sells products that are bought for resale, for making other products, or for general business operations

Limited-Line Wholesalers

McKesson is a limited-line wholesaler providing a wide variety of pharmaceutical supplies.

They can reduce a retailer's burden of looking for and coordinating supply sources. If the wholesaler purchases for several different buyers, expenses can be shared by all customers. Furthermore, whereas a manufacturer's salesperson offers retailers only a few products at a time, independent wholesalers always have a wide range of products available. Thus, through partnerships, wholesalers and retailers can forge successful relationships for the benefit of customers.

The distinction between services performed by wholesalers and those provided by other businesses has blurred in recent years. Changes in the competitive nature of business, especially the growth of strong retail chains like Wal-Mart, Home Depot, and Best Buy, are changing supply-chain relationships. In many product categories, such as electronics, furniture, and even food products, retailers have discovered that they can deal directly with producers, performing wholesaling activities themselves at a lower cost. An increasing number of retailers are relying on computer technology to expedite ordering, delivery, and handling of goods. Technology thus is allowing retailers to take over many wholesaling functions. However, when a wholesaler is eliminated from a marketing channel, wholesaling activities still have to be performed by a member of the supply chain, whether a producer, retailer, or facilitating agency. These wholesaling activities are critical components of supply-chain management.

Types of Wholesalers

Wholesalers are classified according to several criteria. Whether a wholesaler is independently owned or owned by a producer influences how it is classified. Wholesalers also can be grouped according to whether they take title to (own) the products they handle. The range of services provided is another criterion used for classification. Finally, wholesalers are classified according to the breadth and depth of their product lines. Using these criteria, we discuss three general types of wholesaling establishments: merchant wholesalers, agents and brokers, and manufacturers' sales branches and offices.

Merchant Wholesalers. **Merchant wholesalers** are independently owned businesses that take title to goods, assume risks associated with ownership, and generally

merchant wholesalers Independently owned businesses that take title to goods, assume ownership risks, and buy and resell products to other wholesalers, business customers, or retailers

figure 15.1

TYPES OF MERCHANT WHOLESALERS

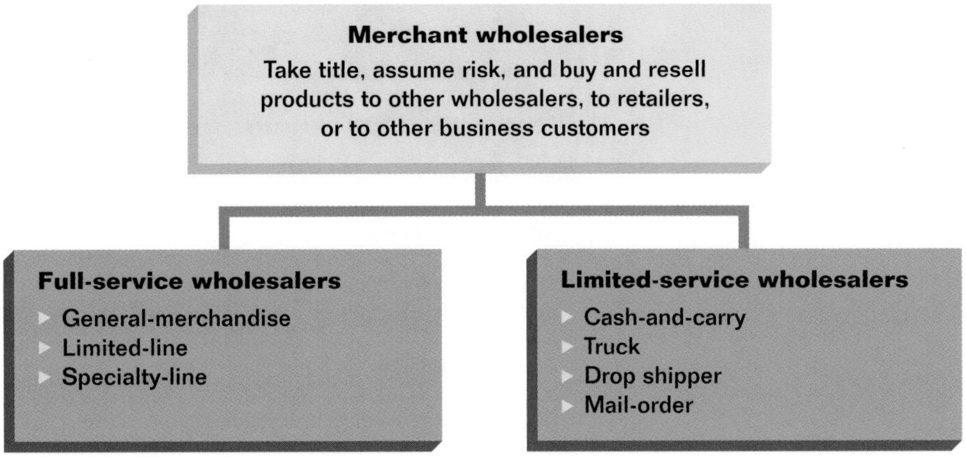

Merchant wholesalers
Take title, assume risk, and buy and resell products to other wholesalers, to retailers, or to other business customers

Full-service wholesalers
▸ General-merchandise
▸ Limited-line
▸ Specialty-line

Limited-service wholesalers
▸ Cash-and-carry
▸ Truck
▸ Drop shipper
▸ Mail-order

buy and resell products to other wholesalers, business customers, or retailers. A producer is likely to rely on merchant wholesalers when selling directly to customers would be economically unfeasible. Merchant wholesalers are also useful for providing market coverage, making sales contacts, storing inventory, handling orders, collecting market information, and furnishing customer support. Some merchant wholesalers are even involved in packaging and developing private brands to help retail customers be competitive. Merchant wholesalers go by various names, including *wholesaler, jobber, distributor, assembler, exporter,* and *importer.* They fall into one of two broad categories: full-service and limited-service (see Figure 15.1).

Full-service wholesalers perform the widest possible range of wholesaling functions. Customers rely on them for product availability, suitable assortments, breaking large quantities into smaller ones, financial assistance, and technical advice and service. Universal Corporation, the world's largest buyer and processor of leaf tobacco, is an example of a full-service wholesaler. Based in Richmond, Virginia, the firm buys, processes, resells, and ships tobacco and provides financing for its customers, which include cigarette manufacturers such as Philip Morris (which accounts for a significant portion of Universal's sales). Universal is also involved in sales of lumber, building products, and other agricultural products and has operations in 40 countries.[32] Full-service wholesalers handle either consumer or business products and provide numerous marketing services to their customers. Many large grocery wholesalers help retailers with store design, site selection, personnel training, financing, merchandising, advertising, coupon redemption, and scanning. Although full-service wholesalers often earn higher gross margins than other wholesalers, their operating expenses are also higher because they perform a wider range of functions.

Full-service wholesalers are categorized as general merchandise, general-line, and specialty-line wholesalers and as rack jobbers. **General merchandise wholesalers** carry a wide product mix but offer limited depth within product lines. They deal in products such as drugs, nonperishable foods, cosmetics, detergents, and tobacco. **General-line wholesalers** carry only a few product lines, such as groceries, lighting fixtures, or oil-well drilling equipment, but offer an extensive assortment of products within those lines. Bergen Brunswig Corporation, for example, is a general-line wholesaler of pharmaceuticals and health and beauty aids. General-line wholesalers provide a range of services similar to those of general merchandise wholesalers. **Specialty-line wholesalers** offer the narrowest range of products, usually a single product line or a few items within a product line. Red River Commodities, Inc., for example, is the leading

full-service wholesalers Merchant wholesalers that perform the widest range of wholesaling functions

general merchandise wholesalers Full-service wholesalers with a wide product mix but limited depth within product lines

general-line wholesalers Full-service wholesalers that carry only a few product lines but many products within those lines

specialty-line wholesalers Full-service wholesalers that carry only a single product line or a few items within a product line

table 15.3	SERVICES THAT LIMITED-SERVICE WHOLE-SALERS PROVIDE			
	Cash-and-Carry	**Truck**	**Drop Shipper**	**Mail-Order**
Physical possession of merchandise	Yes	Yes	No	Yes
Personal sales calls on customers	No	Yes	No	No
Information about market conditions	No	Some	Yes	Yes
Advice to customers	No	Some	Yes	No
Stocking and maintenance of merchandise in customers' stores	No	No	No	No
Credit to customers	No	No	Yes	Some
Delivery of merchandise to customers	No	Yes	No	No

importer (specialty-line wholesaler) of nuts, seeds, and dried fruits in the United States.[33] **Rack jobbers** are full-service, specialty-line wholesalers that own and maintain display racks in supermarkets, drugstores, and discount and variety stores. They set up displays, mark merchandise, stock shelves, and keep billing and inventory records; retailers need furnish only space. Rack jobbers specialize in nonfood items with high profit margins, such as health and beauty aids, books, magazines, hosiery, and greeting cards.

Limited-service wholesalers provide fewer marketing services than do full-service wholesalers and specialize in just a few functions. Producers perform the remaining functions or pass them on to customers or to other intermediaries. Limited-service wholesalers take title to merchandise but often do not deliver merchandise, grant credit, provide marketing information, store inventory, or plan ahead for customers' future needs. Because they offer restricted services, limited-service wholesalers are compensated with lower rates and have smaller profit margins than full-service wholesalers. The decision about whether to use a limited-service or a full-service wholesaler depends on the structure of the marketing channel and the need to manage the supply chain to provide competitive advantage. Although certain types of limited-service wholesalers are few in number, they are important in the distribution of products such as specialty foods, perishable items, construction materials, and coal. Table 15.3 summarizes the services provided by four typical limited-service wholesalers: cash-and-carry wholesalers, truck wholesalers, drop shippers, and mail-order wholesalers.

Cash-and-carry wholesalers are intermediaries whose customers—usually small businesses—pay cash and furnish transportation. Cash-and-carry wholesalers usually handle a limited line of products with a high turnover rate, such as groceries, building materials, and electrical or office supplies. Many small retailers whose accounts are refused by other wholesalers survive because of cash-and-carry wholesalers. **Truck wholesalers,** sometimes called *truck jobbers,* transport a limited line of products directly to customers for on-the-spot inspection and selection. They are often small operators who own and drive their own trucks. They usually have regular routes, calling on retailers and other institutions to determine their needs. **Drop shippers,** also known as *desk jobbers,* take title to products and negotiate sales but never take actual possession of products. They forward orders from retailers, business buyers, or other wholesalers to manufacturers and arrange for carload shipments of items to be delivered directly from producers to these customers. They assume responsibility for products during the entire transaction, including the costs of any unsold goods.

rack jobbers Full-service, specialty-line wholesalers that own and maintain display racks in stores

limited-service wholesalers Merchant wholesalers that provide some services and specialize in a few functions

cash-and-carry wholesalers Limited-service wholesalers whose customers pay cash and furnish transportation

truck wholesalers Limited-service wholesalers that transport products directly to customers for inspection and selection

drop shippers Limited-service wholesalers that take title to products and negotiate sales but never take actual possession of products

figure 15.2

TYPES OF AGENTS AND BROKERS

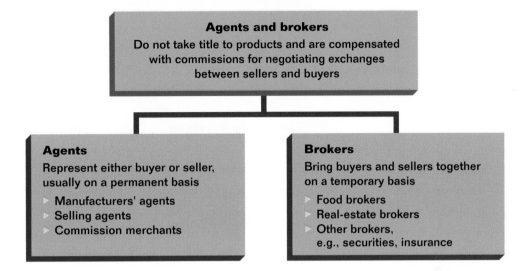

Mail-order wholesalers use catalogs instead of sales forces to sell products to retail and business buyers. Wholesale mail-order houses generally feature cosmetics, specialty foods, sporting goods, office supplies, and automotive parts. Mail-order wholesaling enables buyers to choose and order particular catalog items for delivery through United Parcel Service, the U.S. Postal Service, or other carriers. This is a convenient and effective method of selling small items to customers in remote areas that other wholesalers might find unprofitable to serve. The Internet has provided an opportunity for mail-order wholesalers to sell products over their own websites and have the products shipped by the manufacturers.

Agents and Brokers.   Agents and brokers negotiate purchases and expedite sales but do not take title to products (see Figure 15.2). Sometimes called *functional middlemen,* they perform a limited number of services in exchange for a commission, which generally is based on the product's selling price. **Agents** represent either buyers or sellers on a permanent basis, whereas **brokers** are intermediaries that buyers or sellers employ temporarily.

Although agents and brokers perform even fewer functions than limited-service wholesalers, they are usually specialists in particular products or types of customers and can provide valuable sales expertise. They know their markets well and often form long-lasting associations with customers. Agents and brokers enable manufacturers to expand sales when resources are limited, to benefit from the services of a trained sales force, and to hold down personal selling costs. Table 15.4 (on page 396) summarizes the services provided by agents and brokers.

Manufacturers' agents, which account for more than half of all agent wholesalers, are independent intermediaries that represent two or more sellers and usually offer customers complete product lines. They sell and take orders year round, much as a manufacturer's sales force does. Restricted to a particular territory, a manufacturer's agent handles noncompeting and complementary products. The relationship between the agent and the manufacturer is governed by written contracts that outline territories, selling price, order handling, and terms of sale relating to delivery, service, and warranties. Manufacturers' agents have little or no control over producers' pricing and marketing policies. They do not extend credit and may be unable to provide technical advice. Manufacturers' agents are commonly used in sales of apparel, machinery and equipment, steel, furniture, automotive products, electrical goods, and certain food items.

mail-order wholesalers Limited-service wholesalers that sell products through catalogs

agents Intermediaries that represent either buyers or sellers on a permanent basis

brokers Intermediaries that bring buyers and sellers together temporarily

manufacturers' agents Independent intermediaries that represent two or more sellers and offer complete product lines

table 15.4	SERVICES THAT AGENTS AND BROKERS PROVIDE			
	Manufacturers' Agents	Selling Agents	Commission Merchants	Brokers
Physical possession of merchandise	Some	Some	Yes	No
Long-term relationship with buyers or sellers	Yes	Yes	Yes	No
Representation of competing product lines	No	No	Yes	Yes
Limited geographic territory	Yes	No	No	No
Credit to customers	No	Yes	Some	No
Delivery of merchandise to customers	Some	Yes	Yes	No

Selling agents market either all of a specified product line or a manufacturer's entire output. They perform every wholesaling activity except taking title to products. Selling agents usually assume the sales function for several producers simultaneously and are used often in place of marketing departments. In fact, selling agents are used most often by small producers or by manufacturers that have difficulty maintaining a marketing department because of seasonal production or other factors. In contrast to manufacturers' agents, selling agents generally have no territorial limits and have complete authority over prices, promotion, and distribution. To avoid conflicts of interest, selling agents represent noncompeting product lines. They play a key role in advertising, marketing research, and credit policies of the sellers they represent, at times even advising on product development and packaging.

Commission merchants receive goods on consignment from local sellers and negotiate sales in large, central markets. Sometimes called *factor merchants*, these agents have broad powers regarding prices and terms of sale. They specialize in obtaining the best price possible under market conditions. Most often found in agricultural marketing, commission merchants take possession of truckloads of commodities, arrange for necessary grading or storage, and transport the commodities to auction or markets where they are sold. When sales are completed, the agents deduct commission and the expense of making the sale and then turn over profits to the producer. Commission merchants also offer planning assistance and sometimes extend credit but usually do not provide promotional support.

A broker's primary purpose is to bring buyers and sellers together. Thus brokers perform fewer functions than other intermediaries. They are not involved in financing or physical possession, have no authority to set prices, and assume almost no risks. Instead, they offer customers specialized knowledge of a particular commodity and a network of established contacts. Brokers are especially useful to sellers of certain types of products, such as supermarket products and real estate. Food brokers, for example, sell food and general merchandise to retailer-owned and merchant wholesalers, grocery chains, food processors, and business buyers.

Manufacturers' Sales Branches and Offices.   Sometimes called *manufacturers' wholesalers*, manufacturers' sales branches and offices resemble merchant wholesalers' operations. **Sales branches** are manufacturer-owned intermediaries that sell products and provide support services to the manufacturer's sales force. Situated away from the manufacturing plant, they are usually located where large customers are concentrated and demand is high. They offer credit, deliver goods, give promotional assistance, and furnish other services. Customers include retailers, business buyers, and other

selling agents Intermediaries that market a whole product line or a manufacturer's entire output

commission merchants Agents that receive goods on consignment and negotiate sales in large, central markets

sales branches Manufacturer owned intermediaries that sell products and provide support services to the manufacturer's sales force

wholesalers. Manufacturers of electrical supplies, such as Westinghouse Electric, and of plumbing supplies, such as American Standard, often have branch operations. They are also common in the lumber and automotive parts industries.

Sales offices are manufacturer-owned operations that provide services normally associated with agents. Like sales branches, they are located away from manufacturing plants, but unlike sales branches, they carry no inventory. A manufacturer's sales office (or branch) may sell products that enhance the manufacturer's own product line.

Manufacturers may set up these branches or offices to reach their customers more effectively by performing wholesaling functions themselves. A manufacturer also may set up such a facility when specialized wholesaling services are not available through existing intermediaries. A manufacturer's performance of wholesaling and physical distribution activities through its sales branch or office may strengthen supply-chain efficiency. In some situations, though, a manufacturer may bypass its sales office or branches entirely—for example, if the producer decides to serve large retailer customers directly.

...And Now, Back to Hard Rock Café

Many Hard Rock Café customers are tourists who eat at a Hard Rock Café and then buy T-shirts or other items as souvenirs. Some branded, city-specific items can be purchased only in person, which encourages customers to visit other Hard Rock Cafés when they travel. The company sells more than 12 million logo items annually, and more than 30 percent of annual revenue comes from merchandise sales. Hard Rock also commands an exceptional level of global brand awareness: 81 percent in Tokyo, 91 percent in Mexico City, and 98 percent in the United States. Hard Rock Café merchandise is sought after around the world by satisfied fans wanting to memorialize their visit to a Hard Rock Café. The company also has extremely loyal employees perhaps owing as much to caring managers as to employee benefits that include health and dental insurance, 401(k) plans, tuition reimbursement, bonuses, and prizes such as a Rolex watch after 10 years of employment and a diamond encirclement for the watch face after 20 years on the job. In all, the cost of outfitting a new café can exceed $3 million. This does not include the cost of all the food and merchandise that must be ready for customers on opening day. By making its distribution system more efficient, the company can rock on with continued expansion and added profits.

In 2006, the Seminole Tribe of Florida, in a deal thought to be the largest by a Native American tribe, paid $965 million for 124 Hard Rock Cafés, Four Hard Rock Hotels, two Hard Rock Casino Hotels, and two Hard Rock Live! Concert venues, as well as stakes in three unbranded hotels. The deal excluded the licensed locations, including the casino in Las Vegas. However, the deal added to the two Hard Rock Hotels and Casino resorts and five other casinos the tribe already operated. The tribe, headquartered in Hollywood, Florida, has a population of nearly 3,300; it has experience licensing and running Hard Rock Hotels and Casinos in Florida, which helped the tribe beat 70 other bidders for Hard Rock' assets. The Seminole Tribe has been a pioneer in Native American gaming: It opened the first American Indian–owned casino in the late 1970s, which served as a model for other tribes. Even before the Hard Rock deal, the tribe was among the top players in what is now a nearly $23 billion a year industry. According to Max Osceola, Jr., a tribal council representative, "Our ancestors sold Manhattan for trinkets. . . . We're going to buy Manhattan back, one hamburger at a time."[34]

1. What makes the Hard Rock Café so popular?

2. Would you visit more than one Hard Rock Café? Why or why not?

3. How does Hard Rock market itself?

sales offices Manufacturer owned operations that provide services normally associated with agents

CHAPTER REVIEW

1. Understand the purpose and function of retailers in the marketing channel.

Retailing includes all transactions in which buyers intend to consume products through personal, family, or household use. Retailers, organizations that sell products primarily to ultimate consumers, are important links in the marketing channel because they are both marketers for and customers of wholesalers and producers. They add value, provide services, and assist in making product selections.

2. Identify the major types of retailers.

Retail stores can be classified according to the breadth of products offered. Two broad categories are general merchandise retailers and specialty retailers. The primary types of general merchandise retailers include department stores, which are large retail organizations organized by departments and characterized by wide product mixes in considerable depth; discount stores, which are self-service, low-price, general merchandise outlets; convenience stores, which are small self-service stores that are open long hours and carry a narrow assortment of products, usually convenience items; supermarkets, which are large self-service food stores that carry some nonfood products; superstores, which are giant retail outlets that carry all the products found in supermarkets and most consumer products purchased on a routine basis; hypermarkets, which offer supermarket and discount store shopping at one location; warehouse clubs, which are large-scale, members-only discount operations; and warehouse and catalog showrooms, which are low-cost operations characterized by warehouse methods of materials handling and display, large inventories, and minimal services. Specialty retailers offer substantial assortments in a few product lines. They include traditional specialty retailers, which carry narrow product mixes with deep product lines; category killers, large specialty stores that concentrate on a major product category and compete on the basis of low prices and enormous product availability; and off-price retailers, which sell brand name manufacturers' seconds and product overruns at deep discounts.

3. Explore strategic issues in retailing.

Location, the least flexible of the strategic retailing issues, determines the trading area from which a store draws its customers and therefore should be evaluated carefully. When evaluating potential sites, retailers take into account various factors, including the location of the firm's target market within the trading area, customer characteristics, kinds of products sold, availability of public transportation and/or parking, and competitors' locations. Retailers can choose among several types of locations, including freestanding structures, traditional business districts, traditional planned shopping centers (neighborhood, community, regional, and superregional), or nontraditional shopping centers (lifestyle, power, and outlet).

Retail positioning involves identifying an unserved or underserved market segment and serving it through a strategy that distinguishes the retailer from others in those customers' minds. Store image, which should facilitate positioning, derives not only from atmosphere but also from location, products offered, customer services, prices, promotion, and the store's overall reputation. Atmospherics refers to the physical elements of a store's design that can be adjusted to appeal to consumers' emotions and thus induce them to buy. Scrambled merchandising adds unrelated product lines to an existing product mix and is being used by a growing number of stores to generate sales.

The wheel-of-retailing theory holds that new retail institutions start as low-status, low-margin, and low-price operations. As they develop, they increase service and raise prices and eventually become vulnerable to newer institutions, which enter the market and repeat the cycle.

4. Recognize the various forms of direct marketing and selling.

Direct marketing is the use of telecommunications and nonpersonal media to communicate product and organizational information to consumers, who then can purchase products by mail, telephone, or Internet. Such communication may occur through a catalog (catalog marketing), advertising (direct response marketing), telephone (telemarketing), television (television home shopping), or online (online retailing). Direct selling markets products to ultimate consumers through face-to-face sales presentations at home or in the workplace.

5. Examine franchising and its benefits and weaknesses.

Franchising is an arrangement in which a supplier grants a dealer the right to sell products in exchange for some type of consideration. Franchise arrangements have a number of advantages and disadvantages over traditional business forms, and their use is increasing.

6. Understand the nature and functions of wholesalers.

Wholesaling consists of all transactions in which products are bought for resale, for making other products, or for general business operations. Wholesalers are individuals or organizations that facilitate and expedite exchanges that are primarily wholesale transactions. For producers, wholesalers are a source of financial assistance and information; by performing specialized accumulation and allocation functions, they allow producers to concentrate on manufacturing products. Wholesalers provide retailers with buying expertise, wide product lines, efficient distribution, and warehousing and storage.

7. Understand how wholesalers are classified.

Merchant wholesalers are independently owned businesses that take title to goods and assume ownership risks. They are either full-service wholesalers, offering the widest possible range of wholesaling functions, or limited-service wholesalers, providing only some marketing services and specializing in a few functions. Full-service merchant wholesalers include general merchandise wholesalers, which offer a wide but relatively shallow product mix; general-line wholesalers, which offer extensive assortments within a few product lines; specialty-line wholesalers, which carry only a single product line or a few items within a line; and rack jobbers, which own and service display racks in supermarkets and other stores. Limited-service merchant wholesalers include cash-and-carry wholesalers, which sell to small businesses, require payment in cash, and do not deliver; truck wholesalers, which sell a limited line of products from their own trucks directly to customers; drop shippers, which own goods and negotiate sales but never take possession of products; and mail-order wholesalers, which sell to retail and business buyers through direct mail catalogs.

Agents and brokers negotiate purchases and expedite sales in exchange for a commission, but they do not take title to products. Whereas agents represent buyers or sellers on a permanent basis, brokers are intermediaries employed by buyers and sellers on a temporary basis to negotiate exchanges. Manufacturers' agents market the complete product lines of two or more sellers. Selling agents market a complete product line or a producer's entire output and perform every wholesaling function except taking title to products. Commission merchants are agents that receive goods on consignment from local sellers and negotiate sales in large, central markets.

Manufacturers' sales branches and offices are owned by manufacturers. Sales branches sell products and provide support services for the manufacturer's sales force in a given location. Sales offices carry no inventory and function much as agents do.

ACE self-test

Please visit the student website at **www.prideferrell.com** for ACE Self-Test questions that will help you prepare for exams.

KEY CONCEPTS

retailing
retailer
general merchandise
   retailer
department stores
discount stores
convenience store
supermarkets
superstores
hypermarkets
warehouse clubs
warehouse showrooms
traditional specialty
   retailers
category killer

off-price retailers
neighborhood shopping
   centers
community shopping
   centers
regional shopping centers
superregional shopping
   centers
lifestyle shopping centers
power shopping centers
retail positioning
atmospherics
category management
scrambled merchandising
wheel of retailing

direct marketing
catalog marketing
direct response marketing
telemarketing
television home shopping
online retailing
direct selling
franchising
wholesaling
wholesaler
merchant wholesalers
full-service wholesalers
general merchandise
   wholesalers
general-line wholesalers

specialty-line wholesalers
rack jobbers
limited-service wholesalers
cash-and-carry wholesalers
truck wholesalers
drop shippers
mail-order wholesalers
agents
brokers
manufacturers' agents
selling agents
commission merchants
sales branches
sales offices

ISSUES FOR DISCUSSION AND REVIEW

1. What value is added to a product by retailers? What value is added by retailers for producers and for ultimate consumers?

2. What are the major differences between discount stores and department stores?

3. In what ways are traditional specialty stores and off-price retailers similar? How do they differ?

4. What major issues should be considered when determining a retail site location?

5. Describe the three major types of traditional shopping centers. Give an example of each type in your area.

6. Discuss the major factors that help to determine a retail store's image. How does atmosphere add value to products sold in a store?

7. In what ways does the use of scrambled merchandising affect a store's image?

8. How is door-to-door selling a form of retailing? Some consumers believe that direct response orders bypass the retailer. Is this true?

9. If you were opening a retail business, would you prefer to open an independent store or own a store under a franchise arrangement? Explain your preference.

10. What services do wholesalers provide to producers and retailers?

11. What is the difference between a full-service merchant wholesaler and a limited-service merchant wholesaler?

12. Drop shippers take title to products but do not accept physical possession of them, whereas commission merchants take physical possession of products but do not accept title. Defend the logic of classifying drop shippers as wholesale merchants and commission merchants as agents.

13. Why are manufacturers' sales offices and branches classified as wholesalers? Which independent wholesalers are replaced by manufacturers' sales branches? By sales offices?

MARKETING APPLICATIONS

1. Juanita wants to open a small retail store that specializes in high-quality, high-priced children's clothing. What types of competitors should she be concerned about in this competitive retail environment? Why?

2. Location of retail outlets is an issue in strategic planning. What initial steps would you recommend to Juanita (see Marketing Application 1) when she considers a location for her store?

3. Visit a retail store you shop in regularly or one in which you would like to shop. Identify the store, and describe its atmospherics. Be specific about both exterior and interior elements, and indicate how the store is being positioned through its use of atmospherics.

4. Contact a local retailer you patronize, and ask the store manager to describe the store's relationship with one of its wholesalers. Using your text as a guide, identify the distribution activities performed by the wholesaler. Are any of these activities shared by both the retailer and the wholesaler? How do these activities benefit the retailer? How do they benefit you as a consumer?

Online Exercise

5. Wal-Mart provides a website from which customers can shop for products, search for a nearby store, and even preorder new products. The website lets customers browse what's on sale and view company information. Access Wal-Mart's website at **www.walmart.com**.
   a. How does Wal-Mart attempt to position itself on its website?
   b. Compare the atmospherics of Wal-Mart's website to the atmospherics of a traditional Wal-Mart store. Are they consistent? If not, should they be?
   c. Find Wal-Mart's history on the website. Relate the firm's history to the wheel-of-retailing concept.

globalEDGE™

You are an upper-level manager of a large retailing firm that currently is undertaking a primary initiative of international expansion. In your analysis on this topic, an important factor in choosing which markets to enter is the level of retail development in the countries targeted. Access the Global Retail Development Index website by using the search term "retail development" at **http://globaledge.msu.edu/ibrd** (and check the box "Resource Desk only"). What are four components that may assist in assessing the retail readiness of a country based on information provided by the Global Retail Development Index website? Can you name the top five emerging markets as ranked by an index on the topic? Are there any markets on your list that surprised you? Which three countries have the greatest market potential? Which market is the most stable?

Video CASE

Adventures in Retailing at REI

Few retailers allow customers to test ride mountain bikes on special indoor trails or let them pour water through different filtration devices before they decide which model to purchase. An open invitation to "try it before you buy it" is just one reason Recreational Equipment, Inc. (REI), stands out in the world of retailing. REI was founded in 1938 by 25 mountain climbers who pooled their buying power to get a better deal on ice axes and other climbing gear. From the start, REI was a consumer cooperative, a retail business that shares some of its profits with members. Today, the Kent, Washington, retailer sells a vast array of outdoor sporting goods and apparel through 80 stores in 27 states, a printed catalog, two websites, and telephone sales. It also operates REI Adventures, a travel service for those who want to paddle, climb, cycle, ski, hike, or enjoy a combination of outdoor activities while on vacation.

REI's store atmospherics are unique, making the shopping experience an adventure in itself. Most stores have a two-story climbing wall that customers are invited to scale when trying out gear before buying. For example, the store in Sandy, Utah, features a 22-foot-high climbing wall modeled after the granite walls of a local canyon. Like other stores in the chain, the Sandy store has demonstration areas devoted to camp stoves, water filter testing, and hiking boots. Surrounding these special areas are acres and acres of items that one employee calls "grown-up toys," from kayaks and canteens to snow shoes and sleeping bags.

Store employees are enthusiastic about the merchandise they sell because they share their customers' love of the active life. "A passion for the outdoors comes first throughout REI and is a natural bond between employees and customers," observes REI's vice president of direct sales. "That passion and commitment to quality are reflected whether you're in an REI store, shopping online, or placing a catalog order on the phone." This may help to explain REI's annual ranking in *Fortune* magazine's "100 Best Companies to Work for in America." Employees are trained to determine their customers'

needs, demonstrate appropriate products, and help customers make informed buying decisions.

REI's two retail websites feature page after page of product details, product comparisons, and how-to articles about outdoor sports and equipment. These sites are accessible from Internet kiosks set up in each REI store so that customers can order any of 50,000 products for home delivery. If they prefer, customers can eliminate shipping fees by having online orders sent to any REI store for pickup—an option chosen by more than 30 percent of REI-Outlet.com's customers.

Customers can become members of the REI cooperative by paying a one-time fee of $15. They are then eligible for refund vouchers of up to 10 percent on their total annual purchases from REI stores, catalogs, and websites. They also pay lower prices for equipment rented or repaired in REI stores and for travel packages arranged through REI Adventures.

One of REI's core values is its ongoing commitment to protecting the natural environment by donating to nature centers, open-space projects, youth recreation programs, land conservation, and related activities in local communities. Moreover, as REI's president notes, store employees invest a great deal of "sweat equity" in the local community by volunteering their time to maintain hiking trails, clean up rivers, and preserve the environment in many other ways.

The market for outdoor sporting goods and apparel is increasingly competitive. Bass Pro Shops, headquartered in Missouri, targets customers who like fishing, hunting, and boating with a huge catalog. Its 54 U.S. and Canadian stores offer demonstration areas for fishing and other sports, creating a focal point for customers. Cabela's operates 30 similar stores and an online catalog. Eastern Mountain Sports (EMS), headquartered in New Hampshire, operates 80 stores in eastern and midwestern states. In addition, REI competes with many independent stores and chain retailers that carry clothing and gear for the active lifestyle.

Today, REI generates more than $1 billion in revenue and serves nearly 3 million customers yearly. Its stores range in size from 10,000 to 95,000 square feet, so no two stores carry exactly the same merchandise. "Even though we don't have a lot of stores, we have a lot of variety in our stores," says REI's inventory planning manager, "and that creates merchandising challenges for us." REI's solution: Analyze the profitability and sales per square foot of each product category in each store, and then eliminate the weakest categories to make room for the strongest. This helps the retailer manage inventory more efficiently and choose the most profitable assortment for each store.[35]

Questions for Discussion

1. Why would REI locate many of its stores in freestanding structures rather than in shopping centers?
2. What is the likely effect of REI's consumer cooperative structure on the retailer's ability to build customer relationships?
3. What is REI's retail positioning, and why is it appropriate for the target market?

part

8

Promotion Decisions

Part 8 focuses on communication with target-market members and, at times, other groups. A specific marketing mix cannot satisfy people in a particular target market unless they are aware of the product and know where to find it. Some promotion decisions relate to a specific marketing mix, whereas others are geared toward promoting the entire organization. Chapter 16 discusses integrated marketing communications. It describes the communication process and the major promotional methods that can be included in promotion mixes. Chapter 17 analyzes the major steps in developing an advertising campaign. It also explains what public relations is and how it can be used. Chapter 18 deals with the management of personal selling and the role it can play in a firm's promotional efforts. It also explores the general characteristics of sales promotion and describes sales promotion techniques.

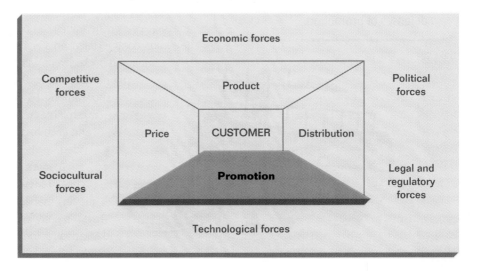

Integrated Marketing Communications

OBJECTIVES

1. Discuss the nature of integrated marketing communications.

2. Describe the process of communication.

3. Understand the role of promotion in the marketing mix.

4. Explain the objectives of promotion.

5. Understand the major elements of the promotion mix.

6. Describe the factors that affect the choice of promotion-mix elements.

7. Explore word-of-mouth communication and how it affects promotion.

8. Understand the criticisms and defenses of promotion.

Toyota Coordinates Promotions Across Many Platforms

Across the United States there are more than 226 million mobile phones in use, and consumers upgrade to more sophisticated handsets at a faster rate each year. During the last two seasons of TV show *American Idol,* Cingular (now AT&T) customers sent more than 100 million text messages in connection with the show; more than 4.8 million consumers access The Weather Channel's mobile Web products each month. The numbers speak for themselves: Mobile marketing has arrived as a serious force, and companies increasingly are using this new advertising medium. Indeed, marketers spent $150 million in mobile advertising in 2006, up from $45 million in 2005. Mobile marketing is the use of wireless media—primarily cellular phones and personal digital assistants (PDAs)—to deliver integrated promotional messages and interact with consumers. It includes text messaging (SMS), video messaging (MMS), video downloads such as "mobisodes"—short television program episodes designed specifically for mobile phones—and banner ads on mobile websites. It also includes content such as ringtones and wallpaper downloaded to mobile phones. So it's no surprise that Toyota, *Advertising Age*'s marketer of the year in 2006, used mobile marketing in its promotional arsenal when it launched its new fuel-efficient subcompact Yaris sedan and hatchback.

Toyota is targeting the Yaris at 18- to-34-year-olds by aiming promotional messages everywhere they can be found. Of course, it employed traditional television commercials and a website to create awareness for the new brand, but it also backed Yaris with the first-ever advertiser-sponsored mobile-phone episodes tied to Fox's *Prison Break,* the number 1 television show among 16- to-35-year-olds. In the first four weeks, the two-minute "mobisodes" were downloaded 255,000 times, and each had a Yaris commercial at the beginning of the video.

Toyota's innovative yet integrated message about the "cheeky, irreverent, and mischievous" Yaris didn't stop with the tiny mobile screen. The Yaris launch also marked Toyota's entry into video gaming. Toyota teamed the Yaris and Microsoft's Xbox360 for the first driving game for Xbox Live Arcade, and the Yaris had a heavy presence at the E3 video game

convention in Los Angeles. The company even offered a $20,000 prize for the best new cell phone game based on the Yaris at the DigiPen School of Technology. Toyota also made sure that the Yaris had its own profile page on social-networking sites such as Facebook and MySpace.com (where it already has 38,000 "friends"). And the Yaris was integrated into a series of sketches on Fox's *MadTV*.[1] ∎

O rganizations such as Toyota employ various promotional methods to communicate with their target markets. Providing information to customers and other stakeholders is vital to initiating and developing long-term relationships with them. In this chapter we look at the general dimensions of promotion. First, we discuss the nature of integrated marketing communications. We then define and examine the role of promotion. Next, we analyze the meaning and process of communication and explore some of the reasons promotion is used. After that, we consider major promotional methods and the factors that influence marketers' decisions to use particular methods. Finally, we examine criticisms and defenses of promotion.

What Is Integrated Marketing Communications?

Integrated marketing communications (IMC) refers to the coordination of promotional efforts to ensure maximum informational and persuasive impact on customers. Coordinating multiple marketing tools to produce this synergistic effect requires a marketer to employ a broad perspective. A major goal of integrated marketing

Communication Channels

Numerous communications tools such as Yahoo are available for use in integrated marketing communication programs.

integrated marketing communications (IMC) Coordination of promotional efforts for maximum informational and persuasive impact

communications is to send a consistent message to customers. When United Airlines launched Ted, a Chicago-based discount carrier catering to its own business customers' vacation needs, it employed a variety of tactics to introduce the new brand and reinforce its identity. For example, a fleet of orange trucks paraded throughout Chicago and appeared at special events, bringing fun activities and treats to get people to think that Ted's low fares would enable them to treat themselves to a vacation. In the "Random Acts of Ted" promotion, special representatives handed out small treats (e.g., glow sticks at a Fourth-of-July celebration and fans after a marathon). Fifteen-second television ads targeted specific Chicago neighborhoods with the simple low-fare message, and radio ads employed a humorous "man-on-the-street" approach. The startup's consistent message across many vehicles helped to boost brand awareness, which quickly translated to full planes.[2]

Because various units both inside and outside most companies traditionally have planned and implemented promotional efforts, customers have not always received consistent messages. Integrated marketing communications allow a firm to coordinate and manage its promotional efforts to transmit consistent messages. This approach fosters not only long-term customer relationships but also the efficient use of promotional resources.

The concept of integrated marketing communications has been increasingly accepted for several reasons. Advertising to a mass audience, a very popular promotional method in the past, is used less today because of its high cost and unpredictable audience size. Marketers now can take advantage of more precisely targeted promotional tools such as cable TV, direct mail, the Internet, special-interest magazines, CDs and DVDs, cell phones, and even iPods. Database marketing is also allowing marketers to target individual customers more precisely. Until recently, suppliers of marketing communications were specialists. Advertising agencies developed advertising campaigns, sales promotion companies provided sales promotion activities and materials, and public relations firms engaged in publicity efforts. Today, several promotion-related companies provide one-stop shopping to the client seeking advertising, sales promotion, and public relations, thus reducing coordination problems for the sponsoring company. Because the overall cost of marketing communications has risen significantly, upper management demands systematic evaluations of communication efforts and a reasonable return on investment.

The specific communication vehicles employed and the precision with which they are used are changing as both information technology and customer interests become increasingly dynamic. For example, an increasing number of companies are running short advertisements during podcasts of TV shows and other videos that users download to their video iPods.[3] Some companies are even creating their own branded content to exploit the many vehicles through which consumers obtain information. Burger King, for example, produced a movie, *Above the King,* about a teenager who lives over a Burger King restaurant and befriends an aristocrat. The company also used its updated king mascot not only in television commercials but also in its own Xbox video games and in a MySpace profile.[4] Mars created an Internet show, *Instant Def,* for its Snickers brand featuring hip-hop performers will.i.am, Fergie, Taboo, and apl.de.ap. Such branded content does not replace traditional advertising but gives marketers new, controlled avenues for reaching consumers who have more entertainment choices today than ever before.[5]

Today, marketers and customers have almost unlimited access to data about each other. Integrating and customizing marketing communications while protecting customer privacy has become a major challenge. Through the Internet, companies can provide product information and services that are coordinated with traditional promotional activities. Communication relationships with customers actually can determine the nature of the product. Reflect.com, an online cosmetics firm, mixes makeup for different skin types based on information exchanges with customers. The sharing of information and use of technology to facilitate communication between buyers and sellers are necessary for successful customer relationship management.

figure 16.1

THE COMMUNICATION PROCESS

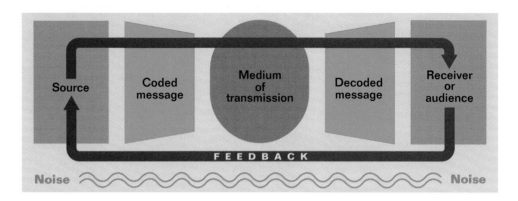

The Communication Process

Communication is essentially the transmission of information. For communication to take place, both the sender and the receiver of information must share some common ground. They must have a common understanding of the symbols, words, and pictures used to transmit information. Thus we define **communication** as a sharing of meaning.[6] Implicit in this definition is the notion of transmission of information because sharing necessitates transmission.

As Figure 16.1 shows, communication begins with a source. A **source** is a person, group, or organization with a meaning it attempts to share with an audience. A source could be a salesperson wishing to communicate a sales message or an organization wanting to send a message to thousands of customers through an advertisement. Developing a strategy can enhance the effectiveness of the source's communication. A **receiver** is the individual, group, or organization that decodes a coded message, and an *audience* is two or more receivers. The intended receivers, or audience, of an advertisement for Kashi's Heart to Heart cereal, for example, might be consumers who are concerned about reducing their cholesterol and blood pressure. Kashi could use this information to target receivers with integrated marketing communications about its products.

To share meaning, a source must convert the meaning into a series of signs or symbols representing ideas or concepts. This is called the **coding process**, or *encoding*. When coding meaning into a message, the source must consider certain characteristics of the receiver or audience. To share meaning, the source should use signs or symbols familiar to the receiver or audience. Research has shown that persuasive messages from a source are more effective when the appeal matches an individual's personality.[7] Marketers who understand this realize the importance of knowing their target market and ensuring that an advertisement, for example, uses language the target market understands. Thus, when General Mills advertises Cheerios, it does not mention in its advertising all the ingredients used to make the cereal because some ingredients would have little meaning to consumers. Some notable problems have occurred in translating English advertisements into other languages to communicate with customers in global markets. For example, Budweiser has been advertised in Spain as the "Queen of Beers," and the Chinese have been encouraged to "eat their fingers off" when receiving KFC's slogan "Finger-Lickin' Good."[8] Clearly, it is important that people understand the language used in promotion.

When coding a meaning, a source needs to use signs or symbols that the receiver or audience uses for referring to the concepts the source intends to convey. Instead of

communication A sharing of meaning

source A person, group, or organization with a meaning it tries to share

receiver The individual, group, or organization that decodes a coded message

coding process Converting meaning into a series of signs or symbols

| table 16.1 | WHERE PEOPLE GET THEIR NEWS AND INFORMATION |

Survey Respondents Who Say They . . . Daily	Percent
Watch television	56.1
Use the Internet	53.3
Listen to the radio	34.3
Read print newspapers	33.5
Read print magazines	5.8

Source: Harris Interactive, Inc., in Ron Alsop, "News, Ads Shape Corporate Images," *The Wall Street Journal,* January 31, 2007, http://online.wsj.com.

technical jargon, explanatory language that helps consumers to understand is more likely to result in positive attitudes and purchase intentions.[9] Marketers try to avoid signs or symbols that may have several meanings for an audience. For example, *soda* as a general term for soft drinks might not work well in national advertisements. Although in some parts of the United States the word means "soft drink," in other regions it may connote bicarbonate of soda, an ice cream drink, or something one mixes with Scotch whiskey.

To share a coded meaning with the receiver or audience, a source selects and uses a medium of transmission. A **communications channel**, the medium of transmission, carries the coded message from the source to the receiver or audience. Transmission media include ink on paper, air-wave vibrations produced by vocal cords, chalk marks on a chalkboard, and electronically produced vibrations of air waves (in radio and television signals, for example). Table 16.1 summarizes the leading communications channels from which people obtain information and news.

When a source chooses an inappropriate communications channel, several problems may arise. The coded message may reach some receivers, but the wrong ones. Coded messages also may reach intended receivers in incomplete form because the intensity of the transmission is weak. For example, radio and broadcast television signals are received effectively only over a limited range, which varies depending on climatic conditions. Members of the target audience living on the fringe of the broadcast area may receive a weak signal; others well within the broadcast area also may receive an incomplete message if, for example, they listen to the radio while driving or studying.

In the **decoding process**, signs or symbols are converted into concepts and ideas. When a receiver finds that a message runs counter to his or her own attitudes, the source may influence the decoding process.[10] Seldom does a receiver decode exactly the same meaning that the source coded. When the result of decoding differs from what was coded, noise exists. **Noise** is anything that reduces the clarity and accuracy of the communication; it has many sources and may affect any or all parts of the communication process. Noise sometimes arises within the communications channel itself. Radio static, poor or slow Internet connections, and laryngitis are sources of noise. Noise also occurs when a source uses signs or symbols that are unfamiliar to the receiver or have a different meaning from the one intended. Noise also may originate in the receiver; a receiver may be unaware of a coded message when perceptual processes block it out.

The receiver's response to a message is **feedback** to the source. The source usually expects and normally receives feedback, although perhaps not immediately. During feedback, the receiver or audience is the source of a message directed toward the

communications channel
The medium of transmission that carries the coded message from the source to the receiver or audience

decoding process Converting signs or symbols into concepts and ideas

noise Anything that reduces a communication's clarity and accuracy

feedback The receiver's response to a message

original source, which then becomes a receiver. Feedback is coded, sent through a communications channel, and decoded by the receiver, the source of the original communication. Thus communication is a circular process, as indicated in Figure 16.1.

During face-to-face communication, such as occurs in personal selling and product sampling, verbal and nonverbal feedback can be immediate. Instant feedback lets communicators adjust messages quickly to improve the effectiveness of their communication. For example, when a salesperson realizes through feedback that a customer does not understand a sales presentation, the salesperson adapts the presentation to make it more meaningful to the customer. This may be why face-to-face sales presentations create higher behavioral intentions to purchase services than do telemarketing sales contacts.[11] In interpersonal communication, feedback occurs through talking, touching, smiling, nodding, eye movements, and other body movements and postures.

When mass communication such as advertising is used, feedback is often slow and difficult to recognize. For example, Coca-Cola is trying to revitalize sales of soft drinks, especially its Coca-Cola Zero product, by expanding its target market and boosting promotional spending on the zero-calorie soft drink to include sponsorship of the Notre Dame football team, national advertising during college football, and an updated product package.[12] It may be several years, however, before the effects of this promotion will be known. Feedback does exist for mass communication in the form of measures of changes in sales volume or in consumers' attitudes and awareness levels.

Each communication channel has a limit on the volume of information it can handle effectively. This limit, called **channel capacity**, is determined by the least efficient component of the communication process. Consider communications that depend on speech. An individual source can speak only so fast, and there is a limit to how much an individual receiver can take in aurally. Beyond that point, additional messages cannot be decoded; thus meaning cannot be shared. Although a radio announcer can read several hundred words a minute, a one-minute advertising message should not exceed about 150 words because most announcers cannot articulate words into understandable messages at a rate beyond 150 words per minute.

The Role and Objectives of Promotion

channel capacity The limit on the volume of information a communication channel can handle effectively

promotion Communication to build and maintain relationships by informing and persuading one or more audiences

Promotion is communication that builds and maintains favorable relationships by informing and persuading one or more audiences to view an organization more positively and to accept its products. While a company may pursue several promotional objectives (discussed later in this chapter), the overall role of promotion is to stimulate product demand. Toward this end, many organizations spend considerable resources on promotion to build and enhance relationships with current and potential customers. For example, the egg ("The Incredible Edible Egg"), pork ("Pork: The Other White Meat"), and milk ("Got Milk?") industries promote the use of these products to stimulate demand. Marketers also indirectly facilitate favorable relationships by focusing information about company activities and products on interest groups (such as environmental and consumer groups), current and potential investors, regulatory agencies, and society in general. For example, some organizations promote responsible use of products criticized by society, such as tobacco, alcohol, and violent movies. Companies sometimes promote programs that help selected groups. Yoplait, for instance, supports the Susan G. Komen Breast Cancer Research Foundation with its "Save Lids to Save Lives" campaign, which contributes 10 cents to the charity for every pink yogurt lid sent in by consumers.[13] Such *cause-related marketing* efforts link the purchase of products to philanthropic efforts for one or more causes. By contributing to causes that its target markets support, cause-related marketing can help marketers to boost sales and generate goodwill. Marketers also sponsor special events, often leading to news coverage and positive promotion of organizations and their brands. Fendi, for example, held a star-studded hip-hop party in Tokyo to promote the designer label's new B.Mix line of bags.[14]

Role of Promotion

Honda stimulates demand for its automobiles by promoting its environmentally friendly models.

For maximum benefit from promotional efforts, marketers strive for proper planning, implementation, coordination, and control of communications. Effective management of integrated marketing communications is based on information about and feedback from customers and the marketing environment, often obtained from an organization's marketing information system (see Figure 16.2). How successfully marketers use promotion to maintain positive relationships depends largely on the quantity and quality of information the organization receives. Because customers derive information and opinions from many different sources, integrated marketing communications planning also takes into account informal methods of communication such as word of mouth and independent information sources on the Internet.

Promotional objectives vary considerably from one organization to another and within organizations over time. Large firms with multiple promotional programs operating simultaneously may have quite varied promotional objectives. For the purpose of analysis, we focus on eight promotional objectives. Although this set of possible promotional objectives is not exhaustive, one or more of these objectives underlie many promotional programs.

Create Awareness

A considerable amount of promotion focuses on creating awareness. For an organization introducing a new product or a line extension, making customers aware of the product is crucial to initiating the product adoption process. A marketer that has invested heavily in product development strives to create product awareness quickly to generate revenues to offset the high costs of product development and introduction. To create awareness of its new Spicy Premium Chicken sandwich, for example, McDonald's passed out samples of the sandwich, coupons, T-shirts, and iPod covers in 14 cities.[15]

Creating awareness is important for existing products, too. Promotional efforts may aim to increase awareness of brands, product features, image-related issues (such as organizational size or socially responsive behavior), or operational characteristics (such as store hours, locations, and credit availability). Some promotional programs are unsuccessful because marketers fail to generate awareness of critical issues among a significant portion of target-market members or because the programs do not target the right audience.

Stimulate Demand

When an organization is the first to introduce an innovative product, it tries to stimulate **primary demand**—demand for a product category rather than for a specific

primary demand Demand for a product category rather than for a specific brand

figure 16.2

INFORMATION FLOWS ARE IMPORTANT IN INTEGRATED MARKETING COMMUNICATIONS

Information about customers and marketing environment forces → Integrated marketing communications plan → Customers

F E E D B A C K

4,000-YEAR-OLD MAN FOUND FROZEN IN ICE, FEET STILL WARM AND DRY.

THE BUGASTORM™ LIGHT WEIGHT SKI SOCK: With 73% non-itch Merino wool for warmth, moisture wicking and breathability • Comfy over-calf length, arch support and selective cushioning • 800-MA BOYLE or columbia.com

TESTED TOUGH
Gert Boyle, Chairman

◆ Columbia
Sportswear Company.

Selective Demand

In this advertisement for ski socks, Columbia attempts to stimulate selective demand.

pioneer promotion Promotion that informs consumers about a new product

selective demand Demand for a specific brand

brand of product—through pioneer promotion. **Pioneer promotion** informs potential customers about the product: what it is, what it does, how it can be used, and where it can be purchased. Because pioneer promotion is used in the introductory stage of the product life cycle, which means there are no competing brands, it neither emphasizes brand names nor compares brands. The first company to introduce the digital video recorder, for instance, initially attempted to stimulate primary demand by emphasizing the benefits of digital video recorders in general rather than the benefit of its specific brand. Primary-demand stimulation is not just for new products. At times, an industry trade association rather than a single firm uses promotional efforts to stimulate primary demand.

To build **selective demand**, demand for a specific brand, a marketer employs promotional efforts that point out the strengths and benefits of a specific brand. Building selective demand also requires singling out attributes important to potential buyers. Selective demand can be stimulated by differentiating the product from competing brands in the minds of potential buyers. It also can be stimulated by increasing the number of product uses and promoting them through advertising campaigns, as well as through price discounts, free samples, coupons, consumer contests and games, and sweepstakes. Bennigan's, for example, launched an advertising campaign and held a 30th anniversary party to coincide with St. Patrick's Day to remind customers that the Irish-themed restaurant chain provides a fun environment where people can share good food.[16] Promotions for large package sizes or multiple-product packages are directed at increasing consumption, which, in turn, can stimulate demand. In addition, selective demand can be stimulated by encouraging existing customers to use more of the product.

Encourage Product Trial

When attempting to move customers through the product adoption process, a marketer may successfully create awareness and interest, but customers may stall during the evaluation stage. In this case, certain types of promotion, such as free samples, coupons, test drives or limited free-use offers, contests, and games, are employed to encourage product trial. Diamond Foods, for example, gave out product samples during the Emerald Bowl football game to promote its new Emerald brand trail mix product.[17] Whether a marketer's product is the first of a new product category, a new brand in an existing category, or simply an existing brand seeking customers, trial-inducing promotional efforts aim to make product trial convenient and low risk for potential customers.

Identify Prospects

Certain types of promotional efforts are directed at identifying customers who are interested in the firm's product and are most likely to buy it. A marketer may use a magazine advertisement with a direct-response information form, requesting the reader to complete and mail the form to receive additional information. Some advertisements have toll-free numbers to facilitate direct customer response. Customers who fill out information blanks or call the organization usually have higher interest in the product, which makes them likely sales prospects. The organization

SIP ENERGY. GULP DATA.

The new Sun Fire™ servers with CoolThreads™ technology.
5x the performance, 1/5 the power, 1/4 the size.

Get a free 60-day trial now at **sun.com.**

Encouraging Product Trial

Sun Microsystems encourages product trial by offering free use for a selected period of time.

can respond with phone calls, follow-up letters, or personal contact by salespeople. Dun & Bradstreet, for example, offered a free article on customer relationship management to businesspeople who mailed in a card or called a toll-free number. This helped the consulting firm identify prospects to sell data used to develop and maintain customer relationships.

Retain Loyal Customers

Clearly, maintaining long-term customer relationships is a major goal of most marketers. Such relationships are quite valuable. Promotional efforts directed at customer retention can help an organization control its costs because the costs of retaining customers are usually considerably lower than those of acquiring new ones. Frequent-user programs, such as those sponsored by airlines, car rental agencies, and hotels, seek to reward loyal customers and encourage them to remain loyal. Moët Hennessy, for example, introduced the Sparkling Circle, a membership club for 15,000 loyal customers.[18] Some organizations employ special offers that only their existing customers can use. To retain loyal customers, marketers not only advertise loyalty programs but also use reinforcement advertising, which assures current users that they have made the right brand choice and tells them how to get the most satisfaction from the product.

Facilitate Reseller Support

Reseller support is a two-way street. Producers generally want to provide support to resellers to maintain sound working relationships, and in turn, they expect resellers to support their products. When a manufacturer advertises a product to consumers, resellers should view this promotion as a form of strong manufacturer support. In some instances, a producer agrees to pay a certain proportion of retailers' advertising expenses for promoting its products. When a manufacturer is introducing a new consumer brand in a highly competitive product category, it may be difficult to persuade supermarket managers to carry this brand. However, if the manufacturer promotes the new brand with free samples and coupon distribution in the retailer's area, a supermarket manager views these actions as strong support and is much more likely to handle the product. To encourage wholesalers and retailers to market its products more aggressively, a manufacturer may provide them with special offers, buying allowances, and contests. In certain industries, a producer's salesperson may provide support to a wholesaler by working with the wholesaler's customers (retailers) in the presentation and promotion of the products. Strong relationships with resellers are important to a firm's ability to maintain a sustainable competitive advantage. The use of various promotional methods can help an organization achieve this goal.

Combat Competitive Promotional Efforts

At times, a marketer's objective in using promotion is to offset or lessen the effect of a competitor's promotional program. This type of promotional activity does not necessarily increase the organization's sales or market share, but it may prevent a sales or market share loss. A combative promotional objective is used most often by firms in extremely competitive consumer markets, such as the fast-food and automobile industries. When some automakers began advertising their automobiles' ability to withstand collisions, as determined by crash tests conducted by various federal and private agencies, Volkswagen, Volvo, and other firms quickly launched their own safety ads to combat their competitors' advertising. Although these ads were trying to promote safety records, the companies also were trying to prevent market share loss in a very competitive market.

Reduce Sales Fluctuations

Demand for many products varies from one month to another because of factors such as climate, holidays, and seasons. A business, however, cannot operate at peak efficiency when sales fluctuate rapidly. Changes in sales volume translate into changes in production, inventory levels, personnel needs, and financial resources. When promotional techniques reduce fluctuations by generating sales during slow periods, a firm can use its resources more efficiently.

Promotional techniques are often designed to stimulate sales during sales slumps. For example, advertisements promoting price reduction of lawn-care equipment can increase sales during fall and winter months. During peak periods, a marketer may refrain from advertising to prevent stimulating sales to the point where the firm cannot handle all the demand. On occasion, an organization advertises that customers can be better served by coming in on certain days. A pizza outlet, for example, might distribute coupons that are valid only Monday through Thursday because on Friday through Sunday the restaurant is extremely busy.

To achieve the major objectives of promotion discussed here, companies must develop appropriate promotional programs. In the next section we consider the basic components of such programs, referred to as the *promotion-mix elements*.

The Promotion Mix

Several promotional methods can be used to communicate with individuals, groups, and organizations. When an organization combines specific methods to manage the integrated marketing communications for a particular product, that combination constitutes the promotion mix for that product. The four possible elements of a **promotion mix** are advertising, personal selling, public relations, and sales promotion (see Figure 16.3). For some products, firms use all four ingredients; for others, they use only two or three.

promotion mix A combination of promotional methods used to promote a specific product

> **figure 16.3**
>
> **THE FOUR POSSIBLE ELEMENTS OF A PROMOTION MIX**

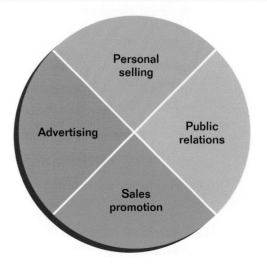

© 2005 Merck & Co., Inc. All rights reserved. 20608303(22)-03/05-PPH

Think cervical cancer isn't an issue until you're much older?

Millions of young women have a virus they don't even know about. It's called human papillomavirus (HPV), and certain types can cause cervical cancer. For most women, HPV clears on its own. But for some, cervical cancer can develop. Ask your doctor about the importance of Pap tests. Cervical cancer, caused by a virus. Now that you know,

Tell someone.

To:

tell-someone.com   1-877-NOW-TELL

Send eCards at tell-someone.com

◇ MERCK

Advertising Aimed at Prevention

Merck & Co., Inc. uses the "Tell Someone" campaign to heighten awareness of cervical cancer and human papillomavirus (HPV).

Advertising

Advertising is a paid nonpersonal communication about an organization and its products transmitted to a target audience through mass media, including television, radio, the Internet, newspapers, magazines, direct mail, outdoor displays, and signs on mass-transit vehicles. Individuals and organizations use advertising to promote goods, services, ideas, issues, and people. Being highly flexible, advertising can reach an extremely large target audience or focus on a small, precisely defined segment. For instance, Wendy's advertising focuses on a large audience of potential fast-food customers, ranging from children to adults, whereas advertising for Gulfstream jets aims at a much smaller and more specialized target market.

Advertising offers several benefits. It is extremely cost-efficient when it reaches a vast number of people at a low cost per person. For example, the cost of a four-color, one-page advertisement in *Time* magazine is $246,000. Because the magazine reaches more than 4 million subscribers, the cost of reaching 1,000 subscribers is only about $62.[19]

Advertising also lets the source repeat the message several times. Levi Strauss, for example, advertises on television, in magazines, and in outdoor displays. Furthermore, advertising a product a certain way can add to its value, and the visibility an organization gains from advertising can enhance its image. For example, research suggests that incorporating touchable elements that generate a positive sensory feedback in mail and print advertising can be a positive persuasive tool.[20] At times, a firm tries to enhance its own or its product's image by including celebrity endorsers in advertisements. For example, the National Fluid Milk Processor Promotion Board's "milk moustache" campaign has featured Beyoncé and Solange Knowles, David Beckham, Alex Rodriguez, and even Superman.[21]

Advertising has disadvantages as well. Even though the cost per person reached may be low, the absolute dollar outlay can be extremely high, especially for commercials during popular television shows. High costs can limit, and sometimes prevent, the use of advertising in a promotion mix. Advertising rarely provides rapid feedback. Measuring its effect on sales is difficult, and it is ordinarily less persuasive than personal selling. In most instances, the time available to communicate a message to customers is limited to seconds because people look at a print advertisement for only a few seconds, and most broadcast commercials are 30 seconds or less long. Of course, the use of "infomercials" can increase exposure time for viewers. We discuss advertising in considerable detail in Chapter 17.

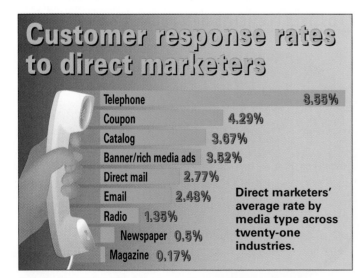

Customer response rates to direct marketers

Telephone	8.55%
Coupon	4.29%
Catalog	3.67%
Banner/rich media ads	3.52%
Direct mail	2.77%
Email	2.48%
Radio	1.35%
Newspaper	0.5%
Magazine	0.17%

Direct marketers' average rate by media type across twenty-one industries.

Source: The DMA 2005 Response Rate Report.

Nielsen Gets Students to Play the Ratings Game

Most of us have heard of the Nielsen television ratings system, but few of us really understand how it works. Now that Nielsen is including away-from-home college students, it's time for a crash course. Nielsen uses a national panel consisting of 10,000 households to determine the country's viewing habits. Before 1987, people living in the randomly chosen households agreed to record the programs that they watched in paper diaries. Today, people in surveyed households agree to press a button on an electronic "people meter" device installed by Nielsen each time they begin to watch a show. Once Nielsen receives these data, it estimates audience size to the nearest thousand and breaks down the data by demographics. For years, the Nielsen system has been criticized widely. One regularly cited flaw has been the fact that college students residing in dorms have not been counted. However, Nielsen recently asked currently surveyed households to include viewing data from members who are living on college campuses. Of those who fall into this category, about a third have agreed to take part in the survey. This means that the 130 participating college students will have a significant impact on Nielsen's description of the overall viewing habits of people aged 18 to 24.

As a result of Nielsen's inclusion of away-from-home college students, ratings for several television shows and networks have jumped dramatically. Comedy Central in particular has seen a huge jump

in ratings. Its *Drawn Together* cartoon boasted a 60 percent ratings increase among men aged 18 to 24. *South Park, The Daily Show with Jon Stewart,* and *The Colbert Report* are also said to have large college audiences. ABC's *Grey's Anatomy* and CW's *Gilmore Girls* are also popular—their ratings have jumped more than 50 percent among those aged 18 to 24.

Nielsen ratings are of critical importance to both networks and advertisers. Simply put, advertisers invest in shows through which they can reach the greatest number of viewers in their target markets. And networks hope that higher ratings for shows popular with the 18- to 24-year-old demographic translate into more money from advertisers targeting the college crowd. While the addition of surveying on-campus college students appears to be a step forward for Nielsen, some still contend that the entire ratings system needs a major overhaul. For example, professors at Northwestern University and California State University, Fullerton, assert that the sample size is simply too small to represent viewing habits accurately. Others worry that Nielsen's system doesn't account for those viewing television outside the home/dorm room. People regularly view TV in less traditional locations—sports bars, hotel rooms, gyms, airport lounges, and so on. And people are increasingly viewing their favorite shows on their computers, iPods, and other devices. Thus many believe that the Nielsen system needs to be significantly updated.

Although Nielsen executives don't feel that its system is highly flawed, they do agree that it needs updating. They are currently working to develop portable people meters and to implement devices that will identify audio signals of radio and television programs without requiring an individual to press a button. The Nielsen system has yet to enter the twenty-first century, but it's taking steps to get there.[a]

Personal Selling

Personal selling is a paid personal communication that seeks to inform customers and persuade them to purchase products in an exchange situation. The phrase *purchase products* is interpreted broadly to encompass acceptance of ideas and issues. Telemarketing, direct selling over the telephone, relies heavily on personal selling.

Personal selling has both advantages and limitations when compared with advertising. Advertising is general communication aimed at a relatively large target audience, whereas personal selling involves more specific communication directed at one or several persons. Reaching one person through personal selling costs considerably more than through advertising, but personal selling efforts often have greater impact on customers. Personal selling also provides immediate feedback, allowing marketers to adjust their messages to improve communication. It helps them to determine and respond to customers' information needs.

When a salesperson and a customer meet face to face, they use several types of interpersonal communication. The predominant communication form is language, both spoken and written. A salesperson and customer frequently use **kinesic communication**, or communication through the movement of head, eyes, arms, hands, legs, or torso. Winking, head nodding, hand gestures, and arm motions are forms of kinesic communication. A good salesperson often can evaluate a prospect's interest in a product or presentation by noting eye contact and head nodding. **Proxemic communication**, a less obvious form of communication used in personal selling situations, occurs when either person varies the physical distance separating them. When a customer backs away from a salesperson, for example, he or she may be displaying a lack of interest in the product or expressing dislike for the salesperson. Touching, or **tactile communication**, is also a form of communication, although less popular in the United States than in many other countries. Handshaking is a common form of tactile communication both in the United States and elsewhere. We discuss personal selling in more detail in Chapter 18.

Public Relations

While many promotional activities are focused on a firm's customers, other stakeholders—suppliers, employees, stockholders, the media, educators, potential investors, government officials, and society in general—are important to an organization as well. To communicate with customers and stakeholders, a company employs public relations. Public relations is a broad set of communication efforts used to create and maintain favorable relationships between an organization and its stakeholders. Maintaining a positive relationship with one or more stakeholders can affect a firm's current sales and profits, as well as its long-term survival.

Public relations uses various tools, including annual reports, brochures, event sponsorship, and sponsorship of socially responsible programs aimed at protecting the environment or helping disadvantaged individuals. Nintendo, for example, is seeking to target older game players by hosting Super Bowl parties with men's magazines *Maxim* and *FHM*, as well as Spring Break parties and music tours, and it sponsored the Burton snowboarding championships.[22] Merrill Lynch sponsored a "Women of the World" art exhibit that featured art by women artists from around the world to help the financial services firm achieve its goal of targeting more affluent women.[23]

Other tools arise from the use of publicity, which is a component of public relations. Publicity is nonpersonal communication in news story form about an organization or its products, or both, transmitted through a mass medium at no charge. A few examples of publicity-based public relations tools are news releases, press conferences, and feature articles. Ordinarily, public relations efforts are planned and implemented to be consistent with and support other elements of the promotion mix. Public relations efforts may be the responsibility of an individual or of a department within the organization, or the organization may hire an independent public relations agency.

Unpleasant situations and negative events such as product tampering or an environmental disaster may provoke unfavorable public relations for an organization. To minimize the damaging effects of unfavorable coverage, effective marketers have policies and procedures in place to help manage any public relations problems. For example, Wal-Mart responded to negative publicity owing to news stories and lawsuits related to its hiring practices, union management, and aggressive expansion

kinesic communication
Communicating through the movement of head, eyes, arms, hands, legs, or torso

proxemic communication
Communicating by varying the physical distance in face-to-face interactions

tactile communication
Communicating through touching

Yesterday, you could only
get your work, at work.

Today, work anywhere you want.

Connect

Getting to your work when you're away from your desk has always been a real pain. Simdesk has changed that. We make your work available wherever you are, whenever you want. So access to your files, messages, and other work information is hassle-free. Simply connect to our secure and private solutions with a click of a button. And it only takes minutes to get started at simdesk.com/signup.

FREE TRIAL!
Get simple and affordable file storage,
sharing, messaging, and more.
simdesk.com/signup
866.Simdesk

SIMDESK
On-demand computing for the world

Offer subject to Simdesk's standard terms and conditions of sale available during the purchase process at simdesk.com/signup. ©2006 Simdesk Technologies, Inc.

Sales Promotion

Simdesk offers a free trial or sample of its services.

policies with a television ad campaign promoting the entrepreneurial vision of its founder, the savings it offers families, and its employee-benefit packages.[24]

Public relations should not be viewed as a set of tools to be used only during crises. To get the most from public relations, an organization should have someone responsible for public relations either internally or externally and should have an ongoing public relations program. We discuss public relations and publicity in considerable detail in Chapter 17.

Sales Promotion

Sales promotion is an activity or material that acts as a direct inducement, offering added value or incentive for the product, to resellers, salespeople, or consumers.[25] Examples include free samples, games, rebates, displays, sweepstakes, contests, premiums, and coupons. For example, to promote its new call-10-friends-for-free plan, Alltel Wireless sponsored a "My Circle 500" sweepstakes asking subscribers to text a particular website in order to compete to win prizes including an all-expense paid trip to the NASCAR Winston Cup.[26] *Sales promotion* should not be confused with *promotion;* sales promotion is just one part of the comprehensive area of promotion. Marketers spend more on sales promotion than on advertising, and sales promotion appears to be a faster-growing area than advertising.

Generally, when companies employ advertising or personal selling, they depend on either continuously or cyclically. However, a marketer's use of sales promotion tends to be irregular. Many products are seasonal. A company such as Toro may offer more sales promotions in August than in the peak selling season of April or May, when more people buy tractors, lawn mowers, and other gardening equipment. Marketers frequently rely on sales promotion to improve the effectiveness of other promotion-mix elements, especially advertising and personal selling. Decisions to cut sales promotion can have significant negative effects on a company. For example, Clorox decided to cut the promotion budget for Glad branded products two years in a row in part to compensate for rising plastic resin prices. When competitors did not decrease their promotional budgets, Glad lost significant market share in trash bags (down 10.3 percent), food storage bags (down 10.6 percent), and lawn and leaf bags (down 23.2 percent).[27] We discuss sales promotion—both consumer and trade promotions—in more detail in Chapter 18.

Selecting Promotion-Mix Elements

Marketers vary the composition of promotion mixes for many reasons. Although a promotion mix can include all four elements, frequently a marketer selects fewer than four. Many firms that market multiple product lines use several promotion mixes simultaneously.

An effective promotion mix requires the right combination of components. To see how such a mix is created, we now examine the factors and conditions affecting the selection of promotion-mix elements that an organization uses for a specific promotion mix.

Promotional Resources, Objectives, and Policies

The size of an organization's promotional budget affects the number and relative intensity of promotional methods included in a promotion mix. If a company's promotional budget is extremely limited, the firm is likely to rely on personal selling because it is easier to measure a salesperson's contribution to sales than to measure the sales effectiveness of advertising. Businesses generally must have sizable promotional budgets to use regional or national advertising. Procter & Gamble, for example, spends $3.34 million a year on advertising its many diverse products in the United States.[28] Organizations with extensive promotional resources generally include more elements in their promotion mixes, but having more promotional dollars to spend does not necessarily mean using more promotional methods. Research indicates that resources spent on promotion activities have a positive influence on shareholder value.[29]

An organization's promotional objectives and policies also influence the types of promotion selected. If a company's objective is to create mass awareness of a new convenience good, such as a breakfast cereal, its promotion mix probably leans heavily toward advertising, sales promotion, and possibly public relations. For example, the Chinese firm Inner Mongolia Mengiu Milk Industry Company advertises its dairy products during Chinese broadcasts of National Basketball Association games and reality shows, participated in an NBA "Jam Van" road show that visited 17 Chinese cities, and donates cartons of milk to 500 Chinese elementary schools every day.[30] If a company hopes to educate customers about the features of a durable good, such as a home appliance, its promotion mix may combine a moderate amount of advertising, possibly some sales promotion designed to attract customers to retail stores, and a great deal of personal selling because this method is an excellent way to inform customers about such products.

Characteristics of the Target Market

Size, geographic distribution, and demographic characteristics of a firm's target market help to dictate the methods to include in a product's promotion mix. To some degree, market size determines composition of the mix. If the size is limited, the promotion mix probably will emphasize personal selling, which can be very effective for reaching small numbers of people. Firms selling to business markets and firms marketing products through only a few wholesalers frequently make personal selling the major component of their promotion mixes. When a product's market consists of millions of customers, businesses rely on advertising and sales promotion because these methods reach masses of people at a low cost per person.

Geographic distribution of a firm's customers also affects the choice of promotional methods. Personal selling is more feasible if a company's customers are concentrated in a small area than if they are dispersed across a vast region. When the company's customers are numerous and dispersed, advertising may be more practical. Distribution of a target market's demographic characteristics, such as age, income, or education, may affect the types of promotional techniques a marketer selects, as well as the messages and images employed.

Characteristics of the Product

Generally, promotion mixes for business products concentrate on personal selling, whereas advertising plays a major role in promoting consumer goods. This generalization should be treated cautiously, though. Marketers of business products use some advertising to promote products. Personal selling is used extensively for consumer durables, such as home appliances, automobiles, and houses, whereas consumer convenience items are promoted mainly through advertising and sales promotion. Public relations appears in promotion mixes for both business and consumer products. Marketers of highly seasonal products often emphasize advertising, and sometimes sales promotion as well, because off-season sales generally

ONE FRESH GROUND BEEF PATTY

SLICE OF AMERICAN

RED RIPE TOMATO

PICKLES AND MORE CRUNCHY PICKLES

WHOLE LEAF LETTUCE

ONIONS

KETCHUP

MUSTARD

NO MAYO, THANK YOU

IVETTE DOES THE IVETTE BURGER,
NOT JUST ANOTHER OFF-THE-RACK BURGER.

Don't compromise. Personalize. Wendy's® makes your hamburger right when you order it
with the fresh toppings you say to put on. Do a hamburger made just for you.

Do what tastes right.™

Product Characteristics

Inexpensive, frequently purchased convenience products require significant levels of advertising.

push policy Promoting a product only to the next institution down the marketing channel

will not support an extensive year-round sales force. Although most toy producers have sales forces to sell to resellers, many of these companies depend chiefly on advertising to promote their products.

A product's price also influences the composition of the promotion mix. High-priced products call for personal selling because consumers associate greater risk with the purchase of such products and usually want information from a salesperson. Few people, for example, are willing to purchase a refrigerator from a self-service establishment. For low-priced convenience items, marketers use advertising rather than personal selling. When products are marketed through intensive distribution, firms depend strongly on advertising and sales promotion. Many convenience products, such as lotions, cereals, and coffee, are promoted through samples, coupons, and money refunds. When marketers choose selective distribution, promotion mixes vary considerably. Items handled through exclusive distribution, such as expensive watches, furs, and high-quality furniture, typically require a significant amount of personal selling. Manufacturers of highly personal products, such as laxatives, nonprescription contraceptives, and feminine hygiene products, depend on advertising because many customers do not want to talk with salespeople about these products.

Costs and Availability of Promotional Methods

Costs of promotional methods are major factors to analyze when developing a promotion mix. National advertising and sales promotion require large expenditures. If these efforts succeed in reaching extremely large audiences, however, the cost per individual reached may be quite small, possibly a few pennies. Some forms of advertising are relatively inexpensive. Many small, local businesses advertise goods and services through local newspapers, radio and television stations, outdoor displays, search engine result ads, and signs on mass-transit vehicles.

Another consideration that marketers explore when formulating a promotion mix is availability of promotional techniques. Despite the tremendous number of media vehicles in the United States, a firm may find that no available advertising medium effectively reaches a certain target market. The problem of media availability becomes more pronounced when marketers advertise in some foreign countries. Some media, such as television, simply may not be available, or it may be illegal to advertise on television. In China, the State Administration for Radio, Film, and Television banned a Nike commercial that featured basketball star LeBron James besting a kung fu master and a pair of dragons in a video game. In recent years, the agency has cracked down on U.S. and Japanese advertisements that fail to "uphold national dignity and interest, and respect the motherland's culture" of China.[31] Available media may not be open to certain types of advertisements. In some countries, advertisers are forbidden to make brand comparisons on television.

Push and Pull Channel Policies

Another element marketers consider when planning a promotion mix is whether to use a push policy or a pull policy. With a **push policy**, the producer promotes the product only to the next institution down the marketing channel. In a marketing channel

figure 16.4   COMPARISON OF PUSH AND PULL PROMOTIONAL STRATEGIES

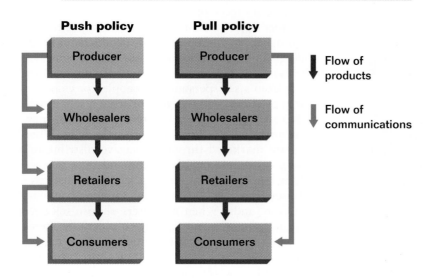

with wholesalers and retailers, the producer promotes to the wholesaler because in this case the wholesaler is the channel member just below the producer (see Figure 16.4). Each channel member, in turn, promotes to the next channel member. A push policy normally stresses personal selling. Sometimes sales promotion and advertising are used in conjunction with personal selling to push the products down through the channel.

As Figure 16.4 shows, a firm using a **pull policy** promotes directly to consumers to develop strong consumer demand for its products. It does so primarily through advertising and sales promotion. Because consumers are persuaded to seek the products in retail stores, retailers, in turn, go to wholesalers or the producers to buy the products. This policy is intended to pull the goods down through the channel by creating demand at the consumer level. Consumers are told that if the stores don't have it, ask them to get it. Push and pull policies are not mutually exclusive. At times, an organization uses both simultaneously.

The Growing Importance of Word-of-Mouth Communications

pull policy Promoting a product directly to consumers to develop strong consumer demand that pulls products through the marketing channel

word-of-mouth communication Personal informal exchanges of communication that customers share with one another about products, brands, and companies

buzz marketing An attempt to incite publicity and public excitement surrounding a product through a creative event

viral marketing A strategy to get consumers to share a marketer's message, often through e-mail or online video, in a way that spreads dramatically and quickly

When making decisions about the composition of promotion mixes, marketers should recognize that commercial messages, whether from advertising, personal selling, sales promotion, or public relations, are limited in the extent to which they can inform and persuade customers and move them closer to making purchases. Depending on the type of customers and the products involved, buyers to some extent rely on word-of-mouth communication from personal sources such as family members and friends. **Word-of-mouth communication** is personal informal exchanges of communication that customers share with one another about products, brands, and companies.[32] Most consumers are likely to seek information from knowledgeable friends, family members, and experts when buying medical, legal, and auto repair services. Word-of-mouth communication is also very important when people are selecting restaurants and entertainment, as well as automotive, banking, and personal services such as hair care. Effective marketers who understand the importance of word-of-mouth communication attempt to identify advice givers and opinion leaders and to encourage them to try their products in the hope that they will spread favorable word about them.

Customers increasingly are going online to share their opinions about goods and services as well as about the companies that market them. At a number of consumer-oriented websites, such as epinions.com and ConsumerReview.com, consumers can learn about other consumers' feelings toward and experiences with specific products. Users also can search within product categories and compare consumers' viewpoints on various brands and models. Buyers can peruse Internet-based newsgroups, forums, and blogs to find word-of-mouth information. A consumer looking for a new cell phone service, for example, might inquire in forums about other participants' experiences and level of satisfaction to gain more information before making a purchase decision. A study by Forrester and Intelliseek found that more than 90 percent of consumers trust such recommendations they get from other consumers.[33]

Electronic word of mouth is particularly important to consumers staying abreast of trends. At Facebook.com, a feature called The Pulse tracks trends relating to each

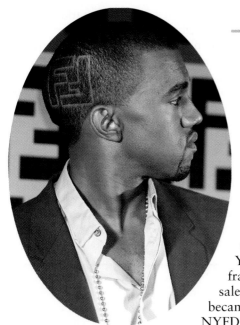

Buzz Marketing
Kanye West created much buzz around Fendi's new B.Mix bags at a promotional party in Tokyo.

school. Students, for instance, can see which band is the most popular on their campus and how it compares with all schools. At "social news" websites such as Digg.com, Reddit.com, and Del.icio.us, trend-setting consumers can share bookmarks of their favorite websites or Internet stories. These sites have become so influential in introducing consumers to new products and shaping their views about them that marketers are increasingly monitoring them to identify new trends; some firms have even attempted to affect users' votes on their favorite items.[34]

Through an approach called **buzz marketing**, marketers attempt to incite publicity and public excitement surrounding a product through a creative event. For example, NYC Marketing, the marketing arm of the City of New York, gave celebrities such as Nick Lachey and Liv Tyler new but seemingly frayed caps with the logo for its sanitation department, which are available for sale online and in city souvenir shops. The tactic worked, and the caps quickly became a must-have fashion item in a line that has in the past included NYPD and NYFD T-shirts and hats.[35] The idea behind buzz marketing is that an accepted member of a social group will always be more credible than any other form of paid communication.[36]

Buzz marketing works best as a part of an integrated marketing communication program that also uses advertising, personal selling, sales promotion, and publicity. However, marketers also should take care that buzz marketing campaigns do not violate any laws or have the potential to be misconstrued and cause undue alarm. Consider that after a buzz effort to promote the Cartoon Network's *Aqua Teen Hunger Force* show using electronic devices with flashing lights caused a widespread terrorism scare in the city of Boston, the performance artists hired to implement the campaign were arrested and charged with disorderly conduct and creating a hoax in such a way as to cause panic. Turner Broadcasting, the corporate parent of the Cartoon Network, ultimately apologized for the incident and agreed to make restitution to the city for the expenses of responding to the apparent bomb threat.[37]

Viral marketing is a strategy to get consumers to share a marketer's message, often through e-mail or online video, in a way that spreads dramatically and quickly. Burger King, for example, created the "Subservient Chicken" website, where Web surfers seem to be able to control a person in a chicken suit by typing in commands. Viral communications resulted in nearly 52 million visitors to the website in less than a year.[38] OfficeMax created 20 holiday websites to promote its stores as a gift-shopping destination. One of the sites, "ElfYourself," where users could create their own e-card with their own photo, garnered 36 million hits in just five weeks and also resulted in significant publicity in the form of news stories.[39]

Word of mouth, no matter how it's transmitted, is not effective in all product categories. It seems to be most effective for new-to-market and more expensive

marketing ENTREPRENEURS

Dave Balter

HIS BUSINESS: BzzAgent

FOUNDED: In 2002, when Balter was 31

SUCCESS: Has grown from 300 to 450,000 "agents" in just four years

Dave Balter believes so strongly in the power of word-of-mouth communications to "turn passionate customers into brand evangelists" that he built a business on it. BzzAgent assembled a volunteer army of "agents" who strive to generate word-of-mouth buzz for products they talk up at parties, events, and in e-mail. The company chooses which agents to enlist for a campaign by the client company's target-market demographics and psychographics. Agents get a sample product (which they get to keep) and a training manual; they are expected to file reports detailing their activities and effectiveness. Clients—including Anheuser-Busch, Levi Strauss, and Ralph Lauren—benefit from the unscripted exposure of their product by BzzAgents who've actually used them, although BzzAgent won't guarantee that all agents' opinions will be positive.[b]

products. Despite the obvious benefits of positive word of mouth, marketers also must recognize the potential dangers of negative word of mouth. This is particularly important in dealing with online platforms that can reach more people and encourage consumers to "gang up" on a company or product. For example, music giant Sony BMG received negative press over a protest campaign that moved from online to the front of its office building. Sony had stopped production on the third album of its artist Fiona Apple after it decided the record was not radio-friendly. A copy of the album was mysteriously "leaked" on the Internet and soon became one of the most downloaded items online. Fans organized at websites and online forums to create petitions and mail apples to Sony's executives every day for several months. Sony agreed to release the album to stores after members of the online campaign picketed Sony's offices in New York and the story reached the mainstream media.[40] In any case, marketers should not underestimate the importance of word-of-mouth communications and personal influence, nor should they have unrealistic expectations about the performance of commercial messages.

Should Procter & Gamble Buzz Minors?

Tremor is a buzz marketing website offered by Procter & Gamble (P&G). The company recruited 250,000 "connectors"—teens with lots of social connections—to talk up its products to other teenagers. P&G does not tell members of the "Tremor Crew" what to say, and it does not pay them, but it does bestow coupons, samples, discounts, and free downloads. Members are not required to disclose their membership to anyone—not even their own parents.

Commercial Alert, a consumer-activist group, filed a complaint with the Federal Trade Commission (FTC) arguing that Tremor inappropriately targets minor children. The group also asked the federal agency to investigate whether such viral and buzz marketing efforts violate laws requiring the disclosure of commercial relationships. Commercial Alert argues that buzz marketing is deceptive, intrusive, takes advantage

of the kindness of strangers, and involves turning people's friends and family against them for profit. P&G, however, contends that "We have been upfront with [our teens] to let them know that we are part of Procter & Gamble and a word-of-mouth marketing program."

Buzz marketing, now a $60 million business, has been controversial from the beginning. Sony Ericsson Mobile deployed "fake tourists" to ask bystanders in New York's Times Square to take their photos with a new camera phone and then chat with them about the phones. However, they did not disclose their relationship to the company. The Word-of-Mouth Marketing Association (WOMMA) has a code of ethics that encourages its members to be open and honest about their relationship with marketers in all communications. The FTC has not signaled its opinion on this growing form of promotion. If marketers fail to act appropriately in this area, the result may be regulations or legislation.

The FTC ultimately declined to issue guidelines related to buzz marketing initiatives, especially in light of self-regulatory efforts by WOMMA, and announced its intention to consider enforcement action with regard to marketing to minors only on a case-by-case basis. P&G later broadened Tremor to include VocalPoint, a similar national group of 450,000 women with children.[c]

table 16.2	TOP TEN BRANDS IN PRODUCT PLACEMENT

Brand	Occurrences
1. Coca-Cola Soft drinks	3,346
2. Chef Revival Apparel	1,592
3. Nike Apparel	1,245
4. 24 Hour Fitness Centers/Clubs	858
5. Chicago Bears Football Team	600
6. Cingular Wireless Telephone Services (wireless)	532
7. Starter Apparel	494
8. Dell Computer Systems	494
9. SLS Electronic Equipment Speakers	489
10. Nike Sport Footwear	471

Source: Nielsen Product Placement, Research for January through December 2006, in "Nielsen Issues Most Popular Lists for 2006," Nielsen Media press release, December 20, 2006, www.prnewswire.com/cgi-bin/stories.pl?ACCT=104&STORY=/www/story/12-20-2006/0004494967&EDATE.

Product Placement

A growing technique for reaching consumers is the selective placement of products within the context of television programs viewed by the target market. **Product placement** is the strategic location of products or product promotions within television program content to reach the product's target market. The hit NBC show, *The Office,* for example, has integrated products from Hewlett-Packard and Staples within storylines. Such product placement has become more important owing to the increasing fragmentation of television viewers who have ever-expanding viewing options and technology that can screen advertisements (e.g., digital video recorders such as TiVo). Research indicates that 60 to 80 percent of digital video recorder users skip the commercials when replaying programming.[41]

In-program product placements have been successful in reaching consumers as they are being entertained rather than in the competitive commercial break time periods. Table 16.2 identifies some of the top ten brands in product placement. After Oprah Winfrey gave 276 audience members new Pontiac G6s, it generated tremendous publicity for both *Oprah* and Pontiac, with more than 600 media outlets commenting on the giveway in the days following the show. The sales of the G6 are higher than its closest competitor by 20 percent.[42] Reality programming in particular has been a natural fit for product placements because of the close interchange between the participants and the product (e.g., Sears and *Extreme Makeover Home Edition;* Levi's, Burger King, Marquis Jet, and Dove and *The Apprentice;* and Coca-Cola and *American Idol*). When Genworth Financial was evaluating this advertising tactic, it found that its target market aligned well with the viewership of *The Apprentice,* which is among the wealthiest and highest educated for network television. Genworth Financial was featured in the last episode of season two and was exposed to 30.4 million *Apprentice* viewers. As a new company, Genworth did not have the prior brand recognition of competitors such as MetLife, Prudential, or Allstate.[43]

Product placement is not limited to U.S. television shows. The European Parliament recently green lighted product placement, but left it up to individual European nations to decide whether and how to permit the practice in their own countries. Moreover, European broadcasters will have to alert viewers that products have been placed in a particular show episode. In general, the notion of product placement has not been viewed favorably in Europe and has been particularly controversial in the

product placement The strategic location of products or product promotions within television program content to reach the product's target market

United Kingdom. However, British viewers have already been exposed to product placement within shows imported from the United States, including *Desperate Housewives, The OC,* and *American Idol.*[44]

Criticisms and Defenses of Promotion

Even though promotional activities can help customers to make informed purchasing decisions, social scientists, consumer groups, government agencies, and members of society in general have long criticized promotion. There are two main reasons for such criticism: Promotion does have some flaws, and it is a highly visible business activity that pervades our daily lives. Although people almost universally complain that there is simply too much promotional activity, several more specific issues have been raised. Promotional efforts have been called deceptive. Promotion has been blamed for increasing prices. Other criticisms of promotion are that it manipulates consumers

table 16.3 CRITICISMS AND DEFENSES OF PROMOTION

Issue	Discussion
Is promotion deceptive?	Although no longer widespread, some deceptive promotion still occurs; laws, government regulations, and industry self-regulation have helped to decrease intentionally deceptive promotion; customers may be unintentionally misled because some words have diverse meanings.
Does promotion increase prices?	When promotion stimulates demand, higher production levels may result in lower per-unit production costs, which keeps prices lower; when demand is not stimulated, however, prices increase owing to the added costs of promotion; promotion fuels price competition, which helps to keep prices lower.
Does promotion create needs?	Many marketers capitalize on people's needs by basing their promotional appeals on these needs; however, marketers do not actually create these needs; if there were no promotion, people would still have basic needs such as those suggested by Maslow.
Does promotion encourage materialism?	Because promotion creates awareness and visibility for products, it may contribute to materialism in the same way that movies, sports, theater, art, and literature may contribute to materialism; if there were no promotion, it is likely that there would still be materialism among some groups, as evidenced by the existence of materialism among some ancient groups of people.
Does promotion help customers without costing too much?	Customers learn about products and services through promotion, allowing them to make more intelligent buying decisions.
Should potentially harmful products be advertised?	Some critics suggest that the promotion of possibly unhealthy products should not be allowed at all; others argue that as long as it is legal to sell such products, promoting those products should be allowed.

into buying products they do not need, that it leads to a more materialistic society, that customers do not benefit sufficiently from promotion to justify its high costs, and that promotion is used to market potentially harmful products. These issues are discussed in Table 16.3.

...And now, back to Toyota

In an age when the traditional Big Three automakers—Ford, GM, and Chrysler—are struggling, Japan's Toyota is thriving. While Ford and GM terminated a combined 46,000 North American employees and anticipated closing 26 North American factories over the next five years, Toyota has never closed a North American factory. Toyota's emphasis on continuous improvement has ensured that it is leaps and bounds ahead of its competition. One of the most significant challenges remaining is for the Japanese automaker to become the number one car manufacturer, which many expect to happen as soon as next year. What many people don't realize is that many of the cars and trucks that Toyota produces for the United States are actually built in the United States with many U.S. parts.

Toyota and its subsidiaries sell more than 7.4 million passenger cars, trucks, and buses worldwide under the Toyota, Scion, Lexus, Daihatsu, and Hino brands. The company manufactures vehicles in 27 countries and regions throughout the world and sells them in more than 170 countries and locations. Of course, Japan accounts for 32.1 percent of Toyota sales, but North America ranks second with 30.7 percent of Toyota sales. The youthful Scion and luxury Lexus lines have contributed to Toyota's sales gains over the past few years, as have its expanded hybrid offerings from the Prius to the Lexus RX400h.

In addition to traditional ad spending, Toyota has increased its use of events advertising and dealer funding dramatically. Toyota believes that its customers are a dynamic group, and it learned from its experience marketing the youth-oriented Scion the power of connecting with consumers on topics that are of great personal interest and then subtly injecting vehicles in an organic way. It used this knowledge when it kicked off a four-city modern art exhibit for the LS-460 launch dubbed the "460 Degrees Gallery" with photography, an architectural installation, and video art. The tour included touch-screen displays with artist interviews and events such as chocolate tastings.

Toyota has split the small sport-utility vehicle (SUV) segment with the FJ Cruiser and RAV4 by connecting with very different buyers. Toyota's brands move off dealer lots much faster than the industry average. Its "days to turn"—the average length of time needed to sell a new vehicle after it arrives on a dealer's lot—is 25 days compared with the industry average of 63; Chrysler's is the worst at 87 days. Mining consumer loyalty is critical to reaching niches. Toyota's brands have high owner-loyalty levels, so the company gets a jump-start on sales for new-model introductions. The financial resources Toyota has for new launches, combined with a focus on events, loyalty programs, and interactive marketing, have paved the way for Toyota to become the number 1 automaker in the United States. Whether it can achieve this goal remains to be seen, but sending an integrated message across all possible communication platforms is giving it a head start.[45]

1. What impact will mobile ads have on marketing?

2. What are the advantages and disadvantages of using "mobisodes" for shows such as *Prison Break* for a product such as the Yaris?

3. Do you think that advertising in video games will take off? Is it effective?

CHAPTER REVIEW

1. Discuss the nature of integrated marketing communications.

Integrated marketing communications is the coordination of promotion and other marketing efforts to ensure the maximum informational and persuasive impact on customers. Sending consistent messages to customers is a major goal of integrated marketing communications. As both information technology and customer interests become increasingly dynamic, the specific communication vehicles employed and the precision with which they are used are changing.

2. Describe the process of communication.

Communication is a sharing of meaning. The communication process involves several steps. First, the source translates meaning into code, a process known as coding or encoding. The source should employ signs or symbols familiar to the receiver or audience. The coded message is sent through a communications channel to the receiver or audience. The receiver or audience then decodes the message and usually supplies feedback to the source. When the decoded message differs from the encoded one, a condition called noise exists.

3. Understand the role of promotion in the marketing mix.

Promotion is communication to build and maintain relationships by informing and persuading one or more audiences. The overall role of promotion is to stimulate product demand, although a company might pursue several promotional objectives. Cause-related marketing efforts link the purchase of products to philanthropic efforts for one or more causes. Marketers strive for proper planning, implementation, coordination, and control of communications for maximum benefit from promotional efforts. Integrated marketing communications planning takes into account informal methods of communication because customers derive information and opinions from many different sources.

4. Explain the objectives of promotion.

Eight primary objectives underlie many promotional programs. Promotion aims to create awareness of a new product, new brand, or existing product; to stimulate primary and selective demand; to encourage product trial through the use of free samples, coupons, limited free-use offers, contests, and games; to identify prospects; to retain loyal customers; to facilitate reseller support; to combat competitive promotional efforts; and to reduce sales fluctuations.

5. Understand the major elements of the promotion mix.

The promotion mix for a product may include four major promotional methods: advertising, personal selling, public relations, and sales promotion. Advertising is paid nonpersonal communication about an organization and its products transmitted to a target audience through a mass medium. Personal selling is paid personal communication that attempts to inform customers and persuade them to purchase products in an exchange situation. Public relations is a broad set of communication efforts used to create and maintain favorable relationships between an organization and its stakeholders. Sales promotion is an activity or material that acts as a direct inducement, offering added value or incentive for the product, to resellers, salespeople, or consumers.

6. Describe the factors that affect the choice of promotion-mix elements.

Major determinants of which promotional methods to include in a product's promotion mix are the organization's promotional resources, objectives, and policies; characteristics of the target market; characteristics of the product; and cost and availability of promotional methods. Marketers also consider whether to use a push policy or a pull policy. With a push policy, the producer promotes the product only to the next institution down the marketing channel. Normally, a push policy stresses personal selling. Firms that use a pull policy promote directly to consumers, with the intention of developing strong consumer demand for the products. Once consumers are persuaded to seek the products in retail stores, retailers go to wholesalers or the producer to buy the products.

7. Explore word-of-mouth communication and how it affects promotion.

Most customers are likely to be influenced by friends and family members when making purchases. Word-of-mouth communication is personal, informal exchanges of communication that customers share with one another about products, brands, and companies. Customers also may choose to go online to find electronic word of mouth about products or companies. Buzz marketing is an attempt to incite publicity and public excitement surrounding a product through a creative event. Viral marketing is a strategy to get consumers to share a marketer's message, often through e-mail or online video, in a way that spreads dramatically and quickly. A related concept, product placement is the strategic location of products or product promotions within television program content to reach the product's target market.

8. Understand the criticisms and defenses of promotion.

Promotional activities can help consumers to make informed purchasing decisions, but they also have evoked many criticisms. Promotion has been accused of deception. Although some deceiving or misleading promotions do exist, laws, government regulation, and industry self-regulation minimize deceptive promotion. Promotion has been blamed for increasing prices, but it usually tends to lower them. When demand is high, production and marketing costs decrease, which can result in lower prices. Promotion also helps to keep prices lower by facilitating price competition. Other criticisms of promotional activity are that it manipulates consumers into buying products they do not need, that it leads to a more materialistic society, and that consumers do not benefit sufficiently from promotional activity to justify its high cost. Finally, some critics of promotion suggest that potentially harmful products, especially those associated with violence, sex, and unhealthy activities, should not be promoted at all.

ACE self-test

Please visit the student website at **www.prideferrell.com** for ACE Self-Test questions that will help you prepare for exams.

KEY CONCEPTS

integrated marketing
  communications
communication
source
receiver
coding process
communications channel

decoding process
noise
feedback
channel capacity
promotion
primary demand
pioneer promotion

selective demand
promotion mix
kinesic communication
proxemic communication
tactile communication
push policy
pull policy

word-of-mouth
  communication
buzz marketing
viral marketing
product placement

ISSUES FOR DISCUSSION AND REVIEW

1. What does *integrated marketing communications* mean?

2. What is the major task of promotion? Do firms ever use promotion to accomplish this task and fail? If so, give several examples.

3. What is communication? Describe the communication process. Is it possible to communicate without using all the elements in the communication process? If so, which ones can be omitted?

4. Identify several causes of noise. How can a source reduce noise?

5. Describe the possible objectives of promotion, and discuss the circumstances under which each objective might be used.

6. Identify and briefly describe the four promotional methods an organization can use in its promotion mix.

7. What forms of interpersonal communication besides language can be used in personal selling?

8. How do target-market characteristics determine which promotional methods to include in a promotion mix? Assume that a company is planning to promote a cereal to both adults and children. Along what major dimensions would these two promotional efforts have to differ from each other?

9. How can a product's characteristics affect the composition of its promotion mix?

10. Evaluate the following statement: "Appropriate advertising media are always available if a company can afford them."

11. Explain the difference between a pull policy and a push policy. Under what conditions should each policy be used?

12. In which ways can word-of-mouth communication influence the effectiveness of a promotion mix for a product? How can marketers use word-of-mouth communication to create "buzz" for a product?

13. Which criticisms of promotion do you believe are the most valid? Why?

14. Should organizations be allowed to promote offensive, violent, sexual, or unhealthy products that can be sold and purchased legally? Support your answer.

MARKETING APPLICATIONS

1. Identify two television commercials, one aimed at stimulating primary demand and one aimed at stimulating selective demand. Describe each commercial, and discuss how each attempts to achieve its objective.

2. Which of the four promotional methods—advertising, personal selling, public relations, or sales promotion—would you emphasize if you were developing the promotion mix for the following products? Explain your answers.
   a. Washing machine
   b. Cereal
   c. Halloween candy
   d. Compact disc

3. Suppose that marketers at Falcon International Corporation have come to you for recommendations on how they should promote their products. They want to develop a comprehensive promotional campaign and have a generous budget with which to implement their plans. What questions would you ask them, and what would you suggest they consider before developing a promotional program?

4. Identify two products for which marketers should use a push policy and a pull policy and a third product that might best be promoted using a mix of the two policies. Explain your answers.

Online Exercise

5. MySpace isn't just for friends—it's also a unique promotional platform for musical artists, especially unsigned and independent artists. By creating a MySpace page, musicians can share their songs, post important dates, or even blog. MySpace music pages are different from record company websites because they feel more personal. Artists also take advantage of MySpace's viral nature by allowing other MySpace members to post their pictures, songs, and music videos on their own MySpace profile pages. Visit the website at **http://music.myspace.com** and look for your favorite artist or explore a new one.
   a. Who is the target market for members?
   b. What is being promoted to these individuals?
   c. What are the promotional objectives of the website?

The readiness of a global market's infrastructure is important for any integrated marketing campaign to communicate a similar message across different media (e.g., newspaper, magazine, radio, television, and Internet) in an effective manner. One report that may be useful here is the Global Information Technology Report, which can be accessed by using the search term "global information technology" at **http://globaledge.msu.edu/ibrd** (and check the box "Resource Desk only"). Once there, find the most recent report. What are the ten markets with the most equipped infrastructures? Are there any surprises among the markets listed? What regions are represented in your report?

Video CASE

Promoting "The Ultimate Driving Machine"

Careful targeting, consistent positioning, and a good match between message and media have all helped Bayerische Motoren Werke (better known as BMW) to accelerate sales revenue on a relatively small advertising budget. The company, based in Munich, Germany, markets such well-known global brands as BMW, Mini Cooper, and Rolls-Royce, as well as BMW Motorcycles. Although other multibrand automobile manufacturers offer a range of vehicles for mass-market and upscale segments, BMW has followed a different route to profitability. The automaker focuses exclusively on high-end vehicles, targeting drivers who are affluent, successful, demanding of themselves and their cars, and interested in the time-saving convenience of automotive technology.

BMW uses television and magazine advertising to reinforce its brand image and to give the target audience a feeling for what the company calls "The Ultimate Driving Machine." Because its advertising budget is not as large as those of its competitors, BMW looks for ways to stand out in the crowd. For example, it likes to air television commercials supported by bursts of newspaper advertising; more than once it has signed on as the lone sponsor of television programs favored by its target audience. "TV advertising plays a vital role for us in building brand awareness, image, and desirability among members of the general public," notes a BMW marketing executive. "Without that type of broad appeal, a brand such as BMW would have less desirability within its target consumer groups."

The aim of every commercial is to help viewers picture themselves on the open road behind the wheel of a BMW; the car, not the driver or the scenery, is the star of the advertisement. The camera lingers on the vehicle's sleek lines, comfortable interior, high-tech features, and the familiar blue-and-white brand symbol. While the vehicle and the scenery may change from commercial to commercial, the ultimate objective is to motivate consumers to test-drive a BMW.

Movies have played a key role in BMW's promotions. The company has garnered huge waves of publicity from having the Mini Cooper featured in *The Italian Job* and for arranging for James Bond to drive new BMWs. To reach Internet-savvy car buyers, BMW also hired top directors to make short films especially for Web viewing. Although the films ran online for only four years, they were viewed more than 100 million times, won numerous awards, and were later issued on DVD for free distribution to prospective buyers.

BMW's sales promotion efforts also include samples—in the form of extended test drives—as well as participation in major automotive trade shows. Eye-catching point-of-purchase displays in dealer showrooms support the overall integrated marketing communications effort by echoing selected images from the company's advertising. Price promotions are rare, although the company held its first end-of-year clearance sale on select U.S. models not long ago. The company also has offered special leasing deals to spark sales of its X3 model.

After a long stretch as head of marketing for BMW of North America, Jim McDowell switched jobs with Jack Pitney, who directed marketing for the company's Mini brand. Pitney has begun infusing BMW's marketing with some of the Mini's most successful promotional ideas. He plans to retain "The Ultimate Driving Machine" slogan for BMW's marketing communications because it resonates with the target audience and differentiates the brand from other premium competitors. BMW's worldwide positioning will not change, but with the launch of new models every year, the company will continue refining the promotion mix to attract new buyers, maintain brand image, and keep profits high.[46]

Questions for Discussion

1. Evaluate BMW's use of movies in its integrated marketing communications program.
2. What types of objectives is BMW attempting to change through its television commercials?
3. How does BMW's extended sampling facilitate the personal selling efforts when customers visit a BMW dealership?

Advertising and Public Relations

Mini Cooper's Alternative Advertising Campaign

In 1956, fuel shortages in a number of countries including Great Britain created a pressing need for a fuel-efficient car. Lord Nuffield of British Motor Corporation charged his chief designer, Sir Alec Issigonis, with creating an "orderly saloon" that nonetheless could compete with the explosion of fuel-efficient microcars on the market. The resulting Classic Mini made its debut on August 26, 1959. The first mass-produced automobile with a transversally placed engine, it fit four adults, was fuel-efficient, handled great, and cost less than $800. Sales began to take off after Queen Elizabeth II and other celebrities were seen at the wheel of Classic Minis. Over the decades, it became the most popular British car ever made, with more than 5.3 million units sold.

In 1961, renowned British race-car driver John Cooper revamped the Classic Mini to craft a high-performance racing model, the Mini Cooper, giving it a more powerful engine, higher and closer gear ratios, better brakes, wider tires, and a color-contrasting roof. Between 1960 and 1967, about 10,000 Classic Minis were sold in the United States. In 1968, however, the U.S. government issued new safety and emissions regulations that British Motor Corporation was not at the time prepared to implement in the Mini, spelling its end in the United States.

In 2001, BMW bought the Mini brand and relaunched it. BMW's Mini is larger than the Classic—about 21.5 inches longer, almost 12 inches wider, and almost 900 pounds heavier. Although some people were angry about the demise of the Classic Mini and resented BMW's taking over the brand, others embraced the new Mini as the logical successor of the Classic Mini, recognizing it as the only way the brand could survive in light of modern safety, emissions, and manufacturing principles. Since the Mini has come under the BMW brand name, its acceptability has increased; BMW also views it as an important addition to its portfolio.

Because of their small size, Minis have long been used in creative advertising

OBJECTIVES

1. Describe the nature and types of advertising.

2. Explain the major steps in developing an advertising campaign.

3. Identify who is responsible for developing advertising campaigns.

4. Recognize the tools used in public relations.

5. Understand how public relations is used and evaluated.

campaigns. Minis have appeared on the roofs of houses, on ski lifts at ski resorts, driving down walls, and even on roof racks of other cars. To maintain its cult following, BMW has had to constantly revamp its advertising campaigns for the Mini to keep its loyal customer base and to attract new customers.[1] ∎

Like BMW's Mini USA, many organizations, both for-profit and nonprofit, use advertising and public relations tools to stimulate demand, launch new products, promote current brands, improve organizational images, or boost awareness of public issues. In this chapter we explore several dimensions of advertising and public relations. First, we focus on the nature and types of advertising. Next, we examine the major steps in developing an advertising campaign and describe who is responsible for developing such campaigns. We then discuss the nature of public relations and how public relations is used. We examine various public relations tools and ways to evaluate the effectiveness of public relations. Finally, we focus on how companies deal with unfavorable public relations.

The Nature and Types of Advertising

Advertising permeates our daily lives. At times, we may view it positively; at other times, we avoid it. Some advertising informs, persuades, or entertains us; some bores and even offends us.

As mentioned in Chapter 16, **advertising** is a paid form of nonpersonal communication transmitted to a target audience through mass media, such as television, radio, the Internet, newspapers, magazines, direct mail, outdoor displays, and signs on mass-transit vehicles. In Boston, for example, some taxicabs are sporting a cup of Starbucks coffee magnetically attached to their roofs.[2] Organizations use advertising to reach different audiences ranging from small, specific groups, such as stamp collectors in Idaho, to extremely large groups, such as all athletic-shoe purchasers in the United States. One goal of advertisers is to have their advertisements well liked; Table 17.1 lists some well-liked advertisements.

When asked to name major advertisers, most people immediately mention business organizations. However, many nonbusiness types of organizations, including governments, churches, universities, and charitable organizations, employ advertising to communicate with stakeholders. For example, the government of the United Kingdom spends more than $350 million a year on advertising to advise, influence, or gently chastise its citizens to act appropriately.[3] In 2005, the U.S. government was the twenty-seventh largest advertiser in the country, spending $1.2 billion on advertising.[4] Although we analyze advertising in the context of business organizations here, much of the material applies to all types of organizations.

Advertising is used to promote goods, services, ideas, images, issues, people, and anything else that advertisers want to publicize or foster. Depending on what is being promoted, advertising can be classified as institutional or product advertising. **Institutional advertising** promotes organizational images, ideas, and political issues. It can be used to create or maintain an organizational image. Institutional advertisements may deal with broad image issues, such as organizational strength or the friendliness of employees. Institutional advertising also may aim to create a more favorable view of an organization in the eyes of stakeholders, such as shareholders, consumer advocacy groups, potential shareholders, or the general public. When a company promotes its position on a public issue—for instance, a tax increase, abortion, gun control, or international trade coalitions—institutional advertising is referred to as **advocacy advertising**. Institutional advertising may be used to promote socially approved behavior such as recycling and moderation in the consumption of alcoholic beverages. Philip Morris, for example, has run television advertisements urging parents to talk to their children about not smoking. This type of advertising not only has societal benefits but also helps to build an organization's image.

advertising Paid nonpersonal communication about an organization and its products transmitted to a target audience through mass media

institutional advertising Promotes organizational images, ideas, and political issues

advocacy advertising Promotes a company's position on a public issue

table 17.1   MOST LIKED ADS

Brand	Description of Ad
1. Budweiser	Two teams of horses line up to play football in a field, sheared sheep streaks, cowboy says, "I didn't need to see that."
2. FedEx	Caveman ties message to leg of pterodactyl, dinosaur snatches it, boss fires him, he exits cave, and dinosaur stomps on him.
3. Tyson	Beef Tips in Gravy–grandmother jumps double-dutch with three other girls; family at table.
4. Ameriquest Mortgage	Doctor kills fly with defibrillator, mother and daughter stare in horror as they hear the doctor say, "That killed him."
5. Budweiser	Horse runs into barn, looks at memorabilia, pulls Bud cart as Dalmatian watches, two horses help push, "I won't tell if you won't."
6. Coca-Cola	NASCAR drivers get points for drinking Coke on camera, discover that money gets donated to charity, appear on all types of programming.
7. FedEx	Caveman ties message to leg of pterodactyl, dinosaur snatches it, boss fires him, he exits cave, and dinosaur stomps on him (30 seconds)
8. ONDCP	AboveTheInfluence.com–Young man offers boy a smoke, "What do you say?" I smoke clowns like you on the basketball court.
9. Pedigree	This is Frankie: dog in cage; 1-800-DOGS RULE.
10. Pedigree	Max needs a good home; when you buy Pedigree, we make a donation for them to find loving homes.

Source: *Advertising Age,* January 1, 2007, p. 14.

product advertising
Promotes products' uses, features, and benefits

pioneer advertising Tries to stimulate demand for a product category rather than a specific brand by informing potential buyers about the product

competitive advertising
Tries to stimulate demand for a specific brand by promoting its features, uses, and advantages

comparative advertising
Compares the sponsored brand with one or more identified brands on the basis of one or more product characteristics

reminder advertising
Reminds consumers about an established brand's uses, characteristics, and benefits

reinforcement advertising
Assures users they chose the right brand and tells them how to get the most satisfaction from it

Product advertising promotes the uses, features, and benefits of products. There are two types of product advertising: pioneer and competitive. **Pioneer advertising** focuses on stimulating demand for a product category (rather than a specific brand) by informing potential customers about the product's features, uses, and benefits. This type of advertising is employed when the product is in the introductory stage of the product life cycle. **Competitive advertising** attempts to stimulate demand for a specific brand by promoting the brand's features, uses, and advantages, sometimes through indirect or direct comparisons with competing brands. To make direct product comparisons, marketers use a form of competitive advertising called **comparative advertising**, which compares the sponsored brand with one or more identified brands on the basis of one or more product characteristics. Quizno's, for example, used comparative advertising to promote the value and size of its cheese-steak sandwich as compared with that offered by rival Subway.[5] Often the brands promoted through comparative advertisements have low market shares and are compared with competitors that have the highest market shares in the product category. Product categories that commonly use comparative advertising include soft drinks, toothpaste, pain relievers, foods, tires, automobiles, and detergents. Under the provisions of the 1988 Trademark Law Revision Act, marketers using comparative advertisements must not misrepresent the qualities or characteristics of competing products. Other forms of competitive advertising include reminder and reinforcement advertising. **Reminder advertising** tells customers that an established brand is still around and still offers certain characteristics, uses, and advantages. **Reinforcement advertising** assures current users they have made the right brand choice and tells them how to get the most satisfaction from that brand.

Developing an Advertising Campaign

An **advertising campaign** involves designing a series of advertisements and placing them in various advertising media to reach a particular target audience. As Figure 17.1 indicates, the major steps in creating an advertising campaign are (1) identifying and analyzing the target audience, (2) defining the advertising objectives, (3) creating the advertising platform, (4) determining the advertising appropriation, (5) developing the media plan, (6) creating the advertising message, (7) executing the campaign, and (8) evaluating advertising effectiveness. The number of steps and the exact order in which they are carried out may vary according to an organization's resources, the nature of its product, and the type of target audience to be reached. Nevertheless, these general guidelines for developing an advertising campaign are appropriate for all types of organizations.

Identifying and Analyzing the Target Audience

The **target audience** is the group of people at whom advertisements are aimed. Advertisements for Barbie cereal are targeted toward young girls who play with Barbie dolls, whereas those for Special K cereal are directed at health-conscious adults. Identifying and analyzing the target audience are critical actions. The information yielded helps to determine other steps in developing the campaign. The target audience for a campaign may include everyone in the firm's target market or only a portion of the target market. For example, General Motors is targeting its Pontiac G5 sports coupe at young men with an online-only campaign of ads on Google, Yahoo! Music, and MySpace.com, where young men in the market for a sports car are likely to look.[6]

Target Audience

Fresh Step targets consumers that want cat litter boxes odor free.

Advertisers research and analyze advertising targets to establish an information base for a campaign. Information commonly needed includes location and geographic distribution of the target group; the distribution of demographic factors such as age, income, race, sex, and education; lifestyle information; and consumer attitudes regarding purchase and use of both the advertiser's products and competing products. The exact kind of information an organization finds useful depends on the type of product being advertised, the characteristics of the target audience, and the type and amount of competition. Generally, the more an advertiser knows about the target audience, the more likely the firm is to develop an effective advertising campaign. When the advertising target is not precisely identified and properly analyzed, the campaign may fail.

Defining the Advertising Objectives

The advertiser's next step is to determine what the firm hopes to accomplish with the campaign. Because advertising objectives guide campaign development, advertisers should define objectives carefully. Advertising objectives should be stated clearly, precisely, and in measurable terms. Precision and measurability allow advertisers to evaluate advertising success at the end of the campaign in terms of whether or not objectives have been met. To provide precision and measurability, advertising objectives should contain benchmarks and indicate how far the advertiser wishes to move from these standards. If the goal is to

figure 17.1

GENERAL STEPS IN DEVELOPING AND IMPLEMENTING AN ADVERTISING CAMPAIGN

8 Evaluate advertising effectiveness

7 Execute campaign

6 Create advertising message

5 Develop media plan

4 Determine advertising appropriation

3 Create advertising platform

2 Define advertising objectives

1 Identify and analyze target audience

increase sales, the advertiser should state the current sales level (the benchmark) and the amount of sales increase sought through advertising. An advertising objective also should specify a time frame so that advertisers know exactly how long they have to accomplish the objective. An advertiser with average monthly sales of $450,000 (the benchmark) might set the following objective: "Our primary advertising objective is to increase average monthly sales from $450,000 to $540,000 within 12 months."

If an advertiser defines objectives on the basis of sales, the objectives focus on increasing absolute dollar sales or unit sales, increasing sales by a certain percentage, or increasing the firm's market share. Even though an advertiser's long-run goal is to increase sales, not all campaigns are designed to produce immediate sales. Some campaigns are designed to increase product or brand awareness, make consumers' attitudes more favorable, or increase consumers' knowledge of product features. These types of objectives are stated in terms of communication.

Creating the Advertising Platform

Before launching a political campaign, party leaders develop a political platform stating the major issues that are the basis of the campaign. Like a political platform, an **advertising platform** consists of the basic issues or selling points that an advertiser wishes to include in the advertising campaign. New Balance, for example, launched a campaign that mocks professional athletes while reminding its 25- to 49-year-old target market about the joys of competing for fun and the love of sports.[7] A single advertisement in an advertising campaign may contain one or several issues from the platform. Although the platform sets forth the basic issues, it does not indicate how to present them.

An advertising platform should consist of issues important to customers. One of the best ways to determine those issues is to survey customers about what they consider most important in the selection and use of the product involved. Selling features must not only be important to customers, but they also should be strongly competitive features of the advertised brand. For example, New Balance's "Love or Money" campaign stemmed in part from Internet research that found that many people have become disturbed by the behavior of well-known professional athletes, some of whom receive millions of dollars a year in endorsements from New Balance's competitors.[8]

advertising campaign Designing a series of advertisements and placing them in various advertising media to reach a particular target audience

target audience The group of people at whom advertisements are aimed

advertising platform Basic issues or selling points to be included in the advertising campaign

THE WALL STREET JOURNAL.

Every journey needs a Journal.

Advertising Platform

Wall Street Journal's advertising platform—"Every journey needs a Journal" documents the philanthropic and professional achievements of successful business people like Kenneth Cole. Many of these achievements appeal to WSJ consumers.

Although research is the most effective method for determining what issues to include in an advertising platform, it is expensive. Therefore, an advertising platform is based most commonly on opinions of personnel within the firm and of individuals in the advertising agency, if an agency is used. This trial-and-error approach generally leads to some successes and some failures.

Because the advertising platform is a base on which to build the advertising message, marketers should analyze this stage carefully. A campaign can be perfect in terms of selection and analysis of its target audience, statement of its objectives, its media strategy, and the form of its message. But the campaign ultimately will fail if the advertisements communicate information that consumers do not deem important when selecting and using the product.

Determining the Advertising Appropriation

The **advertising appropriation** is the total amount of money a marketer allocates for advertising for a specific time period. New Balance, for example, planned to spend $21 million on its "Love or Money" campaign.[9] It is hard to decide how much to spend on advertising for a specific period because the potential effects of advertising are so difficult to measure precisely.

Many factors affect a firm's decision about how much to appropriate for advertising. Geographic size of the market and the distribution of buyers within the market have a great bearing on this decision. As Table 17.2 (on page 438) shows, both the type of product advertised and the firm's sales volume relative to competitors' sales volumes also play their respective parts in determining what proportion of revenue to spend on advertising. Advertising appropriations for business products are usually quite small relative to product sales, whereas consumer convenience items, such as soft drinks, soaps, and cosmetics, generally have large advertising expenditures relative to sales.

Of the many techniques used to determine the advertising appropriation, one of the most logical is the **objective-and-task approach**. Using this approach, marketers determine the objectives a campaign is to achieve and then attempt to list the tasks required to accomplish them. The costs of the tasks are calculated and added to arrive at the total appropriation. This approach has one main problem: Marketers sometimes have trouble accurately estimating the level of effort needed to attain certain objectives. A coffee marketer, for example, may find it extremely difficult to determine how much of an increase in television advertising is needed to raise a brand's market share from 8 to 10 percent.

In the more widely used **percent-of-sales approach**, marketers simply multiply the firm's past sales, plus a factor for planned sales growth or decline, by a standard percentage based on what the firm traditionally spends on advertising and perhaps on the industry average. This approach is flawed because it is based on the incorrect assumption that sales create advertising rather than the reverse. A marketer using this approach during declining sales will reduce the amount spent on advertising, but such

advertising appropriation Advertising budget for a specified period

objective-and-task approach Budgeting for an advertising campaign by first determining its objectives and then calculating the cost of all the tasks needed to attain them

percent-of-sales approach Budgeting for an advertising campaign by multiplying the firm's past or expected sales by a standard percentage

Peyton Manning MVP: Most Marketable Player

Football fans are certainly familiar with 2007 Super Bowl MVP Peyton Manning's skill and records, but did you know that *Sports Business Journal* recently voted the Indianapolis Colts quarterback the NFL's "most marketable player"? *USA Today* also dubbed Manning the NFL's "most valuable pitchman." Indeed, there's little chance that a person watching television could possibly have missed seeing at least one of Peyton Manning's commercials in 2006. In one year he did spots for MasterCard, Sprint, DirecTV, Reebok, and more. Companies love Manning, who pulled in an estimated $11.5 million in 2006 for his advertising gigs, and many viewers do as well.

What makes Peyton Manning so appealing and marketable? Of course, part of it is his record with the NFL. But it also has to do with his off-the-field reputation and his family background. Manning is viewed as having a wholesome reputation and is actively involved in community service. He also comes from a football family: His father, Archie Manning, was an NFL quarterback himself, as is his younger brother Eli (currently quarterback for the New York Giants). Arguably, though, Manning's success in the marketing arena has to do with the likeability factor. He doesn't come across as pretty like Tom Brady or tough like Donovan McNabb, but rather down-to-earth, more approachable. His 2006 lineup of commercials has allowed him to display his goofy, funny side, and this seems to resonate with viewers. Manning claims that he is often approached in public by fans quoting lines from his commercials.

Although many people enjoy Manning's ads, some people, including perhaps Manning's father, feel that he's becoming overexposed. Jokes about "too much Manning" were peppered throughout football commentary for the 2006 season, and blogs ranting about Manning's many ads popped up all over the Internet. But Manning's brands don't appear to be concerned. Chris Jogis, MasterCard's vice-president of brand development, says that the way Manning is portrayed in ads wipes out any concern of overexposure. Manning's record as an advertiser's darling speaks for itself. In addition to his "most marketable player" title, he has received a higher Q Score—a survey measure that marketers use to rate a character's familiarity and appeal—than Dale Earnhardt, Jr., who currently endorses sports advertising's biggest spender, Anheuser-Busch. The Davie Brown Index—a measure that focuses on recognition, although it measures multiple marketing categories—says that Manning ranks high on "influence in today's world" and "trust." It's clear that, right now, most of the world loves Peyton, so we'll just have to see how much of Peyton we get (off the field) in future years![a]

a reduction may further diminish sales. Though illogical, this technique has been used widely because it is easy to implement.

Another way to determine the advertising appropriation is the **competition-matching approach**. Marketers following this approach try to match their major competitors' appropriations in absolute dollars or to allocate the same percentage of sales for advertising that their competitors do. Although a marketer should be aware of what competitors spend on advertising, this technique should not be used alone because the firm's competitors probably have different advertising objectives and different resources available for advertising. Many companies and advertising agencies review competitive spending on a quarterly basis, comparing competitors' dollar expenditures on print, radio, and television with their own spending levels.

At times, marketers use the **arbitrary approach**, which usually means a high-level executive in the firm states how much to spend on advertising for a certain period.

competition-matching approach Determining an advertising budget by trying to match competitors' ad outlays

arbitrary approach Budgeting for an advertising campaign as specified by a high-level executive in the firm

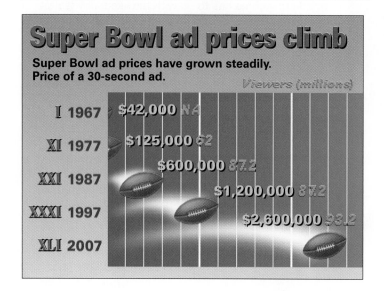

Super Bowl ad prices climb

Super Bowl ad prices have grown steadily.
Price of a 30-second ad.

Viewers (millions)

I	1967	$42,000	NA
XI	1977	$125,000	62
XXI	1987	$600,000	87.2
XXXI	1997	$1,200,000	87.2
XLI	2007	$2,600,000	93.2

The arbitrary approach often leads to underspending or overspending. Although hardly a scientific budgeting technique, it is expedient.

Developing the Media Plan

As Figure 17.2 shows, advertisers spend tremendous amounts on advertising media. These amounts have grown rapidly during the past two decades. To derive maximum results from media expenditures, marketers must develop effective media plans. A **media plan** sets forth the exact media vehicles to be used (specific magazines, television stations, newspapers, and so forth) and the dates and times the advertisements will appear. The plan focuses on how many people in the target audience will be exposed to a message and the frequency of exposure. Table 17.3 (on page 440) lists the leading sources of food information for consumers, which would help food marketers to determine where to allocate their advertising. It also determines, to some degree, the effects of the message on those individuals. Media planning is a complex task requiring thorough analysis of the target audience. Sophisticated computer models have been developed to attempt to maximize the effectiveness of media plans.

To formulate a media plan, the planners select the media for the campaign and prepare a time schedule for each medium. The media planner's primary goal is to reach the largest number of people in the advertising target audience that the budget will allow. A secondary goal is to achieve the appropriate message reach and frequency for

media plan Specifies media vehicles and schedule for running the advertisements

table 17.2   TOP TEN LEADING NATIONAL ADVERTISERS

Organization	Advertising Expenditures ($ millions)	U.S. Sales ($ millions)	Advertising Expenditures as Percentage of Sales
1. Procter & Gamble	4,609	25,342*	18.2
2. General Motors	4,353	127,316	3.4
3. Time Warner	3,494	34,469	10.1
4. Verizon	2,484	72,701	3.4
5. AT&T	2,471	43,852	5.6
6. Ford Motor	2,398	96,764	2.5
7. Walt Disney	2,279	24,806*	9.2
8. Johnson & Johnson	2,209	28,377	7.8
9. GlaxoSmithKline	2,194	16,482	13.3
10. DaimlerChrysler	2,179	82,931	2.6

*North American sales.
Source: *Advertising Age,* June 26, 2006, pp. S-8, S-16–S-103.

figure 17.2

ADVERTISING EXPENDITURES BY MEDIA: 1985 VERSUS 2005

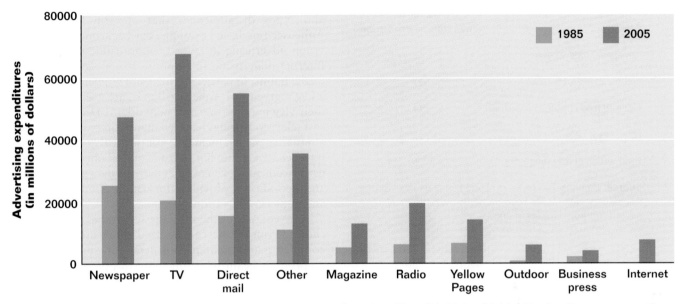

Source: "Ad Spending Totals by Media," *Advertising Age,* June 26, 2006, p. S-5; Robert J. Coen, "Coen: Little Ad Growth," *Advertising Age,* May 6, 1991, pp. 1, 16.

the target audience while staying within budget. *Reach* refers to the percentage of consumers in the target audience actually exposed to a particular advertisement in a stated period. *Frequency* is the number of times these targeted consumers are exposed to the advertisement.

Media planners begin with broad decisions but eventually make very specific ones. They first decide which kinds of media to use: radio, television, the Internet, newspapers, magazines, direct mail, outdoor displays, or signs on mass-transit vehicles. Internet advertising in particular is growing, with companies spending nearly $5 billion to run ads alongside Internet searches in sites such as Google and Yahoo!, an amount projected to grow to nearly $8 billion by 2010.[10] Media planners assess different formats and approaches to determine which are the most effective. Some media plans are quite focused and use just one medium. The media plans of manufacturers of consumer packaged goods can be quite complex and dynamic.

Media planners take many factors into account when devising a media plan. They analyze location and the demographic characteristics of people in the target audience because people's tastes in media differ according to

Media Selection

Media planners have many types of media options from which to choose. Qualitative factors are considered when making media choices, and databases provide quantitative profiles on specific media alternatives.

table 17.3	WHERE SHOPPERS GET INFORMATION ABOUT FOOD	

Category	Percent of Traffic (Visits from Search Engines)
Newspaper food section	53
Website about food	17
Cable TV food channel	14
Food magazine	12
Food section of magazine	5

Source: Gallup & Robinson, in "Food Shoppers Have Strong Appetite for Newspaper Food Sections," advertisement, *Advertising Age,* January 1, 2007.

demographic groups and locations. There are radio stations especially for teenagers, magazines for men ages 18 to 34, and television cable channels aimed at women in various age groups. Media planners also consider the sizes and types of audiences that specific media reach. Anheuser-Busch, for example, cut back on network television advertising in favor of more cable television and Internet advertising in response to changing consumer media habits. In particular, men and women age 21 to 34, a key segment for Anheuser-Busch, are spending more of their viewing time on cable networks.[11] Declining broadcast television ratings have led many companies to explore alternative media, including not only cable television and Internet advertising but also ads on cell phones and product placements in videogames. Several data services collect and periodically provide information about circulations and audiences of various media.

The content of the message sometimes affects media choice. Print media can be used more effectively than broadcast media to present complex issues or numerous details in single advertisements. If an advertiser wants to promote beautiful colors, patterns, or textures, media offering high-quality color reproduction—magazines or television—should be used instead of newspapers. For example, food can be promoted effectively in full-color magazine advertisements but far less effectively in black and white.

The cost of media is an important but troublesome consideration. Planners try to obtain the best coverage possible for each dollar spent. But there is no accurate way to compare the cost and impact of a television commercial with the cost and impact of a newspaper advertisement. A **cost comparison indicator** lets an advertiser compare the costs of several vehicles within a specific medium (such as two magazines) in relation to the number of people each vehicle reaches. The *cost per thousand* (CPM) is the cost comparison indicator for magazines; it shows the cost of exposing a thousand people to a one-page advertisement. Figure 17.2 shows that the extent to which each medium is used varies and how it has changed since 1985. Media are selected by weighing the various advantages and disadvantages of each (see Table 17.4).

Like media selection decisions, media scheduling decisions are affected by numerous factors, such as target-audience characteristics, product attributes, product seasonality, customer media behavior, and size of the advertising budget. There are three general types of media schedules: continuous, flighting, and pulsing. When a *continuous* schedule is used, advertising runs at a constant level with little variation throughout the campaign period. With a *flighting* schedule, advertisements run for set periods of time, alternating with periods in which no ads run. For example, an advertising campaign might have an ad run for two weeks, then suspend it for two weeks, and then run it again for two weeks. A *pulsing* schedule combines continuous and flighting schedules. During the entire campaign, a certain portion of advertising runs continuously, and during specific time periods of the campaign, additional advertising is used to intensify the level of communication with the target audience.

Creating the Advertising Message

The basic content and form of an advertising message are functions of several factors. A product's features, uses, and benefits affect the content of the message. Characteristics of the people in the target audience—gender, age, education, race, income, occupation, lifestyle, and other attributes—influence both content and form. For example, gender affects how people respond to advertising claims that use hedging words such as *may* and *probably* and pledging words such as *definitely* and *absolutely*. Researchers have found that women respond negatively to both types of claims, but pledging claims have little effect on men.[12] When Procter & Gamble

cost comparison indicator A means of comparing the cost of vehicles in a specific medium in relation to the number of people reached

| table 17.4 | ADVANTAGES AND DISADVANTAGES OF MAJOR ADVERTISING MEDIA | |

Medium	Advantages	Disadvantages
Newspapers	Reaches large audience; purchased to be read; geographic flexibility; short lead time; frequent publication; favorable for cooperative advertising, merchandising services.	Not selective for socioeconomic groups or target market; short life; limited reproduction capabilities; large advertising volume limits exposure to any one advertisement.
Magazines	Demographic selectivity; good reproduction; long life; prestige; geographic selectivity when regional issues are available; read in leisurely manner.	High costs; 30- to 90-day average lead time; high level of competition; limited reach; communicates less frequently.
Direct mail	Little wasted circulation; highly selective; circulation controlled by advertiser; few distractions; personal; stimulates actions; use of novelty; relatively easy to measure performance; hidden from competitors.	Very expensive; lacks editorial content to attract readers; often thrown away unread as junk mail; criticized as invasion of privacy; consumers must choose to read the ad.
Radio	Reaches 95% of consumers; highly mobile and flexible; very low relative costs; ad can be changed quickly; high level of geographic and demographic selectivity; encourages use of imagination.	Lacks visual imagery; short life of message; listeners' attention limited because of other activities; market fragmentation; difficult buying procedures; limited media and audience research.
Television	Reaches large audiences; high frequency available; dual impact of audio and video; highly visible; high prestige; geographic and demographic selectivity; difficult to ignore.	Very expensive; highly perishable message; size of audience not guaranteed; amount of prime time limited; lack of selectivity in target market.
Internet	Immediate response; potential to reach a precisely targeted audience; ability to track customers and build databases; highly interactive medium.	Costs of precise targeting are high; inappropriate ad placement; effects difficult to measure; concerns about security and privacy.
Yellow Pages	Wide availability; action and product category oriented; low relative costs; ad frequency and longevity; nonintrusive.	Market fragmentation; extremely localized; slow updating; lack of creativity; long lead times; requires large space to be noticed.
Outdoor	Allows for frequent repetition; low cost; message can be placed close to point of sale; geographic selectivity; operable 24 hours a day; high creativity and effectiveness.	Message must be short and simple; no demographic selectivity; seldom attracts readers' full attention; criticized as traffic hazard and blight on countryside; much wasted coverage; limited capabilities.

Source: Information from William F. Arens, *Contemporary Advertising* (Burr Ridge, IL: Irwin/ McGraw-Hill, 2007); George E. Belch and Michael Belch, *Advertising and Promotion* (Burr Ridge, IL: Irwin/McGraw-Hill, 2006).

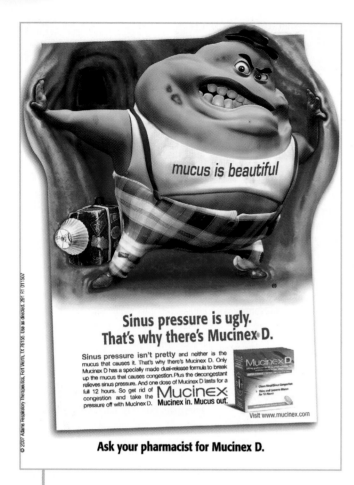

Components of a Print Ad

This Mucinex ad contains all the major components of a print advertisement.

promotes Crest toothpaste to children, the company emphasizes daily brushing and cavity control. When Crest is marketed to adults, tartar and plaque control are emphasized. To communicate effectively, advertisers use words, symbols, and illustrations that are meaningful, familiar, and attractive to people in the target audience.

An advertising campaign's objectives and platform also affect the content and form of its messages. If a firm's advertising objectives involve large sales increases, the message may include hard-hitting, high-impact language and symbols. When campaign objectives aim at increasing brand awareness, the message may use much repetition of the brand name and words and illustrations associated with it.

Choice of media obviously influences the content and form of the message. Effective outdoor displays and short broadcast spot announcements require concise, simple messages. Magazine and newspaper advertisements can include considerable detail and long explanations. Because several kinds of media offer geographic selectivity, a precise message can be tailored to a particular geographic section of the target audience. Some magazine publishers produce **regional issues**, in which advertisements and editorial content of copies appearing in one geographic area differ from those appearing in other areas. For example, *Time* magazine publishes eight regional issues. A company advertising in *Time* might decide to use one message in the New England region and another in the rest of the nation. A company also may choose to advertise in only one region. Such geographic selectivity lets a firm use the same message in different regions at different times.

Copy.   **Copy** is the verbal portion of an advertisement and may include headlines, subheadlines, body copy, and signature. Not all advertising contains all these copy elements. Even handwritten notes on direct-mail advertising that say, "Try this. It works!" seem to increase requests for free samples.[13] The headline is critical because often it is the only part of the copy that people read. It should attract readers' attention and create enough interest to make them want to read the body copy. The subheadline, if there is one, links the headline to the body copy and sometimes is used to explain the headline.

Body copy for most advertisements consists of an introductory statement or paragraph, several explanatory paragraphs, and a closing paragraph. Some copywriters have adopted guidelines for developing body copy systematically: (1) Identify a specific desire or problem, (2) recommend the product as the best way to satisfy that desire or solve that problem, (3) state product benefits and indicate why the product is best for the buyer's particular situation, (4) substantiate advertising claims, and (5) ask the buyer to take action. When substantiating claims, it is important to present the substantiation in a credible manner. The proof of claims should help strengthen the image of the product and company integrity. Typeface selection can help advertisers create a desired impression by using fonts that are engaging, reassuring, or very prominent.[14]

The signature identifies the advertisement's sponsor. It may contain several elements, including the firm's trademark, logo, name, and address. The signature should be attractive, legible, distinctive, and easy to identify in a variety of sizes.

Because radio listeners often are not fully "tuned in" mentally, radio copy should be informal and conversational to attract listeners' attention, resulting in greater impact. Radio messages are highly perishable and should consist of short, familiar

regional issues Versions of a magazine that differ across geographic regions

copy The verbal portion of advertisements

Black and White Versus Color

This example highlights the importance of using color when advertising certain products.

storyboard A mockup combining copy and visual material to show the sequence of major scenes in a commercial

artwork An ad's illustrations and layout

illustrations Photos, drawings, graphs, charts, and tables used to spark audience interest

layout The physical arrangement of an ad's illustration and copy

terms. The length should not require a rate of speech exceeding approximately two and one-half words per second.

In television copy, the audio material must not overpower the visual material, and vice versa. However, a television message should make optimal use of its visual portion, which can be very effective for product demonstrations. Copy for a television commercial is sometimes initially written in parallel script form. Video is described in the left column and audio in the right. When the parallel script is approved, the copywriter and artist combine copy with visual material by using a **storyboard**, which depicts a series of miniature television screens showing the sequence of major scenes in the commercial. Beneath each screen is a description of the audio portion to be used with that video segment. Technical personnel use the storyboard as a blueprint when producing the commercial.

Artwork. **Artwork** consists of an advertisement's illustrations and layout. Although **illustrations** are often photographs, they also can be drawings, graphs, charts, and tables. Illustrations can be more important in capturing attention than text or brand elements, independent of size.[15] They are used to attract attention, encourage audiences to read or listen to the copy, communicate an idea quickly, or communicate ideas that are difficult to put into words.[16] Advertisers use various illustration techniques. They may show the product alone, in a setting, or in use, or they may show the results of its use. Illustrations also can be in the form of comparisons, contrasts, and diagrams.

The **layout** of an advertisement is the physical arrangement of the illustration and the copy—headline, subheadline, body copy, and signature. These elements can be arranged in many ways. The final layout is the result of several stages of layout preparation. As it moves through these stages, the layout promotes an exchange of ideas among people developing the advertising campaign and provides instructions for production personnel.

Executing the Campaign

Execution of an advertising campaign requires extensive planning and coordination because many tasks must be completed on time and many people and firms are involved. Production companies, research organizations, media firms, printers, photo-engravers, and commercial artists are just a few of the people and firms contributing to a campaign.

Implementation requires detailed schedules to ensure that various phases of the work are done on time. Advertising management personnel must evaluate the quality of the work and take corrective action when necessary. Citibank, for example, pulled the plug on ads for its credit card rewards program featuring an annoying pair of fictional eastern Europeans because of criticism in the media and the blog world.[17] In some instances, changes are made during the campaign so that it meets objectives more effectively. Sometimes one firm develops a campaign, and another executes it.

Evaluating Advertising Effectiveness

Advertising can be evaluated before, during, and after the campaign. An evaluation performed before the campaign begins is called a **pretest**. A pretest usually attempts to evaluate the effectiveness of one or more elements of the message. To pretest advertisements, marketers sometimes use a **consumer jury**, a panel of actual or potential buyers of the advertised product. Jurors judge one or several dimensions of two or more advertisements. Such tests are based on the belief that consumers are more likely than advertising experts to know what influences them.

To measure advertising effectiveness during a campaign, marketers sometimes use "inquiries." In a campaign's initial stages, an advertiser may use several advertisements simultaneously, each containing a coupon, form, or toll-free phone number through which potential customers can request information. The advertiser records the number of inquiries returned from each type of advertisement. If an advertiser receives 78,528 inquiries from advertisement A, 37,072 from advertisement B, and 47,932 from advertisement C, advertisement A is judged superior to advertisements B and C.

Evaluation of advertising effectiveness after the campaign is called a **posttest**. Advertising objectives often determine what kind of posttest is appropriate. If the objectives focus on communication—to increase awareness of product features or brands or to create more favorable customer attitudes—the posttest should measure changes in these dimensions. Advertisers sometimes use consumer surveys or experiments to evaluate a campaign based on communication objectives.

For campaign objectives stated in terms of sales, advertisers should determine the change in sales or market share attributable to the campaign. For example, after a tourism campaign by the state of Utah—with the slogan "Utah: Life Elevated"—tourist spending in the state increased by nearly 8 percent to almost $6 billion.[18] However, changes in sales or market share brought about by advertising cannot be measured precisely. Many factors independent of advertisements affect a firm's sales and market share. Competitors' actions, government actions, and changes in economic conditions, consumer preferences, and weather are only a few factors that might enhance or diminish a company's sales or market share. By using data about past and current sales and advertising expenditures, advertisers can make gross estimates of the effects of a campaign on sales or market share.

Because it is difficult to determine the direct effects of advertising on sales, some advertisers evaluate print advertisements according to how well consumers can remember them. Posttest methods based on memory include recognition and recall tests. Such tests usually are performed by research organizations through surveys. In a **recognition test**, respondents are shown the actual advertisement and asked whether they recognize it. If they do, the interviewer asks additional questions to determine how much of the advertisement each respondent read. When recall is evaluated, the respondents are not shown the actual advertisement but instead are asked about what they have seen or heard recently. Recall can be measured through either unaided or aided recall methods. In an **unaided recall test**, respondents identify advertisements they have seen recently but are not shown any clues to help them remember. A similar procedure is used with

pretest Evaluation of ads performed before a campaign begins

consumer jury A panel of a product's actual or potential buyers who pretest ads

posttest Evaluation of advertising effectiveness after the campaign

recognition test A posttest in which individuals are shown the actual ad and asked if they recognize it

unaided recall test A posttest in which respondents identify ads they have recently seen but are given no recall clues

Selling Insurance with a Quack

American Family Life Assurance Company (Aflac) is a multibillion-dollar insurance company that has been in business for 50 years and insures more than 40 million people. A *Fortune* 500 company, it is a major insurance carrier in the United States and the largest life insurer in Japan. Before it launched a campaign featuring its quacking duck, only 12 percent of the people in the United States had ever heard of the company. Now, 90 percent of U.S. consumers are aware of it. Since the duck first appeared on TV four years ago, Aflac's sales have increased by 20 percent, and the "Aflac" quack has become part of the U.S. vernacular.

The resounding success of Aflac's advertising campaign is unique for several reasons. It is rare for a brand icon such as a humorous duck to be used to represent a serious business like life and health insurance. It is also noteworthy that the duck generated such high awareness and popularity in such a short time. Creating a brand icon often takes years and can require a massive ad budget. Aflac spends $45 million on commercial time annually. While not an insignificant sum, it is substantially less than what McDonald's spends promoting Ronald McDonald or Energizer Batteries spends on its drum-banging bunny. Consider that a major portion of McDonald's annual $680 million advertising budget supports Ronald McDonald, who has a lower Q Score than the Aflac duck. A Q Score is a survey measurement that marketers use to rate a character's familiarity and appeal. Energizer Batteries has spent approximately $1 billion on its

veteran Energizer Bunny over the past 15 years, also with lower Q Score results.

Beyond creativity, the duck's advantage can be attributed to the company's successful guerrilla public relations campaign. Aflac's public relations department is constantly looking for opportunities to get free publicity for its web-footed mascot. The Aflac duck has been featured on CNBC, *The Tonight Show with Jay Leno, Saturday Night Live,* and *Live with Regis and Kelly.* Aflac's publicity team has conducted two "Quack Attacks," on NBC's *Today Show* with a group of 15 Aflac executives carrying large plush duck toys and signs on the show's outdoor set to get free media time for the duck. The Aflac duck was even enshrined on Madison Avenue's Walk of Fame recognizing the beloved corporate mascot as one of America's favorite advertising icons. Now that's one hard-quacking duck![b]

an **aided recall test**, but respondents are shown a list of products, brands, company names, or trademarks to jog their memories. For example, the long-running national youth antidrug media campaign by the Office of National Drug Control Policy has nearly 70 percent recognition and recall among youth and 55 percent among parents.[19] Several research organizations, such as Daniel Starch, provide research services that test recognition and recall of advertisements. The major justification for using recognition and recall methods is that people are more likely to buy a product if they can remember an advertisement about it than if they cannot. Researchers also use sophisticated techniques based on *single-source data* to help evaluate advertisements. With this technique, individuals' behaviors are tracked from televisions to checkout counters. Monitors are placed in preselected homes, and computers record when the television is on and which station is being viewed. At the supermarket checkout, the individual in the sample household presents an identification card. Checkers then record the purchases

aided recall test A posttest that asks respondents to identify recent ads and provides clues to jog their memories

by scanner, and data are sent to the research facility. Some single-source data companies provide sample households with scanning equipment for use at home to record purchases after returning from shopping trips. Single-source data provide information that links exposure to advertisements with purchase behavior.

Who Develops the Advertising Campaign?

An advertising campaign may be handled by an individual or by a few persons within a firm, by a firm's own advertising department, or by an advertising agency. In very small firms, one or two individuals are responsible for advertising (and for many other activities as well). Usually these individuals depend heavily on personnel at local newspapers and broadcast stations for copywriting, artwork, and advice about scheduling media.

In certain large businesses—especially large retail organizations—advertising departments create and implement advertising campaigns. Depending on the size of the advertising program, an advertising department may consist of a few multiskilled persons or a sizable number of specialists, such as copywriters, artists, media buyers, and technical production coordinators. Advertising departments sometimes obtain the services of independent research organizations and hire freelance specialists when a particular project requires it.

Many firms employ an advertising agency to develop advertising campaigns. The U.S. Army, for example, contracted with McCann Worldgroup to create an advertising campaign with the theme "Army strong." The recruiting campaign, expected to cost $1.35 billion over five years, included videos on YouTube, a website (goarmy.com), and a profile on MySpace.[20] When an organization uses an advertising agency, the firm and the agency usually develop the advertising campaign jointly. Advertising agencies assist businesses in several ways. An agency, especially a large one, can supply the services of highly skilled specialists—not only copywriters, artists, and production coordinators but also media experts, researchers, and legal advisers. Agency personnel often have broad advertising experience and are usually more objective than a firm's employees about the organization's products. Because an agency traditionally receives most of its compensation from a 15 percent commission paid by the media from which it makes purchases, firms can obtain some agency services at low or moderate costs. If an agency contracts for $400,000 of television time for a firm, it receives a commission of $60,000 from the television station. Although the traditional compensation method for agencies is changing and now includes other factors, media commissions still offset some costs of using an agency. Table 17.5 lists some of the leading ad agencies.

public relations Communication efforts used to create and maintain favorable relations between an organization and its stakeholders

TABLE 17.5   LEADING AD AGENCIES—TRADITIONAL AND MEDIA SPECIALISTS

Traditional Agencies	Percent Billings	Media Specialists	Percent Billings
1. JWT	5.0	1. OMD Worldwide	11.4
2. McCann Erickson Worldwide	4.7	2. MindShare Worldwide	11.2
3. Leo Burnett Worldwide	3.8	3. Starcom USA	9.3
4. BBDO Worldwide	3.0	4. Mediedge:cia	8.6
5. Ogilvy & Mather Worldwide	3.0	5. Initiative	7.9

Source: *Advertising Age,* January 1, 2007, p. 26.

Public Relations

Public relations is a broad set of communication efforts used to create and maintain favorable relationships between an organization and its stakeholders. PepsiCo, for example, publishes a newspaper insert called *Disfrútalo* that not only introduces Spanish-speaking mothers to Pepsi products but also strives to build relationships through coupons, tips, and useful information to help Hispanic moms transition to life in the United States.[21] An organization communicates with various stakeholders, both internal and external, and public relations efforts can be directed toward any and all of these. A firm's stakeholders can include customers, suppliers, employees, stockholders, the media, educators, potential investors, government officials, and society in general.

Public relations can be used to promote people, places, ideas, activities, and even countries. It focuses on enhancing the image of the total organization. Assessing public attitudes and creating a favorable image are no less important than direct promotion of the organization's products. Because the public's attitudes toward a firm are likely to affect the sales of its products, it is very important for firms to maintain positive public perceptions. In addition, employee morale is strengthened if the public perceives the firm positively.[22] Although public relations can make people aware of a company's products, brands, or activities, it also can create specific company images, such as innovativeness or dependability. Companies such as Green Mountain Coffee Roasters, Patagonia, Sustainable Harvest, and Honest Tea have earned reputations for being socially responsible not just because they strive to act in a socially responsible manner but also because their efforts are reported through news stories and other public relations efforts. By getting the media to report on a firm's accomplishments, public relations helps the company maintain positive public visibility.

Annual Report

Annual reports, when appropriately designed, can generate favorable public relations.

Public Relations Tools

Companies use various public relations tools to convey messages and create images. Public relations professionals prepare written materials, such as brochures, newsletters, company magazines, news releases, websites, blogs, and annual reports, that reach and influence their various stakeholders. Procter & Gamble (P&G), for example, created a social-networking website called Capessa where women—who are major consumers of P&G products—can discuss issues such as health, work, weight loss, and pregnancy and share their personal stories.[23] Public relations personnel also create corporate identity materials, such as logos, business cards, stationery, and signs, that make firms immediately recognizable. Speeches are another public relations tool. Because what a company executive says publicly at meetings or to the media can affect the organization's image, his or her speech must convey the desired message clearly.

Event sponsorship, in which a company pays for part or all of a special event, such as a benefit concert or a tennis tournament, is another public relations tool. Examples are Home Depot's sponsorship of NASCAR and the U.S. Olympic teams. Sponsoring special events can be an effective means of increasing company or brand recognition with relatively minimal expenditures.

marketing ENTREPRENEURS

Alex Tew

HIS BUSINESS: MillionDollarHomePage

FOUNDED: In England in 2005, when Tew was 21

SUCCESS: $1 million in sales in 5 months

Alex Tew had an overdrawn bank account and no way to pay for his Nottingham University classes. Determined to avoid years of paying off student loans, he brainstormed the idea to sell 1 million pixels of advertising space on a website for $1 each (actually 100 pixels, the smallest size the eye can see, for $100). He used the funds from selling the first 1,000 pixels to send out press releases to local media. The story of his efforts quickly traveled around the world through news stories, blogs, and e-mail. Thanks to the viral publicity, he sold enough advertising space to pay for his entire college education in two weeks, 100 pixels at a time. Tew plans to use the money from the venture to invest in new marketing ventures and charity.[c]

publicity A news story type of communication transmitted through a mass medium at no charge

news release A short piece of copy publicizing an event or a product

feature article A manuscript of up to 3,000 words prepared for a specific publication

captioned photograph A photo with a brief description of its contents

press conference A meeting used to announce major news events

Event sponsorship can gain companies considerable amounts of free media coverage. For example, corporate sponsors of professional beach volleyball, such as McDonald's, Nissan, and Budweiser, benefited from more than 1 billion media impressions during a single season.[24] An organization tries to make sure that its product and the sponsored event target a similar audience and that the two are easily associated in customers' minds. Public relations personnel also organize unique events to "create news" about the company. These may include grand openings with celebrities, prizes, hot-air balloon rides, and other attractions that appeal to a firm's audience.

Publicity is part of public relations. **Publicity** is communication in news-story form about the organization, its products, or both transmitted through a mass medium at no charge. For example, after Apple chairman Steve Jobs announced that the company would introduce a revolutionary new mobile phone, the iPhone, the story was covered in newspapers and television news shows throughout the world for months afterward. Although public relations has a larger, more comprehensive communication function than publicity, publicity is a very important aspect of public relations. Publicity can be used to provide information about goods or services; to announce expansions, acquisitions, research, or new-product launches; or to enhance a company's image.

The most common publicity-based public relations tool is the **news release**, sometimes called a *press release,* which is usually a single page of typewritten copy containing fewer than 300 words and describing a company event or product. A news release gives the firm's or agency's name, address, phone number, and contact person. News releases can tackle a multitude of specific issues, as suggested in Table 17.6. A **feature article** is a manuscript of up to 3,000 words prepared for a specific publication. A **captioned photograph** is a photograph with a brief description explaining the picture's content. Captioned photographs are effective for illustrating new or improved products with highly visible features.

There are several other kinds of publicity-based public relations tools. A **press conference** is a meeting called to announce major news events. Media personnel are invited to a press conference and are usually supplied with written materials and photographs. Letters to the editor and editorials are sometimes prepared and sent to newspapers and magazines. Videos and audiotapes may be distributed to broadcast stations in the hope that they will be aired.

Publicity-based public relations tools offer several advantages, including credibility, news value, significant word-of-mouth communications, and a perception of being endorsed by the media. The public may consider news coverage more truthful and credible than an advertisement because the media are not paid to provide the information. In addition, stories regarding a new-product introduction or a new environmentally responsible company policy, for example, are handled as news items and are likely to receive notice. Finally, the cost of publicity is low compared with the cost of advertising.[25]

Publicity-based public relations tools have some limitations. Media personnel must judge company messages to be newsworthy if the messages are to be published or broadcast at all. Consequently, messages must be timely, interesting, accurate, and in the public interest. Many communications do not qualify. It may take a great deal of time and effort to convince media personnel of the news value of publicity releases.

TABLE 17.6 POSSIBLE ISSUES FOR NEWS RELEASES	
Changes in marketing personnel	Packaging changes
Support of a social cause	New products
Improved warranties	New slogan
Reports on industry conditions	Research developments
New uses for established products	Company's history and development
Product endorsements	Employment, production, and sales records
Quality awards	Award of contracts
Company name changes	Opening of new markets
Interviews with company officials	Improvements in financial position
Improved distribution policies	Opening of an exhibit
International business efforts	History of a brand
Athletic event sponsorship	Winners of company contests
Visits by celebrities	Logo changes
Reports on new discoveries	Speeches of top management
Innovative marketing activities	Merit awards
Economic forecasts	Anniversary of inventions

Although public relations personnel usually encourage the media to air publicity releases at certain times, they control neither the content nor the timing of the communication. Media personnel alter length and content of publicity releases to fit publishers' or broadcasters' requirements and may even delete the parts of messages that company personnel view as most important. Furthermore, media personnel use publicity releases in time slots or positions most convenient for them. Thus messages sometimes appear in locations or at times that may not reach the firm's target audiences. Although these limitations can be frustrating, properly managed publicity-based public relations tools offer an organization substantial benefits.

Evaluating Public Relations Effectiveness

Because of the potential benefits of good public relations, it is essential that organizations evaluate the effectiveness of their public relations campaigns. Research can be conducted to determine how well a firm is communicating its messages or image to its target audiences. *Environmental monitoring* identifies changes in public opinion affecting an organization. A *public relations audit* is used to assess an organization's image among the public or to evaluate the effect of a specific public relations program. A communications audit may include a content analysis of messages, a readability study, or a readership survey. If an organization wants to measure the extent to which stakeholders view it as being socially responsible, it can conduct a *social audit*.

One approach to measuring the effectiveness of publicity-based public relations is to count the number of exposures in the media. To determine which releases are published in print media and how often, an organization can hire a clipping service, a firm that

Contact: Sean Greenwood
Ben & Jerry's PR Poobah
802-846-1500, ext. 7701
sean.greenwood@benjerry.com

FOR IMMEDIATE RELEASE

BEN & JERRY'S TAKES STALK IN ITS PACKAGING
New Environmentally Friendly Corn Based Cup To Be Used at Scoop Shops Nationwide

Sept 5, 2006 - It's the one combination the Vermont company never tried: ice cream and corn. However, for the environment it could be a field of dreams.

Ben & Jerry's is switching to a new line of 100% corn based cold drink cups for use in their Scoop Shops starting this fall. The ecologically friendly cups are made from American grown corn, are environmentally sustainable and are fully compostable in commercial or industrial facilities. Specialty printed with Ben & Jerry's unmistakable colorful cow and pasture scene, the two sizes of new cups replace traditional petroleum based packaging for smoothies and frozen drinks.

"The cob does the job!" remarked Graham Rigby, Brand Manager at the company's headquarters. "We still have many improvements to make, but this is one switch we can be proud of."

Founded on a sustainable corporate culture, Ben & Jerry's strives to minimize the negative impact of its business practices on the environment. The ice cream maker has undertaken campaigns from helping family farms to offsetting its manufacturing plants emissions. It was the first frozen food business to introduce an unbleached paperboard container in 1998 and the mission continues with the use of Fabri-Kal's Greenware line of cold drink cups.

Headquartered in Kalamazoo, Michigan and in continuous operation since 1950, Fabri-Kal is one of the largest converters of the corn-based material used in the creation of the cups. More information about the Greenware line of products may be found at the company's website at www.f-k.com.

Ben & Jerry's, a wholly-owned autonomous subsidiary of Unilever, operates its business on a three-part mission statement emphasizing product quality, economic reward and a commitment to the community. The company produces a wide variety of super-premium ice cream and ice cream novelties which they distribute through many channels including 580 franchised Scoop Shops and PartnerShops worldwide.

* Greenware is a registered trademark of Fabri-Kal Corporation

Press Release

Press releases are often used as a way to spread news about a company.

clips and sends news releases to client companies. To measure the effectiveness of television coverage, a firm can enclose a card with its publicity releases requesting that the television station record its name and the dates when the news item is broadcast (although station personnel do not always comply). Although some television and radio tracking services exist, they are extremely costly.

Counting the number of media exposures does not reveal how many people actually have read or heard the company's message or what they thought about the message afterward. However, measuring changes in product awareness, knowledge, and attitudes resulting from the publicity campaign does. To assess these changes, companies must measure these levels before and after public relations campaigns. Although precise measures are difficult to obtain, a firm's marketers should attempt to assess the impact of public relations efforts on the organization's sales.

Dealing with Unfavorable Public Relations

We have thus far discussed public relations as a planned element of the promotion mix. However, companies may have to deal with unexpected and unfavorable publicity resulting from an unsafe product, an accident, controversial actions of employees, or some other negative event or situation. For example, an airline that experiences a plane crash faces a very tragic and distressing situation. Unfavorable coverage can have quick and dramatic effects. For example, after JetBlue, a low-cost airline, left nine planes full of passengers stranded for six hours or more while waiting for a weather break during an ice storm, many negative news stories appeared on TV, in print, and online, and the company's stock plummeted.[26] As it did with JetBlue, a single negative event that produces public relations can wipe out a company's favorable image and destroy positive customer attitudes established through years of expensive advertising campaigns and other promotional efforts. Today's mass media, including online services and the Internet, disseminate information faster than ever before, and bad news generally receives considerable media attention.

To protect its image, an organization needs to prevent unfavorable public relations or at least lessen its effect if it occurs. First and foremost, the organization should try to prevent negative incidents and events through safety programs, inspections, and effective quality-control procedures. Experts insist that sending consistent brand messages and images throughout all communications at all times can help a brand maintain its strength even during a crisis.[27] However, because negative events can befall even the most cautious firms, an organization should have predetermined plans in place to handle them when they do occur. Firms need to establish policies and procedures for reducing the adverse impact of news coverage of a crisis or controversy. In most cases, organizations should expedite news coverage of negative events rather than trying to discourage or block it. If news coverage is suppressed, rumors and other misinformation may replace facts and be passed along anyway. An unfavorable event easily can balloon into serious problems or public issues and become quite damaging. By being forthright with the press and public and taking prompt action, firms may be able to convince the public of their honest attempts to deal with the situation, and news personnel may be more willing to help explain complex issues to the public. Dealing effectively with a negative event allows an organization to lessen the unfavorable impact on its image. Consider that after news reports surrounding JetBlue leaving nine planes of passengers stranded on runways, the company offered the passengers full refunds and vouchers for free flights in the future. JetBlue founder and CEO David Neeleman, who said he was "humiliated and mortified" by the incident, immediately implemented plans to add and train staff to remedy communications and operations issues that contributed to the crisis. He also pledged to enact a customer bill of rights that would penalize the airline and reward passengers should such a scenario recur.[28] Experts generally advise that companies confronting negative publicity respond quickly and honestly to the situation and keep the lines of communications with all stakeholders open.

...And now, back to the Mini Cooper

BMW initiated a viral advertising campaign for the Mini disguised as a debate over whether a British engineer had built robots out of Mini car parts. The campaign included postings in chat rooms and booklets inserted in magazines such as *Motor Trend, National Geographic Adventure,* and *Rolling Stone.* The 40-page booklets purported to be passages from a book, *Men of Metal: Eyewitness Accounts of Humanoid Robots,* from a phony London publisher specializing in conspiracy-theory books on topics such as Bigfoot, the Loch Ness Monster, and UFOs. After a few months, Mini revealed wall posters featuring the Mini logo above images of the "motorbots." The goal of the campaign was to generate "buzz" for the car, particularly among mechanical-minded male drivers who might worry about women perceiving the car as "cute." Experts applauded the promotion as a great example of a viral campaign, spread by word of mouth among just the young men BMW wanted to reach. The following year, the company followed suit by launching a spoof website, the Counter Counterfeit Commission (**www.counterfeitmini.org**), that claimed to be "dedicated to putting an end to the victimization associated with purchasing a counterfeit Mini Cooper." It included a video called *Counterfeit Mini Coopers* and even a section on Confiscated Counterfeits. Once again, the creative campaign was widely discussed on blogs and spread mostly by word of mouth.

BMW later initiated another novel viral campaign, this time focused on current Mini owners rather than potential buyers. The campaign included a series of advertisements in magazines such as *Maxim* and *The New Yorker.* The ads were encrypted, decipherable only by the 150,000 U.S. Mini owners; no one else could read what was on the page. Mini USA sent all Mini owners a "covert" kit made to look like an aged book that included special glasses, a decoder, and a "magic window decryptor." Using these tools, Mini owners could find in the ads website URLs that led them to free prizes and invitations to events. One prize was an invitation to join a "Mini Takes the States" cross-country rally. Other prizes included gag switch covers for the Mini dashboard that, following the spy motif, labeled things like the fog-light switch as the "ejector seat." Mini USA executives hoped that the campaign would spur owners to continue to buy Minis and also to tell their friends about the campaign. Many people like the quirky Mini advertising campaigns, and Mini will continue to come up with unique advertising ideas to keep its existing customers and attract new ones.[29]

1. What is Mini tyring to achieve with its advertising campaign aimed at owners?

2. How does putting a Mini on ski lifts accomplish Mini's goals?

3. Do you think the "motorbots" campaign was good? Defend your answer.

CHAPTER REVIEW

1. Describe the nature and types of advertising.

Advertising is a paid form of nonpersonal communication transmitted to consumers through mass media such as television, radio, the Internet, newspapers, magazines, direct mail, outdoor displays, and signs on mass-transit vehicles. Both nonbusiness and business organizations use advertising. Institutional advertising promotes organizational images, ideas, and political issues. When a company promotes its position on a public issue such as taxation, institutional advertising is referred to as advocacy advertising. Product advertising promotes uses, features, and benefits of products. The two types of product advertising are pioneer advertising, which focuses on stimulating demand for a product category rather than a specific brand, and competitive advertising, which attempts to stimulate demand for a specific brand by indicating the brand's features, uses, and advantages. To make direct product comparisons, marketers use comparative advertising, in which two or more brands are compared. Two other forms of competitive advertising are reminder advertising, which tells customers that an established brand is still around, and reinforcement advertising, which assures current users they have made the right brand choice.

2. Explain the major steps in developing an advertising campaign.

Although marketers may vary in how they develop advertising campaigns, they should follow a general pattern. First, they must identify and analyze the target audience, the group of people at whom advertisements are aimed. Second, they should establish what they want the campaign to accomplish by defining advertising objectives. Objectives should be clear, precise, and presented in measurable terms. Third, marketers must create the advertising platform, which contains basic issues to be presented in the campaign. Advertising platforms should consist of issues important to consumers. Fourth, advertisers must decide how much money to spend on the campaign; they arrive at this decision through the objective-and-task approach, percent-of-sales approach, competition-matching approach, or arbitrary approach.

Advertisers then must develop a media plan by selecting and scheduling media to use in the campaign. Some of the factors affecting the media plan are location and demographic characteristics of the target audience, content of the message, and cost of the various media. The basic content and form of the advertising message are affected by product features, uses, and benefits; characteristics of the people in the target audience; the campaign's objectives and platform; and the choice of media. Advertisers use copy and artwork to create the message. The execution of an advertising campaign requires extensive planning and coordination.

Finally, advertisers must devise one or more methods for evaluating advertisement effectiveness. Evaluations performed before the campaign begins are called pretests; those conducted after the campaign are called posttests. Two types of posttests are a recognition test, in which respondents are shown the actual advertisement and asked whether they recognize it, and a recall test. In aided recall tests, respondents are shown a list of products, brands, company names, or trademarks to jog their memories. In unaided tests, no clues are given.

3. Identify who is responsible for developing advertising campaigns.

Advertising campaigns can be developed by personnel within the firm or in conjunction with advertising agencies. When a campaign is created by the firm's personnel, it may be developed by one or more individuals or by an advertising department within the firm. Use of an advertising agency may be advantageous because an agency provides highly skilled, objective specialists with broad experience in advertising at low to moderate costs to the firm.

4. Recognize the tools used in public relations.

Public relations is a broad set of communication efforts used to create and maintain favorable relationships between an organization and its stakeholders. Public relations can be used to promote people, places, ideas, activities, and countries and to create and maintain a positive company image. Public relations tools include written materials, such as brochures, newsletters, and annual reports; corporate identity materials, such as business cards and signs; speeches; event sponsorships; and special events. Publicity is communication in news-story form about an organization, its products, or both transmitted through a mass medium at no charge. Publicity-based public relations tools include news releases, feature articles, captioned photographs, and press conferences. Problems that organizations confront in using publicity-based public relations include reluctance of media personnel to print or air releases and lack of control over timing and content of messages.

5. Understand how public relations is used and evaluated.

To evaluate the effectiveness of their public relations programs, companies conduct research to determine how well their messages are reaching their audiences. Environmental monitoring, public relations audits, and counting the number of media exposures are all means of evaluating public relations effectiveness. Organizations should avoid negative public relations by taking steps to prevent negative events that result in unfavorable publicity. To diminish the impact of unfavorable public relations, organizations should institute policies and procedures for dealing with news personnel and the public when negative events occur.

Please visit the student website at **www.prideferrell.com** for ACE Self-Test questions that will help you prepare for exams.

ACE self-test

KEY CONCEPTS

advertising	target audience	cost comparison indicator	recognition test
institutional advertising	advertising platform	regional issues	unaided recall test
advocacy advertising	advertising appropriation	copy	aided recall test
product advertising	objective-and-task	storyboard	public relations
pioneer advertising	approach	artwork	publicity
competitive advertising	percent-of-sales approach	illustrations	news release
comparative advertising	competition-matching	layout	feature article
reminder advertising	approach	pretest	captioned photograph
reinforcement advertising	arbitrary approach	consumer jury	press conference
advertising campaign	media plan	posttest	

ISSUES FOR DISCUSSION AND REVIEW

1. What is the difference between institutional and product advertising?

2. What is the difference between competitive advertising and comparative advertising?

3. What are the major steps in creating an advertising campaign?

4. What is a target audience? How does a marketer analyze the target audience after identifying it?

5. Why is it necessary to define advertising objectives?

6. What is an advertising platform, and how is it used?

7. What factors affect the size of an advertising budget? What techniques are used to determine an advertising budget?

8. Describe the steps in developing a media plan.

9. What is the function of copy in an advertising message?

10. Discuss several ways to posttest the effectiveness of advertising.

11. What role does an advertising agency play in developing an advertising campaign?

12. What is public relations? Who can an organization reach through public relations?

13. How do organizations use public relations tools? Give several examples that you have observed recently.

14. Explain the problems and limitations associated with publicity-based public relations.

15. In what ways is the effectiveness of public relations evaluated?

16. What are some sources of negative public relations? How should an organization deal with unfavorable public relations?

MARKETING APPLICATIONS

1. Which of the following advertising objectives would be most useful for a company, and why?
   a. The organization will spend $1 million to move from second in market share to market leader.
   b. The organization wants to increase sales from $1.2 million to $1.5 million this year to gain the lead in market share.
   c. The advertising objective is to gain as much market share as possible within the next 12 months.
   d. The advertising objective is to increase sales by 15 percent.

2. Select a print ad and identify how it (a) identifies a specific problem, (b) recommends the product as the best solution to the problem, (c) states the product's advantages and benefits, (d) substantiates the ad's claims, and (e) asks the reader to take action.

3. Look through several recent newspapers and magazines or use an Internet search engine and identify a news release, a feature article, or a captioned photograph used to publicize a product. Describe the type of product.

4. Identify a company that recently was the target of negative public relations. Describe the situation, and discuss the company's response. What did marketers at this company do well? What, if anything, would you recommend that they change about their response?

Online Exercise

5. The LEGO company has been making toys since 1932 and has become one of the most recognized brand names in the toy industry. With the company motto "Only the best is good enough," it is no surprise that the LEGO company has developed such an exciting and interactive website. See how the company promotes the LEGO products as well as encourages consumer involvement with the brand by visiting **www.lego.com.**

a. Which type of advertising is LEGO using on its website?
b. What target audience is the LEGO company intending to reach?
c. Identify the advertising objectives that the LEGO company is attempting to achieve through this website.

globalEDGE™

An essential component of advertising and public relations in marketing is a firm's ability to impart information to the most advanced consumers in a fast and efficient manner. To better focus your firm's communications worldwide in technologically savvy regions, you have been asked to survey the state of mobile technology by examining a report found on the GSM World website. The report required for answering this question can be found by using either the search term "mobile" or "GSM" at **http://globaledge.msu.edu/ibrd** (and check the box "Resource Desk only"). Once you reach the GSM World website, go to the "MediaCenter" option at the top far right and click on GSM statistics. Find the most recent quarterly report. Given the most recent data at the time of publication, the three regions with the most GSM usage are Asia-Pacific, Europe: Western, and Europe: Eastern. By following the "GSM Family" option at the top and then clicking on the GSM link, the definition for GSM is found ("global system for mobile communications").

Video CASE

Vail Resorts Uses Public Relations to Put Out a Fire

Vail Resorts, Inc., is one of the leading resort operators in North America. The company operates four ski resorts in Colorado, including Vail, Keystone, Beaver Creek, and Breckenridge, as well as one in Lake Tahoe. Vail Mountain has become the most popular ski destination in the United States, with 1.6 million skier visits in the 2005–2006 season. *SKI* magazine has ranked Vail as one of the best ski resorts in North America since 1988.

Despite its success, the company experienced a very challenging year in 1998. In October of that year, just two weeks before the beginning of the ski season, the Vail Mountain resort suffered the largest "ecoterrorist" event in U.S. history. Several structures, including Patrol Headquarters, the Two Elk restaurant, and Camp One, were burned to the ground, and four chair lift operator buildings were damaged. Total damages exceeded $12 million. The deliberately and strategically set fires disabled three central lifts and the biggest restaurant and guest service center on the mountain.

Shortly after the fires, the Earth Liberation Front (ELF), a radical environmental organization, claimed responsibility. In an e-mail, ELF, which splintered off the better-known Earth First! organization, claimed to have set the fires to protest a planned expansion of the resort, which, the group argued, would threaten habitat needed to reintroduce the Canada lynx, an endangered wild cat. In the e-mail, ELF said, "Putting profits ahead of Colorado's wildlife will not be tolerated." ELF's communiqué also warned skiers to stay away from the resort "for your safety and convenience." However, Earth First! and many other environmental groups, which had protested Vail's controversial plans to expand into lynx habitat, were quick to condemn ELF's firebombing at Vail. More than eight years later, Stanislas Meyerhoff and Chelsea Gerlach were arrested for and pleaded guilty to committing multiple ecoterrorism attacks including the incident at Vail.

As with most disasters, the mass media quickly swarmed the scene at Vail Mountain, and the resulting stories published around the country were not always beneficial to Vail Mountain and nearby Vail, Colorado—or accurate. Some newspapers reported that all ski lifts had been destroyed and that the resort would be unable to open for the season. A few reported that the nearby town of Vail was on fire, including hotels.

Vail Resorts responded to the misinformation by launching a direct-mail campaign to communicate with everyone who had made reservations for ski vacations through Vail Central Reservations, as well as to travel agents and individual hotels in town. The company reassured skiers that the resort would indeed open and would be a safe place for their families to vacation. Vail Resorts managed to salvage the season and make it successful, despite the havoc wreaked by the fires.

Vail Resorts, like many firms, had a generic crisis plan in place at the time of the incident. However, some analysts contend that the degree to which the company followed that plan was questionable. In hindsight, Vail management has stated that things might have gone more smoothly in the first 48 hours after the crisis if they had adhered more closely to that plan. For example, managers now recognize that they did not use their staff as effectively as possible. Instead of clearly defining responsibilities up front, staff members were called up somewhat randomly, adding to the confusion surrounding the event. The plan also failed to address communication with employees. Resort management quickly decided that keeping employees fully informed was a top priority because they were the best ambassadors to the public.

Crisis management has been defined as preparation for low-probability or unexpected events that could threaten an organization's viability, reputation, or profitability. It has been viewed traditionally as "damage control," with little preplanning taking place. However, with the changing global political climate, events such as terrorist attacks and workplace violence have become more common, increasing the need for crisis management and disaster-recovery planning for businesses. Even small companies are beginning to recognize the need to plan for the unexpected.

Crisis management and disaster recovery are critical for most organizations that deal with large numbers of customers, especially in the recreation and entertainment industries. The negative publicity resulting from a crisis can be potentially more devastating than a natural disaster such as an earthquake or a technologic disruption such as a major power failure. The disruption of routine operations and paralysis of employees and customers in the face of crisis can reduce productivity, destroy long-established reputations, and erode public confidence in a company. Crisis planning can arm a company with tools and procedures to manage a crisis, protect the company's image, and reduce unfavorable publicity. By being forthright with the press and the public and taking prompt action, companies may be able to convince the public of their honest attempts to resolve the situation, and news media may be more willing to help explain complex issues to the public. Effectively dealing with a negative event allows an organization to reduce the unfavorable impact on its image.

In the case of Vail Resorts, managers believe that they could have followed their previously established crisis management plan more closely. During the two days immediately following the fires, management was disorganized, and employees and Vail residents were confused about the future of the resort. Ultimately, Vail chose to be honest and open with the media and its employees, which helped the resort weather the crisis with its image intact. The company's direct-mail campaign to vacationers also helped preserve public trust in the company.

To prepare for unexpected events, all firms should develop a crisis management program, which includes four basic steps: conducting a crisis audit, making contingency plans, assigning a crisis management team, and practicing the plan. Conducting a crisis audit involves assessing the potential impacts of different events, such as the death of an executive or a natural disaster. *Contingency planning* refers to the development of backup plans for emergencies that specify actions to be taken and their expected consequences. Crisis management teams also should be designated so that key areas are covered in case of emergency, such as media relations and legal affairs. Finally, companies should practice the crisis management plan and update it as necessary on a regular basis so that all employees are familiar with the plan.[30]

Questions for Discussion

1. What tools did Vail Resorts use to respond to the crisis?
2. Evaluate Vail Resorts' response to the crisis. What did the firm do right? What else could it have done to relieve public concerns about the safety of the resort as well as its controversial expansion?
3. How can creating a crisis management and disaster-recovery plan help a company to protect its reputation, customer relationships, and profits?

Personal Selling and Sales Promotion

Best Buy Reshapes the World of Selling

Best Buy Company, Inc., is a specialty retailer of consumer electronics, home-office products, entertainment software, appliances, and related services. The innovative company has more than 930 retail stores across the United States and in Canada, and its operations include not only Best Buy (including Best-Buy.com and BestBuyCanada.ca) but also Future Shop (FutureShop.ca), Geek-Squad (GeekSquad.com), and Magnolia Audio Video (Magnoliaav.com), as well as an outlet store on eBay. Best Buy operates in a highly competitive environment in which it must compete not only against other electronics retailers, specialty home-office retailers, mass merchants, home-improvement super-stores, and a growing number of direct-to-consumer alternatives but also independent dealers, regional chain discount stores, wholesale clubs, video rental stores, and other specialty retail stores. There is also an increasing pressure from online sites that offer entertainment as downloads, as well as pay-per-view cable companies.

To improve the efforts of its sales staff, Best Buy has been collecting data since 1996 on nearly every transaction made, rain check issued, and call-center problem resolved for 75 million customers. The company developed a database to incorporate information from 19 customer touch points, including point of sale, and enhanced it with Experians's INSOURCE consumer marketing data to obtain a complete view of its customers. It gained further insight by using purchase histories to build a more complete picture of its customers' current and future needs through segmentation analysis. This permitted executives to develop and identify new customer segments, better understand existing customers, target promotions more precisely, and identify key areas for expansion. Best Buy also retained Larry Selden, a Columbia University professor, as a consultant. Selden argues that profits generated by what he calls "angel" customers can be wiped out by losses produced by "devil" customers. After analyzing its database, Best Buy indeed found that 20 percent of the company's customers generate a significant portion of the revenue and profits.

Through consultation data analysis, Best Buy was able to identify five angel customer segments as well as devil customers. The angel segments were defined as customers who bought high-definition TVs, portable electronics, and newly released DVDs without waiting for markdowns or rebates, whereas the devils bought products, applied for their rebates, then returned the products,

OBJECTIVES

1. Define personal selling and understand its purpose.

2. Describe the basic steps in the personal selling process.

3. Identify the types of sales force personnel.

4. Understand sales management decisions and activities.

5. Explain what sales promotion activities are and how they are used.

6. Recognize specific consumer and trade sales promotion methods.

and bought them back again at returned-merchandise discounts. Best Buy used this information to focus on angel customers (and discourage devils) by converting stores to a "customer-centric" model. Each Best Buy store analyzes its local market to identify which angel segments can be found there and then targets those customers both in store and with specific promotions.[1] ∎

For many organizations, programs that motivate employees, especially sales staff, to find creative ways to maintain long-term, satisfying customer relationships contribute to the company's success. As we saw in Chapter 16, personal selling and sales promotion are two possible elements in a promotion mix. Sales promotion is sometimes a company's sole promotional tool, although it is generally used in conjunction with other promotion-mix elements. It is playing an increasingly important role in marketing strategies. Personal selling is becoming more professional and sophisticated, with sales personnel acting more as consultants and advisers.

In this chapter we focus on personal selling and sales promotion. We first consider the purposes of personal selling and then its basic steps. Next, we look at types of salespeople and how they are selected. We then discuss major sales force management decisions, including setting objectives for the sales force and determining its size; recruiting, selecting, training, compensating, and motivating salespeople; managing sales territories; and controlling and evaluating sales force performance. Then we examine several characteristics of sales promotion, reasons for using sales promotion, and sales promotion methods available for use in a promotion mix.

What Is Personal Selling?

Personal selling is paid personal communication that attempts to inform customers and persuade them to purchase products in an exchange situation. For example, a salesperson describing the benefits of a Toyota Scion to a customer at a dealership is engaging in personal selling. Personal selling goals vary from one firm to another. However, they usually involve finding prospects, persuading prospects to buy, and keeping customers satisfied. Although the public may harbor negative perceptions of personal selling, unfavorable stereotypes of salespeople are changing thanks to the efforts of major corporations, professional sales associations, and academic institutions. Research indicates that personal selling will continue to gain respect as professional sales associations develop and enforce ethical codes of conduct.[2]

Personal selling gives marketers the greatest freedom to adjust a message so that it will satisfy customers' information needs. Compared with other promotion methods, personal selling is the most precise, enabling marketers to focus on the most promising sales prospects. Other promotion-mix elements are aimed at groups of people, some of whom may not be prospective customers. However, personal selling is generally the most expensive element in the promotion mix. The average cost of a business sales call is more than $400.[3]

Salespeople must be aware of their competitors. They must monitor the development of new products and know about competitors' sales efforts in their sales territories, how often and when the competition calls on their accounts, and what the competition is saying about their product in relation to its own. Salespeople must emphasize the benefits that their products provide, especially when competitors' products do not offer those specific benefits.

Few businesses survive solely on profits from one-time customers. For long-run survival, most marketers depend on repeat sales and therefore strive to keep their customers satisfied. Satisfied customers provide favorable word-of-mouth communications, attracting new customers. Even though the whole organization is responsible for achieving customer satisfaction, much of the burden falls on salespeople because they are almost always closer to customers than anyone else in the company and often provide buyers with information and service after the sale. Such contact gives salespeople an opportunity to generate additional sales and offers them a good vantage point for

personal selling Paid personal communication that informs customers and persuades them to buy products

The Ultimate Energy Salesperson

They say that you can sell anything if you put your mind to it, and Jim Headlee, the founder of Summit Energy Services, Inc., likely would agree. After being fired owing to an ethical disagreement, the former national sales manager for a natural gas marketing firm decided to start his own company. He initially set up Summit Energy Services to help corporations obtain better prices for natural gas. In time, the company expanded its services to include helping with electricity pricing as well. Headlee's first clients were small firms that could pay him only about $500 per month. Today, Summit brings in around $30 million in annual revenue from about 130 corporate clients, many of which appear on the *Fortune* 1000 list. The company's success certainly has been earned.

How did Jim Headlee manage to turn a firing into a multimillion-dollar enterprise? With his experience as a sales manager and an idea to help companies save money, Headlee began to sell clients both on himself as a person and on his knowledge of the natural gas and electricity markets. As for selling himself, Headlee promises a high level of integrity and ethics. He always tells clients that they can trust him to follow through on what he says he will do. He believes strongly that his clients must trust him, and he does everything in his power to earn and maintain that trust. Headlee also hires employees based on their character and integrity. Once establishing they have these important traits, he is then willing to teach them about the energy business. As for Headlee's knowledge, he promises clients unbiased advice. Because he does not sell energy for companies, like Enron did, he does not have a vested interest in any one supplier. Indeed, Headlee and his team actually have taken on a number of Enron's former clients. Those at Summit certainly seem to know their stuff—Headlee estimates that his company saved clients well over $1 billion in 2006. Since its inception, Summit has grown to 175 employees and now offers additional services such as hedging strategies, auditing bills for errors, and reviewing plant operations with an eye toward cost savings. Headlee says that one of the reasons for his company's continued success is that many of its competitors do not offer so many services under one roof. With happy customers such as General Motors, Lockheed Martin, and Pfizer, it looks like Jim Headlee's sales pitch of ethics and unbiased knowledge has paid off in a big way.[a]

evaluating the strengths and weaknesses of the company's products and other marketing-mix components. Their observations help to develop and maintain a marketing mix that better satisfies both customers and the firm. Thus marketing managers want salespeople to know as much as possible about the firm's marketing strategy and the customers' perceived value in the products they sell.[4]

The Personal Selling Process

The specific activities involved in the selling process vary among salespeople, selling situations, and cultures. No two salespeople use exactly the same selling methods. Nonetheless, many salespeople move through a general selling process as they sell products. This process consists of seven steps, outlined in Figure 18.1: prospecting, preapproach, approach, making the presentation, overcoming objections, closing the sale, and following up.

Prospecting for Customers. Developing a list of potential customers is called **prospecting**. Salespeople seek names of prospects from company sales records, trade shows, commercial databases, newspaper announcements (of marriages, births, deaths, and so on), public records, telephone directories, trade association directories,

prospecting Developing a list of potential customers

Identifying Prospects

Salesgenie.com helps companies connect with the right potential business customers.

and many other sources. Sales personnel also use responses to traditional and online advertisements that encourage interested persons to send in information request forms. Seminars and meetings targeted at particular types of clients, such as attorneys or accountants, also may produce leads.

Most salespeople prefer to use referrals—recommendations from current customers—to find prospects. Obtaining referrals requires that the salesperson have a good relationship with the current customer and so must have performed well before asking the customer for help. Research shows that one referral is as valuable as 12 cold calls. Also, 80 percent of clients are willing to give referrals, but only 20 percent are ever asked. Sales experts indicate that the advantages of using referrals are that the resulting sales leads are highly qualified, the sales rates are higher, initial transactions are larger, and the sales cycle is shorter.[5]

Consistent activity is critical to successful prospecting. Salespeople must actively search the customer base for qualified prospects who fit the target-market profile. After developing the prospect list, a salesperson evaluates whether each prospect is able, willing, and authorized to buy the product. Based on this evaluation, prospects are ranked according to desirability or potential.

Evaluating Prospects.   Before contacting acceptable prospects, a salesperson finds and analyzes information about each prospect's specific product needs, current use of brands, feelings about available brands, and personal characteristics. In short, salespeople need to know what potential buyers and decision makers consider most important and why they need a specific product.[6] The most successful salespeople are thorough in their evaluations of prospects. This *preapproach* step involves identifying key decision makers, reviewing account histories and problems, contacting other clients for information, assessing credit histories, preparing sales presentations, and identifying product needs. Marketers are increasingly using information technology and customer relationship management (CRM) systems to comb through their databases and identify their most profitable products and customers. CRM systems also can help sales departments manage leads, track customers, forecast sales, and assess performance. A salesperson with a lot of information about a prospect is better equipped to develop a presentation that communicates precisely with the prospect.

Approaching the Customer.   The **approach**, the manner in which a salesperson contacts a potential customer, is a critical step in the sales process. In more than 80 percent of initial sales calls, the purpose is to gather information about the buyer's needs and objectives. Creating a favorable impression and building rapport with prospective clients are important tasks in the approach. During the initial contact, the salesperson strives to develop a relationship rather than just push a product. The salesperson may have to call on a prospect several times before the product is considered. The approach must be designed to deliver value to targeted customers. If the sales approach is inappropriate, the salesperson's efforts are likely to have poor results.

As mentioned earlier, one type of approach is based on referrals: The salesperson approaches the prospect and explains that an acquaintance, associate, or relative suggested the call. Another type of approach is the "cold canvass," in which a salesperson calls on potential customers without prior consent. The exact type of approach depends on the salesperson's preferences, the product being sold, the firm's resources, and the prospect's characteristics.

approach The manner in which a salesperson contacts a potential customer

Making the Presentation.   During the sales presentation, the salesperson must attract and hold the prospect's attention, stimulate interest, and spark a desire for the product. Research indicates that salespersons who carefully monitor the selling situation and adapt their presentations to meet the needs of prospects are associated with effective sales performance.[7] Salespeople should match their influencing tactics—such as information exchange, recommendations, threats, promises, ingratiation, and inspirational appeals—to their prospects. Different types of buyers respond to different tactics, but most prospects respond well to information exchange and recommendations, and virtually no prospects respond to threats.[8] The salesperson should have the prospect touch, hold, or use the product. If possible, the salesperson should demonstrate the product. Audiovisual equipment and software also may enhance the presentation.

During the presentation, the salesperson not only must talk but also listen. Nonverbal modes of communication are especially beneficial in building trust during the presentation.[9] The sales presentation gives the salesperson the greatest opportunity to determine the prospect's specific needs by listening to questions and comments and observing responses. Even though the salesperson plans the presentation in advance, he or she must be able to adjust the message to meet the prospect's informational needs.

Overcoming Objections.   An effective salesperson usually seeks out a prospect's objections so that he or she can address them. If they are not apparent, the salesperson cannot deal with them, and the prospect may not buy. One of the best ways to overcome objections is to anticipate and counter them before the prospect raises them. However, this approach can be risky because the salesperson may mention objections that the prospect would not have raised. If possible, the salesperson should handle objections as they arise. They also can be addressed at the end of the presentation.

Closing the Sale.   **Closing** is the stage of the selling process when the salesperson asks the prospect to buy the product. During the presentation, the salesperson may use a "trial close" by asking questions that assume that the prospect will buy the product. The salesperson might ask the potential customer about financial terms, desired colors or sizes, or delivery arrangements. One questioning approach uses broad questions (*what, how,* and *why*) to probe or gather information and focused questions (*who, when,* and *where*) to clarify and close the sale. Reactions to such questions usually indicate how close the prospect is to buying. A trial close allows

figure 18.1

GENERAL STEPS IN THE PERSONAL SELLING PROCESS

1 Prospecting

2 Preapproach

3 Approach

4 Making the presentation

5 Overcoming objections

6 Closing the sale

7 Following up

Enhancing the Sales Presentation

Many sales teams are using WebEx technology for online sales presentations.

closing The stage in the selling process when the salesperson asks the prospect to buy the product

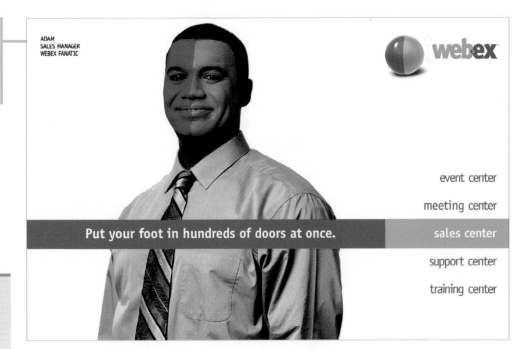

ADAM
SALES MANAGER
WEBEX FANATIC

webex

Put your foot in hundreds of doors at once.

event center

meeting center

sales center

support center

training center

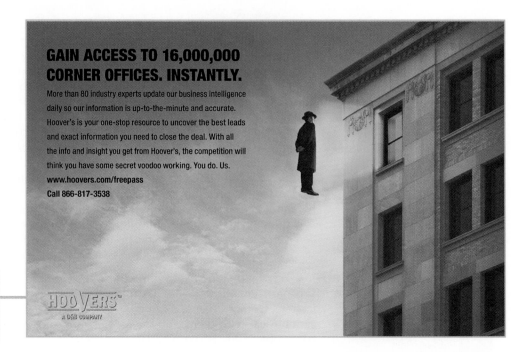

GAIN ACCESS TO 16,000,000 CORNER OFFICES. INSTANTLY.

More than 80 industry experts update our business intelligence daily so our information is up-to-the-minute and accurate. Hoover's is your one-stop resource to uncover the best leads and exact information you need to close the deal. With all the info and insight you get from Hoover's, the competition will think you have some secret voodoo working. You do. Us.

www.hoovers.com/freepass

Call 866-817-3538

HOOVERS™
A D&B COMPANY

Closing the Sale

Hoover's Online provides detailed information that can help close sales.

prospects to indicate indirectly that they will buy the product without having to say those sometimes difficult words, "I'll take it."

A salesperson should try to close at several points during the presentation because the prospect may be ready to buy. One closing strategy involves asking the potential customer to place a low-risk tryout order. An attempt to close the sale may result in objections. Thus, closing can uncover hidden objections, which the salesperson then can address.

Following Up.   After a successful closing, the salesperson must follow up the sale. In the follow-up stage, the salesperson determines whether the order was delivered on time and installed properly, if installation was required. He or she should contact the customer to learn if any problems or questions regarding the product have arisen. The follow-up stage is also used to determine customers' future product needs.

Types of Salespeople

To develop a sales force, a marketing manager decides what kind of salesperson will sell the firm's products most effectively. Most organizations use several different kinds of sales personnel. Based on the functions performed, salespeople can be classified into three groups: order getters, order takers, and support personnel. One salesperson can, and often does, perform all three functions.

Order Getters.   To obtain orders, a salesperson informs prospects and persuades them to buy the product. The role of the **order getter** is to increase sales by selling to new customers and increasing sales to current customers. This task sometimes is called *creative selling*. It requires that salespeople recognize potential buyers' needs and give them necessary information. Order getting is sometimes divided into two categories: current-customer sales and new-business sales.

Order Takers.   Salespeople take orders to perpetuate long-lasting, satisfying customer relationships. **Order takers** seek repeat sales. They generate the bulk of many organizations' total sales. One major objective is to be certain customers that have sufficient product quantities where and when needed. Most order takers handle orders for standardized products purchased routinely and not requiring extensive sales efforts. The role of order takers is evolving, however. In the future they probably will

order getter The salesperson who sells to new customers and increases sales to current ones

order takers Salespersons who primarily seek repeat sales

serve more as identifiers and problem solvers to meet the needs of their customers. There are two groups of order takers: inside order takers and field order takers.

In many businesses, *inside order takers,* who work in sales offices, receive orders by mail, telephone, and the Internet. Certain producers, wholesalers, and retailers have sales personnel who sell from within the firm rather than in the field. This does not mean that inside order takers never communicate with customers face to face. For example, retail salespeople are classified as inside order takers. As more orders are placed through the Internet, the role of the inside order taker will continue to change.

Salespeople who travel to customers are *outside,* or *field, order takers.* Often customers and field order takers develop interdependent relationships. The buyer relies on the salesperson to take orders periodically (and sometimes to deliver them), and the salesperson counts on the buyer to purchase a certain quantity of products periodically. Use of notebook and handheld computers has improved the field order taker's inventory and order-tracking capabilities.

Support Personnel.   **Support personnel** facilitate selling but usually are not involved solely with making sales. They are engaged primarily in marketing industrial products, locating prospects, educating customers, building goodwill, and providing service after the sale. There are many kinds of sales support personnel; the three most common are missionary, trade, and technical salespeople.

Missionary salespeople, usually employed by manufacturers, assist the producer's customers in selling to their own customers. Missionary salespeople may call on retailers to inform and persuade them to buy the manufacturer's products. When they succeed, retailers purchase products from wholesalers, who are the producer's customers. Manufacturers of medical supplies and pharmaceuticals often use missionary salespeople, called *detail reps,* to promote their products to physicians, hospitals, and retail druggists.

Trade salespeople are not strictly support personnel because they usually take orders as well. However, they direct much effort toward helping customers, especially retail stores, promote the product. They are likely to restock shelves, obtain more shelf space, set up displays, provide in-store demonstrations, and distribute samples to store customers. Food producers and processors commonly employ trade salespeople.

Technical salespeople give technical assistance to the organization's current customers, advising them on product characteristics and applications, system designs, and installation procedures. Because this job is often highly technical, the salesperson usually has formal training in one of the physical sciences or in engineering. Technical sales personnel often sell technical industrial products, such as computers, heavy equipment, and steel.

When hiring sales personnel, marketers seldom restrict themselves to a single category because most firms require different types of salespeople. Several factors dictate how many of each type a particular company should have. Product use, characteristics, complexity, and price influence the kind of sales personnel used, as do the number and characteristics of customers. The types of marketing channels and the intensity and type of advertising also affect the composition of a sales force.

Types of Selling

Personal selling has become an increasingly complex process owing in large part to rapid technological innovation. Most important, the focus of personal selling is shifting from selling a specific product to building long-term relationships with customers by finding solutions to their needs, problems, and challenges. As a result, the roles of salespeople are changing. Among the new philosophies for personal selling are team selling and relationship selling.

Many products, particularly expensive high-tech business products, have become so complex that a single salesperson can no longer be expert in every aspect of the product and purchase process. **Team selling**, which involves the salesperson joining with people from the firm's financial, engineering, and other functional areas, is

support personnel Sales staff members who facilitate selling but usually are not involved solely with making sales

missionary salespeople Support salespersons who assist the producer's customers in selling to their own customers

trade salespeople Salespersons involved mainly in helping a producer's customers promote a product

technical salespeople Support salespersons who give technical assistance to a firm's current customers

team selling The use of a team of experts from all functional areas of a firm, led by a salesperson, to conduct the personal selling process appropriate for such products. The salesperson takes the lead in the personal selling process, but other members of the team bring their unique skills, knowledge, and resources to the process to help customers find solutions to their own business challenges. Selling teams may be created to address a particular short-term situation, or they may be formal, ongoing teams. Team selling is advantageous in situations calling for detailed knowledge of new, complex, and dynamic technologies such as jet aircraft and medical equipment. It can be difficult, however, for highly competitive salespersons to adapt to a team-selling environment.

Relationship selling, also known as *consultative* or *solution selling,* involves building mutually beneficial long-term associations with a customer through regular communications over prolonged periods of time. Like team selling, it is used especially in business-to-business (B2B) marketing. Relationship selling involves finding solutions to customers' needs by listening to them, gaining a detailed understanding of their organization, understanding and caring about their needs and challenges, and providing support after the sale. Relationship selling efforts can be enhanced through sales automation technology tools that enhance interactive communication.[10] At Computer Discount Warehouse (CDW), relationship selling is based on helping customers succeed. Before hurricanes struck Florida, for example, some CDW account managers contacted clients in the paths of the storms and suggested computer backup storage and battery solutions that could help their businesses weather the storms with greater confidence.[11]

Managing the Sales Force

The sales force is directly responsible for generating one of an organization's primary inputs—sales revenue. Without adequate sales revenue, businesses cannot survive. In addition, a firm's reputation is often determined by the ethical conduct of its sales force. The morale and ultimately the success of a firm's sales force depend in large part on adequate compensation, room for advancement, adequate training, and management support—all key areas of sales management. Salespeople who are not satisfied with these elements may leave. Evaluating the input of salespeople is an important part of sales force management because of its strong bearing on a firm's success.

We explore eight general areas of sales management: establishing sales force objectives, determining sales force size, recruiting and selecting salespeople, training sales personnel, compensating salespeople, motivating salespeople, managing sales territories, and controlling and evaluating sales force performance.

Establishing Sales Force Objectives. To manage a sales force effectively, sales managers must develop sales objectives. Sales objectives tell salespeople what they are expected to accomplish during a specified time period. They give the sales force direction and purpose and serve as standards for evaluating and controlling the performance of sales personnel. Research indicates that a focus on sales performance increases efforts to achieve sales objectives.[12] Sales objectives should be stated in precise, measurable terms and should specify the time period and geographic areas involved.

Sales objectives usually are developed for both the total sales force and each salesperson. Objectives for the entire force normally are stated in terms of sales volume, market share, or profit. Volume objectives refer to dollar or unit sales. For example, the objective for an electric drill producer's sales force might be to sell $18 million worth of drills, or 600,000 drills, annually. When sales goals are stated in terms of market share, they usually call for an increase in the proportion of the firm's sales relative to the total number of products sold by all businesses in that industry. When sales objectives are based on profit, they generally are stated in terms of dollar amounts or return on investment.

Sales objectives, or quotas, for individual salespeople commonly are stated in terms of dollar or unit sales volume. Other bases used for individual sales objectives include average order size, average number of calls per time period, and ratio of orders to calls.

relationship selling The building of mutually beneficial long-term associations with a customer through regular communications over prolonged periods of time

Where do you want to be?

Find your perfect place. It's easy with RE/MAX.

Whether you're dreaming of a second home in a faraway land – or your very first house right around the corner – just tell RE/MAX what you want.

RE/MAX agents average more experience than other agents. They know their markets and they care enough to get to know you, too.

Equal opportunity employers.   051792
©2006 RE/MAX International, Inc. All rights reserved.
Each RE/MAX® real estate office is independently owned and operated.

Nobody sells more real estate than RE/MAX. So wherever you are or want to be, we'll be there for you.

RE/MAX

Outstanding Agents. Outstanding Results.®
remax.com®

Recruiting a Sales Force

Many organizations, like RE/MAX, recruits salespeople through advertising.

Determining Sales Force Size.   Sales force size is important because it influences the company's ability to generate sales and profits. The size of the sales force affects the compensation methods used, salespeople's morale, and overall sales force management. Sales force size must be adjusted periodically because a firm's marketing plans change along with markets and forces in the marketing environment. One danger in cutting back the size of the sales force to increase profits is that the sales organization may lose strength, preventing it from rebounding when growth occurs or better market conditions prevail.

Several analytical methods can help to determine optimal sales force size. One method involves determining how many sales calls per year are necessary for the organization to serve customers effectively and then dividing this total by the average number of sales calls a salesperson makes annually. A second method is based on marginal analysis, whereby additional salespeople are added to the sales force until the cost of an additional salesperson equals the additional sales generated by that person. Although marketing managers may use one or several analytical methods, they normally temper decisions with subjective judgments.

Recruiting and Selecting Salespeople.   To create and maintain an effective sales force, sales managers must recruit the right type of salespeople. Effective recruiting efforts are a vital part of implementing the strategic sales force plan and can help to ensure successful organizational performance.[13] In recruiting, the sales manager develops a list of qualified applicants for sales positions. To ensure that the recruiting process results in a pool of qualified salespeople from which to hire, a sales manager establishes a set of qualifications before beginning to recruit. Two activities help to establish this set of required attributes. First, the sales manager should prepare a job description listing specific tasks salespeople are to perform. Second, the manager should analyze characteristics of the firm's successful salespeople, as well as those of ineffective sales personnel. From the job description and analysis of traits, the sales manager should be able to develop a set of specific requirements and be aware of potential weaknesses that could lead to failure.

A sales manager generally recruits applicants from several sources: departments within the firm, other firms, employment agencies, educational institutions, respondents to advertisements, and individuals recommended by current employees. The specific sources depend on the type of salesperson required and the manager's experiences with particular sources.

The process of recruiting and selecting salespeople varies considerably from one company to another. Companies intent on reducing sales force turnover are likely to have strict recruiting and selection procedures. Some organizations use the specialized services of other companies to hire sales personnel. Recruitment should not be sporadic. It should be a continuous activity aimed at reaching the best applicants. The selection process should systematically and effectively match applicants' characteristics and needs with the requirements of specific selling tasks. Finally, the selection process should ensure that new sales personnel are available where and when needed.

Training Sales Personnel.   Many organizations have formal training programs; others depend on informal, on-the-job training. Some systematic training programs are quite extensive, whereas others are rather short and rudimentary. Whether the training program is complex or simple, developers must consider what to teach, whom to train, and how to train them.

A sales training program can concentrate on the company, its products, or selling methods. Training programs often cover all three. Such programs can be aimed at newly hired salespeople, experienced salespeople, or both. Training for experienced company salespeople usually emphasizes product information, although salespeople also must be informed about new selling techniques and changes in company plans, policies, and procedures. Honda, for example, designed a sales training program that involved going to 21 cities to train 7,500 sales associates about the automaker's new entry-level auto, the Fit. The training program introduced sales reps not only to the features and benefits of the new car but also to the car's target market: young buyers who are comfortable finding their own car information online.[14] Ordinarily, new sales personnel require comprehensive training, whereas experienced personnel need both refresher courses on established products and training regarding new-product information.

Sales training may be done in the field, at educational institutions, in company facilities, and/or online using Web-based technology. For many companies, training online saves time and money and helps salespeople learn about new products quickly. Some firms train new employees before assigning them to a specific sales position. Others put them in the field immediately, providing formal training only after they have gained some experience. Training programs for new personnel can be as short as several days or as long as three years; some are even longer. Because experienced salespeople usually need periodic retraining, a firm's sales management must determine the frequency, sequencing, and duration of these efforts.

Materials for sales training programs range from videos, texts, online materials, manuals, and cases to programmed learning devices and audio- and videocassettes. Lectures, demonstrations, simulation exercises, and on-the-job training all can be effective teaching methods. Self-directed learning to supplement traditional sales training has the potential to improve sales performance.[15] Choice of methods and materials for a particular sales training program depends on type and number of trainees, program content and complexity, length and location, size of the training budget, number of teachers, and teacher preferences.

Compensating Salespeople.   To develop and maintain a highly productive sales force, a business must formulate and administer a compensation plan that attracts, motivates, and retains the most effective individuals. The plan should give sales management the desired level of control and provide sales personnel with acceptable levels of income, freedom, and incentive. It should be flexible, equitable, easy to administer, and easy to understand. Good compensation programs facilitate and encourage proper treatment of customers. Obviously, it is quite difficult to incorporate all these requirements into a single program.

Developers of compensation programs must determine the general level of compensation required and the most desirable method of calculating it. In analyzing the required compensation level, sales management must ascertain a salesperson's value to the company on the basis of the tasks and responsibilities associated with the sales position. Sales managers may consider a number of factors, including salaries of other types of personnel in the firm, competitors' compensation plans, costs of sales force turnover, and nonsalary selling expenses. The average low-level salesperson earns about $65,000 annually (including commissions and bonuses), whereas a high-level, high-performing salesperson can make as much as $157,000 a year (Figure 18.2).[16]

Sales compensation programs usually reimburse salespeople for selling expenses, provide some fringe benefits, and deliver the required compensation level. To achieve this, a firm may use one or more of three basic compensation methods: straight salary, straight commission, or a combination of salary and commission. Table 18.1 (on page 468) lists the pros and cons of each. In a **straight salary compensation plan,** salespeople are paid a specified amount per time period, regardless of selling effort. This sum remains the same until they receive a pay increase or decrease. Although this method is easy to administer and affords salespeople financial security, it provides little

straight salary compensation plan Paying salespeople a specific amount per time period, regardless of selling effort

straight commission compensation plan Paying salespeople according to the amount of their sales in a given time period

combination compensation plan Paying salespeople a fixed salary plus a commission based on sales volume

Sales Training

Companies like Richardson offer specialized programs to assist the training process either at a physical location or online.

incentive for them to boost selling efforts. In a **straight commission compensation plan,** salespeople's compensation is determined solely by sales for a given period. A commission may be based on a single percentage of sales or on a sliding scale involving several sales levels and percentage rates. While this method motivates salespersonnel to escalate their selling efforts, it offers them little financial security, and it can be difficult for sales managers to maintain control over the sales force. For these reasons, many firms offer a **combination compensation plan** in which salespeople receive a fixed salary plus a commission based on sales volume. Some combination programs require that a salesperson exceed a certain sales level before earning a commission; others offer commissions for any level of sales. Research indicates that higher commissions are the most preferred reward followed by pay increases.[17] The Container Store, which markets do-it-yourself organizing and storage products, prefers to pay its sales staff salaries that are 50 to 100 percent higher than that offered by rivals instead of paying salespeople according to commission plans.[18]

Motivating Salespeople. Although financial compensation is an important incentive, additional programs are necessary for motivating sales personnel. A sales manager should develop a systematic approach for motivating salespeople to be productive. Effective sales force motivation is achieved through an organized set of activities performed continuously by the company's sales management.

Sales personnel, like other people, join organizations to satisfy personal needs and achieve personal goals. Sales managers must identify these needs and goals and strive to create an organizational climate that allows each salesperson to fulfill

figure 18.2

AVERAGE SALARIES FOR SALES REPRESENTATIVES AND EXECUTIVES

Source: From Christine Galea, "Average Salary for Sales Staffers in 2005," *Sales and Marketing Management,* May 2006, p. 30. © 2004 VNU Business Media, Inc. Reprinted with permission from Sales and Marketing Management.

TABLE 18.1   CHARACTERISTICS OF SALES FORCE COMPENSATION METHODS

Compensation Method	Frequency of Use (%)*	When Especially Useful	Advantages	Disadvantages
Straight salary	17.5	Compensating new salespersons; firm moves into new sales territories that require developmental work; sales requiring lengthy presale and postsale services.	Gives salesperson security; gives sales manager control over salespersons; easy to administer; yields more predictable selling expenses.	Provides no incentive; necessitates closer supervision of salespersons; during sales declines, selling expenses remain constant.
Straight commission	14.0	Highly aggressive selling is required; nonselling tasks are minimized; company uses contractors and part-timers.	Provides maximum amount of incentive; by increasing commission rate, sales managers can encourage salespersons to sell certain items; selling expenses relate directly to sales resources.	Salespersons have little financial security; sales manager has minimum control over sales force; may cause salespeople to give inadequate service to smaller accounts; selling costs less predictable.
Combination	68.5	Sales territories have relatively similar sales potential; firm wishes to provide incentive but still control sales force activities.	Provides certain level of financial security; provides some incentive; can move sales force efforts in profitable direction.	Selling expenses less predictable; may be difficult to administer.

*The figures are computed from Dartnell's 30th Sales Force Compensation Survey, Dartnell Corporation, Chicago, 1999.
Source: Charles Futrell, *Sales Management* (Ft. Worth: Dryden Press, 2001), pp. 307–316.

them. Enjoyable working conditions, power and authority, job security, and opportunity to excel are effective motivators, as are company efforts to make sales jobs more productive and efficient. At the Container Store, for example, sales personnel receive hundreds of hours of training every year about the company's products so that they can help customers solve their organization and storage problems.[19] Research has shown that a strong corporate culture leads to higher levels of job satisfaction and organizational commitment and lower levels of job stress.[20] A positive ethical climate, one component of corporate culture, has been associated with decreased role stress and turnover intention and improved job attitudes and job performance in sales.[21] Sales contests and other incentive programs can be effective motivators. Sales contests can motivate salespeople to increase sales or add new accounts, promote special items, achieve greater volume per sales call, and cover territories more thoroughly. However, companies need to understand salespersons' preferences when designing contests in order to make them effective in increasing sales.[22] Some companies find such contests powerful tools for motivating sales personnel to achieve company goals.

Properly designed incentive programs pay for themselves many times over, and sales managers are relying on incentives more than ever. Recognition programs that acknowledge outstanding performance with symbolic awards, such as plaques, can be very effective when carried out in a peer setting. The most common incentive offered by companies is cash, followed by gift cards and travel.[23] Other common awards include meals, merchandise, and recognition through special parking spaces. Travel reward programs can confer a high-profile honor, provide a unique experience that makes recipients feel special, and build camaraderie among award-winning salespeople. However, some recipients of travel awards may feel that they already travel too

HOW DO YOU DEFINE PERFORMANCE AT YOUR ORGANIZATION?

Rewarding people for performance and effectively managing incentive compensation plans allow you to create a performance-driven organization.

With 500 employees, Synygy is the largest provider of Enterprise Incentive Management (EIM) solutions and a leading supplier of software and services that enable companies to align, measure, reward, report, and analyze employee performance. Flexible deployment options. Rapid, fixed-fee implementations—typically in just three to six months. Pay-as-you-go subscription pricing. Guaranteed success—or your money back.

How do you want to deploy your EIM solution?

Installed Software | Hosted Software-as-a-Service | Installed Managed Services | Hosted Managed Services

Register for a free web cast and find out how Synygy can help you drive performance.
www.synygy.com

SYNYGY
Performance Defined. Results Delivered.™

Motivating Salespeople

Synygy provides sales compensation management solutions. Properly managed incentive programs motivate appropriate sales force behaviors, and thus drive sales performance.

much on the job. Cash rewards are easy to administer, are always appreciated by recipients, and appeal to all demographic groups. However, cash has no visible "trophy" value and provides few "bragging rights." The benefits of awarding merchandise are that the items have visible trophy value, recipients who are allowed to select the merchandise feel more control, and merchandise awards can help to build momentum for the sales force. The disadvantages of using merchandise are that employees may have lower perceived value of the merchandise and that the company may experience greater administrative problems. Some companies outsource their incentive programs to companies that specialize in the creation and management of such programs.

Managing Sales Territories.   The effectiveness of a sales force that must travel to customers is somewhat influenced by management's decisions regarding sales territories. When deciding on territories, sales managers must consider size, shape, routing, and scheduling.

Several factors enter into the design of a sales territory's size and shape. First, sales managers must construct territories so that sales potential can be measured. Sales territories often consist of several geographic units, such as census tracts, cities, counties, or states, for which market data are obtainable. Sales managers usually try to create territories with similar sales potential or that require about the same amount of work. If territories have equal sales potential, they almost always will be unequal in geographic size. Salespeople with larger territories have to work longer and harder to generate a certain sales volume. Conversely, if sales territories requiring equal amounts of work are created, sales potential for those territories often will vary. At times, sales managers use commercial programs to help them balance sales territories. Although a sales manager seeks equity when developing and maintaining sales territories, some inequities always prevail. A territory's size and shape also should help the sales force provide the best possible customer coverage and should minimize selling costs. Customer density and distribution are important factors.

The geographic size and shape of a sales territory are the most important factors affecting the routing and scheduling of sales calls. Next in importance are the number and distribution of customers within the territory, followed by sales call frequency and duration. In some firms, salespeople plan their own routes and schedules with little or no assistance from the sales manager; in other organizations, the sales manager draws up the routes and schedules. No matter who plans the routing and scheduling, the major goals should be to minimize salespeople's nonselling time (time spent traveling and waiting) and maximize their selling time. Planners should try to achieve these goals so that a salesperson's travel and lodging costs are held to a minimum.

Controlling and Evaluating Sales Force Performance.   To control and evaluate sales force performance properly, sales managers need information. A sales manager

Sir Richard Branson

HIS BUSINESS: Virgin Group

FOUNDED: In England in 1970, when Branson was 20

SUCCESS: A total of 350 companies yield $8 billion in annual sales

Self-described adrenaline junkie Richard Branson founded the first piece of his multibillion-dollar empire at age 16: a student magazine run out of a basement. Four years later, he launched a mail-order record company and opened his first record store in London. This led to Virgin Music, which recorded many well-known bands, including the Rolling Stones and the Sex Pistols, before being sold in 1992 for $1 billion. Today, Virgin Group's 350 large and small ventures include a successful airline, a pay-as-you-go wireless phone service, health clubs, a winery, a limousine service, and a space travel agency, Virgin Galactic (no flights yet). Knighted in 1999, Branson has generated much publicity for his firm and himself by his record-breaking attempts to circumnavigate the globe in a high-tech hot-air balloon.[b]

can use call reports, customer feedback, and invoices. Call reports identify the customers called on and present detailed information about interaction with those clients. Web-enabled smart phones also can help sales managers to keep abreast of a salesperson's activities. Data about a salesperson's interactions with customers and prospects can be included in the company's CRM system. This information provides insights about the salesperson's performance.

Dimensions used to measure a salesperson's performance are determined largely by sales objectives, normally set by the sales manager. If an individual's sales objective is stated in terms of sales volume, that person should be evaluated on the basis of sales volume generated. Sales managers often evaluate many performance indicators, including average number of calls per day, average sales per customer, actual sales relative to sales potential, number of new-customer orders, average cost per call, and average gross profit per customer.

To evaluate a salesperson, a sales manager may compare one or more of these dimensions with predetermined performance standards. However, sales managers commonly compare a salesperson's performance with that of other employees operating under similar selling conditions or the salesperson's current performance with past performance. Sometimes management judges factors that have less direct bearing on sales performance, such as personal appearance and product knowledge. The positive relationship between organizational commitment and job performance is stronger for sales personnel than for nonsales employees.[24]

After evaluating salespeople, sales managers take any needed corrective action to improve sales force performance. They may adjust performance standards, provide additional training, or try other motivational methods. Corrective action may demand comprehensive changes in the sales force.

What Is Sales Promotion?

sales promotion An activity and/or material meant to induce resellers or salespeople to sell a product or consumers to buy it

Sales promotion is an activity or material, or both, that acts as a direct inducement, offering added value or incentive for the product, to resellers, salespeople, or consumers. It encompasses all promotional activities and materials other than personal selling, advertising, and public relations. For example, to promote newly designed restaurants, McDonald's initiated a "Mobile Whoa" campaign in which consumers could text the word *hunt* to a special phone number or visit a website and answer trivia questions. Participants received coupons, and some early participants received $5 reloadable frequent-user cards.[25] In competitive markets, where products are very similar, sales promotion provides additional inducements that encourage product trial and purchase.

Marketers often use sales promotion to facilitate personal selling, advertising, or both. Companies also employ advertising and personal selling to support sales promotion activities. For example, marketers frequently use advertising to promote contests, free samples, and premiums. The most effective sales promotion efforts are highly interrelated with other promotional activities. Decisions regarding sales promotion often affect advertising and personal selling decisions, and vice versa.

Sales Promotion–Coupons

This Sugar in the Raw coupon is easily recognized and states the offer clearly.

Sales promotion can increase sales by providing extra purchasing incentives. Many opportunities exist to motivate consumers, resellers, and salespeople to take desired actions. Some kinds of sales promotion are designed specifically to stimulate resellers' demand and effectiveness, some are directed at increasing consumer demand, and some focus on both consumers and resellers. Regardless of the purpose, marketers must ensure that sales promotion objectives are consistent with the organization's overall objectives, as well as with its marketing and promotion objectives.

When deciding which sales promotion methods to use, marketers must consider several factors, particularly product characteristics (price, size, weight, costs, durability, uses, features, and hazards) and target-market characteristics (age, gender, income, location, density, usage rate, and shopping patterns). How products are distributed and the number and types of resellers may determine the type of method used. The competitive and legal environments also may influence the choice.

The use of sales promotion has increased dramatically over the last 20 years, primarily at the expense of advertising. This shift in how promotional dollars are used has occurred for several reasons. Heightened concerns about value have made customers more responsive to promotional offers, especially price discounts and point-of-purchase displays. Thanks to their size and access to checkout scanner data, retailers have gained considerable power in the supply chain and are demanding greater promotional efforts from manufacturers to boost retail profits. Declines in brand loyalty have produced an environment in which sales promotions aimed at persuading customers to switch brands are more effective. Finally, the stronger emphasis placed on improving short-term performance results calls for greater use of sales promotion methods that yield quick (albeit perhaps short-lived) sales increases.[26]

In the remainder of this chapter we examine several consumer and trade sales promotion methods, including what they entail and what goals they can help marketers achieve.

Consumer Sales Promotion Methods

Consumer sales promotion methods encourage or stimulate consumers to patronize specific retail stores or try particular products. These methods initiated by retailers often aim to attract customers to specific locations, whereas those used by manufacturers generally introduce new products or promote established brands. In this section we discuss coupons, cents-off offers, money refunds and rebates, frequent-user incentives, demonstrations, point-of-purchase displays, free samples, premiums, consumer contests and games, and consumer sweepstakes.

Coupons and Cents-Off Offers.   **Coupons** reduce a product's price and are used to prompt customers to try new or established products, increase sales volume quickly, attract repeat purchasers, or introduce new package sizes or features. Savings may be deducted from the purchase price or offered as cash. Research indicates that coupons are most effective when a small-face-value coupon is used in conjunction with a lower product price available for all consumers.[27] Coupons are the most widely used consumer sales promotion technique. Consumer packaged-goods manufacturers distribute about 253 billion coupons, of which about 1 percent are redeemed, saving

consumer sales promotion methods Ways of encouraging consumers to patronize specific stores or try particular products

coupons Written price reductions used to encourage consumers to buy a specific product

table 18.2	PRODUCT CATEGORIES WITH THE GREATEST DISTRIBUTION OF COUPONS

Product Category	No. of Coupons Issued
1. Household cleaning	12.4 million
2. Pet food and treats	12.3 million
3. Rug and room deodorizers	10.8 million
4. Cross-category personal care	10.5 million
5. Snacks	7.2 million
6. Cold, allergy, flu care	6.7 million
7. Hair care	6.2 million
8. Vitamins	6 million
9. Dishwashing soap	5.5 million
10. Cereal	5.5 million

Source: Betsy Spethmann, "FSI Coupon Worth Reaches $300 Billion in 2006: MARX," Promo, January 4, 2007, http://promomagazine.com/othertactics/news/fsi_coupon_worth_300_billion_010407/.

consumers an estimated $3 billion. Nearly 80 percent of all consumers use coupons.[28] Table 18.2 shows the product categories with the greatest distribution of coupons.

For best results, the coupons should be easy to recognize and state the offer clearly. The nature of the product (seasonal demand for it, life cycle stage, and frequency of purchase) is the prime consideration in setting up a coupon promotion. Paper coupons are distributed on and in packages, through freestanding inserts (FSIs), in print advertising, and through direct mail (Figure 18.3). Electronic coupons are distributed online, via in-store kiosks, through shelf dispensers in stores, and at checkout counters. When deciding on the distribution method for coupons, marketers should consider strategies and objectives, redemption rates, availability, circulation,

figure 18.3	

SOURCES OF COUPONS

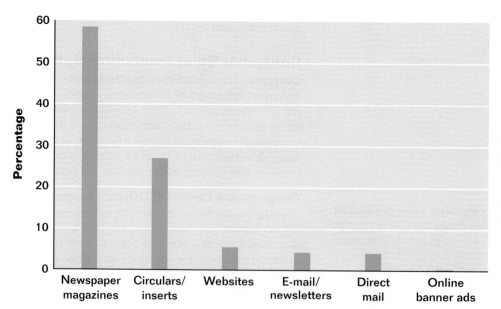

Source: Enid Burns, "Coupons Converge Online," *ClickZ*, October 6, 2005, www.clickz.com/showPage.html?page=3554206.

and exclusivity. The coupon distribution and redemption arena has become very competitive. To draw customers to their stores, some grocers double and sometimes even triple the value of customers' coupons.

Coupons offer several advantages. Print advertisements with coupons are often more effective at generating brand awareness than are print ads without coupons. In China, research has found that coupons positively influence consumer attitudes toward a brand.[29] Generally, the larger the coupon's cash offer, the better is the recognition generated. Coupons reward present product users, win back former users, and encourage purchases in larger quantities. Because they are returned, coupons also help a manufacturer determine whether it reached the intended target market. The advantages of using electronic coupons over paper coupons include lower cost per redemption, greater targeting ability, improved data-gathering capabilities, and improved experimentation capabilities to determine optimal face values and expiration cycles.[30] On the other hand, motivated consumers are likely to consider information in a print coupon more carefully than in an online coupon.[31]

Drawbacks of coupon use include fraud and misredemption, which can be expensive for manufacturers. The Coupon Information Council estimates that coupon fraud—including counterfeit Internet coupons as well as coupons cashed in under false retailer names—amounts to $500 million a year in the United States.[32] Another disadvantage, according to some experts, is that coupons are losing their value; because so many manufacturers offer them, consumers have learned not to buy without some incentive, whether it is a coupon, rebate, or refund. Furthermore, brand loyalty among heavy coupon users has diminished, and many consumers redeem coupons only for products they normally buy. It is believed that about three-fourths of coupons are redeemed by people already using the brand on the coupon. Thus coupons have questionable success as an incentive for consumers to try a new brand or product. An additional problem with coupons is that stores often do not have enough of the coupon item in stock. This situation generates ill will toward both the store and the product.

With a **cents-off offer**, buyers pay a certain amount less than the regular price shown on the label or package. Similar to coupons, this method can serve as a strong incentive for trying new or unfamiliar products. Commonly used in product introductions, cents-off offers can stimulate product sales, yield short-lived sales increases, and promote products in off-seasons. It is an easy method to control and is often used for specific purposes. If used on an ongoing basis, however, cents-off offers reduce the price for customers who would buy at the regular price and also may cheapen a product's image. In addition, the method often requires special handling by retailers who are responsible for giving the discount at the point of sale.

Refunds and Rebates.   With **money refunds**, consumers submit proof of purchase and are mailed a specific amount of money. Usually manufacturers demand multiple product purchases before consumers qualify for refunds. Money refunds, used primarily to promote trial use of a product, are relatively low in cost, but because they sometimes generate a low response rate, they have limited impact on sales. With **rebates**, the customer is sent a specified amount of money for making a single purchase. Rebates generally are given on more expensive products than money refunds and are used to encourage customers. Marketers also use rebates to reinforce brand loyalty, provide promotion buzz for salespeople, and as advertisements for the product. On larger items, such as cars, rebates are often given at the point of sale. Most rebates, however, especially on smaller items, offer a delayed discount because it takes time for the customer to receive the rebate.

One problem with money refunds and rebates is that many people perceive the redemption process as too complicated. Only about 40 percent of individuals who purchase rebated products actually apply for the rebates.[33] Consequently, marketers are increasingly encouraging customers to apply for rebates online, eliminating the need for forms that may confuse customers and frustrate retailers. Consumers also may have

cents-off offer A promotion that lets buyers pay less than the regular price to encourage purchase

money refunds A sales promotion technique offering consumers money when they mail in a proof of purchase, usually for multiple product purchases

rebates A sales promotion technique whereby a customer is sent a specific amount of money for purchasing a single product

snapshot

Redeeming loyalty
What types of rewards do loyal customers prefer?

Gift certificates — Rewards Card **57%**

Cash back, and lower or no fees — Rewards Card **37%**

2.7% Travel

2.6% Merchandise

Source: Maritz Loyalty Marketing.

negative perceptions of manufacturers' reasons for offering rebates. They may believe the products are new, are untested, or haven't sold well. If these perceptions are not changed, rebate offers actually may degrade the image and desirability of the products.

Frequent-User Incentives.   Do you have a "Reward Card" from Border's? Many firms develop incentive programs to reward customers who engage in repeat (frequent) purchases. As mentioned earlier, most major airlines offer frequent flier programs that reward customers who have flown a specified number of miles with free tickets for additional travel. Frequent-user incentives foster customer loyalty to a specific company or group of cooperating companies. They are favored by service businesses, such as airlines, auto rental agencies, hotels, and restaurants. At Neiman Marcus, for example, the InCircle Rewards program rewards loyal shoppers with dollar-for-dollar-spent benefits, but they must spend $5,000 per year to be eligible. Indeed, research shows that 93 percent of consumers with household incomes above $100,000 participate in frequent-user programs, whereas only 58 percent of shoppers with incomes below $50,000 participate.[34]

Samples Stimulate Product Trial

Lunesta offers free samples under its 7-Night Lunesta Challenge in order to stimulate product trial.

Point-of-Purchase Materials and Demonstrations.   Point-of-purchase (P-O-P) materials include outdoor signs, window displays, counter pieces, display racks, and self-service cartons. Innovations in P-O-P displays include sniff-teasers, which give off a product's aroma in the store as consumers walk within a radius of four feet, and computerized interactive displays. These items, often supplied by producers, attract attention, inform customers, and encourage retailers to carry particular products. A retailer is likely to make use of P-O-P materials if they are attractive, informative, well constructed, and in harmony with the store's image.

Demonstrations are excellent attention getters. Manufacturers offer them temporarily to encourage trial use and purchase of a product or to show how a product works. Because labor costs can be extremely high, demonstrations are not used widely. They can be highly effective for promoting certain types of products, such as appliances, cosmetics, and cleaning supplies. Cosmetics marketers, such as Merle Norman and Clinique, sometimes offer potential customers "makeovers" to demonstrate product benefits and proper application.

Free Samples and Premiums.   Marketers use **free samples** to stimulate trial of a product, increase sales volume in the early stages of a product's life cycle, and obtain desirable distribution. Sampling is the most expensive sales promotion method because production and distribution—at local events, by mail or door-to-door delivery, online, in stores, and on packages—entail high costs. Schick, for example, gave away 200,000 Quattro for Women razors outside office buildings in Chicago, New York, Philadelphia, and San Francisco.[35] Many consumers prefer to get their samples by mail. Other consumers like to sample new food products at supermarkets or to try samples of new recipes featuring foods they already like. In designing a free sample, marketers should consider factors such as seasonal demand for the product, market characteristics, and prior advertising. Free samples usually are not appropriate for slow-turnover products. Despite high costs, use of sampling is increasing. In a given year, almost three-fourths of consumer product companies may use sampling. Distribution of free samples through websites such as StartSampling.com and FreeSamples.com is growing.

Premiums are items offered free or at minimal cost as a bonus for purchasing a product. Like the prize in a Cracker Jack box, premiums are used to attract competitors' customers, introduce different sizes of established products, add variety to other promotional efforts, and stimulate consumer loyalty. Creativity is essential when using premiums; to stand out and achieve a significant number of redemptions, the premium must match both the target audience and the brand's image. Premiums also must be easily recognizable and desirable. Premiums are placed on or in packages and also can be distributed by retailers or through the mail. Examples include a service station giving a free carwash with a fill-up, a free toothbrush available with a tube of toothpaste, and a free plastic storage box given with the purchase of Kraft Cheese Singles.

Consumer Games, Contests, and Sweepstakes.   In **consumer contests**, individuals compete for prizes based on analytical or creative skills. This method can be used to generate retail traffic and frequency of exposure to promotional messages. Contestants are usually more highly involved in consumer contests than in games or sweepstakes, even though total participation may be lower. Contests also may be used in conjunction with other sales promotional methods, such as coupons. For example, Borders invited its Reward loyalty club members to submit essays about New Orleans in order to win a trip to the New Orleans Jazz & Heritage Festival.[36]

In **consumer games**, individuals compete for prizes based primarily on chance—often by collecting game pieces such as bottle caps or a sticker on the side of french fries. Because collecting multiple pieces may be necessary to win or increase an individual's chances of winning, the game stimulates repeated business. Games typically are conducted over a long period of time and are commonly used by fast-food chains, soft-drink companies, and hotels to stimulate traffic and repeat business.

point-of-purchase (P-O-P) materials Signs, window displays, display racks, and similar means used to attract customers

demonstrations A sales promotion method manufacturers use temporarily to encourage trial use and purchase of a product or to show how a product works

free samples Samples of a product given out to encourage trial and purchase

premiums Items offered free or at a minimal cost as a bonus for purchasing a product

consumer contests Sales promotion methods in which individuals compete for prizes based on analytical or creative skills

consumer games Sales promotion method in which individuals compete for prizes based primarily on chance

Holy Cow! Promotion at Chick-fil-A

Like most restaurant chains, Chick-fil-A uses sales promotions to bring customers into its restaurants. But unlike other fast-food chains, it doesn't imitate its competitors.

McDonald's, Burger King, and Denny's invest millions of dollars into marketing kid's meals with toys that are popularized through movies, television, and storybook characters. Chick-fil-A puts its money into teaching kids through books and CDs. One of its most successful promotions was a series of children's books that teaches basic money skills. This five-book series covers topics such as work, spending, saving, giving, and contentment. The booklets were free with a kid's meal and an additional 99 cent purchase. Another kid's meal promotion was built around Veggie Tales CDs that teach children life lessons, including the importance of family and forgiveness.

The Atlanta-based Chick-fil-A, Inc., is the nation's second-largest quick-service chicken restaurant chain with more than 1,240 restaurants in 38 states. The chain, which usually adds around 60 locations annually, has a tradition of giving away a free year's supply of Chick-fil-A food to the first 100 customers on the opening day of each new restaurant. This event has attracted fans from across the country who camp out in all types of weather to be among the first in line. Almost $3 million in free Chick-fil-A meals have been given away since this promotion began.

While serious about its children's premiums, the company is not against having fun with its promotions. For the past decade, Chick-fil-A has run its "Eat Mor Chikin" campaign featuring lovable cows that encourage beefeaters to switch to chicken out of self-preservation. The chain has even designated July 15 as Cow Appreciation Day, when customers receive a free combo meal if they arrive at a restaurant dressed as a cow. The self-preserving cows have become the restaurant's mascots, appearing on clothing and other merchandise that can be purchased at Chick-fil-A locations or from its website.

The chain also uses the bovine theme in its annual calendars, dubbed "Cows in Shining Armor," which depicts cows in various heroic situations. Now in its ninth year, the Chik-Fil-A cow calendar has become the largest-selling calendar in the United States—more than doubling the sales of even Sports Illustrated's wildly popular swimsuit calendar.

Like its competition, Chick-fil-A will no doubt continue to use sales promotion to drive its business, but don't expect this company to follow the crowd.[c]

Development and management of consumer games often are outsourced to an independent public relations firm, which can help marketers to navigate federal and state laws applying to games. Although games may stimulate sales temporarily, there is no evidence to suggest that they affect a company's long-term sales. Marketers should exercise care in developing and administering games: Problems or errors may anger customers and could result in lawsuits. Consider that McDonald's' popular Monopoly game promotion, in which customers collect Monopoly real estate pieces on drink and fry packages, has been tarnished by both fraud and lawsuits. After six successful years, McDonald's was forced to end the annual promotion after a crime ring, which included employees of the promotional firm running the game, was convicted of stealing millions of dollars in winning game pieces. After

McDonald's reintroduced the Monopoly game with improved security, it once again came under scrutiny as the focus of a class-action lawsuit filed by Burger King franchisees, who contended that their customers were lured away by the false promises of McDonald's game.[37]

Entrants in a **consumer sweepstakes** submit their names for inclusion in a drawing for prizes. Hostess, for example, sponsored a "Treats and Tracks" online game with trips to see Danica Patrick, Leilani Munter, and Melanie Troxel in auto races in Daytona, Indianapaolis, or Las Vegas as prizes.[38] Sweepstakes are employed more often than consumer contests and tend to attract a greater number of participants. Contests, games, and sweepstakes may be used in conjunction with other sales promotion methods, such as coupons. It is important to know regulations and laws for contests and sweepstakes because some state laws may view some types of events as forms of gambling or lotteries.[39]

Trade Sales Promotion Methods

To encourage resellers, especially retailers, to carry their products and to promote them effectively, producers use sales promotion methods. **Trade sales promotion methods** stimulate wholesalers and retailers to carry a producer's products and market those products more aggressively. These methods include buying allowances, buy-back allowances, scan-back allowances, merchandise allowances, cooperative advertising, dealer listings, free merchandise, dealer loaders, premium or push money, and sales contests.

Trade Allowances.   Many manufacturers offer trade allowances to encourage resellers to carry a product or stock more of it. One such trade allowance is a **buying allowance**, which is a temporary price reduction offered to resellers for purchasing specified quantities of a product. A soap producer, for example, might give retailers $1 for each case of soap purchased. Such offers provide an incentive for resellers to handle new products, achieve temporary price reductions, or stimulate purchase of items in larger than normal quantities. The buying allowance, which takes the form of money, yields profits to resellers and is simple and straightforward. There are no restrictions on how resellers use the money, which increases the method's effectiveness. One drawback of buying allowances is that customers may buy "forward," meaning that they buy large amounts that keep them supplied for many months. Another problem is that competitors may match (or beat) the reduced price, which can lower profits for all sellers.

A **buy-back allowance** is a sum of money that a producer gives to a reseller for each unit the reseller buys after an initial promotional deal is over. This method is a secondary incentive in which the total amount of money that resellers receive is proportional to their purchases during an initial consumer promotion, such as a coupon offer. Buy-back allowances foster cooperation during an initial sales promotion effort and stimulate repurchase afterward. The main disadvantage of this method is expense.

A **scan-back allowance** is a manufacturer's reward to retailers based on the number of pieces moved through the retailers' scanners during a specific time period. To participate in scan-back programs, retailers usually are expected to pass along savings to consumers through special pricing. Scan-backs are becoming widely used by manufacturers because they link trade spending directly to product movement at the retail level.

A **merchandise allowance** is a manufacturer's agreement to pay resellers certain amounts of money for providing promotional efforts such as advertising or P-O-P displays. This method is best suited to high-volume, high-profit, easily handled products. A drawback is that some retailers perform activities at a minimally acceptable level simply to obtain allowances. Before paying retailers, manufacturers usually verify their performance. Manufacturers hope that retailers' additional promotional efforts will yield substantial sales increases.

consumer sweepstakes A sales promotion in which entrants submit their names for inclusion in a drawing for prizes

trade sales promotion methods Ways of persuading wholesalers and retailers to carry a producer's products and market them aggressively

buying allowance A temporary price reduction to resellers for purchasing specified quantities of a product

buy-back allowance A sum of money given to a reseller for each unit bought after an initial promotion deal is over

scan-back allowance A manufacturer's reward to retailers based on the number of pieces scanned

merchandise allowance A manufacturer's agreement to pay resellers certain amounts of money for providing special promotional efforts

Cooperative Advertising and Dealer Listings. **Cooperative advertising** is an arrangement whereby a manufacturer agrees to pay a certain amount of a retailer's media costs for advertising the manufacturer's products. The amount allowed is usually based on the quantities purchased. As with merchandise allowances, a retailer must show proof that advertisements did appear before the manufacturer pays the agreed-on portion of the advertising costs. These payments give retailers additional funds for advertising. Some retailers exploit cooperative advertising agreements by crowding too many products into one advertisement. Not all available cooperative advertising dollars are used. Some retailers cannot afford to advertise, whereas others can afford it but do not want to advertise. A large proportion of all cooperative advertising dollars are spent on newspaper advertisements.

Dealer listings are advertisements promoting a product and identifying participating retailers that sell the product. Dealer listings can influence retailers to carry the product, build traffic at the retail level, and encourage consumers to buy the product at participating dealers.

Free Merchandise and Gifts. Manufacturers sometimes offer **free merchandise** to resellers that purchase a stated quantity of products. Occasionally, free merchandise is used as payment for allowances provided through other sales promotion methods. To avoid handling and bookkeeping problems, the "free" merchandise usually takes the form of a reduced invoice.

A **dealer loader** is a gift to a retailer who purchases a specified quantity of merchandise. Dealer loaders are often used to obtain special display efforts from retailers by offering essential display parts as premiums. For example, a manufacturer might design a display that includes a sterling silver tray as a major component and give the tray to the retailer. Marketers use dealer loaders to obtain new distributors and to push larger quantities of goods.

Premium (Push) Money. **Premium money** (or **push money**) is additional compensation to salespeople offered by the manufacturer as an incentive to push a line of goods. This method is appropriate when personal selling is an important part of the marketing effort; it is not effective for promoting products sold through self-service. The method often helps manufacturers obtain a commitment from the sales force, but it can be very expensive.

Sales Contests. A **sales contest** is designed to motivate distributors, retailers, and sales personnel by recognizing outstanding achievements. To be effective, this method must be equitable for all persons involved. One advantage is that it can achieve participation at all distribution levels. Positive effects may be temporary, however, and prizes are usually expensive.

cooperative advertising An arrangement in which a manufacturer agrees to pay a certain amount of a retailer's media costs for advertising the manufacturer's products

dealer listings An advertisement that promotes a product and identifies the names of participating retailers that sell the product

free merchandise A manufacturer's reward given to resellers for purchasing a stated quantity of products

dealer loader A gift, often part of a display, given to a retailer purchasing a specified quantity of merchandise

premium money (or push money) Also called push money; extra compensation to salespeople for pushing a line of goods

sales contest A promotion method used to motivate distributors, retailers, and sales personnel through recognition of outstanding achievements

... And Now, Back to Best Buy

To improve the effectiveness of its sales force, Best Buy is serious about listening to its employees. Best Buy tries to inspire its 128,000 employees to offer their own ideas to better meet the needs of their customers. For example, Nate Omann, a project manager for Best Buy's service division, noticed that an unusually high number of flat-panel TVs were being damaged during home delivery to the great annoyance of customers. Nate came up with the "TV taco," a reusable device that goes around a television to better protect it during transit. The company expects the idea to save millions of dollars and greatly improve customer satisfaction. When a company such as Best Buy wants to become more innovative, a lot depends on whether managers truly listen to their employees' experience and creativity in finding solutions to workplace issues.

Another effort to improve employee performance and motivation is underway at Best Buy headquarters, where now there are no fixed schedules and no mandatory meetings, and the focus is on results rather than hours at work. This means that employees do not physically have to be at work—they are free to work wherever they want, whenever they want, so long as they accomplish their assigned tasks and achieve their goals. The endeavor, called ROWE, or *results-only work environment,* seeks to bulldoze the decades-old business notion that equates productivity with physical presence. This means that it is acceptable to take conference calls while you hunt, collaborate from your lakeside cabin, or log on after dinner so that you can spend the afternoon with your child. The company also plans to transfer its clockless campaign to its stores—a high-stakes challenge that no company has ever tried before in a retail environment. It is fitting that at Best Buy, the idea for ROWE came from the employees themselves rather than from top management. It started as a covert operation that spread virally and eventually became a revolution. This type of innovation is exactly what Best Buy strives to nurture at its company.

Prior to the ROWE campaign, Best Buy's move into services such as the Geek Squad and its "customer-centricity" initiative was accompanied by employee stress, burnout, and high turnover. The aim of ROWE is to free employees to make their own work-life decisions in order to boost morale and productivity and keep the service initiative on track. So far the program seems to be working. Since its implementation, average voluntary turnover has fallen drastically, and productivity is up an average of 35 percent in departments that have switched to ROWE. It also has had other effects too, such as reducing the need for corporate office space, which, in turn, reduces costs that can then be plowed back into the new "customer-centric" stores. The next step is to test ROWE in retail stores, although how Best Buy will do so in an environment where it would seem that salespeople need to put in regular hours remains to be seen. ROWE's success has so far outweighed its costs, making a successful test an exciting prospect in a competitive retail environment where motivated and effective salespeople make the difference.[40]

1. How has Best Buy's results-only work environment affected the company?

2. By focusing on its angel customers, will Best Buy alienate its devil customers? Is this enough, or does the company need to specifically focus on its devil customers too?

3. Even though the new "customer-centric" stores are more expensive, do you think they will pay off for Best Buy?

CHAPTER REVIEW

1. Define personal selling and understand its purpose.

Personal selling is paid personal communication that attempts to inform customers and persuade them to purchase products in an exchange situation. Three general purposes of personal selling are finding prospects, persuading them to buy, and keeping customers satisfied.

2. Describe the basic steps in the personal selling process.

Many salespeople move through a general selling process when they sell products. In prospecting, the salesperson develops a list of potential customers. Before contacting prospects, the salesperson conducts a preapproach that involves finding and analyzing information about prospects and their needs. The approach is the way in which a salesperson contacts potential customers. During the sales presentation, the salesperson must attract and hold the prospect's attention to stimulate interest in and desire for the product. If possible, the salesperson should handle objections as they arise. During the closing, the salesperson asks the prospect to buy the product or products. After a successful closing, the salesperson must follow up the sale.

3. Identify the types of sales force personnel.

In developing a sales force, marketing managers consider which types of salespeople will sell the firm's products most effectively. The three classifications of salespeople are order getters, order takers, and support personnel. Order getters inform both current customers and new prospects and persuade them to buy. Order takers seek repeat sales and fall into two categories: inside order takers and field order takers. Sales support personnel facilitate selling, but their duties usually extend beyond making sales. The three types of support personnel are missionary, trade, and technical salespeople. The roles of salespeople are changing. Team selling involves the salesperson joining with people from the firm's financial, engineering, and other functional areas. Relationship selling involves building mutually beneficial long-term associations with a customer through regular communications over prolonged periods of time.

4. Understand sales management decisions and activities.

Sales force management is an important determinant of a firm's success because the sales force is directly responsible for generating the organization's sales revenue. Major decision areas and activities include establishing sales force objectives; determining sales force size; recruiting, selecting, training, compensating, and motivating salespeople; managing sales territories; and controlling and evaluating sales force performance.

5. Explain what sales promotion activities are and how they are used.

Sales promotion is an activity or a material (or both) that acts as a direct inducement, offering added value or incentive for the product to resellers, salespeople, or consumers. Marketers use sales promotion to identify and attract new customers, introduce new products, and increase reseller inventories.

6. Recognize specific consumer and trade sales promotion methods.

Sales promotion techniques fall into two general categories: consumer and trade. Consumer sales promotion methods encourage consumers to trade at specific stores or try a specific product. These sales promotion methods include coupons, cents-off offers, money refunds and rebates, frequent-user incentives, point-of-purchase displays, demonstrations, free samples, premiums, and consumer contests, games, and sweepstakes. Trade sales promotion techniques can motivate resellers to handle a manufacturer's products and market those products aggressively. These sales promotion techniques include buying allowances, buy-back allowances, scan-back allowances, merchandise allowances, cooperative advertising, dealer listings, free merchandise, dealer loaders, premium (or push) money, and sales contests.

 ACE self-test   Please visit the student website at **www.prideferrell.com** for ACE Self-Test questions that will help you prepare for exams.

KEY CONCEPTS

personal selling
prospecting
approach
closing
order getter
order takers
support personnel
missionary salespeople
trade salespeople
technical salespeople
team selling
relationship selling

straight salary
    compensation plan
straight commission
    compensation plan
combination compensation
    plan
sales promotion
consumer sales promotion
    methods
coupons
cents-off offer
money refunds

rebates
point-of-purchase (P-O-P)
    materials
demonstrations
free samples
premiums
consumer contests
consumer games
consumer sweepstakes
trade sales promotion
    methods
buying allowance

buy-back allowance
scan-back allowance
merchandise allowance
cooperative advertising
dealer listing
free merchandise
dealer loader
premium money (*or* push
    money)
sales contest

ISSUES FOR DISCUSSION AND REVIEW

1. What is personal selling? How does personal selling relate to other types of promotional activities?

2. Identify the elements of the personal selling process. Must a salesperson include all these elements when selling a product to a customer? Why or why not?

3. How does a salesperson find and evaluate prospects? Do you consider any of these methods to be ethically questionable? Explain.

4. Are order getters more aggressive or creative than order takers? Why or why not?

5. Why are team selling and relationship selling becoming more prevalent?

6. How should a sales manager establish criteria for selecting sales personnel? What do you think are the general characteristics of a good salesperson?

7. What major issues or questions should management consider when developing a training program for the sales force?

8. Explain the major advantages and disadvantages of the three basic methods of compensating salespeople. In general, which method would you prefer? Why?

9. How does a sales manager, who cannot be with each salesperson in the field on a daily basis, control the performance of sales personnel?

10. What is sales promotion? Why is it used?

11. For each of the following, identify and describe three techniques, and give several examples: (a) consumer sales promotion methods and (b) trade sales promotion methods.

MARKETING APPLICATIONS

1. Briefly describe an experience you have had with a salesperson at a clothing store or an automobile dealership. Describe the steps used by the salesperson. Did the salesperson skip any steps? What did the salesperson do well? Not so well?

2. Refer to your answer to Marketing Application 1. Would you describe the salesperson as an order getter, an order taker, or a support salesperson? Why? Did the salesperson perform more than one of these functions?

3. Identify a familiar type of retail store or product. Recommend at least three sales promotion methods that should be used to promote the store or product. Explain why you would use these methods.

4. Identify which method or methods of sales promotion a producer might use in the following situations, and explain why the method would be appropriate.
   a. A golf ball manufacturer wants to encourage retailers to add a new type of golf ball to current product offerings.
   b. A life insurance company wants to increase sales of its universal life products, which have been lagging recently (the company has little control over sales activities).
   c. A light bulb manufacturer with an overproduction of 100-watt bulbs wants to encourage its grocery store chain resellers to increase their bulb inventories.

Online Exercise

5. TerrAlign offers consulting services and software products designed to help a firm maximize control and deployment of its field sales representatives. Review its website at **www.terralign.com.**
   a. Identify three features of TerrAlign software that are likely to benefit salespeople.
   b. Identify three features of TerrAlign software that are likely to benefit sales managers.
   c. Why might field sales professionals object to the use of software from TerrAlign?

globalEDGE™

Your firm has recently developed a revolutionary new chemical that is widely applicable, nearly costless, and does not harm the environment. However, before widespread production, you must identify the largest manufacturing companies worldwide that might be interested in your new product. The *IndustryWeek*'s IW 1000 ranking should prove useful for this task. This can be found using the search term "largest manufacturing companies" at **http://globaledge.msu.edu/ibrd** (and check the box "Resource Desk only"). From there, follow the link to the IW 1000 database and then choose the chemicals industry as a choice criterion. Because your firm is based in the United States and focused on the domestic market, which companies are feasible to target for a comprehensive sales strategy? If you were planning to enter a new market, which would it be?

IBM Sales Force Sells Solutions

In recent years, IBM has worked hard to reposition itself from a supplier of information technology (IT) hardware and software to a company that provides business solution services. Although IBM is still the world's largest provider of IT hardware and software, its executives regard this as the means to an end and not the end. In their own words, ". . . we measure ourselves today by how well we help clients solve their biggest and most pressing problems." Obviously, successful problem solving leads to an increase in customers and an increase in goods and services sold.

The company has relied heavily on its global sales force in making the transition from goods to a solutions service provider. Personal selling always has been a fundamental aspect of IBM's business philosophy. Historically, it has been one of the foundations of the company's success. The enormous task of changing the company's focus from selling hardware and software to selling solutions cannot be overstated. IBM has customers in 174 countries who speak 165 languages. The company's sales force makes 18 billion client contacts a year and addresses 350,000 sales opportunities per day.

As in all organizations, IBM's change comes from the top. Samuel J. Palmisano, IBM's chairman, president, and chief executive officer, led a process of examining and redefining the company's core values. One of the first core values identified was "dedication to every client's success." From a sales perspective, this is achieved through consultative selling—also known as solutions or relationship selling—which brings all of IBM's resources and expertise together to solve customer problems. This requires that the sales force thoroughly understand their customers' business environment and deliver the correct answers to their questions. As Palmisano pointed out, the company's business model has changed. It used to be: "Invent, build, and sell"—today it is "Craft, solve, and deliver the solution."

Not surprisingly, solutions selling has brought new challenges to the sales force. IBM believes that salespeople are not born but trained. The company puts its salespeople through an extensive training program lasting over five months and encompasses three major areas of focus: IBM's commitment to its customers, techniques of collaborative selling, and techniques for gaining understanding of a company's resources and infrastructure. For large projects, salespeople often work in teams consisting of one sales leader and four to five sales specialists who have expertise relevant to the project.

For the most part, IBM salespeople use the Socratic method of selling, which involves asking open-ended questions to better understand their customers' problems, desires, and needs. As might be expected, solution (or pull selling) is more complex than product (or push selling). The salesperson's role in solutions selling is to gather information concerning the customer's business problem, provide a point of view, solve the problem (with the help of other team members), and determine the potential impact on the customer's business once the recommended solution is implemented.

The most accurate and important indicator of the success of the solutions service is customer reaction. An example of IBM achieving its sales objective of "ensuring our clients are successful" is the Sales Connections Program. Actuate, an independent software vendor and IBM customer, used the Sales Connection website to express concerns about a customer dragging its feet on an applications deal. IBM discovered that the person Actuate was working with lacked the authority to close the deal. IBM provided Actuate with the correct contact person, and the sale was closed quickly.

Another example is IBM's Software-as-a-Service Program. Software-as-a-Service delivers software via the Internet. This eliminates the need for companies to buy, build, manage, and maintain applications such as accounting, human resources, customer relationship management, and enterprise resource planning. Companies benefit from this concept because it can reduce their operational costs and maintenance expenses, therefore increasing profits. In an effort to sell this service more broadly, an IBM sales team designed a sales incentive that awards a 10 percent referral fee and additional marketing incentives to IBM customers that submit leads resulting in business for IBM. The marketing incentives include direct mail, telemarketing, advertising, and technical resources to help businesses generate leads. This program enabled one of IBM's customers to generate 800 sales leads in one year.

With this kind of dedication, there is little doubt that IBM's solutions service will continue its success.[41]

Questions for Discussion

1. What are the advantages for IBM in selling solutions rather than goods?
2. Why is solutions selling more complex than hardware and software selling? Identify the sales skills needed for each approach?
3. What are some ways that IBM can measure the effectiveness of its solutions or consultative selling?

Changes in the Workplace

Between one-fourth and one-third of the civilian work force in the United States is employed in marketing-related jobs. Although the field offers a multitude of diverse career opportunities, the number of positions in each area varies. For example, millions of workers are employed in many facets of sales, but relatively few people work in public relations and marketing research.

Many nonbusiness organizations now recognize that they perform marketing activities. For that reason, the number of marketing positions in government agencies, hospitals, charitable and religious groups, educational institutions, and similar organizations is increasing. Today's nonprofit organizations are competitive and better managed, with job growth rates often matching those of private-sector firms. Another area ripe with opportunities is online. With so many businesses setting up websites, demand will rise for people who have the skills to develop and design marketing strategies for the Internet.

Many workers laid off from large corporations are choosing an entrepreneurial path, creating still more new opportunities for first-time job seekers. Even some of those who have secure managerial positions are leaving corporations and heading to smaller companies, toward greater responsibility and autonomy. The traditional career path used to be graduation from college, then a job with a large corporation, and a climb up the ladder to management. This pattern has changed, however. Today people are more likely to experience a career path of sideways "gigs" rather than sequential steps up a corporate ladder.

Career Choices Are Major Life Choices

Many people think career planning begins with an up-to-date résumé and a job interview.[1] In reality, it begins long before you prepare your résumé. It starts with *you* and what you want to become. In some ways, you have been preparing for a career ever since you started school. Everything you have experienced during your lifetime you can use as a resource to help you define your career goals. Since you will likely spend more time at work than at any other single place during your lifetime, it makes sense to spend that time doing something you enjoy. Some people just work at a *job* because they need money to survive. Other people choose a *career* because of their interests and talents or commitment to a particular profession. Whether you are looking for a job or a career, you should examine your priorities.

Personal Factors Influencing Career Choices

Before choosing a career, you need to consider what motivates you and what skills you can offer an employer. The following questions may help you define what you consider important in life.

1. *What types of activities do you enjoy?* Although most people know what they enjoy in a general way, a number of interest inventories exist. By helping you determine specific interests and activities, these inventories can help you land a job that will lead to a satisfying career. In some cases, it may be sufficient just to list the activities you enjoy, along with those you dislike. Watch for patterns that may influence your career choices.

2. *What do you do best?* All jobs and all careers require employees to be able to "do something." It is extremely important to assess what you do best. Be honest with yourself about your ability to succeed in a specific job. It may help to make a list of your strongest job-related skills. Also, try looking at your skills from an

employer's perspective: What can you do that an employer would be willing to pay for?

3. *What kind of education will you need?* The amount of education you need is determined by the type of career you choose. In some careers, it is impossible to get an entry-level position without at least a college degree. In other careers, technical or hands-on skills may also be important. Generally, more education increases your potential earning power.

4. *Where do you want to live?* Initially some college graduates will want to move to a different part of the country before entering the job market, whereas others may prefer to reside close to home, friends, and relatives. In reality, successful job applicants must be willing to go where the jobs are. The location of an entry-level job may be influenced by the type of marketing career selected. For example, some of the largest advertising agencies are in New York, Chicago, and Los Angeles. Likewise, large marketing research organizations are based in metropolitan areas. On the other hand, sales positions and retail management jobs are available in medium-size as well as large cities.

Job Search Activities

When people begin to search for a job, they often first go online or turn to the classified ads in their local newspaper. Those ads are an important source of information about jobs in a particular area, but they are only one source. Many other sources can lead to employment and a satisfying career. Because there is a wealth of information about career planning, you should be selective in both the type and the amount of information you use to guide your job search.

In recent years the library, a traditional job-hunting tool, has been joined by the Internet. Both the library and the Internet are sources of everything from classified newspaper ads and government job listings to detailed information on individual companies and industries. You can use either resource to research an area of employment or a particular company that interests you. In addition, the Internet allows you to check electronic bulletin boards for current job information, exchange ideas with other job seekers through online discussion groups or e-mail, and get career advice from professional counselors. You can also create your own webpage to inform prospective employers of your qualifications. You may even have a job interview online. Many companies use their websites to post job openings, accept applications, and interview candidates.

As you start your job search, you may find the following websites helpful. (Addresses of additional career-related websites can be accessed through the Student Career Center at **www.prideferrell.com.**)

America's Job Bank: **www.ajb.dni.us**

This massive site contains information on more than 2 million jobs. Listings come from 1,800 state employment offices around the country and represent every line of work, from professional and technical to blue-collar, and from entry level on up.

CareerBuilder: **www.careerbuilder.com**

This site is one of the largest on the Internet, with more than 900,000 jobs to view. The site allows a job seeker to find jobs, post résumés, get advice and career resources, and obtain information on career fairs.

Hoover's Online: **www.hoovers.com**

Hoover's offers a variety of job search tools, including information on potential employers and links to sites that post job openings.

Monster: **www.monster.com**

Monster carries hundreds of pages of job listings and offers links to related sites, such as company homepages and a site with information about job fairs.

Federal jobs: **www.fedworld.gov/jobs/jobsearch.html**

If you are interested in working for a government agency, this site lists positions across the country. You can limit your search to specific states or do a general cross-country search for job openings. Other web addresses for job seekers include:

www.careers-in-marketing.com

www.marketingjobs.com

www.careermag.com

www.salary.com

In addition to the library and the Internet, the following sources can be of great help when trying to find the "perfect job":

1. *Campus placement offices.* Colleges and universities have placement offices staffed by trained personnel specialists. In most cases, these offices serve as clearinghouses for career information. The staff may also be able to guide you in creating a résumé and preparing for a job interview.

2. *Professional sources and networks.* A network is a group of people—friends, relatives, and professionals—who are in a position to exchange information, including information about job openings. According to many job applicants, networking is one of the best sources of career information and job leads. Start with as many people as you can think of to establish your network. (The Internet can be very useful in this regard.) Contact these people and ask specific questions about job opportunities they may be aware of. Also, ask each individual to introduce or refer you to someone else who may be able to help you in your job search.

3. *Private employment agencies.* Private employment agencies charge a fee for helping people find jobs. Typical fees can be as high as 15 to 20 percent of an employee's first-year salary. The fee may be paid by the employer or the employee. Like campus placement offices, private employment agencies provide career counseling, help create résumés, and provide preparation for job interviews. Before you use a private employment agency, be sure you understand the terms of any contract or agreement you sign. Above all, make sure you know who is responsible for paying the agency's fee.

4. *State employment agencies.* The local office of your state employment agency is a source of information about job openings in your immediate area. Some job applicants are reluctant to use state agencies because most jobs available through them are for semiskilled or unskilled workers. From a practical standpoint, though, it can't hurt to consult state employment agencies. They will have information about some professional and managerial positions available in your area, and you will not be charged a fee if you obtain a job through one of these agencies.

Many graduates want a job immediately and are discouraged at the thought that an occupational search can take months. But people seeking entry-level jobs should expect their job search to take considerable time. Of course, the state of the economy and whether or not employers are hiring can shorten or extend a job search.

During a job search, you should use the same work habits that effective employees use on the job. Resist the temptation to "take the day off" from job hunting. Instead, make a master list of the activities you want to accomplish each day. If necessary, force yourself to make contacts, do job research, or schedule interviews that might lead to job opportunities. (In fact, many job applicants look at the job hunt as their actual job and "work" full time at it until they find the job they want.) Above all, realize that an occupational search requires patience and perseverance. According to many successful applicants, perseverance may be the job hunter's most valuable trait.

Planning and Preparation

The key to landing the job you want is planning and preparation—and planning begins with goals. In particular, it is important to determine your *personal* goals, decide on the role your career will play in reaching those goals, and then develop your *career* goals. Once you know where you are going, you can devise a feasible plan for getting there.

The time to begin planning is as early as possible. You must, of course, satisfy the educational requirements for the occupational area you desire. Early planning will give you the opportunity to do so. However, some of the people who will compete with you for the better jobs will also be fully prepared. Can you do more? Company recruiters say the following factors give job candidates a definite advantage:

- *Work experience.* You can get valuable work experience in cooperative work/school programs, during summer vacations, or in part-time jobs during the school year. Experience in your chosen occupational area carries the most weight, but even unrelated work experience is useful.

- *The ability to communicate well.* Verbal and written communications skills are increasingly important in all aspects of business. Yours will be tested in your letters to recruiters, in your résumé, and in interviews. You will use these same communication skills throughout your career.

- *Clear and realistic job and career goals.* Recruiters feel most comfortable with candidates who know where they are headed and why they are applying for a specific job.

Again, starting early will allow you to establish well-defined goals, sharpen your communication skills (through elective courses, if necessary), and obtain solid work experience. To develop your own personal career plan, go to the **www.prideferrell.com** student site and access the Student Career Center. There you will find personal career plan worksheets.

The Résumé

An effective résumé is one of the keys to being considered for a good job. Because your résumé states your qualifications, experiences, education, and career goals, a potential employer can use it to assess your compatibility with the job requirements. The résumé should be accurate and current.

In preparing a résumé, it helps to think of it as an advertisement. Envision yourself as a product and the company, particularly the person or persons doing the hiring, as your customer. To interest the customer in buying the product—hiring you—your résumé must communicate information about your qualities and indicate how you can satisfy the customer's needs—that is, how you can help the company achieve its objectives. The information in the résumé should persuade the organization to take a closer look at you by calling you in for an interview.

To be effective, the résumé should be targeted at a specific position, as Figure A.1 shows. This document is just one example of an acceptable résumé. The job target section is specific and leads directly to the applicant's qualifications for the job. The qualifications section details capabilities—what the applicant can do—and also shows that the applicant has an understanding of the job's requirements. Skills and strengths that relate to the specific job should be emphasized. The achievement section ("Experiences" in Figure A.1) indicates success at accomplishing tasks or goals on the job and at school. The work experience section in Figure A.1 includes an unusual listing, which might pique the interest of an interviewer: "helped operate relative's blueberry farm in Michigan for three summers." That is something that could help launch an interview discussion. It tends to inspire, rather than satisfy curiosity, thus inviting further inquiry.

Another type of résumé is the chronological résumé, which lists work experience and educational history in order by date. This type of résumé is useful for those just entering the job market because it helps highlight education and work experience. In

Figure A.1

A RÉSUMÉ TARGETED AT A SPECIFIC POSITION

LORRAINE MILLER
2212 WEST WILLOW
PHOENIX, AZ 12345
(416) 862-9169

EDUCATION: B.A. Arizona State University, 2005, Marketing, achieved a 3.4 on a 4.0 scale throughout college

POSITION DESIRED: Product manager with an international firm providing future career development at the executive level

QUALIFICATIONS:

- Communicates well with individuals to achieve a common goal
- Handles tasks efficiently and in a timely manner
- Understands advertising sales, management, marketing research, packaging, pricing, distribution, and warehousing
- Coordinates many activities at one time
- Receives and carries out assigned tasks or directives
- Writes complete status or research reports

EXPERIENCES:

- Assistant Editor of college paper
- Treasurer of the American Marketing Association (student chapter)
- Internship with 3-Cs Advertising, Berkeley, CA
- Student Assistantship with Dr. Steve Green, Professor of Marketing, Arizona State University
- Solo cross-Canada canoe trek, summer 2003

WORK RECORD:

2004–Present	Blythe and Company Advertising —Assistant Account Executive
2002–2003	Student Assistant for Dr. Steve Green —Research Assistant
2000–2001	The Men —Retail sales and consumer relations
1998–1999	Farmer —Helped operate relative's blueberry farm in Michigan for three summers

some cases, education is more important than unrelated work experience because it indicates the career direction you desire despite the work experience you have acquired thus far.

Common suggestions for improving résumés include: use a clear and easily read (not elaborate) format, delete outdated information, improve organization, use high-quality paper and printer, ensure correct grammar and spelling, and provide a detailed description of work experiences. Keep in mind that the person who will look at your résumé may have to sift through hundreds in the course of the day in addition to handling other duties. Consequently it is important to keep your résumé short (one page is best, never more than two), concise, and neat. Moreover, you want your résumé to be distinctive so it will stand out from all the others. You may need to prepare a plain-text or computer-friendly version of your résumé that can be submitted via e-mail or filled in on a website if that is required by a prospective employer.

In addition to having the proper format and content, a résumé should be easy to read. It is best to use only one or two kinds of type, and plain white paper. When sending a résumé to a large company, several copies may be made and distributed. Textured, gray, or colored paper may make a good impression on the first person who sees the résumé, but it will not reproduce well for the others, who will see only a poor copy. You should also proofread your résumé with care. Typos and misspellings will grab attention—the wrong kind.

Along with the résumé itself, always submit a cover letter. In the letter, you can include somewhat more information than in your résumé and convey a message that expresses your interest and enthusiasm about the organization and the job.

The Job Interview

In essence, your résumé and cover letter are an introduction. The deciding factor in the hiring process is the interview (or several interviews) with representatives of the firm. It is through the interview that the firm gets to know you and your qualifications. At the same time, the interview gives you a chance to learn about the firm.

Here again, preparation is the key to success. Research the firm before your first interview. Learn all you can about its products, its subsidiaries, the markets in which it operates, its history, the locations of its facilities, and so on. If possible, obtain and read the firm's most recent annual report. Be prepared to ask questions about the firm and the opportunities it offers. Interviewers welcome such questions. They expect you to be interested enough to spend some time thinking about your potential relationship with their organization.

Also, prepare to respond to questions the interviewer may ask. Table A.1 lists typical interview questions that job applicants often find difficult to answer. But don't expect interviewers to stick to the list given in the table or to the items appearing in your résumé. They will be interested in anything that helps them decide what kind of person and worker you are.

Make sure you are on time for your interview and are dressed and groomed in a businesslike manner. Interviewers take note of punctuality and appearance just as they do of other personal qualities. Bring a copy of your résumé, even if you already sent one to the firm. You may also want to bring a copy of your course transcript and letters of recommendation. If you plan to furnish interviewers with the names and addresses of references rather than with letters of recommendation, make sure you have your references' permission to do so.

Consider the interview itself as a two-way conversation rather than a question-and-answer session. Volunteer any information that is relevant to the interviewer's questions. If an important point is skipped in the discussion, don't hesitate to bring it up. Be yourself, but emphasize your strengths. Good eye contact and posture are also important; they should come naturally if you take an active part in the interview. At the conclusion of the interview, thank the recruiter for taking the time to see you.

In most cases, the first interview is used to *screen* applicants, or choose those who are best qualified. These applicants are then given a second interview, and perhaps a

table A.1	INTERVIEW QUESTIONS JOB APPLICANTS OFTEN FIND DIFFICULT TO ANSWER

1. Tell me about yourself.

2. What do you know about our organization?

3. What can you do for us? Why should we hire you?

4. What qualifications do you have that make you feel you will be successful in your field?

5. What have you learned from the jobs you've held?

6. If you could write your own ticket, what would be your ideal job?

7. What are your special skills, and where did you acquire them?

8. Have you had any special accomplishments in your lifetime that you are particularly proud of?

9. Why did you leave your most recent job?

10. How do you spend your spare time? What are your hobbies?

11. What are your strengths and weaknesses?

12. Discuss five major accomplishments.

13. What kind of boss would you like? Why?

14. If you could spend a day with someone you've known or known of, who would it be?

15. What personality characteristics seem to rub you the wrong way?

16. How do you show your anger? What types of things make you angry?

17. With what type of person do you spend the majority of your time?

Source: Adapted from *The Ultimate Job Hunter's Guidebook*. 4th ed., Susan D. Greene and Melanie C. L. Martel. Copyright © 2004 by Houghton Mifflin Company.

third, usually with one or more department heads. If the job requires relocation to a different area, applicants may be invited there for these later interviews. After the interviewing process is complete, applicants are told when to expect a hiring decision.

After the Interview

Attention to common courtesy is important as a follow-up to your interview. You should send a brief note of thanks to the interviewer and give it as much care as you did your résumé and cover letter. A short, typewritten letter is preferred to a handwritten note or card, or an e-mail. Avoid not only typos but also overconfident statements such as "I look forward to helping you make Universal Industries successful over the next decade." Even in the thank-you letter, it is important to show team spirit and professionalism, as well as convey proper enthusiasm. Everything you say and do reflects on you as a candidate.

After the Hire

Clearly, performing well in a job has always been a crucial factor in keeping a position. In a tight economy and job market, however, a person's attitude, as well as his or her performance, counts greatly. People in their first jobs can commit costly political blunders by being insensitive to their environments. Politics in the business world includes how you react to your boss, how you react to your coworkers, and your general demeanor. Here are a few rules to live by:

1. *Don't bypass your boss.* One major blunder an employee can make is to go over the boss's head to resolve a problem. This is especially hazardous in a bureaucratic organization. You should become aware of the generally accepted chain of

command, and when problems occur, follow that protocol, beginning with your immediate superior. No boss likes to look incompetent, and making him or her appear so is sure to hamper or even crush your budding career. However, there may be exceptions to this rule in emergency situations. It is wise to discuss with your supervisor what to do in an emergency, before an emergency occurs.

2. *Don't criticize your boss.* Adhering to the old adage, "praise in public and criticize in private," will keep you out of the line of retaliatory fire. A more sensible and productive alternative is to present the critical commentary to your boss in a diplomatic way during a private session.

3. *Don't show disloyalty.* If dissatisfied with the position, a new employee may start a fresh job search, within or outside the organization. However, it is not advisable to begin a publicized search within the company for another position unless you have held your current job for some time. Careful attention to the political climate in the organization should help you determine how soon to start a new job campaign and how public to make it. In any case, it is not a good idea to publicize that you are looking outside the company for a new position.

4. *Don't be a naysayer.* Employees are expected to become part of the organizational team and to work together with others. Behaviors to avoid, especially if you are a new employee, include being critical of others; refusing to support others' projects; always playing devil's advocate; refusing to help others when a crisis occurs; and complaining all the time, even about such matters as the poor quality of the food in the cafeteria, the crowded parking lot, or the temperature in the office.

5. *Learn to correct mistakes appropriately.* No one likes to admit having made a mistake, but one of the most important political skills you can acquire is minimizing the impact of a blunder. It is usually advantageous to correct the damage as soon as possible to avoid further problems. Some suggestions: be the first to break the bad news to your boss; avoid being defensive; stay poised and don't panic; and have solutions ready for fixing the blunder.[2]

Types of Marketing Careers

In considering marketing as a career, the first step is to evaluate broad categories of career opportunities in the areas of marketing research, sales, industrial buying, public relations, distribution management, product management, advertising, retail management, direct marketing, and e-marketing and customer relationship management. Keep in mind that the categories described here are not all-inclusive and that each encompasses hundreds of marketing jobs.

Marketing Research

Clearly, marketing research and information systems are vital aspects of marketing decision making. Marketing researchers survey customers to determine their habits, preferences, and aspirations. The information about buyers and environmental forces that research and information systems provide improves a marketer's ability to understand the dynamics of the marketplace and therefore make effective decisions.

Marketing research firms are usually employed by a client organization such as a provider of goods or services, a nonbusiness organization, a research consulting firm, or an advertising agency. The activities performed include concept testing, product testing, package testing, advertising testing, test-market research, and new-product research.

Marketing researchers gather and analyze data relating to specific problems. A researcher may be involved in one or several stages of research depending on the size of the project, the organization of the research unit, and the researcher's experience.

Marketing research trainees in large organizations usually perform a considerable amount of clerical work, such as compiling secondary data from the firm's accounting and sales records and from periodicals, government publications, syndicated data services, the Internet, and unpublished sources. A junior analyst may edit and code questionnaires or tabulate survey results. Trainees may also participate in gathering primary data through mail and telephone surveys, personal interviews, and observation. As a marketing researcher gains experience, he or she may become involved in defining problems and developing research questions; designing research procedures; and analyzing, interpreting, and reporting findings. Exceptional personnel may assume responsibility for entire research projects.

Although most employers consider a bachelor's degree sufficient qualification for a marketing research trainee, many specialized positions require a graduate degree in business administration, statistics, or other related fields. Today trainees are more likely to have a marketing or statistics degree than a liberal arts degree. Courses in statistics, information technology, psychology, sociology, communications, economics, and technical writing are valuable preparation for a career in marketing research.

The Bureau of Labor Statistics indicates that marketing research provides abundant employment opportunities, especially for applicants with graduate training in marketing research, statistics, economics, and the social sciences. Generally, the value of information gathered by marketing information and research systems rises as competition increases, thus expanding opportunities for prospective marketing research personnel.

The major career paths in marketing research are with independent marketing research agencies/data suppliers and marketing research departments in advertising agencies and other businesses. In a company in which marketing research plays a key role, the researcher is often a member of the marketing strategy team. Surveying or interviewing customers is the heart of the marketing research firm's activities. A statistician selects the sample to be surveyed, analysts design the questionnaire and synthesize the gathered data into a final report, data processors tabulate the data, and the research director controls and coordinates all these activities so each project is completed to the client's satisfaction.

Salaries in marketing research depend on the type, size, and location of the firm, as well as the nature of the position. Generally, starting salaries are somewhat higher and promotions somewhat slower than in other occupations requiring similar training. The typical salary for a market analyst is $24,000 to $50,000; a marketing research director can earn $75,000 to $200,000.[3]

Sales

Millions of people earn a living through personal selling. Chapter 18 defined personal selling as paid personal communication that attempts to inform customers and persuade them to purchase products in an exchange situation. Although this definition describes the general nature of sales positions, individual selling jobs vary enormously with respect to the types of businesses and products involved, the educational background and skills required, and the specific activities sales personnel perform. Because the work is so varied, it offers numerous career opportunities for people with a wide range of qualifications, interests, and goals. The two types of career opportunities we discuss relate to business-to-business sales.

Sales Positions in Wholesaling   Wholesalers buy products intended for resale, for use in making other products, and for general business operations and sell them directly to business markets. Wholesalers thus provide services to both retailers and producers. They can help match producers' products to retailers' needs and provide services that save producers time, money, and resources. Some activities a sales representative for a wholesaling firm is likely to perform include planning and negotiating transactions; assisting customers with sales, advertising, sales promotion, and publicity; facilitating transportation and storage; providing customers with inventory control and data processing assistance; establishing prices; and giving customers technical, managerial, and merchandising assistance.

The background needed by wholesale personnel depends on the nature of the product handled. A sales representative for a drug wholesaler, for example, needs extensive technical training and product knowledge, and may have a degree in chemistry, biology, or pharmacology. A wholesaler of standard office supplies, on the other hand, may find it more important that its sales staff be familiar with various brands, suppliers, and prices than have technical knowledge about the products. A person just entering the wholesaling field may begin as a sales trainee or hold a nonselling job that provides experience with inventory, prices, discounts, and the firm's customers. A college graduate usually enters a wholesaler's sales force directly. Competent salespeople also transfer from manufacturer and retail sales positions.

The number of sales positions in wholesaling is expected to grow about as rapidly as the average for all occupations. Earnings for wholesale personnel vary widely because commissions often make up a large proportion of their incomes.

Sales Positions in Manufacturing   A manufacturer's sales personnel sell the firm's products to wholesalers, retailers, and industrial buyers; they thus perform many of the same activities as a wholesaler's representatives. As in wholesaling, educational requirements for a sales position depend largely on the type and complexity of the products and markets. Manufacturers of nontechnical products usually hire college graduates who have a liberal arts or business degree and train them so they become knowledgeable about the firm's products, prices, and customers. Manufacturers of highly technical products generally prefer applicants who have degrees in fields associated with the particular industry and market.

Sales positions in manufacturing are expected to increase at an average rate. Manufacturers' sales personnel are well compensated and earn above-average salaries; most are paid a combination of salary and commission. Commissions vary according to the salesperson's efforts, abilities, and sales territory, as well as the type of products sold. Annual salary and/or commission for sales positions range from $63,000 to $78,000 for a sales manager and $30,000 to $52,000 for a field salesperson. A sales trainee would start at about $35,000 in business sales positions.[4]

Industrial Buying

Industrial buyers, or purchasing agents, are responsible for maintaining an adequate supply of the goods and services an organization requires for its operations. In general, industrial buyers purchase all items needed for direct use in producing other products and for use in day-to-day operations. Industrial buyers in large firms often specialize in purchasing a single, specific class of products—for example, all petroleum-based lubricants. In smaller organizations, buyers may be responsible for many different categories of purchases, including raw materials, component parts, office supplies, and operating services.

An industrial buyer's main job is to select suppliers that offer the best quality, service, and price. When the products to be purchased are standardized, buyers may base their purchasing decisions on suppliers' descriptions of their offerings in catalogs and trade journals. Buyers who purchase highly homogeneous products often meet with salespeople to examine samples and observe demonstrations. Sometimes buyers must inspect the actual product before purchasing it; in other cases, they invite suppliers to bid on large orders. Buyers who purchase equipment made to specifications often deal directly with manufacturers. After choosing a supplier and placing an order, an industrial buyer usually must trace the shipment to ensure on-time delivery. Sometimes the buyer is also responsible for receiving and inspecting an order and authorizing payment to the shipper.

Training requirements for a career in industrial buying relate to the needs of the firm and the types of products purchased. A manufacturer of heavy machinery may prefer an applicant who has a background in engineering. A service company, on the other hand, may recruit liberal arts majors. Although not generally required, a college degree is becoming increasingly important for industrial buyers who wish to advance to management positions.

Employment prospects for industrial buyers are expected to increase faster than average. Opportunities will be excellent for individuals with a master's degree in business administration or a bachelor's degree in engineering, science, or business administration. Companies that manufacture heavy equipment, computer equipment, and communications equipment will need buyers with technical backgrounds.

Public Relations

Public relations encompasses a broad set of communication activities designed to create and maintain favorable relationships between an organization and its stakeholders—customers, employees, stockholders, government officials, and society in general. Public relations specialists help clients create the image, issue, or message they wish to present and communicate it to the appropriate audience. According to the Public Relations Society of America, about 120,000 people work in public relations in the United States. Half the billings of the nation's 4,000 public relations agencies and firms come from Chicago and New York. The highest starting salaries are also found there. Communication is basic to all public relations programs. To communicate effectively, public relations practitioners must first gather data about the firm's stakeholders to assess their needs, identify problems, formulate recommendations, implement new plans, and evaluate current activities.

Public relations personnel disseminate large amounts of information to the organization's stakeholders. Written communication is the most versatile tool of public relations; thus, good writing skills are essential. Public relations practitioners must be adept at writing for a variety of media and audiences. It is not unusual for a person in public relations to prepare reports, news releases, speeches, broadcast scripts, technical manuals, employee publications, shareholder reports, and other communications aimed at both organizational personnel and external groups. In addition, a public relations practitioner needs a thorough knowledge of the production techniques used in preparing various communications. Public relations personnel also establish distribution channels for the organization's publicity. They must have a thorough understanding of the various media, their areas of specialization, the characteristics of their target audiences, and their policies regarding publicity. Anyone who hopes to succeed in public relations must develop close working relationships with numerous media personnel to enlist their interest in disseminating clients' communications.

A college education combined with writing or media-related experience is the best preparation for a career in public relations. Most beginners have a college degree in journalism, communications, or public relations, but some employers prefer a business background. Courses in journalism, business administration, marketing, creative writing, psychology, sociology, political science, economics, advertising, English, and public speaking are recommended. Some employers ask applicants to present a portfolio of published articles, scripts written for television or radio programs, slide presentations, and other work samples. Other agencies require written tests that include such tasks as writing sample press releases. Manufacturing firms, public utilities, transportation and insurance companies, and trade and professional associations are the largest employers of public relations personnel. In addition, sizable numbers of public relations personnel work for health-related organizations, government agencies, educational institutions, museums, and religious and service groups.

Although some larger companies provide extensive formal training for new personnel, most new public relations employees learn on the job. Beginners usually perform routine tasks such as maintaining files about company activities and searching secondary data sources for information to be used in publicity materials. More experienced employees write press releases, speeches, and articles and help plan public relations campaigns.

Employment opportunities in public relations are expected to increase faster than the average for all occupations. One caveat is in order, however: competition for beginning jobs is keen. The prospects are best for applicants who have solid academic preparation and some media experience. Abilities that differentiate candidates, such as an understanding of information technology, are becoming increasingly important. Public relations account executives can earn from $24,000 to $42,000. Public relations agency managers earn in the $38,000 to $51,000 range.[5]

Distribution Management

A distribution manager arranges for transportation of goods within firms and through marketing channels. Transportation is an essential distribution activity that permits a firm to create time and place utility for its products. It is the distribution manager's job to analyze various transportation modes and select the combination that minimizes cost and transit time while providing acceptable levels of reliability, capability, accessibility, and security.

To accomplish this task, a distribution manager performs many activities. First, the individual must choose one or a combination of transportation modes from the five major modes available: railroads, trucks, waterways, airways, and pipelines. The distribution manager must then select the specific routes the goods will travel and the particular carriers to be used, weighing such factors as freight classifications and regulations, freight charges, time schedules, shipment sizes, and loss and damage ratios. In addition, this person may be responsible for preparing shipping documents, tracing shipments, handling loss and damage claims, keeping records of freight rates, and monitoring changes in government regulations and transportation technology.

Distribution management employs relatively few people and is expected to grow about as fast as the average for all occupations in the near future. Manufacturing firms are the largest employers of distribution managers, although some distribution managers work for wholesalers, retail stores, and consulting firms. Salaries of experienced distribution managers vary, but generally are much higher than the average for all nonsupervisory personnel. Entry-level positions are diverse, ranging from inventory control and traffic scheduling to operations or distribution management. Inventory management is an area of great opportunity because of increasing global competition. While salaries in the distribution field vary depending on the position and information technology skill requirements, entry salaries start at about $40,000.[6]

Most employers of distribution managers prefer to hire graduates of technical programs or people who have completed courses in transportation, logistics, distribution management, economics, statistics, computer science, management, marketing, and commercial law. A successful distribution manager is adept at handling technical data and is able to interpret and communicate highly technical information.

Product Management

The product manager occupies a staff position and is responsible for the success or failure of a product line. Product managers coordinate most of the activities required to market a product. However, because they hold a staff position, they have relatively little actual authority over marketing personnel. Nevertheless, they take on a large amount of responsibility and typically are paid quite well relative to other marketing employees. Being a product manager can be rewarding both financially and psychologically, but it can also be frustrating because of the disparity between responsibility and authority.

What jobs pay today

Median salaries for entry-level positions in the U.S.:

PAY TO:	
Customer Service Rep	$28,381
Sales Assistant	$30,991
Advertising Assistant	$35,002
Public Relations Assistant	$39,221
Assistant Merchandise Buyer	$40,042

Source: Data from Monster Salary Center, htttp://salary.monster.com (accessed June 24, 2005)

A product manager should have a general knowledge of advertising, transportation modes, inventory control, selling and sales management, sales promotion, marketing research, packaging, pricing, and warehousing. The individual must be knowledgeable enough to communicate effectively with personnel in these functional areas and to make suggestions and help assess alternatives when major decisions are being made.

Product managers usually need college training in an area of business administration. A master's degree is helpful, although a person usually does not become a product manager directly out of school. Frequently, several years of selling and sales management experience are prerequisites for a product management position, which often is a major step in the career path of top-level marketing executives. Product managers can earn $60,000 to $120,000, while an assistant product manager starts at about $40,000.[7]

Advertising

Advertising pervades our daily lives. Business and nonbusiness organizations use advertising in many ways and for many reasons. Advertising clearly needs individuals with diverse skills to fill a variety of jobs. Creativity, imagination, artistic talent, and expertise in expression and persuasion are important for copywriters, artists, and account executives. Sales and managerial abilities are vital to the success of advertising managers, media buyers, and production managers. Research directors must have a solid understanding of research techniques and human behavior. A related occupation is an advertising salesperson, who sells newspaper, television, radio, or magazine advertising to advertisers.

Advertising professionals disagree on the most beneficial educational background for a career in advertising. Most employers prefer college graduates. Some employers seek individuals with degrees in advertising, journalism, or business; others prefer graduates with broad liberal arts backgrounds. Still other employers rank relevant work experience above educational background.

"Advertisers look for generalists," says a staff executive of the American Association of Advertising Agencies. "Thus, there are just as many economics or general liberal arts majors as M.B.A.'s." Common entry-level positions in an advertising agency are found in the traffic department, account service (account coordinator), or the media department (media assistant). Starting salaries in these positions are often quite low, but to gain experience in the advertising industry, employees must work their way up in the system. Assistant account executives start at $25,000 to $30,000, while a typical account executive earns $30,000 to $55,000. Copywriters earn $30,000 to $55,000 a year.[8]

A variety of organizations employ advertising personnel. Although advertising agencies are perhaps the most visible and glamorous employers, many manufacturing firms, retail stores, banks, utility companies, and professional and trade associations maintain advertising departments. Advertising jobs are also available with television and radio stations, newspapers, and magazines. Other businesses that employ advertising personnel include printers, art studios, letter shops, and package design firms. Specific advertising jobs include advertising manager, account executive, research director, copywriter, media specialist, and production manager.

Retail Management

Although a career in retailing may begin in sales, there is more to retailing than simply selling. Many retail personnel occupy management positions. Besides managing the sales force, they focus on selecting and ordering merchandise, promotional activities, inventory control, customer credit operations, accounting, personnel, and store security.

Organization of retail stores varies. In many large department stores, retail management personnel rarely engage in actual selling to customers; these duties are performed by retail salespeople. Other types of retail organizations may require management personnel to perform selling activities from time to time.

Large retail stores offer a variety of management positions, including assistant buyers, buyers, department managers, section managers, store managers, division managers, regional managers, and vice president of merchandising. The following list describes the general duties of four of these positions; the precise nature of these duties may vary from one retail organization to another.

A section manager coordinates inventory and promotions and interacts with buyers, salespeople, and ultimate consumers. The manager performs merchandising, labor relations, and managerial activities, and usually works more than a 40-hour workweek.

The buyer's task is more focused. This fast-paced occupation involves much travel and pressure, and the need to be open-minded with respect to new, potentially successful items.

The regional manager coordinates the activities of several stores within a given area, usually monitoring and supporting sales, promotions, and general procedures.

The vice president of merchandising has a broad scope of managerial responsibility and reports to the organization's president.

Most retail organizations hire college graduates, put them through management training programs, and then place them directly in management positions. They frequently hire candidates with backgrounds in liberal arts or business administration. Sales positions and retail management positions offer the greatest employment opportunities for marketing students.

Retail management positions can be exciting and challenging. Competent, ambitious individuals often assume a great deal of responsibility very quickly and advance rapidly. However, a retail manager's job is physically demanding and sometimes entails long working hours. In addition, managers employed by large chain stores may be required to move frequently during their early years with the company. Nonetheless, positions in retail management often offer the chance to excel and gain promotion. Growth in retailing, which is expected to accompany the growth in population, is likely to create substantial opportunities during the next ten years. While a trainee may start in the $20,000 to $35,000 range, a store manager may earn an excess of $100,000 depending on the size of the store.[9]

Direct Marketing

One of the most dynamic areas in marketing is direct marketing, in which the seller uses one or more direct media (telephone, online, mail, print, or television) to solicit a response. The telephone is a major vehicle for selling many consumer products. Telemarketing is direct selling to customers using a variety of technological improvements in telecommunications. Direct mail catalogs appeal to such market segments as working women and people who find going to retail stores difficult or inconvenient. Newspapers and magazines offer great opportunity, particularly in special market segments. *Golf Digest,* for example, is obviously a good medium for selling golfing equipment. Cable television provides many opportunities for selling directly to consumers. Home shopping channels, for instance, have been very successful. The Internet offers numerous direct marketing opportunities.

The most important asset in direct marketing is experience. Employers often look to other industries to locate experienced professionals. This preference means that if you can get an entry-level position in direct marketing, you will have an advantage in developing a career.

Jobs in direct marketing include buyers, such as department store buyers, who select goods for catalog, telephone, or direct mail sales. Catalog managers develop marketing strategies for each new catalog that goes into the mail. Research/mail-list management involves developing lists of products that will sell in direct marketing and lists of names of consumers who are likely to respond to a direct mail effort. Order fulfillment managers direct the shipment of products once they are sold. The effectiveness of direct marketing is enhanced by periodic analysis of advertising and communications at all phases of contact with the consumer. Direct marketing involves all aspects of marketing decision making. Most positions in direct marketing involve planning and market analysis. Some direct marketing jobs involve the use of databases that include customer information, sales history, and other tracking data. A database manager might receive a salary of $54,000 to $89,000. A telemarketing director in business-to-business sales could receive a salary of $35,000.[10]

E-Marketing and Customer Relationship Management

Today only about 2.5 percent of all retail sales are conducted on the Internet, although experts project that figure will eventually reach 10–15 percent of all retail sales.[11] Currently, approximately one-half of all businesses order online. One characteristic of firms engaged in e-marketing is a renewed focus on relationship marketing by building customer loyalty and retaining customers—in other words, on customer relationship management (CRM). This focus on CRM is possible because of e-marketers' ability to target individual customers. This effort is enhanced over time as the customer invests more time and effort in "teaching" the firms what he or she wants.

Opportunities abound to combine information technology expertise with marketing knowledge. By providing an integrated communication system of websites, fax and telephone numbers, and personal contacts, marketers can personalize customer relationships. Careers exist for individuals who can integrate the Internet as a touch point with customers as part of effective CRM.

The use of laptops, cellular phones, digital music players, e-mail, voice mail, and other devices is necessary to maintain customer relationships and allow purchases on the Internet. A variety of jobs exist for marketers who have integrated technology into their work and job skills. Job titles include e-marketing manager, customer relationship manager, and e-services manager, as well as jobs in dot-coms.

Salaries in this rapidly growing area depend on technical expertise and experience. For example, a CRM customer service manager receives a salary in the $40,000 to $45,000 range. Database managers receive higher salaries of approximately $71,000 to $90,000. With five years of experience in e-marketing, individuals who are responsible for online product offerings can earn from $50,000 to $100,000.[12]

accessibility The ability to obtain information available on the Internet

accessory equipment Equipment that does not become part of the final physical product but is used in production or office activities

addressability A marketer's ability to identify customers before they make a purchase

advertising Paid nonpersonal communication about an organization and its products transmitted to a target audience through mass media

advertising appropriation Advertising budget for a specified period

advertising campaign Designing a series of advertisements and placing them in various advertising media to reach a particular target audience

advertising platform Basic issues or selling points to be included in the advertising campaign

advocacy advertising Promotes a company's position on a public issue

aesthetic modifications Changes to the sensory appeal of a product

agents Intermediaries that represent either buyers or sellers on a permanent basis

aided recall test A posttest that asks respondents to identify recent ads and provides clues to jog their memories

allowance A concession in price to achieve a desired goal

approach The manner in which a salesperson contacts a potential customer

arbitrary approach Budgeting for an advertising campaign as specified by a high-level executive in the firm

artwork An ad's illustrations and layout

Asia-Pacific Economic Cooperation (APEC) An alliance that promotes open trade and economic and technical cooperation among member nations throughout the world

atmospherics The physical elements in a store's design that appeal to consumers' emotions and encourage buying

attitude An individual's enduring evaluation of, feelings about, and behavioral tendencies toward an object or idea

attitude scale Means of measuring consumer attitudes by gauging the intensity of individuals' reactions to adjectives, phrases, or sentences about an object

average fixed cost The fixed cost per unit produced

average total cost The sum of the average fixed cost and the average variable cost

average variable cost The variable cost per unit produced

bait pricing Pricing an item in the product line low with the intention of selling a higher-priced item in the line

balance of trade The difference in value between a nation's exports and its imports

barter The trading of products

base-point pricing Geographic pricing combining factory price and freight charges from the base point nearest the buyer

benchmarking Comparing the quality of the firm's goods, services, or processes with that of the best-performing competitors

benefit segmentation The division of a market according to benefits that customers want from the product

Better Business Bureau A local, nongovernmental regulatory agency, supported by the local businesses, that helps settle problems between customers and specific business firms

blogs Web-based journals in which people can editorialize and interact with other Internet users

brand A name, term, design, symbol, or any other feature that identifies one marketer's product as distinct from those of other marketers

brand competitors Firms that market products with similar features and benefits to the same customers at similar prices

brand equity The marketing and financial value associated with a brand's strength in a market

brand extension Using an existing brand to brand a new product in a different product category

brand insistence The degree of brand loyalty in which a customer strongly prefers a specific brand and will accept no substitute

brand licensing An agreement whereby a company permits another organization to use its brand on other products for a licensing fee

brand loyalty A customer's favorable attitude toward a specific brand

brand manager The person responsible for a single brand

brand mark The part of a brand not made up of words

brand name The part of a brand that can be spoken

brand preference The degree of brand loyalty in which a customer prefers one brand over competitive offerings

brand recognition A customer's awareness that the brand exists and is an alternative purchase

breakdown approach Measuring company sales potential based on a general economic forecast for a specific period and the market potential derived from it

breakeven point The point at which the costs of producing a product equal the revenue made from selling the product

brokers Intermediaries that bring buyers and sellers together temporarily

buildup approach Measuring company sales potential by estimating how much of a product a potential buyer in a specific geographic area will purchase in a given period, multiplying the estimate by the number of potential buyers, and adding the totals of all the geographic areas considered

bundle pricing Packaging together two or more complementary products and selling them for a single price

business (organizational) buying behavior The purchase behavior of producers, government units, institutions, and resellers

business analysis Evaluating the potential contribution of a product idea to the firm's sales, costs, and profits

business cycle A pattern of economic fluctuations that has four stages: prosperity, recession, depression, and recovery

business market Individuals or groups that purchase a specific kind of product for resale, direct use in producing other products, or use in general daily operations

business products Products bought to use in an organization's operations, to resell, or to make other products

business services   The intangible products that many organizations use in their operations

buy-back allowance   A sum of money given to a reseller for each unit bought after an initial promotion deal is over

buying allowance   A temporary price reduction to resellers for purchasing specified quantities of a product

buying behavior   The decision processes and acts of people involved in buying and using products

buying center   The people within an organization, including users, influencers, buyers, deciders, and gatekeepers, who make business purchase decisions

buying power   Resources, such as money, goods, and services, which can be traded in an exchange

buzz marketing   An attempt to incite publicity and public excitement surrounding a product through a creative event

captioned photograph   A photo with a brief description of its contents

captive pricing   Pricing the basic product in a produce line low while pricing related items at a higher level

cash discount   A price reduction given to buyers for prompt payment or cash payment

cash-and-carry wholesalers   Limited-service wholesalers whose customers pay cash and furnish transportation

catalog marketing   A type of marketing in which an organization provides a catalog from which customers make selections and place orders by mail, telephone, or the Internet

category killer   A very large specialty store concentrating on a major product category and competing on the basis of low prices and product availability

category management   A retail strategy of managing groups of similar, often substitutable products produced by different manufacturers

cause-related marketing   The practice of linking products to a particular social cause on an ongoing or short-term basis

centralized organization   A structure in which top management delegates little authority to levels below it

cents-off offer   A promotion that lets buyers pay less than the regular price to encourage purchase

channel capacity   The limit on the volume of information a communication channel can handle effectively

channel power   The ability of one channel member to influence another member's goal achievement

client-based relationships   Interactions that result in satisfied customers who use a service repeatedly over time

closing   The stage in the selling process when the salesperson asks the prospect to buy the product

co-branding   Using two or more brands on one product

codes of conduct   Formalized rules and standards that describe what the company expects of its employees

coding process   Converting meaning into a series of signs or symbols

cognitive dissonance   A buyer's doubts shortly after a purchase about whether the decision was the right one

combination compensation plan   Paying salespeople a fixed salary plus a commission based on sales volume

commercialization   Deciding on full-scale manufacturing and marketing plans and preparing budgets

commission merchants   Agents that receive goods on consignment and negotiate sales in large, central markets

Common Market of the Southern Cone   An alliance that promotes the free circulation of goods, services, and production factors and has a common external tariff and commercial policy among member nations in South America

communication   A sharing of meaning

communications channel   The medium of transmission that carries the coded message from the source to the receiver or audience

community   A sense of group membership or feeling of belonging

community shopping centers   Shopping centers with one or two department stores, some specialty stores, and convenience stores

company sales potential   The maximum percentage of market potential that an individual firm can expect to obtain for a specific product

comparative advertising   Compares the sponsored brand with one or more identified brands on the basis of one or more product characteristics

comparison discounting   Setting a price at a specific level and comparing it with a higher price

competition   Other firms that market products that are similar to or can be substituted for a firm's products in the same geographic area

competition-based pricing   Pricing influenced primarily by competitors' prices

competition-matching approach   Determining an advertising budget by trying to match competitors' ad outlays

competitive advantage   The result of a company's matching a core competency to opportunities in the marketplace

competitive advertising   Tries to stimulate demand for a specific brand by promoting its features, uses, and advantages

component parts   Items that become part of the physical product and are either finished items ready for assembly or products that need little processing before assembly

concentrated targeting strategy   A strategy in which an organization targets a single market segment using one marketing mix

concept testing   Seeking potential buyers' responses to a product idea

conclusive research   Research designed to verify insights through objective procedures and to help marketers in making decisions

consideration set   A group of brands that a buyer views as alternatives for possible purchase

consistency of quality   The degree to which a product has the same level of quality over time

consumer buying behavior   Buying behavior of people who purchase products for personal or household use and not for business purposes

consumer buying decision process   A five-stage purchase decision process that includes problem recognition, information search, evaluation of alternatives, purchase, and postpurchase evaluation

consumer contests   Sales promotion methods in which individuals compete for prizes based on analytical or creative skills

consumer games   Sales promotion method in which individuals compete for prizes based primarily on chance

consumer jury   A panel of a product's actual or potential buyers who pretest ads

consumer market   Purchasers and household members who intend to consume or benefit from the purchased products and do not buy products to make profits

consumer products   Products purchased to satisfy personal and family needs

consumer sales promotion methods Ways of encouraging consumers to patronize specific stores or try particular products

consumer socialization The process through which a person acquires the knowledge and skills to function as a consumer

consumer sweepstakes A sales promotion in which entrants submit their names for inclusion in a drawing for prizes

consumerism Organized efforts by individuals, groups, and organizations to protect consumers' rights

contract manufacturing The practice of hiring a foreign firm to produce a designated volume of product to specification

control Customers' ability to regulate the information they view and the rate and sequence of their exposure to that information

convenience products Relatively inexpensive, frequently purchased items for which buyers exert minimal purchasing effort

convenience store A small self-service store that is open long hours and carries a narrow assortment of products, usually convenience items

cookie An identifying string of text stored on a website visitor's computer

cooperative advertising An arrangement in which a manufacturer agrees to pay a certain amount of a retailer's media costs for advertising the manufacturer's products

copy The verbal portion of advertisements

core competencies Things a firm does extremely well, which sometimes give it an advantage over its competition

corporate strategy A strategy that determines the means for using resources in the various functional areas to reach the organization's goals

cost comparison indicator A means of comparing the cost of vehicles in a specific medium in relation to the number of people reached

cost-based pricing Adding a dollar amount or percentage to the cost of the product

cost-plus pricing Adding a specified dollar amount or percentage to the seller's cost

coupons Written price reductions used to encourage consumers to buy a specific product

cultural relativism The concept that morality varies from one culture to another and that business practices are therefore differentially defined as right or wrong by particular cultures

culture The values, knowledge, beliefs, customs, objects, and concepts of a society

cumulative discounts Quantity discounts aggregated over a stated period

customary pricing Pricing on the basis of tradition

customer advisory boards Small groups of actual customers who serve as sounding boards for new-product ideas and offer insights into their feelings and attitudes toward a firm's products and other elements of marketing strategy

customer contact The level of interaction between provider and customer needed to deliver the service

customer forecasting survey A survey of customers regarding the types and quantities of products they intend to buy during a specific period

customer relationship management (CRM) Using information about customers to create marketing strategies that develop and sustain desirable customer relationships

customer services Human or mechanical efforts or activities that add value to a product

customers The purchasers of organizations' products; the focal point of all marketing activities

cycle analysis An analysis of sales figures for a period of three to five years to ascertain whether sales fluctuate in a consistent, periodic manner

cycle time The time needed to complete a process

database A collection of information arranged for easy access and retrieval

dealer listings An advertisement that promotes a product and identifies the names of participating retailers that sell the product

dealer loader A gift, often part of a display, given to a retailer purchasing a specified quantity of merchandise

decentralized organization A structure in which decision-making authority is delegated as far down the chain of command as possible

decline stage The stage of a product's life cycle when sales fall rapidly

decoding process Converting signs or symbols into concepts and ideas

Delphi technique A procedure in which experts create initial forecasts, submit them to the company for averaging, and then refine the forecasts

demand curve A graph of the quantity of products expected to be sold at various prices if other factors remain constant

demand-based pricing Pricing based on the level of demand for the product

demonstrations A sales promotion method manufacturers use temporarily to encourage trial use and purchase of a product or to show how a product works

department stores Large retail organizations characterized by wide product mixes and organized into separate departments to facilitate marketing and internal management

depth of product mix The average number of different product items offered in each product line

derived demand Demand for industrial products that stems from demand for consumer products

descriptive research Research conducted to clarify the characteristics of certain phenomena and thus solve a particular problem

differential pricing Charging different prices to different buyers for the same quality and quantity of product

differentiated targeting strategy A strategy in which an organization targets two or more segments by developing a marketing mix for each

digitalization The ability to represent a product, or at least some of its benefits, as digital bits of information

direct marketing The use of telecommunications and nonpersonal media to introduce products to consumers, who then can purchase them via mail, telephone, or the Internet

direct ownership A situation in which a company owns subsidiaries or other facilities overseas

direct response marketing A type of marketing that occurs when a retailer advertises a product and makes it available through mail or telephone orders

direct selling The marketing of products to ultimate consumers through face-to-face sales presentations at home or in the workplace

discount stores Self-service, general merchandise stores offering brand name and private brand products at low prices

discretionary income Disposable income available for spending and saving after an individual has purchased the basic necessities of food, clothing, and shelter

disposable income   After-tax income

distribution   The decisions and activities that make products available to customers when and where they want to purchase them

distribution centers   Large, centralized warehouses that focus on moving rather than storing goods

drop shippers   Limited-service wholesalers that take title to products and negotiate sales but never take actual possession of products

dual distribution   The use of two or more channels to distribute the same product to the same target market

dumping   Selling products at unfairly low prices

early adopters   Careful choosers of new products

early majority   Those adopting new products just before the average person

electronic commerce (or e-commerce)   Business exchanges conducted over the Internet using telecommunications tools such as web pages, e-mail, and instant/text messaging

electronic data interchange (EDI)   A computerized means of integrating order processing with production, inventory, accounting, and transportation

electronic marketing (or e-marketing)   The strategic process of creating, distributing, promoting, and pricing products for targeted customers in the virtual environment of the Internet

embargo   A government's suspension of trade in a particular product or with a given country

empowerment   Giving customer-contact employees authority and responsibility to make marketing decisions on their own

environmental analysis   The process of assessing and interpreting the information gathered through environmental scanning

environmental scanning   The process of collecting information about forces in the marketing environment

ethical issue   An identifiable problem, situation, or opportunity requiring a choice among several actions that must be elevated as right or wrong, ethical or unethical

European Union (EU)   An alliance that promotes trade among its member countries in Europe

evaluative criteria   Objective and subjective characteristics that are important to a buyer

everyday low prices (EDLP)   Setting a low price for products on a consistent basis

exchange controls   Government restrictions on the amount of a particular currency that can be bought or sold

exchanges   The provision or transfer of goods, services, or ideas in return for something of value

exclusive distribution   Using a single outlet in a fairly large geographic area to distribute a product

executive judgment   Sales forecasting based on the intuition of one or more executives

experimental research   Research that allows marketers to make causal inferences about relationships

expert forecasting survey   Sales forecasts prepared by experts such as economists, management consultants, advertising executives, college professors, or other persons outside the firm

exploratory research   Research conducted to gather more information about a problem or to make a tentative hypothesis more specific

exporting   The sale of products to foreign markets

extended problem solving   A type of consumer problem-solving process employed when purchasing unfamiliar, expensive, or infrequently bought products

external customers   Individuals who patronize a business

external reference price   A comparison price provided by others

external search   An information search in which buyers seek information from outside sources

F.O.B. destination   A price indicating the producer is absorbing shipping costs

F.O.B. factory   The price of the merchandise at the factory, before shipment

family branding   Branding all of a firm's products with the same name

family packaging   Using similar packaging for all of a firm's products or packaging that has one common design element

feature article   A manuscript of up to 3,000 words prepared for a specific publication

Federal Trade Commission (FTC)   An agency that regulates a variety of business practices and curbs false advertising, misleading pricing, and deceptive packaging and labeling

feedback   The receiver's response to a message

fixed costs   Costs that do not vary with changes in the number of units produced or sold

focus-group interview   A research method involving observation of group interaction when members are exposed to an idea or a concept

franchising   A form of licensing in which a franchiser, in exchange for a financial commitment, grants a franchisee the right to market its product in accordance with the franchiser's standards

franchising   An arrangement in which a supplier (franchiser) grants a dealer (franchisee) the right to sell products in exchange for some type of consideration

free merchandise   A manufacturer's reward given to resellers for purchasing a stated quantity of products

free samples   Samples of a product given out to encourage trial and purchase

freight absorption pricing   Absorption of all or part of actual freight costs by the seller

freight forwarders   Organizations that consolidate shipments from several firms into efficient lot sizes

full-service wholesalers   Merchant wholesalers that perform the widest range of wholesaling functions

functional modifications   Changes affecting a product's versatility, effectiveness, convenience, or safety

General Agreement on Tariffs and Trade (GATT)   An agreement among nations to reduce worldwide tariffs and increase international trade

general merchandise retailer   A retail establishment that offers a variety of product lines that are stocked in considerable depth

general merchandise wholesalers   Full-service wholesalers with a wide product mix but limited depth within product lines

general-line wholesalers   Full-service wholesalers that carry only a few product lines but many products within those lines

generic brands   Brands indicating only the product category

generic competitors   Firms that provide very different products that solve the same problem or satisfy the same basic customer need

geodemographic segmentation   Marketing segmentation that clusters people in zip code areas and smaller neighborhood units based on lifestyle and demographic information

geographic pricing   Reductions for transportation and other costs related to the physical distance between buyer and seller

globalization The development of marketing strategies that treat the entire world (or its major regions) as a single entity

good A tangible physical entity

government markets Federal, state, county, and local governments that buy goods and services to support their internal operations and provide products to their constituencies

green marketing The specific development, pricing, promotion, and distribution of products that do not harm the natural environment

gross domestic product (GDP) The market value of a nation's total output of goods and services for a given period; an overall measure of economic standing

growth stage The stage of a product's life cycle when sales rise rapidly and profits reach a peak and then start to decline

heterogeneity Variation in quality

heterogeneous markets Markets made up of individuals or organizations with diverse needs for products in a specific product class

homogeneous market A market in which a large proportion of customers have similar needs for a product

horizontal channel integration Combining organizations at the same level of operation under one management

hypermarkets Stores that combine supermarket and discount store shopping in one location

hypothesis An informed guess or assumption about a certain problem or set of circumstances

idea A concept, philosophy, image, or issue

idea generation Seeking product ideas to achieve objectives

illustrations Photos, drawings, graphs, charts, and tables used to spark audience interest

import tariff A duty levied by a nation on goods bought outside its borders and brought in

importing The purchase of products from a foreign source

impulse buying An unplanned buying behavior resulting from a powerful urge to buy something immediately

individual branding A policy of naming each product differently

industrial distributor An independent business that takes title to business products and carries inventories

inelastic demand Demand that is not significantly altered by a price increase or decrease

information inputs Sensations received through the sense organs

in-home (door-to-door) interview A personal interview that takes place in the respondent's home

innovators First adopters of new products

inseparability Being produced and consumed at the same time

installations Facilities and nonportable major equipment

institutional advertising Promotes organizational images, ideas, and political issues

institutional markets Organizations with charitable, educational, community, or other nonbusiness goals

intangibility A service that is not physical and cannot be touched

integrated marketing communications (IMC) Coordination of promotional efforts for maximum informational and persuasive impact

intended strategy The strategy the company decides on during the planning phase

intensive distribution Using all available outlets to distribute a product

interactivity The ability to allow customers to express their needs and wants directly to the firm in response to the firm's marketing communications

intermodal transportation Two or more transportation modes used in combination

internal customers A company's employees

internal marketing Coordinating internal exchanges between the firm and its employees to achieve successful external exchanges between the firm and its customers

internal reference price A price developed in the buyer's mind through experience with the product

internal search An information search in which buyers search their memories for information about products that might solve their problem

international marketing Developing and performing marketing activities across national boundaries

introduction stage The initial stage of a product's life cycle—its first appearance in the marketplace—when sales start at zero and profits are negative

inventory management Developing and maintaining adequate assortments of products to meet customers' needs

joint demand Demand involving the use of two or more items in combination to produce a product

joint venture A partnership between a domestic firm and a foreign firm or government

just-in-time (JIT) An inventory-management approach in which supplies arrive just when needed for production or resale

kinesic communication Communicating through the movement of head, eyes, arms, hands, legs, or torso

labeling Providing identifying, promotional, or other information on package labels

laggards The last adopters, who distrust new products

late majority Skeptics who adopt new products when they feel it is necessary

layout The physical arrangement of an ad's illustration and copy

learning Changes in an individual's thought processes and behavior caused by information and experience

level of involvement An individual's degree of interest in a product and the importance of the product for that person

level of quality The amount of quality a product possesses

licensing An alternative to direct investment requiring a licensee to pay commissions or royalties on sales or supplies used in manufacturing

lifestyle An individual's pattern of living expressed through activities, interests, and opinions

lifestyle shopping centers A type of shopping center that is typically open air and features upscale specialty, dining, and entertainment stores

limited problem solving A type of consumer problem-solving process that buyers use when purchasing products occasionally or when they need information about an unfamiliar brand in a familiar product category

limited-service wholesalers Merchant wholesalers that provide some services and specialize in a few functions

line extension Development of a product that is closely related to existing products in the line but meets different customer needs

mail survey A research method in which respondents answer a questionnaire sent through the mail

mail-order wholesalers Limited-service wholesalers that sell products through catalogs

manufacturer brands Brands initiated by producers

manufacturers' agents Independent intermediaries that represent two or more sellers and offer complete product lines

marginal cost (MC) The extra cost a firm incurs by producing one more unit of a product

marginal revenue (MR) The change in total revenue resulting from the sale of an additional unit of a product

market A group of individuals and/or organizations that have needs for products in a product class and have the ability, willingness, and authority to purchase those products

market density The number of potential customers within a unit of land area

market manager The person responsible for managing the marketing activities that serve a particular group of customers

market opportunity A combination of circumstances and timing that permits an organization to take action to reach a target market

market potential The total amount of a product that customers will purchase within a specified period at a specific level of industrywide marketing activity

market segment Individuals, groups, or organizations with one or more similar characteristics that cause them to have similar product needs

market segmentation The process of dividing a total market into groups with relatively similar product needs to design a marketing mix that matches those needs

market share The percentage of a market that actually buys a specific product from a particular company

market test Making a product available to buyers in one or more test areas and measuring purchases and consumer responses

market-growth/market-share matrix A strategic planning tool based on the philosophy that a product's market growth rate and market share are important in determining marketing strategy

marketing The process of creating, distributing, promoting, and pricing goods, services, and ideas to facilitate satisfying exchange relationships with customers and to develop and maintain favorable relationships with stakeholders in a dynamic environment

marketing channel A group of individuals and organizations directing the flow of products from producers to customers

marketing citizenship The adoption of a strategic focus for fulfilling the economic, legal, ethical, and philanthropic social responsibilities expected by stakeholders

marketing concept A managerial philosophy that an organization should try to satisfy customers' needs through a coordinated set of activities that also allows the organization to achieve its goals

marketing control process Establishing performance standards and trying to match actual performance to those standards

marketing decision support system (MDSS) Customized computer software that aids marketing managers in decision making

marketing environment The competitive, economic, political, legal and regulatory, technological, and sociocultural forces that surround the customer and affect the marketing mix

marketing ethics Principles and standards that define acceptable marketing conduct as determined by various stakeholders

marketing implementation The process of putting marketing strategies into action

marketing information system (MIS) A framework for the management and structuring of information gathered regularly from sources inside and outside an organization

marketing intermediary A middleman linking producers to other middlemen or ultimate consumers through contractual arrangements or through the purchase and resale of products

marketing management The process of planning, organizing, implementing, and controlling marketing activities to facilitate exchanges effectively and efficiently

marketing mix Four marketing activities—product, pricing, distribution, and promotion—that a firm can control to meet the needs of customers within its target market

marketing objective A statement of what is to be accomplished through marketing activities

marketing orientation An organizationwide commitment to researching and responding to customer needs

marketing plan A written document that specifies the activities to be performed to implement and control an organization's marketing activities

marketing planning The process of assessing opportunities and resources, determining objectives, defining strategies, and establishing guidelines for implementation and control of the marketing program

marketing research The systematic design, collection, interpretation, and reporting of information to help marketers solve specific marketing problems or take advantage of marketing opportunities

marketing strategy A plan of action for identifying and analyzing a target market and developing a marketing mix to meet the needs of that market

markup pricing Adding to the cost of the product a predetermined percentage of that cost

Maslow's hierarchy of needs The five levels of needs that humans seek to satisfy, from most to least important

materials handling Physical handling of tangible goods, supplies, and resources

maturity stage The stage of a product's life cycle when the sales curve peaks and starts to decline as profits continue to fall

media plan Specifies media vehicles and schedule for running the advertisements

megacarriers Freight transportation firms that provide several modes of shipment

memory The ability to access databases or data warehouses containing individual customer profiles and past purchase histories and to use these data in real time to customize a marketing offer

merchandise allowance A manufacturer's agreement to pay resellers certain amounts of money for providing special promotional efforts

merchant wholesalers Independently owned businesses that take title to goods, assume ownership risks, and buy and resell products to other wholesalers, business customers, or retailers

micromarketing An approach to market segmentation in which organizations focus precise marketing efforts on very small geographic markets

mission statement A long-term view of what the organization wants to become

missionary salespeople Support salespersons who assist the producer's customers in selling to their own customers

modified-rebuy purchase A new-task purchase that is changed on subsequent orders or when the requirements of a straight-rebuy purchase are modified

money refunds A sales promotion technique offering consumers money when they mail in a proof of purchase, usually for multiple product purchases

monopolistic competition A competitive structure in which a firm has many potential competitors and tries to develop a marketing strategy to differentiate its product

monopoly A competitive structure in which an organization offers a product that has no close substitutes, making that organization the sole source of supply

motive An internal energizing force that directs a person's behavior toward satisfying needs or achieving goals

MRO supplies Maintenance, repair, and operating items that facilitate production and operations but do not become part of the finished product

multinational enterprise Firms that have operations or subsidiaries in many countries

multiple sourcing An organization's decision to use several suppliers

multiple-unit pricing Packaging together two or more identical products and selling them for a single price

National Advertising Review Board (NARB) A self-regulatory unit that considers challenges to issues raised by the National Advertising Division (an arm of the Council of Better Business Bureaus) about an advertisement

negotiated pricing Establishing a final price through bargaining

neighborhood shopping centers Shopping centers usually consisting of several small convenience and specialty stores

new-product development process A seven-phase process for introducing products

news release A short piece of copy publicizing an event or a product

new-task purchase An initial purchase by an organization of an item to be used to perform a new job or solve a new problem

noise Anything that reduces a communication's clarity and accuracy

noncumulative discounts One-time reductions in price based on specific factors

nonprice competition Emphasizing factors other than price to distinguish a product from competing brands

nonprobability sampling A sampling technique in which there is no way to calculate the likelihood that a specific element of the population being studied will be chosen

North American Free Trade Agreement (NAFTA) An alliance that merges Canada, Mexico, and the United States into a single market

North American Industry Classification System (NAICS) An industry classification system that will generate comparable statistics among the United States, Canada, and Mexico

objective-and-task approach Budgeting for an advertising campaign by first determining its objectives and then calculating the cost of all the tasks needed to attain them

odd-even pricing Ending the price with certain numbers to influence buyers' perceptions of the price or product

off-price retailers Stores that buy manufacturers' seconds, overruns, returns, and off-season merchandise for resale to consumers at deep discounts

oligopoly A competitive structure in which a few sellers control the supply of a large proportion of a product

online retailing Retailing that makes products available to buyers through computer connections

online survey A research method in which respondents answer a questionnaire via e-mail or on a website

opinion leader A reference group member who provides information about a specific sphere that interests reference group participants

order getter The salesperson who sells to new customers and increases sales to current ones

order processing The receipt and transmission of sales-order information

order takers Salespersons who primarily seek repeat sales

outsourcing The practice of contracting manufacturing or other tasks to companies in countries where labor and supplies are less expensive

outsourcing The contracting of physical distribution tasks to third parties who do not have managerial authority within the marketing channel

patronage motives Motives that influence where a person purchases products on a regular basis

penetration pricing Setting prices below those of competing brands to penetrate a market and gain a significant market share quickly

percent-of-sales approach Budgeting for an advertising campaign by multiplying the firm's past or expected sales by a standard percentage

perception The process of selecting, organizing, and interpreting information inputs to produce meaning

performance standard An expected level of performance

periodic discounting Temporary reduction of prices on a patterned or systematic basis

perishability The inability of unused service capacity to be stored for future use

personal selling Paid personal communication that informs customers and persuades them to buy products

personal-interview survey A research method in which participants respond to survey questions face to face

personality A set of internal traits and distinct behavioral tendencies that result in consistent patterns of behavior

physical distribution Activities used to move products from producers to consumers and other end users

pioneer advertising Tries to stimulate demand for a product category rather than a specific brand by informing potential buyers about the product

pioneer promotion Promotion that informs consumers about a new product

point-of-purchase (P-O-P) materials Signs, window displays, display racks, and similar means used to attract customers

population All the elements, units, or individuals of interest to researchers for a specific study

portal A multiservice website that serves as a gateway to other websites

posttest Evaluation of advertising effectiveness after the campaign

power shopping centers A type of shopping center that combines off-price stores with category killers

premium money (or push money) Also called push money; extra compensation to salespeople for pushing a line of goods

premium pricing Pricing the highest-quality or most versatile products higher than other models in the product line

premiums Items offered free or at a minimal cost as a bonus for purchasing a product

press conference A meeting used to announce major news events

prestige pricing Setting prices at an artificially high level to convey prestige or a quality image

prestige-sensitive Drawn to products that signify prominence and status

pretest Evaluation of ads performed before a campaign begins

price Value exchanged for products in a marketing transaction

price competition Emphasizing price and matching or beating competitors' prices

price discrimination Providing price differentials that injure competition by giving one or more buyers a competitive advantage

price elasticity of demand A measure of the sensitivity of demand to changes in price

price leaders Product priced below the usual markup, near cost, or below cost

price lining Setting a limited number of prices for selected groups or lines of merchandise

price skimming Charging the highest possible price that buyers who most desire the product will pay

price-conscious Striving to pay low prices

pricing objectives Goals that describe what a firm wants to achieve through pricing

primary data Data observed and recorded or collected directly from respondents

primary demand Demand for a product category rather than for a specific brand

private distributor brands Brands initiated and owned by resellers

private warehouses Company-operated facilities for storing and shipping products

probability sampling A sampling technique in which every element in the population being studied has a known chance of being selected for study

process materials Materials that are used directly in the production of other products but are not readily identifiable

producer markets Individuals and business organizations that purchase products to make profits by using them to produce other products or using them in their operations

product A good, a service, or an idea

product adoption process The stages buyers go through in accepting a product

product advertising Promotes products' uses, features, and benefits

product competitors Firms that compete in the same product class but market products with different features, benefits, and prices

product deletion Eliminating a product from the product mix

product design How a product is conceived, planned, and produced

product development Determining if producing a product is technically feasible and cost effective

product differentiation Creating and designing products so that customers perceive them as different from competing products

product features Specific design characteristics that allow a product to perform certain tasks

product item A specific version of a product that can be designated as a distinct offering among a firm's products

product life cycle The progression of a product through four stages: introduction, growth, maturity, and decline

product line A group of closely related product items viewed as a unit because of marketing, technical, or end-use considerations

product manager The person within an organization responsible for a product, a product line, or several distinct products that make up a group

product mix The total group of products that an organization makes available to customers

product modification Change in one or more characteristics of a product

product placement The strategic location of products or product promotions within television program content to reach the product's target market

product positioning Creating and maintaining a certain concept of a product in customers' minds

product-line pricing Establishing and adjusting prices of multiple products within a product line

professional pricing Fees set by people with great skill or experience in a particular field

promotion Communication to build and maintain relationships by informing and persuading one or more audiences

promotion mix A combination of promotional methods used to promote a specific product

prospecting Developing a list of potential customers

proxemic communication Communicating by varying the physical distance in face-to-face interactions

psychological influences Factors that partly determine people's general behavior, thus influencing their behavior as consumers

psychological pricing Pricing that attempts to influence a customer's perception of price to make a product's price more attractive

public relations Communication efforts used to create and maintain favorable relations between an organization and its stakeholders

public warehouses Businesses that lease storage space and related physical distribution facilities to other firms

publicity A news story type of communication transmitted through a mass medium at no charge

pull policy Promoting a product directly to consumers to develop strong consumer demand that pulls products through the marketing channel

pure competition A market structure characterized by an extremely large number of sellers, none strong enough to significantly influence price or supply

push policy Promoting a product only to the next institution down the marketing channel

quality Characteristics of a product that allow it to perform as expected in satisfying customer needs

quality modifications Changes relating to a product's dependability and durability

quantity discounts Deductions from list price for purchasing large quantities

quota A limit on the amount of goods an importing country will accept for certain product categories in a specific time period

quota sampling   A nonprobability sampling technique in which researchers divide the population into groups and then arbitrarily choose participants from each group

rack jobbers   Full-service, specialty-line wholesalers that own and maintain display racks in stores

random discounting   Temporary reduction of prices on an unsystematic basis

random factor analysis   An analysis attempting to attribute erratic sales variation to random, nonrecurrent events

random sampling   A type of probability sampling in which all units in a population have an equal chance of appearing in a sample

raw materials   Basic natural materials that become part of a physical product

realized strategy   The strategy that actually takes place

rebates   A sales promotion technique whereby a customer is sent a specific amount of money for purchasing a single product

receiver   The individual, group, or organization that decodes a coded message

reciprocity   An arrangement unique to business marketing in which two organizations agree to buy from each other

recognition test   A posttest in which individuals are shown the actual ad and asked if they recognize it

reference group   Any group that positively or negatively affects a person's values, attitudes, or behavior

reference pricing   Pricing a product at a moderate level and displaying it next to a more expensive model or brand

regional issues   Versions of a magazine that differ across geographic regions

regional shopping centers   A type of shopping center with the largest department stores, the widest product mix, and the deepest product lines of all shopping centers

regression analysis   A method of predicting sales based on finding a relationship between past sales and one or more variables, such as population or income

reinforcement advertising   Assures users they chose the right brand and tells them how to get the most satisfaction from it

relationship marketing   Establishing long-term, mutually satisfying buyer-seller relationships

relationship selling   The building of mutually beneficial long-term associations with a customer through regular communications over prolonged periods of time

reliability   A condition existing when a research technique produces almost identical results in repeated trials

reminder advertising   Reminds consumers about an established brand's uses, characteristics, and benefits

research design   An overall plan for obtaining the information needed to address a research problem or issue

reseller markets   Intermediaries who buy finished goods and resell them for profit

retail positioning   Identifying an unserved or underserved market segment and serving it through a strategy that distinguishes the retailer from others in the minds of consumers in that segment

retailer   An organization that purchases products for the purpose of reselling them to ultimate consumers

retailing   All transactions in which the buyer intends to consume the product through personal, family, or household use

role   Actions and activities that a person in a particular position is supposed to perform based on expectations of the individual and surrounding persons

routinized response behavior   A type of consumer problem-solving process used when buying frequently purchased, low-cost items that require very little search and decision effort

sales branches   Manufacturer owned intermediaries that sell products and provide support services to the manufacturer's sales force

sales contest   A promotion method used to motivate distributors, retailers, and sales personnel through recognition of outstanding achievements

sales force forecasting survey   A survey of a firm's sales force regarding anticipated sales in their territories for a specified period

sales forecast   The amount of a product a company expects to sell during a specific period at a specified level of marketing activities

sales offices   Manufacturer owned operations that provide services normally associated with agents

sales promotion   An activity and/or material meant to induce resellers or salespeople to sell a product or consumers to buy it

sample   A limited number of units chosen to represent the characteristics of the population

sampling   The process of selecting representative units from a total population

scan-back allowance   A manufacturer's reward to retailers based on the number of pieces scanned

scrambled merchandising   The addition of unrelated products and product lines to an existing product mix, particularly fast-moving items that can be sold in volume

screening   Choosing the most promising ideas for further review

seasonal analysis   An analysis of daily, weekly, or monthly sales figures to evaluate the degree to which seasonal factors influence sales

seasonal discount   A price reduction given to buyers for purchasing goods or services out of season

secondary data   Data compiled both inside and outside the organization for some purpose other than the current investigation

secondary-market pricing   Setting one price for the primary target market and a different price for another market

segmentation variables   Characteristics of individuals, groups, or organizations used to divide a market into segments

selective demand   Demand for a specific brand

selective distortion   An individual's changing or twisting of information when it is inconsistent with personal feelings or beliefs

selective distribution   Using only some available outlets to distribute a product

selective exposure   The process of selecting inputs to be exposed to our awareness while ignoring others

selective retention   Remembering information inputs that support personal feelings and beliefs and forgetting inputs that do not

self-concept   Perception or view of oneself

selling agents   Intermediaries that market a whole product line or a manufacturer's entire output

service   An intangible result of the application of human and mechanical efforts to people or objects

shopping products   Items for which buyers are willing to expend considerable effort in planning and making purchases

shopping-mall intercept interviews   A research method that involves interviewing a percentage of persons passing by "intercept" points in a mall

single-source data   Information provided by a single marketing research firm

situational influences   Influences resulting from circumstances, time, and location that affect the consumer buying decision process

social class   An open group of individuals with similar social rank

social influences   The forces other people exert on one's buying behavior

social responsibility   An organization's obligation to maximize its positive impact and minimize its negative impact on society

sociocultural forces   The influences in a society and its culture(s) that change people's attitudes, beliefs, norms, customs, and lifestyles

sole sourcing   An organization's decision to use only one supplier

source   A person, group, or organization with a meaning it tries to share

spam   Unsolicited commercial e-mail

special-event pricing   Advertised sales or price cutting linked to a holiday, season, or event

specialty products   Items with unique characteristics that buyers are willing to expend considerable effort to obtain

specialty-line wholesalers   Full-service wholesalers that carry only a single product line or a few items within a product line

stakeholders   Constituents who have a "stake" or claim in some aspect of a company's products, operations, markets, industry, and outcomes

statistical interpretation   Analysis of what is typical or what deviates from the average

storyboard   A mockup combining copy and visual material to show the sequence of major scenes in a commercial

straight commission compensation plan   Paying salespeople according to the amount of their sales in a given time period

straight salary compensation plan   Paying salespeople a specific amount per time period, regardless of selling effort

straight-rebuy purchase   A routine purchase of the same products under approximately the same terms of sale by a business buyer

strategic alliances   Partnerships formed to create a competitive advantage on a worldwide basis

strategic business unit (SBU)   A division, product line, or other profit center within a parent company

strategic channel alliance   An agreement whereby the products of one organization are distributed through the marketing channels of another

strategic philanthropy   The synergistic use of organizational core competencies and resources to address key stakeholders' interests and achieve both organizational and social benefits

strategic planning   The process of establishing an organizational mission and formulating goals, corporate strategy, marketing objectives, marketing strategy, and a marketing plan

strategic windows   Temporary periods of optimal fit between the key requirements of a market and a firm's capabilities

stratified sampling   A type of probability sampling in which the population is divided into groups according to a common attribute, and a random sample is then chosen within each group

styling   The physical appearance of a product

subculture   A group of individuals whose characteristic values and behavior patterns are similar to and differ from those of the surrounding culture

supermarkets   Large, self-service stores that carry a complete line of food products, along with some nonfood products

superregional shopping centers   A type of shopping center with the widest and deepest product mixes that attracts customers from many miles away

superstores   Giant retail outlets that carry food and nonfood products found in supermarkets, as well as most routinely purchased consumer products

supply-chain management   Long-term partnerships among marketing-channel members that reduce inefficiencies, costs, and redundancies and develop innovative approaches to satisfy customers

support personnel   Sales staff members who facilitate selling but usually are not involved solely with making sales

sustainable competitive advantage   An advantage that the competition cannot copy

SWOT analysis   A tool that marketers use to assess an organization's strengths, weaknesses, opportunities, and threats

tactile communication   Communicating through touching

target audience   The group of people at whom advertisements are aimed

target market   A specific group of customers on whom an organization focuses its marketing efforts

team selling   The use of a team of experts from all functional areas of a firm, led by a salesperson, to conduct the personal selling process

technical salespeople   Support salespersons who give technical assistance to a firm's current customers

technology   The application of knowledge and tools to solve problems and perform tasks more efficiently

telemarketing   The performance of marketing-related activities by telephone

telephone depth interview   An interview that combines the traditional focus group's ability to probe with the confidentiality provided by telephone surveys

telephone survey   A research method in which respondents' answers to a questionnaire are recorded by interviewers on the phone

television home shopping   A form of selling in which products are presented to television viewers, who can buy them by calling a toll-free number and paying with a credit card

test marketing   Introducing a product on a limited basis to measure the extent to which potential customers will actually buy it

time-series analysis   A forecasting method that uses historical sales data to discover patterns in the firm's sales over time and generally involves trend, cycle, seasonal, and random factor analyses

total budget competitors   Firms that compete for the limited financial resources of the same customers

total cost   The sum of average fixed and average variable costs times the quantity produced

total quality management (TQM)   A philosophy that uniform commitment to quality in all areas of the organization will promote a culture that meets customers' perceptions of quality

trade (functional) discount   Also known as functional discount; a reduction off the list price given by a producer to an intermediary for performing certain functions

trade name Full legal name of an organization

trade sales promotion methods Ways of persuading wholesalers and retailers to carry a producer's products and market them aggressively

trade salespeople Salespersons involved mainly in helping a producer's customers promote a product

trademark A legal designation of exclusive use of a brand

traditional specialty retailers Stores that carry a narrow product mix with deep product lines

transfer pricing Prices charged in sales between an organization's units

transportation The movement of products from where they are made to intermediaries and end users

trend analysis An analysis that focuses on aggregate sales data over a period of many years to determine general trends in annual sales

truck wholesalers Limited-service wholesalers that transport products directly to customers for inspection and selection

unaided recall test A posttest in which respondents identify ads they have recently seen but are given no recall clues

undifferentiated targeting strategy A strategy in which an organization designs a single marketing mix and directs it at the entire market for a particular product

uniform geographic pricing Charging all customers the same price, regardless of geographic location

unsought products Products purchased to solve a sudden problem, products of which customers are unaware, and products that people do not necessarily think about buying

validity A condition existing when a research method measures what it is supposed to measure

value A customer's subjective assessment of benefits relative to costs in determining the worth of a product

value analysis An evaluation of each component of a potential purchase

value-conscious Concerned about price and quality of a product

variable costs Costs that vary directly with changes in the number of units produced or sold

vendor analysis A formal, systematic evaluation of current and potential vendors

venture team A cross-functional group that creates entirely new products that may be aimed at new markets

vertical channel integration Combining two or more stages of the marketing channel under one management

vertical marketing systems (VMSs) A marketing channel managed by a single channel member

viral marketing A strategy to get consumers to share a marketer's message, often through e-mail or online video, in a way that spreads dramatically and quickly

warehouse clubs Large-scale members-only establishments that combine features of cash-and-carry wholesaling with discount retailing

warehouse showrooms Retail facilities in large, low-cost buildings with large on-premises inventories and minimal services

warehousing The design and operation of facilities for storing and moving goods

wheel of retailing A hypothesis holding that new retailers usually enter the market as low-status, low-margin, low-price operators but eventually evolve into high-cost, high-price merchants

wholesaler An individual or organization that sells products that are bought for resale, for making other products, or for general business operations

wholesaling Transactions in which products are bought for resale, for making other products, or for general business operations

width of product mix The number of product lines a company offers

wikis Software that create an interface that enables users to add or edit the content of some types of websites (also called wikis or wikipages)

willingness to spend An inclination to buy because of expected satisfaction from a product, influenced by the ability to buy and numerous psychological and social forces

word-of-mouth communication Personal informal exchanges of communication that customers share with one another about products, brands, and companies

World Trade Organization (WTO) An entity that promotes free trade among member nations

zone pricing Pricing based on transportation costs within major geographic zones

Notes

CHAPTER 1

1. Eric Bangeman, "Sirius CEO Talks Merger," *Ars Technica,* November 27, 2006, http://arstechnica.com/news.ars/post/20061127-8293.html; Dan Thanh Dang, "Satellite Radio Industry Continues to Grow, Enter Mainstream," *The Baltimore Sun,* November 16, 2003, www.sunspot.net; Stephen Holden, "High-Tech Quirkiness Restores Radio's Magic," *The New York Times,* December 26, 2003, p. E1; "In Brief, Radio: XM Radio Ends '03 with 1.36 Million Users," *The Los Angeles Times,* January 8, 2004, p. C3; Kevin Kingsbury, "Howard Stern Gets More Shares of Sirius after Subscriber Growth," *The Wall Street Journal,* January 9, 2007, http://online.wsj.com; David Pogue, "Satellite Radio Extends Its Orbit," *The New York Times,* December 18, 2003, p. G1; "Satellite Scramble," *The Wall Street Journal,* http://online.wsj.com/documents/info-satellite04.html?printVersion=true (accessed January 18, 2007); "Sirius Satellite Radio Hits Three Million Subscribers," *The Wall Street Journal,* December 27, 2005, http://online.wsj.com; Brad Stone, "Greetings, Earthlings: Satellite Radio for Cars Is Taking Off and Adding New Features—Now Broadcasters Are Starting to Fight Back," *Newsweek,* January 26, 2003, p. 55; David Welch, "Satellite Radio: Two for the Road," *BusinessWeek,* November. 24, 2003, p. 144; Guy Wire, "Satellite in Trouble as HD Grows," *RW Online,* August 23, 2006, www.rwonline.com/pages/s.0048/t.258.html; XM Radio Fast Facts, www.xmradio.com/about/fast-facts/consumer.xmc (accessed January 18, 2007).

2. *Dictionary of Marketing Terms,* American Marketing Association, www.marketingpower.com/mg-dictionary.php?SearchFor=marketing&Searched=1 (accessed January 18, 2007).

3. Julie Schlosser, "DeWalt," in "Breakaway Brands," *Fortune,* October 31, 2005, pp. 156–158.

4. Mark Jewell, "Dunkin' Donuts Eyes Turn Westward: Chain Evolves from No Frills," *The [Fort Collins] Coloradoan,* January 17, 2005, p. E1.

5. Tom Lowry, "Wow! Yao!" *BusinessWeek,* October 25, 2004, pp. 86–90.

6. Kelly K. Spors, "Beyond Flowers: New Funeral Options Proliferate," *The Wall Street Journal,* October 19, 2005, p. D2, http://online.wsj.com/.

7. Lorrie Grant, "Scrimping to Splurge," *USA Today,* January 28, 2005, p. 1B.

8. Janet Adamy, "For Subway, Every Nook and Cranny on the Planet Is Possible Site for a Franchise," *The Wall Street Journal,* September 1, 2006, p. A11, http://online.wsj.com/.

9. Sauce Co., www.greatsauce.com (accessed May 16, 2007).

10. Mike Beirne, "Kibbles 'n Bits Freshens Poochie Smooches," *BrandWeek,* September 11, 2006, www.brandweek.com/bw/news/packaged/article_display.jsp?vnu_content_id=1003119801.

11. Eric Bontrager, "U.S. to Consumers: Turn Down Heat," *The Wall Street Journal,* October 4, 2005, p. D2, http://online.wsj.com/; Matthew L. Wald, "Shifting Message, Energy Officials Announce Conservation Plan," *The New York Times,* October 4, 2005, www.nytimes.com.

12. Joseph B. White, "Detroit Finally Learns Tough Lesson," *The Wall Street Journal,* September 11, 2006, http://online.wsj.com.

13. Chad Terhune, "Pepsi Outlines Ad Campaign for Healthy Food," *The Wall Street Journal,* October 15, 2005, p. A4, http://online.wsj.com/.

14. Ajay K. Kohli and Bernard J. Jaworski, "Market Orientation: The Construct, Research Propositions, and Managerial Implications," *Journal of Marketing,* April 1990, pp. 1–18; O. C. Ferrell, "Business Ethics and Customer Stakeholders," *Academy of Management Executive* 18 (May 2004): 126–129.

15. Eugene W. Anderson, Claes Fornell, and Sanal K. Mazvancheryl, "Customer Satisfaction and Shareholder Value," *Journal of Marketing,* October 2004, pp. 172–185.

16. Kohli and Jaworski, "Market Orientation: The Construct, Research Propositions, and Managerial Implications."

17. Kwaku Atuahene-Gima, "Resolving the Capability-Rigidity Paradox in New Product Innovation," *Journal of Marketing* 69 (October 2005): 61–83.

18. Gary F. Gebhardt, Gregory S. Carpenter, and John F. Sherry, Jr., "Creating a Marketing Orientation," *Journal of Marketing* 70 (October 2006), www.marketingpower.com.

19. Sunil Gupta, Donald R. Lehmann, and Jennifer Ames Stuart, "Valuing Customers," *Journal of Marketing Research,* February 2004, pp. 7–18.

20. Jacquelyn S. Thomas, Robert C. Blattberg, and Edward J. Fox, "Recapturing Lost Customers," *Journal of Marketing Research,* February 2004, pp. 31–45.

21. Alan Grant and Leonard Schlesinger, "Realize Your Customers' Full Profit Potential," *Harvard Business Review,* September/October 1995, p. 59.

22. Jagdish N. Sheth and Rajendras Sisodia, "More Than Ever Before, Marketing Is under Fire to Account for What It Spends," *Marketing Management,* Fall 1995, pp. 13–14.

23. Lynette Ryals and Adrian Payne, "Customer Relationship Management in Financial Services: Towards Information-Enabled Relationship Marketing," *Journal of Strategic Marketing,* March 2001, p. 3.

24. Mya Frazier, James Tenser, and Tricia Despres, "Retail Lesson: Small Programs Best," *Advertising Age,* March 20, 2006, pp. S-2–S-3.

25. Werner J. Reinartz and V. Kumar, "On the Profitability of Long-Life Customers in a Noncontractual Setting: An Empirical Investigation and Implications for Marketing," *Journal of Marketing,* October 2000, pp. 17–35.

26. Roland T. Rust, Katherine N. Lemon, and Valarie A. Zeithaml, "Return on Marketing: Using Customer Equity to Focus Marketing Strategy," *Journal of Marketing,* January 2004, pp. 109–127.

27. Rajkumar Venkatesan and V. Kumar, "A Customer Lifetime Value Framework for Customer Selection and Resource Allocation Strategy," *Journal of Marketing,* October 2004, pp. 106–125.

28. O. C. Ferrell and Michael Hartline, *Marketing Strategy* (Mason, OH: South-Western, 2005), p. 108.

29. "Kids' Food Pyramid Launched," CNN, September 28, 2005, www.cnn.com.

30. "Charitable Giving Rises 6 Percent to More than $160 Billion in 2005, Giving USA Foundation press release, June 7, 2006, www.aafrc.org/press_releases/trustreleases/0606_PR.pdf.

31. Andrew LaVallee, "Now, Virtual Fashion," *The Wall Street Journal,* September 22, 2006, p. B1, http://online.wsj.com; Gavin O'Malley, "Virtual Worlds: The Latest Fashion," *Advertising Age,* July 10, 2006, pp. 3+.

32. Enid Burns, "Online Retail Sales Grew in 2005," *ClickZ,* January 5, 2006, www.clickz.com/showPage.html?page=3575456.

33. "A Perfect Fit: Staples and Kids in Need," *Chain Store Age,* October 2005, p. 78.

34. Eric Bangeman, "Sirius CEO Talks Merger," *Ars Technica,* November 27, 2006, http://arstechnica.com/news.ars/post/20061127-8293.html; Dan Thanh Dang, "Satellite Radio Industry Continues to Grow, Enter Mainstream," *The Baltimore Sun,* November 16, 2003, www.sunspot.net; Stephen Holden, "High-Tech Quirkiness Restores Radio's Magic," *The New York Times,* December 26, 2003, p. E1; "In Brief, Radio: XM Radio Ends '03 with 1.36 Million Users," *The Los Angeles Times,* January 8, 2004, p. C3; Kevin Kingsbury, "Howard Stern Gets More Shares of Sirius after Subscriber Growth," *The Wall Street Journal,* January 9, 2007, http://online.wsj.com; David Pogue, "Satellite Radio Extends Its Orbit," *The New York Times,* December 18, 2003, p. G1; "Satellite Scramble," *The Wall Street Journal,* http://online.wsj.com/documents/info-satellite04.html?printVersion=true (accessed January 18, 2007); "Sirius Satellite Radio Hits Three Million Subscribers," *The Wall Street Journal,* December 27, 2005, http://online.wsj.com; Brad Stone, "Greetings, Earthlings: Satellite Radio for Cars Is Taking Off and Adding New Features—Now Broadcasters Are Starting to Fight Back," *Newsweek,* January 26, 2003, p. 55; David Welch, "Satellite Radio: Two for the Road," *BusinessWeek,* November 24, 2003, p. 144; Guy Wire, "Satellite in Trouble as HD Grows," *RW Online,* August 23, 2006, www.rwonline.com/pages/s.0048/t.258.html; XM Radio Fast Facts, www.xmradio.com/about/fast-facts/consumer.xmc (accessed January 18, 2007).

35. Donna Hood Crecca, "Higher Calling," *Chain Leader,* December 2002, p. 14; Finagle A Bagel, www.finagleabagel.com/home.htm (accessed January 18, 2007); "Finagle Sees a Return to More Normal Business Mode," *Foodservice East,* Fall 2002, pp. 1, 17; interview with Laura B. Trust and Alan Litchman, February 25, 2003; "Sloan Grads Bet Their Money on Bagels," *Providence Business News,* October 25, 1999, p. 14; "State Fare: Finagle A Bagel, Boston," *Restaurants and Institutions,* October 1, 2002, www.rimag.com/ 1902/sr.htm; Matt Viser, "Small, But Thinking Big," *The Boston Globe,* October 27, 2005, www.boston.com/news/local/articles/2005/10/27/small_but_thinking_big/.

a Kerry A. Dolan, "The Soda with Buzz," *Forbes,* March 28, 2005; Burt Helm, "The Sport of Extreme Marketing," *BusinessWeek,* March 14, 2005; Melanie Ho, "For Red Bull, It's Here, There and Everywhere," *The Washington Post,* August 23, 2006, p. E1, www.washingtonpost.com/; Bruce Horovitz, "Energy Drinks Take a Chill," *USA Today,* May 6, 2007, www.usatoday; Kathryn Masterson, "Crank Juice—As Energy Drinks Gain on Sodas in THR Market Selection Grows Too," *Chicago Tribune,* December 5, 2005; Red Bull, www.redbull.com (accessed January 19, 2007).

b "About Facebook," Facebook.com, www.facebook.com/about.php (accessed May 16, 2007); David Kushner, "The Web's Hottest Site: Facebook.com," *Rolling Stone,* April 7, 2006, www.rollingstone.com/news/story/9597735/the_webs_hottest_site_facebookcom; Angus Loten, "The Great Communicator," Inc., www.inc.com/30under30/zuckerberg.html (accessed January 19, 2007); Rachel Rosmarin, "Facebook's Makeover," *Forbes,* September 5, 2006, www.forbes.com/technology/2006/09/01/facebook-myspace-internet_cx_rr_0905facebook.html.

c "About IKEA," IKEA, www.ikea.com/ms/en_US/about_ikea/splash.html (accessed January 19, 2007); Kerry Capell, "IKEA: How the Swedish Retailer Became a Global Brand," *BusinessWeek,* November 14, 2005, pp. 96–106; "IKEA's Growth Limited by Style Issues, Says CEO," *Nordic Business Report,* January 21, 2004, www.nordicbusinessreport.com.

CHAPTER 2

1. Sharon Silke Carty and James R. Healey, "Ford Risks It with Outsider," *USA Today,* September 6, 2006, pp. B1–B2; Mark Fields, Ford Motor Company Executive Vice President, "Fields: Ford Fights Back," speech delivered January 23, 2006, http://media.ford.com/article_display.cfm?article_id=22464; Daren Fonda, "Ford: Just Fix the Car; New Boss, Same Old Problem: The Automaker Has to Build Better, Exciting Autos to Make a Comeback," *Time,* September 18, 2006, p. 46; James R. Healey, "Bill Ford Hands Keys to New CEO," *USA Today,* September 6, 2006, p. A1; Mark Phelan, "New Ford CEO Upbeat, but Says We're 'Not Competitive' Yet," *USA Today,* November 11, 2006, www.usatoday.com/money/autos/2006-11-10-ford-ceo-interview_x.htm; Sarah A. Webster, "A Chat with Ford's New CEO: Upbeat but Realistic," *Detroit Free Press,* November 11, 2006, www.freep.com/apps/pbcs.dll/article?AID=2006611110353; James P. Womack, "Why Toyota Is Better than GM and Ford," *Economists' View,* February 13, 2006, http://economistsview.typepad.com/economistsview/2006/02/why_toyota_is_b.html.

2. O. C. Ferrell and Michael Hartline, *Marketing Strategy* (Mason, OH: South-Western, 2008), p. 10.

3. Christian Homburg, Karley Krohmer, and John P. Workman, Jr., "A Strategy Implementation Perspective of Market Orientation," *Journal of Business Research* 57 (2004): 1331–1340.

4. Ferrell and Hartline, *Marketing Strategy,* p. 10.

5. Abraham Lustgarten, "iPod," in "Breakaway Brands," *Fortune,* October 31, 2005, pp. 154–156.

6. Ferrell and Hartline, *Marketing Strategy,* p. 51.

7. Graham J. Hooley, Gordon E. Greenley, John W. Cadogan, and John Fahy, "The Performance Impact of Marketing Resources," *Journal of Business Research* 58 (2005): 18–27.

8. Steven Gray, "Wendy's Stumbles with Baja Fresh," *The Wall Street Journal,* January 4, 2005, p. B7, http://online.wsj.com.

9. Derek F. Abell, "Strategic Windows," *Journal of Marketing,* July 1978, p. 21.

10. "eBay Registers 212 Million Users," BBC News, October 18, 2006, http://news.bbc.co.uk/1/hi/business/6064718.stm; Michael Krauss, "EBay 'Bids' on Small-Biz Firms to Sustain Growth," *Marketing News,* December 8, 2003, p. 6.

11. Catherine Holahan, "Will Less Be More for AOL?" *BusinessWeek Online,* July 31, 2006, www.busineweek.com.

12. Ibid.

13. Jack Ewing, "Music Phones Tackle the iPod," *BusinessWeek Online,* July 11, 2006, www.businessweek.com.

14. Ibid.

15. Douglas Bowman and Hubert Gatignon, "Determinants of Competitor Response Time to a New Product Introduction," *Journal of Marketing Research,* February 1995, pp. 42–53.

16. "Our Mission," Celestial Seasonings, www.celestialseasonings.com/whoweare/corporatehistory/mission.php (accessed May 16, 2007).

17. Cláudia Simões, Sally Dibb, and Raymond P. Fisk, "Managing Corporate Identity," *Journal of the Academy of Marketing Science* 33 (April 2005): 154–168.

18. Peter Asmus, "17th Annual Business Ethics Awards," *Business Ethics,* Fall 2005, pp. 18–20.

19. Jefferson Graham, "Google Cues up with YouTube," *USA Today,* October 10, 2006, p. 1A.

20. Thomas Ritter and Hans Georg Gemünden, "The Impact of a Company's Business Strategy on Its Technological Competence, Network Competence and Innovation Success," *Journal of Business Research* 57 (2004): 548–556.

21. Information Resouces, Inc., reported in Stephanie Thompson, "Nestlé, Hershey Figure Sticks Will Be Big Sellers," *Advertising Age,* October 3, 2005, p. 3.

22. Robert D. Buzzell, "The PIMS Program of Strategy Research: A Retrospective Appraisal," *Journal of Business Research* 57 (2004): 478–483.

23. Joseph P. Guiltinan and Gordon W. Paul, *Marketing Management: Strategies and Programs* (New York: McGraw-Hill, 1991), p. 43.

24. George S. Day, "Diagnosing the Product Portfolio," *Journal of Marketing,* April 1977, pp. 30–31.

25. Isabelle Maignan, O. C. Ferrell, and Linda Ferrell, "A Stakeholder Model for Implementing Social Responsibility in Marketing," *European Journal of Marketing* 39 (September/October 2005): 956–977.

26. Kate MacCarthur, "Franchisees Turn on Crispin's King," *Advertising Age,* October 24, 2005, pp. 1, 42.

27. Maignan, Ferrell, and Ferrell, "A Stakeholder Model for Implementing Social Responsibility in Marketing."

28. G. Tomas, M. Hult, David W. Cravens, and Jagdish Sheth, "Competitive Advantage in the Global Marketplace: A Focus on Marketing Strategy," *Journal of Business Research,* January 2001, pp. 1–3.

29. Kwaku Atuahene-Gima and Janet Y. Murray, "Antecedents and Outcomes of Marketing Strategy Comprehensiveness," *Journal of Marketing,* October 2004, pp. 33–46.

30. Marc Graser, "Toyota Hits Touch Points as It Hawks Yaris to Youth," *Advertising Age,* May 1, 2006, p. 28.

31. Nancy Einhart, "How the New T-Bird Went Off Course," *Business 2.0,* November 2003, pp. 74–76.

32. Christian Homburg, John P. Workman, and Ove Jensen, "Fundamental Changes in Marketing Organization: The Movement Toward a Customer-Focused Organizational Structure," *Journal of the Academy of Marketing Science,* Fall 2000, pp. 459–478.

33. Jack Neff, "Tissues Fit for the Toilet," *Advertising Age,* November 27, 2006, pp. 3+.

34. Rajdeep Grewal and Patriya Tansuhaj, "The Chain of Effects from Brand Trust and Brand Affect to Brand Performance: The Role of Brand Loyalty," *Journal of Marketing,* April 2001, pp. 67–80.

35. Steve Watkins, "Marketing Basics: The Four P's Are as Relevant Today as Ever," *Investor's Business Daily,* February 4, 2002, p. A1.

36. Bent Dreyer and Kjell Grønhaug, "Uncertainty, Flexibility, and Sustained Competitive Advantage," *Journal of Business Research* 57 (2004): 484–494.

37. Hemant C. Sashittat and Avan R. Jassawalla, "Marketing Implementation in Smaller Organizations: Definition, Framework, and Propositional Inventory," *Journal of the Academy of Marketing Science,* Winter 2001, pp. 50–69.

38. Ferrell and Hartline, *Marketing Strategy,* p. 257.

39. Michael J. Weiss, "To Be About to Be," *American Demographics,* September 2003, pp. 28–36.

40. Adapted from Nigel F. Piercy, *Market-Led Strategic Change* (Newton, MA: Butterworth-Heinemann, 1992), pp. 374–385.

41. Ian N. Lings, "Internal Market Orientation: Construct and Consequences," *Journal of Business Research* 57 (2004): 405–413.

42. Sybil F. Stershic, "Internal Marketing Campaign Reinforces Service Goals," *Marketing News,* July 31, 1998, p. 11.

43. Betsy Spethmann, "Internal Affairs," *Promo,* March 1, 2006, http://promotmagazine.com.

44. Kee-hung Lee and T. C. Edwin Cheng, "Effects of Quality Management and Marketing on Organizational Performance," *Journal of Business Research* 58 (2005): 446–456; Wuthichai Sittimalakorn and Susan Hart, "Market Orientation Versus Quality Orientation: Sources of Superior Business Performance," *Journal of Strategic Marketing,* December 2004, pp. 243–253.

45. Philip B. Crosby, *Quality Is Free: The Art of Making Quality Certain* (New York: McGraw-Hill, 1979), pp. 9–10.

46. Piercy, *Market-Led Strategic Change.*

47. Douglas W. Vorhies and Neil A. Morgan, "Benchmarketing Marketing Capabilities for Sustainable Competitive Advantage," *Journal of Marketing,* January 2005, pp. 80–94.

48. Kenneth W. Thomas and Betty A. Velthouse, "Cognitive Elements of Empowerment: An 'Interpretive' Model of Intrinsic Task Motivation," *Academy of Management Review,* October 1990, pp. 666–681.

49. Ferrell and Hartline, *Marketing Strategy.*

50. Rohit Deshpande and Frederick E. Webster, Jr., "Organizational Culture and Marketing: Defining the Research Agenda," *Journal of Marketing,* January 1989, pp. 3–15.

51. REI, www.rei.com (accessed January 18, 2007).

52. Kathleen Cholewka, "CRM: Lose the Hype and Strategize," *Sales & Marketing Management,* June 2001, pp. 27–28.

53. Eric M. Olson, Stanley F. Slater, and G. Tomas Hult, "The Performance Implications of Fit Among Business Strategy, Marketing Organization Structure, and Strategic Behavior," *Journal of Marketing* 69 (July 2005): 49–65.

54. Bernard J. Jaworski, "Toward a Theory of Marketing Control: Environmental Context, Control Types, and Consequences," *Journal of Marketing,* July 1988, pp. 23–39.

55. Christie Schweinsberg, "Toyota Sets Prius Sales Goal at 175,000 for 2007," WardsAuto.com, September 22, 2006, http://wardsauto.com/ar/toyota_prius_goal/.

56. "Lexus Ranks Highest in Customer Satisfaction with Dealer Service," J. D. Powers & Associates press release, July 20, 2006, www.jdpower.com/corporate/news/releases/pressrelease.asp?ID=2006119.

57. Sharon Silke Carty and James R. Healey, "Ford Risks It with Outsider," *USA Today,* September 6, 2006, pp. B1–B2; Mark Fields, Ford Motor Company Executive Vice President, "Fields: Ford Fights Back," speech delivered January 23, 2006, http://media.ford.com/article_display.cfm?article_id=22464; Daren Fonda, "Ford: Just Fix the Car; New Boss, Same Old Problem: The Automaker Has to Build Better, Exciting Autos to Make a Comeback," *Time,* September 18, 2006, p. 46; James R. Healey, "Bill Ford Hands Keys to New CEO," *USA Today,* September 6, 2006, p. A1; Mark Phelan, "New Ford CEO Upbeat, but Says We're 'Not Competitive' Yet," *USA Today,* November 11, 2006, www.usatoday.com/money/autos/2006-11-10-ford-ceo-interview_x.htm; Sarah A. Webster, "A Chat with Ford's New CEO: Upbeat but Realistic," *Detroit Free Press,* November 11, 2006, www.freep.com/apps/pbcs.dll/article?AID=2006611110353; James P. Womack, "Why Toyota Is Better than GM and Ford," *Economists View,* February 13, 2006, http://economistsview.typepad.com/economistsview/2006/02/why_toyota_is_b.html.

58. "100 Best Corporate Citizens 2006," *Business Ethics,* Spring 2006, www.business-ethics.com/whats_new/100best.html; "200 Best Small Companies in America," *Forbes,* October 14, 2005, www.forbes.com/lists/2005/23/GMAE.html; Green Mountain Coffee, www.greenmountaincoffee.com (accessed January 18, 2007); Green Mountain Coffee Annual Report 10-K; "Green Mountain Coffee Roasters," Hoover's Online, www.hoovers.com/green-mountain-coffee/—ID__45721—/free-co-factsheet.xhtml?cm_ven=PAID&cm_cat=BUS&cm_pla=CO1&cm_ite=Green_Mountain_Coffee_Roasters_Inc (accessed January 18, 2007).

 a "Arby's to Cut Trans Fat From Fries," *CBS News: Health Watch,* November 29, 2006, cbs4boston.com/food/local_story_334115006.html; Bruce Horovitz, "KFC Plans 'Important' *Trans* Fat 'Milestone,'" *USA Today,* October 30, 2006, p. 1B; "KFC, Taco Bell Complete Swith to Oil with No Trans Fat, CNN, April 30, 2007, www.cnn.com; Kate MacArthur, "Why McD's Hasn't Cut the Fat," *Advertising Age,* November 6, 2006, pp. 4, 80; "Popeyes® Chicken & Biscuits Selects Fogarty Klein Monroe as National Advertising Agency of Record," Popeyes press release, January 23, 2006, www.popeyes.com/news/news.asp?n=79; Raymond Sokolov, "A Chicken to Die For," *The Wall Street Journal,* November 11–12, 2006, p. 6.

 b Donny Deutsch, "The BIG IDEA with Donny Deutsch," CNBC, December 18, 2006, www.cereality.com/bigideapop.html; Joann Louiglio, "Totally Cereal-ous: All-Cereal Restaurant," *The Coloradoan,* December 2004, pp. E1, E2; Cereality, www.cereality.com (accessed January 18, 2007); "A Cereal Store for Cereal (Seriously)," *Business 2.0,* October 2004, p. 42; "Carb Appeal," *Fortune Small Business,* October 2004, p. 28.

 c Laura Blue, "Let's Talk Trash," *Time,* November 2006, pp. A37+; Bo Burlingham, "The Coolest Little Startup in America," *Inc.,* July 2006, www.inc.com/magazine/20060701/coolest-startup.html; TerraCycle, www.terracycle.net/ (accessed January 18, 2007).

CHAPTER 3

1. "100 Best Corporate Citizens 2006," *Business Ethics,* Spring 2006, pp. 22–24; Anne Fifield, "Starbucks and Global Exchange," *Tuck Today,* Summer 2003, pp. 17–18, http://mba.tuck.dartmouth.edu/pdf/2002-1-0023.pdf; "'Fortune' 100 Best Companies to Work for 2006," *Fortune,* January 20, 2006, http://money.cnn.com/magazines/fortune/bestcompanies/snapshots/1267.html; "Health Care Takes Its Toll on Starbucks," MSNBC.com, Sept 14, 2005, http://www.msnbc.msn.com/id/9344634/; Bruce Horovitz, "Starbucks Aims Beyond Lattes to Extend Brand to Films, Music and Books," *USA Today,* May 19, 2006, pp. A1, A2; Starbucks Annual Report 10-K, www.starbucks.com (accessed January 19, 2007); "Starbucks Company Fact Sheet November 2006," Starbucks, www.starbucks.com/aboutus/Company_Factsheet.pdf (accessed January 19, 2007).

2. Gina Chon, "Sales of SUVs Fall Sharply," *The Wall Street Journal,* October 4, 2005, p. D1, http://online.wsj.com/.

3. P. Varadarajan, Terry Clark, and William M. Pride, "Controlling the Uncontrollable: Managing Your Market Environment," *Sloan Management Review,* Winter 1992, pp. 39–47.

4. "Carbonated Soft-Drinks Suffer Setback in 2005, Beverage Marketing Corporation Reports," Beverage Marketing Corporation press release, April 2006, www.beveragemarketing.com/news2zz.htm.

5. O. C. Ferrell and Michael D. Hartline, *Marketing Strategy* (Mason, OH: South-Western, 2008), p. 58.

6. Ibid.

7. Rodolfo Vazquez, Maria Leticia Santos, and Luis Ignacio Álvarez, "Market Orientation, Innovation and Competitive Strategies in Industrial Firms," *Journal of Strategic Marketing,* March 2001, pp. 69–90.

8. Lorrie Grant, "Scrimping to Splurge," *USA Today,* January 28, 2005, p. 1B.

9. Patrick Barta and Anne Marie Chaker, "Consumers Voice Rising Dissatisfaction with Companies," *The Wall Street Journal,* May 21, 2001, p. A2.

10. Paula Lyon Andruss, "Staying in the Game: Turning an Economic Dip into Opportunity," *Marketing News,* May 7, 2001, pp. 1, 9.

11. Federal Election Commission, October 10, 2006, data via the Center for Responsive Politics, www.opensecrets.org/orgs/list.asp?.

12. Nannette Byrnes, "Big Tobacco's Showdown in the West," *BusinessWeek,* September 11, 2006, p. 38.

13. "Marketers of 'Smoke Away' Pay $1.3 Million to Settle FTC Charges," Federal Trade Commission press release, August 23, 2005, www.ftc.gov/opa/2005/08/emerson.htm.
14. Sarah Ellison, "Why Kraft Decided to Ban Some Food Ads to Children," *The Wall Street Journal*, October 31, 2005, p. A1, http://online.wsj.com/public/us.
15. David Tyler, "BBB Hangs Up on Cingular," *Rochester Democrat & Chronicle*, September 10, 2005, www.rochesterdandc.com/apps/pbcs.dll/article?AID=/20050910/BUSINESS/509100309&SearchID=73220665966305.
16. "NAD Refers BIE Health Products to the FTC and FDA," National Advertising Division press release, July 17, 2006, www.nadreview.org.
17. "New Subscribers to Telecom Services Continues Growing in 2005," Cellular-News.com, October 5, 2005, www.cellular-news.com/story/12792.php.
18. Gwen Moran, "Top New Marketing Trends," MSNBC, August 7, 2006, www.msnbc.msn.com/id/14231013/.
19. McAlister, Ferrell, and Ferrell, *Business and Society*.
20. Ibid.
21. Ibid.
22. U.S. Bureau of the Census, *Statistical Abstract of the United States, 2007* (Washington: U.S. Government Printing Office, 2006), p. 13.
23. Ibid., pp. 50, 53.
24. Ibid., p. 12.
25. U.S. Bureau of the Census, "U.S. Interim Projections by Age, Sex, Race, and Hispanic Origin," March 18, 2004, www.census.gov/ipc/www/usinterimproj/natprojtab01a.pdf.
26. Isabelle Maignan and O. C. Ferrell, "Corporate Social Responsibility and Marketing: An Integrative Framework," *Journal of the Academy of Marketing Science*, January 2004, pp. 3–19.
27. Peter Loftus, "Number of Vioxx-Related Lawsuits Tops 22,000 as Deadline Nears," *The Wall Street Journal*, September 29, 2006, http://online.wsj.com; "Report: Merck Aware of Vioxx Problems," *The Austin American-Statesman*, November 2, 2004, http://statesman.com.
28. "At a Glance," Avon, www.avoncompany.com/about/ (accessed January 19, 2007); "The Avon Breast Cancer Crusade," Avon, www.avoncompany.com/women/avoncrusade/index.html (accessed January 19, 2007).
29. McAlister, Ferrell, and Ferrell, *Business and Society*.
30. O. C. Ferrell, "Business Ethics and Customer Stakeholders," *Academy of Management Executive*, May 2004, pp. 126–129.
31. "2005 Corporate Citizenship Report," Pfizer, www.pfizer.com/pfizer/subsites/corporate_citizenship/report/stakeholders_table.jsp (accessed January 19, 2007).
32. Archie Carroll, "The Pyramid of Corporate Social Responsibility: Toward the Moral Management of Organizational Stakeholders," *Business Horizons*, July/August 1991, p. 42.
33. William T. Neese, Linda Ferrell, and O. C. Ferrell, "An Analysis of Federal Mail and Wire Fraud Cases Related to Marketing," *Journal of Business Research* 58 (2005): 910–918.
34. Don Clark, "Transmeta Sues Intel Over Chip Patents," *The Wall Street Journal*, October 12, 2006, p. A8, http://online.wsj.com/.
35. *Business Ethics*, January/February 1995, p. 13.
36. Claudia Grisales, "Sony Settles with Texas Consumers," *The Austin American-Statesman*, December 20, 2006, www.statesman.com; Mark Lisheron, "Texas Sues Sony Over Hidden Software That Can Hurt PCs," *The Austin American-Statesman*, November 22, 2005, www.statesman.com; Ethan Smith, "Sony BMG Pulls Millions of CDs Amid Antipiracy-Software Flap," *The Wall Street Journal*, November 17, 2005, p. D5, http://online.wsj.com/.
37. "Consumer Cries Foul over Kraft Dip," *The Austin American-Statesman*, November 30, 2006, www.statesman.com.
38. Tim Barnett and Sean Valentine, "Issue Contingencies and Marketers' Recognition of Ethical Issues, Ethical Judgments and Behavioral Intentions," *Journal of Business Research* 57 (2004): 338–346.
39. "Charitable Giving Rises 6 Percent to More than $160 Billion in 2005," Giving USA Foundation press release, June 7, 2006, www.aafrc.org/press_releases/trustreleases/0606_PR.pdf.
40. Jessica Stannard-Friel, "Corporate Giving Responds to Hurricane Katrina," *OnPhilanthropy*, August 30, 2005, www.onphilanthropy.com/onthescene/os2005-08-30.html.
41. Stacy Perman, "Scones and Social Responsibility," *BusinessWeek*, August 21/28, 2006, p. 38.
42. "Take Charge of Education," Target, http://sites.target.com/site/en/corporate/page.jsp?contentId=PRD03-001825 (accessed January 19, 2007).
43. Marianne Wilson, "Doing Good Is More Than a Feel-Good Option," *Chain Store Age*, October 2005, pp. 77+.
44. McAlister, Ferrell, and Ferrell, *Business and Society*.
45. Peter Asmus, "17th Annual Business Ethics Awards," *Business Ethics*, Fall 2005, pp. 18–20.
46. Isabelle Maignan and Debbie Thorne McAlister, "Socially Responsible Organizational Buying: How Can Stakeholders Dictate Purchasing Policies?" *Journal of Macromarketing*, December 2003, pp. 78–89.
47. Stephanie Thompson, "Aveda Pressures Mags to Go Green," *Advertising Age*, November 29, 2004, p. 19.
48. Jill Gabrielle Klein, N. Craig Smith, and Andrew John, "Why We Boycott: Consumer Motivations for Boycott Participation," *Journal of Marketing*, July 2004, pp. 92–109.
49. Bruce R. Gaumnitz and John C. Lere, "Contents of Codes of Ethics of Professional Business Organizations in the United States," *Journal of Business Ethics* 35 (2002): 35–49.
50. Jeff Leeds, "2 Are Fired at Clear Channel after a Misconduct Inquiry," *The New York Times*, October 12, 2005, www.nytimes.com.
51. Ferrell and Hartline, *Marketing Strategy*.
52. Marjorie Kelly, "Holy Grail Found: Absolute, Definitive Proof that Responsible Companies Perform Better Financially," *Business Ethics*, Winter 2005, www.business-ethics.com/current_issue/winter_2005_holy_grail_article.html; Xueming Luo and C.B. Bhattacharya,

"Corporate Social Responsibility, Customer Satisfaction, and Market Value," *Journal of Marketing* 70 (October 2006), www.marketingpower.com; Isabelle Maignan, O. C. Ferrell, and Linda Ferrell, "A Stakeholder Model for Implementing Social Responsibility in Marketing," *European Journal of Marketing* 39 (September/October 2005): 956–977.

53. "Multi-Year Study Finds 21% Increase in Americans Who Say Corporate Support of Social Issues Is Important in Building Trust," Cone, Inc., press release, December 8, 2004, www.coneinc.com/Pages/pr_30.html.

54. Maignan, Ferrell, and Ferrell, "A Stakeholder Model for Implementing Social Responsibility in Marketing."

55. "100 Best Corporate Citizens 2006," *Business Ethics*, Spring 2006, pp. 22–24; Anne Fifield, "Starbucks and Global Exchange," *Tuck Today*, Summer 2003, pp.17–18, http://mba.tuck.dartmouth.edu/pdf/2002-1-0023.pdf; "'Fortune' 100 Best Companies to Work for 2006," *Fortune*, January 20, 2006, http://money.cnn.com/magazines/fortune/bestcompanies/snapshots/1267.html; "Health Care Takes Its Toll on Starbucks," MSNBC.com, September 14, 2005, http://www.msnbc.msn.com/id/9344634/; Bruce Horovitz, "Starbucks Aims Beyond Lattes to Extend Brand to Films, Music and Books," *USA Today*, May 19, 2006, pp. A1, A2; Starbucks Annual Report 10-K, www.starbucks.com (accessed January 19, 2007); "Starbucks Company Fact Sheet November 2006," Starbucks, www.starbucks.com/aboutus/Company_Factsheet.pdf (accessed January 19, 2007).

56. "About PETCO," PETCO, www.petco.com (accessed May 16, 2007); Corporate Governance—Code of Ethics, PETCO, http://ir.petco.com/phoenix.zhtml?c=93935&p=irol-govConduct (accessed January 19, 2007); "Fortune 500 2006," CNN Money.com, http://money.cnn.com/magazines/fortune/fortune500/snapshots/2154.html (accessed January 19, 2007); "Health and Services Drive Pet Industry Sales," American Pet Products Manufacturers Association, press release, February 22, 2007, www.appma.org/press_releasedetail.asp?id=101; Michelle Higgins, "When the Dog's Hotel Is Better than Yours," *The Wall Street Journal*, June 30, 2004, p. D1; "Just Say No! PETCO—the Place Where Pets Die," Kind Planet, www.kindplanet.org/petno.html (accessed January 19, 2007); Ilene Lelchuk, "San Francisco Alleges Cruelty at 2 PETCOs," *San Francisco Chronicle*, June 19, 2002, www.anapsid.org/pettrade/petcocit2.html; "Lifestyle Trends Affect Pet Markets," *PET AGE*, January 2006, www.petage.com/News010607.asp; Chris Penttila, "Magic Markets," *Entrepreneur*, September 2004, www.entrepreneur.com/article/0,4621,316866-2,00.html; "PETA and PETCO Announce Agreement," PETA press release, April 12, 2005, www.peta.org/feat/PETCOAgreement/default.asp; "PETCO Pays Fine to Settle Lawsuit," PETA Annual Review, 2004, www.peta.org/feat/annual_review04/notToAbuse.asp; "PETCO Foundation to 'Round-up' Support for Spay/Neuter Programs," PETCO press release, July 13, 2005, www.forbes.com/prnewswire/feeds/prnewswire/2005/07/13/prnewswire200507131335PR_NEWS_B_WES_LA_LAW067.html; "PETCO Lawsuit—Mistreating Animals San Diego, CA," Pet-Abuse.com, May 28, 2004, www.pet-abuse.com/cases/2373/CA/US; "PETCO Looks to the Web to Enhance Multi-Channel Marketing" *Internet Retailer*, January 16, 2006; "PETCO's Bad Business Is Bad for Animals," *PETA Animal Times*, Spring 2003, www.peta.org/living/at-spring2003/comp2.html; "PETCO Settles FTC Charges," Federal Trade Commission press release, November 17, 2004, www.ftc.gov/opa/2004/11/petco.htm; "PETCO Settles Suit Alleging Abuse, Overcharging," CBSNews.com, May 27, 2004, www.anapsid.org/pettrade/petcocit2.html; "PETCO 'Spring a Pet'," PETCO http://www.petco.com/petco_Page_PC_springapet_Nav_379.aspx (accessed May 16, 2007); "The Pet Market—Market Assessment 2005," *Research and Markets*, April 2005, www.researchandmarkets.com/reports/c26485/; "Pet Portion Control," *Prevention*, February 2006, p. 201; "Pet Store Scandal: PETA Uncovers Shocking Back-Room Secrets," *PETA Animal Times*, Summer 2000, www.peta.org/living/at-summer2000/petco.html; "Say No to PETCO," *PETA Animal Times*, Spring 2002, www.peta.org/living/at-spring2002/specialrep/; Julie Schmidt, "Pet Bird Buyers Asking Sellers about Avian Flu," *USA Today*, November 28, 2005; Jessica Stannard-Freil, "Corporate Philanthropy: PR or Legitimate News?" *OnPhilanthropy*, May 20, 2005, www.onphilanthropy.com/tren_comm/tc2005-05-20.html "'Tree of Hope' Fundraiser Gives Pets a Second Chance," PETCO press release, November 14, 2006, www.petco.com/Content/PressRelease.aspx?PC=pr111406&Nav=146&=.

a "Hottest New Pet Products Unleashed at Global Pet Expo," *Business Wire*, March 29, 2005, www.businesswire.com; Laura Koss-Feder, "Critter Comforts: The Boom in Pet Businesses Has Entrepreneurs Vying for Their Spots as Top Dog," *Entrepreneur*, November 2005, p. 124; Kathleen M. Mangan, "Perks for Pets: Nutritional Supplements for Fluffy and Fido," *E: The Enforcement Magazine*, November/December 2004, www.emagazine.com.

b Amy's Ice Cream, www.amysicecream.com (accessed January 18, 2007); Renuka Rayasam, "Amy's Grows Up," *Austin American-Statesman*, September 29, 2005, www.statesman.com; Jim Swift, "Amy's Ice Cream," KXAN, September 2006, www.kxan.com/Global/story.asp?S=2510107.

c Shoemart, www.shoemart.com (accessed January 22, 2006); "The Timberland Company CEO and CFO to Present at the Companies for Social Responsibility Investor Conference," *Business Wire*, April 28, 2005, www.businesswire.com; "Any Company Can Create a Great Workplace, Our Mission Is to Help Them Do It," Great Place to Work Institute, www.greatplacetowork.com (accessed January 19, 2007); The Timberland Company, www.timberland.com (accessed January 19, 2007).

CHAPTER 4

1. Ben Elgin, "Can Google Go Glossy?" *BusinessWeek.com*, December 12, 2005, www.businessweek.com/magazine/content/05_50/b3963130.htm?chan=search; Jon Fine, "Google's New Frontier: Print Ads," *BusinessWeek.com*, November 6, 2006, www.businessweek.com/technology/content/nov2006/tc20061105_572061.htm?chan=search; Sara Kehaulani Goo, "Building a 'Googley' Workforce: Corporate Culture Breeds Innovation," *Washington Post Online*, October 21, 2006, p. D01, www.washingtonpost.com/wp-dyn/content/article/2006/10/20/AR2006102001461.html; Adam Lashinsky, "Chaos By Design," *Fortune*, October 2, 2006, pp. 86–98; Michael Liedtke, "Google Stock Price Rises Above $500," *BusinessWeek.com*, November 21, 2006, www.businessweek.com/ap/financialnews/D8LHN81G0.htm?chan=search..

2. Ruby P. Lee and Rajdeep Grewal, "Strategic Responses to New Technology and Their Impact on Performance, *Journal of Marketing*, October 2004, pp. 157–171.

3. "Shop Around the Clock," *American Demographics*, September 2003, p. 18.

4. Eli's Cheesecake Company, www.elicheesecake.com/default.aspx (accessed January 2, 2007).

5. David W. Stewart and Qin Zhao, "Internet Marketing, Business Models, and Public Policy," *Journal of Public Policy & Marketing,* Fall 2000, pp. 287–296.

6. Christopher Hart and Pete Blackshaw, "Internet Inferno," *Marketing Management,* January/February 2006, p. 19.

7. John Eaton, "E-Word-of-Mouth Marketing," custom module for William M. Pride and O. C. Ferrell, *Marketing,* 14th ed. (Boston: Houghton Mifflin, 2007), www.prideferrell.com.

8. Hart and Blackshaw, "Internet Inferno," p. 21.

9. Mary Wagner, "From the Customer's Mouth to the Retailer's Ear," *Internet Retailer,* October 2006, www.internetretailer.com/printArticle.asp?id=20017.

10. Jon Mark Giese, "Place Without Space, Identity Without Body: The Role of Cooperative Narrative in Community and Identity Formation in a Text-Based Electronic Community," unpublished dissertation, Pennsylvania State University, 1996.

11. Robert D. Hof, with Seanna Browder and Peter Elstrom, "Internet Communities," *BusinessWeek,* May 5, 1997, pp. 64–80.

12. Heather Green, "It Takes a Web Village," *BusinessWeek,* September 4, 2006, p. 66.

13. David Kirkpatrick and Daniel Roth, "Why There's No Escaping the Blog," *Fortune,* January 10, 2005, pp. 44–50.

14. "About Dell," Dell, www.dell.com/content/topics/global.aspx/corp/en/home?c=us&l=en&s=corp (accessed January 3, 2007).

15. "Southwest Airlines Fact Sheet," Southwest Airlines, www.iflyswa.com/about_swa/press/factsheet.html (accessed January 2, 2007).

16. Andrew Park, "Imperial Sugar," *BusinessWeek,* November 24, 2003, p. 98.

17. "Connecting Buyers and Sellers," *Inbound Logistics,* November 2004, p. 24.

18. "Jupiter Research Forecasts Online Retail Spending Will Be $144 Billion in 2010, a CAGR of 12% from 2005," Jupiter Media press release, February 6, 2006, www.jupitermedia.com/corporate/releases/06.02.06-newjupresearch.html.

19. "Amazon.com Announces Free Cash Flow Surpasses $500 Million for the First Time; Customers Joined Amazon Prime at an Accelerated Rate," Amazon.com press release, February 2, 2006, http://phx.corporate-ir.net/phoenix.zhtml?c=176060&p=irol-newsArticle&ID=812301&highlight=.

20. Enid Burns, "Online Ads: A Source of Further Learning for Consumers,' *ClickZ,* November 7, 2006, http://clickz.com/showPage.html?page=3623878.

21. Enid Burns, "Online Ads Influence Collegiate Set," *ClickZ,* February 10, 2006, www.clickz.com/stats/sectors/demographics/article.php/3584441.

22. Puneet Manchanda, Jean-Pierre Dubé, Khim Yong Goh, and Pradeep K. Chintagunta, "The effect of Banner Advertising on Internet Purchasing," *Journal of Marketing Research* 43 (February 2006): 98–108, www.marketingpower.com.

23. Enid Burns, "Online Seizes More of the Advertising Mix," *ClickZ,* February 13, 2006, www.clickz.com/stats/sectors/advertising/article.php/3584801.

24. Francesca Sotgiu and Fabio Ancarani, "Exploiting the Opportunities of Internet and Multi-Channel Pricing: An Exploratory Research," *Journal of Product and Brand Management,* 13 (2004): 125–136.

25. Martin Spann and Gerard J. Tellis, "Does the Internet Promote Better Consumer Decisions? The Case of Name-Your-Own Price Auctions," *Journal of Marketing* 70 (January 2006): 65–78, www.marketing-power.com.

26. Stephanie Stahl and John Soat, "Feeding the Pipeline: Procter & Gamble Uses IT to Nurture New Product Lines," *Information Week,* February 24, 2003, www.informationweek.com.

27. V. Kumar, "Customer Relationship Management," custom module for William M. Pride and O. C. Ferrell, *Marketing,* 14th ed. (Boston: Houghton Mifflin, 2006), www.prideferrell.com.

28. Werner Reinzrtz, Jackquelyn S. Thomas, and V. Kumar, "Balancing Acquisition and Retention Resources to Maximize Customer Profitability," *Journal of Marketing,* January 2005, pp. 63–79.

29. D. Aaker, V. Kumar, and G. Day, *Marketing Research,* 8th ed. (New York: Wiley, 2004).

30. Marlus Wübben and Florian von Wangenheim, "Predicting Customer Lifetime Duration and Future Purchase Levels: Simple Heuristics vs. Complex Models," in Jean L. Johnson and John Hulland (eds.), *2006: AMA Winter Educators' Conference,* published in *Marketing Theory and Applications* 17 (Winter 2006): 83–84.

31. Kumar, "Customer Relationship Management."

32. Christine McManus, "'Micro-Cheesery' Closes," *The [Fort Collins] Coloradoan,* February 10, 2006, www.coloradoan.com.

33. V. Kumar, J. Andrew Peterson, and Robert P. Leone, "The Power of Customer Advocacy," in Jean L. Johnson and John Hulland (eds.), *2006: AMA Winter Educators' Conference,* publihed in *Marketing Theory and Applications* 17 (Winter 2006): 81–82.

34. O. C. Ferrell and Michael D. Hartline, *Marketing Strategy* (Mason, OH: South-Western, 2008), p. 72.

35. Kumar, "Customer Relationship Management."

36. Jessica Sabor, "Tools for Gold: Marketing that Mines Best Customers," *DestinationCRM,* October 16, 2006, www.destinationcrm.com/print/default.asp?ArticleID=6424.

37. Ruby Roy Dholakia and Nikhilesh Dholakia, "Mobility and Markets: Emerging Outlines of M-Commerce," *Journal of Business Research* 57 (2004): 1391–1396.

38. J. Bonasia, "Eyeing Growth in Customer Relationship Management," *Investors Business Daily,* January 8, 2002, p. 7.

39. "Cisco Systems' Best Practice Customer Care," CustomerServiceWorld.com, www.ecustomerservice-world.com/earticlesstore_articles.asp?type=article&id=523 (accessed January 4, 2007).

40. Michael Krauss, "At Many Firms, Technology Obscures CRM," *Marketing News,* March 18, 2002, p. 5.

41. Edward Prewitt, "How to Build Customer Loyalty in an Internet World," *CIO,* January 1, 2002, www.cio.com/archive/ 010102/loyalty_content.html.

42. Ibid.
43. Itamar Simonson, "Determinants of Customers Responses to Customized Offers: Conceptual Framework and Research Propositions," *Journal of Marketing,* January 2005, pp. 32–45.
44. David Pottruck and Terry Peace, "Listening to Customers in the Electronic Age," *Fortune,* May 2000, www.business2.com/articles/mag/0,1640,7700,00.html.
45. Stephenie Steitzer, "Commercial Web Sites Cut Back on Collections of Personal Data" *The Wall Street Journal,* March 28, 2002, http://online.wsj.com.
46. Enid Burns, "Top Corporations Clean up Web Sites, Privacy Policies," *ClickZ,* September 11, 2006, www.clickz.com/showPage.html?page=3623398.
47. "BBBOnline Privacy Seal," www.BBBOnline.org/privacy/index.asp (accessed January 4, 2007).
48. "European Union Directive on Privacy," E-Center for Business Ethics, www.e-businessethics.com/eud.htm (accessed January 4, 2007).
49. "Study: Spam Costing Companies $22 Billion a Year," CNN, February 4, 2005, www.cnn.com
50. Brad Stone, "Spam Doubles, Finding New Ways to Deliver Itself, *The New York Times,* December 6, 2006, www.nytimes.com.
51. "Consumers Lose $8 Billion to Online Fraud," ConsumerAffairs.com, August 8, 2006, www.consumeraffairs.com/news04/2006/08/cr_online_fraud.html.
52. Kate Macarthur, "Phishers Switch Their Brand Bait," *Advertising Age,* December 11, 2006, pp. 3, 38.
53. "Global Software Piracy Study," Business Software Alliance, www.bsa.org/globalstudy/ (accessed January 4, 2007).
54. Patrick Goldstein, "The People's Republic of YouTube," *The Los Angeles Times,* October 17, 2006, www.latimes.com/entertainment/news/cl-et-goldstein17oct17,0,1592781.story?coll=la-home-entertainment.
55. William T. Neese and Charles R. McManis, "Summary Brief: Law Ethics, and the Internet: How Recent Federal Trademark Law Prohibits a Remedy Against Cyber-squatters," *Proceedings from the Society of Marketing Advances,* November 4–7, 1998.
56. Ben Elgin, "Can Google Go Glossy?" *BusinessWeek.com,* December 12, 2005, www.businessweek.com/magazine/content/05_50/b3963130.htm?chan=search; Jon Fine, "Google's New Frontier: Print Ads," *BusinessWeek.com,* November 6, 2006, www.businessweek.com/technology/content/nov2006/tc20061105_572061.htm?chan=search; Sara Kehaulani Goo, "Building a 'Googley' Workforce: Corporate Culture Breeds Innovation," *Washington Post Online,* October 21, 2006, p. D01, www.washingtonpost.com/wp-dyn/content/article/2006/10/20/AR2006102001461.html; Adam Lashinsky, "Chaos By Design," *Fortune,* October 2, 2006, pp. 86–98; Michael Liedtke, "Google Stock Price Rises above $500," *BusinessWeek.com,* November 21, 2006, www.businessweek.com/ap/financialnews/D8LHN81G0.htm?chan=search.
57. Marty Gast, "Travelocity.com: A Glimpse Through History," *Travel News,* December 23, 2003, www.breakingtravelnews.com/article.php?story=20031222221110443&mode=print; Josh Roberts, "Travelocity, Expedia Aim to Prove Their Differences," *USA Today,* May 11, 2005, www.usatoday.com/travel/deals/inside/2005-05-11-column_x.htm; Travelocity, www.travelocity.com (accessed January 4, 2007); "Travelocity.com LP," Hoovers, www.hoovers.com/travelocity/—ID__100249—/free-co-factsheet.xhtml (accessed January 4, 2007).
a Dana Brown, "Fast Food, Faster," *The Hamilton Spectator,* October 27, 2006, www.hamiltonspectator.com/; GoMobo, http://gomobo.com/ (accessed January 2, 2007); "Young, Fearless, and Smart: America's Best Young Entrepreneurs: Noah Glass," *BusinessWeek Online,* October 2006, http://images.business.com/ss/06/10/bestunder25/source/9.htm.
b "About YouTube," www.youtube.com/t/about (accessed January 3, 2007); Allison Enright, "The M-BlawG: Law, Regulation, & Economy," *Marketing News,* November 15, 2006, p. 4; Jennifer Gill, "Contagious Commercials; How to Get in on the YouTube Craze," *Inc.,* November 2006, pp. 31–32; Tom Lowry and Robert D. Hof, "Smart Move or Silly Money 2.0?" *BusinessWeek,* October 23, 2006, pp. 34–37; Peter Grant, "Coming to Your TV—Homemade Hamster Videos?" *The Wall Street Journal,* November 8, 2006, p. B1, http://online.wsj.com; "YouTube Fact Sheet," www.youtube.com/t/fact_sheet (accessed January 3, 2007).
c "Arctic Monkeys Make Chart History," *BBC News,* January 29, 2006, http://news.bbc.co.uk/go/pr/fr/-/1/hi/entertainment/4660394.stm; Jac Chebatoris, "More Monkeyshines? Or the Real Deal?" *Newsweek,* February 6, 2006, p. 10; Carl Ellison, "Fever Pitch," *DestinationCRM,* September 2006, http://destinationcrm.com/articles/default.asp?ArticleID=6248; Paul Sexton, "Arctic Monkeys Earn Fastest-Selling U.K. Debut," *Billboard.com,* January 30, 2006, www.billboard.com/bbcom/news/article_display.jsp?vnu_content_id=1001920504.

CHAPTER 5

1. Rekha Balu, "Hop Faster, Energizer Bunny: Rayovac Batteries Roll On," *The Wall Street Journal,* June 15, 1999, p. B4; "Battle of the Blades Draws Corporate Blood," *The New York Times,* October 12, 2003, sec. 3, p. 1; The Gillette Company, www.gillette.com (accessed January 8, 2007); Gillette 1999–2005 Annual Reports; "Gillette's Edge," *BusinessWeek,* January 19, 1998, pp. 70–77; "Gillette, Schick End Legal War, but Battle in Market Rages On," *The Boston Globe,* February 17, 2006, www.boston.com/business/healthcare/articles/2006/02/17/gillette_schick_end_legal_war_but_battle_in_market_rages_on; P&G/Gillette Questions and Answers, www.pg.com/images/homepage/pg_gillette_faq.pdf (accessed January 8, 2007); "Wal-Mart Selling Its Own Brand of Alkaline Batteries," *The Wall Street Journal,* December 10, 1999, pp. C4–5.
2. Johnnie L. Roberts, "World Tour," *Newsweek,* June 6, 2005, pp. 34–35.
3. "Company Profile," Starbucks, November 2006, www.starbucks.com/aboutus/Company_Profile.pdf; "Latest Counts of Wal-Mart," Wal-Mart.com, www.wal-martchina.com/english/news/stat.htm (accessed January 5, 2007).
4. "The U.S. Commercial Service, Export.gov, www.export.gov/comm_svc/about_us/about_home.html (accessed January 5, 2007).
5. Gary A. Knight and S. Tamer Cavusgil, "Innovation, Organizational Capabilities, and the Born-Global Firm," *Journal of International Business Studies,* March 2004, pp. 124–141.

6. Amy Guthrie, "Mexico's Snack Stores Are Expanding," *The Wall Street Journal,* February 2, 2005, http://online.wsj.com.

7. Gordon Fairclough and Janet Adamy, "Sex, Skin, Fireworks, Licked Fingers—It's a Quarter Pounder Ad in China," *The Wall Street Journal,* September 21, 2006, p. B1, http://online.wsj.com; "What Made McDonald's Click in India?" *Hindustan Times.com,* September 7, 2006, via http://content.msn.co.in/Lifestyle/Work/LifeStyleHT_070906_1906.htm.

8. Anton Piësch, "Speaking in Tongues," *Inc.,* June 2003, p. 50.

9. "Product Pitfalls Proliferate in Global Cultural Maze," *The Wall Street Journal,* May 14, 2001, p. B11.

10. George Balabanis and Adamantios Diamantopoulos, "Domestic Country Bias, Country-or-Origin Effects, and Consumer Ethnocentrism: A Multidimensional Unfolding Approach," *Journal of the Academy of Marketing Science,* January 2004, pp. 80–95.

11. Ming-Huel Hsieh, Shan-Ling Pan, and Rudy Setiono, "Product-, Corporate-, and Country-Image Dimensions and Purchase Behavior: A Multicountry Analysis," *Journal of the Academy of Marketing Science,* July 2004, pp. 251–270.

12. Janet Adamy, "Eyeing a Billion Tea Drinkers, Starbucks Pours It On in China," *The Wall Street Journal,* November 29, 2006, p. A1, http://online.wsj.com.

13. CIA, *The World Fact Book,* www.cia.gov/cia/publications/factbook/index.html (accessed January 8, 2007).

14. "Cell Phones Reshaping Africa," CNN, October 17, 2005, www.cnn.com.

15. "Will the New Congress Shift Gears on Free Trade?" *The Wall Street Journal,* November 18–19, 2006, p. A7.

16. Ibid.

17. "U.S. Trade in Goods and Services," U.S. Bureau of the Census, Foreign Trade Statistics, March 9, 2007, www.census.gov/foreign-trade/statistics/historical/gands.pdf.

18. Charles R. Taylor, George R. Franke, and Michael L. Maynard, "Attitudes Toward Direct Marketing and Its Regulation: A Comparison of the United States and Japan," *Journal of Public Policy & Marketing,* Fall 2000, pp. 228–237.

19. Frederik Balfour, "Fakes!," *Business Week,* Feb. 7, 2005, pp. 54–64.

20. "Major U.S. Film Companies File Lawsuit in China," *Forbes.com,* September 13, 2006, www.forbes.com/home/feeds/afx/2006/09/13/afx3012637.html.

21. Adapted from O. C. Ferrell, John Fraedrich, and Linda Ferrell, *Business Ethics: Ethical Decision Making and Cases,* 6th ed. (Boston: Houghton Mifflin, 2005), pp. 217–221.

22. Dave Izraeli and Mark S. Schwartz, "What We Can Learn from the Federal Sentencing Guidelines for Organizational Ethics," *Journal of Business Ethics,* July 1998, pp. 9–10.

23. "This Is Systembolaget," Systembolaget www.systembolaget.se/Applikationer/Knappar/InEnglish/Swedish_alcohol_re.htm (accessed January 8, 2007).

24. CIA, *The World Fact Book.*

25. Enid Burns, "Euro Teens Respond to Online Advertising," *ClickZ,* February 23, 2006, www.clickz.com/stats/sectors/demographics/article.php/3586966.

26. "Report: Mobile Phone Users Double Since 2000," CNN, December 9, 2004, www.cnn.com.

27. Ting Shi, "A Gas Pump for 300 Million Phones," *Business 2.0,* June 2005, p. 78.

28. U.S. Bureau of the Census, *Statistical Abstract of the United States, 2007* (Washington, DC: U.S. Government Printing Office, 2006), pp. 833–835, 845; "NAFTA: A Decade of Success," Office of the United States Trade Representative, July 1, 2004, http://ustr.gov/Document_Library/Fact_Sheets/2004/NAFTA_A_Decade_of_Success.html.

29. CIA, *The World Fact Book.*

30. "Trade with Canada: 2005," U.S. Bureau of the Census, www.census.gov/foreign-trade/balance/c1220.html (accessed January 8, 2007).

31. William C. Symonds, "Meanwhile, to the North, NAFTA Is a Smash," *BusinessWeek,* February 27, 1995, p. 66.

32. "Will the New Congress Shift Gears on Free Trade?"

33. CIA, *The World Fact Book*; U.S. Bureau of the Census, *Statistical Abstract,* p. 810.

34. globalEDGE, Country Insights, http://globaledge.msu.edu (accessed January 8, 2007).

35. "The European Union at a Glance," Europa (European Union) online, http://europa.eu.int/abc/index_en.htm# (accessed January 8, 2007).

36. Ibid.

37. Stanley Reid, with Ariane Sains, David Fairlamb, and Carol Matlack, "The Euro: How Damaging a Hit?" *BusinessWeek,* September 29, 2003, p. 63; "The Single Currency," CNN, www.cnn.com/SPECIALS/2000/eurounion/story/currency/ (accessed September 27, 2006).

38. T. R. Reid, "The New Europe," *National Geographic,* January 2002, pp. 32–47.

39. "Common Market of the South (MERCOSUR): Agri-Food Regional Profile Statistical Overview," Agriculture and Agrifood Canada, March 2005, http://atn-riae.agr.ca/latin/3947_e.htm; "Mercosur," Export Virginia, June 2003, www.exportvirginia.org/FastFacts_2004/FF%20Issues%20Mercosur.pdf; "Profile: Mercosur—Common Market of the South," *BBC News,* December 15, 2006, http://news.bbc.co.uk/2/hi/americas/5195834.stm.

40. "About APEC," Asia-Pacific Economic Cooperation, www.apecsec.org.sg/apec/about_apec.html, (accessed January 8, 2007).

41. "South Korean Auto Exports to U.S. Hit Record High in 2001," *Inbound Logistics,* March 2002, p. 26.

42. Xu Dashan, "China's Economy to Grow 8% Annually from 2006 to 2010," *China Daily,* March 21, 2005, http://www.chinadaily.com.cn/english/doc/2005-03/21/content_426718.htm.

43. Janet Adamy, "One U.S. Chain's Unlikely Goal: Pitching Chinese Food in China," *The Wall Street Journal,* October 20, 2006, p. A1, http://online.wsj.com.

44. "What Is the WTO?" World Trade Organization, www.wto.org/ (accessed January 8, 2007).

45. Leigh Thomas, "E.U., U.S., Canada Haul China Before WTO over Auto Parts Dispute," *Yahoo! News,* September 15, 2006, http://news.yahoo.com/s/afp/20060915/bs_afp/euuscanadachinawto_060915221834.

46. George Chryssochoidis and Vasilis Theoharakis, "Attainment of Competitive Advantage by the Exporter-Importer Dyad: The Role of Export Offering and Import Objectives," *Journal of Business Research,* April 2004, pp. 329–337.

47. Gerry Khermouch, "'Whoa, Cool Shirt.' 'Yeah, It's a Pepsi,'" *BusinessWeek,* September 10, 2001, p. 84.

48. Farok J. Contractor and Sumit K. Kundu. "Franchising versus Company-Run Operations: Model Choice in the Global Hotel Sector," *Journal of International Marketing,* November 1997, pp. 28–53.

49. "Tribune Outsourcing Customer Service, Cutting 250 Jobs," *USA Today,* August 28, 2006, www.usatoday.com/money/media/2006-08-28-tribune-cuts_x.htm.

50. Katie Hafner, "EBay Is Expected to Close Its Auction Site in China," *The New York Times,* December 19, 2006, www.nytimes.com.

51. Andrew Kupfer, "How to Be a Global Manager," *Fortune,* March 14, 1988, pp. 52–58.

52. Kathryn Rudie Harrigan, "Joint Ventures and Competitive Advantage," *Strategic Management Journal,* May 1988, pp. 141–158.

53. "What We're About," NUMMI, www.nummi.com/co_info.html (accessed January 8, 2007).

54. Loretta Chao, "Claiborne to Bring Juicy Apparel Line to China Market," *The Wall Street Journal,* September 20, 2006, p. A20, http://online.wsj.com.

55. Jagdish N. Sheth, "From International to Integrated Marketing," *Journal of Business Research,* January 2001, pp. 5–9.

56. Ronald Paul Hill and Kanwalroop Kathy Dhanda, "Globalization and Technological Advancement: Implications for Macromarketing and the Digital Divide," *Journal of Macromarketing,* December 2004, pp. 147–155.

57. Deborah Owens, Timothy Wilkinson, and Bruce Kellor, "A Comparison of Product Attributes in a Cross-Cultural/Cross-National Context," *Marketing Management Journal,* Fall/Winter 2000, pp. 1–11.

58. William E. Kilbourne, "Globalization and Development: An Expanded Macromarketing View," *Journal of Macromarketing,* December 2004, pp. 122–135.

59. Anil K. Gupta and Vijay Govindarajan, "Converting Global Presence into Global Competitive Advantage," *Academy of Management Executive,* May 2001, pp. 45–58.

60. Rekha Balu, "Hop Faster, Energizer Bunny: Rayovac Batteries Roll On," *The Wall Street Journal,* June 15, 1999, p. B4; "Battle of the Blades Draws Corporate Blood," *The New York Times,* October 12, 2003, sec. 3, p. 1; The Gillette Company, www.gillette.com (accessed January 8, 2007); Gillette 1999–2005 Annual Reports; "Gillette's Edge," *BusinessWeek,* January 19, 1998, pp. 70–77; "Gillette, Schick End Legal War, but Battle in Market Rages On," *The Boston Globe,* February 17, 2006, www.boston.com/business/healthcare/articles/2006/02/17/gillette_schick_end_legal_war_but_battle_in_market_rages_on; P&G/Gillette Questions and Answers, www.pg.com/images/homepage/pg_gillette_faq.pdf (accessed Jan. 8, 2007); "Wal-Mart Selling Its Own Brand of Alkaline Batteries," *The Wall Street Journal,* December 10, 1999, pp. C4–5.

61. About IDG," International Data Group, www.idg.com/www/home.nsf/AboutIDGForm?OpenForm&region=WW (accessed January 8, 2007); Catherine Arnst, "Patrick J. McGovern: Insights for Dummies," *BusinessWeek,* May 1, 2006, www.businessweek.com/magazine/content/06_18/b3982034.htm?chan=search; Sam Perkins and Neal Thornberry, "Corporate Entrepreneurship for Dummies," Harvard Business School Publishing (Case BAB114).

a Apple Computer, Inc., www.apple.com (accessed January 19, 2007); Mary Bellis, "Inventors of the Modern Computer," *About,* http://inventors.about.com/library/weekly/aa121598.htm (accessed May 29, 2007); Carol Glatz, "Vatican Radio Employees Present Pope with Specially Loaded iPod Nano," Catholic News Service press release, March 3, 2006, www.catholicnews.com/data/stories/cns/0601282.htm; iPod, www.apple.com/ipod/ipod.html (accessed January 5, 2007); Leander Kahney, "The Cult of iPod," *Playlist,* http://playlistmag.com (accessed January 18, 2006); Louise Lee, "Sewing Up the iPod Market," *BusinessWeek,* January 12, 2006.

b Madhusmita Bora, "Bottled Mexican Coca-Cola Offers a Sweet Taste of Home," *The Indianapolis Star,* May 5, 2005, www.indystar.com/apps/pbcs.dll/article?AID=/20050505/LIVING/505050378; Louise Chu, "Is Mexican Coke the Real Thing?" *The San Diego Union-Tribune,* November 9, 2004, www.signonsandiego.com/uniontrib/20041109/news_1b9mexcoke.html; Tom Ragan, "Mexican Coke: The 'Real Thing?'" *Santa Cruz Sentinel,* March 19, 2006, www.santacruzsentinel.com/archive/2006/March/19/local/stories/01local.htm; Chad Terhune, "U.S. Thirst for Mexican Cola Poses Sticky Problem for Coke," *The Wall Street Journal,* January 11, 2006, pp. A1, A10.

c O. C. Ferrell, personal visit to Thailand, January 2007; Pitsinee Jitpleecheep, "Challenging the Goliath," *Bangkok Post,* January 8, 2007, p. B1.

CHAPTER 6

1. Allison Enright, "Gian Fulgani: When Consumer Habits Yield Real-World Results," *Marketing News,* November 1, 2006, pp. 20, 22; Gabriel M. Gelb, "Online Options Change Biz a Little—and a Lot," *Marketing News,* November 1, 2006, p. 23; Jared Heyman, "Net Research: Looks Easy, But It's Not: Know When It's Time to Hire the Professionals," *Marketing News,* November 1, 2006, p. 25; "Search Engines," *IT Facts,* October 20, 2006, www.itfacts.biz/index.php?id5P7477 (accessed January 15, 2007).

2. Anne L. Souchon, John W. Cadogan, David B. Procter, and Belinda Dewsnap, "Marketing Information Use and Organisational Performance: The Mediating Role of Responsiveness," *Journal of Strategic Marketing,* December 2004, pp. 231–242.

3. Bradley Johnson, "Understanding the 'Generation Wireless' Demographic," *Advertising Age,* March 20, 2006.

4. Ellen Byron, "New Penney: Chain Goes for 'Missing Middle,'" *The Wall Street Journal,* February 14, 2005, http://online.wsj.com.

5. Catherine Arnold, "Self-Examination: Researchers Reveal State of MR in Survey," *Marketing News,* February 1, 2005, pp. 55, 56.

6. Kenneth Chang, "Enlisting Science's Lessons to Entice More Shoppers to Spend More," *The New York Times,* September 19, 2006, www.nytimes.com.

7. Jamie Lareau, "Hummer's H3 Thrives in Slow SUV Market Despite Higher Gas Prices," *AutoWeek,* October 11, 2005, www.autoweek.com/news.cms?newsId5103335.
8. A. Parasuraman, Dhruv Grewal, and R. Krishnan, *Marketing Research* (Boston: Houghton Mifflin, 2007), p. 63.
9. Ken Manning, O. C. Ferrell, and Linda Ferrell, "Consumer Expectations of Clearance vs. Sale Prices," University of Wyoming working paper, 2007.
10. Parasuraman, Grewal, and Krishnan, *Marketing Research,* p. 64.
11. Ibid., p. 73.
12. Vikas Mittal and Wagner A. Kamakura, "Satisfaction, Repurchase Intent, and Repurchase Behavior: Investigating the Moderating Effects of Customer Characteristics," *Journal of Marketing Research,* February 2001, pp. 131–142.
13. Haya El Nasser, "Census Bureau No Longer Waiting 10 Years for Data," *The Coloradoan,* January 17, 2005, p. A2.
14. "Information Resources, Inc.," *Marketing News,* August 15, 2006, pp. H22–24.
15. "External Secondary Market Research," *CCH Business Owner's Toolkit,* www.toolkit.cch.com/text/P03_3011.asp (accessed January 23, 2007).
16. Arnold, "Self-Examination."
17. Jack Neff, "Consumers Rebel Against Marketers' Endless Surveys," *Advertising Age,* October 2, 2006, www.adage.com.
18. Ibid.
19. Maria Grubbs Hoy and Avery M. Abernethy, "Nonresponse Assessment in Marketing Research: Current Practice and Suggested Improvements," in *Marketing Theory and Applications,* American Marketing Association Winter Educators' Conference Proceedings, 2002.
20. David Jobber, John Saunders, and Vince-Wayne Mitchell, "Prepaid Monetary Incentive Effects on Mail Survey Response," *Journal of Business Research,* January 2004, pp. 347–350.
21. John Harwood and Shirley Leung, "Hang-Ups: Why Some Pollsters Got It So Wrong This Election Day," *The Wall Street Journal,* November 8, 2003, pp. A1, A6.
22. Ibid.
23. Robert V. Kozinets, "The Field Behind the Screen: Using Netnography for Marketing Research in Online Communities," *Journal of Marketing Research,* February 2002, pp. 61–72.
24. Glen L. Urban and John R. Hauser, "'Listening In' to Find and Explore New Combinations of Customer Needs," *Journal of Marketing,* April 2004, pp. 72–87.
25. Alissa Quart, "Ol' College Pry," *Business 2.0,* April 3, 2001.
26. "Where the Stars Design the Cars," *Business 2.0,* July 2005, p. 32.
27. Peter DePaulo, "Sample Size for Qualitative Research," *Quirk's Marketing Research Review,* December 2000, www.quirks.com.
28. Theodore T. Allen and Kristen M. Maybin, "Using Focus Group Data to Set New Product Prices," *Journal of Product and Brand Management,* January 2004, pp. 15–24.
29. Sean Geehan and Stacy Sheldon, "Connecting to Customers," *Marketing Management,* November/December 2005, pp. 37–42.
30. Kenneth Hein, "KFC Cooks Up Moms Panel," *BrandWeek,* August 22, 2006, www.brandweek.com.
31. Barbara Allan, "The Benefits of Telephone Depth Sessions," *Quirk's Marketing Research Review,* December 2000, www.quirks.com.
32. David Kiley, "Shoot the Focus Group," *BusinessWeek Online,* November 14, 2005, www.businessweek.com.
33. Judy Strauss and Donna J. Hill, "Consumer Complaints by E-mail: An Exploratory Investigation of Corporate Responses and Customer Reactions," *Journal of Interactive Marketing,* Winter 2001, pp. 63–73.
34. Kevin Kelleher, "66,207,986 Bottles of Beer on the Wall," *Business 2.0,* via CNN, February 25, 2004, www.cnn.com.
35. Thomas Mucha, "The Builder of Boomtown," *Business 2.0,* September 2005, www.business2.com.
36. "Group Warns of Grocery Grab for Data," *Marketing News,* April 15, 2002, p. 7.
37. Noah Rubin Brier, John McManus, David Myron, and Christopher Reynolds, "'Zero-In' Heroes," *American Demographics,* October 2004, pp. 36–45.
38. Laurence N. Goal, "High Technology Data Collection for Measurement and Testing," *Marketing Research,* March 1992, pp. 29–38.
39. Behrooz Noori and Mohammad Hossein Salimi, "A Decision-Support System for Business-to-Business Marketing," *Journal of Business & Industrial Marketing* 20 (2005): 226–236.
40. Carlos Denton, "Time Differentiates Latino Focus Groups," *Marketing News,* March 15, 2004, p. 52.
41. "Top 50 U.S. Research Organizations: VNU," *Marketing News,* August 5, 2006, pp. H6–H8.
42. Lambeth Hochwald, "Are You Smart Enough to Sell Globally?" *Sales & Marketing Management,* July 1998, pp. 52–56.
43. Ibid.
44. Allison Enright, "Gian Fulgani: When Consumer Habits Yield Real-World Results," *Marketing News,* November 1, 2006 pp. 20, 22; Gabriel M. Gelb, "Online Options Change Biz a Little—and a Lot," *Marketing News,* November 1, 2006, p. 23; Jared Heyman, "Net Research: Looks Easy, But It's Not: Know When It's Time to Hire the Professionals," *Marketing News,* November 1, 2006, p. 25; "Search Engines," *IT Facts,* October 20, 2006, www.itfacts.biz/index.php?id5P7477 (accessed January 15, 2007).
45. Steve Bassill, "How to Implement a Winning Segment Strategy," Marketing Profs.com, February 21, 2006, www.marketingprofs.com/6/bassill1.asp; Lake Snell Perry Mermin & Associations, www.lakesnellperry.com/ (accessed January 23, 2007); "Leading Democratic Poling Firm Celebrates 10th Anniversary with New Partner," Lake Snell Perry Mermin & Associations press release, March 11, 2005, www.lakesnellperry.com/new/Mermin0311.htm.
a. "On Any Day, PepsiCo 2005," PepsiCo Annual Report 2005, pp. 10–12, http://ccbn.mobular.net/ccbn/7/1250/1337/; "Coca-Cola North America Marketing and Innovation Focuses on Full Portfolio of Brands," Coca-Cola Company press release, February 3, 2006, www2.coca-cola.com/presscenter/nr_20060203_

americas_portfolio_of_brands.html; Kate MacArthur and Stephanie Thompson, "Pepsi, Coke: We Satisfy Your 'Need States,'" *Advertising Age*, November 27, 2006, pp. 3, 23.

b Stephanie Kang, "Trying to Connect with a Hip Crowd," *The Wall Street Journal*, October 13, 2005, p. B3, http://online.wsj.com; "Quest for Cool," Time, September 2003, via www.look-look.com/look-look/ html/Test_Drive_Press_Time.html; "What We Do," Look-Look.com, www.look-look.com/dynamic/looklook/jsp/What_We_Do.jsp (accessed January 23, 2007); "Who We Are," Look-Look.com, www.look-look.com/looklook/html/Test_Drive_Who_We_Are.html (accessed January 23, 2007).

c Robert Frank, "How One Entrepreneur Lives Large—For Free," *The Wall Street Journal Online*, June 11, 2003, www.startupjournal.com/ideas/services/20030611-frank.html; Matthew Heimer, "Mystery Shopper," *Smart Money*, December 2005, pp. 96–101; "Krispy Kreme Doughnuts Hires Mystery Shopping Firm," *Market Research Bulletin*, October 23, 2006, www.brandrepublic.com/bulletins/marketresearch/article/599753/krispy-kreme-doughnuts-hires-mystery-shopping-firm/; "Mystery Shopping Industry Estimated at Nearly $600 Million in United States, According to Market Size Report," Mystery Shopper Providers Association press release, November 29, 2005, www.mysteryshop.org/news/article_pr.php?art_ID569; "Our Programs: Digital On-Site Mystery Shopping," Pacific Research Group, http://65.119.21.227/programs/digital_onsite_shopping.asp (accessed May 29, 2007).

CHAPTER 7

1. Scott Allen, "Ingvar Kamprad—IKEA Founder and One of the World's Richest Men," About: Entrepreneurs, http://entrepreneurs.about.com/cs/famousentrepreneur/p/ingvarkamprad.htm (accessed January 2, 2007); Kerry Capell, "IKEA: How the Swedish Retailer Became a Global Brand," *BusinessWeek*, November 14, 2005, pp. 96–106; "Facts and Figures," IKEA, www.ikea.com/ms/en_US (accessed January 2, 2007); "IKEA's Growth Limited by Style Issues, Says CEO," *Nordic Business Report*, January 21, 2004, www.nordicbusinessreport.com; "IKEA Sets New Heights with Cat," *Printing World*, August 21, 2003, p. 3; "Stylish, Swedish, 60-ish: IKEA's a Global Phenomenon," *Western Mail*, May 20, 2003, p. 1; "Verticalnet's Supply Chain Software Upgrade, Packaging Wins Customers," *InternetWeek*, September 3, 2003, www.internetworld.com.

2. Marc Graser, "Toyota Hits Touch Points as It Hawks Yaris to Youth," *Advertising Age*, May. 1, 2006, p. 28.

3. Marie Swift, "Niche Masters," *Financial Planning*, September 2006, pp. 105–106.

4. Andrew Blum, with Louise Lee, "It Sure Ain't Old Navy," *BusinessWeek*, October 17, 2005, pp. 62–64; Sandra O'Loughlin, "It's First Down, Goal to Go for Gap's Forth & Towne," *Brandweek*, September 11, 2006, www.brandweek.com.

5. Suzanne Vranica, "In Haggar's Bold Ad Blitz, Middle-Aged Is the New Young," *The Wall Street Journal*, November 6, 2006, p. B1, http://online.wsj.com.

6. Service Corporation International, www.hoovers.com/service-corporation-international/—ID__11341—/free-co-factsheet.xhtml (accessed January 25, 2007).

7. Constantine von Hoffman, "K-C Is Rolling Out Toilet Paper for Tykes," *Brandweek*, March 13, 2006, p. 4, www.brandweek.com.

8. Stephanie Kang, "Chasing Generation Y," *The Wall Street Journal*, September 1, 2006, p. A11, http://online.wsj.com.

9. U.S. Bureau of the Census, *Statistical Abstract of the United States, 2007* (Washington, DC: U.S. Government Printing Office, 2006), p. 12.

10. Lisa Sanders, "How to Target Blacks? First You Gotta Spend," *Advertising Age*, July 3, 2006, p. 19.

11. Laura Heller, "Sears Targets Ethnic Customers with New Lines, Bilingual Associates," *DSN Retailing Today*, October 25, 2004, p. 69.

12. Constantine von Hoffman, "For Some Marketers, Low Income Is Hot," *Brandweek*, September 11, 2006, www.brandweek.com.

13. Jason Fields, "America's Families and Living Arrangements: 2003," *Current Population Reports* (Washington, DC: U.S. Census Bureau, November 2004), pp. 1–20.

14. "Clients and Case Studies," MicroMarketing, Inc., www.micromarketing.com/clients/index.html (accessed January 24, 2007).

15. Ann Zimmerman, "To Boost Sales, Wal-Mart Drops One-Size Fits-All Approach," *The Wall Street Journal*, September 7, 2006, p. A1, http://online.wsj.com.

16. "Yum, Bally Fitness Team Up for Promo," *Advertising Age*, January 3, 2005, p. 2.

17. Joseph T. Plummer, "The Concept and Application of Life Style Segmentation," *Journal of Marketing*, January 1974, p. 33.

18. "Catching Up with the Next Generation: They're Not Slackers Anymore," *PR Newswire*, October 26, 2004.

19. Rebecca Piirto Heath, "You Can Buy a Thrill: Chasing the Ultimate Rush," *American Demographics*, June 1997, pp. 47–51.

20. Beverage World, "Beverage Market Index 2003," June 15, 2003, VNU Business Media.

21. Stephanie Thompson, "Want That Perfect Body? Have Some More Danon," *Advertising Age*, September 25, 2006, pp. 3+.

22. Philip Kotler, *Marketing Management: Analysis, Planning, Implementation, and Control*, 7th ed. (Englewood Cliffs, NJ: Prentice Hall, 2003), p. 144.

23. "Analysis: Huge Cardiovascular Market Potential in Aging Baby Boomers," *Heart Disease Weekly*, via NewsRX.com and NewsRX.net, April 11, 2004, p. 92.

24. Charles W. Chase, Jr., "Selecting the Appropriate Forecasting Method," *Journal of Business Forecasting*, Fall 1997, pp. 2, 23, 28–29.

25. "ACNielsen Market Decisions: Controlled Market Testing," ACNielsen, http://us.acnielsen.com/products/rms_amd_controlledmktest.shtml (accessed November 8, 2006).

26. Constantine von Hoffman, "P&G Plans to Shrink Line of Detergents," *Brandweek*, October 16, 2006, p. 6, www.brandweek.com.

27. Scott Allen, "Ingvar Kamprad—IKEA Founder and One of the World's Richest Men," About: Entrepreneurs, http://entrepreneurs.about.com/cs/famousentrepreneur/p/ingvarkamprad.htm (accessed January 2, 2007);

Kerry Capell, "IKEA: How the Swedish Retailer Became a Global Brand," *BusinessWeek,* November 14, 2005, pp. 96–106; "Facts and Figures," IKEA, www.ikea.com/ms/en_US (accessed January 2, 2007); "IKEA's Growth Limited by Style Issues, Says CEO," *Nordic Business Report,* January 21, 2004, www.nordicbusinessreport.com; "IKEA Sets New Heights with Cat," *Printing World,* Auguat 21, 2003, p. 3; "Stylish, Swedish, 60-ish: IKEA's a Global Phenomenon," *Western Mail,* May 20, 2003, p. 1; "Verticalnet's Supply Chain Software Upgrade, Packaging Wins Customers," *InternetWeek,* September 3, 2003, www.internetworld.com

28. Janet Groeber, "That's Entertainment," *Display & Design Ideas,* May 2005, p. 22; Jordan's Furniture, www.jordans.com (accessed November 8, 2006); "Jordan's Furniture, Inc.," Hoovers, www.hoovers.com/jordan's-furniture/—ID__99028—/free-co-factsheet.xhtml (accessed January 25, 2007); "Jordan's Makes Furniture Shopping a Fun Event," *Metro Report Boston,* July 2005, p. 30; "Three Customer-Centric Retailers," *Chain Store Age,* October 2005, pp. 26–29.

a "Whole Baby Program Introduces New Moms to Advantages of Natural and Organic Lifestyle for Their Growing Families, Whole Foods Market and Mothering Magazine Partner to Launch Informational Lecture Tour About Benefits of Natural Parenting," *PR Newswire,* August 11, 2005, www.prnewswire.com/; "Whole Foods Market Survey Reveals Expectant Moms Are Hungry for Natural and Organic Nutrition Guidance, Whole Baby Lecture Series Kicks Off in New York City Sept. 22, National Experts Promote Health to Growing Families," *PR Newswire,* September 19, 2005, www.prnewswire.com/; Whole Foods Market, www.wholefoodsmarket.com (accessed January 24, 2007); Whole Baby Lecture Series, www.wholebaby lecture.com (accessed January 24, 2007).

b "About Us," Samantá Shoes, www.samantashoes.com/ (accessed January 24, 2007); Sonia Alleyne, "On the Right Footing: Samanta Shoes Offers More than Just a Good Look," *Black Enterprise,* June 2006, http://findarticles.com/p/articles/mi_m1365/is_11_36/ai_n16533093; "Samantá Joseph, President and CEO, Samanta Shoes," *Essence,* September 2005, p. 114.

c Brian Grow, "Tapping a Market That Is Hot, Hot, Hot," *BusinessWeek,* January 17, 2005, p. 36; "Innovations in Personal Finance for the Unbanked: Emerging Practices from the Field; Case Study; Cash & Save—Union Bank of California," Fannie Mae Foundation, www.fanniemaefoundation.org/programs/pdf/fscs_CashSave.pdf (accessed January 24, 2007); Shaheen Pasha, "Banks Woo Hispanic Market," *CNN/Money,* November 22, 2005, http://money.cnn.com.

CHAPTER 8

1. Monica Davey, "Harley at 100," *The New York Times,* September 1, 2003, p. A1; Jonathan Fahey, "Love into Money," *Forbes,* January 7, 2002, pp. 60–65; Harley-Davidson Company, www.harley-davidson.com (accessed Janyary 12, 2007); "Harley-Davidson Reports Record Second Quarter," Harley-Davidson news release, July 16, 2003, www.harley-davidson.com; Abraham Lustgarten, "The 100 Best Companies to Work For: Harley-Davidson," *Fortune,* January 12, 2004, p. 76; Ryan Nakashima, "Harley-Davidson Plans China Dealership," Forbes.com, January 18, 2006, www.forbes.com/business/energy/feeds/ap/2006/01/18/ap2458631.html; Joseph Weber, "Harley Just Keeps On Cruisin'," *BusinessWeek,* November 6, 2006, p. 71–72; Mark Yost, "Harley-Davidson Centenary Bash Brings Out Armchair 'Rebels,'" *The Wall Street Journal,* September 3, 2003, p. D4.

2. Wayne D. Hoyer and Deborah J. MacInnis, *Consumer Behavior,* 3rd ed. (Boston: Houghton Mifflin, 2004), pp. 57–59.

3. Andrew D. Gershoff and Gita Venkataramani Johar, "Do You Know Me? Consumer Calibration of Friends' Knowledge," *Journal of Consumer Research* 32 (March 2006): 496+.

4. Russell W. Belk, "Situational Variables and Consumer Behavior," *Journal of Consumer Research,* December 1975, pp. 157–164.

5. "Sorry Cupid, Santa's the One Handing Out Engagement Rings This Year—and He's Buying Them Online," *PR Newswire,* December 6, 2004.

6. Chien-Huang Lin, HsiuJu Rebecca Yen, and Shin-Chieh Chuang, "The Effects of Emotion and Need for Cognition on Consumer Choice Involving Risk," *Marketing Letters* 17 (January 2006): 47–60.

7. Jeremy Caplan, "Scents and Sensibility," *Time,* October 16, 2006, pp. 66–67.

8. Kim Ann Zimmermann, "Safeway Enters Online Grocery Turnstile," *E-Commerce Times,* January 16, 2002, www.ecommercetimes.com/perl/story/?id=5809.

9. Margaret Sheridan, "Made to Measure: Patient Satisfaction Surveys Provide Hospitals with Paths to Improvement," *Restaurants & Institutions,* November 1, 2003, p. 69.

10. Laura Q. Hughes and Alice Z. Cuneo, "Lowe's Retools Image in Push Toward Women," *Advertising Age,* February 26, 2001, www.adage.com/news_and_features/features/20010226/article7.html.

11. Maria Mooshil, "More Retailers Take Steps to Capture Women's Consumer Allegiance," *Chicago Tribune,* June 15, 2005, http://web.lexis-nexis.com/.

12. Gigi Suhanic, "What's Green and Purple and Grows in the Fridge?" *Financial Post,* August 23, 2004, p. FP4.

13. David B. Wooten, "From Labeling Possessions to Possessing Labels: Ridicule and Socialization Among Adolescents," *Journal of Consumer Research* 33 (September 2006): 188+.

14. Donnel A. Briley and Jennifer L. Aaker, "When Does Culture Matter? Effects of Personal Knowledge on the Correction of Culture-Based Judgments," *Journal of Marketing Research* 33 (August 2006), via marketingpower.com.

15. "2005 American Community Survey Data Profile Highlights," U.S. Census Bureau, http://factfinder.census.gov/servlet/ACSSAFFFacts?_submenuId=factsheet_0&_sse=on (accessed January 26, 2007).

16. Jeffrey M. Humphreys, "The Multicultural Economy 2006," *Georgia Business and Economic Conditions* 66 (Third Quarter 2006), www.selig.uga.edu/forecast/GBEC/GBEC063Q.pdf.

17. Lisa Sanders, "How to Target Blacks? First, You Gotta Spend," *Advertising Age,* July 3, 2006, p. 19.

18. Stuart Elliott, "Campaigns for Black Consumers," *The New York Times,* June 13, 2003, www.nytimes.com.

19. Sanders, "How to Target Blacks?"; Ann Zimmerman, "To Boost Sales, Wal-Mart Drops One-Size-Fits-All Approach," *The Wall Street Journal,* September 7, 2006, p. A1, http://online.wsj.com.

20. "Target Dreams in Color for King Day and Beyond," Target press release, January 11, 2007, http://news.target.com/phoenix.zhtml?c=196187&p=irol-newsArticle&ID=949530.

21. DaimlerChrysler Corporation press release, www.csrwire.com (accessed May 20, 2004).

22. "2005 American Community Survey Data Profile Highlights," U.S. Census Bureau; Humphreys, "The Multicultural Economy 2006," *Georgia Business and Economic Conditions.*

23. "Ethnic Analysis," www.databankusa.com/Services/Ethnic.asp (accessed January 26, 2007).

24. Humphreys, "The Multicultural Economy 2006," *Georgia Business and Economic Conditions.*

25. Laurel Wentz, "Reebok Launches Web Site for U.S. Hispanic Market," *Advertising Age,* November 15, 2005, www.adage.com/news.cms?newsId=46764; Samar Farah, "Latino Marketing Goes Mainstream," *The Boston Globe,* July 9, 2006, www.boston.com/business/articles/2006/07/09/latino_marketing_goes_mainstream/.

26. Greta Guest, "Analysts Commend New Kmart Ads; Campaign to Capitalize on Store's Strengths," *Detroit Free Press,* October 17, 2003.

27. Elliott, "Campaigns for Black Consumers."

28. Noel C. Paul, "Advertisers Slip into Spanish," *The Christian Science Monitor,* June 2, 2003, www.csmonitor.com/2003/0602/p16s01-wmcn.html.

29. Ibid.

30. "2005 American Community Survey Data Profile Highlights," U.S. Census Bureau.; Christina Hoag, "Asian-Americans Are Fastest Growing Group," *Miami Herald,* April 7, 2003, www.miami.com/mld/miamiherald/.

31. Humphreys, "The Multicultural Economy 2006," *Georgia Business and Economic Conditions.*

32. The 'Invisible' Market," *BrandWeek,* February 1, 2006, www.brandweek.com.

33. Monica Davey, "Harley at 100," *The New York Times,* September 1, 2003, p. A1; Jonathan Fahey, "Love into Money," *Forbes,* January 7, 2002, pp. 60–65; Harley-Davidson Company, www.harley-davidson.com (accessed January 12, 2007); "Harley-Davidson Reports Record Second Quarter," Harley-Davidson news release, July 16, 2003, www.harley-davidson.com; Abraham Lustgarten, "The 100 Best Companies to Work For: Harley-Davidson," *Fortune,* January 12, 2004, p. 76; Ryan Nakashima, "Harley-Davidson Plans China Dealership," Forbes.com, January 18, 2006, www.forbes.com/business/energy/feeds/ap/2006/01/18/ap2458631.html; Joseph Weber, "Harley Just Keeps on Cruisin'," *BusinessWeek,* November 6, 2006, p. 71–72; Mark Yost, "Harley-Davidson Centenary Bash Brings Out Armchair 'Rebels,'" *The Wall Street Journal,* September 3, 2003, p. D4.

34. "Child Safety Seat Warning Withdrawn," CBS News, January 18, 2007, www.cbsnews.com/stories/2007/01/18/tech/main2371839.shtml; Consumer Reports, www.consumerreports.com (accessed January 29, 2007); "Consumer Reports Fries Wendy's Claims of Less Trans Fat," WRAL, November 6, 2006, www.wral.com/money/10258468/detail.html; "Consumer Reports: Refuse Extended Warranties," MSNBC, November 13, 2006, http://msnbc.msn.com/id/15704495/; "Holiday Shopping Made Easy: Consumer Reports ShopSmart Mobile Subscription Service Helps On-the-Go Holiday Shoppers Buy the Best Gifts at the Best Prices," AScribe Newswire, December 12, 2005, www.highbeam.com; Roger Parloff, "The Ionic Breeze Is No Match for Consumer Reports," *Fortune,* December 13, 2004; "Winner: Consumer Reports Staff," *The Quill,* June/July 2005.

a Samantha Critchell, "Designer Marc Eckos Building a Fashion Empire," *The [Massachusetts] Standard-Times,* May 12, 2004, p. B1, www.southcoasttoday.com/daily/05-04/05-12-04/b01li040.htm; Ecko Unlimited, www.eckounltd.com/ (accessed January 29, 2007); Mark Ecko Enterprises, www.marceckoenterprises.com/ (accessed January 29, 2007); "Marc Ecko Fashion Collections," *First View,* www.firstview.com/alldesigners/MarcEcko.html#Anchor3 (accessed September12, 2006); Jordan Robertson, "Toe the Line Between Corporate and Cool," *Business* 2.0, November 2004.

b Andrew LaVallee, "Now, Virtual Fashion," *The Wall Street Journal,* September 22, 2006, online.wsj.com/article/SB115888412923570768.html; "Living a Second Life," *The Economist,* September 30, 2006, via Business Source Complete database; Jennifer Mears and Ann Bednarz, "You Know It's Cool When Vendors Want In," *NetworkWorld,* October 10, 2006, www.networkworld.com; Richard Siklos, "A Virtual World but Real Money," *The New York Times,* October 19, 2006, http://select.nytimes.com/gst/abstract.html; Arun Sudhaman, "The Virtual World of Second Life," *Media Asia,* November 3, 2006, via Business Source Complete database; "What Is Second Life?" Second Life, secondlife.com/whatis/ (accessed January 29, 2007); Dan Zehr, "Dell Gets Virtual with Second Life Island," *The Austin American-Statesman,* November 15, 2006, www.statesman.com/business/content/business/stories/technology/11/15/15dell.html.

c Kathleen Hays, Gerri Willis, and Valerie Morris, "Teen Moguls & Spotting Teen Buying Trends," *The Flipside,* March 18, 2004; "Teen Clout Shows No Sign of Diminishing, Everyone Takes Note," *Business and Industry,* July 18, 2005; Jan Eisner, "Putting Brakes on Materialism: Teen Buying Power," *Knight Ridder Newspapers,* September 20, 2004; Becky Sisco, "Sweet Buy and By; Research Finds a Few Changes in Teens' Purchasing Habits," *Telegraph Herald,* January 9, 2005; "Teen Market Profile," Mediamark Research, Inc., www.magazine.org/content/files/teenprofile04.pdf (accessed January 29, 2007).

CHAPTER 9

1. "It's the Mirrors," Texas Instruments DLP, www.itsthemirrors.com/ (accessed January 15, 2007); Peter Lewis, "Texas Instruments' Lunatic Fringe," *CNNMoney,* November 14, 2006, http://money.cnn.com/; Gene Marcial, "Texas Instruments: In Electronic Paradise," *BusinessWeek Online,* March 13, 2006, www.businessweek.com/print/magazine/content/06_11/b3975124.htm?chan=gl; Joe Osha, "Merrill: Texas Instruments Faces Wireless Woes," *BusinessWeek Online,* December 11, 2006, www.businessweek.com/print/investor/content/dec2006/pi20061211_045991.htm; Andrew Park, "Texas Instruments Inside?" *BusinessWeek Online,* December 6, 2004, www.businessweek.com/print/magazine/content/04_49/b3911045_mz011.htm?chan=gl; Texas Instruments Annual Report 10-K, "Designing for the Environment," "Working with Suppliers," "Workplace Safety," "TI, the Law and You: A Survival Guide for Changing Times," Texas Instruments training materials, www.ti.com (accessed January 15, 2007).

2. "STP: Segmentation, Targeting, Positioning," American Marketing Association, www.marketingpower.com/content1488C381S3.php (accessed January 30, 2007).

3. Ibid.

4. Matt Kelly, "Consortium Finds a Happy Ending," *eWeek,* September 19, 2005, pp. C1, C4.

5. Michael D. Hutt and Thomas W. Speh, *Business Marketing Management* (Mason, OH: Thomson/South-Western, 2004), p. 93.

6. Bureau of the Census, *Statistical Abstract of the United States, 2007* (Washington, DC: U.S. Government Printing Office, 2006), pp. 649–650.

7. Ibid, p. 649.

8. Ibid., p. 308.

9. Ibid., p. 264.

10. "Identix Wins the U.S. Department of State Facial Recognition Solicitation," *Business Wire,* September 29, 2004.

11. "Adina Genn, "E-Deals Even Small-Biz Playing Field," *Long Island Business News,* July 9, 2004.

12. Hussey Seating, www.husseyseating.com (accessed January 29, 2007).

13. Boeing, RyanAir Agree to Order for 32 Additional 737-800s," Boeing press release, September 29, 2006, www.boeing.com/news/releases/2006/q3/060929a_nr.html.

14. Das Narayandas and V. Kasturi Rangan, "Building and Sustaining Buyer-Seller Relationships in Mature Industrial Markets," *Journal of Marketing,* July 2004, p. 63.

15. Ellen Byron, "Aiming to Clean Up, P&G Courts Business Customers," *The Wall Street Journal,* January 26, 2007, p. B1, http://online.wsj.com.

16. Alex R. Zablah, Wesley J. Johnston, and Danny N. Bellenger, "Transforming Partner Relationships Through Technological Innovation," *Journal of Business & Industrial Marketing* 20 (August 2005): 355–363.

17. Cindy Claycomb and Gary L. Frankwick, "Dynamics of Buyers' Perceived Costs during a Relationship Development Process: An Empirical Assessment," *Journal of Business Research* 58 (2005): 1662–1671.

18. Lisa Harrington, "Right Moves," *Inbound Logistics,* November 2005, pp. 37–40.

19. Leonidas C. Leonidou, "Industrial Buyers' Influence Strategies: Buying Situation Differences," *Journal of Business & Industrial Marketing* 20 (January 2005): 33–42.

20. Joseph O'Reilly, "A Ready-Mix Transport Solution," *Inbound Logistics,* November 2005, pp. 70–71.

21. Jeffrey Burt, "Gateway Eyes Small Businesses," *eWeek,* September 5, 2005, www.eweek.com.

22. Frederick E. Webster, Jr., and Yoram Wind, "A General Model for Understanding Organizational Buyer Behavior," *Marketing Management,* Winter/Spring 1996, pp. 52–57.

23. Robert D. McWilliams, Earl Naumann, and Stan Scott, "Determining Buying Center Size," *Industrial Marketing Management* 21 (1992): 43–49.

24. Doug Bartholomew, "CEO of the Year—The King of Customer," *Industry Week,* February 1, 2002, www.industryweek.com/CurrentArticles/Asp/articles.asp?ArticleId+180.

25. Laura Heller, *DSN Retailing Today,* January 10, 2005, pp. 13–14.

26. George S. Day and Katrina J. Bens, "Capitalizing on the Internet Opportunity," *Journal of Business & Industrial Marketing* 20 (2005): 160–168.

27. Steve Hamm, "GM's Way or the Highway," *BusinessWeek,* December 19, 2005, pp. 48–49.

28. Niklas Myhr and Robert E. Spekman, "Collaborative Supply-Chain Partnerships Built upon Trust and Electronically Mediated Exchange," *Journal of Business & Industrial Marketing* 20 (2005): 179–186.

29. "Development of NAICS," U.S. Census Bureau, www.census.gov/epcd/www/naicsdev.htm (accessed January 30, 2007).

30. "It's the Mirrors," Texas Instruments DLP, www.itsthemirrors.com/ (accessed January 15, 2007); Peter Lewis, "Texas Instruments' Lunatic Fringe," *CNNMoney,* November 14, 2006, http://money.cnn.com/; Gene Marcial, "Texas Instruments: In Electronic Paradise," *BusinessWeek Online,* March 13, 2006, www.businessweek.com/print/magazine/content/06_11/b3975124.htm?chan=gl; Joe Osha, "Merrill: Texas Instruments Faces Wireless Woes," *BusinessWeek Online,* December 11, 2006, www.businessweek.com/print/investor/content/dec2006/pi20061211_045991.htm; Andrew Park, "Texas Instruments Inside?" *BusinessWeek Online,* December 6, 2004, www.businessweek.com/print/magazine/content/04_49/b3911045_mz011.htm?chan=gl; Texas Instruments Annual Report 10-K, "Designing for the Environment," "Working with Suppliers," "Workplace Safety," "TI, the Law and You: A Survival Guide for Changing Times," Texas Instruments training materials, www.ti.com (accessed January 15, 2007).

31. Lextant, www.lextant.com (accessed January 30, 2007); "Wyatt Starosta, 34," *C-Bus,* September/October 2006, pp. 13, 16; Jon Udell, "Art and Science of Usability Analysis," *InfoWorld,* June 4, 2004, www.infoworld.com/article/04/06/04/23FEuser-sb_1.html?INTEGRATED%20DEVELOPMENT%20ENVIRONMENT%20-%20IDE.

a "About Naturally Potatoes," Naturally Potatoes, www.naturallypotatoes.com/about.html (accessed January 30, 2007); "Potatoes: Finding the Perfect Potato," Michael Foods, www.michaelfoods.com/products/potatoes.cfm (accessed January 30, 2007); "Products: Potato Express," Reser's Fine Foods, www.resers.com/products/potatoexpress (accessed January 30, 2007); "Retail," Naturally Potatoes, www.naturallypotatoes.com/retail.html (accessed January 30, 2007); David Sharp, "Spuds Go the Way of Salad: Right Out of the Package," *The [Fort Collins] Coloradoan,* August 28, 2005, p. E2.

b "Entrepreneur of the Year," Inc., January 5, 2005, www.inc.com/entrepreneur/profile/index.php?mcn-abb56; Hilary Potkewitz, "Geek Support," *Los Angeles Business Journal,* June 13, 2005, www.geeksontime.com/labusiness.pdf; "Who We Are," 1-800-GeeksOnTime, www.geeksontime.com/founder.html (accessed January 30, 2007); "Women Entrepreneurs: Venus McNabb," *ABCNews,* December 19, 2005, http://abcnews.go.com/GMA/story?id51405873.

c "Press Room: Background," IBM, www-03.ibm.com/press/us/en/background.wss (accessed January 30, 2007); Steve Hamm, "GM's Way or the Highway," *BusinessWeek,* December 19, 2005, pp. 48–49; IBM Annual Report 2004, IBM, pp. 1–7 ; Understanding Our Company, An IBM Prospectus, IBM, March 2005, www.ibm.com/annualreport/2004/prospectus/index.shtml.

CHAPTER 10

1. "Consumers Get Chance to 'Have Their Say' on Heinz Ketchup Bottles; Heinz Launches Myheinz.com to Offer 'Create-Your-Own' Talking Labels That Speak for Themselves at Birthdays, Weddings and Every Occasion in Between," Heinz press release, August 2, 2006, http://home.businesswire.com/portal/site/heinz/index.jsp?epi-content=GENERIC&newsId=20060802005575&ndmHsc=v2*A1136120400000*B1165537418000*C4102491599000*DgroupByDate*J2*M691*N1003052&newsLang=en&beanID=748445763&viewID=news_view; "Heinz's New 'Fridge Door Fit' Ketchup 'Fits in' with Peak of Summer Cookout Season; Designed as the Most Convenient, Large-Sized Bottle Ever, Heinz's Latest Innovation is an Easy to Pour, Easy to Store Bottle of Ketchup," Heinz press release, June 29, 2006, http://home.businesswire.com/portal/site/heinz/index.jsp?epi-content=GENERIC&newsId=20060629005517&ndmHsc=v2*A1136120400000*B1165537418000*C4102491599000*DgroupByDate*J2*M691*N1003052&newsLang=en&beanID=748445763&viewID=news_view; "Heinz Zeros in on Innovation; Set to Launch 100 new products," FoodProcessing.com, July 3, 2006, www.foodprocessing.com/industrynews/2006/096.html; Russell Jackson, "Beans Means Heinz Winz Prize for Television's Most Memorable Ad," *The Scotsman*, May 27, 2006, http://thescotsman.scotsman.com/index.cfm?id=783502006; Teresa F. Lindeman, "Consumer Goods Companies Turn to 'Talkative' and Offbeat Labels to Stick out in Crowded Aisles," *Pittsburgh Post-Gazette*, January 7, 2007, www.post-gazette.com/pg/07007/751693-28.stm; Sonia Reyes, "Heinz Goes Back to the '80s in Trivial Pursit Promo," *Adweek*, November 30, 2006, www.adweek.com/aw/search/article_display.jsp?vnu_content_id=1003466434.
2. "Netflix Stock Sinks, Blockbuster Blooms," *BusinessWeek Online*, January 4, 2007, www.businessweek.com.
3. Greg Moss, "Starbucks Sees Growing Demand for Drive-Thrus," 9News.com, December 27, 2005, www.9news.com.
4. Debbie Howell, "HEB Plus! Is at It Again—Turning Heads with a NEW GM Line," *DSN Retailing Today*, December 19, 2005, pp. 3+.
5. Steve Hargreaves, "Calming Ethanol-Crazed Corn Prices," *CNNMoney*, January 30, 2007, http://money.cnn.com/.
6. Joann Muller, "Parts for the Sensitive Car," *Forbes*, November 28, 2005, pp. 204–208.
7. Ellen Byron, "Aiming to Clean Up, P&G Courts Business Customers," *The Wall Street Journal*, January 26, 2007, http://online.wsj.com
8. Traci Pardum, "Procter & Gamble: Adding More Goods to Its Bag," *IndustryWeek*, October 13, 2005, www.industryweek.com/ReadArticle.aspx?ArticleID=10862&SectionID=5.
9. Muller, "Parts for the Sensitive Car."
10. Michael D. Johnson, Andreas Herrmann, and Frank Huber, "Evolution of Loyalty Intentions," *Journal of Marketing* 70 (April 2006), via www.marketingpower.com.
11. "Who Is Dr. Gadget?" The Dettman Group, www.doctorgadget.com/Who_Is_Dr._Gadget.html (accessed January 31, 2007).
12. Elizabeth Esfahani, "Finding the Sweet Spot," *Business 2.0*, November 2005, www.business2.com.
13. James R. Healey and Jayne O'Donnell, "Popularity of Crossovers Leaves SUVs in Dust," *USA Today*, December 8, 2005, pp. 1B, 3B.
14. Dennis K. Berman and Ellen Byron, "P&G Sells Sure Deodorant Label to Private Firm Innovative Brands," *The Wall Street Journal*, September 26, 2006, p. B2, http://online.wsj.com.
15. Adapted from Everett M. Rogers, *Diffusion of Innovations* (New York: Macmillan, 1962), pp. 81–86.
16. Ibid., pp. 247–250.
17. "Dictionary of Marketing Terms," American Marketing Association, www.marketingpower.com/mg-dictionary.php (accessed January 31, 2007).
18. Warren Church, "Investment in Brand Pays Large Dividends," *Marketing News*, November 15, 2006, p. 21.
19. U.S. Bureau of the Census, *Statistical Abstract of the United States, 2007* (Washington, DC: U.S. Government Printing Office, 2006), p. 507.
20. C. D. Simms and P. Trott, "The Perception of the BMW Mini Brand: The Importance of Historical Associations and the Development of a Model," *Journal of Product & Brand Management* 15 (2006): 228–238.
21. Douglas B. Holt, *How Brands Become Icons: The Principles of Cultural Branding* (Boston: Harvard Business School Press, 2004).
22. Nigel Hollis, "Branding Unmasked," *Marketing Research*, Fall 2005, pp. 24–29.
23. David A. Aaker, *Managing Brand Equity: Capitalizing on the Value of a Brand Name* (New York: Free Press, 1991), pp. 16–17.
24. Don E. Schultz, "The Loyalty Paradox," *Marketing Management*, September/October 2005, pp. 10–11.
25. Janet Adamy, "New Food, New Look," *The Wall Street Journal*, November 21, 2005, p. R8, http://online.wsj.com.
26. Chiranjeev S. Kohli, Katrin R. Harich, and Lance Leuthesser, "Creating Brand Identity: A Study of Evaluation of New Brand Names," *Journal of Business Research* 58 (2005): 1506–1515.
27. Dionne Searcey, "Bye, Cingular, in AT&T Rebranding," *The Wall Street Journal*, January 12, 2007, p. B3, http://online.wsj.com.
28. Kitty Bean Yancey, "Could You Name a New Hotel Chain?" *USA Today*, September 22, 2006, p. 11D.
29. Allison Fass, "Animal House," *Forbes*, February 12, 2007, pp. 72–75.
30. Dorothy Cohen, "Trademark Strategy," *Journal of Marketing*, January 1986, p. 63.
31. Chiranjev Kohli and Rajheesh Suri, "Brand Names That Work: A Study of the Effectiveness of Different Brand Names," *Marketing Management Journal*, Fall/Winter 2000, pp. 112–120.
32. U.S. Trademark Association, "Trademark Stylesheet," no. 1A, n.d.
33. Dan Weeks, "Bacardi to Defend 'Vigorously' in Havana Club Lawsuit," *Caribbean Net News*, August 17, 2006, www.caribbeannetnews.com/cgi-script/csArticles/articles/000028/002823.htm.
34. Dorothy Cohen, "Trademark Strategy Revisited," *Journal of Marketing*, July 1991, pp. 46–59.
35. Stephanie Thompson, "Kellogg Has Megabrand Ambitions for Special K," *Advertising Age*, November 6, 2006, p. 6.

36. Vicki R. Lane, "The Impact of Ad Repetition and Ad Content on Consumer Perceptions of Incongruent Extensions," *Journal of Marketing,* April 2000, pp. 80–91.

37. Shantini Munthree, Geoff Bick, and Russell Abratt, "A Framework for Brand Revitalization," *Journal of Product & Brand Management* 15 (2006): 157–167.

38. Chris Pullig, Carolyn J. Simmons, and Richard G. Netemeyer, "Brand Dilution: When Do New Brands Hurt Existing Brands?" *Journal of Marketing* 70 (April 2006), via marketingpower.com.

39. "Kohl's Inks Exclusive Deal for Tony Hawk Footwear," *Los Angeles Business,* January 29, 2007, http://losangeles.bizjournals.com/losangeles/stories/2007/01/29/daily38.html?surround=lfn.

40. Deborah Ball, "The Perils of Packaging: Nestlé Aims for Easier Openings," *The Wall Street Journal,* November 17, 2005, p. B1, http://online.wsj.com.

41. Thomas J. Madden, Kelly Hewett, and Martin S. Roth, "Managing Images in Different Cultures: A Cross-National Study of Color Meanings and Preferences," *Journal of International Marketing,* Winter 2000, p. 90.

42. Gary Grossman, "Put Some Pizzazz in Your Packaging," *Brandweek,* January 17, 2005, p. 17.

43. Smucker's Annual Report, 2005, The J.M. Smucker Company.

44. Deborah Ball, "The Perils of Packaging: Nestlé Aims for Easier Openings," *The Wall Street Journal,* November 17, 2005, p. B1, http://online.wsj.com.

45. Valerie Folkes and Shashi Matta, "The Effect of Package Shape on Consumers' Judgment of Product Volume: Attention as a Mental Contaminant," *Journal of Consumer Research,* September 2004, p. 390.

46. "Consumers Get Chance to 'Have Their Say' on Heinz Ketchup Bottles; Heinz Launches Myheinz.com to Offer 'Create-Your-Own' Talking Labels That Speak for Themselves at Birthdays, Weddings and Every Occasion in Between," Heinz press release, August 2, 2006, http://home.businesswire.com/portal/site/heinz/index.jsp?epi-content=GENERIC&newsId=20060802005575&ndmHsc=v2*A1136120400000-*B1165537418000*C4102491599000*DgroupByDate*J2*M691*N1003052&newsLang=en&beanID=748445763&viewID=news_view; "Heinz's New 'Fridge Door Fit' Ketchup 'Fits in' with Peak of Summer Cookout Season; Designed as the Most Convenient, Large-Sized Bottle Ever, Heinz's Latest Innovation is an Easy to Pour, Easy to Store Bottle of Ketchup," Heinz press release, June 29, 2006, http://home.businesswire.com/portal/site/heinz/index.jsp?epi-content=GENERIC&newsId=20060629005517&ndmHsc=v2*A1136120400000*B1165537418000*C4102491599000*DgroupByDate*J2*M691*N1003052&newsLang=en&beanID=748445763&viewID=news_view; "Heinz Zeros in on Innovation; Set to Launch 100 New Products," FoodProcessing.com, July 3, 2006, www.foodprocessing.com/industrynews/2006/096.html; Russell Jackson, "Beans Means Heinz Winz Prize for Television's Most Memorable Ad," *The Scotsman,* May 27, 2006, http://thescotsman.scotsman.com/index.cfm?id=783502006; Teresa F. Lindeman, "Consumer Goods Companies Turn to 'Talkative' and Offbeat Labels to Stick Out in Crowded Aisles," *Pittsburgh Post-Gazette,* January 7, 2007, www.post-gazette.com/pg/07007/751693-28.stm; Sonia Reyes, "Heinz Goes Back to the '80s in Trivial Pursit Promo," *Adweek,* November 30, 2006, www.adweek.com/aw/search/article_display.jsp?vnu_content_id=1003466434.

47. Peter Asmus, "Goodbye Coal, Hello Wind," *Business Ethics,* July/Aug. 1999, pp. 10–11; Robert Baun, "New Belgium Hits Top 5 Among U.S. Specialty Brewers," *The [Fort Collins] Coloradoan,* February 21, 2002, p. 9; Robert Baun, "What's in a Name? Ask the Makers of Fat Tire," *The [Fort Collins] Coloradoan,* October 8, 2000, pp. E1, E3; Rachel Brand, "Colorado Breweries Bring Home 12 Medals in Festival," *Rocky Mountain [Denver] News,* www.insidedenver.com/news/1008beer6.shtml (accessed November 6, 2000); Stevi Deter, "Fat Tire Amber Ale," The Net Net, www.thenetnet.com/reviews/fat.html (accessed February 1, 2007); Robert F. Dwyer and John F. Tanner, Jr., *Business Marketing* (Burr Ridge, IL: Irwin/McGraw-Hill, 1999), p. 104; "Four Businesses Honored with Prestigious International Award for Outstanding Marketplace Ethics," Better Business Bureau press release, September 23, 2002, www.bbb.org/alerts/ 2002torchwinners.asp; Julie Gordon, "Lebesch Balances Interests in Business, Community," *The [Fort Collins] Coloradoan,* February 26, 2003; Del I. Hawkins, Roger J. Best, and Kenneth A. Coney, *Consumer Behavior: Building Marketing Strategy,* 8th ed. (Burr Ridge, IL: Irwin/McGraw-Hill, 2001); David Kemp, Tour Connoisseur, New Belgium Brewing Company, personal interview by Nikole Haiar, November 21, 2000; New Belgium Brewing Company, Ft. Collins, CO, www.newbelgium.com (accessed February 1, 2007); New Belgium Brewing Company Tour by Nikole Haiar, November 20, 2000; "New Belgium Brewing Wins Ethics Award," *Denver Business Journal,* January 2, 2003, http://denver.bizjournals.com/denver/ stories/2002/12/30/daily21.html; Dan Rabin, "New Belgium Pours It on for Bike Riders," *Celebrator Beer News,* August/September 1998, www.celebrator.com/9808/rabin.html; Lisa Sanders, "This Beer Will Reduce Your Anxiety," *Advertising Age,* January 17, 2005, p. 25; Bryan Simpson, "New Belgium Brewing: Brand Building Through Advertising and Public Relations," http://college.hmco.com/instructors/catalog/misc/new_ belgium_brewing.pdf (accessed February 1, 2007). This case was prepared by Nikole Haiar for classroom discussion rather than to illustrate either effective or ineffective handling of an administrative, ethical, or legal decision by management.

a Emily Holt, "A Pair of Odd Socks," *Women's Wear Daily,* Aug. 9, 2004; Brendan I. Koerner, "A Salute to the Stray Sock," *The New York Times,* October 3, 2004, sec. 3, p. 2; LittleMissMatched, www.littlemissmatched.com (accessed January 31, 2007); "A Successful Mismatch," CNN, May 9, 2005, www.cnn.com; "The Sock of the New," *Boston Globe,* October 14, 2004.

b Sewell Chan, "Honoring Robinson Is Part of Citi Field Plans," *The New York Times,* November 14, 2006 www.nytimes.com/2006/11/14/sports/baseball/14stadium.html?ex51321160400&en5 90020d8b2d8fe77f&ei55090&partner5rssuserland&emc5rss; Stuart Elliott, "The Mets' New Marquee Name," *The New York Times,* November 14, 2006, p. C5; David Lennon and Chau Lam, "Mets Break Ground on Citi Field," Newsday, November 13, 2006, www.newsday.com/sports/baseball/mets/ny-spground1114,0,5116647.story?coll5ny-mets-print; "Mets and Citigroup Announce Landmark Strategic Partnership at Ceremonial Groundbreaking for Citi Field," New York Mets press release, November 13, 2006, http://newyork.mets.mlb.com/NASApp/mlb/news/press_releases/press_release.jsp?ymd520061113 &content_id51739655&vkey5pr_nym&fext5.jsp&c_id5nym.

c Julie Gordon, "Churning up Cheese," *MouCo News,* June 24, 2001, http://mouco.com/sitecms/content/view/50/2/; Christine McManus, "Bingham Hill Returns," *The Coloradoan,* November 11, 2005, p.

D8; Christine McManus, "'Micro-Cheesery' Closes," *The Coloradoan*, February 10, 2006, www.coloradoan.com; Kate Sander, "Rustic Blue Won Bingham Hill Its Fame; Now Company Delves into New Cheeses," *Cheese Market News*, September 2, 2005, www.cheesemarketnews.com/articlearch/retailwatch/2005/rw02sept05.html; Kate Sander, "Bingham Hill Builds on Microbreweries' Success with Colorado 'Microcessery,'" *Cheese Market News*, June 15, 2001, www.cheesemarketnews.com/ articlearch/retail-watch/2001/rw13jul01.html; Anna Wolfe, "Bingham Hill Quadruples Production Capacity," Gourmet News, August 2005, via www.looksmartitalianfood.com/p/articles/mi_qa4024/is_200508/ ai_n14851846.

CHAPTER 11

1. "Brands," Binney & Smith, www.binney-smith.com/page.cfm?id=10 (accessed February 5, 2007); "Company Profile," Binney & Smith, www.binney-smith.com/page.cfm?id=30 (accessed February 5, 2007); "History," Binney & Smith, www.binney-smith.com/page.cfm?id=11 (accessed February 5, 2007); Bruce Horovitz, "Crayoloa Draws on New Ideas as Crayons Make Room for 'Mess-Less' Toys," *USA Today*, December 12, 2006, pp. 1B–2B, www.usatoday.com/money/industries/retail/2006-12-06-crayola-revamp_x.htm; Reena Jana, "Crayola Brightens a Brand," *BusinessWeek Online*, January 26, 2007, www.businessweek.com/innovate/content/jan2007/id20070126_338855.htm; Denise O'Neal, "New Products Brighten Crayola's Rainbow," *Chicago Sun Times*, April 14, 2006, www.findarticles.com/p/articles/mi_qn4155/is_20060414/ai_n16169784.
2. Stephanie Thompson, "Kellogg Positions Special K as Megabrand," *Advertising Age*, November 7, 2006, www.adage.com.
3. Steven Gray, "Hormel Struggles to Add Upscale Foods Without Alienating Lovers of Its Spam," *The Wall Street Journal*, November 29, 2006, p. B1, http://online.wsj.com.
4. Kate MacArthur, "Drink Your Fruits, Veggies: Water's the New Fitness Fad," *Advertising Age*, January 3, 2005, p. 4.
5. Maria Sääksjärvi and Minttu Lampinen, "Consumer Perceived Risk in Successive Product Generations," *European Journal of Innovation Management* 8 (June 2005): 145–156.
6. Jean Halliday, "Bet Your Luxury Car Can't Do This," *Advertising Age*, November 13, 2006, www.adage.com.
7. Jeff Sabatini, "An SUV with Sports-Car Envy," *The Wall Street Journal*, December 1, 2006, p. W11C, http://online.wsj.com.
8. Frank Franzak and Dennis Pitta, "New Product Development at Eastern Spice & Flavorings," *Journal of Product & Brand Management* 14 (2005): 462–467.
9. Gray, "Hormel Struggles to Add Upscale Foods Without Alienating Lovers of Its Spam."
10. Scott Sprinzen and Robert Schulz, "Running on Empty in Detroit," *BusinessWeek Online*, December 9, 2005, www.businessweek.com.
11. Kate Macarthur, "Coke, Nestlé Offer a Workout in a Can," *Advertising Age*, October 16, 2006, p. 8.
12. "Making Headway with Helmets," *BusinessWeek*, January 15, 2007, p. 75.
13. Lee G. Cooper. "Strategic Marketing Planning for Radically New Products," *Journal of Marketing*, January 2000, pp. 1–16.
14. Lisa C. Troy, David M. Szymanski, and P. Rajan Varadarajan, "Generating New Product Ideas: An Initial Investigation of the Role of Market Information and Organizational Characteristics," *Journal of the Academy of Marketing Science*, January 2001, pp. 89–101.
15. Janet Adamy, "For McDonald's It's a Wrap," *The Wall Street Journal*, January 30, 2007, p. B1, http://online.wsj.com.
16. A. G. Lafley, "Procter & Gamble," *BusinessWeek*, December 19, 2005, p. 62.
17. Ann Zimmerman, "Home Depot Bets on Design of Store Brand to Fire Up Sales," *The Wall Street Journal*, November 29, 2006, p. B3, http://online.wsj.com.
18. "Inside a White-Hot Idea Factory," *BusinessWeek*, January 15, 2007, pp. 72–73.
19. Stephen J. Carson, "When to Give Up Control of Outsourced New Product Development," *Journal of Marketing* 71 (January 2007): 49–66.
20. Dennis A. Pitta and Danielle Fowler, "Online Consumer Communities and Their Value to New Product Developers," *Journal of Product & Brand Management* 14 (2005): 283–291.
21. Jathon Sapsford, "Honda Caters to Japan's Pet Population Boom," *The Wall Street Journal*, October 5, 2005, p. B1, http://online.wsj.com.
22. Deborah Ball, "As Chocolate Sags, Cadbury Gambles on a Piece of Gum," *The Wall Street Journal*, January 12, 2006, p. A1, http://online.wsj.com.
23. Lisa Sanders, "Berlin Cameron Wins Heineken Light Beer Ad Campaign," *Advertising Age*, December 27, 2005, www.adage.com.
24. Alexander E. Reppel, Isabelle Szmigin, and Thorsten Gruber, "The iPod Phenomenon: Identifying a Market Leader's Secrets through Qualitative Marketing Research," *Journal of Product & Brand Management* 15 (2006): 239–249.
25. "P&G Ends Test of Impress Plastic Wrap," *Advertising Age*, www.adage.com.
26. Sanders, "Berlin Cameron Wins Heineken Light Beer Ad Campaign."
27. Jack Neff, "Swiffer by Another Name," *Advertising Age*, April 11, 2005, p. 11.
28. Faye Rice, "How to Deal with Tougher Customers," *Fortune*, December 3, 1990, pp. 39–48.
29. Adapted from Michael Levy and Barton A. Weitz, *Retailing Management* (Burr Ridge, IL: Irwin/McGraw-Hill, 2001), p. 585.
30. Sidra Durst, "How Zappos Became No. 1 in Online Shoes," *Business 2.0*, January 15, 2007, http://money.cnn.com/magazines/business2/business2_archive/2006/12/01/8394993/index.htm?postversion=2007011508.
31. Stephanie Thompson, "Pepsi Dons Disguise in Attempt to Seduce Whole Foods Devotees," *Advertising Age*, November 9, 2006, www.adage.com.
32. Steve Miller, "Ford Rises to a (Driving) Challenge," *BrandWeek*, January 5, 2007, www.brandweek.com/bw/news/autos/article_display.jsp?vnu_content_id=1003528228.

33. "Want a Cause with That?" *Forbes,* January 8, 2007, p. 83.

34. "Nikon Will Stop Making Most Film Cameras," CNN, January 12, 2006, www.cnn.com.

35. "Delta to Eliminate Discount Carrier Song," *The New York Times,* October 28, 2005, www.nytimes.com.

36. Stephanie Thompson, "Mars to Scale Back M-Azing Brand," *Advertising Age,* October 26, 2006, www.adage.com.

37. "Nikon Will Stop Making Most Film Cameras."

38. "Ruckus Expands Music Download Service to All College Students," *The Wall Street Journal,* January 22, 2007, http://online.wsj.com.

39. Michelle Conlin, "Call Centers in the Rec Room," *BusinessWeek,* January 23, 2006, www.businessweek.com.

40. The information in this section is based on K. Douglas Hoffman and John E. G. Bateson, *Essentials of Services Marketing* (Mason, OH: South-Western, 2001); and Valarie A. Zeithaml, A. Parasuraman, and Leonard L. Berry, *Delivering Quality Service: Balancing Customer Perceptions and Expectations* (New York: Free Press, 1990).

41. Jeremy J. Sierra and Shaun McQuitty, "Service Providers and Customers: Social Exchange Theory and Service Loyalty," *Journal of Services Marketing* 19 (October 2005): 392–400.

42. J. Paul Peter and James H. Donnelly, *A Preface to Marketing Management* (Burr Ridge, IL: Irwin/McGraw-Hill, 2003), p. 212.

43. Sarah Nassauer, "Eliminating the Human Element," *The Wall Street Journal,* November 14, 2006, p. D7, http://online.wsj.com.

44. Robert Moore, Melissa L. Moore, and Michael Capella, "The Impact of Customer-to-Customer Interactions in a High Personal Contact Service Setting," *Journal of Services Marketing* 19 (July 2005): 482–491.

45. Michael D. Hartline and O. C. Ferrell, "Service Quality Implementation: The Effects of Organizational Socialization and Managerial Actions of Customer Contact Employee Behavior," *Marketing Science Institute Report,* no. 93–122 (Cambridge, MA: Marketing Science Institute, 1993).

46. Gretchen Weber, "Preserving the Starbucks Counter Culture," *Workforce Management,* February 2005, pp. 28–34, www.workforce.com/section/06/feature/23/94/44/index.html.

47. Raymond P. Fisk, Stephen J. Grove, and Joby John, *Interactive Services Marketing* (Boston: Houghton Mifflin, 2003), p. 91.

48. Ahmed Taher and Hanan El Basha, "Hetergeneity of Consumer Demand: Opportunities for Pricing of Services," *Journal of Product & Brand Management* 15 (2006): 331–340.

49. Sam Schechner, "Testing Out Airline Web Sites," *The Wall Street Journal,* February 15, 2005, p. D5.

50. International Smart Tan Network Educational Institute, http://saloncertification.com/ (accessed February 6, 2007).

51. Lesley Kump, "Teaching the Teachers," *Forbes,* December 12, 2005, p. 121.

52. Pavel Strach and André M. Everett, "Brand Corrosion: Mass-Marketing's Threat to Luxury Automobile Brands after Merger and Acquisition," *Journal of Product & Brand Management* 15 (2006): 106–120.

53. Rajesh Sethi, "New Product Quality and Product Development Teams," *Journal of Marketing,* April 2000, pp. 1–14.

54. "Brands," Binney & Smith, www.binney-smith.com/page.cfm?id=10 (accessed February 5, 2007); "Company Profile," Binney & Smith, www.binney-smith.com/page.cfm?id=30 (accessed February 5, 2007); "History," Binney & Smith, www.binney-smith.com/page.cfm?id=11 (accessed February 5, 2007); Bruce Horovitz, "Crayoloa Draws on New Ideas as Crayons Make Room for 'Mess-Less' Toys," *USA Today,* December 12, 2006, pp. 1B–2B, www.usatoday.com/money/industries/retail/2006-12-06-crayola-revamp_x.htm; Reena Jana, "Crayola Brightens a Brand," *BusinessWeek Online,* January 26, 2007, www.businessweek.com/innovate/content/jan2007/id20070126_338855.htm; Denise O'Neal, "New Products Brighten Crayola's Rainbow," *Chicago Sun Times,* April 14, 2006, www.findarticles.com/p/articles/mi_qn4155/is_20060414/ai_n16169784.

55. "100 Best Corporate Citizens 2006," *Business Ethics,* Spring 2006, www.business-ethics.com/whats_new/100best.html; "Brewing up a Strong Starbucks Alternative," MSNBC, February 5, 2006, www.msnbc.msn.com/id/4163701/; "Coca-Cola may Take on Starbucks," MSNBC, January 30, 2006, www.msnbc.msn.com/id/11101825/; "Company Fact Sheet," Starbucks, Winter 2006, www.starbucks.com/aboutus/Company_Factsheet.pdf; "'Fortune 100 Best Companies to Work for 2006," *Fortune,* http://money.cnn.com/magazines/fortune/bestcompanies/snapshots/1267.html (accessed February 6, 2007); "Health Care Takes Its Toll on Starbucks," MSNBC, September 14, 2005, www.msnbc.msn.com/id/9344634/; Adam Horowitz, David Jacobson, Mark Lasswell, and Owen Thomas, "101 Dumbest Moments in Business," *Business 2.0,* February 1, 2006, http://money.cnn.com/magazines/business2/101dumbest/full_list/page6.html; "In Rare Flop, Starbucks Scraps Chocolate Drink," MSNBC, February 10, 2006, www.msnbc.msn.com/id/11274445/; "Robust Innovations Pipeline Continues to Surprise and Delight Starbucks Customers Both In and Out of Stores," Starbucks press release, October 5, 2006, http://investor.starbucks.com/phoenix.zhtml?c=99518&p=irol-newsArticle&ID=912916&highlight=; Starbucks, www.starbucks.com (accessed February 6, 2007); Starbucks Annual Report 10-K; Winter, "Starbucks Everywhere," www.starbuckseverywhere.net/ (accessed February 6, 2007).

a Planet Dog, www.planetdog.com (accessed Febraury 6, 2007); "Raise the Woof," CNN, November 4, 2005, www.cnn.com/2005/US/03/28/otr.planet.dog/index.html; Stephanie Volo, "Unleash Your Commitment," *Fast Company,* March 2003, www.fastcompany.com/fast50_02/people/culture/volo.html.

b Brooks Barnes, "How 'Wicked' Cast Its Spell," *The Wall Street Journal,* October 22, 2005, p. A1, http://online.wsj.com; Michael Kuchwara, "One Woman Stands Behind Broadway's Best," MSNBC.com, August 21, 2005, http://msnbc.com/id/8974469/page/2/; "Wicked," Internet Broadway Database, www.ibdb.com/production.asp?id=13485 (accessed February 6, 2007), Wicked, www.wickedthemusical.com/ (accessed February 6, 2007).

c Candace Jackson and Peter Sanders, "The New Hotel Name Game," *The Wall Street Journal,* September 9–10, 2006, pp. P4, P6; Barbara De Lollis, "Hotels Train Employees to Think Fast," *USA Today,* November 29, 2006, pp. 1B–2B.

CHAPTER 12

1. Mark Berman, "Cuban: Steph Shoes on Mark," *New York Post,* January 16, 2007, www.nypost.com/seven/01162007/sports/knicks/cuban__steph_shoes_on_mark_knicks_marc_berman.htm; Stanley Holmes, ""Changing the Game on Nike," *BusinessWeek,* January 22, 2007, www.businessweek.com/print/magazine/content/07_04/b4018080.htm?chan=gl; LaMont Jones, "Knicks Star Introduces Low Price Athletic Shoes," *Pittsburgh Post-Gazette,* June 25, 2006, www.post-gazette.com/pg/06176/700465-314.stm; NBA.com, www.nba.com/playerfile/stephon_marbury/bio.html (accessed January 19, 2007); Michael Precker, "2006 Good News Roundup," *Detroit Free Press,* www.freep.com/apps/pbcs.dll/article?AID=/20061225/FEATURES01/612250311/1025 (accessed January 19, 2007); Ed Stannard, "Net Worth: Popular Sneaks Run Cheap," *New Haven Register,* http://zwire.townnews.biz/site/news.cfm?notn=1&ncdr=1&newsid=17617656&BRD=1281&PAG=461 &dept_id=31007&rfi=6 (accessed January 19, 2007); Starbury, www.starbury.com/ (accessed January 19, 2007); Steve & Barry's, www.steveandbarrys.com/website/starburyfaq.htm (accessed January 19, 2007).

2. Rajneesh Suri and Kent B. Monroe, "The Effects of Time Constraints on Consumers' Judgments of Prices and Products," *Journal of Consumer Research,* June 2003, pp. 92+.

3. Kelly K. Spors, "Trade You a Laptop? Online Sites Promote the Art of the Barter," *The Wall Street Journal,* November 14, 2006, p. B1, http://online.wsj.com.

4. "Hewlett-Packard," Professional Pricing Society, case study, www.pricingsociety.com/case_studies_details4.asp (accessed February 7, 2007).

5. Michael Arndt, "Frontier: Not About to Pack Its Bags," *BusinessWeek Online,* February 20, 2006.

6. David Krechevsky, "Target Ups Ante in Drug War," *Republican American,* November 23, 2006, www.rep-am.com/story.php?id=15785; "Wal-Mart Tests in Florida Its $4 Generic-Drug Plan," *The Wall Street Journal,* September 21, 2006, http://online.wsj.com.

7. Lauren Young, "Candy's Getting Dandy," *BusinessWeek,* February 13, 2006, pp. 88–89.

8. David Aaker and Erich Joachimsthaler, "An Alternative to Price Competition," *American Demographics,* September 2000, p. 11.

9. Frank Byrt, "Vermont Pure Seeks to Deliver Higher Margins by Shifting Focus," *The Wall Street Journal,* February 16, 2005, p. 1.

10. "Dictionary of Marketing Terms," American Marketing Association, www.marketingpower.com/mg-dictionary.php (accessed February 7, 2007).

11. Gary McWilliams and Evan Ramstad, "Where the TV Bargains Are," *The Wall Street Journal,* January 17, 2006, p. D1, http://online.wsj.com/.

12. "Dictionary of Marketing Terms."

13. Nicole C. Wong, "Sun Turning Around to See Profits Ahead," *The Mercury News,* February 6, 2007, www.mercurynews.com/mld/mercurynews/news/16637931.htm.

14. Donald Lichtenstein, Nancy M. Ridgway, and Richard G. Netemeyer, "Price Perceptions and Consumer Shopping Behavior: A Field Study," *Journal of Marketing Research,* May 1993, pp. 234–245.

15. Linda Halstad-Acharya, "Stuck in a Sea of Surcharges: Fuel Prices Abate, But the Add-Ons Keep Coming On," *Billings Gazette,* January 27, 2007, www.billingsgazette.net/articles/2007/01/27/news/local/25-stuck.txt.

16. "Investing," *BusinessWeek,* February 13, 2006, p. 90.

17. Russell S. Winer, *Pricing* (Cambridge, MA: Marketing Science Institute, 2005), p. 20.

18. Bruce L. Alford and Brian T. Engelland, "Advertised Reference Price Effects on Consumer Price Estimates, Value Perception, and Search Intention," *Journal of Business Research,* May 2000, pp. 93–100.

19. Lichtenstein, Ridgway, and Netemeyer, "Price Perceptions and Consumer Shopping Behavior."

20. Peter Burrows, "Apple's Down Market Gamble; By Launching a Much Cheaper Mac and iPod, Steve Jobs Is Appealing to Hordes of Price-Conscious Consumers," *BusinessWeek Online,* January 12, 2005, www.businessweek.com.

21. Lichtenstein, Ridgway, and Netemeyer, "Price Perceptions and Consumer Shopping Behavior."

22. Ibid.

23. Michal Lev-Ram, "This $310,000 Phone Blings, Then Rings," *Business 2.0,* December 20, 2006, http://money.cnn.com/2006/12/13/magazines/business2/special_phones.biz2/index.htm.

24. Linda Tischler, "The Price Is Right," *Fast Company,* November 2003, pp. 83+.

25. "Six Guilty in Synthetic Rubber Pricing Fixing," *The Tire Review,* November 29, 2006, www.tirereview.com/default.aspx?type=wm&module=4&id=2&state=DisplayFullText&item=6752.

26. David Perry, "Simmons Sets Fast Pace in Allowances Category," *Furniture Today,* July 10, 2006, p. 36.

27. Leonard Klie, "DSD in Reverse," *Food Logistics,* April 2005, pp. 14–17.

28. Mark Berman, "Cuban: Steph Shoes on Mark," *New York Post,* January 16, 2007, www.nypost.com/seven/01162007/sports/knicks/cuban__steph_shoes_on_mark_knicks_marc_berman.htm; Stanley Holmes, ""Changing the Game on Nike," *BusinessWeek,* January 22, 2007, www.businessweek.com/print/magazine/content/07_04/b4018080.htm?chan=gl; LaMont Jones, "Knicks Star Introduces Low Price Athletic Shoes," *Pittsburgh Post-Gazette,* June 25, 2006, www.post-gazette.com/pg/06176/700465-314.stm; NBA.com, www.nba.com/playerfile/stephon_marbury/bio.html (accessed January 19, 2007); Michael Precker, "2006 Good News Roundup," *Detroit Free Press,* www.freep.com/apps/pbcs.dll/article?AID=/20061225/FEATURES01/612250311/1025 (accessed January 19, 2007); Ed Stannard, "Net Worth: Popular Sneaks Run Cheap," *New Haven Register,* http://zwire.townnews.biz/site/news.cfm?notn=1&ncdr=1&newsid=17617656&BRD=1281&PAG=461 &dept_id=31007&rfi=6 (accessed January 19, 2007); Starbury, www.starbury.com/ (accessed January 19, 2007); Steve & Barry's, www.steveandbarrys.com/website/starburyfaq.htm (accessed January 19, 2007).

29. "Blue Skies: Is JetBlue the Next Great Airline-Or Just a Little Too Good to Be True?" *Time,* July 30, 2001, pp. 24+; Amy Goldwasser, "Something Stylish, Something Blue," *Business 2.0,* February 2002, pp. 94–95; JetBlue, www.jetblue.com (accessed February 7, 2007); "JetBlue Thinks Turnaround Taking Off," Forbes.com, November 15, 2006, www.forbes.com/markets/feeds/ap/2006/11/15/ap3178834.html; Alexan-

dra Marks, "New Fare War Adds to Pressure on Airlines," *Christian Science Monitor,* January 10, 2005, p. 2; Jeremy W. Peters, "Rougher Times Amid Higher Costs at JetBlue," *The New York Times,* November 11, 2004, pp. C1+; Chuck Salter, "And Now the Hard Part," *Fast Company,* May 2004, pp. 66+; Darren Shannon, "Three of a Kind," *Travel Agent,* July 23, 2001, pp. 60+.

a Robert D. Hof, "Netflix 1, Wal-Mart 0," *BusinessWeek Online,* May 20, 2005, via EBSCO Host Research Database; Tara Lemmey, "Push the Positive for Customers," *BusinessWeek Online,* September 13, 2005, via EBSCO Host Research Database; Jena McGregor, "High-Tech Achiever: Netflix, At Netflix, the Secret Sauce Is Software," *Fast Company,* October 2005, p. 48, http://pf.fastcompany.com/magazine/99/ open_customer-netflix.html; "Movies to Go," Economist, July 9, 2005, p. 57, via EBSCO Host Research Database; Timothy J. Mullaney and Robert Hof, "Netflix: Starring in Merger Story?" BusinessWeek Online, November 10, 2005, via EBSCO Host Research Database; Netflix, www.netflix.com (accessed February 7, 2007); Julie Schlosser, "Netflix Makes it Big in Hollywood," *Fortune,* June 13, 2005, p. 34, via EBSCO Host Research Database.

b Amie Street, http://amiestreet.com/home.php (accessed February 7, 2007); "Best Entrepreneurs under 25: Elliott Breece, Joshua Boltuch, Elias Roman," *BusinessWeek Online,* October 2006, http://images.business-week.com/ss/06/10/bestunder25/source/3.htm; Jamin Warren, "Online: Music," The Wall Street Journal, October 14, 2006, p. P2, http://online.wsj.com.

c Marilyn Adams and Dan Reed, "Delta, Northwest File Chapter 11," *USA Today,* September 15, 2005, p. 1B; "As One Airline Emerges, 2 Still in Bankruptcy," WCCO, January 31, 2006, http://wcco.com/business/local_story_031071357.html; Barbara De Lollis and Barbara Hansen, "Airlines Gear up for Ultralong Haul," *USA Today,* June 27, 2005, p. 1B; David Grossman, "10 Reasons Why Airline Woes Aren't Over Yet," *USA Today,* December 3, 2006, www.usatoday.com/travel/columnist/grossman/2006-12-03-grossman_x.htm; Dan Reed and Marilyn Adams, "Northwest on Brink of Filing for Bankruptcy," *USA Today,* September 14, 2005, p. 1B.

CHAPTER 13

1. Jim Hu, "Microsoft Opens MSN Music Store," CNet, September 1, 2004, http://news.com.com/2100-1027_ 3-5342795.html; "IFPI: 07: The Digital Music Report," IFPI, www.ifpi.org/content/library/digital-music-report-2007.pdf (accessed February 8 2007); Stephen Hinkle, "RIAA, Surrender Now!" Dmusic.com, http://news.dmusic.com/print/5026 (accessed November 20, 2003); iTunes, www.apple.com/itunes/store/ (accessed January 18, 2007); Bob Keefe, "Music File-Shares Hit by New Round of Lawsuits," *The Austin American-Statesman,* January 22, 2004, www.statesman.com; Napster, www.napster.com (accessed January 18, 2007); George Szalai, "Napster Uploads AOL Music Subscriptions," *Brandweek,* January 15, 2007, www.brandweek.com/bw/news/recent_display.jsp?vnu_content_id=1003532446; Wal-Mart, www.wal-mart .com (accessed January 18, 2007).
2. Lori Hawkins, "If Price Is Right," *The Austin American-Statesman,* February 13, 2006, www.statesman.com.
3. William C. Symonds and Robert Bernes, "Gillette's New Edge," *BusinessWeek Online,* February 6, 2006.
4. Kevin Schweitzer, "Hybrid Potential Limited Only by Price," *Chicago Tribune,* February 11, 2005, p. 10.
5. "New Bentley Pricing," Automotive.com, www.automotive.com/new-cars/pricing/01/bentley/index.html (accessed February 8 2007).
6. Robert J. Frank, Jeffrey P. George, and Laxman Narasimhan, "When Your Competitor Delivers More for Less," *McKinsey Quarterly,* www.mckinseyquarterly.com.
7. Barry J. Babin, David M. Hardesty, and Tracy A. Suter, "Color and Shopping Intentions: The Intervening Effect of Price Fairness and Perceived Affect," *Journal of Business Research,* July 2003, pp. 541–551.
8. David Moin, "Category Killers' Concerns: Overgrowth and Extinction," *WWD,* January 6, 2005, p. 17.
9. "Fairchild Dynamic Pricing Team," Professional Pricing Society, case study, www.pricingsociety.com/case_studies_details1.asp (accessed February 8, 2007).
10. George J. Avlonitis and Kostis A. Indounas, "Pricing Objectives and Pricing Methods in the Services Sector," *Journal of Services Marketing* 19 (January 2005): 47–57.
11. Allan Hall, "Berlin Taxis Offer Half-Price 'Happy-Hours,'" *Evening Standard,* February 22, 2002, www.thisislondon.co.uk.
12. "Cutler-Hammon/Eaton Corporation," Professional Pricing Society, case study, www.pricingsociety.com/case_studies_details2.asp (accessed February 8, 2007).
13. Marla Royne Stafford and Thomas F. Stafford, "The Effectiveness of Tensile Pricing Tactics in the Advertising of Services," *The Journal of Advertising,* Summer 2000, pp. 45–56.
14. Dan Gallagher, "iPhone Price Raises Issue for Apple," *The Seattle Times,* January 15, 2007, http://seattletimes.nwsource.com/html/businesstechnology/2003525467_btapplepricing15.html.
15. "Arctic Monkeys Play on Web Hype," *CNN/Money,* February 2, 2006, www.cnnmoney.com.
16. Amanda Cantrell, "iPod Add-Ons: Boombox Purses, and More," *CNN/Money,* January 12, 2006, www.cnnmoney.com.
17. Lee Gomes, "A Peek under PlayStation 3's Hood Shows Sony Is Selling Units at a Loss," *The Wall Street Journal,* November 21, 2006, http://online.wsj.com.
18. Mike Ricciuti, "Microsoft Sets Vista Prices, Expands Testing," CNet, September 5, 2006, http://news.com .com/2100-1016_3-6112260.html.
19. Simona Romani, "Price Misleading Advertising: Effects on Trustworthiness Toward the Source of Information and Willingness to Buy," *Journal of Product & Brand Management* 15 (2006): 130–138.
20. Daniel A. Sheinin and Janet Wagner, "Pricing Store Brands Across Categories and Retailers," *Journal of Product & Brand Management* 12, no. 4 (2003): 201–220.
21. Jaihak Chung and Vithala R. Rao, "A General Choice Model for Bundles with Multiple-Category Products: Application to Market Segmentation and Optimal Pricing for Bundles," *Journal of Marketing Research,* May 2003, pp. 115–130.
22. George Mannes, "The Urge to Unbundle," *Fast Company,* February 2005, pp. 23–25.

23. Doug Halonen, "Watchdog Sets Sights on à la Carte," *TelevisionWeek*, January 10, 2005, p. 8.

24. Mannes, "The Urge to Unbundle."

25. Kris Hudson, "Competing Retailers Dispute Wal-Mart Trademark Request," *The Wall Street Journal*, November 7, 2006, http://online.wsj.com.

26. "'Made in USA' Means Little to Furniture Buyers," MSNBC, February 10, 2006, www.msnbc.com.

27. Ralk Wagner and Kai-Stefan Beinke, "Identifying Patterns of Customer Response to Price Endings," *Journal of Product & Brand Management* 15, no. 5 (2006): 341–351.

28. Sajeev Varki, Sanjiv Sabherwal, Albert Della Bitta, and Keith M. Moore, "Price-End Biases in Financial Products," *Journal of Product & Brand Management* 15, no. 6 (2006): 394–401.

29. "Price Promotions Give ASDA a Lift and Multibuys Boost Sainsbury," *Grocer*, February 2, 2002, p. 30.

30. Bruce L. Alford and Brian T. Engelland, "Advertised Reference Price Effects on Consumer Price Estimates, Value Perception, and Search Intention," *Journal of Business Research*, May 2000, pp. 93–100.

31. "Blockbuster Plans to Eliminate 300 Jobs," *BusinessWeek Online*, February 8, 2006.

32. Nigel Cox, "Amex Charges Ahead," *Smart Business*, April 2001, pp. 123–128.

33. Jim Hu, "Microsoft Opens MSN Music Store," CNet, September 1, 2004, http://news.com.com/2100-1027_3-5342795.html; "IFPI: 07: The Digital Music Report," IFPI, www.ifpi.org/content/library/digital-music-report-2007.pdf (accessed February 8 2007); Stephen Hinkle, "RIAA, Surrender Now!" Dmusic.com, http://news.dmusic.com/print/5026 (accessed November 20, 2003); iTunes, www.apple.com/itunes/store/ (accessed January 18, 2007); Bob Keefe, "Music File-Shares Hit by New Round of Lawsuits," *The Austin American-Statesman*, January 22, 2004, www.statesman.com; Napster, www.napster.com (accessed January 18, 2007); George Szalai, "Napster Uploads AOL Music Subscriptions," *Brandweek*, January 15, 2007, www.brandweek.com/bw/news/recent_display.jsp?vnu_content_id= 1003532446; Wal-Mart, www.wal-mart.com (accessed January 18, 2007).

34. "Fact Sheet: New Balance Athletic Shoe, Inc.," New Balance, March 2006, www.newbalance.com/cms-service/stream/pdf/?pdf_id=4642506; Daren Fonda, "Sole Survivor," *Time*, November 8, 2004, p. 48; Donna Goodison, "New Balance in Race for High Performers," *Boston Herald*, February 7, 2007, http://business.bostonherald.com/businessNews/view.bg?articleid=181458; interviews with Jim Sciabarrasi, Christine Epplett, and Paul Heffernan of New Balance, video, Houghton Mifflin Company, 2003; Kathy Lally, "Marketers in Full Bloom: As the Biggest Generation Passes 50, Retailers Refit Their Appeal," *Washington Post*, January 9, 2005, p. F6; Thomas J. Ryan, "The Price Is Right," *Footwear Business*, February 2004, n.p.

a Sarah Duxbury, "Levi's Planning Pair of Snazzy Denim Spots," *San Francisco Business Times*, May 9, 2005, http://sanfrancisco.bixjournals.com/sanfrancisco/stories/2005/05/09/story6.html; Theresa Howard, "Levi's Charms Buyers Back," *USA Today*, October 24, 2004, www.usatoday.com/money/advertising/ad-track/2004-10-21-levis_x.htm; Jana Reena, "How Green Are My Blue Jeans," *BusinessWeek*, September 18, 2006, p. 12; Stephanie Thompson, "Levi's Struggles to Redefine Itself as a Premium-Denim Purveyor," *Advertising Age*, July 11, 2005, p. 12.

b Express Drop, www.expressdrop.com/ (accessed February 8, 2007); "Fast Forward," *Entrepreneur*, May 2006, http://entrepreneur.com/magazine/entrepreneur/2006/may/159808.html; Wendy Navratil, "eBay Made Easy," *Chicago Tribune*, March 28, 2004, via www.expressdrop.com/press/chicago_tribune/ebay_made_easy/ebay_made_easy.htm.

c Dina Bass, "Sony PlayStation 3 Sales Fall Short, *Denver Post*, December 8, 2006, www.denverpost.com/business/ci_4804952; Arik Hesseldahl, "For Every Xbox, A Big Fat Loss," *UPFront*, December 5, 2005, p. 13; Thomas Jackson, "War of the New Machines," *Forbes*, December 13, 2005, pp. 81–83, via EBSCO Host Research Database; Stephen Manes, "Generation X," *Forbes*, December 12, 2005, pp. 70–72, via EBSCO Host Research Database; Frank Michael Russell, "Xbox 360 Pricing Strategy: Less than the Sum of Its Parts?" *Mercury News*, November 23, 2005; Stephen H. Wildstrom, "Xbox: A Winner Only at Games," *Business Week*, December 12, 2005, via EBSCO Host Research Database.

CHAPTER 14

1. Cisco Systems, "Cisco Helps FedEx Make On-Time Delivery," www.cisco.com/en/US/products/ps5854/products_case_study0900aecd80364838.shtml (accessed January 19, 2007); FedEx Facts, www.fedex.com/us/about/today/companies/corporation/facts.html?link=4 (accessed February 9, 2007); "December 18, 2006 to be Busiest Day in FedEx History," FedEx press release, October 23, 2006, http://peak.van.fedex.com/images/PeakPressRelease2006.pdf; FedEx History, www.fedex.com/us/about/today/history/?link=4 (accessed January 19, 2007); Ellen Florian Kratz, "For FedEx, It was Time to Deliver," *Fortune*, October 3, 2005, p. 65; Kate MacArthur, "Visa, FedEx Pony Up for Future Fund," *Advertising Age*, November 14, 2005, pp.1, 37; "Pass the Parcel," *Economist*, February 11, 2006, p. 61.

2. "eBay: The World's Online Marketplace," eBay.com, http://pages.ebay.com/aboutebay/thecompany/companyoverview.html (accessed February 12, 2007).

3. Lisa Harrington, "Getting Service Parts Logistics Up to Speed," *Inbound Logistics*, November 2006, www.inboundlogistics.com/articles/features/1106_feature02.shtml.

4. "From Planning to Control: Improving the High-Tech Supply Chain," Valdero Corporation white paper, January 4, 2002, accessible via www.manufacturing.net.

5. "Trendspotting," *Intelligent Enterprises*, March 2005, p. 17; Doug Henschen, "Content and CRM: Completing the Picture Intelligent Enterprise," *Intelligent Enterprise*, March 2005, pp. 34+.

6. Anthony J. Dukes, Esther Gal-Or, and Kannan Srinivasan, "Channel Bargaining with Retailer Asymmetry," *Journal of Marketing Research* 43 (February 2006), via www.marketingpower.com.

7. Stewart Scharf, "Grainger: Tooled Up for Growth," *BusinessWeek*, April 25, 2006, p. 8.

8. "Ocean Spray and PepsiCo Form Strategic Alliance," Ocean Spray press release, July 13, 2006, www.oceanspray.com/news/pr/pressrelease104.aspx.

9. Wroe Alderson, *Dynamic Marketing Behavior* (Homewood, IL: Irwin, 1965), p. 239.

10. Andrew Martin, "The Package May Say Healthy, but This Grocer Begs to Differ," *The New York Times*, November 6, 2006, www.nytimes.com

11. Scott Kilman, "Smithfield to Buy Hog Farmer Premium Standard," *The Wall Street Journal*, September 19, 2006, p. A12, http://online.wsj.com.

12. Hans Greimel, "Japan Tobacco Buying Gallaher for $14.7B," *BusinessWeek Online*, December 15, 2006, www.businessweek.com/; Andrew Morse and Jason Singer, "Japan Returns to Global Stage as an Acquirer," *The Wall Street Journal*, December 16, 2006, p. A1, http://online.wsj.com.

13. Leo Aspinwall, "The Marketing Characteristics of Goods," *Four Marketing Theories* (Boulder, CO: University of Colorado Press, 1961), pp. 27–32.

14. Pete Engardio, with Michael Arndt and Dean Foust, "The Future of Outsourcing," *BusinessWeek*, January 30, 2006, pp. 50–58.

15. Lee Pender, "The Basic Links of SCM," Supply Chain Management Research Center, www.cio.com/research/scm/edit/020501_basic.html (accessed February 12, 2007).

16. William Atkinson, "E-Logistics and E-Procurement: Here to Stay," *Supply Chain Management Review*, November 15, 2001,www.manufacturing.net.

17. Dominic Gates, "Boeing 7E7 Site Winner Will Get Second Plant Bonus," *Seattle Times*, November 19, 2003.

18. Merrill Douglas, "From Doughnuts to Dollars," *Inbound Logistics*, November 2006, pp. 85–87.

19. "Starbucks Keeps Fresh with RFID," *RFIDJournal*, December 13, 2006, www.rfidjournal.com/article/articleview/2890/1/1/.

20. Amanda Loudin, "Giving Voice to Warehouse Productivity," *Inbound Logistics*, November 2006, pp. 81–83.

21. Anne T. Coughlan, Erin Anderson, Louis W. Stern, and Adel I. El-Ansary, *Marketing Channels* (Upper Saddle River, NJ: Prentice-Hall, 2001), p. 510.

22. Leslie Hansen Harps, "Best Practics in Today's Distribution Center," *Inbound Logistics*, May 2005, www.inboundlogistics.com/articles/features/0505_feature01.shtml.

23. Daniel Machalaba, "Trucker Rewards Customers for Good Behavior," *The Wall Street Journal*, September 9, 2003, http://online.wsj.com/article/0,,SB106306613229256300,00.html.

24. Anne Stuart, "Express Delivery," *Inc. Tech 2001*, March 15, 2001, pp. 54–56.

25. Cisco Systems, "Cisco Helps FedEx Make On-Time Delivery," www.cisco.com/en/US/products/ps5854/products_case_study0900aecd80364838.shtml (accessed January 19, 2007); FedEx Facts, www.fedex.com/us/about/today/companies/corporation/facts.html?link=4 (accessed February 9, 2007); "December 18, 2006 to be Busiest Day in FedEx History," FedEx press release, October 23, 2006, http://peak.van.fedex.com/images/PeakPressRelease2006.pdf; FedEx History, www.fedex.com/us/about/today/history/?link=4 (accessed January 19, 2007); Ellen Florian Kratz, "For FedEx, It Was Time to Deliver," *Fortune*, October 3, 2005, p. 65; Kate MacArthur, "Visa, FedEx Pony Up for Future Fund," *Advertising Age*, November 14, 2005, pp.1, 37; "Pass the Parcel," *Economist*, February 11, 2006, p. 61.

26. Katrina Brooker, "The Pepsi Machine," *Fortune*, February 6, 2006, pp. 68–72; Coca-Cola Company, www2.coca-cola.com/ourcompany/aroundworld.html (accessed February 12, 2007); "Coca-Cola Company: Crisis and Reputation Management," in Debbie Thorne McAlister, O. C. Ferrell, and Linda Ferrell, *Business and Society: A Strategic Approach to Social Responsibility*, 2nd ed. (Boston: Houghton Mifflin, 2005), pp. 394–401; T. C. Doyle, "Channel Stuffing Rears Its Ugly Head," *VARBusiness*, May 6, 2003, www.varbusiness.com/showArticle.jhtml;jsessionid=PCVHTC51ICHQ0QSNDBCSKHSCJUMEKJVN?articleID=18823602; "Grand Jury to Investigate Coke on Channel Stuffing Allegations," *Atlanta Business Chronicle*, May 3, 2004 http://atlanta.bizjournals.com/atlanta/stories/2004/05/03/daily2.html; Majorie Kelly, "100 Best Corporate Citizens," *Business Ethics*, Spring 2005, pp. 20–23; Betsy McKay and Chad Terhune, "Coca-Cola Settles Regulatory Probe; Deal Resolves Allegations by SEC That Firm Padded Profit by 'Channel Stuffing,'" *The Wall Street Journal*, via http://proquest.umi.com/pqdweb?did=823831501&sid=1&Fmt=3&clientld=2945&RQT=309&Vname=PQD (accessed November 8, 2005); Stephen Taub, "SEC Probing Harley Statements," CFO.com, July 13, 2005, www.cfo.com/article.cfm/4173321/c_4172651?f=archives&origin=archive.

a Clay Chandler, "Full Speed Ahead," *Fortune*, February 7, 2005, p. 78; Philip Evans and Bob Wolf, "Collaboration Rules," *Harvard Business Review*, July/August 2005, p. 96; Toyota.com, www.toyota.co.jp/en/index_company.html (accessed February 9, 2007); Kate Vitasek, Karl B. Manrodt, and Jeff Abbott, "What Makes a Supply Chain Lean?" *Supply Chain Management*, October 1, 2005, p. 39.

b Kitty Crider, "Off the Bike, the Soup Peddler Expands," *The Austin American-Statesman*, September 14, 2005, www.statesman.com; Julie Powell, "Tale of the Soup Peddler," *Food & Wine*, November 2005, pp. 204–214; The Soup Peddler, www.souppeddler.com/ (accessed February 9, 2007).

c Jonathan Birchall, "Radio Shack Seeks the Right Retail Wavelength," *Financial Times* (U.S. Edition), May 31, 2005, Business Life Section, p. 9 Laura Heller, "Radio Shack Inks Two Wireless Deals," *DSN Retailing Today*, October 25, 2004, p. 5; Radio Shack, www.radioshackcorporation.com (accessed February 9, 2007).

CHAPTER 15

1. "Acquiring a Hard Rock Franchise," Hard Rock Café International, www.hardrock.com/corporate/contactus/grfx/WhatisaFranchise.pdf (accessed January 23, 2007); "Avicon Leads Hard Rock Café's Successful Transition to Outsourced Logistics, Fulfillment and Distribution," *Business Wire*, December 1, 2003, www.businesswire.com; Kelly L. Carter, "Hard Rock Café Falls Hard for Detroit," *The Detroit Free Press*, November 7, 2003, www.freep.com; Wade Daniels, "Kelly Marshall: Not Just Another Starstruck Fan, GM Keeps Her Casual Cool at this Celebrity-Focused Restaurant—Hard Rock Café," January 26, 2004, www.findarticles.com/p/articles/mi_m3190/is_4_38/ai_113097209/print; "Hard Rock Announces Plans for a Unique Rock 'n' Roll Park in Myrtle Beach, South Carolina, in 2008," Hard Rock Café International press release, March 31, 2006, www.hardrock.com/corporate/press/content.aspx?id=149; Adrian Sainz, "Seminole Tribe of Fla. Buying Hard Rock," *Yahoo! Finance*, December 7, 2006, http://biz.yahoo.com/ap/061207/hard_rock_cafe_seminole_tribe.html?.v=29.

2. U.S. Bureau of the Census, *Statistical Abstract of the United States, 2007* (Washington, DC: U.S. Government Printing Office, 2006), p. 649.

3. Ann Zimmerman and Kris Hudson, "Looking Upscale, Wal-Mart Begins a Big Makeover," *The Wall Street Journal,* September 17, 2005, p. A1, http://online.wsj.com; Robert Berner, "Watch Out, Best Buy and Circuit City," *BusinessWeek,* November 21, 2005, pp. 46–48.

4. Amy Merrick, Jeffrey A. Trachtenberg, and Ann Zimmerman, "Department Stores Fight to Save a Model That May Be Outdated," *The Wall Street Journal,* March 12, 2002, http://online.wsj.com/.

5. Wal-Mart Fact Sheet, Hoover's Online, www.hoovers.com/free (accessed February 13, 2007).

6. "A Different Type of Sears Store," *The New York Times,* February 9, 2005, p. C5.

7. "Testing Ground, Why the Convenience Channel Is the Ideal Environment to Spur Consumer Trial," *Stagnito's New Products Magazine,* May 2005, p. 38.

8. National Association of Convenience Stores, July 2006, www.nacsonline.com/NACS/Resource/PRToolkit/FactSheets/prtk_fact_nacs.htm.

9. Elizabeth Esfahani, "7-Eleven Gets Sophisticated," *Business 2.0,* January/February 2005, pp. 93–100.

10. Stanley Holmes, "The Jack Welch of the Meat Aisle; Former GE Exec Larry Johnston Brings High-Tech to Troubled Albertson's," *BusinessWeek,* January 24, 2005, p. 60.

11. Richard C. Morais, "One Hot Tamale," *Forbes,* December 27, 2004, p. 137.

12. Sam's Club Fact Sheet, Costco Wholesale Corporation Fact Sheet, B.J.'s Wholesale Club Fact Sheet, Hoover's Online, www.hoovers.com/free (accessed February 13, 2007).

13. Janet Adamy, "For Subway, Every Nook and Cranny on the Planet Is Possible Site for a Franchise," *The Wall Street Journal,* September 1, 2006, p. A11, http://online.wsj.com.

14. Merrick, Trachtenberg, and Zimmerman, "Department Stores Fight to Save a Model That May Be Outdated."

15. Mall of America, www.mallofamerica.com/ (accessed February 14, 2007).

16. Kurt Blumenau, "Are Target, Best Buy Really Upscale? Owners of 'Lifestyle' Shopping Centers Still Signing Retail Tenants," *The [Allentown, Pennsylvania] Morning Call,* May 29, 2005, via LexisNexis; Debra Hazel, "Wide-Open Spaces," *Chain Store Age,* November 2005, p. 120; "ICSC Shopping Center Definitions," International Council of Shopping Centers, http://icsc.org/srch/lib/USDefinitions.pdf (accessed December 18, 2006); Greg Lindsay, "Say Goodbye to the Mall," *Advertising Age,* October 2, 2006, p. 13.

17. Stephanie Kang, "After a Slump, Payless Tries on Fashion for Size," *The Wall Street Journal,* February 10, 2007, p. A1, http://online.wsj.com.

18. Merrick, Trachtenberg, and Zimmerman, "Department Stores Fight to Save a Model That May Be Outdated."

19. Velitchka D. Kaltcheva and Barton A. Weitz, "When Should a Retailer Create an Exciting Store Environment?" *Journal of Marketing* 70 (January 2006), www.marketingpower.com.

20. Mindy Fetterman and Jayne O'Donnell, "Just Browsing at the Mall? That's What You Think," *USA Today,* September 1, 2006, http://usatoday.com.

21. Anick Bosmans, "Scents and Sensibility: When Do (In)Congruent Ambient Scents Influence Product Evaluations?" *Journal of Marketing* 70 (July 2006), www.marketingpower.com.

22. "Store Atmospherics Provide Competitive Edge," *Chain Store Age,* December 2005, p. 74.

23. Stephen Brown, "The Wheel of Retailing: Past and Future," *Journal of Retailing,* Summer 1990, pp. 143–149.

24. Scott Frey, "Complying with Do-Not-Call," *National Underwriter Life & Health—Financial Services Edition,* December 8, 2003, p. 17.

25. "National Do-Not-Call Registry," Federal Trade Commission, www.ftc.gov/donotcall/ (accessed February 14, 2007).

26. "Jupiter Research Forecasts Online Retail Spending Will Be $144 Billion in 2010, a CAGR of 12% from 2005," Jupiter Media press release, February 6, 2006, www.jupitermedia.com/corporate/releases/06.02.06-newjupresearch.html.

27. Lucinda Hahn, "Pampered Life," *Chicago Tribune,* January 18, 2005, p. 1.

28. "Fact Sheet: U.S. Direct Selling in 2005," *Direct Selling Association,* www.dsa.org/pubs/numbers/calendar05factsheet.pdf (accessed February 14, 2007).

29. International Franchise Association, www.franchise.org (accessed February 13, 2007).

30. U.S. Bureau of the Census, *Statistical Abstract of the United States, 2007,* p. 649.

31. "Genuine Parts Company," Hoover's Online, www.hoovers.com/free (accessed February 14, 2007).

32. "Universal Corporation," Hoover's Online, www.hoovers.com/free (accessed February 14, 2007).

33. "Red River Commodities, Inc.," Hoover's Online, www.hoovers.com/free (accessed February 14, 2007); Red River Commodities, Inc., www.redriv.com (accessed December 18, 2006).

34. "Acquiring a Hard Rock Franchise," Hard Rock Café International, www.hardrock.com/corporate/contactus/grfx/WhatisaFranchise.pdf (accessed January 23, 2007); "Avicon Leads Hard Rock Café's Successful Transition to Outsourced Logistics, Fulfillment and Distribution," *Business Wire,* December 1, 2003, www.businesswire.com; Kelly L. Carter, "Hard Rock Café Falls Hard for Detroit," *The Detroit Free Press,* November 7, 2003, www.freep.com; Wade Daniels, "Kelly Marshall: Not Just Another Starstruck Fan, GM Keeps Her Casual Cool at this Celebrity-Focused Restaurant—Hard Rock Café," January 26, 2004, www.findarticles.com/p/articles/mi_m3190/is_4_38/ai_113097209/print; "Hard Rock Announces Plans for a Unique Rock 'n' Roll Park in Myrtle Beach, South Carolina in 2008," Hard Rock Café International press release, March 31, 2006, www.hardrock.com/corporate/press/content.aspx?id=149; Adrian Sainz, "Seminole Tribe of Fla. Buying Hard Rock," *Yahoo! Finance,* December 7, 2006, http://biz.yahoo.com/ap/061207/hard_rock_cafe_seminole_tribe.html?.v=29.

35. "About REI," REI, www.rei.com/aboutrei/about_rei.html (accessed February 14, 2007); Bass Pro Shops, www.basspro.com (accessed February 14, 2007); Cabela's, www.cabelas.com (accessed February 14, 2007); Ken Clark, "REI Scales New Heights," *Chain Store Age,* July 2004, pp. 26A+; Stephane Fitch, "Uphill Battle," *Forbes,* April 25, 2005, pp. 62+; Mike Gorrell, "New REI Store Opens in Salt Lake City Area," *Salt Lake Tribune,* March 28, 2003, www.sltrib.com; "REI Named to *Fortune*'s 100 Best Companies List," *Business Wire,* January 10, 2005, www.businesswire.com; "REI Climbs to New Heights Online," *Chain Store Age,* October 2003, pp. 72+.

a "Destinations: Mixed-Use Retail Restaurants," Cuningham Group, www.cuningham.com/portfolio/destination/rainforest.html (accessed February 13, 2007); Judith Dobrzynski, "Jungle Canopy In America's Mall," *The New York Times,* July 31, 1996, pp. C4, C17; Alan Dorich, "One of a Kind," *Food and Drink Magazine,* January/February 2006, www.fooddrink-magazine.com/content_archives/JanFeb06/06.html; Ken Hoover, "Rainforest Made a Fast Swing, Then Faded," *Investor's Business Daily,* February 22, 2005, p. B20; "Landry's Restaurants Announces First International Expansion of Its Most Popular Concept," Landry's Restaurants press release, March 15, 2006, www.prnewswire.com/cgi-bin/stories.pl?ACCT=104&STORY=/www/story/03-15-2006/0004320517&EDATE=; "Landry's Saves Rainforest," *CNNMoney.com,* September 26, 2000, money.cnn.com/2000/09/26/deals/rainforest.

b Paul Grimaldi, "Out of the Woods—After 93 years in Freeport, Maine, L.L. Bean Says It Has to Open a String of Retail Stores to Fend Off Its Competitors," *The Providence Journal,* July 24, 2005; Tux Terkel, "L.L. Bean Considers Retail, Distribution Expansion in Freeport, Maine," Portland Press Herald, September 22, 2005; Clarke Canfield, "L.L. Bean Reports 17 Percent Surge in Holiday Sales," The Associated Press State and Local Wire, January 9, 2006; L.L. Bean, www.llbean.com (accessed February 14, 2007).

c Les Christie, "The Sweet Smell of Success," *CNN/Money,* June 6, 2006, http://money.cnn.com/2005/06/01/smbusiness/perfume_bay/index.htm; Ryan J. McCarthy, "The Next Generation," *Inc.,* www.inc.com/30under30/tran.html (accessed February 14, 2007); Pefume Bay, www.perfumebay.com (accessed February 14, 2007).

CHAPTER 16

1. Marc Graser, "Toyota Hits Touch Points as It Hawks Yaris to Youth," *Advertising Age,* May 1, 2006, p. 28; Jean Halliday, "Marketer of the Year Toyota," *Advertising Age,* December 13, 2006, pp. M-1–5, S-2; Julie Liesse, "Hitting the Target: Mobile Makes Its Mark," *2006 Mobile Marketing Association Annual Mobile Marketing Guide,* December 4, 2006, pp. 4, 5; Steve McClellan, "Will Mobile Ads Take Off in '07, or Be Put on Hold?" *Adweek,* January 1, 2007, http://adweek.com/aw/magazine/article_display.jsp?vnu_content_id=1003526234&imw=Y; Toyota, www.toyota.com/about/shareholder/services/index.html (accessed January 29, 2007); Toyota Investor Fact Sheet, www.toyota.com/about/shareholder/images/2005factsheet.pdf (accessed January 29, 2007).

2. Martin Wodarz, "Paint the Town Ted: Launching an Airline Using IMC Principles," *Journal of Integrated Marketing Communications,* 2006, pp. 28–33.

3. Suzanne Vranica, "Marketers Aim New Ads at Video iPod Users," *The Wall Street Journal,* January 31, 2006, p. B1, http://online.wsj.com.

4. Allison Fass, "A Kingdom Seeks Magic," *Forbes,* October 16, 2006, pp. 68–70.

5. Louise Story, "Programmed to Sell," *The New York Times,* November 10, 2006, pp. C1, C4.

6. Terence A. Shimp, *Advertising, Promotion, and Supplemented Aspects of Integrated Marketing Communications* (Fort Worth: Dryden Press, 2000), p. 117.

7. Salvador Ruiz and María Sicilia, "The Impact of Cognitive and/or Affective Processing Styles on Consumer Response to Advertising Appeals," *Journal of Business Research* 57 (2004): 657–664.

8. John S. McClenahen, "How Can You Possibly Say That?" *Industry Week,* July 17, 1995, pp. 17–19; Anton Piësch, "Speaking in Tongues," *Inc.,* June 2003, p. 50.

9. Samuel D. Bradley III and Robert Meeds, "The Effects of Sentence-Level Context, Prior Word Knowledge, and Need for Cognition on Information Processing of Technical Language in Print Ads," *Journal of Consumer Psychology* 14, no. 3 (2004): 291–302.

10. Zakary L. Tormala and Richard E. Petty, "A Source Credibility and Attitude Certainty: A Metacognitive Analysis of Resistance to Persuasion," *Journal of Consumer Psychology,* 14, no. 4 (2004): 427–442.

11. David M. Szymanski, "Modality and Offering Effects in Sales Presentations for a Good Versus a Service," *Journal of the Academy of Marketing Science* 29, no. 2 (2001): 179–189.

12. Kate Macarthur, "Coke Bets on Zero to Save Cola Category," *Advertising Age,* January 1, 2007, www.adage.com.

13. "Yoplait Is Committed to Fighting Breast Cancer!" Yoplait, www.yoplait.com/breastcancer_commitment.aspx (accessed February 16, 2007).

14. "Monkey Magic," *The Independent,* January 11, 2007, http://news.independent.co.uk/media/article2144921.ece.

15. Amy Johannes, "McDonald's Debuts Coupons, Sampling Effort for Chicken Sandwich," *Promo,* February 8, 2006, http://promomagazine.com/othertactics/mcds_spicychicken_020806/.

16. "Bennigan's Celebrates 30th Anniversary with Irish Bash," *Promo,* January 12, 2006, http://promomagazine.com/eventmarketing/bennigans_30anniversary_011206/.

17. "Diamond Suits Up for Emerald Bowl," *Promo,* December 8, 2006, http://promomagazine.com/news/diamond_emerald_bowl_120806/.

18. Betsy Spethmann, "Moët Fine Tunes Loyalty Premiums," *Promo,* February 8, 2006,http://promomagazine.com/interactivemarketing/moet_loyaltypremiums_020806/.

19. "2006 Rates and Editions," *Time,* www.time.com/time/mediakit/editions/national/index.html (accessed February 16, 2007).

20. Joann Peck and Jennifer Wiggins, "It Just Feels Good: Customers' Affective Response to Touch and Its Influence in Persuasion," *Journal of Marketing* 70 (October 2006), via www.marketingpower.com.

21. "Got Milk," National Fluid Milk Processor Promotion Board, www.milknewsroom.com/index.htm, (accessed February 16, 2007).

22. Beth Snyder Bulik, "Nintendo 'Maximi'-izes to Lure Older Generation of Gamers," *Advertising Age,* February 7, 2005, p. 8.

23. Colleen DeBaise, "To Draw Women Investors, Firms Appeal to Senses," *Marketing News,* February 15, 2005, p. 14.

24. Mya Frazier, "Wal-Mart Looks to Refurbish Image with Political-Style Ads," *Advertising Age,* January 8, 2007, http://adage.com/article?article_id=114179.

25. John J. Burnett, *Promotion Management* (Boston: Houghton Mifflin, 1993), p. 7.

26. "Alltel Sweeps Promotes Friends Calling Feature," *Promo Magazine,* February 16, 2007, http://promomagazine.com/news/alltel_friends_calling_features_021607/.

27. Jack Neff, "Clorox Gives in on Glad, Hikes Trade Promotion," *Advertising Age,* July 19, 2001, www.adage.com.

28. "TNS Media Intelligence Reports U.S. Advertising Expenditures Increased 4.1% in 2006," www.tns-mi.com/news/03132007.htm, accessed October 8, 2007.

29. Xueming Luo and Naveen Donthu, "Marketing's Credibility: A Longitudinal Investigation of Marketing Communications Productivity and Shareholder Value," *Journal of Marketing* 70 (October 2006), via www.marketingpower.com.

30. Normandy Madden, "How a Chinese Dairy Plans to Become a Global Brand," *Advertising Age,* January 29, 2007, p. 31.

31. Geoffrey A. Fowler, "China Bans Nike's LeBron Ad as Offensive to Nation's Dignity," *The Wall Street Journal,* December 7, 2004, http://online.wsj.com.

32. John Eaton, "e-Word-of-Mouth Marketing," *Teaching Module* (Boston: Houghton Mifflin Company, 2006).

33. "The New Realities of a Low-Trust World," *Advertising Age,* February 13, 2006, www.adage.com.

34. Jamin Warren and John Jurgensen, "The Wizards of Buzz," *The Wall Street Journal,* February 10–11, 2007, pp. P1, P4.

35. Sarah Kugler, "Hats Off to NY Fashion," *Houston Chronicle,* January 9, 2007, www.chron.com/disp/story.mpl/life/4458016.html.

36. Gerry Khermouch and Jeff Green, "Buzz Marketing," *BusinessWeek,* July 30, 2001, pp. 50–51.

37. Pam Belluck, "Company Will Pay Boston After Scare Over Ads," *The New York Times,* February 2, 2007, www.nytimes.com.

38. Allison Fass, "A Kingdom Seeks Magic," *Forbes,* October 16, 2006, pp. 68–70.

39. T. L. Stanley, "Eat That, Subservient Chicken: OfficeMax Site Draws 36M," *Advertising Age,* January 29, 2007, pp. 4, 35.

40. Scott D. Lewis, "Fiona Apple vs. Sony," *The Oregonian,* April 15, 2005, p. D1.

41. Lynna Goch, "The Place to Be," *Best's Review,* February 2005, pp. 64–65.

42. Andrew Tilin, "The G6 Does Oprah," *Business 2.0,* January/February 2005, p. 47.

43. Goch, "The Place to Be."

44. Emma Hall, "Product Placement Faces Wary Welcome in Britain," *Advertising Age,* January 8, 2007, p. 27.

45. Marc Graser, "Toyota Hits Touch Points as It Hawks Yaris to Youth," *Advertising Age,* May 1, 2006, p. 28; Jean Halliday, "Marketer of the Year Toyota," *Advertising Age,* December 13, 2006, pp. M-1–5, S-2; Julie Liesse, "Hitting the Target: Mobile Makes Its Mark," *2006 Mobile Marketing Association Annual Mobile Marketing Guide,* December 4, 2006, pp. 4, 5; Steve McClellan, "Will Mobile Ads Take Off in '07, or Be Put on Hold?" *Adweek,* January 1, 2007, http://adweek.com/aw/magazine/article_display.jsp?vnu_content_id=1003526234&imw=Y; Toyota, www.toyota.com/about/shareholder/services/index.html (accessed January 29, 2007); Toyota Investor Fact Sheet, www.toyota.com/about/shareholder/images/2005factsheet.pdf (accessed January 29, 2007).

46. Based on information from Matthew Creamer and Lisa Sanders, "BMW Seeks a 'Holistic' Ad Approach," *Automotive News,* November 21, 2005, p. 10; "50 Years of Fame," *Marketing,* September 21, 2005, p. 25; Neal E. Boudette, "Navigating Curves," *The Wall Street Journal,* January 10, 2005, pp. A1+; Neal E. Boudette, "BMW's CEO Just Says 'No' to Protect Brand," *The Wall Street Journal,* November 26, 2003, pp. B1+; "The Psychology of Luxury," *USA Today,* December 15, 2003, www.usatoday.com; BMW North America, www.bmwusa.com (accessed January 11, 2007).

a Carl Bialik, "Nielsen's New College Numbers," *The Wall Street Journal,* February 9, 2007, http://wsj.com; "Nielsen Begins Including College Students Away From Home in Its National People Meter Sample," Nielsen Media Research press release, January 29, 2007, www.nielsen.com/media/pr_070129_a.html; Louise Story, "At Last, Television Ratings Go to College," *The New York Times,* January 29, 2007, www.nytimes.com/.

b "BzzAgent Word of Mouth Reaches 10.5 MM Consumers in 2006," BzzAgent press release, December 11, 2006, http://home.businesswire.com/portal/site/google/index.jsp?ndmViewId=news_view&newsId=20061211005225&newsLang=en; Ken Schafer, "Five Questions for Dave Balter," *One Degree,* May 23, 2006, www.onedegree.ca/2006/05/23/five-questions-for-dave-balter-bzzagent; Linda Tischler, "What's the Buzz?" *Fast Company,* May 2004, p. 76, www.fastcompany.com/magazine/82/buzz.html.

c About Us," *Tremor,* http://business.tremor.com//about_us.html (accessed January 11, 2007); Claire Atkinson, "Commercial Alert Seeks FTC Buzz Marketing Investigation," *Advertising Age,* October 18, 2005, www.adage.com; "Buzz Marketing," *Commercial Alert,* www.commercialalert.org/issues/culture/buzz-marketing (accessed January 11, 2007); Matthew Creamer, "Is Buzz Marketing Illegal?" *Advertising Age,* October 4, 2005, www.adage.com; Mary K. Engle, FTC associate director of advertising practices, letter to Gary Ruskin, executive director of *Commercial Alert,* December 7, 2006, www.ftc.gov/os/closings/staff/061211staffopiniontocommercialalert.pdf; Jeff Gelles, "New Buzz Tactic: Manipulating Teens," *Philadelphia Enquirer,* October 31, 2005, via www.commercialalert.org/issues-article.php?article_id=816&subcategory_id=90&category=1; Kate Kaye, "FTC Response to WOM Issue Won't Change Much," ClickZ blog, December 13, 2006, http://blog.clickz.com/061213-172739.html; Andy Sernovitz, "'Is Buzz Marketing Illegal? Story Rebutted," Letter to the Editor, *Advertising Age,* October 10, 2005, www.adage.com.

CHAPTER 17

1. "Counter Counterfeit Commission," www.counterfeitmini.org (accessed January 15, 2007); Stuart Elliott, "Pursuing Marketing Buzz," *The New York Times,* May 10, 2004, www.nytimes.com/2004/05/10/business/media/10adco.html?ex51399608000&en5b9adab23dbcd24f8&ei55007&partner5USE RLAND; "Full Collection of Crazy Mini Ads," *Marketallica,* April 30, 2006, http://marketallica.wordpress.

com/2006/04/30/collection-of-alternative-mini-ads/; Burt Helm, "For Your Eyes Only: Mini Cooper's Campaign, Aimed Just at Owners, Looks to Enhance the Car's Cachet," *Business Week,* July 31, 2006; "Mini History," MINI USA, www.miniusa.com/#/contactFaq/faq/history-I (accessed January 15, 2007).

2. "Starbucks Revs Up Advertising with Taxi Rooftop Campaign," *Marketing News,* February 1, 2005, p. 12.

3. Aaron O. Patrick, "U.K. Spends Millions Nagging Its Citizens," *The Wall Street Journal,* January 24, 2006, p. B1, http://online.wsj.com.

4. "100 Leading National Advertisers," *Advertising Age,* June 23, 2006, p. S-8.

5. Kate Macarthur, "Quiznos Launches 'Aggressive' Ad Effort Against Subway," *Advertising Age,* September 20, 2006, www.adage.com.

6. Jean Halliday, "Pontiac G5 Blazes Trail to Internet-Only Advertising," *Advertising Age,* August 27, 2006, www.adage.com/.

7. Joe Pereira, "New Balance Sneaker Ads Jab at Pro Athletes' Pretentions," *The Wall Street Journal,* March 10, 2005, p. B1.

8. Ibid.

9. Ibid.

10. "U.S. Search Marketing Spending to 2010," *Advertising Age, Special Marketing Fact Pack,* November 6, 2006, p. 6.

11. Sarah Ellison, "Anheuser Will Raise Spending on Cable, Internet," *The Wall Street Journal,* November 30, 2005, p. B3, http://online.wsj.com.

12. Ilona A. Berney-Reddish and Charles S. Areni, "Sex Differences in Responses to Probability Markers in Advertising Claims," *Journal of Advertising* 35 (Summer 2006): 7–17.

13. Daniel J. Howard and Roger A. Kerin, "The Effects of Personalized Product Recommendations on Advertisement Response Rates: The 'Try This. It Works!' Technique," *Journal of Consumer Psychology* 14, no. 3 (2004): 271–279.

14. Pamela W. Henderson, Joan L. Giese, and Joseph A. Cote, "Impression Management Using Typeface Design," *Journal of Marketing,* October 2004, pp. 60–72.

15. Rik Pieters and Michel Wedel, "Attention Capture and Transfer in Advertising: Brand, Pictorial, and Text-Size Effects," *Journal of Marketing,* April 2004, pp. 36–50.

16. William F. Arens, *Contemporary Advertising* (Burr Ridge, IL: Irwin/McGraw-Hill, 2007).

17. Jeremy Mullman, "Citibank Yanks Spots Starring Pair of Oddballs," *Advertising Age,* January 22, 2007, p. 25.

18. Brock Vergakis, "Utah Tourism Spike Stifles Critics of Campaign," *Marketing News,* February 1, 2007, p. 16.

19. "Media Campaign Fact Sheets," Office of National Drug Control Policy, www.mediacampaign.org/newsroom/factsheets/accomplishments.html (accessed February 19, 2007).

20. Stuart Elliott, "Army's New Battle Cry Aims at Potential Recruits," *The New York Times,* November 9, 2006, www.nytimes.com.

21. "Martha Bermudez: Senior Marketing Manager Pepsi-Cola North America," *Advertising Age,* January 29, 2007, p. C10.

22. George E. Belch and Michael A. Belch, *Advertising and Promotion* (Burr Ridge, IL: Irwin/McGraw-Hill, 2001), pp. 576–577.

23. Lisa Cornwell, "P&G Launches Two Social Networking Sites," *Marketing News,* February 1, 2007, p. 21.

24. Deborah L. Vence, "Serves Them Right," *Marketing News,* February 1, 2005, pp. 13, 16.

25. Belch and Belch, *Advertising and Promotion,* p. 598.

26. Jeff Bailey, "JetBlue's CEO Is 'Mortified' After Fliers Are Stranded," *The New York Times,* February 19, 2007, http://www.nytimes.com/; Rich Thomaselli, "Management's Misjudgment gives JetBlue a Black Eye," *Advertising Age,* February 19, 2007, www.adage.com.

27. Deborah L. Vence, "Stand Guard: In Bad Times, An Ongoing Strategy Keeps Image Intact," *Marketing News,* November 15, 2006, p. 15.

28. Bailey, "JetBlue's CEO Is 'Mortified' After Fliers Are Stranded"; Thomaselli, "Management's Misjudgment gives JetBlue a Black Eye."

29. "Counter Counterfeit Commission," www.counterfeitmini.org (accessed January 15, 2007); Stuart Elliott, "Pursuing Marketing Buzz," *The New York Times,* May 10, 2004, www.nytimes.com/2004/05/10/business/media/10adco.html?ex51399608000&en5b9adab23dbcd24f8&ei55007&partner5USERLAND; "Full Collection of Crazy Mini Ads," *Marketallica,* April 30, 2006, http://marketallica.wordpress.com/2006/04/30/collection-of-alternative-mini-ads/; Burt Helm, "For Your Eyes Only: Mini Cooper's Campaign, Aimed Just at Owners, Looks to Enhance the Car's Cachet," *Business Week,* July 31, 2006; "Mini History," Mini USA, www.miniusa.com/#/contactFaq/faq/history-I (accessed January 15, 2007).

30. Jeff Benard, "'Prime Suspect' Named in Two Elk Fire," *Summit Daily News,* December 13, 2005, www.summitdaily.com/article/20051213/NEWS/112130036; Robert S. Boynton, "Powder Burn," *Outside,* January 1999, http://outside.away.com/magazine/0199/9901vail.html; "Destination Vail," Vail Resorts, www.vailresorts.com/ourresorts.cfm?mode5vail (accessed January 12, 2007); "Earth Liberation Front Sets Off Incendiary at Vail Colorado," FactNet, www.factnet.org/cults/earth_liberation_front/vail_fire.html (accessed January 12, 2007); Joe Garner, "2 Guilty in Vail Arson," *Rocky Mountain News,* December 14, 2006, www.rockymountainnews.com/drmn/local/article/0,1299,DRMN_15_5213529,00.html; Robert Kreitner, *Management,* 9th ed. (Boston: Houghton Mifflin, 2004), p. 572; Sarah Love, "Investigation into Vail Fires Continues," *Mountain Zone,* November 4, 1998, http://classic.mountainzone.com/news/vail10-21.html.

a Jarrett Bell, "Even in Timeouts, Manning Scores," *USA Today,* November 16, 2006, pp. 1C–2C; Mark Alesia, "Commercial Exposure May Be Making P. Manning NFL's Biggest Star," *USA Today,* October 23, 2006, www.usatoday.com/sports/football/nfl/colts/2006-10-23-pmanning-endorsements_x.htm?POE=SPOISVA; Jon Show, "Exclusive Survey Names Peyton Manning Most Marketable NFLer," *Sports Business Daily,* www.sportsbusinessdaily.com/index.cfm?fuseaction=page.feature&FeatureID=202 (accessed January 15, 2007).

b Aflac, www.aflac.com (accessed January 12, 2007); "Aflac Duck Enshrined on Advertising Walk of Fame—The Aflac Duck Receives Honor as a Favorite Icon During New York City's Second Annual Celebration of the Advertising Industry," *PR Newswire*, September 26, 2005; "Aflac Takes Next Step in Defining Brand—Brand Evolution of Aflac—The Duck to Do More Than Just Quack Company Name," *PR Newswire*, December 2, 2004; Lewis Lazarre, "Duck Swoops to the Rescue," *Chicago Sun-Times*, December 18, 2006, www.suntimes.com/business/lazare/176269,CST-FIN-lew18.article; Suzanne Vranica, "Aflac Duck's Stardom: Creativity On The Cheap," *Ventura County Star*, August 1, 2004.

   c Steve Boggan, "Million Dollar Boy," *The Times*, October 14, 2005, www.timesonline.co.uk/article/0,,3223-1824063,00.html; MillionDollarHomePage.com (accessed January 12, 2007); Sarah Pierce, "The Million-Dollar Home Page," *Entrepreneur*, January 13, 2006, www.entrepreneur.com/worklife/successstories/article82936.html.

CHAPTER 18

1. Best Buy, www.BestBuy.com (accessed January 24, 2007); Best Buy 2005 Annual Report; Ariana Eunjung Chu "In Retail Profiling for Profit. Best Buy Stores Cater to Specific Customer Types," *The Washington Post*, August 17, 2005, p. A1, www.WashingtonPost.com; Stacey Collett, "Turning Data into Dollars," *ComputerWorld*, September 24, 2004, www.Computerworld.com; Michelle Conlin, "Smashing the Clock," *Business Week*, December 11, 2006, pp. 60–68; "INSOURCE Data Contributes to Best Buy's Successful Customer Relationship Management Strategy," Experian case study, www.experian.com/case_studies/best_buy.pdf, (accessed January 24, 2007); Gary McWilliams, "Analyzing Customers, Best Buy Decides Not All Are Welcome," *The Wall Street Journal*. August 11, 2004, http://online.wsj.com; "Shari Ballard, Executive Vice President of Human Resources and Legal, with Nate Omann and His 'TV Taco' Best Buy, Minneapolis, Minnesota," *Fast Talk*, November 2006, pp. 66–67.

2. Jon M. Hawes, Anne K. Rich, and Scott M. Widmier, "Assessing the Development of the Sales Profession," *Journal of Personal Selling & Sales Management*, Winter 2004, pp. 27–37.

3. "Research and Markets: The Cost of the Average Sales Call Today is More Than 400 Dollars," *M2 Presswire*, February 28, 2006.

4. Bob Donath, "Chief Customer Officers Integrate Operations," *Marketing News*, November 1, 2004, p. 5.

5. Sarah Lorge, "The Best Way to Prospect," *Sales & Marketing Management*, January 1998, p. 80.

6. Bob Donath, "Tap Sales 'Hot Buttons' to Stay Competitive," *Marketing News*, March 1, 2005, p. 8.

7. Ralph W. Giacobbe, Donald W. Jackson, Jr., Lawrence A. Crosby, and Claudia M. Bridges, "A Contingency Approach to Adaptive Selling Behavior and Sales Performance: Selling Situations and Salesperson Characteristics," *Journal of Personal Selling & Sales Management* 26 (Spring 2006): 115–142.

8. Richard G. McFarland, Goutam N. Challagalla, and Tasadduq A. Shervani, "Influence Tactics for Effective Adaptive Selling," *Journal of Marketing* 70 (October 2006), via www.marketingpower.com.

9. John Andy Wood, "NLP Revisted: Nonverbal Communications and Signals of Trustworthiness," *Journal of Personal Selling & Sales Management* 26 (Spring 2006): 198–204.

10. Gary K Hunter and William D. Perreault, Jr., "Making Sales Technology Effective," *Journal of Marketing* 71 (January 2007): 16–34.

11. Chuck Salter, "The Soft Sell," *Fast Company*, January 2005, pp. 72+.

12. Eric G. Harris, John C. Mowen, and Tom J. Brown, "Re-examining Salesperson Goal Orientations: Personality, Influencers, Customer Orientation, and Work Satisfaction," *Journal of the Academy of Marketing Science* 33, no. 1 (2005): 19–35.

13. Michael A. Wiles and Rosann L. Spiro, "Research Notes: Attracting Graduates to Sales Positions and the Role of Recruiter Knowledge: A Reexamination," *Journal of Personal Selling & Sales Management*, Winter 2004, pp. 39–48.

14. Jacqueline Durett, "Road Warriors: Making Honda a Fit for Gen-Y," *Sales & Marketing Management*, September 2006, pp. 46–48.

15. Andrew B. Artis and Eric G. Harris, "Self-Directed Learning and Sales Force Performance: An Integrated Framework," *Journal of Personal Selling & Sales Management* 27 (Winter 2007), via www.marketingpower.com.

16. Christine Galea, "Average Salary for Sales Staffers in 2005," *Sales & Marketing Management*, May 2006, p. 30.

17. Tara Burnthorne Lopez, Christopher D. Hopkins, and Mary Anne Raymond, "Reward Preferences of Salespeople: How Do Commissions Rate?" *Journal of Personal Selling & Sales Management* 26 (Fall 2006): 381–390.

18. Kirk Shinkle, "All of Your People Are Salesmen: Do They Know? Are They Ready?" *Investor's Business Daily*, February 6, 2002, p. A1.

19. Ibid.

20. John W. Barnes, Donald W. Jackson, Jr., Michael D. Hutt, and Ajith Kumar, "The Role of Culture Strength in Shaping Salesforce Outcomes," *Journal of Personal Selling & Sales Management* 26 (Summer 2006): 255–270.

21. Fernando Jaramillo, Jay Prakash Mulki, and Paul Solomon, "The Role of Ethical Climate on Salesperson's Role Stress, Job Attitudes, Turnover Intention, and Job Performance," *Journal of Personal Selling & Sales Management* 26 (Summer 2006): 272–282.

22. William H. Murphy, Peter A. Dacin, and Neil M. Ford, "Sales Contest Effectiveness: An Examination of Sales Contest Design Preferences of Field Sales Forces," *Journal of the Academy of Marketing Science* 32, no. 2 (2004): 127–143.

23. Patricia Odell, "Motivating the Masses," *Promo*, September 1, 2005, http://promomagazine.com.

24. Fernando Jaramillo, Jay Prakash Mulki, and Greg W. Marshall, "A Meta-Analysis of the Relationship Between Organizational Commitment and Salesperson Job Performance: 25 Years of Research," *Journal of Business Research* 58 (2005): 705–714.

25. "Trivial Pursuits," *Marketing Research*, Winter 2006, p. 5.

26. George E. Belch and Michael A. Belch, *Advertising and Promotion* (Burr Ridge, IL: Irwin/McGraw-Hill, 2001), pp. 526–532.

27. Eric T. Anderson and Inseong Song, "Coordinating Price Reductions and Coupon Events," *Journal of Marketing Research,* November 2004, pp. 411–422.

28. "All About Coupons," Coupon Council, www.couponmonth.com/pages/allabout.htm (accessed January 16, 2007); "Coupons Add Value: Eductation as Well," Coupon Council press release, August 23, 2006, www.couponmonth.com/pages/news.htm; Betsy Spethmann, "FSI Coupon Worth Reaches $300 Billion in 2006: MARX," *Promo,* January 4, 2007, http://promomagazine.com/othertactics/news/fsi_coupon_worth_300_billion_010407/.

29. Michel Laroche, Maria Kalamas, and Qinchao Huang, "Effects of Coupons on Brand Categorization and Choice of Fast Foods in China," *Journal of Business Research,* May 2005, pp. 674–686.

30. Arthur L. Porter, "Direct Mail's Lessons for Electronic Couponers," *Marketing Management Journal,* Spring/Summer 2000, pp. 107–115.

31. Rajneesh Suri, Srinivasan Swaminathan, and Kent B. Monroe, "Price Communications in Online and Print Coupons: An Empirical Investigation," *Journal of Interactive Marketing,* Autumn 2004, pp. 74–86.

32. Karen Holt, "Coupon Crimes," *Promo,* April 1, 2004, http://promomagazine.com/mag/marketing_coupon_crimes/.

33. Brian Grow, "The Great Rebate Runaround," *BusinessWeek,* December 5, 2005, pp. 34–37.

34. Mya Frazier, James Tenser, and Tricia Despres, "Retail Lesson: Small Programs Best," *Advertising Age,* March 20, 2006, pp. S2–S3.

35. Betsy Spethmann, "Schick Revved Quattro with Sampling," *Promo,* December 26, 2005, http://promomagazine.com/sampling/schick_sampling_122705/.

36. Amy Johanes, "Borders Launches Contests for Reward Members," *Promo,* February 7, 2007, http://promomagazine.com/contests/borders_contests_reward_members_020707/.

37. Amy Garber, "BK Franchisees File Class Action Suit Against McD," *Nation's Restaurant News,* August 29, 2005, p. 1.

38. "Hostess Rallies Around Racing Divas," *Promo,* February 8, 2006, http://promomagazine.com/contests/hostess_racingdivas_020806/.

39. Burt A. Lazar, "Agencies Held Liable for Client Ads, Promos," *Marketing News,* February 15, 2005, p. 6.

40. Best Buy, www.BestBuy.com (accessed January 24, 2007); Best Buy 2005 Annual Report; Ariana Eunjung Chu "In Retail Profiling for Profit. Best Buy Stores Cater to Specific Customer Types," *The Washington Post,* August 17, 2005, p. A1, www.WashingtonPost.com; Stacey Collett, "Turning Data into Dollars," *ComputerWorld,* September 24, 2004, www.Computerworld.com; Michelle Conlin, "Smashing the Clock," *BusinessWeek,* December 11, 2006, pp. 60–68; "INSOURCE Data Contributes to Best Buy's Successful Customer Relationship Management Strategy," Experian case study, www.experian.com/case_studies/best_buy.pdf, (accessed January 24, 2007); Gary McWilliams, "Analyzing Customers, Best Buy Decides Not All Are Welcome," *The Wall Street Journal.* August 11, 2004, http://online.wsj.com; "Shari Ballard, Executive Vice President of Human Resources and Legal, with Nate Omann and His 'TV Taco' Best Buy, Minneapolis, Minnesota," *Fast Talk,* November 2006, pp. 66–67.

41. IBM, www.ibm.com (accessed January 17, 2007); "IBM Steps up Efforts to Drive the Adoption of Software as a Service—Offers Broadest Range of Resources Enabling Business Partners to Transition to Rapid Delivery Model," *Market Wire,* February 23, 2006, http://new.marketwire.com/2.0/rel.jsp?id=681290&sourceType=1; Dan Neel, "IBM Connects the Partner Dots," *Computer Reseller News,* November 7, 2005, www.crn.com/it-channel/173403181; video interviews with IBM employees: Dan Pelino, Greg Pushalla, Karen Lowe, Monica Chambers (accessed February 28, 2006).

a Dean Foust, "A Real Power Negotiator," BusinessWeek, November 20, 2006, p. 74; Jason Singer, "Summit Energy Expands in Europe by Acquiring GfE," *The Wall Street Journal,* September 1, 2006, www.summitenergy.com/news/summit_in_wsj_09.01.06.pdf; Bill Wolfe, "Fired But Not Beaten," *The Courier-Journal,* January 30, 2006, www.summitenergy.com/news/summit_in_cj_01.30.06.pdf.

b Alan Deutschman, "The Enlightenment of Richard Branson," *Fast Company,* September 2006, p. 48, www.fastcompany.com/subscr/108/open_customers-branson.html; "All About Virgin," Virgin Group, www.virgin.com/aboutvirgin/allaboutvirgin/default.asp (accessed January 17, 2007); Michael S. Hopkins, "Richard Branson, Virgin Group," Inc., April 2005, www.inc.com/magazine/20050401/26-branson.html.

c Kristina Buchthal, "The Ten-Minute Manager's Guide To . . . Being Child-Friendly," *Restaurants and Institutions,* February 15, 2006; Chick-fil-A, www.chickfila.com (accessed January 17, 2007); "Chick-fil-A President to Camp Out at San Antonio's Third Chick-fil-A Opening This Year—Nov. 17 Opening to Include a Free One-Year Supply of Chick-fil-A to the First 100 People in Line," *Market Wire,* November 15, 2005, www.marketwire.com/2.0/release.do?id=666083&k=Chick-fil-A; "Herds of Customers Expected to Stampede Chick-fil-A Restaurants Nationwide on Cow Appreciation Day July 15," *Chick-fil-A press release,* July 8, 2005, www.chickfilapressroom.com/news.asp; "Thanksgiving Comes Early as Chick-fil-A Celebrates Restaurant Grand Opening in Chandler on Nov. 17," *Market Wire,* November 16, 2005, www.marketwire.com/2.0/release.do?id=667861&k=Chick-fil-A.

APPENDIX

1. This section and the three that follow are adapted from William M. Pride, Robert J. Hughes, and Jack R. Kapoor, *Business* (Boston: Houghton Mifflin, 2002), pp. A1–A9.

2. Andrew J. DuBrin, "Deadly Political Sins," *Wall Street Journal's Managing Your Career,* Fall 1993, pp. 11–13.

3. "Market Research: Salaries," Careers in Marketing, www.careers-in-marketing.com/mrsal.htm (accessed Feb. 28, 2007).

4. Salary Center, Monster.com, http://monster.salary.com/ (accessed Feb. 28, 2007).

5. "Advertising & Public Relations: Salaries," Careers in Marketing, www.careers-in-marketing.com/adsal.htm (accessed Feb. 28, 2007).

6. Monster.com.

7. "Product Management: Salaries," Careers in Marketing, www.careers-in-marketing.com/pmsal.htm (accessed Feb. 28, 2007).

8. "Advertising & Public Relations: Salaries."

9. "Retailing: Salaries," *Careers in Marketing*, www.careers-in-marketing.com/rtsal.htm (accessed Feb. 28, 2007).

10. Monster.com.

11. Antone Gonsalves, "An Eventual Plateau Seen for Online Retail Sales," *Information Week,* Jan. 16, 2007, www.informationweek.com/internet/showArticle.jhtml?articleID=196901232&subSection=E-Business.

12. Monster.com.

Credits

Chapter 1

Page 2: Michael Dunning/Photographer's Choice/Getty Images. Page 4: Reprinted with permission of ESPN. Page 5: Getty Images Publicity. Page 10: Copyright State Farm Automobile Insurance Company 2005. Used by permission. Page 13: Reprinted with permission of Accenture. Page 16: Reprinted with permission of The American Red Cross. Page 17: Royalty-Free/CORBIS. Page 18: These materials have been reproduced with the permission of eBay Inc. © 2007 EBAY INC. ALL RIGHTS RESERVED. Page 22: Susan Van Etten/PhotoEdit, Inc.

Chapter 2

Page 25: AP Images/Roland Weihrauch. Page 27: Reprinted with permission of POM WONDERFUL (www.pomtea.com). Page 28: Reprinted with permission of Veterinary Pet Insurance. Page 29: Spencer Grant/PhotoEdit, Inc. Page 30: Reprinted with permission of Leupold and Stevens, Inc. Page 34: Reprinted with permission of Siemens Corporation. Page 35: Reprinted with permission of Dyson. Page 37: Courtesy of Unilever. Used by permission. Page 38: © Stefanie Grewel/zefa/Corbis. Page 43: Reprinted with permission of *BusinessWeek*. Page 48: Fotosearch.com.

Chapter 3

Page 49: AP Images/Robert F. Bukaty. Page 51: Reprinted with permission of Saatchi & Saatchi LA. Courtesy of Toyota. Page 52: Reprinted with permission of AMI Brands, LLC. Page 59: Copyright 2006 - Monster, Inc. All Rights Reserved. Page 60: Image Source/FotoSearch.com. Page 61: Reprinted with permission of Allianz Life Insurance Company of North America. Page 65: Reprinted with permission from the Prostate Cancer Foundation. Page 68: Photodisc Green/Getty Images. Page 74: Royalty-Free/CORBIS.

Chapter 4

Page 76: Torsten Silz/AFP/Getty Images. Page 78: Reprinted from REAL SIMPLE ® © Time, Inc. All rights reserved. Page 80: Reprinted with permission of SCORE "Counselors to America's Small Business." Page 82: © Jerry Arcieri/CORBIS. Page 83: Reprinted with permission of Napster, LLC. Page 84: Reprinted with permission of Southwest Airlines. Page 87: AP Images/Sang Tan. Page 88: Reprinted with permission of Informatica Software. Page 91: Reprinted with permission of Sage Software, Inc. © 2006–2007 Sage Software, Inc. All Rights Reserved. Page 92: Reprinted with permission of Sharp Electronics Corporation. Page 99: Image Source/Getty Images.

Chapter 5

Page 101: Michael Newman/PhotoEdit, Inc. Page 103: Reprinted with permission of Xerox Corporation. All rights reserved. Page 104: Courtesy of American Indian College Fund. Page 105: AP Images/Paul Sakuma. Page 108: Reprinted with permission of Cargill, Incorporated. Page 110: Reprinted with permission of DataPipe and Robb Allen, Richard Dolan, Pat. James Longo. Page 112: Courtesy of Continental Airlines. Page 113: © Anders Ryman/CORBIS. Page 117: Courtesy of The Patron Spirits Company. Page 118: Reprinted with permission of RE/MAX International, Inc. Page 122: Reprinted with permission of Bruce Peterson.com and EDS. Page 126: Comstock/Jupiter Images.

Chapter 6

Page 128: © Comstock/CORBIS. Page 129: Reprinted with permission of Claritas. Page 130: Jeff Greenberg/PhotoEdit, Inc. Page 133: Reprinted with permission of BITDEFENDER. Page 135: Reprinted with permission of GMI (Global Market Insite, Inc.). Page 138: © 2007 AOL LLC. All Rights Reserved. Opinion Place is a registered trademark of AOL LLC. Used with permission. Page 142: Courtesy of McMillion Research/Mindfield Online Panels. Page 144: Gary S, Chapman/Photographer's Choice/Getty Images. Page 143: Reprinted with permission of Burke, Inc. Page 146: Reprinted with permission of Blackbaud, Inc. Photo copyright Eureka/Alamy. Page 152: Image 100/Jupiter Images.

Chapter 7

Page 155: Michael Newman/PhotoEdit, Inc. Page 157: Reprinted with permission of New Belgium Brewing Co. Page 160: Courtesy of MontBlanc NA, LLC. Page 161: Royalty-Free/CORBIS. Page 162: Reprinted with permission of The Dial Corporation. Photo copyright Benjamin Kende Photography. Page 165: Bill Aron/PhotoEdit, Inc. Page 167: Reprinted with permission of GoRving.com. Page 170: Reprinted with permission of Linksys ®, A division of Cisco Systems, Inc. Page 175: Courtesy of MapInfo Corporation. Page 179: China Photos/Getty Images News.

Chapter 8

Page 182: AP Images/Douglas C. Pizac, File. Page 184: Reprinted with permission of Pepsi-Cola North America. Page 186: Reprinted with permission of KHS Bicycles, Inc. Page 188: Reprinted with permission of AVG Internet Security. Page 190: SKY AND WATER I by M./C. Escher. Used by Permission. Page 192: Courtesy of the ASPCA. Page 194: Reprinted with permission of Mothers Against Drunk Driving © 2002. Page 195: Courtesy of The Creative Circus. Used by permission. Page 196: AP Images. Page 199: George Doyle/Stockbyte Platinum/Getty Images. Page 201: Reprinted with permission of Univision Communications Inc. Page 207: Randy Faris/CORBIS.

Chapter 9

Page 209: Scott Olson/Getty Images. Page 210: Reprinted with permission of Siemens Corporation. Page 212: Jonelle Weaver/Photodisc Green/Getty Images. Page 213: Reprinted with permission of Gifts In Kind International. Page 215: Reprinted with permissions of Cargill, Incorporated. Page 217: Poulides/Thatcher/Stone/Getty Images. Page 218: Courtesy of Magma Design Automation. Page 220: Reprinted with permission of Sprint. Page 222: Reprinted with permission of American Airlines. Page 223: Reprinted with permission of Leliam de Castro Rana. Courtesy of EMBRAER. Page 228: Louie Psihoyos/Science Faction/Getty Images.

Chapter 10

Page 232: David Young-Wolff/PhotoEdit, Inc. Page 234: Reprinted with permission of Splintek P.P. Inc. Page 236: Reprinted with permission of Seven Cycles and MIBA Design. Page 238: Reprinted with permission of Newman's Own, Inc. Page 241: AQUAFINA and AQUAFINA SPARKLING are registered trademarks of PepsiCo, Inc. Used with permission. Page 245: Ad used by permission of Napster, LLC. Page 246: David Saffron/Icon SMI/

CORBIS. Page 247: Reprinted with permission of The Quaker Oats Company. Page 249: Ryan McVay/Photodisc/Getty Images. Page 250: Reprinted with permission of Sears Brand, LLC. Page 253: Susan Van Etten/PhotoEdit, Inc. Page 256: Courtesy of The Procter & Gamble Company. Used by permission. Page 262: David Young-Wolff/PhotoEdit, Inc.

Chapter 11

Page 263: AP Images/Dan Loh. Page 265: Courtesy of Frito-Lay, Inc. Used by permission. Page 266: M&M'S ® and the M&M'S® Characters are trademarks of Mars, Incorporated and its affiliates. The M&M'S Characters are also registered with the U.S. Copyright Office. These trademarks and copyrights are used with permission. Mars, Incorporated is not associated with Houghton Mifflin Company. Advertisements printed with permission of Mars, Incorporated. © Mars, Inc. 2009. Page 270: Reprinted with permission of The Stanley Works. Page 273: Reprinted by permission of Equal Exchange. Page 275: Reprinted with permission of GEICO. Page 278: Reprinted with permission of FSC Securities Corporation. Page 279: Darren Kirk/Alamy. Page 280: Courtesy of FRINGE SALON and Amy Schiappa. Page 285: Reprinted with permission of The Endurance International Group, Inc.; Artwork by Jason Fragoso, Concept by Joshua McGinnis, http://www.powweb.com. Page 291: Michael Newman/PhotoEdit, Inc.

Chapter 12

Page 294: AP Images/Mary Altaffer. Page 296: Courtesy of The Dial Corporation. Used by permission. Page 297: AP Images/Paul Sakuma. Page 298: Reprinted with permission of ROLEX. Page 305: AP Images/Paul Sakuma. Page 306: Courtesy of American Ironhorse Motorcycle Company, Inc. Used by permission. Page 308: Reprinted with permission of The Gillette Company. Page 309: Reprinted with permission of Avantair ®. Page 318: Image Source/Getty Images.

Chapter 13

Page 321: Eriko Koga/Taxi Japan/Getty Images. Page 324: Reprinted with permission of Merck & Co., Inc. Page 325: PORSCHE, CAYENNE and the PORSCHE CREST are registered trademarks and the distinctive shapes of PORSCHE automoibiles are trade dress of Dr. Ing. H. c. F. Porsche AG. Used with permission of Porsche Cars North America, Inc. Copyrighted by Porsche Cars North America, Inc. Photographer: Stephan Romer. Page 325: Corbis Royalty-Free/Jupiter Images. Page 329: Reprinted with permission of The Woodstock Inn & Resort. Page 332: Reprinted with permission of 1&1 Internet, Inc. Page 333: Joan Joannides/Alamy. Page 334: Courtesy of The Kohler Company. Used by permission. Page 336: Reprinted with permission of Dorfman Sterling. Page 342: James Leynse/CORBIS.

Chapter 14

Page 344: Robert Sullivan/AFP/Getty Images. Page 345: Reprinted with permission of Luther Brown. Used by Permission of nVision Global Technology Solutions, Inc. Page 347: Cut and Deal/Gambling Stock Photography/Alamy. Page 351: Use of the AT&T print ad is granted under permission by AT&T Knowledge Ventures. All rights reserved. Page 352: Reprinted with permission of Procter & Gamble. All rights reserved. Page 355: Reprinted with permission of Steve Madden LTD. Page 357: AP Images/Reed Saxon. Page 359: Reprinted with permission of WM. Wrigley Jr. Company. Page 360: Reprinted with permission of Data2Logistics,

LLC. Page 363: Reprinted with permission of Ryder System, Inc. Page 367: Reprinted with permission of Odyssey Logistics & Technology Corporation. Page 371: © Andy Rain/epa/CORBIS.

Chapter 15

Page 373: Richard Cummins/CORBIS. Page 375: AP Images/Mark Lennihan. Page 377: AP Images/David Zalubowski. Page 380: Reprinted with permission of Lowe's Companies. Page 381: Reprinted with permission of Corporate Marketing Department of MapInfo Corporation. Page 382: Reprinted with permission of Wrentham Village Premium Outlets. Page 383: Richard Cummins/CORBIS. Page 384: Reprinted with permission of Pier 1 Imports. Page 386: Reprinted with permission of DirectoryNET, LLC. Page 387: © Goodshoot/CORBIS. Page 388: Reprinted with permission of Expedia, Inc. Page 390: Reprinted with permission of Merry Maid L.P. Page 392: Courtesy of McKesson Corp./www.mckesson.com. Page 401: Kimball Andrew Schmidt/Stock Connection Blue/Alamy.

Chapter 16

Page 404: Roberto Schmidt/AFP/Getty Images. Page 405: © 2006 Yahoo! Inc. YAHOO! and the YAHOO! logo are trademarks of Yahoo! Inc. Page 410: Used by permission of American Honda Motor Corporation and RPA. Page 411: Reprinted with permission of Columbia Sportswear Company. Page 412: Copyright 2006 Sun Microsystems Inc. All rights reserved. Reprinted with permission of Sun Microsystems Inc. Page 414: Reprinted with permission of Merck & Co., Inc. Page 417: Reprinted with permission of Simdesk Technologies, Inc. Page 419: Used by permission of Wendy's International, Inc. All rights reserved. Page 421: Junko Kimura/Getty Images Entertainment. Page 422: Peter Lowe/Stock Image/Pixland/Alamy. Page 429: Frank Whitney/Brand X Pictures/Alamy.

Chapter 17

Page 431: Sion Touhig/Getty Images. Page 434: FRESH STEP ® is a registered trademark of The Clorox Pet Products Company. Used by permission. © 2006, The Clorox Pet Products Company. Reprinted with permission. Photo © Jill Greenberg. Page 436: Copyright © 2008 Dow Jones & Company, Inc. All rights reserved. Page 437: AP Images/Ronen Zilberman. Page 439: Courtesy of Clear Channel Radio. Page 442: © 2007 Adams Respiratory Operations, Inc., Ft. Worth, TX 76155. Page 443: Reprinted with permission of Carolina Turkeys. Page 445: Brand X Pictures/Alamy. Page 447: Reprinted with permission of Steinway Musical/The Wyant Simboli Group. Page 450: Reprinted with permission of Ben & Jerry's Homemade, Inc. Page 455: Jonathan Nourak/PhotoEdit, Inc.

Chapter 18

Page 457: Dennis Kitchen/Stone/Getty Images. Page 459: Alexander Caminada/Alamy. Page 460: Reprinted with permission of InfoUSA. Page 461: Reprinted with permission of WebEx Communications, Inc. Page 462: Reprinted with permission of Hoover's, Inc., a D&B Company. Page 465: Reprinted with pemrission of RE/MAX International, Inc. Photo by Ed Dosien. Page 467: Reprinted with permission of Richardson. Page 469: Reprinted with permission of Synygy, Inc. Page 471: Reprinted with permission of Cumberland Packing Corporation. Page 474: Reprinted with permission of Sepracor, Inc. Page 476: Swerve/Alamy. Page 482: AP Images/Fabian Bimmer.

Subject Index

Accessibility, 83, 87–88
Accessory equipment, 237
Actual full cost, 314
Addressability, 79–81
Administered vertical marketing system (VMS), 358
Advertising. *See also* Integrated marketing communications (IMC)
    advantages and disadvantages of, 414
    careers in, 446, 497
    cooperative, 478
    expenditures for, 436–438
    explanation of, 414, 432
    institutional, 432
    Internet, 86
    objectives for, 434–435
    product, 433
    for services, 285–286
    types of, 432–435
Advertising agencies, 446
Advertising appropriations, 436–438
Advertising campaigns
    allocating money for, 436–438
    creating message for, 440, 442–443
    creating platform for, 435–436
    developing media plan for, 438–440
    evaluation of, 444–446
    execution of, 444
    explanation of, 434
    individuals involved in, 446
    target audience for, 434
Advertising media, 441, 442
Advertising platform, 435–436
Advocacy advertising, 432
Aesthetic modifications, 265
Africa, 106
African American subculture, 202
Age, as segmentation variable, 158, 163, 164
Agents, 395
Aided recall test, 445
Allowances, 312, 313
American Consumer Satisfaction Index, 54, 55
Antitrust Improvements Act (1976), 56
Approach, 460
Arbitrary approach, 437–438
Artwork, 443
Asian American subculture, 203
Asia-Pacific Economic Cooperation (APEC), 114–115
Atmospherics, 383–384
Attitudes, 193–194
Attitude scale, 194
Average fixed costs, 301
Average total costs, 301, 302
Average variable costs, 301
Awareness
    creation of, 410–411
    product, 243

Baby boomers, 36, 61, 168
Bait pricing, 333
Balance of trade, 108
Banner ads, 86
Barter, 295
Base-point pricing, 314
Behavioristic variables, 163, 168–169
Benchmarking, 41
Benefit segmentation, 168–169
Better Business Bureau, 58
Birdyback, 367
Blogs, 77, 78
Bonded storage, 364
Boston Consulting Group (BCG) approach, 33–34
Brand competitors, 51
Brand counterfeiting, 251
Brand equity, 247–248
Brand extensions, 252–253
Brand insistence, 247
Brand loyalty, 247–248
Brand managers, 286
Brand mark, 245
Brand name
    explanation of, 244–245
    protection of, 251
    selection of, 250
Brand preference, 247
Brand recognition, 247
Brands/branding
    co-, 253
    cultural, 246
    explanation of, 244–245
    family, 252
    generic, 250
    individual, 252
    licensing of, 253
    manufacturer, 248–249
    policies regarding, 252
    private distributor, 249–250
    protection of, 251–252
    types of, 248–250
    value of, 245–246
Breakdown approach, 171–172
Breakeven analysis, 304–305
Breakeven point, 304, 306
Breast Cancer Awareness Crusade, 63
Brokers, 395
Buildup approach, 172
Bundle pricing, 284, 334–335
Business analysis, 268
Business buying
    explanation of, 216
    methods of, 216–217
    purchase types and, 217–218
Business buying behavior
    buying center and, 219–220
    decision process stages and, 221–222
    influences on, 222–223

Business customers
    attributes of, 214
    characteristics of transactions with, 214
    primary concerns of, 215–216
    product demand by, 218–219
    purchase methods of, 216–217
    types of purchases by, 217–218
Business cycles
    in developing countries, 105–106
    explanation of, 54–55
Business markets
    explanation of, 156, 210–211
    government, 213
    industrial classification systems and, 223–225
    institutional, 213–214
    marketing to business customers in, 214–219
    pricing for, 312–315
    producer, 211
    reseller, 211–213
    segmentation variables for, 169–170
Business products
    demand for, 218–219
    explanation of, 237
    marketing channels for, 351–352
    types of, 237–238
Business purchases
    methods of, 216–217
    types of, 217–218
Business services, 238
Business-to-business (B2B) markets, 156, 210. *See also* Business markets
Business-to-consumer (B2C) markets, 156. *See also* Consumer markets
Business-unit strategy, 33–34
Button ads, 86
Buy-back allowance, 477
Buyers, 220
Buying allowance, 477
Buying behavior, 183. *See also* Business buying behavior; Consumer buying behavior
Buying centers, 219–220
Buying clubs. *See* Warehouse clubs
Buying decision process
    business, 219–223
    consumer, 183–203
Buying power, 53–54
Buzz marketing, 421

Call-center software, 91
Campus placement offices, 487
Canada
    economic conditions in, 106
    gross domestic product in, 106
    NAFTA and, 111, 112
Captioned photographs, 448
Captive pricing, 332
Career-related websites, 486–487

explanation of, 27, 38
implementation of, 15, 39
Marketing research
benefits of using, 130–131
careers in, 492–493
data collection for, 134–143
data interpretation for, 143–144
ethical, 147
explanation of, 129–131
international issues in, 147–148
on Internet, 128, 136
reliability and validity of, 134
reporting research findings for, 144–145
steps in process of, 131–132
types of, 132–134
using technology for, 145–147
Marketing strategies. *See also* Strategic planning
business cycle and, 55
development of, 34–37
explanation of, 27
implementation of, 39–44
packaging and, 255–256
Marketing units, 42
Market managers, 286
Market opportunities, 28
Market potential, 171
Markets. *See also* Business markets; Consumer markets; Target markets
business, 156
consumer, 156
explanation of, 33, 156
heterogeneous, 159
Market segmentation
concentrated targeting strategy through, 159–160
differentiated strategy through, 160–161
explanation of, 159
Market segmentation variables
behavioristic, 168–169
for business markets, 169–170
for consumer markets, 162, 163
demographic, 163–166
explanation of, 161–162
geographic, 166–167
psychographic, 167–168
Market segments
developing profiles of, 170–171
evaluation of relevant, 171–172
explanation of, 159
Market share
explanation of, 33
pricing objectives and, 324
Market tests, 175
Markup pricing, 327–328
Maslow's hierarchy of needs, 191–192
Mass communication, 409
Materials handling, 363
Maturity stage of product life cycle, 241–242
M-commerce, 90
Media. *See* Advertising media

Media plan, 438–440
Media planners, 438–440
Megacarriers, 366, 367
Memory, 81–82
Men, median marrying age for, 166
Merchandise allowance, 477
Merchant wholesalers, 392–393
Mexico
Coca-Cola in, 113
NAFTA and, 111, 112
recession in, 55
Micromarketing, 167
Missionary salesperson, 463
Mission statement, 31, 32
Modified-rebuy purchase, 218
Money refunds, 473
Monopolies, 52, 311
Monopolistic competition, 53
Motives, 191–192
MRO supplies, 238
Multinational enterprise, 119
Multinational marketing, 116
Multiple-choice questions, 142
Multiple packaging, 256
Multiple sourcing, 222
Multiple-unit pricing, 335

NAFTA. *See* North American Free Trade Agreement (NAFTA)
Natural environment, 66–67
Needs, Maslow's hierarchy of, 191–192
Negotiated contracts, 217
Negotiated pricing, 330
Negotiation, 217
Neighborhood shopping centers, 381
Netiquette, 96
Networking, 487
New-product development process
business analysis in, 268
commercialization in, 270–272
concept testing in, 267–268
development phase in, 268–269
explanation of, 266
idea generation for, 266–267
screening in, 267
test marketing in, 269–270
New products
explanation of, 266
ideas for, 267
pricing of, 331–332
Newspaper advertising, 441, 442
News releases, 448, 449
New-task purchases, 217–218, 220
Noise, 408
Noncumulative discounts, 313
Nonprice competition, 296–297
Nonprobability sampling, 138
Nonprofit organizations, marketing in, 16
North American Free Trade Agreement (NAFTA), 111–112, 223
North American Industry Classification System (NAICS), 223–224, 226
Nutrition Labeling and Education Act (1990), 56

Objective-and-task approach, 436
Observation methods, 143
Odd-even pricing, 336
Off-peak demand, 284
Off-price retailers, 379–380
Oligopolies, 52–53, 311
Online forums, 78
Online retailing, 374, 375, 388
Online sales training, 466
Online surveys, 140
Open-ended questions, 142
Opinion leaders, 198–199
Order getters, 462
Order lead time, 362
Order processing, 361–362
Order takers, 462–463
Organizations
assessing resources and opportunities of, 28–30
centralized, 42
decentralized, 42
importance of marketing for, 16
mission as goals of, 31–32
nonprofit, 16
segmentation by type of, 170
socially responsible, 62–64
Outdoor advertising, 441
Outlet malls, 382
Outside order takers, 462
Outsourcing, 118, 359–360

Packaging
category-consistent, 255–256
color preferences in, 255
considerations for, 254–255
family, 254
function of, 254
handling-improved, 256
innovative, 256
marketing strategy and, 255–256
multiple, 256
second-use, 255
Partnerships, 214
Patronage motives, 192
Peak demand, 284
Penetration pricing, 331–332
Percent-of-sales approach, 436–437
Perception, 189–191
Perceptual maps, 274
Performance, evaluation of, 44
Performance standards, 43, 44
Periodic discounting, 330
Perishability, 279, 282
Personal digital assistants (PDAs), 90
Personal interview surveys, 141
Personality, 167–168, 194
Personal selling. *See also* Selling
advantages and disadvantages of, 416
explanation of, 415–416
process of, 459–462
sales force for, 462–463
types of, 463–464
Phase-out, 277
Philanthropy, 65–66